Dan Plesac   Harold Reynolds   Matt Vasgersian

Peter Gammons   Jim Kaat   Bob Costas   Chris Rose   Kevin Millar

Brian Kenny   Mitch Williams   Al Leiter

ALL THE ANALYSIS   ALL THE HIGHLIGHTS
ALL THE GAMES   ALL THE INSIGHTS

ALL OF
BASEBALL®

Baseball's best team is ready to suit up again for the 2012 season.
MLB Network has live games, MLB Tonight, Intentional Talk™
and Quick Pitch™ all season long. MLB Network means more
games, more highlights and more of everything you love
about baseball.

MLB NETWORK

 f To find MLB Network in your area, log on to mlbnetwork.com

OUR NATIONAL PASTIME
ALL THE TIME®

SHOP.BASEBALLHALL.ORG
NATIONAL BASEBALL HALL OF FAME OFFICIAL ONLINE STORE

BaseBall america
2012 DIRECTORY

Editor
JOSH LEVENTHAL

Assistant Editors
BEN BADLER, J.J. COOPER, TIM EDNOFF, AARON FITT, CONOR GLASSEY, WILL LINGO, NATHAN RODE, JIM SHONERD, BILL WOODWARD

Database and Application Development
BRENT LEWIS

Photo Editor
NATHAN RODE

Design & Production
SARA HIATT MCDANIEL, LINWOOD WEBB

Programming & Technical Development
BRENT LEWIS

Cover Photo
ED WOLFSTEIN

DISTRIBUTED BY SIMON & SCHUSTER ISBN-13: 978-1-932391-41-1

BaseBall america

PRESIDENT/PUBLISHER Lee Folger

EDITORIAL
EDITORS IN CHIEF Will Lingo, John Manuel
EXECUTIVE EDITOR Jim Callis
MANAGING EDITOR J.J. Cooper
NEWS EDITOR Josh Leventhal
NATIONAL WRITER Aaron Fitt
ASSOCIATE EDITOR Matt Eddy
ASSISTANT EDITORS Ben Badler, Conor Glassey, Nathan Rode, Jim Shonerd
EDITORIAL ASSISTANT Bill Woodward
EDITORIAL INTERN Tim Ednoff

PRODUCTION
DESIGN & PRODUCTION DIRECTOR Sara Hiatt McDaniel
MULTIMEDIA MANAGER Linwood Webb

ADVERTISING
DISPLAY ADVERTISING EXECUTIVE George Shelton
DIRECT MARKETING MANAGER Ximena Caceres
MARKETPLACE MANAGER Kristopher M. Lull
ADVERTISING SALES EXECUTIVE Edward Richards

BUSINESS
CHIEF OPERATING OFFICER Cara Callanan
ECONOMIST Bill Porter
CUSTOMER SERVICE Ronnie McCabe, Dave Slade
MANAGER, FINANCE Susan Callahan
FINANCIAL ADMINISTRATOR Hailey Carpenter
TECHNOLOGY MANAGER Brent Lewis
TECHNOLOGY ASSISTANT Tim Collins
LEGAL COUNSEL Michael P. Ring

WHERE TO DIRECT QUESTIONS
ADVERTISING: advertising@baseballamerica.com
BUSINESS BEAT: joshleventhal@baseballamerica.com
COLLEGES: aaronfitt@baseballamerica.com
DESIGN/PRODUCTION: production@baseballamerica.com
DRAFT: johnmanuel@baseballamerica.com
HIGH SCHOOLS: nathanrode@baseballamerica.com
INDEPENDENT LEAGUES: jjcooper@baseballamerica.com
MAJOR LEAGUES: jimcallis@baseballamerica.com
MINOR LEAGUES: willlingo@baseballamerica.com
PHOTOS: photos@baseballamerica.com
PROSPECTS: benbadler@baseballamerica.com
REPRINTS: production@baseballamerica.com
SUBSCRIPTIONS/CUSTOMER SERVICE: customerservice@baseballamerica.com
WEBSITE: customerservice@baseballamerica.com

GrindMedia

GRINDMEDIA MANAGEMENT
SVP, GROUP PUBLISHER Norb Garrett
norb.garrett@grindmedia.com
VP, DIGITAL Greg Morrow
greg.morrow@grindmedia.com
PRODUCTION DIRECTOR Kasey Kelley
kasey.kelley@grindmedia.com
EDITORIAL DIRECTOR–DIGITAL Chris Mauro
chris.mauro@grindmedia.com
FINANCE DIRECTOR Adam Miner
adam.miner@grindmedia.com

ADVERTISING SALES
SALES STRATEGY MGR/PRINT & EVENTS
Chris Engelsman chris.engelsman@grindmedia.com
SALES STRATEGY MGR/DIGITAL Elisabeth Murray
elisabeth.murray@grindmedia.com

DIGITAL
DIRECTOR OF ENGINEERING Jeff Kimmel
jeff.kimmel@grindmedia.com
SENIOR PRODUCT MANAGER Rishi Kumar
rishi.kumar@grindmedia.com
SENIOR PRODUCT MANAGER Marc Bartell
marc.bartell@grindmedia.com
CREATIVE DIRECTOR Peter Tracy
peter.tracy@grindmedia.com

MARKETING AND EVENTS
MARKETING DIRECTOR Jamey Stone
jamey.stone@grindmedia.com
DIRECTOR OF EVENT OPERATIONS Sean Nielsen
sean.nielsen@grindmedia.com

FACILITIES
MANAGER Randy Ward randy.ward@grindmedia.com
OFFICE COORDINATOR Ruth Hosea
ruth.hosea@grindmedia.com
ARCHIVIST Thomas Voehringer
thomas.voehringer@sorc.com

SOURCE INTERLINK MEDIA

OFFICERS OF SOURCE INTERLINK COMPANIES, INC.
PRESIDENT AND CHIEF EXECUTIVE OFFICER
Michael Sullivan
EVP, CHIEF FINANCIAL OFFICER John Bode
EVP, CHIEF ADMINISTRATIVE OFFICER
Stephanie Justice

SOURCE INTERLINK MEDIA, LLC
PRESIDENT Chris Argentieri
CHIEF CREATIVE OFFICER Alan Alpanian
SVP, FINANCE Dan Bednar
EVP, ENTHUSIAST AUTOMOTIVE Doug Evans
SVP, NEW PRODUCT DEVELOPMENT Howard Lim
CHIEF CONTENT OFFICER Angus MacKenzie
SVP, MANUFACTURING AND PRODUCTION
Kevin Mullan
SVP, CONSUMER MEDIA AND INTEGRATED SALES
Eric Schwab
VP AND GENERAL MANAGER, BRAND DEVELOPMENT
Julie Smartz

DIGITAL MEDIA
CHIEF TECHNOLOGY OFFICER, DIGITAL MEDIA
Raghu Bala
SVP, DIGITAL MARKETING Craig Buccola
SVP, DIGITAL PRODUCT DEVELOPMENT Todd Busby
SVP, DIGITAL PRODUCT DEVELOPMENT Tom Furukawa
VP, DIGITAL PRODUCT DEVELOPMENT Dan Hong
VP, DIGITAL ADVERTISING PRODUCTS AND OPERATIONS Jung Park

CONSUMER MARKETING, SOURCE INTERLINK MEDIA, LLC
VP, SINGLE COPY SALES AND MARKETING Chris Butler

CONSUMER MARKETING, ENTHUSIAST MEDIA SUBSCRIPTION COMPANY, INC.
VP, CONSUMER MARKETING Tom Slater
VP, RETENTION AND OPERATIONS FULFILLMENT
Donald T. Robinson III

TABLE OF CONTENTS

Joseph L. Bruno Stadium, Troy, New York

MARK MORAND

WHAT'S NEW IN 2012

MAJOR LEAGUES

Name Change: Florida Marlins become Miami Marlins.
Ballpark: Marlins Park.

TRIPLE-A

Schedule: Triple-A Scranton-Wilkes/Barre will play 2012 season on the road as ballpark undergoes renovations. Yankees will play home games at International League affiliates Buffalo, Lehigh Valley, Pawtucket, Rochester and Syracuse, and New York-Penn League affiliate Batavia.

DOUBLE-A

Affiliate: Pensacola Blue Wahoos replace Carolina Mudcats in the Southern League.
Ballpark: Pensacola Blue Wahoos—Maritime Park.

HIGH CLASS A

Affiliate: Carolina Mudcats replace Kinston Indians in the Carolina League.

ROOKIE

Affiliate: Grand Junction Rockies replace Casper Ghosts in the Pioneer League.

Stalker has **twice the range and performance** of other "toy" radar products!

Nearly every Major League Baseball team's scouting organization uses Stalker Sport radar. Stalker radars are the most rugged, reliable, and accurate speed radars in the field.

Stalker Pro II
High Performance Sport Radar

- The industry standard
- 500 foot range
- Accurate to +/- 0.1 MPH
- Fastest acquisition
- Measures pitch, plate, and batted ball speeds

Stalker Sport 2
Baseball Radar Gun

- 300 foot range
- Accurate to +/- 0.1 MPH
- Stadium performance
- Measure pitcher and runner

StalkerSportsRadar.com

STALKER® Sports Radar
The Choice of Professionals
888-STALKER

applied concepts, inc.
2609 Technology Drive ■ Plano, Texas 75074
972.398.3780 ■ Fax 972.398.3781

Map illustrations by Paul Trap

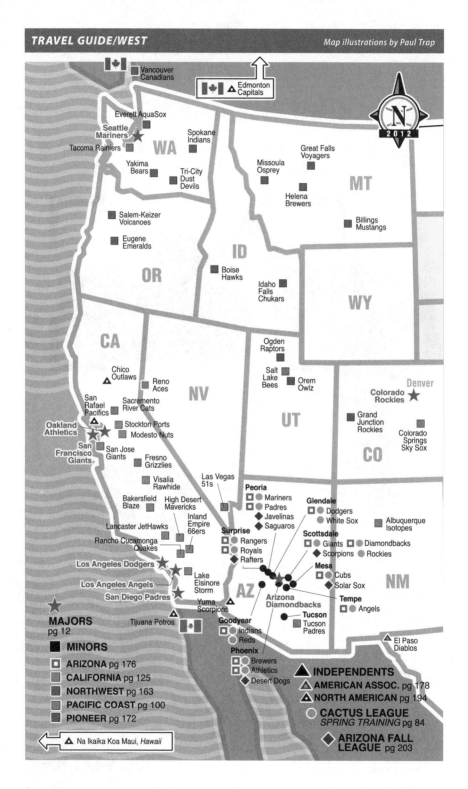

Vancouver Canadians

Edmonton Capitals

Everett AquaSox

Seattle Mariners

Tacoma Rainiers

Spokane Indians

Yakima Bears

Tri-City Dust Devils

WA

Great Falls Voyagers

Missoula Osprey

MT

Helena Brewers

Billings Mustangs

Salem-Keizer Volcanoes

Eugene Emeralds

OR

Boise Hawks

ID

Idaho Falls Chukars

WY

Ogden Raptors

CA

Chico Outlaws

Reno Aces

NV

Salt Lake Bees

Orem Owlz

Denver

Colorado Rockies

San Rafael Pacifics

Sacramento River Cats

UT

Grand Junction Rockies

Colorado Springs Sky Sox

CO

Oakland Athletics

Stockton Ports

Modesto Nuts

San Francisco Giants

San Jose Giants

Fresno Grizzlies

Visalia Rawhide

Las Vegas 51s

Peoria
- Mariners
- Padres
- Javelinas
- Saguaros

Glendale
- Dodgers
- White Sox

Albuquerque Isotopes

Bakersfield Blaze

High Desert Mavericks

Inland Empire 66ers

Surprise
- Rangers
- Royals
- Rafters

Scottsdale
- Giants
- Scorpions

- Diamondbacks
- Rockies

Lancaster JetHawks

Rancho Cucamonga Quakes

Los Angeles Dodgers

Los Angeles Angels

San Diego Padres

Lake Elsinore Storm

AZ

Mesa
- Cubs
- Solar Sox

NM

Arizona Diamondbacks

Tempe
- Angels

Yuma Scorpions

Goodyear
- Indians
- Reds

Tucson
Tucson Padres

Tijuana Potros

Phoenix
- Brewers
- Athletics
- Desert Dogs

El Paso Diablos

MAJORS
pg 12

MINORS

☐ **ARIZONA** pg 176
☐ **CALIFORNIA** pg 125
☐ **NORTHWEST** pg 163
☐ **PACIFIC COAST** pg 100
☐ **PIONEER** pg 172

▲ **INDEPENDENTS**

▲ **AMERICAN ASSOC.** pg 178
▲ **NORTH AMERICAN** pg 194

○ **CACTUS LEAGUE**
SPRING TRAINING pg 84

◆ **ARIZONA FALL LEAGUE** pg 203

▲ Na Ikaika Koa Maui, *Hawaii*

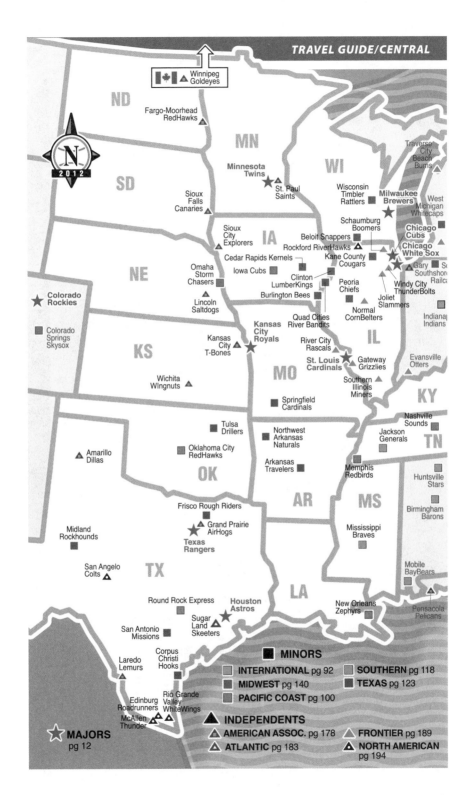

Winnipeg Goldeyes

ND

Fargo-Moorhead RedHawks

MN

WI

Traverse City Beach Bums

Minnesota Twins

St. Paul Saints

Wisconsin Timber Rattlers

Milwaukee Brewers

West Michigan Whitecaps

SD

Sioux Falls Canaries

Schaumburg Boomers

Chicago Cubs

Sioux City Explorers

IA

Beloit Snappers

Chicago White Sox

Rockford RiverHawks

Kane County Cougars

Gary Southshore Railca

Cedar Rapids Kernels

NE

Omaha Storm Chasers

Iowa Cubs

Clinton LumberKings

Peoria Chiefs

Windy City ThunderBolts

Joliet Slammers

Indiana Indians

Colorado Rockies

Lincoln Saltdogs

Burlington Bees

Quad Cities River Bandits

Normal CornBelters

Colorado Springs Skysox

Kansas City Royals

Kansas City T-Bones

IL

River City Rascals

Evansville Otters

KS

MO

St. Louis Cardinals

Gateway Grizzlies

Wichita WIngnuts

KY

Southern Illinois Miners

Springfield Cardinals

Nashville Sounds

TN

Tulsa Drillers

Northwest Arkansas Naturals

Jackson Generals

Amarillo Dillas

Oklahoma City RedHawks

Huntsville Stars

OK

Arkansas Travelers

Memphis Redbirds

AR

MS

Birmingham Barons

Frisco Rough Riders

Midland Rockhounds

Grand Prairie AirHogs

Texas Rangers

Mississippi Braves

Mobile BayBears

San Angelo Colts

TX

LA

Round Rock Express

Houston Astros

New Orleans Zephyrs

Pensacola Pelicans

San Antonio Missions

Sugar Land Skeeters

Laredo Lemurs

Corpus Christi Hooks

Edinburg Roadrunners

Rio Grande Valley WhiteWings

McAllen Thunder

MINORS

INTERNATIONAL pg 92	**SOUTHERN** pg 118
MIDWEST pg 140	**TEXAS** pg 123
PACIFIC COAST pg 100	

INDEPENDENTS

☆ **MAJORS** pg 12

AMERICAN ASSOC. pg 178	**FRONTIER** pg 189
ATLANTIC pg 183	**NORTH AMERICAN** pg 194

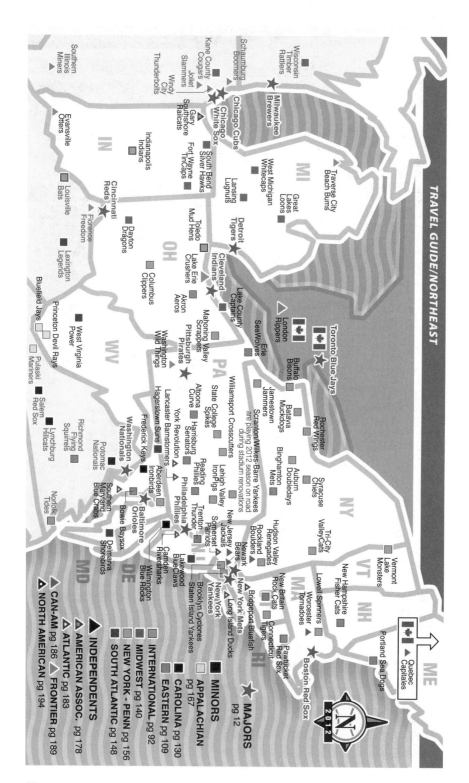

Southern Illinois Miners
Wisconsin Timber Rattlers
Schaumburg Boomers
Kane County Cougars
Joliet Slammers
Windy City Thunderbolts
Chicago White Sox
Milwaukee Brewers
Chicago Cubs
Gary Southshore Railcats
Evansville Otters
Indianapolis Indians
South Bend Silver Hawks
Fort Wayne TinCaps
Traverse City Beach Bums
West Michigan Whitecaps
Great Lakes Loons
Lansing Lugnuts
Cincinnati Reds
Louisville Bats
Florence Freedom
Dayton Dragons
Toledo Mud Hens
Detroit Tigers
Lake Erie Crushers
Cleveland Indians
Lake County Captains
Columbus Clippers
Akron Aeros
Lexington Legends
Bluefield Jays
Princeton Devil Rays
West Virginia Power
Pulaski Mariners
Salem Red Sox
Lynchburg Hillcats
Richmond Flying Squirrels
Hagerstown Suns
Frederick Keys
Washington Wild Things
Pittsburgh Pirates
Mahoning Valley Scrappers
Altoona Curve
Harrisburg Senators
Lancaster Barnstormers
York Revolution
Reading Phillies
Lehigh Valley IronPigs
State College Spikes
Williamsport Crosscutters
Erie SeaWolves
London Rippers
Buffalo Bisons
Batavia Muckdogs
Jamestown Jammers
Rochester Red Wings
Scranton/Wilkes-Barre Yankees are playing 2012 season on road during stadium renovations
Auburn Doubledays
Binghamton Mets
Syracuse Chiefs
Toronto Blue Jays
Potomac Nationals
Washington Nationals
Bowie Baysox
Aberdeen Ironbirds
Baltimore Orioles
Philadelphia Phillies
Trenton Thunder
New Jersey Jackals
Somerset Patriots
Camden Riversharks
Lakewood BlueClaws
Newark Bears
Rockland Boulders
Hudson Valley Renegades
Tri-City ValleyCats
Southern Maryland Blue Crabs
Delmarva Shorebirds
Wilmington Blue Rocks
Norfolk Tides
Brooklyn Cyclones
Staten Island Yankees
New York Yankees
New York Mets
Long Island Ducks
Bridgeport Bluefish
Connecticut Tigers
New Britain Rock Cats
New Hampshire Fisher Cats
Vermont Lake Monsters
Lowell Spinners
Worcester Tornadoes
Pawtucket Red Sox
Portland Sea Dogs
Boston Red Sox
Quebec Capitales

MINORS pg 12

★ **MAJORS** pg 12

■ **INTERNATIONAL** pg 92
■ **EASTERN** pg 109
■ **CAROLINA** pg 130
■ **APPALACHIAN** pg 167
■ **MIDWEST** pg 140
□ **NEW YORK • PENN** pg 156
■ **SOUTH ATLANTIC** pg 148

INDEPENDENTS
▲ **AMERICAN ASSOC.** pg 178
▲ **ATLANTIC** pg 183
△ **CAN-AM** pg 186
△ **FRONTIER** pg 189
▲ **NORTH AMERICAN** pg 194

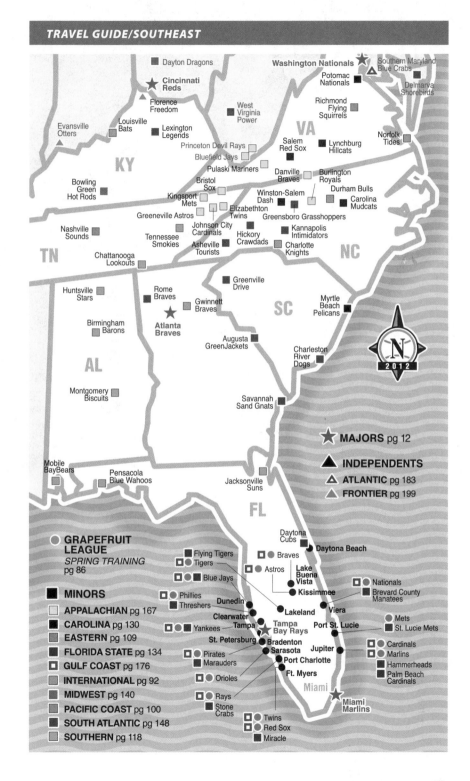

Dayton Dragons
Washington Nationals
Southern Maryland Blue Crabs
Cincinnati Reds
Potomac Nationals
Delmarva Shorebirds
Florence Freedom
West Virginia Power
Richmond Flying Squirrels
Evansville Otters
Louisville Bats
Lexington Legends
Salem Red Sox
Lynchburg Hillcats
Norfolk Tides
Princeton Devil Rays
Bluefield Jays
Pulaski Mariners
Danville Braves
Burlington Royals
Bowling Green Hot Rods
Bristol Sox
Kingsport Mets
Winston-Salem Dash
Durham Bulls
Carolina Mudcats
Greeneville Astros
Elizabethton Twins
Greensboro Grasshoppers
Nashville Sounds
Johnson City Cardinals
Hickory Crawdads
Kannapolis Intimidators
Tennessee Smokies
Asheville Tourists
Charlotte Knights
Chattanooga Lookouts
Huntsville Stars
Rome Braves
Greenville Drive
Gwinnett Braves
Myrtle Beach Pelicans
Birmingham Barons
Atlanta Braves
Augusta GreenJackets
Charleston River Dogs
Montgomery Biscuits
Savannah Sand Gnats
Mobile BayBears
Pensacola Blue Wahoos
Jacksonville Suns

MAJORS pg 12
INDEPENDENTS
ATLANTIC pg 183
FRONTIER pg 199

GRAPEFRUIT LEAGUE
SPRING TRAINING pg 86

Daytona Cubs
Daytona Beach
Flying Tigers
Braves
Tigers
Astros
Lake Buena Vista
Nationals
Brevard County Manatees
Blue Jays
Kissimmee
Phillies
Viera
MINORS
Threshers
Dunedin
Lakeland
APPALACHIAN pg 167
Clearwater
Mets
CAROLINA pg 130
Yankees
Tampa
Port St. Lucie
St. Lucie Mets
EASTERN pg 109
Tampa Bay Rays
FLORIDA STATE pg 134
St. Petersburg
Bradenton
Cardinals
GULF COAST pg 176
Pirates
Sarasota
Jupiter
Marlins
Marauders
Port Charlotte
Hammerheads
INTERNATIONAL pg 92
Orioles
Ft. Myers
Palm Beach Cardinals
MIDWEST pg 140
PACIFIC COAST pg 100
Rays
SOUTH ATLANTIC pg 148
Stone Crabs
Miami Marlins
SOUTHERN pg 118
Twins
Red Sox
Miracle

MAJOR LEAGUES

MAJOR LEAGUE BASEBALL

Mailing Address: 245 Park Ave. New York, NY 10167.
Telephone: (212) 931-7800.
Website: www.mlb.com.
Commissioner: Allan H. "Bud" Selig.
Executive Vice President, Business: Tim Brosnan. **Executive VP, Labor Relations/Human Resources:** Robert Manfred. **Executive VP, Finance/Chief Financial Officer:** Jonathan Mariner. **Executive VP, Administration/Chief Information Officer:** John McHale. **Executive VP, Baseball Development:** Jimmie Lee Solomon.

Bud Selig

BASEBALL OPERATIONS

Senior VP, Baseball Operations: Joe Garagiola Jr, Kim Ng, Peter Woodfork.
VP, International Baseball Operations: Lou Melendez. **VP, Youth/Facility Development:** Darrell Miller. **Senior Director, Major League Operations:** Roy Krasik. **Director, Baseball Operations Initiatives:** Sylvia Lind.
Director, International Baseball Operations: Chris Haydock. **Senior Manager, Baseball Operations:** Jeff Pfeifer. **Senior Manager, Minor League Operations:** Fred Seymour. **Senior Specialist, On-Field Operations:** Unavailable. **Specialist, Amateur Player Administration:** Chuck Fox. **Specialist, Umpire Administration:** Cathy Davis. **Specialist, International Game Development:** Joel Araujo. **Specialist, International Baseball Operations:** Oz Ocampo.
Coordinator, Major League Operations: Gina Liento. **Coordinator, Minor League Operations:** Ben Baroody. **Administrator, International Baseball Operations:** Rebecca Seesel. **Senior Administrative Assistant:** Llubia Bussey, Ana Cariello. **Administrator, Baseball Operations:** Scott Harris.
Director, Major League Umpiring: Randy Marsh. **Director, Umpiring Development:** Rich Rieker. **Director, Umpire Administration:** Matt McKendry. **Director, Umpire Medical Services:** Mark Letendre. **Umpiring Supervisors:** Cris Jones, Chuck Meriwether, Ed Montague, Steve Palermo, Charlie Reliford, Larry Young. **Special Assistant, Umpiring:** Bruce Froemming. **Sure Administrator:** Steve Mara.
Video Coordinator: Freddie Hernandez. **Baseball Systems:** Nancy Crofts. **Director, Dominican Operations:** Rafael Perez. **Assistant Manager:** Osiris Ramirez. **Manager, International Registration:** Juan DeJesus. **Director, Arizona Fall League:** Steve Cobb. **Director, Major League Scouting Bureau:** Frank Marcos. **Assistant Director, Scouting Bureau:** Rick Oliver.

Security
VP, Security/Facility Management: Bill Bordley.
Senior Manager, Facility Operations: Bob Campbell. **Supervisor, Executive Offices Security Operations:** William Diaz. **Manager, Latin America Security Operations:** Tom Reilly. **Supervisor, Executive Protection:** Charles Hargrove. **Security Analyst:** Christopher Ellis. **Supervisor, Security/Facility Management:** Yenifer Nunez. **Assistant to VP, Security/Facility Management:** Danielle Beckom.

Investigations
Senior VP, Investigations: Dan Mullin.
VP, Investigations: George Hanna. **VP, Educational Programming/Investigative Services:** Earnell Lucas. **Senior Administrative Assistant:** Stephanie Valentinetti. **Manager, Investigations:** Nancy Zamudio. **Manager, Investigations/ DR-DOI Office:** Nelson Tejada. **Senior Investigators:** Ed Dominguez, Victor Burgos, Ricardo Burnham, Awilda Santana, Tom J. Reilly. **Research Analysts:** Kevin Cepelak, Ariadne Bonano. **Managing Director, NAPBL:** John Skinner.

Public Relations
Telephone: (212) 931-7878. **Fax:** (212) 949-5654.
Senior VP, Public Relations: Patrick Courtney.
VP, Business Public Relations: Matt Bourne. **Director, Media Relations:** John Blundell. **Director, Public Relations:** Michael Teevan. **Manager, Media Relations:** Donald Muller. **Managers, Business Public Relations:** Jeff Heckelman, Daniel Queen, Lauren Verrusio. **Specialist, Business Public Relations:** Steven Arocho. **Coordinator, Media Relations:** Lydia Panayotidis. **Coordinators, Business Public Relations:** Sarah Leer, Ariel Williams. **Coordinator, Public Relations:** Jennifer Zudonyi. **Administrative Assistant:** Raquel Ramos.

Club Relations
Senior VP, Scheduling/Club Relations: Katy Feeney.
Senior Administrative Assistant, Scheduling/Club Relations: Raxel Concepcion. **Coordinator, Club Relations:** Bennett Shields. **Senior VP, Club Relations:** Phyllis Merhige. **Senior Administrative Assistant, Club Relations:** Angelica Cintron. **Administrator, Club Relations:** Ian Johns.

Licensing
Senior VP, Licensing: Howard Smith.
VP, Domestic Licensing: Steve Armus. **Senior Director, Consumer Products, Retail Marketing:** Adam Blinderman. **Director, Licensing/Minor Leagues:** Eliot Runyon. **Senior Director, Gifts/Novelties:** Maureen Mason. **Senior Director, Hard Goods:** Mike Napolitano. **Senior Director, Non-Authentics:** Greg Sim. **Director, Authentic Collection:** Ryan Samuelson. **Senior Manager, Presence Marketing:** Robin Jaffe.

Publishing/Photographs
VP, Publishing/Photographs: Don Hintze.
Editorial Director: Mike McCormick. **Art Director, Publications:** Faith Rittenberg. **MLB Photographs:** Jessica Foster.

Special Events
Senior VP, Special Events: Marla Miller.
Senior Directors, Special Events: Brian O'Gara, Eileen Buser. **Directors, Special Events:** Jacqueline Secaira-Cotto, Rob Capilli. **Managers, Special Events:** JB Hacking, Jennifer Jacobson, Keri Harris.

Broadcasting
Senior VP, Broadcasting: Chris Tully.
VP, Broadcast Administration/Operations: Bernadette McDonald. **Senior Director, Broadcasting Business Affairs:** Susanne Hilgefort. **Director, Broadcast Administration/Operations:** Chuck Torres. **Manager, Broadcasting:** Dewey Gong.

Corporate Sales/Marketing
Senior VP, Corporate Sales/Marketing: Lou Koskovolis.
VP, Corporate Sales/Marketing: Jeremy Cohen. **VP, National Sales:** Chris Marciani.

Advertising
Senior VP/Chief Marketing Officer: Jacqueline Parkes.
Vice President, Research/Strategic Planning: Dan Derian. **Director, Research:** Marc Beck. **VP, Design Services:** Anne Occi.

Community Affairs
VP, Community Affairs: Tom Brasuell.
Director, Community Affairs: Celia Bobrowsky. **Director, Reviving Baseball in Inner Cities:** David James.

General Administration
Senior VP, Accounting/Treasurer: Bob Clark. **Senior VP/General Counsel, Labor Relations:** Dan Halem. **Senior VP/General Counsel, Business:** Ethan Orlinsky. **Senior VP/General Counsel, BOC:** Tom Ostertag. **Senior VP, Finance:** Kathleen Torres. **Senior VP, Chief Technology Officer:** Mike Morris. **VP, Deputy General Counsel:** Domna Candido. **Senior VP, Diversity/Strategic Alliances:** Wendy Lewis. **VP, Human Resources:** Ray Scott. **VP/Deputy General Counsel:** Jennifer Simms. **VP, Operations/Tech Support:** Peter Surhoff. **Director, Baseball Assistance Team:** Joe Grippo.
VP, Office Operations: Donna Hoder. **Senior Director, Quality Control:** Peggy O'Neill-Janosik. **VP, Recruitment:** John Quinones. **Director, Risk Management/Financial Reporting:** Anthony Avitabile. **Senior Manager, Records:** Mildred Delgado. **Director, Retirement Services:** Rich Hunt. **Director, Benefits/HRIS:** Diane Cuddy.

International
Mailing Address: 245 Park Ave., 31st Floor, New York, NY 10167. **Telephone:** (212) 931-7500. **Fax:** (212) 949-5795.
Senior VP, International Business Operations: Paul Archey.
VP, International Licensing: Denis Nolan. **VP/Executive Producer, International Broadcasting:** Russell Gabay. **VP, Sponsorship/Market Development:** Dominick Balsamo. **VP, World Baseball Classic:** James Pearce. **VP, International Broadcast Sales:** Frank Uddo. **VP, Asia/Managing Director, Japan Operations:** Jim Small. **Managing Director, China Operations:** Leon Xie. **Director, Australian Operations:** Thomas Nicholson. **Managing Director, European Operations:** Clive Russell.

MLB Western Operations
Office Address: 2415 East Camelback Rd., Suite 850, Phoenix, AZ 85016. **Telephone:** (602) 281-7300. **Fax:** (602) 281-7313.
VP, Western Operations/Special Projects: Laurel Prieb. **Office Coordinator:** Valerie Dietrich.

Major League Baseball Productions
Office Address: One MLB Network Plaza, Secaucus, NJ 07094-2403.
Telephone: (201) 751-8500. **Fax:** (201) 751-8568.
VP, Executive In Charge of Production: David Gavant.
Executive Producer: David Check. **Senior Director, Operations:** Shannon Valine. **Senior Manager, Media Management/Tech Ops:** Chris Monico. **Senior Manager, Programming:** John O'Sheal. **Senior Manager, Library Licensing:** Nick Trotta. **Senior Writer:** Jeff Scott. **Coordinating Producers:** Adam Schlackman, Robert Haddad.

Umpires
Lance Barksdale, Ted Barrett, Wally Bell, Dan Bellino, C.B. Bucknor, Mark Carlson, Gary Cederstrom, Eric Cooper, Derryl Cousins, Fieldin Culbreth, Phil Cuzzi, Kerwin Danley, Gary Darling, Bob Davidson, Gerry Davis, Dana DeMuth, Laz Diaz, Mike DiMuro, Rob Drake, Bruce Dreckman, Doug Eddings, Paul Emmel, Mike Everitt, Chad Fairchild, Andy Fletcher, Marty Foster, Greg Gibson, Brian Gorman, Chris Guccione, Tom Hallion, Angel Hernandez, Ed Hickox, John Hirschbeck, Sam Holbrook, James Hoye, Marvin Hudson, Dan Iassogna, Adrian Johnson, Jim Joyce, Jeff Kellogg, Brian Knight, Ron Kulpa, Jerry Layne, Alfonso Marquez, Tim McClelland, Jerry Meals, Bill Miller, Paul Nauert, Jeff Nelson, Brian O'Nora, Tony Randazzo, Ed Rapuano, Jim Reynolds, Brian Runge, Paul Schrieber, Dale Scott, Todd Tichenor, Tim Timmons, Tim Tschida, Larry Vanover, Mark Wegner, Bill Welke, Tim Welke, Hunter Wendelstedt, Joe West, Mike Winters, Jim Wolf.

Events
2012 All-Star Game: July 10 at Kauffman Stadium, Kansas City, MO. **2012 World Series:** Unavailable.

AMERICAN LEAGUE

Year League Founded: 1901.
2012 Opening Date: March 28. **Closing Date:** Oct. 3.
Regular Season: 162 games.
Division Structure: East—Baltimore, Boston, New York, Tampa Bay, Toronto. **Central**—Chicago, Cleveland, Detroit, Kansas City, Minnesota. **West**—Los Angeles, Oakland, Seattle, Texas.
Playoff Format: Unavailable.
All-Star Game: July 10, Kauffman Stadium, Kansas City (National League vs American League).
Roster Limit: 25, through Aug. 31 when rosters expand to 40.
Brand of Baseball: Rawlings.
Statistician: MLB Advanced Media, 75 Ninth Ave., 5th Floor, New York, NY 10011.

STADIUM INFORMATION

Team	Stadium	Dimensions			Capacity	2011 Att.
		LF	CF	RF		
Baltimore	Oriole Park at Camden Yards	333	410	318	45,971	1,755,461
Boston	Fenway Park	310	390	302	37,493	3,054,001
Chicago	U.S. Cellular Field	330	400	335	40,615	2,001,117
Cleveland	Progressive Field	325	405	325	43,545	1,840,835
Detroit	Comerica Park	345	420	330	41,782	2,642,045
Kansas City	Kauffman Stadium	330	410	330	37,903	1,724,450
Los Angeles	Angel Stadium	333	404	333	45,050	3,166,321
Minnesota	Target Field	339	404	328	39,504	3,168,107
New York	Yankee Stadium	318	408	314	52,325	3,653,680
Oakland	The Coliseum	330	400	367	34,077	1,476,792
Seattle	Safeco Field	331	405	326	47,447	1,896,331
Tampa Bay	Tropicana Field	315	404	322	41,315	1,529,188
Texas	Rangers Ballpark in Arlington	332	400	325	48,194	2,946,949
Toronto	Rogers Centre	328	400	328	49,539	1,818,103

NATIONAL LEAGUE

Year League Founded: 1876.
2012 Opening Date: April 4. **Closing Date:** Oct. 3.
Regular Season: 162 games.
Division Structure: East—Atlanta, Miami, New York, Philadelphia, Washington. **Central**—Chicago, Cincinnati, Houston, Milwaukee, Pittsburgh, St. Louis. **West**—Arizona, Colorado, Los Angeles, San Diego, San Francisco.
Playoff Format: Unavailable.
All-Star Game: July 10, Kauffman Stadium, Kansas City (National League vs. American League).
Roster Limit: 25, through Aug. 31 when rosters expand to 40.
Brand of Baseball: Rawlings.
Statistician: MLB Advanced Media, 75 Ninth Ave., 5th Floor, New York, NY 10011.

STADIUM INFORMATION

Team	Stadium	Dimensions			Capacity	2011 Att.
		LF	CF	RF		
Arizona	Chase Field	330	407	334	49,033	2,105,432
Atlanta	Turner Field	335	400	330	49,743	2,372,940
Chicago	Wrigley Field	355	400	353	41,160	3,017,966
Cincinnati	Great American Ball Park	328	404	325	42,319	2,213,498
Colorado	Coors Field	347	415	350	50,499	2,909,777
Houston	Minute Maid Park	315	435	326	40,976	2,067,016
Los Angeles	Dodger Stadium	330	395	330	56,000	2,935,139
Miami	Marlins Park	344	422	335	37,000	1,520,562
Milwaukee	Miller Park	344	400	345	41,900	3,071,373
New York	Citi Field	335	408	330	42,000	2,378,549
Philadelphia	Citizens Bank Park	329	401	330	647	3,680,718
Pittsburgh	PNC Park	325	399	320	38,362	1,940,429
St. Louis	Busch Stadium	336	400	335	43,975	3,093,954
San Diego	Petco Park	336	396	322	42,685	2,143,018
San Francisco	AT&T Park	339	399	309	41,503	3,387,303
Washington	Nationals Park	336	402	335	41,546	1,940,478

Arizona Diamondbacks

Office Address: Chase Field, 401 E. Jefferson St, Phoenix, AZ 85004.
Mailing Address: P.O. Box 2095, Phoenix, AZ 85001.
Telephone: (602) 462-6500. **Fax:** (602) 462-6599. **Website:** www.dbacks.com

OWNERSHIP

Managing General Partner: Ken Kendrick.
General Partners: Mike Chipman, Jeff Royer.

Business Operations
President/CEO: Derrick Hall.
Executive Vice President, Business Operations: Cullen Maxey. **Special Assistants to President/CEO:** Luis Gonzalez, Roland Hemond. **Military Affairs Specialist:** Captain Jack Ensch. **Executive Assistant to President/CEO:** Brooke Mitchell. **Executive Assistant to Executive VP, Business Operations:** Katy Bernham.

Broadcasting
VP, Broadcasting: Scott Geyer. **Senior Director, Game Operations/Multi-Media Productions:** Rob Weinheimer. **Senior Manager, Multi-Media Productions:** Jon Willey.

Ken Kendrick

Corporate Partnerships/Marketing
VP, Corporate Partnerships: Steve Mullins. **Director, Corporate Partnership Services:** Kerri White. **Senior Director, Marketing:** Karina Bohn. **Senior Manager, Marketing/Promotions:** Dustin Payne. **Senior Marketing Media Specialist:** Rayme Lofgren. **Ticket Sales/Marketing Analyst I:** John Prewitt.

Finance
Executive VP/CFO: Tom Harris. **VP, Finance:** Craig Bradley. **Director, Financial Management/Purchasing:** Jeff Jacobs. **Director, Accounting:** Chris James. **Executive Assistant to Managing General Partner/CFO:** Sandy Cox.

Legal
Senior VP/General Counsel: Nona Lee. **Senior Director, Legal Affairs/Associate General Counsel:** Caleb Jay.

Community Affairs
VP, Corporate/Community Impact: Debbie Castaldo. **Manager, Community Programs:** Tara Trzinski. **Manager, Community Events:** Robert Itzkowitz.

Communications/Media Relations
Senior VP, Communications: Josh Rawitch. **Director, Publications:** Josh Greene. **Director, Player/Media Relations:** Casey Wilcox. **Manager, Player/Media Relations:** Patrick O'Connell. **Coordinator, Communications:** Jim Myers.

Special Projects/Fan Experience
Senior Director, Special Projects: Graham Rossini. **Director, Baseball Outreach/Development:** Jeff Rodin.

2012 SCHEDULE

Standard Game Times: 6:40 p.m.; Sun. 1:10.

APRIL	21-23 . . . Los Angeles (NL)	5-8. . . . . Los Angeles (NL)
6-8. . . . . . . San Francisco	25-27 . . . . Milwaukee	13-15 . . . .at Chicago (NL)
10-12 . . . . . at San Diego	28-30 . . . at San Francisco	16-19 . . . . . .at Cincinnati
13-15 . . . . . . at Colorado		20-22 . . . . Houston
16-18 . . . . Pittsburgh	**JUNE**	23-25 . . . . Colorado
19-22 . . . . Atlanta	1-3. . . . . . . at San Diego	26-29 . . . . New York (NL)
23-25 . . . . . Philadelphia	5-7. . . . . Colorado	30-31 . at Los Angeles (NL)
27-30 . . . . . . at Miami	8-10 . . . . Oakland	
	12-14 . . . . .at Texas	**AUGUST**
MAY	15-17 . at Los Angeles (AL)	1 . . . . at Los Angeles (NL)
1-3. . . . . at Washington	18-20 . . . . Seattle	3-5. . . . . at Philadelphia
4-6. . . . at New York (NL)	22-24 . . . . Chicago (NL)	6-9. . . . . . at Pittsburgh
7-9. . . . . St. Louis	26-28 . . . . . . at Atlanta	10-12 . . . . . Washington
11-13 . . . . . San Francisco	29-30 . . . . . at Milwaukee	14-16 . . . . . .at St. Louis
14-15 . at Los Angeles (NL)		17-19 . . . . . .at Houston
16-17 . . . . . at Colorado	**JULY**	20-23 . . . . .Miami
18-20 . . . . .at Kansas City	2-4. . . . . San Diego	24-26 . . . . San Diego
		27-29 . . . . . . Cincinnati
		30-31 . at Los Angeles (NL)
		SEPTEMBER
		1-2. . . at Los Angeles (NL)
		3-5. . . . . at San Francisco
		7-9. . . . . . at San Diego
		11-12 . . .Los Angeles (NL)
		14-16 . . . . . San Francisco
		18-20 . . . . San Diego
		21-24 . . . . . at Colorado
		25-27 . . . at San Francisco
		28-30 . . . . Chicago (NL)
		OCTOBER
		1-3. . . . . .Colorado

GENERAL INFORMATION

Stadium (year opened): Chase Field (1998).
Team Colors: Sedona Red, Sonoran Sand and Black.
Player Representative: Ian Kennedy.
Home Dugout: Third Base.
Playing Surface: Grass.

Manager, Spring Training Operations/GM, Salt River Fields: David Dunne.

Human Resources/Information Technology
Senior VP, Chief Human Resources/Diversity Officer: Marian Rhodes. **HR Coordinator:** Diana Rodriguez. **VP, Chief Information Officer:** Bob Zweig. **Director, Business Systems/Applications:** Craig Pozen.

Stadium Operations
VP, Facility Operations/Event Services: Russ Amaral. **Senior Director, Security:** Sean Maguire. **Senior Manager, Security:** Greg Green. **Director, Facility Services:** Jim Hawkins. **Director, Engineering:** Jim White. **Director, Event Services:** Bryan White. **Event Coordinator:** Jeff Gomez. **Head Groundskeeper:** Grant Trenbeath.

Ticket Sales
Telephone: (602) 514-8400. **Fax:** (602) 462-4141.
Senior VP, Ticket Sales/Marketing: John Fisher. **VP, Business Development:** Jason Howard. **Director, Season Ticket Services:** Cory Parsons. **Senior Director, Business Strategy/Operations:** Kenny Farrell. **Senior Manager, Ticket Operations:** Luis Calderon. **Senior Manager, Ticket Operations:** Josh Simon.

Travel/Clubhouse
Senior Director, Team Travel/Home Clubhouse Manager: Roger Riley. **Manager, Equipment/Visiting Clubhouse:** Bob Doty.

BASEBALL OPERATIONS
Executive VP/General Manager: Kevin Towers. **Assistant GM:** Billy Ryan. **VP/Special Assistant to GM:** Bob Gebhard. **Special Assistant to GM/Major League Scout:** Bill Bryk. **Special Assistant to GM:** Jerry Krause. **Special Assistant to GM/Advance Scout:** Mark Weidemaier. **VP, Latin America Operations:** Junior Noboa. **Director, Baseball Operations:** Ryan Isaac. **Baseball Operations Assistant:** Sam Eaton. **Major League Video Coordinator:** Allen Campbell. **Administrative Assistant:** Kristyn Pierce.

Major League Staff
Manager: Kirk Gibson.
Coaches: Bench—Alan Trammell; **Pitching**—Charles Nagy; **Batting**—Don Baylor; **First Base**—Eric Young; **Third Base**—Matt Williams; **Bullpen**—Glenn Sherlock.

Medical/Training
Club Physicians: Dr. Michael Lee, Dr. Roger McCoy. **Head Trainer:** Ken Crenshaw. **Assistant Trainer:** P.J. Mainville. **Strength/Conditioning Coordinator:** Nate Shaw. **Manual/Performance Therapist:** Neil Rampe.

Kevin Towers

Minor Leagues
Telephone: (602) 462-6500. **Fax:** (602) 462-6425.
Director, Player Development: Mike Bell. **Assistant Director, Player Development:** Quinton McCracken. **Director, Minor League Administration:** Susan Webner.
Coordinators: Jeff Pico (field), Mel Stottlemyre, Jr. (pitching), Alan Cockrell (hitting), Tony Perezchica (infield), Joel Youngblood (outfield/baserunning), Bill Plummer (catching), Carlos Hernandez (short-season catching), Hatuey Mendoza (Latin Liaison), Luis Urueta (short-season field), Ryan DiPanfilo (medical), David Rivera (assistant medical), Brett McCabe (strength), Andrew Hauser (manual performance), Jim Currigan (video), Bob Bensinger (complex).

Farm System
Class	Club (League)	Manager	Hitting Coach	Pitching Coach
Triple-A	Reno (PCL)	Brett Butler	Rick Burleson	Mike Parrott
Double-A	Mobile (SL)	Turner Ward	Jay Bell	Dan Carlson
High A	Visalia (CAL)	Jason Hardtke	Jacob Cruz	Doug Drabek
Low A	South Bend (MWL)	Mark Haley	Bobby Smith	Wellington Cepeda
Short-season	Yakima (NWL)	Audo Vicente	Jason Camilli	Doug Bochtler
Rookie	Missoula (PIO)	Andy Green	JR House	Gil Heredia
Rookie	Diamondbacks (AZL)	Hector de la Cruz	Robby Hammock	Jeff Bajenaru

Scouting
Telephone: (602) 462-6500. **Fax:** (602) 462-6425.
Director, Scouting: Ray Montgomery. **Director, International Scouting:** Carlos Gomez. **Director, Pacific Rim Operations:** Mack Hayashi. **Special Assistant, Pacific Rim Operations:** Jim Marshall. **Scouting Coordinator:** Brendan Domaracki. **Major League Scouts/Special Assistants to GM:** Bill Bryk (Schererville, IN), Todd Greene (Alpharetta, GA), Mike Berger (Oakmont, PA). **Pro Scouts:** Brian Boehringer (Fenton, MO), Mike Brown (Naples, FL), Bob Cummings (Oak Lawn, IL), Mike Fetters (Chandler, AZ), Pat Murtaugh (West Lafayette, IN), Mike Piatnik (Winter Haven, FL), Tom Romenesko (Santee, CA), Brad Kelley (Scottsdale, AZ), Bill Gayton (San Diego, CA), Clay Daniel (Jacksonville, FL). **Independent Leagues Coordinator:** Mal Fichman (Boise, ID). **Regional Supervisors:** Spencer Graham (Gresham, OR), Greg Lonigro (Connellsville, PA), Steve McAllister (Chillicothe, IL), Howard McCullough (Greenville, NC). **Area Scouts:** Rick Matsko (Davidsville, PA), John Bartsch (Rocklin, CA), Nathan Birtwell (Nashville, TN), Rusty Pendergrass (Missouri City, MO), Todd Donovan (East Lyme, CT), Hal Kurtzman (Lake Balboa, CA), TR Lewis (Marietta, GA), Joe Mason (Millbrook, AL), Jeff Mousser (Huntington Beach, CA), James Mouton (Missouri City, TX), Donnie Reynolds (Portland, OR), Joe Robinson (St Louis, MO), JR Salinas (Dallas, TX), Rick Short (Peoria, IL), Matt Smith (Surprise, AZ), George Swain (Wilmington, NC), Frankie Thon Jr (Miami, FL), Luke Wrenn (Lakeland, FL). **International Scouts: Supervisor**—Luis Baez (Santo Domingo, DR). **Dominican Republic**—Gabriel Berroa, José Ortiz, Rafael Mateo. **Panama**—José Díaz Perez. **Nicaragua**—Julio Sanchez. **Colombia**—Luis Gonzalez. **Venezuela**—Ubaldo Heredia, Marlon Urdaneta. **Europe**—Rene Saggiadi.

Atlanta Braves

Office Address: 755 Hank Aaron Dr, Atlanta, GA 30315.
Mailing Address: PO Box 4064, Atlanta, GA 30302.
Telephone: (404) 522-7630. **Website:** www.braves.com.

Ownership
Operated/Owned By: Liberty Media.
Chairman/CEO: Terry McGuirk. **Chairman Emeritus:** Bill Bartholomay. **President:** John Schuerholz. **Senior Vice President:** Henry Aaron.

BUSINESS OPERATIONS
Executive VP, Business Operations: Mike Plant. **Senior VP/General Counsel:** Greg Heller.

Finance
Senior VP/Chief Financial Officer/Controller: Chip Moore.

Marketing, Sales
Executive VP, Sales/Marketing: Derek Schiller. **Executive Director, Marketing:** Gus Eurton. **Senior Director, Ticket Sales:** Paul Adams. **Senior Director, Corporate Sales:** Jim Allen.

Media Relations/Public Relations
Telephone: (404) 614-1556. **Fax:** (404) 614-1391.
Director, Media Relations: Brad Hainje. **Director, Public Relations:** Beth Marshall.
Publications Manager: Andy Pressley. **Public Relations Manager:** Meagan Swingle. **Media Relations Manager:** Adrienne Midgley. **Media Relations Coordinator:** Jim Misudek.

Terry McGuirk

Stadium Operations
Senior Director, Stadium Operations/Security: Larry Bowman. **Field Director:** Ed Mangan. **Director, Game Entertainment:** Scott Cunningham. **PA Announcer:** Casey Motter. **Official Scorers:** Mike Stamus, Jack Wilkinson.

Ticketing
Telephone: 404) 577-9100. **Fax:** (404) 614-2480.
Director, Ticket Sales: Paul Adams. **Director, Ticket Operations:** Anthony Esposito.

Travel, Clubhouse
Director, Team Travel/Equipment Manager: Bill Acree. **Visiting Clubhouse Manager:** John Holland.

2012 SCHEDULE
Standard Game Times: 7:10 p.m.; Fri. 7:35; Sun. 1:35.

APRIL
5 . . . . . . at New York (NL)
7-8 . . . . . at New York (NL)
9-11 . . . . . .at Houston
13-15 . . . . . . .Milwaukee
16-18 . . . .New York (NL)
19-22 . . . . at Arizona
23-25 . at Los Angeles (NL)
27-30 . . . . Pittsburgh

MAY
1-3 . . . . .Philadelphia
4-6 . . . . at Colorado
7-9 . . . . .at Chicago (NL)
11-13 . . . . . . .at St. Louis
14-15 . . . . Cincinnati
16-17 . . . . .Miami

18-20 . . . . . at Tampa Bay
21-24 . . . . . .at Cincinnati
25-27 . . . . . . Washington
28-30 . . . . St. Louis

JUNE
1-3 . . . . . . at Washington
5-7 . . . . at Miami
8-10 . . . . .Toronto
11-13 . . . . .New York (AL)
15-17 . . . . . . Baltimore
18-20 . . at New York (AL)
22-24 . . . . . . .at Boston
26-28 . . . . .Arizona
29-30 . . . . . Washington

JULY
1 . . . . Washington

2-5 . . . . . . Chicago (NL)
6-8 . . . . . at Philadelphia
13-15 . . . .New York (NL)
17-19 . . . .San Francisco
20-22 . . . . at Washington
23-25 . . . . at Miami
27-29 . . . . .Philadelphia
30-31 . . . . .Miami

AUGUST
1-2 . . . . .Miami
3-5 . . . . Houston
6-8 . . . . . at Philadelphia
10-12 . . . at New York (NL)
13-16 . . . . San Diego
17-19 . . . Los Angeles (NL)
20-22 . . . . at Washington

23-26 . . . at San Francisco
27-29 . . . . . at San Diego
31 . . . . .Philadelphia

SEPTEMBER
1-2 . . . . .Philadelphia
3-6 . . . . .Colorado
7-9 . . . . at New York (NL)
10-12 . . . . . at Milwaukee
14-16 . . . . . . Washington
17-19 . . . . at Miami
21-23 . . . . at Philadelphia
25-27 . . . . .Miami
28-30 . . . .New York (NL)

OCTOBER
1-3 . . . . at Pittsburgh

GENERAL INFORMATION
Stadium (year opened): Turner Field (1997).
Team Colors: Red, white and blue.

Player Representative: Unavailable.
Home Dugout: First Base.
Playing Surface: Grass.

BASEBALL OPERATIONS

Telephone: (404) 522-7630. **Fax:** (404) 614-3308.
Executive VP/General Manager: Frank Wren.
Assistant GM: Bruce Manno. **Executive Assistants:** Annie Lee, Chris Rice.

Frank Wren

Major League Staff
Manager: Fredi Gonzalez
Coaches: Bench—Carlos Tosca; **Pitching**—Roger McDowell; **Hitting**—Greg Walker; **First Base**—Terry Pendleton; **Third Base**—Brian Snitker; **Bullpen**—Eddie Perez.

Medical, Training
Head Team Physician: Dr. Xavier Duralde.
Trainer: Jeff Porter. **Assistant Trainer:** Jim Lovell. **Strength/Conditioning Coach:** Phil Falco.

Player Development
Telephone: (404) 522-7630. **Fax:** (404) 614-1350.
Director, Minor League Operations: Ronnie Richardson. **Special Assistant to the GM, Player Development:** Jose Martinez. **Baseball Operations Assistants:** Matt Grabowski, Ron Knight
Minor League Field Coordinator: Dave Trembley. **Pitching Coordinator:** Dave Wallace. **Hitting Coordinator:** Don Long, Roving Instructors: Joe Breeden (catching), Doug Dascenzo (outfield/baserunning), Luis Lopez (infield), Rick Slate (strength/conditioning).

Farm System

Class	Club (League)	Manager	Coach	Pitching Coach
Triple-A	Gwinnett (IL)	Dave Brundage	Jamie Dismuke	Marty Reed
Double-A	Mississippi (SL)	Aaron Holbert	Garey Ingram	Mike Alvarez
High A	Lynchburg (CL)	Luis Salazar	Bobby Moore	Derek Botelho
Low A	Rome (SAL)	Randy Ingle	Carlos Mendez	Derrick Lewis
Rookie	Danville (APP)	Jonathan Schuerholz	D.J. Boston	Gabriel Luckert
Rookie	Braves (GCL)	Rocket Wheeler	Rick Albert	Vladimir Nunez
Rookie	Braves (DSL)	Francisco Santiesteban	Tommy Herrera	William Martinez

Scouting
Telephone: (404) 522-7630. **Fax:** (404) 614-1350.
Director, Pro Scouting: John Coppolella.
Special Assistants to GM/Major League Scouts: Dick Balderson (Englewood, CO), Dom Chiti (Auburndale, FL), Matt Carroll (Erdenheim, PA), Jim Fregosi (Tarpon Springs, FL), Bob Johnson (University Park, FL), Jeff Wren (Senoia, GA). **Professional Scouts:** Rod Gilbreath (Lilburn, GA), Lloyd Merritt (Myrtle Beach, SC), John Stewart (Granville, NY).
Director, Scouting: Tony DeMacio. **Office Coordinator, Scouting:** Dixie Keller.
National Crosscheckers: John Flannery (Austin, TX), Deron Rombach (Mansfield, TX). **Regional Crosscheckers: West**—Tom Davis (Ripon, CA), **Southwest**—James "Bump" Merriweather (Glendale, AZ), **East**—Steve Fleming (Louisa, VA), **Midwest**—Terry R. Tripp (Harrisburg, IL), **Southeast**—Brian Bridges (Rome, GA).
Area Scouts: John Barron (Cameron, TX), Kevin Barry (Kinmundy, IL), Billy Best (Holly Spings, NC), Bill Bliss (Phoenix, AZ), Erwin Bryant (Lexington, KY), Hugh Buchanan (Snellville, GA), Brett Evert (Salem, OR), Ralph Garr (Richmond, TX), Buddy Hernandez (Orlando, FL), Gene Kerns (Hagerstown, MD), Chris Knabenshue (Fort Collins, CO), Steve Leavitt (Huntington Beach, CA), Dennis Sheehan (Glasco, NY), Don Thomas (Geismar, LA), Terry C. Tripp (Raleigh, IL), Gerald Turner (Bedford, TX). **Part-Time Scouts:** Dick Adams (Lincoln, CA), Stu Cann (Bradley, IL), Dewayne Kitts (Moncks Corner, SC), Abraham Martinez (Santa Isabel, PR), Lou Sanchez (Miami, FL).
Director, International Scouting: Johnny Almaraz.
Assistant Director, International Scouting/Operations: Jose Martinez. **International Coordinators: Central American Supervisor**—Luis Ortiz (San Antonio, TX), **Eastern Rim**—Phil Dale (Victoria, Australia).
International Area Supervisors: Matias Laureano (Dominican Republic), Hiroyuki Oya (Japan), Rolando Petit (Venezuela), Manuel Samaniego (Mexico). **Part-Time Scouts:** Neil Burke (Australia), Nehomar Caldera (Venezuela), Junior Carrion (Dominican Republic), Jeremy Chou (Taiwan), Carlos Garcia Roque (Colombia), Raul Gonzalez (Panama), Remmy Hernandez (Dominican Republic), Alfredo Molina (Ecuador), Rafael Motooka (Brazil), Nestor Perez (Spain), Jefferson Romero D'Lima (Venezuela), Eduardo Rosario (Colombia), Miguel Theran (Colombia), Marvin Throneberry (Nicaragua), Carlos Torres (Venezuela).

Baltimore Orioles

Office Address: 333 W Camden St, Baltimore, MD 21201.
Telephone: (888) 848-BIRD. **Fax:** (410) 547-6272.
E-mail Address: birdmail@orioles.com. **Website:** www.orioles.com.

Ownership

Operated By: The Baltimore Orioles Limited Partnership Inc.
Chairman/CEO: Peter Angelos.

BUSINESS OPERATIONS

Executive Vice President: John Angelos. **Executive VP, Business Operations:** Doug Duennes. **VP/Special Liaison to Chairman:** Lou Kousouris. **VP, Planning/Development:** Janet Marie Smith. **General Legal Counsel:** Russell Smouse. **Director, Human Resources:** Lisa Tolson. **Director, Information Systems:** James Kline.

Peter Angelos

Finance

VP/CFO: Robert Ames. **Director, Finance:** Michael D. Hoppes, CPA.

Public Relations/Communications

Telephone: (410) 547-6150. **Fax:** (410) 547-6272.
Director, Communications: Greg Bader. **Director, Public Relations:** Monica Barlow. **Manager, Media Relations:** Jeff Lantz. **Coordinator, Baseball Information:** Jay Moskowitz. **Director, Promotion/Community Initiatives:** Kristen Schultz.

Ballpark Operations

Director, Ballpark Operations: Kevin Cummings. **Head Groundskeeper:** Nicole Sherry.
PA Announcer: Unavailable. **Official Scorers:** Jim Henneman, Marc Jacobson.

Ticketing

Telephone: (888) 848-BIRD. **Fax:** (410) 547-6270.
Director, Sales/Fan Services: Neil Aloise. **Assistant Director, Sales:** Mark Hromalik. **Ticket Manager:** Audrey Brown.

Travel/Clubhouse

Coordinator, Team Travel: Kevin Buck.
Equipment Manager (Home): Jim Tyler. **Equipment Manager (Road):** Fred Tyler.

2012 SCHEDULE

Standard Game Times: 7:05 p.m; Sun. 1:35

APRIL		
6-8 . . . . Minnesota	18-20 . . . . at Washington	2-4 . . . . .at Seattle
9-11 . . . . .New York (AL)	21-23 . . . . Boston	5-8 . . . at Los Angeles (AL)
13-15 . . . . . . at Toronto	25-27 . . . . . . Kansas City	13-15 . . . . Detroit
16-19 . . . .at Chicago (AL)	28-30 . . . . at Toronto	16-19 . . . . . at Minnesota
20-22 . at Los Angeles (AL)		20-23 . . . . . .at Cleveland
24-26 . . . . .Toronto	JUNE	24-26 . . . . . . .Tampa Bay
27-29 . . . . Oakland	1-3 . . . . . . at Tampa Bay	27-29 . . . . Oakland
30 . . . . . at New York (AL)	5-7 . . . . .at Boston	30-31 . . . at New York (AL)
	8-10 . . . . . .Philadelphia	
MAY	12-14 . . . . Pittsburgh	AUGUST
1-2 . . . . . at New York (AL)	15-17 . . . . at Atlanta	1 . . . . . . at New York (AL)
4-6 . . . . .at Boston	18-20 . . .at New York (NL)	3-5 . . . . . . at Tampa Bay
7-10 . . . . Texas	22-24 . . . . . .Washington	6-8 . . . . Seattle
11-13 . . . . . .Tampa Bay	26-27 . . . Los Angeles (AL)	9-12 . . . . Kansas City
14-15 . . . .New York (AL)	28-30 . . . . Cleveland	14-16 . . . . Boston
16-17 . . . .at Kansas City		17-19 . . . . . . .at Detroit
	JULY	20-22 . . . . .at Texas
	1 . . . . Cleveland	

2-4 . . . . .at Seattle	SEPTEMBER
24-26 . . . . .Toronto	1-2 . . . . at New York (AL)
27-30 . . . . Chicago (AL)	3-5 . . . . at Toronto
31 . . . . . at New York (AL)	6-9 . . . . . . .New York (AL)
	11-13 . . . . . . .Tampa Bay
	14-16 . . . . . . .at Oakland
	17-19 . . . . . . .at Seattle
	21-23 . . . . .at Boston
	24-26 . . . . .Toronto
	28-30 . . . . Boston
	OCTOBER
	1-3 . . . . . . at Tampa Bay

GENERAL INFORMATION

Stadium (year opened): Oriole Park at Camden Yards (1992).
Team Colors: Orange, black and white.

Player Representative: Unavailable.
Home Dugout: First Base.
Playing Surface: Grass.

BASEBALL OPERATIONS

Telephone: (410) 547-6107. **Fax:** (410) 547-6271.
Executive Vice President, Baseball Operations: Dan Duquette.
Special Assistants to the Executive VP, Baseball Operations: Brady Anderson, Lee Thomas. **Director, Baseball Administration:** Tripp Norton. **Assistant Director, Major League Operations:** Ned Rice. **Coordinator, Baseball Operations:** Bill Wilkes. **Coordinator, Baseball Analytics:** Sarah Gelles. **Video Coordinator:** Michael Silverman. **Advance Scouting Coordinator:** Ben Werthan.

Dan Duquette

Major League Staff
Manager: Buck Showalter.
Coaches: Bench—John Russell; **Pitching**—Rick Adair; **Batting**—Jim Presley; **First Base**—Wayne Kirby; **Third Base**—Demarlo Hale; **Bullpen**—Bill Castro.

Medical, Training
Club Physician: Dr. William Goldiner. **Club Physician, Orthopedics:** Dr. John Wilckens. **Head Athletic Trainer:** Richie Bancells. **Assistant Athletic Trainer:** Brian Ebel. **Strength/Conditioning Coach:** Joe Hogarty.

Player Development
Telephone: (410) 547-6120. **Fax:** (410) 547-6298.
Director, Player Personnel: John Stockstill. **Assistant Director, Player Development/Scouting:** Mike Snyder. **Coordinator, Minor League Administration:** J Maria Arellano. **Coordinator, Minor League Instruction:** Brian Graham. **Director, Pitching Development:** Rick Peterson. **Coordinator, Minor League Hitting:** Mike Boulanger. **Coordinator, Infield/Baserunning:** Mike Bordick. **Organizational Hitting Instructor/Evaluator:** Terry Crowley. **Coordinator, Sarasota Operations:** Dave Schmidt. **Administrator, Sarasota Operations:** Dave Schmidt.
Roving Instructors: Butch Davis (outfield), Eric Cormell, Bobby Dickerson, Don Werner (catching). **Medical Coordinator:** Dave Walker. **Latin American Medical Coordinator:** Manny Lopez. **Strength/Conditioning Coordinator:** Ryan Driscoll. **Rehab Coordinators:** Scott McGregor (pitchers), Cesar Devarez (position players). **Minor League Equipment Manager:** Jake Parker.

Farm System

Class	Club (League)	Manager	Hitting Coach	Pitching Coach
Triple-A	Norfolk (IL)	Ron Johnson	Denny Walling	Mike Griffin
Double-A	Bowie (EL)	Gary Kendall	Denny Hocking	Kennie Steenstra
High A	Frederick (CL)	Orlando Gomez	Jose Hernandez	Blaine Beatty
Low A	Delmarva (SAL)	Ryan Minor	Einar Diaz	Troy Mattes
Short-season	Aberdeen (NYP)	Gary Allenson	Brad Komminsk	Alan Mills
Rookie	Orioles (GCL)	Ramon Sambo	Milt May	Larry Jaster
Rookie	Orioles (DSL)	Miguel Jabalera	B. Adames/R. Lubo	R. Perez/D. Pascual

Professional Scouting
Major League Scouts: Dave Engle (San Diego, CA), Bruce Kison (Bradenton, FL), Lee MacPhail IV, (Shaker Heights, OH), Fred Uhlman Sr (Baltimore, MD).

Amateur Scouting
Telephone: (410) 547-6187. **Fax:** (410) 547-6298.
Director, Scouting: Gary Rajsich. **Scouting Administrator:** Marcy Zerhusen.
National Crosschecker: Ron Hopkins (Seattle WA). **National Crosschecker:** Dan Haas (Ft Myers, FL). **Midwest Crosschecker:** Jim Richardson (Marlow, OK). **West Coast Crosschecker:** David Blume (Elk Grove, CA). **Area Scouts:** Dean Albany (Baltimore, MD), Juan Alvarez (Miami, FL), Adrian Dorsey (Florence, KY), Thom Dreier (Houston, TX), Todd Frohwirth (Waukesha, WI), Christopher Gale (Raleigh, NC), John Gillette (Gilbert, AZ), Jim Howard (Clifton Park, NY), Ernie Jacobs (Wichita, KS), David Jennings (Spanish Fort, AL), James Keller (Sacramento, CA), Ted Lekas (Brewster, MA), Arthur McConnehead (Atlanta, GA), Rich Morales (Pacifica, CA), Mark Ralston (Carlsbad, CA), Bob Szymkowski (Chicago, IL), Jim Thrift (Sarasota, FL), Brandon Verley (Portland, OR), Scott Walter (Manhattan Beach, CA).
Part-Time Scouts: Darin Blair (Lawrenceville, IL), Larry Chase (Pearcy, AR), Ellis Dungan (Charlotte, NC), Kendal Guthrie (Flower Mound, TX), Tim Norris (Baltimore, MD), Harvey Shapiro (Bloomfield, CT).

International Operations
Exececutive Director, International Recruiting: Fred Ferreira. **Executive Director, International Baseball:** Ray Poitevint.
Director, International Operations: David Stockstill. **Director, Dominican Academy:** Felipe Alou Jr.
International Scouts: Jesus Alfaro (Venezuela), Carlos Bernhardt (Dominican), Calvin Maduro (Caribbean), Ernst Meyer (Curacao), Salvador Ramirez (Dominican), Brett Ward (Australia). **International Part-Time Scouts:** Enrique Constante (Dominican Republic), Amaro Costa (Argentina), Domingo DeLaCruz (Dominican Republic), Jorge Franco (Colombia), Ton Hofstede (Curacao/Netherlands/Europe), Ronald Hurtarte (Guatemala), Juan Linares (Dominican Republic), William Morales (Colombia), Carlos Moreno (Venezuela), Kristian Perreira (Venezuela), Ramon Rivera (Dominican Republic).

Boston Red Sox

Office Address: Fenway Park, 4 Yawkey Way, Boston, MA 02215.
Telephone: (617) 226-6000. **Fax:** (617) 226-6416.
Website: www.redsox.com

Ownership
Principal Owner: John Henry.
Chairman: Thomas C. Werner. **President/CEO:** Larry Lucchino. **Vice Chairmen:** David Ginsberg, Phillip Morse.

BUSINESS OPERATIONS
Executive Vice President/COO: Sam Kennedy. **Executive VP, Business Affairs:** Jonathan Gilula. **Senior VP, Fenway Affairs:** Larry Cancro. **Manager, Fenway Affairs:** Beth Krudys. **Senior VP/Executive Director, Red Sox Foundation:** Meg Vaillancourt. **Director, Business Development:** Tim Zue. **Senior Advisor, Baseball Projects:** Jeremy Kapstein. **General Counsel, Fenway Sports Group:** Ed Weiss. **Senior VP/Assistant General Counsel:** Jennifer Flynn. **Senior VP/Special Counsel:** David Friedman. **VP/Club Counsel:** Elaine Weddington Steward.

Larry Lucchino

Finance/Human Resources/Information Technology
Senior VP/CFO: Steve Fitch. **VP/Controller:** Mark Solitro. **Financial Advisor to CEO:** Jeff White. **Senior Advisor, Finance/Accounting:** Bob Furbush. **Director, Finance:** Ryan Oremus. **Payroll Administrator:** Mauricio Rosas. **Senior Manager, Accounting:** Cathy Fahy. **Senior Accountant:** Mark Sirota. **Manager, Financial Planning/Analysis:** Ryan Scafidi. **VP, Human Resources/Office Administration:** Amy Waryas. **Senior Human Resources Manager:** Patty Vattes. **Director, IT:** Steve Conley. **Director, Business Applications:** Heidi Labritz.

Sales/Corporate Marketing/Fenway Enterprises
Senior VP, Corporate Partnerships: Troup Parkinson. **Director, Client Services:** Marcell Bhangoo. **Director, Fenway Enterprises:** Carrie Campbell. **Assistant Director, Fenway Enterprises:** Marcita Thompson. **Event Services Manager:** Chris Jordan. **Senior Manager, Client Services:** Carole Alkins. **Senior Manager, EMC/Dugout Services:** Erin Donovan.

Public Affairs/Media/Broadcasting/Marketing/Community Relations
Director, Media Relations: Pam Ganley. **Manager, Media Relations:** Leah Tobin. **Senior Manager, Public Affairs:** Zineb Curran. **Manager, Public Affairs:** Mike Olano. **Manager, Photography:** Mike Ivins. **VP/Team Historian Emeritus:** Dick Bresciani. **Director, Publications:** Debbie Matson. **Senior VP, Marketing/Brand Development:** Adam Grossman. **Director, Marketing/Broadcast Services:** Colin Burch. **Manager, Social Media/Marketing:** Ann Unger. **Assistant Director, Community Relations/Player Relations:** Sarah Narracci

Business/Ballpark Operations/Development
Director, Planning/Development: Paul Hanlon. **Director, Ballpark Operations:** Pete Nesbit. **Director, Concessions/Merchandise Operations:** Jeff Goldenberg. **Director, Grounds:** Dave Mellor. **Director, Security:** Charlie Cellucci.

2012 SCHEDULE
Standard Game Times: 7:10 p.m.; Sun. 1:35

APRIL		
5 . . . . .at Detroit	18-20 . . . . at Philadelphia	2-4. . . . . .at Oakland	28-30 . at Los Angeles (AL)
7-8. . . . . .at Detroit	21-23 . . . . .at Baltimore	6-8. . . . . .New York (AL)	31 . . . . .at Oakland
9-11 . . . . at Toronto	25-27 . . . . . .Tampa Bay	13-15 . . . . at Tampa Bay	
13-16 . . . . . . .Tampa Bay	28-31 . . . . Detroit	16-19 . . . . Chicago (AL)	**SEPTEMBER**
17-18 . . . . Texas		20-22 . . . . .Toronto	1-2. . . . . . . .at Oakland
20-22 . . . . .New York (AL)	**JUNE**	23-25 . . . . .at Texas	3-5. . . . . .at Seattle
23-25 . . . at Minnesota	1-3. . . . . at Toronto	27-29 . . . at New York (AL)	7-9. . . . . .Toronto
26-29 . . . at Chicago (AL)	5-7. . . . . Baltimore	30-31 . . . . Detroit	11-13 . . . . .New York (AL)
30 . . . . Oakland	8-10 . . . . . . Washington		14-16 . . . . . at Toronto
	11-13 . . . . at Miami	**AUGUST**	17-20 . . . . at Tampa Bay
MAY	15-17 . . . .at Chicago (NL)	1 . . . . Detroit	21-23 . . . . Baltimore
1-2. . . . . Oakland	19-21 . . . . .Miami	2-5. . . . . .Minnesota	25-26 . . . . . .Tampa Bay
4-6. . . . . Baltimore	22-24 . . . . Atlanta	6-8. . . . . Texas	28-30 . . . .at Baltimore
7-9. . . . . .at Kansas City	25-27 . . . . .Toronto	9-12 . . . . . .at Cleveland	
10-13 . . . . Cleveland	28-30 . . . . . . .at Seattle	14-16 . . . . .at Baltimore	**OCTOBER**
14-15 . . . . Seattle		17-19 . . . at New York (AL)	1-3. . . . . at New York (AL)
16-17 . . . . at Tampa Bay	**JULY**	21-23 . . . Los Angeles (AL)	
	1 . . . . .at Seattle	24-27 . . . . . . Kansas City	

GENERAL INFORMATION

Stadium (year opened): Fenway Park (1912).
Team Colors: Navy blue, red and white.
Player Representative: Unavailable.
Home Dugout: First Base.
Playing Surface: Grass.

Director Emeritus, Grounds: Joe Mooney. Assistant Director, Grounds: Jason Griffeth. Manager, Grounds: Chris Williams. Facilities Superintendent: Donnie Gardner. Director, Florida Business Operations: Katie Haas.

VP, Fan Services/Entertainment: Sarah McKenna. Manager, Entertainment/Special Event Operations: Dan Lyons. Manager, Fan Services/Entertainment: Stephanie Maneikis. Manager, Special Projects: Marty Ray. Senior Manager, Television Production: John Carter. Senior Manager, Video/Scoreboard Operations: Sarah Logan. Manager, Game/ TV Production: Matt Bair. PA Announcer: Carl Beane.

Ticketing Services/Operations
Telephone: 888-REDSOX6.

Senior VP, Ticketing: Ron Bumgarner. VP, Ticketing: Richard Beaton. Director, Ticketing: Naomi Calder. Assistant Director, Ticketing/Season Ticket Services: Joe Matthews. Manager, Ticket Operations: Gary Goldberg. Manager, Ticket Services: Jenean Rombola. Manager, Ticket Accounting/ Administrations: Sean Carragher. Manager, Ticket Fulfillment/Systems: Peter Fahey. Senior Manager, Premium Sales/New Business Development: Corey Bowdre.

BASEBALL OPERATIONS
Telephone: (617) 226-6000.
Executive VP/General Manager: Ben Cherington.

VP/Assistant GM: Mike Hazen. VP/Assistant GM: Brian O'Halloran. VP/Player Personnel: Allard Baird. Director, Player Personnel: Dave Finley. Director, Major League Operations: Zack Scott. Director, Baseball Information Services: Tom Tippett. Assistant, Baseball Operations: Mike Murov. Software Developer: Shawn O'Rourke. Traveling Secretary: Jack McCormick. Executive Assistant: Erin Cox. Senior Advisor: Bill James.

Ben Cherington

Major League Staff
Manager: Bobby Valentine.

Coaches: Bench—Tim Bogar; Pitching—Bob McClure; Hitting—Dave Magadan; First Base—Alex Ochoa; Third Base—Jerry Royster; Bullpen—Gary Tuck; Staff Assistant—Randy Niemann.

Medical/Training
Head Athletic Trainer: Rick Jameyson. Head Physical Therapist: Mike Reinold. Head Team Internist: Dr. Larry Ronan. Head Team Orthopedist: Dr. Peter Asnis. Medical Operations Coordinator: Jim Rowe. Strength/Conditioning Coach: Pat Sandora.

Player Development
Senior Director, Minor League Operations: Raquel Ferreira. Director, Player Development: Ben Crockett. Assistant Director, Florida Baseball Operations: Ethan Faggett. Field Coordinator: David Howard. Director, Dominican Academy: Jesus Alou. Latin American Field Coordinator: Jose Zapata. Latin American Pitching Coordinator: Goose Gregson. Minor League Physical Therapist: Chip Simpson. Minor League Athletic Training Coordinator: Paul Buchheit. Sports Psychology Coach: Bob Tewksbury. Coordinator, Player Development Programs: Duncan Webb. Roving Instructors: Andy Fox (infield), Chad Epperson (catching), Victor Rodriguez (hitting), Ralph Treuel (pitching).

Farm System

Class	Club (League)	Manager	Coach(es)	Pitching Coach
Triple-A	Pawtucket (IL)	Arnie Beyeler	Gerald Perry	Rich Sauveur
Double-A	Portland (EL)	Kevin Boles	Dave Joppie	Bob Kipper
High A	Salem (CL)	Billy McMillon	Rich Gedman	Kevin Walker
Low A	Greenville (SAL)	Carlos Febles	Darren Fenster	Dick Such
Short-season	Lowell (NYP)	Bruce Crabbe	Nelson Paulino	Paul Abbott
Rookie	Red Sox (GCL)	George Lombard	UL Washington/D Tomlin	Walter Miranda
Rookie	Red Sox (DSL)	Jose Zapata	Unavailable	A Telemaco/O Lira

Scouting
Director, Amateur Scouting: Amiel Sawdaye. Assistant Director, Amateur Scouting: Gus Quattlebaum. Director, Professional Scouting: Jared Porter. Advance Scouting Coordinator: Steve Langone. Coordinator, Amateur Scouting: Jared Banner. Special Assignment Scouts: Galen Carr (Burlington, VT), Mark Wasinger (El Paso, TX). Major League Advance Scout: Dana LeVangie (East Bridgewater, MA). Major League Scouts: Bob Hamelin (Charlotte, NC), Steve Peck (Scottsdale, AZ). Professional Scouts: Jaymie Bane (Parrish, FL), Nate Field (Denver, CO), David Keller (Houston, TX), Dave Klipstein (Roanoke, TX), John Lombardo (Grand Prairie, TX), Matt Mahoney (Scottsdale, AZ). Professional Scouting Consultants: Joe McDonald (Lakeland, FL), Joe Nelson (West Palm Beach, FL).

National Crosschecker: Mike Rikard (Durham, NC). Regional Crosscheckers: Midwest—Fred Petersen (Horshoe Bay, TX), Tom Allison (Phoenix, AZ), West—Dan Madsen (Murrieta, CA). Area Scouts: Jon Adkins (Wayne, WV), Tom Battista (Thousand Oaks, CA), Steve Bowden (Kingwood, TX), Quincy Boyd (Harrisburg, NC), Chris Calciano (Ocean View, DE), Raymond Fagnant (East Granby, CT), Laz Gutierrez (Miramar, FL), Blair Henry (Naperville, IL), Tim Hyers (Loganville, GA), Chris Mears (Oklahoma City, OK), Edgar Perez (Vega Baja, PR), Pat Portugal (Seattle, WA), Chris Pritchett (Vancouver, BC), Jim Robinson (Arlington, TX), Demond Smith (Sacramento, CA), Anthony Turco (Tampa, FL), Danny Watkins (Tuscaloosa, AL), Vaughn Williams (Phoenix, AZ), Jim Woodward (Claremont, CA).

Director, International Scouting: Eddie Romero. Coordinator, Latin American Scouting/International Crosschecker: Todd Claus. International Crosschecker: Rolando Pino. Dominican Republic Scouting Supervisor: Manny Nanita. Coordinator, Pacific Rim Scouting: Jon Deeble. International Scouts: Angel Escobar (Venezuela), Ernesto Gomez (Venezuela), Fernando Veracierto (Venezuela), Victor Torres (Dominican Republic), Victor Rodriguez Jr, (Dominican Republic).

Chicago Cubs

Office Address: Wrigley Field, 1060 W. Addison St, Chicago, IL 60613.
Telephone: (773) 404-2827. **Fax:** (773) 404-4129.
E-mail Address: cubs@cubs.com. **Website:** www.cubs.com.

Ownership
Chairman: Tom Ricketts. **Board Members:** Laura Ricketts, Pete Ricketts, Todd Ricketts. **President:** Crane Kenney.

BUSINESS OPERATIONS
Phone: (773) 404-2827. **Fax:** (773) 404-4111.
Executive Vice President, Business Operations: Mark McGuire. **Executive VP, Chief Sales/Marketing Officer:** Wally Hayward. **Executive VP, Community Affairs/General Counsel:** Michael Lufrano. **VP, Ticket Sales/Service:** Colin Faulkner. **VP, Communications/Community Affairs:** Julian Green. **VP/Chief Financial Officer:** Jon Greifenkamp. **VP, Ballpark Operations:** Carl Rice. **VP, Business Development:** Alex Sugarman. **Executive Assistant to the Chairman:** Lorraine Swiatly. **Executive Coordinator, Business Operations:** Sarah Poontong.

Accounting/Human Resources
Director, Finance: Jodi Reischl. **Assistant Director, Business Development:** Jason Sondag. **Finance Manager:** Jamie Norton. **Accounting Manager:** Mike Van Poucke. **Manager, Distributions/Collections:** Theresa Bacholzky. **Senior Accountants:** Marian Greene, Aimee Sison. **Senior Director, Human Resources:** Jenifer Surma.

Tom Ricketts

Event Operations/Security
Director, Event Operations/Security: Mike Hill. **Manager, Event Operations/Security:** Julius Farrell. **Human Resources Ballpark Operations Manager:** Danielle Alexa. **Ballpark Operations Supervisor:** Bill Scott. **Head Groundskeeper:**Roger Baird. **Coordinator, Exterior Operations:** Mary Kusmirek. **Ballpark Operations Management Assistant:** Russell Johnson. **Coordinator, Office Services:** Randy Skocz. **Ballpark Events Assistant:** Stephanie Shaw.

Information Technology
Director, Information Technology: Andrew McIntyre. **Manager, Information Technology:** Sean True.

Legal/Community Affairs/Marketing
Assistant General Counsel: Lydia Wahlke. **Manager, Community Outreach/Grants/Donations:** Jennifer Dedes-Nowak. **Manager, Community Affairs/Funding/Development:** Connie Falcone. **Managing Director, Corporate Partnerships:** Samantha Coghill. **Director, Corporate Partnerships:** Michael Kirschner.

Media Relations
Director, Media Relations: Peter Chase. **Assistant Director, Media Relations:** Jason Carr. **Coordinator, Media Relations:** Dani Holmes-Kirk. **Public Relations/Marketing Specialist:** Kevin Saghy. **Assistant, Media Relations:** Dusty Harrington.

2012 SCHEDULE
Standard Game Times: 7:05 p.m., Sun. 1:20.

APRIL		
5 . . . . Washington	18-20 . . . . . Chicago (AL)	2-5 . . . . at Atlanta	24-26 . . . . Colorado
7-8 . . . . Washington	21-23 . . . . . . .at Houston	6-8 . . . . . at New York (NL)	27-30 . . . . . . .Milwaukee
9-12 . . . . . . .Milwaukee	25-27 . . . . at Pittsburgh	13-15 . . . . Arizona	31 . . . . .San Francisco
13-15 . . . . . . .at St. Louis	28-30 . . . . San Diego	17-19 . . . . .Miami	
17-19 . . . . at Miami		20-22 . . . . . . .at St. Louis	**SEPTEMBER**
20-22 . . . . Cincinnati	**JUNE**	23-25 . . . . . at Pittsburgh	1-2 . . . . . . San Francisco
23-25 . . . . St. Louis	1-4 . . . . . at San Francisco	27-29 . . . . St. Louis	3-6 . . . . . at Washington
27-30 . . . . at Philadelphia	5-7 . . . . . . at Milwaukee	30-31 . . . . Pittsburgh	7-9 . . . . . . at Pittsburgh
	8-10 . . . . . at Minnesota		10-12 . . . . . .at Houston
MAY	12-14 . . . . Detroit	**AUGUST**	14-17 . . . . . . Pittsburgh
1-3 . . . . . . .at Cincinnati	15-17 . . . . Boston	1 . . . . Pittsburgh	18-20 . . . . Cincinnati
4-6 . . . . Los Angeles (NL)	18-20 . . . .at Chicago (AL)	3-5 . . . at Los Angeles (NL)	21-23 . . . . St. Louis
7-9 . . . . Atlanta	22-24 . . . . at Arizona	6-8 . . . . . . at San Diego	25-27 . . . . . at Colorado
11-13 . . . . at Milwaukee	25-27 . . . . .New York (NL)	9-12 . . . . Cincinnati	28-30 . . . . . . at Arizona
14-15 . . . . . .at St. Louis	29-30 . . . . Houston	13-15 . . . . Houston	
16-17 . . . . .Philadelphia		17-19 . . . . .at Cincinnati	**OCTOBER**
	JULY	20-22 . . . . at Milwaukee	1-3 . . . . Houston
	1 . . . . Houston		

GENERAL INFORMATION
Stadium (year opened): Wrigley Field (1914).
Team Colors: Royal blue, red and white.

Player Representative: Unavailable.
Home Dugout: Third Base.
Playing Surface: Grass.

Ticket Operations

Assistant Director, Premier Seats/Services: Andy Blackburn. **Assistant Director, Ticket Sales:** Brian Garza. **Assistant Director, Ticket Services:** Joe Kirchen. **Assistant Director, Ticket Services:** Cale Vennum. **Manager, Premier Seats/Services:** Louis Artiaga. **Vault Room Supervisor:** Cherie Blake. **Coordinator, Ticket Sales:** Karry Kerness.

Game Day Operations

Public Address Announcer: Andrew Belleson. **Organist:** Gary Pressy. **Umpires Room Attendant:** Tom Farinella.

BASEBALL OPERATIONS

Theo Epstein

Telephone: (773) 404-2827. **Fax:** (773) 404-4111.

President/Baseball Operations: Theo Epstein. **Exec. Vice President/General Manager:** Jed Hoyer. **Assistant GM:** Randy Bush. **Assistant to the GM:** Shiraz Rehman. **Director, Pro Scouting:** Joe Bohringer. **Director, Baseball Operations:** Scott Nelson. **Assistant Director, Video/Advance Scouting:** Kyle Evans. **Senior Advisor, Baseball Operations:** Billy Williams.

Special Assistants: Ken Kravec, Dave Littlefield, Louie Eljaua. **Manager, Baseball Information:** Chuck Wasserstrom. **Manager, Statistical Analysis:** Ari Kaplan. **Traveling Secretary:** Jimmy Bank. **Executive Assistant:** Hayley DeWitte. **Major League Video Coordinator:** Naoto Masamoto. **Coordinator, Pro Scouting:** Jake Ciarrachi.

Major League Staff

Manager: Dale Sveum.

Coaches: Pitching—Chris Bosio; **Hitting**—Rudy Jaramillo; **Bench**—Jamie Quirk; **Third Base**—Pat Listach; **First Base**—Dave McKay; **Bullpen**—Lester Strode. **Staff Assistants:** Mike Borzello, Franklin Font. **Bullpen Catcher:** Andy Lane.

Medical/Training

Team Physician: Dr. Stephen Adams. **Team Orthopedist:** Dr. Stephen Gryzlo.

Orthopedic Consultant: Dr. Michael Schafer. **Director, Athletic Training:** Mark O'Neal. **Assistant Athletic Trainers:** Ed Halbur, Matt Johnson. **Major League Strength/Conditioning Coordinator:** Tim Buss.

Player Development

Telephone: (773) 404-4035. **Fax:** (773) 404-4147.

Senior VP, Scouting/Player Development: Jason McLeod. **VP, Player Personnel:** Oneri Fleita. **Manager, Player Development Administration:** Patti James. **Coordinator, Player Development/International Scouting:** Alex Suarez. **Baseball Operations Assistant:** Safdar Khan. **Field Coordinator:** Brandon Hyde. **Coordinators:** Dennis Lewallyn (pitching), James Rowson (hitting), Tom Beyers (hitting), Bill Dancy (infield), Marty Pevey (catching), Lee Tinsley (outfield/baserunning), Carmelo Martinez (Latin American field coordinator). **Minor League Training Coordinator:** Justin Sharpe. **Strength/Conditioning Coordinator:** Doug Jarrow. **Equipment Manager:** Dana Noeltner.

Farm System

Class	Club (League)	Manager	Hitting Coach	Pitching Coach
Triple-A	Iowa (PCL)	Dave Bialas	Dave Keller	Mike Mason
Double-A	Tennessee (SL)	Buddy Bailey	Mariano Duncan	Jeff Fassero
High Class A	Daytona (FSL)	Brian Harper	Desi Wilson	Marty Mason
Low Class A	Peoria (MWL)	Casey Kopitzke	Barbaro Garbey	Tom Pratt
Short-season	Boise (NWL)	Mark Johnson	Bill Buckner	David Rosario
Rookie	Cubs (AZL)	Bobby Mitchell	Jason Dubois	Rick Tronerud/Frank Castillo
Rookie	Cubs I (DSL)	Juan Cabreja	Ricardo Medina	Anderson Tavares
Rookie	Cubs II (DSL)	Yudith Ozorio	Leo Perez/Franklin Blanco	Leo Hernandez

Scouting

Telephone: (773) 404-2827. **Fax:** (773) 404-4147.

Director, Amateur Scouting: Tim Wilken (Dunedin, FL).

Director, Professional Scouting: Joe Bohringer (Dekalb, IL). **Director, International Scouting:** Paul Weaver (Phoenix,AZ). **Special Assistant:** Steve Hinton (Mather, CA). **Senior Advisor:** Jim Crawford (Madison, MS). **Coordinator, Player Development/International Operations:** Alex Suarez. **Coordinator, Pro Scouting:** Jake Ciarrachi. **Amateur Scouting Assistant:** Scott Lonergan. **Administrative Assistant:** Patricia Honzik.

Pro Scouts: Mark Adair (Phoenix, AZ), Billy Blitzer (Brooklyn, New York), Tom Bourque (Cambridge, MA), Joe Housey (Hollywood, FL), Bob Lofrano (Woodland Hills, CA), Mark Servais (LaCrosse, WI), Tom Shafer (Lockport, IL), Keith Stohr (Viera, FL), Richie Zisk (Lighthouse Point, FL). **National Crosscheckers:** Matt Dorey (Houston, TX), Sam Hughes (Atlanta, GA). **Crosscheckers: Southeast**—Charles Aliano (Land O'Lakes, FL), **Central**—Steve Riha (Houston, TX), **West**—Tim Kissner (Kirkland, WA), **Northeast**—Lukas McKnight (Safety Harbour, FL), **Canadian/U.S./International**—Ron Tostenson (El Dorado Hills, CA). **Area Scouts:** Tim Adkins (Huntington, WV), John Ceprini (Massapequa, NY), Tom Clark (Lake City, FL), Ramser Correa (Caguas, PR), Scott Fairbanks (Issaquah, WA), Trey Forkerway (Houston, TX), Al Geddes (Canby, OR), Denny Henderson (Orange, CA), John Koronka (Clairmont, FL), Keith Lockhart (Dacula, GA), Lazaro Llanes (Miami, FL), Steve McFarland (Scottsdale, AZ), Tom Myers (Santa Barbara, CA), Ty Nichols (Broken Arrow, OK), Keith Ryman (Jefferson City, TN), Rick Schroeder (Pleasanton, CA), Eric Servais (St. Louis Park, MN), Matt Sherman (Norwell, MA), Billy Swoope (Norfolk, VA), Stan Zielinski (Winfield, IL).

International Scouts: Hector Ortega (Venezuela), Jose Serra (Dominican Republic), Steve Wilson (Pacific Rim).

Chicago White Sox

Office Address: U.S. Cellular, Field, 333 W. 35th St., Chicago, IL 60616.
Telephone: (312) 674-1000. **Fax:** (312) 674-5116.
Website: www.whitesox.com.

Ownership
Chairman: Jerry Reinsdorf. **Vice Chairman:** Eddie Einhorn.
Board of Directors: Robert Judelson, Judd Malkin, Robert Mazer, Allan Muchin, Jay Pinsky, Larry Pogofsky, Lee Stern, Burton Ury, Charles Walsh.
Special Assistant to Chairman: Dennis Gilbert. **Assistant to Chairman:** Barb Reincke.

BUSINESS OPERATIONS
Executive Vice President: Howard Pizer.
Senior Director, Information Services: Don Brown. **Senior Director, Human Resources:** Moira Foy. **Administrators, Human Resources:** Leslie Gaggiano.

Finance
Senior VP, Administration/Finance: Tim Buzard. **Senior Director, Finance:** Bill Waters.
Accounting Manager: Chris Taylor.

Marketing/Sales
Senior VP, Sales/Marketing: Brooks Boyer. **Senior Director, Business Development/Broadcasting:** Bob Grim. **Manager, Scoreboard Operations/Production:** Jeff Szynal. **Director, Game Operations:** Nichole Manning. **Manager, Game Operations:** Amy Sheridan. **Manager, In-Game Entertainment:** Dan Mielke.

Jerry Reinsdorf

Director, Corporate Partnerships Sales Development: George McDoniel. **Director, Corporate Partnerships Activation:** Gail Tucker. **Managers, Corporate Partnerships:** Jeff Floerke, Beth Cunningham. **Coordinators, Client Services:** Kendele Carney, Lucy Rath. **Account Executive, Corportate Partnerships:** Hank Johnston.
Director, Ticket Sales: Tom Sheridan. **Manager, Premium Seating Sales:** Rob Boaz. **Senior Director, Community Relations:** Christine O'Reilly.
Director, Mass Communications: Maggie Luellen. **Manager, Design Services:** Gareth Breunlin. **Senior Coordinator, Design Services:** Matt Peterson. **Manager, Community Relations:** Danielle Disch. **Manager, Community Relations:** Laina Myers. **Coordinators, Community Relations:** Stacy Tsihlopoulos, Dan Puente.

Media Relations
Telephone: (312) 674-5300. **Fax:** (312) 674-5116.
Senior VP, Communications: Scott Reifert.
Director, Media Relations: Bob Beghtol. **Director, Public Relations:** Lou Hernandez. **Manager, Media Relations:** Ray Garcia. **Manager, Public Relations:** Marty Maloney. **Coordinators, Media Relations/Services:** Leni Depoister, Joe Roti.

2012 SCHEDULE
Standard Game Times: 7:10 p.m.; Sun. 1:10.

APRIL		
6-8 . . . . .at Texas		
9-11 . . . . . .at Cleveland		
13-15 . . . . Detroit		
16-19 . . . . Baltimore		
20-22 . . . . . . .at Seattle		
23-25 . . . . . .at Oakland		
26-29 . . . . Boston		

MAY
1-3 . . . . Cleveland
4-6 . . . . .at Detroit
7-9 . . . . . .at Cleveland
11-13 . . . . . . Kansas City
14-15 . . . . Detroit
16-17 . at Los Angeles (AL)
18-20 . . . .at Chicago (NL)

22-24 . . . . . .Minnesota
25-27 . . . . . . Cleveland
28-30 . . . . . at Tampa Bay

JUNE
1-3 . . . . Seattle
5-7 . . . . .Toronto
8-10 . . . . Houston
12-14 . . . . . . .at St. Louis
15-17 . at Los Angeles (NL)
18-20 . . . . . Chicago (NL)
22-24 . . . . . .Milwaukee
25-27 . . . . at Minnesota
28-30 . . . at New York (AL)

JULY
1 . . . . . . at New York (AL)

3-5 . . . . Texas
6-8 . . . . .Toronto
13-15 . . . .at Kansas City
16-19 . . . . .at Boston
20-22 . . . . . . .at Detroit
23-25 . . . . . .Minnesota
27-29 . . . . . . .at Texas
30-31 . . . . at Minnesota

AUGUST
1 . . . . at Minnesota
3-5 . . . . Los Angeles (AL)
6-8 . . . . Kansas City
10-12 . . . . Oakland
13-16 . . . . . . at Toronto
17-19 . . . . .at Kansas City
20-22 . . . . .New York (AL)

24-26 . . . . Seattle
27-30 . . . . . .at Baltimore
31 . . . . .at Detroit

SEPTEMBER
1-2 . . . . .at Detroit
3-5 . . . . .Minnesota
7-9 . . . . Kansas City
10-13 . . . . Detroit
14-16 . . . . at Minnesota
18-20 . . . .at Kansas City
21-23 . at Los Angeles (AL)
24-26 . . . . Cleveland
27-30 . . . . . .Tampa Bay

OCTOBER
1-3 . . . . .at Cleveland

GENERAL INFORMATION
Stadium (year opened): U.S. Cellular Field (1991).
Team Colors: Black, white and silver.

Player Representative: Unavailable.
Home Dugout: Third Base.
Playing Surface: Grass.

Stadium Operations

Senior VP, Stadium Operations: Terry Savarise. **Senior Director, Event Operations:** Troy Brown. **Senior Director, Guest Services/Diamond Suite Operations:** Julie Taylor. **Head Groundskeeper:** Roger Bossard. **PA Announcer:** Gene Honda. **Official Scorers:** Bob Rosenberg, Don Friske.

Ticketing

Telephone: (312) 674-1000. **Fax:** (312) 674-5102.
Director, Ticket Operations: Mike Mazza. **Manager, Ticket Accounting Administration:** Ken Wisz.

Travel/Clubhouse

Director, Team Travel: Ed Cassin.
Manager, White Sox Clubhouse: Vince Fresso. **Manager, Visiting Clubhouse:** Gabe Morell. **Manager, Umpires Clubhouse:** Joe McNamara Jr.

BASEBALL OPERATIONS

Senior VP/General Manager: Ken Williams.
VP/Assistant GM: Rick Hahn. **Special Assistants:** Bill Scherrer, Dave Yoakum, Marco Paddy.
Executive Assistant to GM: Nancy Nesnidal. **Director, Baseball Operations:** Dan Fabian.
Assistant Director, Baseball Operations: Daniel Zien. **Special Assignment Scout:** Alan Regier.

Ken Williams

Major League Staff

Manager: Robin Ventura
Coaches: Bench—Mark Parent; **Pitching**—Don Cooper; **Batting**—Jeff Manto; **First Base**—Harold Baines; **Third Base**—Joe McEwing; **Bullpen**—Juan Nieves.

Medical, Training

Senior Team Physician: Dr. Charles Bush-Joseph.
Head Athletic Trainer: Herm Schneider. **Assistant Athletic Trainer:** Brian Ball.
Director, Conditioning: Allen Thomas.

Player Development

Telephone: (312) 674-1000. **Fax:** (312) 674-5105.
VP, Player Development/Special Assignments: Buddy Bell.
Senior Director, Minor League Operations: Grace Guerrero Zwit. **Director, Player Development:** Nick Capra.
Assistant Director, Player Development/Scouting: Del Matthews. **Senior Coordinator, Minor League Administration:** Kathy Potoski. **Manager, Clubhouse/Equipment:** Dan Flood.
Minor League Field Coordinator: Kirk Champion. **Roving Instructors:** Daryl Boston (outfield), Curt Hasler (pitching), Everado Magallanes (infield), Timothy Laker (hitting), John Orton (catching), Dale Torborg (conditioning coordinator), Devon White (baserunning/bunting). **Latin Cultural Coordinator:** Geronimo Mendoza. **Dominican Player Development/Scouting Supervisor:** Rafael Santana. **Coordinator, Minor League Trainers/Rehabilitation:** Scott Takao. **Coaching Assistant:** Robbie Cummings. **Dominican Coordinator:** Julio Valdez.

Farm System

Class	Club (League)	Manager	Coach	Pitching Coach
Triple-A	Charlotte (IL)	Joel Skinner	Andy Tomberlin	Richard Dotson
Double-A	Birmingham (SL)	Bobby Magallanes	Bobby Thigpen	Brandon Moore
High A	Winston-Salem (CL)	Tommy Thompson	Gary Ward	J.R. Perdew
Low A	Kannapolis (SAL)	Julio Vinas	Robert Sasser	Jose Bautista
Rookie	Bristol (APP)	Pete Rose Jr.	Greg Briley	Larry Owens
Rookie	Great Falls (PIO)	Ryan Newman	Charlie Poe	Brian Drahman
Rookie	White Sox (DSL)	Guillermo Reyes	Angel Gonzalez	Efrain Valdez

Scouting

Telephone: (312) 674-1000. **Fax:** (312) 674-5105.
Pro Scouts: Kevin Bootay (Sacramento, CA), Joe Butler (Long Beach, CA), Gary Pellant (Chandler, AZ), Paul Provas (Arlington, TX), Daraka Shaheed (Vallejo, CA), Bill Young (Scottsdale, AZ), John Tumminia (Newburgh, NY).
Director, Amateur Scouting: Doug Laumann (Florence, KY).
Assistant Director, Scouting/Player Development: J.J. Lally. **National Crosscheckers:** Nathan Durst (Sycamore, IL), Ed Pebley (Brigham City, UT). **Regional Crosscheckers: East**—Nick Hostetler (Union, KY), **West**—Derek Valenzuela (Temecula, CA). **Crosschecker:** Mike Shirley (Anderson, IN). **Advisor to Baseball Department:** Larry Monroe (Schaumburg, IL).
Area Scouts: Mike Baker (Santa Ana, CA), Kevin Burrell (Sharpsburg, GA), Alex Cosmidis (Raleigh, NC), Ryan Dorsey (Frederick, MD), Dan Durst (Rockford, IL), Phil Gulley (Morehead, KY), Warren Hughes (Mobile, AL), George Kachigian (Coronado, CA), John Kazanas (Phoenix, AZ), Jose Ortega (Fort Lauderdale, FL), Bryan Maloney (Las Vegas, NV), Clay Overcash (Oologan, OK), Andrew Pinter (Raleigh, NC), Joe Siers (Wesley Chapel, FL), Keith Staab (College Station, TX), Adam Virchis (Modesto, CA), Gary Woods (Solvang, CA).
Part-Time Scouts: Tommy Butler (East Rancho Dominguez, CA), Karl Carswell (Kansas City, MO), Javier Centeno (Guaynabo, PR), John Doldoorian (Whitinsville, MA), Trent Eckstaine (Lemars, IA), Cade Griffis (Addison, TX), Jack Jolly (Murfreeboro, TN), Glenn Murdock (Livonia, MI), Howard Nakagama (Salt Lake City, UT), Al Otto (Schaumburg, IL), Mike Paris (Boone, IA).
International Scouts: Marino DeLeon (Dominican Republic), Miguel Peguero (Dominican Republic), Fermin Ubri (Dominican Republic), Amador Arias (Venezuela), Omar Sanchez (Venezuela).

Cincinnati Reds

Office Address: 100 Joe Nuxhall Way, Cincinnati, OH 45202.
Telephone: (513) 765-7000. **Fax:** (513) 765-7342.
Website: www.reds.com.

Ownership

Operated by: The Cincinnati Reds LLC.
President/CEO: Robert Castellini. **Chairman:** Joseph Williams Jr. **Vice Chairman/Treasurer:** Thomas Williams. **COO:** Phillip Castellini. **Executive Assistant to COO:** Diana Busam. **Secretary:** Christopher Fister.

BUSINESS OPERATIONS

Senior Vice President, Business Operations: Karen Forgus. **Senior Director, Business Development:** Lauren Werner. **Business Operations Assistant/Speakers Bureau:** Emily Mahle. **Senior Director, Diversity/Strategic Initiatives:** Joe Morgan. **Special Events Manager:** Sally Greytak.

Finance/Administration

VP, Finance/CFO: Doug Healy. **VP/General Counsel:** James Marx. **Controller:** Bentley Viator. **Assistant to General Counsel/CFO:** Teena Schweier. **Director, Human Resources:** Teddi Mangas-Coon. **Human Resources Manager:** Allison Stortz. **Employee Relations Manager:** Garry McGuire.

Sales

VP, Ticket Sales: John Davis. **Director, Ticket Initiatives:** David Ziegler. **Director, Client Services:** Craig Warman. **Ticket Development Manager:** Jodi Czanik. **Client Services Manager:** Nancy Bloss. **Director, Group Sales/Inside Sales:** Sarah Contardo. **Group Sales Manager:** Ryan Niemeyer. **Inside Sales Manager:** Chris Bausano. **Director, Season/Premium Sales:** Mark Schueler. **Season Sales Manager:** Chris Herrell. **Suite/Premium Services Manager:** Shelley Volpenhein. **Premium Sales Managers:** Patrick Montague, Ryan Rizzo.

Bob Castellini

Ticket Operations

Senior Director, Ticket Operations: John O'Brien. **Assistant Director, Ticket Operations:** Ken Ayer. **Season Ticket Manager:** Bev Bonavita. **Group Ticket Manager:** Brad Callahan.

Media Relations

Director, Media Relations: Rob Butcher. **Assistant Directors, Media Relations:** Larry Herms, Jamie Ramsey.

Communications/Marketing

VP, Communications/Marketing: Ralph Mitchell. **Communications Manager:** Jarrod Rollins. **Design/Production Manager:** Jansen Dell. **Director, Promotional Events:** Zach Bonkowski. **Promotional Events Manager:** Kathryn Braun. **Director, Digital Marketing/Consumer Clubs:** Lisa Braun. **Director, Entertainment/Productions:** Adam Lane. **Public Relations Manager:** Michael Anderson. **Advertising Manager:** Audra Sordyl.

2012 SCHEDULE

Standard Game Times: 7:10 p.m.; Sun. 1:10

APRIL		
5 . . . . .Miami	18-20 . . . at New York (AL)	2-4. . . at Los Angeles (NL)	24-26 . . . . St. Louis

APRIL
5 . . . . .Miami
7-8 . . . . .Miami
9-11 . . . . St. Louis
12-15 . . . . at Washington
17-19 . . . . .at St. Louis
20-22 . . . .at Chicago (NL)
24-26 . . . . . San Francisco
27-29 . . . . Houston

MAY
1-3. . . . . . . Chicago (NL)
4-6. . . . . . . at Pittsburgh
7-9. . . . . . . at Milwaukee
11-13 . . . . . . Washington
14-15 . . . . at Atlanta
16-17 . . . at New York (NL)

JUNE
18-20 . . . at New York (AL)
21-24 . . . . Atlanta
25-27 . . . . . . .Colorado
28-30 . . . . . at Pittsburgh

1-3. . . . . .at Houston
5-7. . . . . Pittsburgh
8-10 . . . . Detroit
12-14 . . . . Cleveland
15-17 . . at New York (NL)
18-20 . . . . .at Cleveland
22-24 . . . . . . Minnesota
25-27 . . . . . .Milwaukee
28-30 . . . at San Francisco

JULY
1 . . . . . . at San Francisco

2-4. . . at Los Angeles (NL)
5-8. . . . . . . at San Diego
13-15 . . . . St. Louis
16-19 . . . . Arizona
20-22 . . . . . .Milwaukee
23-25 . . . . . .at Houston
27-29 . . . . at Colorado
30-31 . . . . . . San Diego

AUGUST
1-2. . . . . San Diego
3-5. . . . . Pittsburgh
6-8. . . . . . at Milwaukee
9-12 . . . . .at Chicago (NL)
14-16 . . . .New York (NL)
17-19 . . . . Chicago (NL)
20-23 . . . . at Philadelphia

24-26 . . . . St. Louis
27-29 . . . . at Arizona
31 . . . . .at Houston

SEPTEMBER
1-2. . . . . .at Houston
3-5. . . . . . . .Philadelphia
7-9. . . . . Houston
10-12 . . . . . . Pittsburgh
14-16 . . . . at Miami
18-20 . . .at Chicago (NL)
21-23 . . .Los Angeles (NL)
25-27 . . . . . .Milwaukee
28-30 . . . . at Pittsburgh

OCTOBER
1-3. . . . . . . .at St. Louis

GENERAL INFORMATION

Stadium (year opened): Great American Ball Park (2003).
Home Dugout: First Base.

Playing Surface: Grass.
Team Colors: Red, white and black.
Player Representative: Mike Leake.

Community Relations
Executive Director: Charley Frank. **Director, Community Relations:** Lorrie Platt. **Manager, Program/Events:** Lindsey Lander. **Manager, Finance/Operations:** Matthew Wagner. **Executive Director, Reds Hall of Fame:** Rick Walls. **Operations Manager/Curator, Reds Hall of Fame:** Chris Eckes.

Corporate Sales
VP, Corporate Sales: Bill Reinberger. **Corporate Sales Managers:** Dave Collins, Casandra Ersel, Dan Lewis, Mark Scherer.

Ballpark Operations
VP, Ballpark Operations: Declan Mullin. **Director, Ballpark Operations:** Sean Brown.Ballpark Operations Manager: Colleen Rodenberg. **Ballpark Operations Superintendent:** Bob Harrison. **Guest Relations Manager:** Jan Koshover. **Manager, Technology Business Center:** Chris Campbell. **Director, Safety/Security:** Kerry Rowland. **Chief Engineer:** Roger Smith. **Head Groundskeeper:** Doug Gallant. **Assistant Head Groundskeeper:** Derrik Grubbs. **Grounds Supervisor:** Robbie Dworkin.

BASEBALL OPERATIONS

President, Baseball Operations/GM: Walt Jocketty.
VP/Assistant GM: Bob Miller. **VP, Scouting/Player Development/International Operations:** Bill Bavasi. **VP/Special Assistant:** Jerry Walker. **VP, Baseball Operations:** Dick Williams. **Senior Advisor, Baseball Operations:** Joe Morgan. **Special Assistants:** Eric Davis, Mario Soto. **Assistant Director, Baseball Operations:** Nick Krall. **Manager, Baseball Systems Development:** Brett Elkins. **Manager, Baseball Research/Analysis:** Sam Grossman. **Manager, Video Scouting:** Rob Coughlin. **Baseball Operations Assistant:** Stephanie Ben.

Medical/Training
Medical Director: Dr. Timothy Kremchek. **Head Athletic Trainer:** Paul Lessard. **Assistant Athletic Trainer:** Steve Baumann. **Strength/Conditioning Coordinator:** Matthew Krause.

Walt Jocketty

Major League Staff
Manager: Dusty Baker.
Coaches: Bench—Chris Speier; **Pitching**—Bryan Price; **Batting**—Brook Jacoby; **First Base**—Billy Hatcher; **Third Base**—Mark Berry; **Bullpen**—Juan Lopez.

Player Development
Telephone: (513) 765-7700. **Fax:** (513) 765-7799.
Assistant Director, Player Development: Jeff Graupe. **Director, Minor League Administration:** Lori Hudson. **Arizona Operations Manager:** Mike Saverino. **Assistant to Arizona Operations Manager:** Charlie Rodriguez. **Minor League Equipment Manager:** Jonathan Snyder. **Field Coordinator:** Freddie Benavides. **Assistant Field Coordinator, Instruction:** Bill Doran. **Assistant Field Coordinator, Latin Focus:** Joel Noboa. **Coordinators:** Ronnie Ortegon (hitting), Mark Riggins (pitching), Darren Bragg (outfield/baserunning), Rick Sweet (catching). **Strength/Conditioning Coordinator:** Sean Marohn. **Medical Coordinator:** Richard Stark. **Medical Administrator:** Patrick Serbus.
Rehab Coordinator/Physical Therapist: Brad Epstein. **Strength/Conditioning Coaches:** Zach Gjestvang, Rigo Febles. **Director, Dominican Republic Academy:** Juan Peralta.

Farm System

Class	Club (League)	Manager	Coach	Pitching Coach
Triple-A	Louisville (IL)	David Bell	Ryan Jackson	Ted Power
Double-A	Pensacola (SL)	Jim Riggleman	Tony Jaramillo	Tom Brown
High A	Bakersfield (CAL)	Ken Griffey	Eli Marrero	Rigo Beltran
Low A	Dayton (MWL)	Delino DeShields	Alex Pelaez	Tom Browning
Rookie	Billings (PIO)	Pat Kelly	Ray Martinez	Tony Fossas
Rookie	Reds (AZL)	Jose Miguel Nieves	Jorge Orta	Derrin Ebert
Rookie	Reds (DSL)	Joel Noboa	Nilson Antiqua	Unavailable

Senior Director, Amateur Scouting: Chris Buckley. **Assistant Director, Amateur Scouting:** Paul Pierson. **Senior Director, Pro/Global Scouting:** Terry Reynolds. **Special Assistant, Player Personnel:** Cam Bonifay. **Special Assistants:** J Harrison, Marty Maier, Mike Squires. **Major League Advance Scout:** Shawn Pender. **Professional Scouts:** Jeff Morris, John Morris, Steve Roadcap, Jeff Taylor, Dominic Viola.
National Crosscheckers: Jeff Barton (Gilbert, AZ), Bill Byckowski (Ontario, Canada), Jerry Flowers (Cypress, TX), Mark McKnight (Tega Cay, SC), Mark Snipp (Humble, TX). **Scouting Supervisors:** Tony Arias (Miami Lakes, FL), Rich Bordi (Rohnert Park, CA), Jeff Brookens (Chambersburg, PA), Clark Crist (Tucson, AZ), Rex De La Nuez (Burbank, CA), Rick Ingalls (Long Beach, CA), Ben Jones (Alexandria, LA), Joe Katuska (Cincinnati, OH), Mike Keenan (Manhattan, KS), Brad Meador (Cincinnati, OH), Mike Misuraca (Murrieta, CA), John Poloni (Tarpon Springs, FL), Lee Seras (Flanders, NJ), Perry Smith (Charlotte, NC), Andy Stack (Hartford, WI), Greg Zunino (Cape Coral, FL). **Scouts:** Jim Grief (Paducha, KY), Bill Killian (Stanwood, MI), David Lander (Los Angeles, CA), Denny Nagel (Cincinnati, OH), Marlon Styles (Cincinnati, OH), Mike Wallace (Escondido, CA), John Walsh (Windsor, CT), Roger Weberg (Bemidji, MN).
Director, Latin America Scouting: Tony Arias. **Assistant Director, Latin American Scouting:** Miguel Machado. **Director, Global Scouting:** Jim Stoeckel. **Scouting Coordinator, Dominican Republic:** Richard Jimenez. **Scout/Administrator:** Jose Fuentes (Venezuela) International Scouts: Jason Hewitt (Australia), Luke Prokopec (Australia), Geronimo Blanco (Colombia), Carlos Batista (Dominican Republic), Edward Bens (Dominican Republic), Cesar Castro (Dominican Republic), Jose Manuel Pujols (Dominican Republic), Sal Varriale (Italy), Anibal Vega (Nicaragua), Anibal Reluz (Panama), Nick Dempsey (South Africa), Victor Oramas (Venezuela).

Cleveland Indians

Office Address: Progressive Field, 2401 Ontario St, Cleveland, OH 44115.
Telephone: (216) 420-4200. **Fax:** (216) 420-4396.
Website: www.indians.com.

Ownership
Owner/CEO: Lawrence Dolan. **Chairman/Chief Executive Officer:** Paul Dolan.

BUSINESS OPERATIONS
President: Mark Shapiro.
Assistant to the President: Andrew Miller. **Executive Administrative Assistant:** Marlene Lehky. **Executive Vice President, Business:** Dennis Lehman. **Executive Administrative Assistant, Business:** Dru Kosik.

Corporate Partnerships/Finance
Director, Corporate Partnerships: Ted Baugh. **Manager, New Business Development:** Sheff Webb. **Manager, Corporate Partnership Services:** Sam Zelasko. **Senior Account Executive, Corporate Partnerships:** Bryan Hoffart. **Senior VP, Finance/CFO:** Ken Stefanov. **VP/General Counsel:** Joe Znidarsic. **Controller:** Sarah Taylor.
Senior Director, Planning/Analysis/Reporting: Rich Dorffer. **Manager, Accounting:** Karen Menzing. **Manager, Payroll Accounting:** Mary Forkapa. **Concessions Controller:** Marj Ruhl. **Concessions Accounting Manager:** Diane Turner. **Senior Staff Accountant:** Kim Haist.

Larry Dolan

Human Resources
VP, Human Resources/Diversity: Sara Lehrke. **Manager, Training:** Mailynh Vu. **Technology Trainer:** Jennifer Gibson. **Coordinator, Benefits:** Crystal Basile. **Human Resource Generalist:** David Mraz.

Marketing
Senior VP, Sales/Marketing: Vic Gregovits. **Director, Marketing:** Sanaa Julien. **Manager, Promotions:** Jason Kidik. **Manager, Productions:** Annie Merovich. **Coordinator, Marketing/Copywriting:** Anne Madzelan. **Senior Director, Merchandising:** Kurt Schloss. **Merchandise Manager:** Karen Fox.

Communications/Baseball Information
Telephone: (216) 420-4380. **Fax:** (216) 420-4430.
Senior VP, Public Affairs: Bob DiBiasio. **Senior Director, Communications:** Curtis Danburg. **Coordinator, Communications:** Danielle Cherry. **Director, Baseball Information:** Bart Swain. **Manager, Administration/Credentials:** Susie Giuliano. **Coordinator, Digital Media:** Rob Campbell. **Manager, Digital Asset Creation/Team Photographer:** Dan Mendlik.

Ballpark Operations
VP, Ballpark Operations: Jim Folk.

2012 SCHEDULE
Standard Game Times: 7:05 p.m.; Sun. 1:05.

APRIL		
5 . . . . .Toronto	18-20 . . . . .Miami	2-4. . . . Los Angeles (AL)	24-26 . . . . .New York (AL)
7-8. . . . . .Toronto	22-24 . . . . Detroit	5-8. . . . . . . .Tampa Bay	27-30 . . . . Oakland
9-11. . . . . Chicago (AL)	25-27 . . . .at Chicago (AL)	13-15 . . . . . . at Toronto	31 . . . . Texas
13-15 . . . .at Kansas City	28-30 . . . . . Kansas City	16-19 . . . . at Tampa Bay	
17-19 . . . . . . .at Seattle		20-23 . . . . . . Baltimore	SEPTEMBER
20-22 . . . . . .at Oakland	JUNE	24-26 . . . . Detroit	1-2. . . . . Texas
24-26 . . . . . Kansas City	1-3. . . . . .Minnesota	27-29 . . . . at Minnesota	3-5. . . . . .at Detroit
27-29 . . . Los Angeles (AL)	5-7. . . . . .at Detroit	31 . . . . . .at Kansas City	7-10. . . . . at Minnesota
	8-10. . . . . . .at St. Louis		11-13 . . . . .at Texas
MAY	12-14 . . . . .at Cincinnati	AUGUST	14-16 . . . . Detroit
1-3. . . . .at Chicago (AL)	15-17 . . . . . .Pittsburgh	1-2. . . . . .at Kansas City	18-20 . . . . . .Minnesota
4-6. . . . . Texas	18-20 . . . . . . Cincinnati	3-5. . . . . .at Detroit	21-23 . . . .at Kansas City
7-9. . . . . . Chicago (AL)	22-24 . . . . . .at Houston	6-8. . . . . . . .Minnesota	24-26 . . . .at Chicago (AL)
10-13 . . . . . . .at Boston	25-27 . . at New York (AL)	9-12. . . . . Boston	28-30 . . . . . Kansas City
14-15 . . . . at Minnesota	28-30 . . . . . .at Baltimore	13-15 . at Los Angeles (AL)	
16-17 . . . . Seattle		17-19 . . . . . .at Oakland	OCTOBER
	JULY	20-22 . . . . . . .at Seattle	1-3. . . . . . Chicago (AL)
	1 . . . . .at Baltimore		

GENERAL INFORMATION
Stadium (year opened): Progressive Field (1994).
Team Colors: Navy blue, red and silver.

Player Representative: Justin Masterson.
Home Dugout: Third Base.
Playing Surface: Grass.

Director, Facility Maintenance: Chris Donahoe. **Head Groundskeeper:** Brandon Koehnke. **Senior Director, Ballpark Operations:** Jerry Crabb. **Assistant Director, Ballpark Operations:** Brad Mohr. **Assistant Director, Facility Maintenance:** Seth Cooper. **Coordinator, Game Day Staff:** Renee VanLaningham. **Coordinator, Ballpark Services:** Steve Walters.

Information Systems
Senior Director, Information Systems: Dave Powell. **Director, Software Development/Support:** Matt Tagliaferri. **Manager, End-User Support:** Matthew Smith. **Director, Information Technology:** Whitney Kuszmaul. **Programmer Analyst:** Plamen Kouzov.

Ticketing
Telephone: (216) 420-4487. **Fax:** (216) 420-4481.
Director, Ticket Services: Gene Connelly. **Manager, Ticket Services:** Andrea Jirousek. **Manager, Ticket Office:** Katie Smith. **Manager, Ticket Operations:** Eric Fronczek. **Director, Fan Services:** Dave Murray.

Spring Training/Arizona Operations
Manager, Arizona Operations: Ryan Lantz. **Manager, Home Clubhouse:** Fletcher Wilkes.
Director, Team Travel: Mike Seghi. **Home Clubhouse/Equipment Manager:** Tony Amato. **Manager, Video Operations:** Bob Chester. **Visiting Clubhouse Manager:** Willie Jenks.

BASEBALL OPERATIONS

Telephone: (216) 420-4200. **Fax:** (216) 420-4321.
Executive Vice President/General Manager: Chris Antonetti.
VP, Baseball Operations/Assistant GM: Mike Chernoff.
Director, Player Personnel: Steve Lubratich. **Director, Baseball Administration:** Wendy Hoppel. **Directors, Baseball Operations:** Derek Falvey, David Stearns. **Director, Baseball Analytics:** Keith Woolner. **Assistant to the President:** Andrew Miller. **Major League Advance Coach:** Alex Eckelman. **Scouting Operations Assistant:** Jason Lynn. **Executive Administrative Assistant:** Marlene Lehky. **Sports Psychologist:** Dr. Charles Maher.

Major League Staff
Manager: Manny Acta.
Coaches: Bench—Sandy Alomar, Jr., **Pitching**—Scott Radinsky, **Hitting**—Bruce Fields, **First Base**—Tom Wiedenbauer, **Third Base/Infield**—Steve Smith, **Bullpen**—Dave Miller.
Assistants, Major League Staff: Armando Camacaro, Francisco Morales.

Chris Antonetti

Medical/Training
Head Team Physician: Dr. Mark Schickendantz. **Director, Medical Services/Head Trainer:** Lonnie Soloff. **Assistant Athletic Trainer:** Jeff Desjardins. **Strength/Conditioning Coach:** Joe Kessler.

Player Development
Telephone: (216) 420-4308. **Fax:** (216) 420-4321.
VP, Player Development: Ross Atkins.
Assistant Director, Player Development: Carter Hawkins. **Administrative Assistant:** Nilda Taffanelli. **Advisor, Player Development:** Johnny Goryl. **Director, Latin America Operations:** Ramon Pena. **Field Coordinator:** Rob Leary. **Coordinators:** Travis Fryman (infield), Mickey Callaway (pitching), Alan Zinter (hitting), Ken Rowe (advisor), Jake Beiting (strength/conditioning), James Quinlan (rehabilitation), Julio Rangel (mental skills), Lino Diaz (cultural development). **Advisor, Latin America:** Minnie Mendoza. **Latin America Strength/Conditioning Coordinator:** Nelson Perez.

Farm System

Class	Club	Manager	Coach	Pitching Coach
Triple-A	Columbus (IL)	Mike Sarbaugh	Phil Clark	Ruben Niebla
Double-A	Akron (EL)	Chris Tremie	Rouglas Odor	Tony Arnold
High A	Carolina (CL)	Edwin Rodriguez	Scooter Tucker	Scott Erickson
Low A	Lake County (MWL)	Dave Wallace	Jim Rickon	Jeff Harris
Short-season	Mahoning Valley (NYP)	Ted Kubiak	Tony Mansolino	Greg Hibbard
Rookie	Indians (AZL)	Anthony Medrano	Junior Betances/Dennis Malave	Steve Karsay
Rookie	Indians (DSL)	Wilfredo Tejeda	Francisco Cabrera/Carlos Fermin	Mario Brito

Scouting
Telephone: (216) 420-4200. **Fax:** (216) 420-4321.
Vice President, Scouting Operations: John Mirabelli.
Director, Amateur Scouting: Brad Grant. **Assistant Director, Scouting:** Paul Gillispie. **Assistant Director, Professional Scouting:** Alex Eckelman. **Major League Scouts:** Dave Malpass (Huntington Beach, CA), Don Poplin (Norwood, NC), Chris Smith (Montgomery, TX). **Pro Scouts:** Doug Carpenter (North Palm Beach, FL), Jim Cuthbert (Summit, NJ), Steve Lyons (Lake Mary, FL).
National Crosschecker: Chuck Ricci (Greencastle, PA). **Regional Crosscheckers:** Kevin Cullen (Frisco, TX), Paul Cogan (Rocklin, CA), Scott Meaney (Apex, NC), Derrick Ross (Lake Orion, MI). **Crosschecker:** Scott Barnsby (Huntsville, AL). **Area Scouts:** Steve Abney (Lawrence, KS), Mark Allen (Gainesville, TX), Chuck Bartlett (Starkville, MS), Kyle Van Hook (Brenham, TX), Ryan Thompson (Scottsdale, AZ), Don Lyle (Sacramento, CA), Bob Mayer (Somerset, PA), Junie Melendez (North Ridgeville, OH), Les Pajari (Angora, MN), Vince Sagisi (Encino, CA), Jason Smith (Long Beach, CA), Mike Soper (Tampa, FL), Brad Tyler (Bishop, GA), Jack Uhey (Ridgefiled, WA), Brent Urcheck (Philadelphia, PA).

Colorado Rockies

Office Address: 2001 Blake St., Denver, CO 80205.
Telephone: (303) 292-0200. **Fax:** (303) 312-2116.
Website: www.coloradorockies.com.

Ownership

Operated by: Colorado Rockies Baseball Club Ltd.
Owner/General Partner: Charles K. Monfort. **Owner/Chairman/Chief Executive Officer:** Richard L. Monfort.
Executive Assistant to the Owner/General Partner: Patricia Penfold. **Executive Assistant to the Owner/Chairman/Chief Executive Officer:** Terry Douglass.

BUSINESS OPERATIONS

Executive Vice President/Chief Operating Officer: Greg Feasel. **Assistant to Executive VP/Chief Operating Officer:** Kim Olson. **VP, Human Resources:** Elizabeth Stecklein.

Finance

Executive VP/CFO/General Counsel: Hal Roth. **VP, Finance:** Michael Kent. **Senior Director, Purchasing:** Gary Lawrence. **Coordinator, Purchasing:** Gloria Giraldi. **Director, Accounting:** Phil Emerson. **Accountants:** Joel Binfet, Laine Campbell. **Payroll Administrator:** Juli Daedelow.

Marketing/Sales

Charles Monfort

VP, Corporate Sales: Marcy Glasser. **Assistant to VP, Corporate Sales:** Jenny Roope. **Senior Account Executive, Corporate Sales:** Kari Anderson. **Account Executives:** Dan Lentz, Nate VanderWal. **VP, Community/Retail Operations:** James P. Kellogg. **Director, Retail Operations:** Aaron Heinrich. **Director, Information Systems:** Bill Stephani. **Director, Promotions/Special Events:** Jason Fleming. **Director, In-Game Entertainment/Broadcasting:** Kent Krosbakken. **Senior Director, Advertising, Marketing/Publications:** Jill Campbell. **Supervisor, Advertising/Marketing:** Sarah Topf. **Coordinator, Multicultural Marketing/Advertising:** Marisol Villagomez.

Public Relations/Communications

Telephone: (303) 312-2325. **Fax:** (303) 312-2319.
VP, Communications/Public Relations: Jay Alves. **Manager, Communications/Public Relations:** Nick Piburn. **Coordinator, Communications/Public Relations:** Mike Kennedy. **Assistant, Communications/Public Relations/Baseball Operations:** Irma Castaneda.

Ballpark Operations

VP, Ballpark Operations: Kevin Kahn. **Senior Director, Food Service Operations/Development:** Albert Valdes. **Manager, Ballpark Services:** Mary Beth Benner. **Senior Director, Guest Services:** Steven Burke. **Head Groundskeeper:** Mark Razum. **Groundskeeping Assistants:** James Sowl, Charles Starkovich. **Senior Director, Engineering/Facilities:**

2012 SCHEDULE

Standard Game Times: 6:40 p.m.; Sat. 6:10; Sun. 1:10.

APRIL		
6-8 . . . . .at Houston	18-20 . . . . Seattle	2-5 . . . . .at St. Louis
9 . . . . San Francisco	21-23 . . . . at Miami	6-8 . . . . . at Washington
11-12 . . . . San Francisco	25-27 . . . . .at Cincinnati	13-15 . . . . .Philadelphia
13-15 . . . . .Arizona	28-31 . . . . . . Houston	16-18 . . . . . . Pittsburgh
16-18 . . . . . . San Diego		20-22 . . . . . at San Diego
20-22 . . . . at Milwaukee	JUNE	23-25 . . . . . . at Arizona
23-25 . . . . at Pittsburgh	1-3 . . . .Los Angeles (NL)	27-29 . . . . . . Cincinnati
27-29 . . . .New York (NL)	4-6 . . . . at Arizona	31 . . . . St. Louis
30 . . . . Los Angeles (NL)	8-10 . . Los Angeles (AL)	
	12-14 . . . . Oakland	AUGUST
MAY	15-17 . . . . . . .at Detroit	1-2 . . . . St. Louis
1-2 . . Los Angeles (NL)	19-21 . . . at Philadelphia	3-5 . . . . . . San Francisco
4-6 . . . . Atlanta	22-24 . . . . . . .at Texas	6-8 . . at Los Angeles (NL)
7-9 . . . . . . at San Diego	25-28 . . . . .Washington	10-12 . . at San Francisco
11-13 . at Los Angeles (NL)	29-30 . . . . . . San Diego	13-15 . . . . . .Milwaukee
14-15 . . . at San Francisco		16-19 . . . . .Miami
16-17 . . . . .Arizona	JULY	20-23 . . .at New York (NL)
	1 . . . . San Diego	24-26 . . . .at Chicago (NL)

27-29 . . . Los Angeles (NL)	
31 . . . . San Diego	
SEPTEMBER	
1-2 . . . . San Diego	
3-6 . . . . at Atlanta	
7-9 . . . at Philadelphia	
10-12 . . . San Francisco	
14-16 . . . . at San Diego	
17-20 . . at San Francisco	
21-24 . . . . Arizona	
25-27 . . . . Chicago (NL)	
28-30 . at Los Angeles (NL)	
OCTOBER	
1-3 . . . . at Arizona	

GENERAL INFORMATION

Stadium (year opened): Coors Field (1995).
Team Colors: Purple, black and silver.

Player Representative: Troy Tulowitzki.
Home Dugout: First Base.
Playing Surface: Grass.

James Wiener. **Director, Engineering:** Randy Carlill. **Director, Facilities:** Oly Olsen. **Official Scorers:** Dave Einspahr, Dave Plati. **Public Address Announcer:** Reed Saunders.

Ticketing
Telephone: (303) 762-5437, (800) 388-7625. **Fax:** (303) 312-2115.

VP, Ticket Operations/Sales/Services: Sue Ann McClaren. **Senior Director, Ticket Operations/Sales/Services:** Kevin Fenton. **Director, Ticket Operations/Finances:** Kent Hakes. **Assistant Director, Ticket Operations:** Scott Donaldson. **Director, Season Tickets/Group Sales:** Jeff Benner. **Director, Outbound Sales/Suites:** Matt Haddad. **Supervisor, Suites/Party Facilities:** Traci Sauerteig. **Senior Account Executive:** Todd Thomas. **Senior Account Representative, Ticket Sales:** Grayson Beatty. **Senior Account Representative, Outbound Sales:** Justin Bennett.

Travel/Clubhouse
Director, Major League Operations: Paul Egins. **Director, Clubhouse Operations:** Keith Schulz. **Visiting Clubhouse Manager:** Alan Bossart.

BASEBALL OPERATIONS
Telephone: (303) 292-0200. **Fax:** (303) 312-2320.

Dan O'Dowd

Executive VP/Chief Baseball Officer/General Manager: Dan O'Dowd. **Assistant to Executive VP/Chief Baseball Officer/GM:** Adele Armagost. **Assistant GM/VP, Baseball Operations:** Bill Geivett. **Manager, Baseball Operations/Assistant General Counsel:** Zack Rosenthal. **Assistants, Baseball Operations:** Kent McKendry, Walter Sylvester. **Special Assistants to GM:** Pat Daugherty (Aurora, CO), Dave Holliday (Tulsa, OK).

Major League Staff
Manager: Jim Tracy.

Coaches: Bench—Tom Runnells; **Pitching**—Bob Apodaca; **Hitting**—Carney Lansford; **First Base**—Glenallen Hill; **Third Base**—Rich Dauer; **Bullpen**—Jim Wright; **Catching**—Jerry Weinstein; **Bullpen Catcher**—Pat Burgess; **Strength/Conditioning**—Brian Jordan; **Video**—Brian Jones.

Medical/Training
Senior Director, Medical Operations/Special Projects: Tom Probst. **Medical Director:** Dr. Thomas Noonan. **Club Physicians:** Dr. Allen Schreiber, Dr. Douglas Wyland. **Head Trainer:** Keith Dugger. **Assistant Athletic Trainer:** Scott Gehret.

Player Development
Telephone: (303) 292-0200. **Fax:** (303) 312-2320.

Senior Director, Player Development: Jeff Bridich. **Assistant Director, Player Development:** Zach Wilson. **Assistant, Player Development:** Walker Monfort. **Field Coordinator:** Ron Gideon. **Pitching Coordinator:** Doug Linton. **Hitting Coordinator:** Jimmy Johnson. **Catching Coordinator:** Marv Foley. **Infield Coordinator:** Dave Hajek. **Outfield/ Baserunning Coordinator:** Trenidad Hubbard.

Senior Advisor, Player Development: Bobby Knoop. **Strength/Conditioning Coordinator:** Gabe Bauer. **Assistant Video Coordinator:** Scott Alves. **Mental Skills Coach:** Ronn Svetich. **Rehabilitation Coordinator:** Scott Murayama. **Equipment Manager:** Jerry Bass.

Farm System

Class	Club (League)	Manager	Coach	Pitching Coach
Triple-A	Colorado Springs (PCL)	Stu Cole	Rene Lachemann	Bo McLaughlin
Double-A	Tulsa (TL)	Duane Espy	Kevin Riggs	Dave Schuler
High A	Modesto (CAL)	Lenn Sakata	Jon Stone	Darryl Scott
Low A	Asheville (SAL)	Joe Mikulik	Mike Devereaux	Joey Eischen
Short-season	Tri-City (NWL)	Fred Ocasio	Anthony Sanders	Dave Burba
Rookie	Grand Junction (PIO)	Tony Diaz	Drew Saylor	Craig Bjornson
Rookie	Rockies (DSL)	Mauricio Gonzalez	F. Nunez/E. Jose	Edison Lora

Scouting
Telephone: (303) 292-0200. **Fax:** (303) 312-2320.

VP, Scouting: Bill Schmidt. **Assistant Director, Scouting:** Danny Montgomery. **Senior Director, Scouting Operations:** Marc Gustafson. **Director, Pro Scouting:** Jon Weil.

Advance Scout: Chris Warren. **Pro Scouts:** Ty Coslow (Louisville, KY), Will George (Woolwich Township, NJ), Jack Gillis (Sarasota, FL), Mike Hamilton (Dallas, TX), Rick Mathews (Centerville, IA), Mike Paul (Tucson, AZ). **Special Assignment Scout:** Terry Wetzel (Overland Park, KS).

National Crosschecker: Mike Ericson (Phoenix, AZ). **Scouting Adviser:** Dave Snow (Seal Beach, CA).

Area Scouts: John Cedarburg (Fort Myers, FL), Scott Corman (Lexington, KY), Jeff Edwards (Missouri City, TX), Chris Forbes (AZ), Mike Garlatti (Edison, NJ), Mark Germann (Atkins, IA), Matt Hattabaugh (Westminster, CA), Darin Holcomb (Seattle, WA), Damon Iannelli (Brandon, MS), Jon Lukens (Dana Point, CA), Alan Matthews (Atlanta, GA), Jay Matthews (Concord, NC), Jesse Retzlaff (Dallas, TX), Rafeal Reyes (Miami, FL), Ed Santa (Powell, OH), Gary Wilson (Sacramento, CA). **Part-Time Scouts:** Norm DeBriyn (Fayetteville, AR), Marc Johnson (Centennial, CO), Dave McQueen (Bossier City, LA), Greg Pullia (Plymouth, MA).

Senior Director, International Operations: Rolando Fernandez. **Manager, Dominican Operations:** Jhonathan Leyba. **Supervisor, Venezuelan Scouting:** Orlando Medina. **Manager, Pacific Rim Operations:** Ming Harbor. **International Scouts:** Phil Allen (Australia), Martin Cabrera (Dominican Republic), Carlos Gomez (Venezuela), Frank Roa (Dominican Republic), Chi-Sheng Tsai (Taiwan), Josher Suarez (Venezuela).

Detroit Tigers

Office Address: 2100 Woodward Ave, Detroit, MI 48201.
Telephone: (313) 471-2000. **Fax:** (313) 471-2138. **Website:** www.tigers.com

Ownership
Operated By: Detroit Tigers Inc. **Owner:** Michael Ilitch.
President/CEO/General Manager: David Dombrowski. **Special Assistants to President:** Al Kaline, Willie Horton.
Executive Assistant to President/CEO/GM: Marty Lyon. **Senior VP:** Jim Devellano.

BUSINESS OPERATIONS
Executive Vice President, Business Operations: Duane McLean.
Executive Assistant to Senior VP, Business Operations: Peggy Thompson.

Finance
VP/CFO: Stephen Quinn. **Senior Director, Finance:** Kelli Kollman. **Director, Purchasing/Supplier Diversity:** DeAndre Berry. **Accounting Manager:** Sheila Robine. **Financial Analyst:** Kristin Jorgensen. **Accounts Payable Coordinator:** Debbi Sword. **Accounts Receivable Coordinator:** Sharon Szkarlat. **Administrative Assistant:** Tracy Rice. **Senior Director, Human Resources:** Karen Gruca. **Director, Payroll Administration:** Maureen Kraatz.

Public/Community Affairs
VP, Community/Public Affairs: Elaine Lewis. **Director, Tigers Foundation:** Jordan Field. **Manager, Player Relations:** Sam Abrams. **Manager, Community Affairs:** Alexandrea Thrubis. **Community Affairs Coordinator:** Kristen Joe. **Administrative Assistant:** Audrey Zielinski/Donna Bernardo.

Sales/Marketing
VP, Corporate Partnerships: Steve Harms. **Senior Director, Corporate Partnerships:** Zach Wagner. **Senior Director, Corporate Sales:** Kurt Buhler. **Corporate Sales Managers:** Soula Burns, John Wolski. **Manager, Sponsorship Services/Assistant Legal Counsel:** Amy Peterson. **Sponsorship Services Coordinator:** Ashley Ransey. **VP, Marketing:** Ellen Hill Zeringue. **Director, Marketing:** Ron Wade. **Social Media Coordinator:** Nicole Blaszczyk. **Director, Promotions/In-Game Entertainment:** Eli Bayless. **Promotions Manager:** Jared Karner. **VP, Ticket/Suite Sales:** Scot Pett.

Media Relations/Communications
Telephone: (313) 471-2114. **Fax:** (313) 471-2138.
VP, Communications: Ron Colangelo. **Director, Baseball Media Relations:** Brian Britten. **Manager, Baseball Media Relations:** Rick Thompson. **Coordinator, Baseball Media Relations:** Aileen Villarreal. **Director, Broadcasting:** Molly Betensley.

Ballpark Operations
VP, Park Operations: Michael Healy. **Director, Park Operations:** Brian Skipinski. **Head Groundskeeper:** Heather Nabozny. **Assistant Groundskeeper:** Gail DeGennaro. **Senior Manager, Park Operations:** Ed Goward. **Manager, Event/**

Mike Ilitch

2012 SCHEDULE
Standard Game Times: 7:05 p.m.; Sun. 1:05.

APRIL			
5 . . . . Boston	18-20 . . . . Pittsburgh	2-5 . . . . Minnesota	28-30 . . . . .at Kansas City
7-8 . . . . Boston	22-24 . . . . . .at Cleveland	6-8 . . . . Kansas City	31 . . . . Chicago (AL)
10-12 . . . . . . .Tampa Bay	25-27 . . . . . at Minnesota	13-15 . . . . . .at Baltimore	
13-15 . . . .at Chicago (AL)	28-31 . . . . .at Boston	16-19 . . . Los Angeles (AL)	SEPTEMBER
16-18 . . . . .at Kansas City		20-22 . . . . . Chicago (AL)	1-2 . . . . Chicago (AL)
19-22 . . . . Texas	JUNE	24-26 . . . . . .at Cleveland	3-5 . . . . Cleveland
24-26 . . . . Seattle	1-3 . . . . .New York (AL)	27-29 . . . . at Toronto	7-9 . . at Los Angeles (AL)
27-29 . . . at New York (AL)	5-7 . . . . Cleveland	30-31 . . . . .at Boston	10-13 . . . .at Chicago (AL)
30 . . . . Kansas City	8-10 . . . . . .at Cincinnati		14-16 . . . . . .at Cleveland
	12-14 . . . .at Chicago (NL)	AUGUST	18-20 . . . . Oakland
MAY	15-17 . . . . Colorado	1 . . . . .at Boston	21-23 . . . . Minnesota
1-2 . . . . Kansas City	19-21 . . . . St. Louis	3-5 . . . . Cleveland	25-27 . . . . . . Kansas City
4-6 . . . . Chicago (AL)	22-24 . . . . at Pittsburgh	6-9 . . . . . . .New York (AL)	28-30 . . . . . at Minnesota
7-9 . . . . .at Seattle	25-27 . . . . .at Texas	10-12 . . . . .at Texas	
10-13 . . . . . . .at Oakland	28-30 . . . . . at Tampa Bay	13-15 . . . . . at Minnesota	OCTOBER
14-15 . . . .at Chicago (AL)		17-19 . . . . Baltimore	1-3 . . . . .at Kansas City
16-17 . . . . Minnesota	JULY	21-23 . . . . .Toronto	
	1 . . . . at Tampa Bay	24-26 . . . Los Angeles (AL)	

GENERAL INFORMATION
Stadium (year opened): Comerica Park (2000).
Team Colors: Navy blue, orange and white.

Player Representative: Justin Verlander.
Home Dugout: Third Base.
Playing Surface: Grass.

Guest Services: Jill Baran. Park Operations Manager: Allan Carrise. Scoreboard Operations Manager: Robb Wilson.

Ticketing
Telephone: (313) 471-2255.
Director, Ticket Sales: Steve Fox. Director, Group Sales: Dwain Lewis. Director, Ticket Services: Grant Anderson.

Travel, Clubhouse
Director, Team Travel: Tyson Steele. Advisor, Team Travel: Bill Brown. Manager, Home Clubhouse: Jim Schmakel. Assistant Manager, Visiting Clubhouse: John Nelson. Baseball Video Operations Coordinator: Jeremy Kelch. Assistant, Baseball Video Operations: Andy Bjornstad, Tim Janicki.

BASEBALL OPERATIONS

Telephone: (313) 471-2000. Fax: (313) 471-2099.
General Manager: David Dombrowski.
VP/Assistant GM: Al Avila. VP/Legal Counsel: John Westhoff. VP, Player Personnel: Scott Reid. Special Assistant: Dick Egan. Director, BaseballOperations: Mike Smith. Executive Assistant to President/GM: Marty Lyon. Executive Assistant: Eileen Surma.

Major League Staff
Manager: Jim Leyland.
Coaches: Pitching—Jeff Jones; Batting—Lloyd McClendon; Infield—Rafael Belliard; First Base—Tom Brookens; Third Base—Gene Lamont; Bullpen—Mike Rojas.

Medical, Training

Dave Dombrowski

Director, Medical Services/Head Athletic Trainer: Kevin Rand. Assistant Athletic Trainers: Steve Carter, Doug Teter. Strength/Conditioning Coach: Javair Gillett. Team Physicians: Dr. Michael Workings, Dr. Stephen Lemos, Dr. Louis Saco (Florida). Coordinator, Medical Services: Gwen Keating.

Player Development
Telephone: (863) 413-4107. Fax: (863) 413-1954.
Director, Minor League Operations: Dan Lunetta. Director, Player Development: Dave Owen. Director, Minor League/Scouting Administration: Cheryl Evans. Director, Latin American Player Development: Manny Crespo.
Minor League Operations Coordinator: Avi Becher. Administrative Assistant, Minor League Operations: Marilyn Acevedo. Minor League Field Coordinator: Kevin Bradshaw. Minor League Medical Coordinator: Dustin Campbell. Minor League Strength/Conditioning Coordinator: Chris Walter. Assistant Minor League Strength/Conditioning Coordinator: Steve Chase.
Roving Instructors: Toby Harrah (hitting), Al Nipper (pitching), Joe DePastino (catching), Gene Roof (outfield/baserunning), Brian Peterson (performance enhancement), Robert "Ghost" Frutchey (minor league clubhouse manager).

Farm System

Class	Club	Manager	Coach	Pitching Coach
Triple-A	Toledo (IL)	Phil Nevin	Leon Durham	A.J. Sager
Double-A	Erie (EL)	Chris Cron	Jerry Martin	Ray Burris
High A	Lakeland (FSL)	Dave Huppert	Larry Herndon	Mike Maroth
Low A	West Michigan (MWL)	Ernie Young	Scott Dwyer	Mark Johnson
Short-season	Connecticut (NYP)	Andrew Graham	Mike Rabelo	Jorge Cordova
Rookie	Tigers (GCL)	Basilio Cabrera	Nelson Santovenia	Greg Sabat

Scouting
Telephone: (863) 413-4112. Fax: (863) 413-1954.
VP, Amateur Scouting/Special Assistant to GM: David Chadd. Director, Amateur Scouting: Scott Pleis. Director, Minor League/Scouting Administration: Cheryl Evans. Assistant, Amateur Scouting: Julian Shabazz.
Major League Scouts: Eddie Bane (Encinitas, CA), Jim Olander (Vail, AZ), Mike Russell (Gulf Breeze, FL), Bruce Tanner (New Castle, PA), Jeff Wetherby (Wesley Chapel, FL).
National Crosscheckers: Ray Crone (Cedar Hill, TX), Tim Hallgren (Cape Girardeau, MO). Regional Crosscheckers: East—James Orr (Orlando, FL); Central—Tom Osowski (Franklin, WI); Midwest—Mike Hankins (Lee's Summit, MO); West—Tim McWilliam (San Diego, CA).
Area Scouts: Bryson Barber (Pensacola, FL), Grant Brittain (Hickory, NC), Bill Buck (Manassas, VA), Rolando Casanova (Miami, FL), Scott Cerny (Rocklin, CA), Murray Cook (Orlando, FL), Tim Grieve (New Braunfels, TX), Garrett Guest (Lockport, IL), Ryan Johnson (Oregon City, OR), Matt Lea (Burbank, CA), Marty Miller (Chicago, IL), Steve Pack (San Marcos, CA), Brian Reid (Gilbert, AZ), Jim Rough (Sharpsburg, GA), Chris Wimmer (Yukon, OK), Harold Zonder (Louisville, KY).
Director, International Operations: Tom Moore. Director, Latin American Development: Manny Crespo. Director, Latin American Scouting: Miguel Garcia. Coordinator, Pacific Rim Scouting: Kevin Hooker. Director, Dominican Operations: Ramon Perez. Coordinator, Dominican Academy: Oliver Arias. Venezuelan Scouting Supervisor: Pedro Chavez. Coordinator, Venezuelan Academy: Oscar Garcia. Scouting Assistant, International Operations: Giovanni Hernandez.

Houston Astros

Office Address: Minute Maid Park, Union Station, 501 Crawford, Suite 400, Houston, TX 77002.
Mailing Address: PO Box 288, Houston, TX 77001.
Telephone: (713) 259-8000. **Fax:** (713) 259-8981.
E-mail Address: fanfeedback@astros.mlb.com. **Website:** www.astros.com.

Ownership

Owner/Chairman: Jim Crane.

BUSINESS OPERATIONS

President/CEO: George Postolos.

President, Business Operations: Pam Gardner. **Executive Assistant:** Eileen Colgin.

Senior VP, Finance/Administration: Jackie Traywick. **Senior Director, Risk Management:** Monica Rusch. **Controller:** Jonathan Germer. **Director, Treasury:** Damian Babin. **Senior Accountant:** Monique Sam. **Accounts Payable Coordinator:** Nestor Lopez.

VP, Human Resources/Stadium Security: Larry Stokes. **Senior Director, Payroll/Employee Benefits:** Ruth Kelly. **Director, Security/Safety:** Chad Ludkey. **Payroll Manager:** Jessica Horton. **Benefits Coordinator:** Cyndi Cook. **Manager, Recruitment/Internships Program:** Chanda Lawdermilk. **Receptionists:** Helen Washington, Heather Kuehn.

Senior VP, Premium Sponsorships: Jamie Hildreth. **VP, Sponsorship Sales:** Matt Brand. **VP, Marketing/Ticket Sales:** Jennifer Germer. **VP, Corporate Partnerships:** Rosi Hernandez. **VP, Sponsorships/Business Development:** John Sorrentino. **VP, Finance:** Doug Steckel. **Director, Marketing:** Clint Pasche. **Director, Sponsorship Sales:** Shane Hildreth. **Marketing Manager:** Chris Hunsaker. **Senior Graphics Designer:** Chris Garcia.

Coordinator, Promotions/Special Events: Christie Miller. **Market Development Coordinator:** Nicky Patriarca. **Assistant Director, Sponsorship Sales:** Joe Furmanski. **Sponsorships Coordinators:** Melissa Garibay, Lacey Clayton.

Jim Crane

Public Relations/Communications

Telephone: (713) 259-8900. **Fax:** (713) 259-8025.

Senior VP, Communications: Jay Lucas. **Senior Director, Media Relations:** Gene Dias. **Media Relations Manager:** Stephen Grande. **Media Relations Coordinator:** MJ Trahan. **Senior Director, Digital Media:** Alyson Footer.

VP, Foundation Development: Marian Harper. **Director, Community Affairs:** Shawn Bertani.

Stadium Operations

Senior VP, Special Events/Guest Services: Marty Price. **VP, Building Operations:** Bobby Forrest. **VP, Special Events:** Kala Sorenson. **Director, Engineering/Maintenance:** David McKenzie. **Director, Building Operations:** Austin Malone. **Senior Director, Creative Services:** Kirby Kander. **Director, Ballpark Entertainment:** Brock Jessel. **Director, Telecommunications/Purchasing:** Tracy Faucette. **Director, Guest Services:** Michael Kenny. **Assistant Director, Guest Services:** Cedrick Edwards. **Authentications Manager:** Mike Acosta. **Assistant Director, Sales/Special Events:** Katy

---

2012 SCHEDULE

Standard Game Times: 7:05 p.m.; Sat. 6:05; Sun. 1:05.

APRIL			
6-8 . . . . .Colorado	18-20 . . . . Texas	2-5. . . . . . at Pittsburgh	24-26 . . . at New York (NL)
9-11 . . . . Atlanta	21-23 . . . . . Chicago (NL)	6-8. . . . . . . .Milwaukee	28-30 . . . . . San Francisco
13-15 . . . . at Miami	25-27 . at Los Angeles (NL)	13-15 . . . at San Francisco	31 . . . . Cincinnati
16-19 . . . at Washington	28-31 . . . . . . at Colorado	16-19 . . . . at San Diego	
20-22 . . . Los Angeles (NL)		20-22 . . . . . . at Arizona	SEPTEMBER
23-25 . . . . . at Milwaukee	JUNE	23-25 . . . . . . Cincinnati	1-2. . . . . Cincinnati
27-29 . . . . . .at Cincinnati	1-3 . . . . Cincinnati	26-29 . . . . . . Pittsburgh	3-5. . . . . . . at Pittsburgh
30 . . . . . . .New York (NL)	5-7 . . . . St. Louis	30-31 . . . . . at Milwaukee	7-9. . . . . . .at Cincinnati
	8-10 . . . .at Chicago (AL)		10-12 . . . . . Chicago (NL)
MAY	12-14 . . . at San Francisco	AUGUST	13-16 . . . . .Philadelphia
1-2. . . . . . .New York (NL)	15-17 . . . . .at Texas	1 . . . . at Milwaukee	18-20 . . . . . . .at St. Louis
4-6. . . . . St. Louis	18-20 . . . . . Kansas City	3-5. . . . . at Atlanta	21-23 . . . . Pittsburgh
7-9. . . . . .Miami	22-24 . . . . . . Cleveland	6-9. . . . . . . Washington	24-26 . . . . St. Louis
11-13 . . . . at Pittsburgh	25-28 . . . . . . San Diego	10-12 . . . . . .Milwaukee	28-30 . . . . . at Milwaukee
14-15 . . . at Philadelphia	29-30 . . . .at Chicago (NL)	13-15 . . . .at Chicago (NL)	
16-17 . . . . . .Milwaukee		17-19 . . . . .Arizona	OCTOBER
	JULY	21-23 . . . . . . .at St. Louis	1-3. . . . . .at Chicago (NL)
	1 . . . . . .at Chicago (NL)		

GENERAL INFORMATION

Stadium (year opened): Minute Maid Park (2000).

Team Colors: Brick red, sand and black.

Player Representative: Unavailable.

Home Dugout: First Base.

Playing Surface: Grass.

Preisler. **Assistant Director, Special Events:** Jonathan Sterchy.
Senior Director, Major League Field Operations: Dan Bergstrom. **First Assistant Groundskeeper:** Kyle Lewis.
Second Assistant Groundskeeper: Joe Johannsen. **Groundskeepers:** Willie Berry, Eric Jaramillo, Chris Wolfe.

Ticketing
Senior Director, Ticket Sales: Bill Goren. **Senior Director, Ticket Services:** Brooke Ellenberger. **Director, Ticket Operations:** Marcia Coronado. **Director, Box Office Operations:** Bill Cannon. **Manager, Premium Sales:** Clay Kowalski. **Manager, Ticket Systems/Customer Retention:** Jolene Sherman. **Premium Sales Account Executive:** Kelsey Matherne. **Senior Account Executive:** Brent Brousssard. **Manager, Ticket Sales:** Carl Grider. **Manager, Ticket Service:** Mark Cole. **Ticket Service Coordinator:** Kristen Lundgren. **Administrative Assistant, Ticket Sales:** Joannie Cobb.

Travel/Clubhouse
Director, Team Travel: Barry Waters.
Clubhouse Manager: Carl Schneider. **Visiting Clubhouse Manager:** Steve Perry. **Umpire Attendant/Clubhouse Assistant:** Chuck New. **Clubhouse Attendants:** David Burd, Stacey Gallagher. **Video Coordinator:** Jim Summers.

BASEBALL OPERATIONS
Telephone: (713) 259-8000. **Fax:** (713) 259-8600.
General Manager: Jeff Luhnow.
Assistant GM/Player Relations: David Gottfried. **Director, Decision Sciences:** Sig Mejdal.
Special Assistant to the GM: Enos Cabell. **Special Assistant to the GM, Scouting:** Mike Elias.
Special Assistant to the GM, Latin America: Felix Francisco. **Special Assistant to the GM, Player Development:** Dan Radison. **Executive Assistant:** Traci Dearing. **Baseball Operations Assistant:** Pete Putila.

Jeff Luhnow

Major League Staff
Manager: Brad Mills.
Coaches: Bench—Joe Pettini; **Pitching**—Doug Brocail; **Hitting**—Mike Barnett; **First Base**—Bobby Meacham, Sr.; **Third Base**—Dave Clark; **Bullpen**—Craig Bjornson. Catching Coordinator /Advance Scout: Matt Sinatro.

Medical, Training
Medical Director: Dr. David Lintner. **Team Physicians:** Dr. Tom Mehlhoff, Dr. Jim Muntz, Dr. Pat McCulloch.
Head Trainer: Nathan Lucero. **Assistant Trainer:** Rex Jones. **Strength/Conditioning Coach:** Dr. Gene Coleman.

Player Development
Telephone: (713) 259-8920. **Fax:** (713) 259-8600.
Director Player Development: Fred Nelson. **Special Assistant to the GM:** Julio Linares. **Senior Advisor, Baseball Operations:** Matt Galante. **Director, Florida Operations:** Jay Edmiston. **Coordinator, Player Development:** Allen Rowin. **Field Coordinator:** Paul Runge. **Minor League Coordinators:** Jamey Snodgrass (medical), Frank Renner (strength/conditioning), Daniel Roberts (rehab), Ty Van Burkleo (hitting), Jon Matlack (pitching). **Roving Instructors:** Milt Thompson (outfield/baserunning), Danny Sheaffer (catching), Tom Lawless (infield).

Farm System

Class	Club	Manager	Hitting Coach	Pitching Coach
Triple-A	Oklahoma City (PCL)	Tony DeFrancesco	Leon Roberts	Burt Hooton
Double-A	Corpus Christi (TL)	Keith Bodie	Joel Chimelis	Gary Ruby
High A	Lancaster (CAL)	Rodney Linares	Darryl Robinson	Don Alexander
Low A	Lexington (SAL)	Ivan DeJesus	Josh Bonifay	Dave Borkowski
Short-season	Tri-City (NYP)	Stubby Clapp	Marc Bailey	Rick Aponte
Rookie	Greeneville (APP)	Omar Lopez	Cesar Cedeno	Hector Mercado
Rookie	Astros (GCL)	Ed Romero	Edgar Alfonzo	Jaime Garcia/Charley Taylor
Rookie	Astros (DSL)	Luis Martinez	Luis Mateo	Jose Martinez

Scouting
Telephone: (713) 259-8925. **Fax:** (713) 259-8600.
Assistant GM, Amateur Scouting: Bobby Heck. **Director, Major League Scouting:** Ricky Bennett. **Coordinator, Amateur Scouting:** Stephanie Wilka. **Major League Scouts:** Paul Ricciarini (Pittsfield, MA), Ken Califano (Stafford, VA). **Professional Scouts:** Hank Allen (Upper Marlboro, MD), Ruben Amaro Sr (Weston, FL), Kenny Baugh (Houston, TX), Ken Califano (Stafford, VA), Bryan Lambe (N Massapequa, NY), Jack Lind (Mesa, AZ), Bob Rossi (Baton Rouge, LA), Josh Miller (Houston, TX), Tad Slowik (Arlington Heights, IL), Scipio Spinks (Missouri City, TX).
National Crosschecker: David Post (Canton, GA). **Regional Supervisors: Midwest**—Ralph Bratton (Dripping Springs, TX); **West**—Mark Ross (Tucson, AZ); **East**—JD Alleva (Charlotte, NC). **Area Scouts:** Tim Bittner (Mechanicsville, VA), Keith Bogan (Ridgeland, MS), Mike Brown (Chandler, AZ), Brad Budzinski (Huntington Beach, CA), Tim Costic (Stevenson Ranch, CA), Gavin Dickey (Houston, TX), Paul Gale (Keizer, OR), Joe Graham (Sacramento, CA), Troy Hoerner (Middleton, WI), John Kosciak (Milford, MA), John Martin (Tampa, FL), Larry Pardo (Miami, FL), Jim Stevenson (Tulsa, OK), Everett Stull (Richmond, VA), Nick Venuto (Newton Falls, OH).
Senior Advising Scouts: Bob King (La Mesa, CA), Bob Poole (Redwood City, CA). **Part-Time Scouts:** Ed Fastaia (Lake Ronkonkoma, NY), Joey Sola (Caguas, PR).
International Scouts: Venezuela—Daniel Acuna, Oscar Alvarado, Miguel Chacoa, Jose Palacios; **Dominican Republic**—Rafael Belen, Julio De La Cruz, Jose Lima, Francis Mojica, Jose Ortiz, Melvi Ortega; **Colombia**—Carlos Martinez; **Panama**—Jose Luis Santos; **Nicaragua**—Leocadio Guevara; **Curacao**—Wellington Herrera; **Australia**—Greg Morriss.

Kansas City Royals

Office Address: One Royal Way, Kansas City, MO 64129.
Mailing Address: P.O. Box 419969, Kansas City, MO 64141.
Telephone: (816) 921-8000. **Fax:** (816) 924-0347. **Website:** www.royals.com

Ownership

Operated By: Kansas City Royals Baseball Club, Inc.
Chairman/CEO: David Glass. **President:** Dan Glass. **Board of Directors:** Ruth Glass, Don Glass, Dayna Martz, Julia Kauffman. **Executive Administrative Assistant (Executive Staff):** Ginger Salem.

BUSINESS OPERATIONS

Senior Vice President, Business Operations: Kevin Uhlich. **Executive Administrative Assistant:** Cindy Hamilton. **Director, Royals Hall of Fame:** Curt Nelson.

David Glass

Finance/Administration

VP, Finance/Administration: David Laverentz. **Director, Finance:** Adam Tyhurst. **Director, Human Resources:** Johnna Meyer. **Director, Renovation Accounting/Risk Management:** Patrick Fleischmann. **Senior Director, Payroll:** Tom Pfannenstiel. **Senior Director, Information Systems:** Brian Himstedt. **Director, Information Systems Operations:** Scott Novak. **Senior Director, Ticket Operations:** Larry Chu. **Director, Ticket Operations:** Chris Darr.

Communications/Broadcasting

VP, Communications/Broadcasting: Mike Swanson. **Director, Broadcast Services/Royals Alumni:** Fred White. **Director, Media Relations:** David Holtzman. **Coordinator, Media Services:** Dina Blevins. **Coordinator, Communications/Broadcasting:** Colby Curry.

Publicity/Community Relations

VP, Community Affairs/Publicity: Toby Cook. **Senior Director, Community Relations:** Ben Aken. **Senior Director, Publicity:** Lora Grosshans. **Senior Director, Royals Charities:** Joy Sedlacek. **Director, Community Outreach:** Betty Kaegel.

Ballpark Operations

VP, Ballpark Operations/Development: Bob Rice. **Director, Event Operations/Fan Experience:** Carrie Bligh. **Director, Groundskeeping/Landscaping:** Trevor Vance. **Director, Ballpark Services:** Johnny Williams. **Director, Stadium Engineering/Maintenance:** Todd Burrow.

Marketing/Business Development

VP, Marketing/Business Development: Michael Bucek.
Senior Director, Event Presentation/Production: Don Costante. **Director, Event Presentation/Production:** Chris DeRuyscher. **Director, Online/Target Marketing:** Erin Sleddens. **Senior Director, Corporate Sponsorships/Broadcast Sales:** Wes Engram. **Senior Director, Client Services:** Michele Kammerer. **Director, Special Event Sales:** Ashley Voss.

2012 SCHEDULE

Standard Game Times: 7:10 p.m.; Sat. 6:10; Sun. 1:10.

APRIL
6-8. . . at Los Angeles (AL)
9-11 . . . . .at Oakland
13-15 . . . . Cleveland
16-18 . . . . Detroit
20-23 . . . . .Toronto
24-26 . . . . .at Cleveland
27-29 . . . . at Minnesota
30 . . . . .at Detroit

MAY
1-2. . . . . .at Detroit
3-6. . . . . .New York (AL)
7-9. . . . . Boston
11-13 . . . .at Chicago (AL)
14-15 . . . . .at Texas
16-17 . . . . Baltimore

18-20 . . . . .Arizona
21-23 . . at New York (AL)
25-27 . . . . . .at Baltimore
28-30 . . . . . .at Cleveland

JUNE
1-3. . . . . Oakland
4-6. . . . . Minnesota
8-10 . . . . . at Pittsburgh
12-14 . . . . . .Milwaukee
15-17 . . . . . .at St. Louis
18-20 . . . . . .at Houston
22-24 . . . . St. Louis
25-27 . . . . . .Tampa Bay
20-30 . . . . . at Minnesota

JULY
1 . . . . at Minnesota

2-5. . . . . at Toronto
6-8. . . . . .at Detroit
13-15 . . . . Chicago (AL)
16-19 . . . . Seattle
20-22 . . . . . . .Minnesota
23-25 . at Los Angeles (AL)
26-29 . . . . . . .at Seattle
31 . . . . Cleveland

AUGUST
1-2. . . . . Cleveland
3-5. . . . . Texas
6-8. . . . .at Chicago (AL)
9-12 . . . . . .at Baltimore
14-16 . . . . Oakland
17-19 . . . . Chicago (AL)
20-22 . . . . at Tampa Bay

24-27 . . . . . . .at Boston
28-30 . . . . Detroit
31 . . . . .Minnesota

SEPTEMBER
1-2. . . . . .Minnesota
3-6. . . . . Texas
7-9. . . . .at Chicago (AL)
11-13 . . . . . at Minnesota
14-16 . . . Los Angeles (AL)
18-20 . . . . Chicago (AL)
21-23 . . . . Cleveland
25-27 . . . . .at Detroit
28-30 . . . . .at Cleveland

OCTOBER
1-3. . . . . Detroit

GENERAL INFORMATION

Stadium (year opened): Ewing M. Kauffman Stadium (1973).
Team Colors: Royal blue and white.

Player Representative: Billy Butler.
Home Dugout: First Base.
Playing Surface: Grass.

Senior Director, Sales/Service: Steve Shiffman. Director, Sales: Theodore Hodges. Director, Ticket Services: Scott Wadsworth.

BASEBALL OPERATIONS

Dayton Moore

Telephone: (816) 921-8000. **Fax:** (816) 924-0347.
Senior VP, Baseball Operations/General Manager: Dayton Moore.
VP, Baseball Operations/Assistant GM: Dean Taylor. **Assistant GM, Scouting/Player Development:** J.J. Picollo. **Senior Advisor to GM/Scouting/Player Development:** Mike Arbuckle. **Director, Baseball Administration:** Jin Wong. **Assistant to Baseball Operations:** Mike Groopman. **Baseball Operations Assistant:** John Williams. **Administrative Assistant to Baseball Operations:** Emily Penning.
　Manager, Arizona Operations: Nick Leto. **Coordinator, Pro Scouting:** Gene Watson. **Senior Advisors:** Art Stewart, Donnie Williams, John Boles. **Special Assistant to GM, International Operations:** Rene Francisco. **Special Assistant, Player Personnel:** Louie Medina. **VP, Baseball Operations:** George Brett. **Special Assistants to GM:** Pat Jones, Rusty Kuntz, Mike Toomey, Mike Pazik, Jim Fregosi, Jr., Tim Conroy, Mitch Webster. **Team Travel:** Jeff Davenport. **Video Coordinator:** Mark Topping.

Major League Staff
　Manager: Ned Yost.
　Coaches: Bench—Chino Cadahia; **Pitching**—Dave Eiland; **Batting**—Kevin Seitzer; **First Base**—Doug Sisson; **Third Base**—Eddie Rodriguez; **Bullpen**—Steve Foster.

Medical/Training
　Team Physician: Dr. Vincent Key. **Athletic Trainer:** Nick Kenney. **Assistant Athletic Trainer:** Kyle Turner. **Strength/Conditioning:** Ryan Stoneberg.

Player Development
　Telephone: (816) 921-8000. **Fax:** (816) 924-0347.
　Director, Minor League Operations: Scott Sharp.
　Special Assistant: Jack Maloof (hitting). **Special Assistant, Player Development/Scouting:** John Wathan. **Coordinators:** Tony Tijerina (field), Rick Knapp (pitching), Glenn Hubbard (infield), Garrett Sherrill (strength/conditioning), Sean McQueeney (rehab).

Farm System

Class	Club (League)	Manager	Hitting Coach	Pitching Coach
Triple-A	Omaha (PCL)	Mike Jirschele	Tommy Gregg	Doug Henry
Double-A	Northwest Arkansas (TL)	Brian Poldberg	Terry Bradshaw	Larry Carter
High A	Wilmington (CL)	Vance Wilson	Damon Hollins	Steve Luebber
Low A	Kane County (MWL)	Brian Buchanan	Julio Bruno	Jim Brower
Rookie	Idaho Falls (PIO)	Omar Ramirez	Justin Gemoll	Jerry Nyman
Rookie	Burlington (APP)	Tommy Shields	Jon Williams	Carlos Martinez
Rookie	Royals (AZL)	Darryl Kennedy	A. David/N. Liriano	M. Davis/C. Reyes
Rookie	Royals (DSL)	Jose Mejia	Abraham Nunez	Rafael Roque

Scouting
　Telephone: (816) 921-8000. **Fax:** (816) 924-0347.
　Director, Scouting: Lonnie Goldberg.
　Assistant, Scouting/Player Development: Kyle Vena. **Manager, Scouting Operations:** Linda Smith.
　Coordinator, Professional Scouting: Gene Watson (Georgetown, TX). **Major League Scouts:** Charles Bolton (Indianapolis, IN), Mike Pazik (Bethesda, MD), Alec Zumwalt (Winston-Salem, NC).
　National Supervisors: Paul Gibson (Center Moriches, NY), Junior Vizcaino (Raleigh, NC). **Regional Supervisors: Canada & Junior Colleges**—Keith Connolly (Fair Haven, NJ), **Midwest**—Blake Davis (Plano, TX), **Southeast**—Gregg Kilby (Tampa, FL.), **West**—Dan Ontiveros (Laguna Niguel, CA), **Northeast**—Sean Rooney (Pompton Lake, NJ).
　Area Scouts: Rich Amaral (Huntington Beach, CA), Jason Bryans (Windsor, Canada), Dennis Cardoza (Boyd, TX), Keith Connolly (Fair Haven, NJ), Travis Ezi (Baton Rouge, LA), Casey Fahy (Apex, NC), Jim Farr (Williamsburg, VA), Sean Gibbs (Canton, GA), Colin Gonzales (Orlando, FL), Scott Groot (Mission Viejo, CA), Scott Melvin (Quincy, IL), Alex Mesa (Miami, FL), Ken Munoz (Scottsdale, AZ), Matt Price (Overland Park, KS), Scott Ramsay (Valley, WA), Brian Rhees (Live Oak, TX), Max Valencia (Chico, CA).
　Part Time Scouts: Rick Clendenin (Clendenin, WV), Louis Collier (Chicago, IL), Dan Drake (Riverside, CA), Brian Hiler (Cincinnati, OH), Jerry Lafferty (Kansas City, MO), Brittan Motley (Grandview, MO), Chad Raley (Baton Rouge, LA), Johnny Ramos (Carolina, PR)
　Latin America Supervisor: Orlando Estevez. **International Scouts:** Richard Castro (Venezuela), Alvin Cuevas (Dominican Republic), Taizo Date (Japan), Alberto Garcia (Venezuela) Juan Indriago (Venezuela), Jose Gualdron (Venezuela); Joelvis Gonzalez (Venezuela), Edson Kelly (Aruba), Charlie Kim (Korea), Juan Lopez (Nicaragua), Nathan Miller (Taiwan), Rafael Miranda (Colombia), Fausto Morel (Dominican Republic), Ricardo Ortiz (Panama), Edis Perez (Dominican Republic), Rafael Vasquez (Dominican Republic), Franco Wawoe (Curacao).

Los Angeles Angels

Office Address: 2000 Gene Autry Way, Anaheim, CA 92806.
Mailing Address: P.O. Box 2000, Anaheim, CA 92803.
Telephone: (714) 940-2000. **Fax:** (714) 940-2205.
Website: www.angelsbaseball.com.

Ownership
Owner: Arte Moreno. **Chairman:** Dennis Kuhl. **President:** John Carpino.

BUSINESS OPERATIONS

Arte Moreno

Chief Financial Officer: Bill Beverage. **Vice President, Finance/Administration:** Molly Taylor Jolly. **Controller:** Cris Fisher. **Accountants:** Lorelei Largey, Kylie McManus, Jennifer Whynott. **Financial Analyst:** Jennifer Jeanblanc. **Assistant, Accounting:** Linda Chubak. **Director, Human Resources:** Jenny Price. **Benefits Coordinator:** Cecilia Schneider.

Human Resources Representative: Arianna Fernandez. **Manager, Recruitment/Training:** Brittany Johnson. **Director, Legal Affairs/Risk Management:** David Cohen. **Manager, Information Services:** Al Castro. **Senior Network Engineer:** Neil Farris. **Senior Customer Support Analyst:** David Yun. **Assistant Network Administrator:** Paramjit Singh. **Travel Account Manager:** Chantelle Ball.

Marketing/Corporate Sales
Director, Sales: Neil Viserto. **Senior Director, Business Development:** Michael Fach. **Corporate Sales Account Executives:** Derek Ohta, Nicole Provansal, Erin Ross, Rick Turner. **Senior Sponsorship Services Coordinator:** Maria Dinh. **Sponsorship Services Coordinators:** Bobby Kowan, Jackie Perkins, Drew Zinser.

VP, Marketing/Ticket Sales: Robert Alvarado. **Senior Marketing Manager:** Matt Artin. **Marketing Manager:** Ernie Prukner. **Promotions Representative:** John Rozak. **Marketing Coordinator/Graphic Designer:** Jeff Lee. **Ticket Sales Manager:** Tom DeTemple.

Director, Client Services: Brian Sanders. **Client Services Representatives:** Arthur Felix, Ashley Green, Justin Hallenbeck, Shawn Meyer, Alisa Moreno, Adrieanna Ryan, Matt Swanson. **Group Sales Account Executive:** Angel Rodriguez. **Premium Sales/Service Manager:** Brian Lawrence. **Ticket Sales Account Executives:** Clint Blevins, Jeff Leuenberger, Jasmin Matthews, Scott Tarlo. **Administrative Assistant, Marketing:** Monica Campanis.

Public/Media Relations/Communications
Telephone: (714) 940-2014. **Fax:** (714) 940-2205.
VP, Communications: Tim Mead. **Communications Manager:** Eric Kay. **Media Relations Representative:** Ryan Cavinder. **Community Relations Coordinator:** Lindsay McHolm. **Publications Manager:** Doug Ward. **Traveling Secretary:** Tom Taylor. **Maintenance Supervisor:** Steve Preston. **Club Photographers:** Debora Robinson, John Cordes, Bob Binder.

2012 SCHEDULE
Standard Game Times: 7:05 p.m.; Sun. 12:35.

APRIL
6-8 . . . . Kansas City
9 . . . . at Minnesota
11-12 . . . at Minnesota
13-15 . . . at New York (AL)
16-19 . . . . Oakland
20-22 . . . . . . Baltimore
24-26 . . . . . at Tampa Bay
27-29 . . . . . at Cleveland
30 . . . . Minnesota

MAY
1-2 . . . . Minnesota
3-6 . . . . .Toronto
7-9 . . . . . . at Minnesota
11-13 . . . . . . at Rangers
14-15 . . . . Athletics
16-17 . . . . Chicago (AL)

18-20 . . . . . at San Diego
21-23 . . . . . .at Oakland
24-27 . . . . . . .at Seattle
28-30 . . . . New York (AL)

JUNE
1-3 . . . . Texas
4-6 . . . . Seattle
8-10 . . . . . at Colorado
11-13 . at Los Angeles (NL)
15-17 . . . . Arizona
18-20 . . . . San Francisco
22-24 . . . Los Angeles (NL)
26-27 . . . . .at Baltimore
28-30 . . . . . . at Toronto

JULY
1 . . . . at Toronto

2-4 . . . . .at Cleveland
5-8 . . . . Baltimore
13-15 . . . at New York (AL)
16-19 . . . . . .at Detroit
20-22 . . . . Texas
23-25 . . . . . Kansas City
27-29 . . . . .Tampa Bay
30-31 . . . . .at Texas

AUGUST
1-2 . . . . .at Texas
3-5 . . . . . .at Chicago (AL)
6-8 . . . . .at Oakland
10-12 . . . . Seattle
13-15 . . . . . . Cleveland
16-19 . . . . . .Tampa Bay
21-23 . . . . . . .at Boston
24-26 . . . . . . .at Detroit

28-30 . . . . Boston
31 . . . . .at Seattle

SEPTEMBER
1-2 . . . . .at Seattle
3-5 . . . . .at Oakland
7-9 . . . . Detroit
10-13 . . . . Oakland
14-16 . . . .at Kansas City
18-20 . . . . Texas
21-23 . . . . Chicago (AL)
25-27 . . . . Seattle
28-30 . . . . .at Texas

OCTOBER
1-3 . . . . .at Seattle

GENERAL INFORMATION
Stadium (year opened): Angel Stadium (1966).
Team Colors: Red, dark red, blue and silver.

Player Representative: Unavailable.
Home Dugout: Third Base.
Playing Surface: Grass.

Ballpark Operations/Facilities
Director, Ballpark Operations: Sam Maida. **Director, Facility Services:** Mike McKay. **Event Manager:** Calvin Ching. **Maintenance Manager, Field/Ground:** Barney Lopas. **Assistant Manager, Facility Services:** Linda Fitzgerald. **Purchasing Assistant:** Suzanne Peters. **Receptionists:** Sandy Sanford, Margie Walsh.
Manager, Entertainment/Production: Peter Bull. **Producer, Video Operations:** David Tsuruda. **Associate Producer:** Danny Pitts. **Entertainment Supervisor:** Heather Capizzi. **PA Announcer:** David Courtney.

Ticketing
Manager, Ticket Operations: Sheila Brazelton. **Assistant Ticket Manager:** Susan Weiss. **Ticketing Supervisor:** Ryan Vance. **Ticketing Representatives:** Cyndi Nguyen, Clancy Holligan.

Travel/Clubhouse
Clubhouse Manager: Keith Tarter.
Assistant Clubhouse Manager: Shane Demmitt. **Visiting Clubhouse Manager:** Brian Harkins. **Senior Video Coordinator:** Diego Lopez. **Video Coordinator:** Ruben Montano.

BASEBALL OPERATIONS

Jerry Dipoto

General Manager: Jerry Dipoto.
Assistant GM, Baseball Operations: Matt Klentak. **Assistant GM, Player Development/ Scouting:** Scott Servais. **Special Advisor:** Bill Stoneman. **Special Assistant to GM:** Marcel Lachemann. **Director, Baseball Operations:** Justin Hollander. **Director, Pro Scouting:** Hal Morris.

Major League Staff
Manager: Mike Scioscia. **Coaches: Bench**—Rob Picciolo; **Pitching**—Mike Butcher; **Batting**—Mickey Hatcher; **First Base**—Alfredo Griffin; **Third Base**—Dino Ebel; **Bullpen**—Steve Soliz; **Bullpen Catcher**—Tom Gregorio.

Medical/Training
Medical Director: Dr. Lewis Yocum. **Team Physician:** Dr. Craig Milhouse. **Head Athletic Trainer:** Adam Nevala. **Assistant Athletic Trainer:** Rick Smith. **Minor League Head Athletic Trainer:** Geoff Hostetter. **Strength/Conditioning Coach:** T.J. Harrington. **Minor League Strength/Conditioning Coordinator:** Seth Walsh.

Player Development
Manager, Minor League Operations: Mike LaCassa. **Administrative Assistant:** Kathy Mair. **Administration Manager, Arizona:** Eric Blum. **Field Coordinator:** Gary Disarcina. **Hitting Instructor:** Todd Takayoshi. **Roving Instructors:** Orlando Mercado (catching), Bill Lachemann (catching/special assignment), Tyrone Boykin (outfield/baserunning/bunting), Dick Schofield (infield), Kernan Ronan (pitching), Eric Munson (rehab trainer).

Farm System

Class	Club	Manager	Hitting Coach	Pitching Coach
Triple-A	Salt Lake (PCL)	Keith Johnson	Jim Eppard	Erik Bennett
Double-A	Arkansas (TL)	Mike Micucci	Francisco Matos	Trevor Wilson
High A	Inland Empire (CAL)	Bill Hasselman	Paul Sorrento	Brandon Emmanuel
Low A	Cedar Rapids (MWL)	Jamie Burke	Mike Eylward	Chris Gissell
Rookie	Orem (PIO)	Tom Kotchman	Tom Evans	Zeke Zimmerman
Rookie	Angels (AZL)	Brenton Del Chiaro	Nathan Haynes	Jim Gott/Matt Wise
Rookie	Angels (DSL)	Charlie Romero	Edgal Rodriguez	Santos Alcala

Scouting
Director, Amateur Scouting: Ric Wilson. **Assistant, Scouting:** Kathy Mair.
Major League/Special Assignment Scouts: Larry Corrigan (Mendota, IL), Timothy Schmidt (San Bernardino, CA), Jeff Schugel (Denver, CO).
Major League Scouts: Jeff Cirillo (Medina, WA), Willie Fraser (Hopewell Junction, NY), Mike Koplove (Philadelphia, PA), Brad Sloan (Brimfield, IL). **Advance Scout:** Gary Varsho (Chili, WI).
National Crosscheckers: Jeff Malinoff (Lopez, WA), Greg Morhardt (S. Windsor, CT). **Regional Supervisors: Northeast**—Jason Baker (Lynchburg, VA); **Southeast**—Chris McAlpin (Moultrie, GA); **Midwest**—Kevin Ham (Cypress, TX); **West**—Bo Hughes (Sherman Oaks, CA).
Area Scouts: John Burden (Fairfield, OH), Drew Chadd (Wichita, KS), Tim Corcoran (LaVerne, CA), Bobby DeJardin (San Clemente, CA), Jason Ellison (Issaquah, WA), Nick Gorneault (Springfield, MA), John Gracio (Mesa, AZ), Tom Kotchman (Seminole, FL), Brandon McArthur (Kennesaw, GA), Joel Murrie (Evergreen, CO), Dan Radcliff (Palmyra, VA), Ralph Reyes (Miami, FL), Scott Richardson (Sacramento, CA), Rudy Vasquez (San Antonio, TX), Rob Wilfong (San Dimas, CA), J.T. Zink (Hoover, AL).
Director, International Scouting: Marc Russo. **International Scouts:** Jason Dunn (Asia), Lebi Ochoa (Venezuela), Roman Ocumarez (Dominican Republic), Grant Weir (Australia).

Los Angeles Dodgers

Office Address: 1000 Elysian Park Ave, Los Angeles, CA 90090.
Telephone: (323) 224-1500. **Fax:** (323) 224-1269. **Website:** www.dodgers.com

Ownership
Owner and Chairman: Frank McCourt.
Special Advisors to Chairman: Tommy Lasorda, Dr. Frank Jobe, Don Newcombe.

BUSINESS OPERATIONS
Vice Chairman: Jeff Ingram. **Senior Vice President/General Counsel:** Sam Fernandez.
Senior VP, Public Affairs: Howard Sunkin. **CFO:** Peter Wilhelm. **Chief Revenue Officer:** Michael Young.

Frank McCourt

Administration/Finance
Director, Office Administration for the McCourt Group: Hannah Shearer. **VP, Finance:** Marlo Vandemore. **Controller:** Eric Hernandez.

Sales/Partnership
Senior Director, Ticket Sales: David Siegel. **Director, Partnership Administration:** Jenny Oh. **Director, Corporate Partnerships:** Lorenzo Sciarrino. **Director, Business Development:** Schuyler Hoversten. **Director, Premium Sales/Services:** Antonio Morici.

Marketing/Broadcasting
Senior Director, Marketing/Broadcasting: Erik Braverman. **Director, Advertising/Promotions:** Shelley Wagner. **Director, Production:** Greg Taylor. **Director, Graphic Design:** Ross Yoshida.

Human Resources/Legal
Senior Director, Human Resources/Deputy General Counsel: Warren Leonard. **Director, Human Resources:** Leonor Romero. **Senior Counsel:** Chad Gunderson.

Communications
Assistant Directors, Public Relations: Joe Jareck, Yvonne Carrasco. **Director, Publications:** Jorge Martin.

Community Relations
Senior Manager, Community/Alumni Relations: Cindi Adler.

Information Technology/Stadium Operations/Security
Senior Director, Information Technology: Ralph Esquibel. **VP, Stadium Operations:** Francine Hughes. **Senior Director, Security:** Rich Wemmer. **Assistant Director, Turf/Grounds:** Eric Hansen. **PA Announcer:** Eric Smith. **Official Scorers:** Don Hartack, Ed Munson. **Organist:** Nancy Bea Hefley.

Ticketing
Telephone: (323) 224-1471. **Fax:** (323) 224-2609.

2012 SCHEDULE
Standard Game Times: 7:10 p.m.; Sun. 1:10

APRIL
5-8 . . . . at San Diego
9-12 . . . . Pittsburgh
13-15 . . . . . . San Diego
17-19 . . . . . at Milwaukee
20-22 . . . . .at Houston
23-25 . . . . Atlanta
27-29 . . . . . Washington
30 . . . . at Colorado

MAY
1-2 . . . . at Colorado
4-6 . . . . .at Chicago (NL)
7-9 . . . . . San Francisco
11-13 . . . . . . Colorado
14-15 . . . . . . Arizona
16-17 . . . . at San Diego

18-20 . . . . St. Louis
21-23 . . . . . at Arizona
25-27 . . . . . . Houston
28-31 . . . . . .Milwaukee

JUNE
1-3 . . . . at Colorado
4-7 . . . . . at Philadelphia
8-10 . . . . .at Seattle
11-13 . . Los Angeles (AL)
15-17 . . . . Chicago (AL)
19-21 . . . . . .at Oakland
22-24 . at Los Angeles (AL)
25-27 . . at San Francisco
28-30 . . . . .New York (NL)

JULY
1 . . . . .New York (NL)

2-4 . . . . Cincinnati
5-8 . . . . at Arizona
13-15 . . . . . . San Diego
16-18 . . . . .Philadelphia
20-22 . . at New York (NL)
23-26 . . . . . .at St. Louis
27-29 . . . at San Francisco
30-31 . . . . .Arizona

AUGUST
1 . . . . .Arizona
3-5 . . . . . . Chicago (NL)
6-8 . . . . .Colorado
10-12 . . . . at Miami
13-16 . . . . at Pittsburgh
17-19 . . . . . at Atlanta
20-22 . . . . San Francisco

24-26 . . . . .Miami
27-29 . . . . . at Colorado
30-31 . . . . .Arizona

SEPTEMBER
1-2 . . . . .Arizona
3-5 . . . . San Diego
7-9 . . . . at San Francisco
11-12 . . . . . . at Arizona
13-16 . . . . St. Louis
18-20 . . . . at Washington
21-23 . . . . .at Cincinnati
25-27 . . . . at San Diego
28-30 . . . . . . .Colorado

OCTOBER
1-3 . . . . . . San Francisco

GENERAL INFORMATION
Stadium (year opened): Dodger Stadium (1962).
Team Colors: Dodger blue and white.
Player Representative: Clayton Kershaw.
Home Dugout: Third Base.
Playing Surface: Grass.

VP, Ticket Operations: Billy Hunter. Senior Director, Ticket Operations: Seth Bluman.

BASEBALL OPERATIONS

Ned Colletti

Telephone: (323) 224-1500. Fax: (323) 224-1463.
General Manager: Ned Colletti.
Director, Player Personnel: Vance Lovelace. Special Assistants to GM: Ken Bracey, Toney Howell. Special Assistants, Baseball Operations/Player Development: Juan Castro, Bill Mueller, Aaron Sele, Mark Sweeney, Jose Vizcaíno. Director, Baseball Operations: Ellen Harrigan. Director, Baseball Contracts/Research/Operations: Alex Tamin. Director, Team Travel: Scott Akasaki.
Major League Video Coordinator: John Pratt. Assistant, Player Development/International Operations: Roman Barinas. Assistants, Baseball Operations: Matt Marks, Jordan Peikin. Assistant, Pro Scouting/Baseball Operations: Will Sharp. Assistant, Scouting: Artie Harris.
Director, Team Travel: Scott Akasaki. Advisor, Team Travel: Billy DeLury. Home Clubhouse Manager: Mitch Poole. Visiting Clubhouse Manager: Jerry Turner. Assistant Manager, Dodger Clubhouse: Alex Torres. Clubhouse Attendant: Jose Castillo. Major League Video Coordinator: John Pratt.

Major League Staff

Manager: Don Mattingly.
Coaches: Bench—Trey Hillman; Pitching—Rick Honeycutt; Hitting—Dave Hansen; First Base—Davey Lopes; Third Base—Tim Wallach; Bullpen—Ken Howell.
Instructor: Manny Mota, Steve Yeager. Bullpen Catcher: Rob Flippo.

Medical/Training

Senior Director, Medical Services: Stan Conte.
Head Athletic Trainer: Sue Falsone. Assistant Athletic Trainers: Nancy Patterson, Greg Harrel. Strength/Conditioning Coach: Stephen Downey. Massage Therapist: Ichiro Tani. Team Physicians: Dr. Neal ElAttrache, Dr. John Plosay.

Player Development

Telephone: (323) 224-1500. Fax: (323) 224-1359.
Assistant GM, Player Development: De Jon Watson.
Senior Advisors to Player Development: PJ Carey, Gene Clines, Charlie Hough. Latin America Special Advisor: Ramon Martinez. Senior Manager, Player Development: Chris Madden. Coordinator, Minor League Administration: Adriana Urzua. Instructor: Maury Wills. Field Coordinator: Bruce Hines. Coordinators: Eric Owens (hitting), Rafael Chaves (pitching), Damon Mashore (outfield/baserunning), Jody Reed (infield), Travis Barbary (catching). Campo Las Palmas Coordinator: Henry Cruz. Field Coordinator, Campo Las Palmas: Antonio Bautista. Coordinator, Instruction Camelback Ranch: Matt Martin.

Farm System

Class	Club (League)	Manager	Coach	Pitching Coach
Triple-A	Albuquerque (PCL)	Lorenzo Bundy	John Valentin	Glenn Dishman
Double-A	Chattanooga (SL)	Carlos Subero	Franklin Stubbs	Chuck Crim
High-A	Rancho Cucamonga (CAL)	Juan Bustabad	Michael Boughton	Matt Herges
Low-A	Great Lakes (MWL)	John Shoemaker	Razor Shines	Hector Berrios
Rookie	Ogden (PIO)	Damon Berryhill	Doug Mientkiewicz	Bill Simas
Rookie	Dodgers (AZL)	Matt Martin	Leo Garcia	Kremlin Martinez
Rookie	Dodgers (DSL)	Pedro Mega	Keyter Collado	Alejandro Pena

Scouting

Assistant GM, Amateur/International Scouting: Logan White.
Global Crosschecker: Paul Fryer (Calabasas, CA). National Crosschecker: John Green (Tucson, AZ). Eastern Regional Supervisor: Gary Nickels (Naperville, IL). Western Regional Supervisor: Brian Stephenson (Chandler, AZ). Special Advisor, Amateur Scouting/National Crosschecker: Gib Bodet (San Clemente, CA).
Special Assistant, Amateur Scouting: Larry Barton (Leona Valley, CA). Manager, Scouting/Travel Administration: Jane Capobianco. Coordinator, Scouting: Trey Magnuson. Area Scouts: Clint Bowers (The Woodlands, TX), Bobby Darwin (Corona, CA), Rich Delucia (Reading, PA), Scott Hennessey (Ponte Verde, FL), Orsino Hill (Sacramento, CA), Calvin Jones (Highland Village, TX), Henry Jones (Vancouver, WA), Lon Joyce (Spartanburg, SC), Marty Lamb (Nicholasville, KY), Scott Little (Cape Girardeau, MO), Dennis Moeller (Stevenson Ranch, CA), Matthew Paul (Slidell, LA), Clair Rierson (Wake Forest, NC), Chet Sergo (Stoughton, WI), Rob Sidwell (Windermere, FL), Dustin Yount (Paradise Valley, AZ). Part-Time Scouts: Artie Harris, Luis Faccio, Greg Goodwin, Jimmy Johnston, Jeffrey Lachman. Scouting Consultant: George Genovese. Director, Professional Scouting: Rick Ragazzo. Advance Scout: Wade Taylor. Professional Scouts: Bill Latham, Carl Loewenstine, Tydus Meadows, Steve Pope, John Sanders.
Executive Director, Asian Operations: Acey Kohrogi. Senior Manager, Asian Operations: Yayoi Sato. Director, International and Minor League Relations: Joseph Reaves. Senior Advisor, Dominican Republic: Ralph Avila.
International Scouts: Gustavo Zapata (Central America), Rolando Chirino (Curacao), Maximo Gross (Dominican), Wilton Guerrero (Dominican), Rafael Rijo (Dominican), Ezequiel Sepulveda (Dominican), Bienvenido Tavarez (Dominican), Keiichi Kojima (Japan), Byung-Hwan An (Korea), Mike Brito (Mexico), Francisco Cartaya (Venezuela), Camilo Pascual (Venezuela), Bernardino Torres (Venezuela), Oswaldo Villalobos (Venezuela).

Miami Marlins

Office Address: Marlins Park, 501 Marlins Way, Miami, FL 33125
Telephone: (305) 480-1300. **Fax:** (305) 480-3012.
Website: www.marlins.com.

Ownership
Owner/CEO: Jeffrey Loria. **Vice Chairman:** Joel Mael.
President: David Samson. **Special Assistants to Owner:** Jack McKeon, Bill Beck. **Special Assistants to President:** Andre Dawson, Tony Perez, Jeff Conine. **Executive Assistants:** Elizabeth McConville, Lisa Milk, Teresita Garcia.

BUSINESS OPERATIONS

Executive Vice President/CFO: Michel Bussiere. **Executive VP, Ballpark Development:** Claude Delorme. **VP, Ballpark Operations:** Steve Ethier. **VP, Facilities:** Jeff King. **Director, Parking:** Michael McKeon. **Manager, Game Services:** Antonio Torres-Roman.
Senior Director, Human Resources: Ana Hernandez. **Benefits Administrator:** Ruby Mattei. **Manager, Human Resources:** Brian Estes. **Coordinator, Human Resources:** Michelle Casanova. **Supervisor, Office Services:** Karl Heard. **Assistant Office Services:** Donna Kirton.

Finance
Senior VP, Finance: Susan Jaison. **Controller:** Alina Trigo. **Administrator, Payroll:** Carolina Calderon. **Accountant:** Alina Goni. **Coordinator, Accounts Payable:** Marva Alexander. **Coordinator, Finance:** Diana Jorge.

Jeffrey Loria

Marketing
Senior VP, Marketing: Sean Flynn. **Director, Multicultural Marketing:** Juan Martinez. **Director, Marketing/Promotions:** Matt Britten. **Coordinator, Marketing:** Boris Menier. **Coordinator, Promotions:** Rafael Capdevila. **Director, Creative Services:** Alfred Hernandez. **Manager, Creative Services:** Robert Vigon.

Legal
VP/General Counsel: Derek Jackson. **Associate Counsel:** Ashwin Krishnan. **Associate Counsel, Ballpark Affairs:** Chelsea Hirschhorn. **Executive Assistant to VP/General Counsel:** A'kyra Hamilton.

Sales/Ticketing
VP, Business Development: Dale Hendricks. **Senior VP, Corporate Sales:** Brendan Cunningham. **Directors, Corporate Sales:** Tony Tome, Heath Price-Khan. **Managers, Client Services:** Sheri Fanucci, Christina Portice. **Senior VP, Sales/Service:** Andy Silverman. **Senior Account Executives:** Orestes Hernandez, Anthony Jabara. **Senior Account Executives, Group Sales/Special Events:** Mario Signorello, Bray LaDow, Kathleen Massolio, Brian Long. **Senior Director, New Ballpark Suites:** Chad Johnson. **Manager, Inside Sales:** Sean Flood. **Director, Season Ticket Services:** Spencer Linden. **Director, Premium Services:** Amy Chwick. **Manager, Season Ticket Services:** John-Albert Rodriuez. **Director, Retail Operations:** Roger Kitch. **Director, Ticket Operations:** Orvandis Jimenez.

2012 SCHEDULE

Standard Game Times: 7:10 p.m.; Sun. 1:10

APRIL		
4 . . . . St. Louis	16-17 . . . . . . at Atlanta	20-23 . . . . . . at Arizona
5 . . . . .at Cincinnati	18-20 . . . . .at Cleveland	24-26 . at Los Angeles (NL)
7-8 . . . . . . .at Cincinnati	21-23 . . . . . . .Colorado	28-29 . . . . . Washington
9 . . . . . . at Philadelphia	24-27 . . . San Francisco	31 . . . . . .New York (NL)
11-12 . . . . at Philadelphia	28-30 . . . . . Washington	
13-15 . . . . Houston		SEPTEMBER
17-19 . . . . . Chicago (NL)	JUNE	1-2 . . . . . .New York (NL)
20-22 . . . . at Washington	1-3 . . . at Philadelphia	3-6 . . . . .Milwaukee
24-26 . . . at New York (NL)	5-7 . . . . Atlanta	7-9 . . . . . at Washington
27-30 . . . . .Arizona	8-10 . . . . .Tampa Bay	10-12 . . . at Philadelphia
	11-13 . . . . Boston	14-16 . . . . Cincinnati
MAY	15-17 . . . . at Tampa Bay	17-19 . . . . Atlanta
1-3 . . . . . at San Francisco	19-21 . . . . . .at Boston	21-23 . . . at New York (NL)
4-6 . . . . at San Diego	22-24 . . . . .Toronto	25-27 . . . . . . at Atlanta
7-9 . . . . .at Houston	25-27 . . . . St. Louis	28-30 . . . . . Philadelphia
11-13 . . . . .New York (NL)	29-30 . . . . . Philadelphia	
14-15 . . . . . . Pittsburgh		OCTOBER

JULY	
1 . . . . .Philadelphia	
2-5 . . . . . . at Milwaukee	
6-8 . . . . .at St. Louis	
13-16 . . . . . Washington	
17-19 . . . .at Chicago (NL)	
20-22 . . . . at Pittsburgh	
23-25 . . . . Atlanta	
27-29 . . . . San Diego	
30-31 . . . . . at Atlanta	

AUGUST	
1-2 . . . . at Atlanta	
3-5 . . . . . . at Washington	
7-9 . . . .at New York (NL)	
10-12 . . . Los Angeles (NL)	
13-15 . . . . .Philadelphia	
16-19 . . . . . . at Colorado	

OCTOBER	
1-3 . . . . . .New York (NL)	

GENERAL INFORMATION
Stadium (year opened): Marlins Park (2012).
Team Colors: Red-Orange, Yellow, Blue, Black, White.
Player Representative: Unavailable.
Home Dugout: Third Base.
Playing Surface: Grass.

Media Relations/Communications

    Senior VP, Communications/Broadcasting: P.J. Loyello. **Director, Media Relations:** Matthew Roebuck. **Director, Business Communications:** Carolina Perrina de Diego. **Manager, Media Relations:** Marty Sewell. **Supervisor, Media Relations:** Joe Vieira. **Administrative Assistant, Media Relations:** Maria Armella. **Director, Broadcasting:** Emmanuel Munoz. **Manager, Broadcasting:** Nelson Sealy.

    Director, Community Outreach: Angela Smith. **Manager, Community Outreach:** Alex Morin. **Coordinator, Community Outreach/Youth Baseball:** Juan Garciga. **Coordinator, Community Outreach:** Adrian Mora. **Executive Director, Community Foundation:** Alfredo Mesa. **Director, Foundation Partnerships:** Joanne Messing.

In-Game Entertainment

    Director, Game Presentation/Events: Larry Blocker. **Manager, Game Presentation/Events:** Eric Ramirez. **Engineering Director, Game Presentation/Events:** Randy Cousar. **Coordinator, Mascot:** John DeCicco. **PA Announcer:** Dick Sanford.

Travel/Clubhouse

    Director, Team Travel: Manny Colon. **Equipment Manager:** John Silverman. **Visiting Clubhouse Manager:** Michael Hughes. **Assistant Clubhouse Attendant:** Domenic Camarda.

BASEBALL OPERATIONS

Larry Beinfest

    Telephone: (305) 480-1300. **Fax:** (305) 480-3032.
    President, Baseball Operations: Larry Beinfest.
    VP/General Manager: Michael Hill.
    Executive Assistant to the President, Baseball Operations/VP/GM: Rita Filbert. **Special Assistant to President, Baseball Operations:** Jim Fleming. **VP, Player Personnel/Assistant GM:** Dan Jennings. **Senior Advisor to Player Personnel:** Orrin Freeman. **Director, Baseball Operations:** Mike Wickham. **Director, Team Travel:** Manny Colon. **Video Coordinator:** Cullen McRae.

Major League Staff

    Manager: Ozzie Guillen.
    Coaches: Bench—Joey Cora; **Pitching**—Randy St. Claire; **Hitting**—Eduardo Perez; **First Base/Infield**—Gary Thurman; **Third Base**—Joe Espada; **Bullpen**—Reid Cornelius; **Bullpen Coordinator**—Jeff Urgelles; **Pre-Game Instructor**—Omer Muñoz.

Medical, Training

    Head Trainer: Sean Cunningham. **Assistant Trainer:** Mike Kozak. **Strength/Conditioning Coach:** Ty Hill. **Team Psychologist:** Robert Seifer, Ph.D.

Player Development

    VP, Player Development: Marty Scott. **Director, Player Development:** Brian Chattin. **Assistant Director, Player Development/International Operations:** Marc Lippman. **Supervisor, Player Development/Scouting:** Michael Youngberg. **Baseball Operations Assistant:** Brett West. **Player Development Assistant:** Jesse Mills. **Field Coordinator:** John Pierson. **Coordinators:** Gene Basham (training/rehabilitation), Tarrik Brock (outfield/baserunning), Tim Cossins (catching), Wayne Rosenthal (pitching), Tim Leiper (infield), Barry Moss (hitting), Mark Brennan (strength/conditioning). **Minor League Equipment Manager:** Mark Brown. **Rehab Coach:** Jeff Schwarz.

Farm System

Class	Club (League)	Manager	Hitting Coach	Pitching Coach
Triple-A	New Orleans (PCL)	Ron Hassey	Damon Minor	Charlie Corbell
Double-A	Jacksonville (SL)	Andrew Barkett	Kevin Randel	John Duffy
High A	Jupiter (FSL)	Andy Haines	Corey Hart	Joe Coleman
Low A	Greensboro (SAL)	David Berg	Frank Moore	Blake McGinley
Short-season	Jamestown (NYP)	Angel Espada	Unavailable	Brendan Sagara
Rookie	Jupiter (GCL)	Jorge Hernandez	Robert Bell	Jeremy Powell
Rookie	Marlins (DSL)	Ray Nunez	Luis Brito	Edison Santana

Scouting

    Telephone: (561) 630-1816/Pro (561) 630-1809.
    VP, Scouting: Stan Meek. **Assistant Director, Scouting:** Gregg Leonard. **Assistant Director, Pro Scouting:** Dan Noffsinger. **Advance Scout:** Joel Moeller (San Clemente, CA).
    Pro Scouts: Brendan Hause (Scottsdale, AZ), Dave Roberts (Fort Worth, TX), Phil Rossi (Jessup, PA), Tommy Thompson (Greenville, NC), Pierre Arsenault (Pierrefonds, QC), Matt Kinzer (Fort Wayne, IN), Mark Wiley (Boca Raton, FL).
    National Crosschecker: David Crowson (College Station, TX). **Regional Supervisors: East**—Matt Haas (Cincinnati, OH); **Central**—Ray Hayward (Norman, OK); **West**—Scott Goldby (Yuba City, CA); **Canada**—Steve Payne (Barrington, RI).
    Area Scouts: Carlos Berroa (Caguas, PR), Mike Cadahia (Miami, FL), Carmen Carcone (Canton, GA), Robby Corsaro (Victorville, CA), Matt Gaski (Greensboro, NC), John Hughes (Walnut Creek, CA), Kevin Ibach (Arlington Heights, IL), Brian Kraft (Auburndale, FL), Joel Matthews (Concord, NC), Tim McDonnell (Westminster, CA), Bob Oldis (Iowa City, IOWA), Gabe Sandy (Damascus, OR), Scott Stanley (Peoria, AZ), Steve Taylor (Shawnee, OK), Ryan Wardinsky (The Woodlands, TX), Mark Willoughby (Hammond, LA), Nick Zumsande (Fairfax, IA).
    Director, International Operations: Albert Gonzalez. **International Supervisors:** Sandy Nin (Santo Domingo, Dominican Republic), Wilmer Castillo (Maracay, VZ). **International Scouts:** A Hugo Aquero (Dominican Republic), Carlos Avila, Luis Cordoba (Panama), Edgarluis J Fuentes, Alix Martinez (San Pedro de Macoris, DR), Domingo Ortega (Santo Domingo, DR), Robin Ordonez (Zulia, VZ).

Milwaukee Brewers

Office Address: Miller Park, One Brewers Way, Milwaukee, WI 53214.
Telephone: (414) 902-4400. **Fax:** (414) 902-4053.
Website: www.brewers.com.

Ownership
Operated By: Milwaukee Brewers Baseball Club.
Chairman/Principal Owner: Mark Attanasio.

BUSINESS OPERATIONS

Mark Attanasio

Chief Operating Officer: Rick Schlesinger. **Executive Vice President, Finance/Administration:** Bob Quinn. **VP, General Counsel:** Marti Wronski. **Senior Director, Business Operations:** Teddy Werner. **Executive Assistant:** Adela Reeve. **Executive Assistant, Ownership Group:** Samantha Ernest. **Executive Assistant/Paralegal:** Kate Rock.

Finance/Accounting
VP/Controller: Joe Zidanic. **Director, Reporting/Special Projects:** Steve O'Connell. **Accounting Manager:** Vicki Wise. **Accounting Manager:** Vicki Wise. **Payroll Manager:** Vickie Gowan. **VP, Human Resources/Office Management:** Sally Andrist.
VP, Technology/Information Systems: Nick Watson. **Director, Network Services:** Corey Kmichik. **System Support Specialist:** Adam Bauer. **Application Developer:** Josh Krowiorz.

Marketing/Corporate Sponsorships
VP, Corporate Marketing: Tom Hecht. **Senior Director, Corporate Marketing:** Andrew Pauls. **Director, Corporate Marketing:** Sarah Holbrook. **VP, Consumer Marketing:** Jim Bathey. **Senior Director, Merchandise Branding:** Jill Aronoff. **Senior Director, Marketing:** Kathy Schwab. **Director, Merchandise Branding:** Jill Aronoff. **Director, Suite Services:** Kristin Loeser. **Senior Manager, Advertising/Marketing:** Caitlin Moyer. **Coordinator, Marketing/Promotions:** Kelly Candotti.
VP, Broadcasting/Entertainment: Aleta Mercer. **Director, Audio/Video Productions:** Deron Anderson. **Manager, Entertainment/Broadcasting:** Andrew Olson. **Coordinator, Audio/Video Production:** Scott Powell.

Media Relations/Communications
VP, Communications: Tyler Barnes. **Director, Media Relations:** Mike Vassallo. **Manager, Media Relations:** John Steinmiller. **Coordinator, Media Relations:** Ken Spindler. **Publications Assistant:** Robbin Barnes. **Senior Director, Community Relations:** Katina Shaw. **Director, Alumni Relations:** Dave Nelson. **Coordinator, Community Relations:** Erica Bowring. **Executive Director, Brewers Foundation:** Cecelia Gore.

Stadium Operations
Senior Director, Stadium Operations: Bob Hallas. **Senior Director, Event Services:** Matt Kenny. **Director, Grounds:** Gary VandenBerg. **Supervisor, Warehouse:** Patrick Rogo. **VP, Brewers Enterprises:** Jason Hartlund. **Manager, Event Services:** Jennacy Cruz. **Receptionists:** Willa Oden, Jody McBee.

2012 SCHEDULE
Standard Game Times: 7:10 p.m.; Sun. 1:10.

APRIL		
6-8 . . . . St. Louis	18-20 . . . . . . Minnesota	2-5 . . . . Miami	24-26 . . . . . at Pittsburgh
9-12 . . . . . at Chicago (NL)	21-13 . . . . . San Francisco	6-8 . . . . at Houston	27-30 . . . . at Chicago (NL)
13-15 . . . . at Atlanta	25-27 . . . . at Arizona	13-15 . . . . Pittsburgh	31 . . . . Pittsburgh
17-19 . . . Los Angeles (NL)	28-31 . at Los Angeles (NL)	16-18 . . . . St. Louis	
20-22 . . . . Colorado		20-22 . . . . . at Cincinnati	**SEPTEMBER**
23-25 . . . . Houston	**JUNE**	23-25 . . . . at Philadelphia	1-2 . . . . Pittsburgh
27-29 . . . . . .at St. Louis	1-3 . . . . Pittsburgh	26-29 . . . . . Washington	3-6 . . . . at Miami
30 . . . . . . at San Diego	5-7 . . . . . . Chicago (NL)	30-31 . . . . Houston	7-9 . . . . .at St. Louis
	8-10 . . . . San Diego		10-12 . . . . Atlanta
MAY	12-14 . . . .at Kansas City	**AUGUST**	14-16 . . . .New York (NL)
1-2 . . . . . . at San Diego	15-17 . . . . at Minnesota	1 . . . . Houston	18-20 . . . . at Pittsburgh
4-6 . . . . at San Francisco	18-20 . . . . .Toronto	3-5 . . . . .at St. Louis	21-24 . . . . at Washington
7-9 . . . . Cincinnati	22-24 . . . at Chicago (AL)	6-8 . . . . Cincinnati	25-27 . . . . .at Cincinnati
11-13 . . . . Chicago (NL)	25-27 . . . . .at Cincinnati	10-12 . . . . . .at Houston	28-30 . . . . Houston
14-15 . . . at New York (NL)	29-30 . . . . Arizona	13-15 . . . . . at Colorado	
16-17 . . . . . .at Houston		16-19 . . . . .Philadelphia	**OCTOBER**
	JULY	20-22 . . . . . Chicago (NL)	1-3 . . . . San Diego
	1 . . . . .Arizona		

GENERAL INFORMATION
Stadium (year opened): Miller Park (2001).
Team Colors: Navy blue, gold and white.
Player Representative: Unavailable.
Home Dugout: First Base.
Playing Surface: Grass.

Ticketing
Telephone: (414) 902-4000. **Fax:** (414) 902-4100.
Senior Director, Ticket Operations: Regis Bane. **Senior Director, Season Ticket Sales:** Billy Freiss. **Director, Group Ticket Sales:** Chris Barlow. **Administrative Assistant:** Irene Bolton.

BASEBALL OPERATIONS
Telephone: (414) 902-4400. **Fax:** (414) 902-4515.
Executive VP/General Manager: Doug Melvin.
VP/Assistant GM: Gord Ash.
Special Assistant to GM/Baseball Operations: Dan O'Brien. **Special Assistant to GM/Pro Scouting/Player Development:** Dick Groch. **Special Assistant to GM:** Craig Counsell.
Director, Baseball Operations: Tom Flanagan. **Director, Video Scouting/Baseball Research for Pro Scouting:** Karl Mueller. **Coordinator, Advance Scouting/Baseball Research:** Scott Campbell. **Manager/Coaching Assistant/Digital Media Coordinator:** Joe Crawford. **Senior Administrator, Baseball Operations:** Barb Stark.

Doug Melvin

Major League Staff
Manager: Ron Roenicke.
Coaches: Bench—Jerry Narron; **Pitching**—Rick Kranitz; **Hitting**—Johnny Narron; **First Base**—Garth Iorg; **Third Base**—Ed Sedar; **Bullpen**—Stan Kyles; **Outfield Coach**—John Shelby.

Medical/Training
Head Team Physician: Dr. William Raasch. **Head Athletic Trainer:** Dan Wright. **Assistant Athletic Trainer:** Dave Yeager. **Strength/Conditioning Specialist:** Josh Seligman. **Medical Coordinator:** Roger Caplinger.

Player Development
Special Assistant to GM/Director, Player Development: Reid Nichols (Phoenix, AZ).
Business Manager, Player Development/Minor League Operations: Scott Martens. **Assistant Director, Player Development:** Tony Diggs. **Coordinator, Administration/Player Development:** Mark Mueller. **Field/Catching Coordinator:** Charlie Greene. **Coordinators:** Frank Neville (athletic training), Lee Tunnell (pitching), Sandy Guerrero (hitting). **Roving Instructors:** Bob Miscik (infield), Reggie Williams (outfield/baserunning).

Farm System

Class	Club (League)	Manager	Coach	Pitching Coach
Triple-A	Nashville (PCL)	Mike Guerrero	Al LeBoeuf	Fred Dabney
Double-A	Huntsville (SL)	Darnell Coles	Dwayne Hosey	John Curtis
High A	Brevard County (FSL)	Joe Ayrault	Ned Yost IV	Fred Dabney
Low A	Wisconsin (MWL)	Matt Erickson	Dusty Rhodes	Chris Hook
Rookie	Helena (PIO)	Jeff Isom	Don Money	Elvin Nina
Rookie	Brewers (AZL)	Tony Diggs	Kenny Dominguez	Steve Cline
Rookie	Brewers (DSL)	Nestor Corredor	Luis De Los Santos	Jose Nunez

Scouting
Telephone: (414) 902-4400. **Fax:** (414) 902-4059.
Special Assistant to GM/Pro Scouting/Player Personnel: Dick Groch (St. Claire, MI).
Director, Professional Scouting: Zack Minasian. **Director, Amateur Scouting:** Bruce Seid. **Manager, Administration/Amateur Scouting:** Amanda Kropp. **Assistant Director, Baseball Research for Scouting:** Tod Johnson. **Assistant, Pro Scouting:** Ben McDonough.
National Crosschecker: Joe Ferrone (Marine City, MI). **National Pitching Crosschecker:** Jim Rooney (Scottsdale, AZ). **Regional Supervisors:** West—Corey Rodriguez (Redondo Beach, CA); East—Doug Reynolds (Tallahassee, FL).
Pro Scouts: Lary Aaron (Atlanta, GA), Brad Del Barba (Ft. Mitchell, KY), Bryan Gale (Chicago, IL), Joe Kowal (Yardley, PA), Cory Melvin (Tampa, FL), Ben McLure (Hummelstown, PA), Tom Mooney (Pittsfield, MA), Andy Pratt (Peoria, AZ), Marv Thompson (West Jordan, UT), Ryan Thompson (Scottsdale, AZ), Derek Watson (Charlotte, NC), Tom Wheeler (Martinez, CA), Leon Wurth (Paducah, KY).
Area Scouts: Drew Anderson (Cold Spring, MN), Josh Belovsky (Orange, CA), Tim Collinsworth (McKinney, TX), Mike Farrell (Indianapolis, IN), Manolo Hernandez (Puerto Rico), Dan Huston (Westlake Village, CA), Harvey Kuenn, Jr (New Berlin, WI), Marty Lehn (White Rock, British Columbia, Canada), Justin McCray (Davis, CA), Tim McIlvaine (Tampa, FL), Dan Nellum (Crofton, MD), Scott Nichols (Richland, MS), Brian Sankey (The Hills, TX), Jeff Scholzen (Santa Clara, UT), Jeff Simpson (Scottsdale, AZ), Steve Smith (Kennesaw, GA), Charles Sullivan (Weston, FL), Steffan Wilson (Springfield, PA), Shawn Whalen (Vancouver, WA).
Supervisor, Canada: Jay Lapp (London, Ontario, Canada).
Part-Time Scouts: John Bushart (West Hills, CA), Richard Colpaert (Shelby Township, MI), Don Fontana (Pittsburgh, PA), Joe Hodges (Rockwood, TN), Roger Janeway (Englewood, OH), Johnny Logan (Milwaukee, WI), Ernie Rogers (Chesapeake, VA), JP Roy (Saint Nicolas, Quebec, Canada), Lee Seid (Huntington Beach, CA), Brad Stoll (Lawrence, KS), Nathan Trosky (Carmel, CA).
Director, Scouting—Dominican Republic: Fernando Arango (Davie, FL). **Director, Scouting—Venezuela:** Manny Batista (Vega Alta, PR). **Latin America Scouts:** Freddy Torres (Venezuela), Rafael Espinal (Dominican Republic), Pedro Hernandez (Dominican Republic), Reinaldo Hidalgo (Venezuela), Juan Martinez (Dominican Republic).

Minnesota Twins

Office Address: Target Field, 1 Twins Way, Minneapolis, MN 55403.
Telephone: (612) 659-3400. **Fax:** 612-659-4025. **Website:** www.twinsbaseball.com.

Ownership
Operated By: The Minnesota Twins.
Chief Executive Officer: Jim Pohlad.
Chairman, Executive Board: Jerry Bell. **Executive Board:** Jim Pohlad, Bob Pohlad, Bill Pohlad, Dave St. Peter.

BUSINESS OPERATIONS

Jim Pohlad

President, Minnesota Twins: Dave St. Peter. **Executive Vice President, Business Development:** Laura Day. **Executive VP, Business Administration/CFO:** Kip Elliott.
Special Assistant to the President/GM: Bill Smith. **Director, Ballpark Development/Planning:** Dan Starkey. **Executive Assistants:** Joan Boeser, Lynette Gittens. **Administrative Assistant:** Danielle Bungarden.

Human Resources/Finance/Technology
VP, Human Resources/Diversity: Raenell Dorn. **Senior Manager, Payroll:** Lori Beasley. **Senior Manager, Benefits:** Leticia Silva. **Human Resources Generalist:** Holly Corbin. **Senior Director, Finance:** Andy Weinstein. **Senior Manager, Ticket Accounting:** Jerry McLaughlin. **Senior Manager, Accounting:** Lori Windschitl. **Manager, Financial Planning/Analysis:** Mike Kramer. **Director, Purchasing:** Bud Hanley. **Manager, Purchasing:** Luis Lozada.
Vice President, Technology: John Avenson. **Senior Director, Technology:** Wade Navratil.

Marketing/Broadcasting
VP, Marketing: Patrick Klinger. **Senior Director, Advertising:** Nancy O'Brien. **Director, Event Marketing:** Heidi Sammon. **Promotions Manager:** Julie Okland. **Marketing Specialist:** Joe Pohlad. **Director, Emerging Markets:** Miguel Ramos. **Senior Director, Broadcasting/Game Presentation:** Andy Price. **Radio Network Producer:** Mark Genosky.

Corporate Partnerships
Director, Client Services: Bodil Forsling. **Senior Account Executives:** Doug Beck, Brock Maiser. **Account Executives:** Karen Cleary, Jordan Woodcroft. **Coordinators, Corporate Client Services:** Paulette Cheatham, Amelia Johnson, Kayleen Alexson, Joe Morin. **Coordinator, Broadcast Traffic/Service:** Amy Johnson.

Communications
Telephone: (612) 659-3475. **Fax:** (612) 659-3472.
Director, Baseball Communications: Mike Herman. **Senior Manager, Baseball Communications:** Dustin Morse. **Manager, Publications/Media Services:** Molly Gallatin. **Coordinator, Baseball Communications:** Mitch Hestad.

Public Affairs
Executive Director, Public Affairs/Twins Community Fund: Kevin Smith. **Director, Community Relations:** Bryan

2012 SCHEDULE
Standard Game Times: 7:10 p.m.; Sun 1:10.

APRIL			
6-8 . . . . .at Baltimore	18-20 . . . . . at Milwaukee	2-5 . . . . .at Detroit	27-30 . . . . .at Seattle
9 . . . . . Los Angeles (AL)	22-24 . . . .at Chicago (AL)	6-8 . . . . .at Texas	31 . . . . . .at Kansas City
11-12 . . . Los Angeles (AL)	25-27 . . . . Detroit	13-15 . . . . Oakland	
13-15 . . . . Texas	28-30 . . . . Oakland	16-19 . . . . . . Baltimore	SEPTEMBER
16-19 . . . at New York (AL)		20-22 . . . .at Kansas City	1-2 . . . . . . .at Kansas City
20-22 . . . . . at Tampa Bay	JUNE	23-25 . . . .at Chicago (AL)	3-5 . . . . . .at Chicago (AL)
23-25 . . . . Boston	1-3 . . . . . . .at Cleveland	27-29 . . . . . . Cleveland	7-10 . . . . Cleveland
27-29 . . . . . Kansas City	4-6 . . . . . .at Kansas City	30-31 . . . . Chicago (AL)	11-13 . . . . . Kansas City
30 . . . at Los Angeles (AL)	8-10 . . . . . Chicago (NL)		14-16 . . . . Chicago (AL)
	12-14 . . . . .Philadelphia	AUGUST	18-20 . . . . . .at Cleveland
MAY	15-17 . . . . . .Milwaukee	1 . . . . Chicago (AL)	21-23 . . . . . . .at Detroit
1-2 . . at Los Angeles (AL)	19-21 . . . . . at Pittsburgh	2-5 . . . . .at Boston	24-26 . . .New York (AL)
4-6 . . . . .at Seattle	22-24 . . . .at Cincinnati	6-8 . . . . . .at Cleveland	28-30 . . . . Detroit
7-9 . . . . Los Angeles (AL)	25-27 . . . . Chicago (AL)	10-12 . . . . . .Tampa Bay	
10-13 . . . . .Toronto	29-30 . . . . . Kansas City	13-15 . . . . Detroit	OCTOBER
14-15 . . . . . . Cleveland		17-19 . . . . . . .at Seattle	1-3 . . . . at Toronto
17-17 . . . . . . .at Detroit	JULY	20-22 . . . . . .at Oakland	
	1 . . . . Kansas City	23-26 . . . . .at Texas	

GENERAL INFORMATION
Stadium (year opened): Target Field (2010).
Team Colors: Red, navy blue and white.

Player Representative: Nick Blackburn.
Home Dugout: First Base.
Playing Surface: Natural Grass.

Donaldson. **Manager, Corporate Communications:** Chris Iles. **Manager, Community Relations:** Stephanie Johnson. **Manager, Community Programs:** Josh Ortiz. **Coordinator, Community Relations:** Gloria Westerdahl.

Ticket Sales/Service
    Telephone: 1-800-33-TWINS. **Fax:** (612) 659-4030.
    VP, Ticket Sales/Service: Steve Smith. **Director, Ticket Sales/Service:** Mike Clough. **Director, Suite/Premium Seat Sales/Service:** Scott O'Connell.

Ticket Operations/Target Field Events
    Senior Director, Ticket Operations: Paul Froehle. **Senior Manager, Box Office:** Mike Stiles. **Senior Manager, Facility/Event Sales:** David Christie.

Ballpark Operations
    Senior VP, Operations: Matt Hoy. **Senior Director, Ballpark Operations:** Dave Horsman. **Director, Ballpark Systems:** Gary Glawe. **Director, Guest Services:** Patrick Forsland. **Head Groundskeeper:** Larry DiVito. **Assistant Groundskeepers:** Jared Alley, Al Kuehner. **Supervisor, Maintenance:** Dana Minion. **Manager, Ballpark Operations:** John McEvoy. **Manager, Guest Services:** Dan Smoliak. **Manager, Premium Services:** Jeffrey Kroll. **Manager, Event Security:** Dick Dugan. **PA Announcer:** Adam Abrams. **Equipment Manager:** Rod McCormick. **Visitors Clubhouse:** Troy Matchan. **Manager, Major League Video:** Sean Harlin.

BASEBALL OPERATIONS
    Telephone: (612) 659-3485. **Fax:** (612) 659-4026.
    Executive VP/General Manager: Terry Ryan.
    VP, Player Personnel: Mike Radcliff. **Assistant GM:** Rob Antony. **Special Assistants:** Wayne Krivsky, Tom Kelly. **Director, Baseball Operations:** Brad Steil. **Manager, Major League Administration/Baseball Research:** Jack Goin. **Administrative Assistant to the GM:** Katie Van Der Linden. **Senior Director, Team Travel:** Remzi Kiratli.

Terry Ryan

Major League Staff
    Manager: Ron Gardenhire.
    Coaches: Bench—Steve Liddle; **Pitching**—Rick Anderson; **Batting**—Joe Vavra; **First Base**—Jerry White; **Third Base**—Scott Ullger; **Bullpen**—Rick Stelmaszek.

Medical/Training
    Club Physicians: Dr. John Steubs, Dr. Dan Buss, Dr. Vijay Eyunni, Dr. Tom Jetzer, Dr. Gustavo Navarrete. **Head Trainer:** Rick McWane. **Assistant Trainers:** Dave Pruemer, Tony Leo. **Strength/Conditioning Coach:** Perry Castellano.

Player Development
    Telephone: (612) 659-3480. **Fax:** (612) 659-4026.
    Director, Minor Leagues: Jim Rantz. **Manager, Minor League Administration:** Kate Townley. **Minor League Coordinators:** Joel Lepel (field), Eric Rasmussen (pitching), Bill Springman (hitting), Paul Molitor (infield/baserunning).

Farm System

Class	Club	Manager	Coach	Pitching Coach
Triple-A	Rochester (IL)	Gene Glynn	Tom Brunansky/R. Ingram	Bobby Cuellar
Double-A	New Britain (EL)	Jeff Smith	Rudy Hernandez	Stu Cliburn
High A	Fort Myers (FSL)	Jake Mauer	Jim Dwyer	Steve Mintz
Low A	Beloit (MWL)	Nelson Prada	Tommy Watkins	Gary Lucas
Rookie	Elizabethton (APP)	Ray Smith	Jeff Reed	Ivan Arteaga
Rookie	Twins (GCL)	Ramon Borrego	M. Cuyler/R. Hernandez	Henry Bonilla
Rookie	Twins (DSL)	Jimmy Alvarez	Unavailable	Manuel Santana
Rookie	Twins (VSL)	Asdrubal Estrada	Unavailable	Luis Ramirez

Scouting
    Telephone: (612) 659-3490. **Fax:** (612) 659-4026.
    Director, Scouting: Deron Johnson. **Coordinator, Professional Scouting:** Vern Followell.
    Major League Scouts: Ken Compton, Earl Frishman, Bob Hegman, Bill Milos. **Pro Scouts:** Bill Harford, Earl Winn. **Advance Scout:** Shaun McGinn.
    Scouting Supervisors: East—Mark Quimuyog, **West**—Sean Johnson, **Mideast**—Tim O'Neil, **Midwest**—Mike Ruth. **Area Scouts:** Trevor Brown (OR), Taylor Cameron (CA), Billy Corrigan (FL), JR DiMercurio (KS), Marty Esposito (TX), John Leavitt (CA), Hector Otero (FL), Jeff Pohl (IN), Jack Powell (TN), Greg Runser (TX), Rick Sellers (KY), Elliott Strankman (CA), Ricky Taylor (NC), Jay Weitzel (PA), Ted Williams (AZ), John Wilson (NJ), Mark Wilson (MN). **Part-Time Scout:** Alan Sandberg (NJ).
    Coordinator, International Scouting: Howard Norsetter. **Coordinator, Latin American Scouting:** Jose Marzan.
    International Scouts—Full-Time: Cary Broder (Taiwan), Glenn Godwin (Europe, Africa), Fred Guerrero (Dominican Republic), David Kim (Pacific Rim), Jose Leon (Venezuela, Panama), Francisco Tejeda (Dominican Republic).
    International Scouts—Part-Time: Vicente Arias (Dominican Republic), John Cortese (Italy), Eric Espinosa (Panama), Eurey Luis Haslen (Dominican Republic), Andy Johnson (Europe), Manuel Luciano (Dominican Republic), Nelson Meneses (Venezuela), Juan Padilla (Venezuela), Franklin Parra (Venezuela), Yan-Yu "Kenny" Su (Taiwan), Koji Takahashi (Japan), Pablo Torres (Venezuela), Lester Victoria (Curacao), Troy Williams (Germany).

New York Mets

Office Address: Citi Field, 126th Street, Flushing, NY 11368.
Telephone: (718) 507-6387. **Fax:** (718) 507-6395. **Website:** www.mets.com, www.losmets.com. **Twitter:** @mets

Ownership
Operated By: Sterling Mets LP.
Chairman/Chief Executive Officer: Fred Wilpon. **President:** Saul Katz. **Chief Operating Officer:** Jeff Wilpon. **Board of Directors:** Fred Wilpon, Saul Katz, Jeff Wilpon, Richard Wilpon, Michael Katz, David Katz, Tom Osterman, Arthur Friedman, Steve Greenberg, Stuart Sucherman.

BUSINESS OPERATIONS
Executive Vice President, Business Operations: Dave Howard. **Executive VP/General Counsel:** David Cohen. **VP/Deputy General Counsel:** Neal Kaplan.

Finance
CFO: Mark Peskin. **VP/Controller:** Len Labita. **Assistant Controller/Senior Director:** Rebecca Landau Mahadeva. **Assistant Controller/Senior Director:** Robert Gerbe.

Marketing/Sales
Senior VP, Marketing/Communications: David Newman. **Executive Director, Marketing Productions:** Tim Gunkel. **Executive Director, Marketing:** Tina Mannix. **Senior Director, Broadcasting:** Lorraine Hamilton. **Director, Marketing Communications:** Jill Grabill. **Director, Community Outreach:** Jill Knee. **Senior VP, Corporate Sales/Services:** Paul Asencio. **Senior Director, Corporate Partnerships:** Catherine Marquette. **Director, Corporate Sales:** Matthew Soloff. **Senior Director, Suite Sales/Services:** Patrick Jones.

Fred Wilpon

Media Relations
Telephone: (718) 565-4330. **Fax:** (718) 639-3619.
VP, Media Relations: Jay Horwitz. **Senior Director, Media Relations:** Shannon Forde. **Director, Communications:** Danielle Parillo. **Assistant Director, Media Relations:** Ethan Wilson. **Manager, Media Relation:** Robert Hines. **Media Relations Assistant:** Jon Kerber.

Ballpark Operations
VP, Operations: Pat McGovern. **Senior Director, Ballpark Operations:** Sue Lucchi. **Manager, Ballpark Operations:** Mike Dohnert. **Director, Landscaping/Field Operations:** Bill Deacon. **VP, Technology Tom Festa.**

Ticketing
Telephone: (718) 507-8499. **Fax:** (718) 507-6369.
VP, Ticket Sales/Services: Leigh Castergine. **Executive Director, Ticket Sales/Services:** Joseph Barber. **Assistant Director, Group Sales:** Kirk King. **Senior Director, Season Ticket Account Services:** Jamie Ozure. **Director, Ticket Sales:** Katie Mahon.

2012 SCHEDULE
Standard Game Times: 7:10 p.m.; Sun. 1:10.

APRIL		
5 . . . . Atlanta	18-20 . . . . . . at Toronto	3-5 . . . . Philadelphia	28-30 . . . . at Philadelphia
7-8 . . . . Atlanta	21-23 . . . . . at Pittsburgh	6-8 . . . . . . Chicago (NL)	31 . . . . at Miami
9-11 . . . . . Washington	24-27 . . . . . . San Diego	13-15 . . . . . . at Atlanta	
13-15 . . . at Philadelphia	28-30 . . . . . .Philadelphia	17-19 . . . . at Washington	SEPTEMBER
16-18 . . . . at Atlanta		20-22 . . . Los Angeles (NL)	1-2 . . . . at Miami
20-23 . . . . San Francisco	JUNE	23-25 . . . . . Washington	3-5 . . . . .at St. Louis
24-26 . . . . .Miami	1-4 . . . . St. Louis	26-29 . . . . . . at Arizona	7-9 . . . . Atlanta
27-29 . . . . . at Colorado	5-7 . . . . . at Washington	30-31 . . . at San Francisco	10-12 . . . . . Washington
30 . . . . .at Houston	8-10 . . . at New York (AL)		14-16 . . . . . at Milwaukee
	12-14 . . . . at Tampa Bay	AUGUST	17-19 . . . . .Philadelphia
MAY	15-17 . . . . . . Cincinnati	1-2 . . . . at San Francisco	21-23 . . . . .Miami
1-2 . . . . .at Houston	18-20 . . . . . . Baltimore	3-5 . . . . . . at San Diego	24-27 . . . . . Pittsburgh
4-6 . . . . .Arizona	22-24 . . . .New York (AL)	7-9 . . . . .Miami	28-30 . . . . at Atlanta
7-9 . . . . . at Philadelphia	25-27 . . .at Chicago (NL)	10-12 . . . . Atlanta	
11-13 . . . . at Miami	28-30 . at Los Angeles (NL)	14-16 . . . . .at Cincinnati	OCTOBER
14-15 . . . . . .Milwaukee		17-19 . . . . at Washington	1-3 . . . . at Miami
16-17 . . . . . . Cincinnati	JULY	20-23 . . . . .Colorado	
	1 . . . . at Los Angeles (NL)	24-26 . . . . Houston	

GENERAL INFORMATION
Stadium (year opened): Citi Field (2009).
Team Colors: Blue and orange.

Player Representative: Unavailable.
Home Dugout: First Base.
Playing Surface: Grass.

Venue Services
VP, Venue Services: Mike Landeen. **Senior Director, Venue Services:** Paul Schwartz. **Director, Venue Services:** Tyrel Kirkham. **Senior Director, Metropolitan Hospitality:** Heather Collamore.
VP, Guest Experience: Craig Marino. **Director, Guest Experience:** Chris Brown. **Manager, Guest Experience:** Kieran Nulty. **Director, Partner Services:** Andy Horner.

Travel/Clubhouse
Clubhouse Manager: Kevin Keirst. **Assistant Equipment Manager:** Dave Berni. **Visiting Clubhouse Manager:** Tony Carullo. **Manager, Team Travel:** Brian Small. **Video Editors:** Joe Scarola, Sean Haggans.

BASEBALL OPERATIONS
Telephone: (718) 803-4013, (718) 565-4339. **Fax:** (718) 507-6391.
General Manager: Sandy Alderson.
VP/Assistant GM: John Ricco. **Special Assistant to GM:** J.P. Ricciardi.
Executive Assistant to GM: June Napoli. **Manager, Baseball Operations:** Adam Fisher.
Statistical Analyst: Ben Baumer.

Major League Staff
Manager: Terry Collins.
Coaches: Bench—Bob Geren; **Pitching**—Dan Warthen; **Batting**—Dave Hudgens; **First Base**—Tom Goodwin; **Third Base**—Tim Teufel; **Bullpen**—Ricky Bones.

Sandy Alderson

Medical, Training
Medical Director: Dr. David Altchek. **Physician:** Dr. Struan Coleman. **Trainer:** Ray Ramirez.

Player Development
Telephone: (718) 565-4302. **Fax:** (718) 205-7920.
VP, Scouting/Player Development: Paul DePodesta.
Director, Minor League Operations: Adam Wogan. **Assistant Director, Minor League Operations:** Jon Miller. **Assistant, Minor League Operations:** Michele Holmes. **Video Coordinator:** TJ Barra. **Florida Complex Administrator:** Ronny Reyes. **Field Coordinator:** Dick Scott. **Coordinator, Instruction/Infield:** Kevin Morgan. **Hitting Coordinator:** Lamar Johnson. **Pitching Coordinator:** Ron Romanick. **Catching Coordinator:** Bob Natal. **Outfield/Baserunning Coordinator:** Jack Voigt. **Medical Coordinator:** Mike Herbst. **Rehab/Physical Therapist:** Dave Pearson.
Strength/Conditioning: Jason Craig. **Senior Advisor:** Guy Conti. **Pitching Consultant:** Al Jackson. **Special Instructor:** Bobby Floyd. **International Field Coordinator:** Rafael Landestoy. **International Catching Instructor:** Ozzie Virgil. **Short-Season Pitching Coordinator:** Miguel Valdes. **Short-Season Hitting Coordinator:** Luis Rivera.

Farm System

Class	Club	Manager	Coach(es)	Pitching Coach
Triple-A	Buffalo (IL)	Wally Backman	Unavailable	Mark Brewer
Double-A	Binghamton (EL)	Pedro Lopez	Luis Natera	Glenn Abbott
High A	St. Lucie (FSL)	Ryan Ellis	Benny Distefano/Jose Carreno	Phil Regan
Low A	Savannah (SAL)	Luis Rojas	George Greer/Joel Fuentes	Frank Viola
Short-season	Brooklyn (NYP)	Rich Donnelly	Bobby Malek	Marc Valdes
Rookie	Kingsport (APP)	Jon Debus	Yunir Garcia	Jonathan Hurst
Rookie	Mets 1 (DSL)	Jose Leger	M. Martinez/E. Chavez	Francis Martinez
Rookie	Mets 2 (DSL)	Alberto Castillo	L. Hernandez/D. Davalillo	Benjamin Marte

Scouting
Telephone: (718) 565-4311. **Fax:** (718) 205-7920.
Director, Amateur Scouting: Tom Tanous. **Coordinator, Amateur Scouting:** Ian Levin. **Director, Pro Scouting:** Jim D'Aloia. **Professional/International Scouting Assistant:** Diana Parra-Gonzalez. **Professional Scouts:** Bryn Alderson (New York, NY), Mack Babitt (Richmond, CA), Conor Brooks (Plymouth, MA), Thomas Clark (Shrewsbury, MA), Tim Fortugno (Elk Grove, CA), Roland Johnson (Newington, CT), Ashley Lawson (Athens, TN), Shaun McNamara (Worcester, MA), Roy Smith (Chicago, IL), Rudy Terrasas (Santa Fe, TX).
National Crosschecker: David Lakey (Kingwood, TX). **Regional Supervisors: Southeast**—Steve Barningham (Land O'Lakes, FL), **West**—Doug Thurman (San Jose, CA), **Northeast**—Scott Hunter (Mount Laurel, NJ), **Midwest**—Mac Seibert (Cantonment, FL).
Area Supervisors: Jim Blueberg (Carson City, NV), Jim Bryant (Macon, GA), Ray Corbett (College Station, TX), Jarrett England (Murfreesboro, TN), Steve Gossett (Fremont, NE), Jon Heuerman (Fountain Valley, CA), Tommy Jackson (Birmingham, AL), Fred Mazuca (Tustin, CA), Marlin McPhail (Irmo, SC), Claude Pelletier (St. Lazare, Quebec), Art Pontarelli (Lincoln, RI), Jim Reeves (Camas, WA), Kevin Roberson (Scottsdale, AZ), Max Semler (Allen, TX), Mike Silvestri (Davie, FL), Jim Thompson (Philadelphia, PA), Scott Trcka (Hobart, IN).
Director, International Operations: Chris Becerra. **Area Supervisor, Dominican Republic:** Gerardo Cabrera. **Area Supervisor, Venezuela:** Hector Rincones.
International Scouts: Modesto Abreu (Dominican Republic), Marciano Alvarez (Dominican Republic), Alejandro Bautista (Dominican Republic), Carlos Capellan (Dominican Republic), Alexis DeLaCruz (Dominican Republic), Harold Herrera (Colombia), Gabriel Low (Mexico), Daurys Nin (Dominican Republic), Clifford Nuitter (Venezuela), Jorge Sebastian (Dominican Republic), Hilario Soriano (Dominican Republic), Alex Zapata (Panama).

New York Yankees

Office Address: Yankee Stadium, One East 161st Street, Bronx, NY 10451.
Telephone: (718) 293-4300. **Fax:** (718) 293-8431. **Website:** www.yankees.com, www.yankeesbeisbol.com.

OWNERSHIP

Managing General Partner/Co-Chairperson: Harold Z (Hal) Steinbrenner.
General Partner/Co-Chairperson: Henry G (Hank) Steinbrenner. **General Partner/Vice Chairperson:** Jennifer Steinbrenner Swindal. **General Partner/Vice Chairperson:** Jessica Steinbrenner. **Vice Chairperson:** Joan Steinbrenner. **Executive Vice President/Chief International Officer:** Felix Lopez.

Business Operations

President: Randy Levine, Esq.
COO: Lonn A Trost, Esq.
Senior VP, Strategic Ventures: Marty Greenspun. **Senior VP, Chief Security Officer:** Sonny Hight. **Senior VP/Chief Financial Officer, Yankee Global Enterprises:** Anthony Bruno. **Senior VP, Corporate/Community Relations:** Brian Smith. **Senior VP, Corporate Sales/Sponsorship:** Michael Tusiani. **Senior VP, Marketing:** Deborah Tymon. **VP/CFO, Accounting:** Robert Brown. **CFO/VP, Financial Operations:** Scott Krug. **Deputy General Counsel/VP, Legal Affairs:** Alan Chang. **Controller:** Derrick Baio.

Harold Steinbrenner

Communications/Media Relations

Telephone: (718) 579-4460. **Fax:** (718) 293-8414.
Director, Communications/Media Relations: Jason Zillo. **Assistant Director, Media/Player Relations:** Jason Latimer. **Assistant Director, Baseball Information/Public Communications:** Michael Margolis. **Coordinator, Baseball Information:** Lauren Moran. **Coordinator, Media Relations:** Kenny Leandry. **Assistant, Media Relations:** Alexandra Trochanowski. **Administrative Assistant, Media Relations:** Dolores Hernandez.

Ticket Operations

Telephone: (718) 293-6000. **Fax:** (718) 293-4841.
Senior Director, Ticket Operations: Irfan Kirimca. **Executive Director, Ticket Operations:** Kevin Dart.

2012 SCHEDULE

Standard Game Times: 7:05 p.m.; Sat.-Sun. 1:05.

APRIL
6-8 . . . . at Tampa Bay
9-11 . . . . . . .at Baltimore
13-15 . . . Los Angeles (AL)
16-19 . . . . . . .Minnesota
20-22 . . . . . . .at Boston
23-25 . . . . .at Texas
27-29 . . . . Detroit
30 . . . . Baltimore

MAY
1-2 . . . . Baltimore
3-6 . . . . . .at Kansas City
8-10 . . . . . . .Tampa Bay
11-13 . . . . Seattle
14-15 . . . . . .at Baltimore
16-17 . . . . . . at Toronto

18-20 . . . . . . Cincinnati
21-23 . . . . . Kansas City
25-27 . . . . . .at Oakland
28-30 . at Los Angeles (AL)

JUNE
1-3 . . . . .at Detroit
5-7 . . . . .Tampa Bay
8-10 . . . . .New York (NL)
11-13 . . . . . . at Atlanta
15-17 . . . . at Washington
18-20 . . . . Atlanta
22-24 . . at New York (NL)
25-27 . . . . . . Cleveland
28-30 . . . . . Chicago (AL)

JULY
1 . . . . Chicago (AL)

2-4 . . . . . . at Tampa Bay
6-8 . . . . .at Boston
13-15 . . . Los Angeles (AL)
16-18 . . . . .Toronto
19-22 . . . . . .at Oakland
23-25 . . . . . . .at Seattle
27-29 . . . . Boston
30-31 . . . . . . Baltimore

AUGUST
1 . . . . Baltimore
3-5 . . . . Seattle
6-9 . . . . .at Detroit
10-12 . . . . . at Toronto
13-16 . . . . Texas
17-19 . . . . Boston
20-22 . . . .at Chicago (AL)

24-26 . . . . .at Cleveland
27-29 . . . . .Toronto
31 . . . . Baltimore

SEPTEMBER
1-2 . . . . Baltimore
3-5 . . . . . at Tampa Bay
6-9 . . . . . . .at Baltimore
11-13 . . . . . . .at Boston
14-16 . . . . . .Tampa Bay
18-20 . . . . .Toronto
21-23 . . . . Oakland
24-26 . . . . at Minnesota
27-30 . . . . . at Toronto

OCTOBER
1-3 . . . . Boston

GENERAL INFORMATION

Stadium (year opened): Yankee Stadium (2009).
Team Colors: Navy blue and white.

Player Representative: Unavailable.
Home Dugout: First Base.
Playing Surface: Grass.

BASEBALL OPERATIONS

Telephone: (718) 293-4300. **Fax:** (718) 293-0015.

Senior VP/General Manager: Brian Cashman.

Senior VP/Assistant GM: Jean Afterman, Esq. **Assistant GM, Pro Player Personnel:** Billy Eppler. **Senior VP/Special Advisor:** Gene Michael. **Special Advisors:** Reggie Jackson, Yogi Berra. **Special Assistants:** Gordon Blakeley, Tino Martinez, Stump Merrill. **Director, Quantitative Analysis:** Michael Fishman. **Director, Mental Conditioning:** Chad Bohling. **Coordinator, Mental Conditioning:** Chris Passarella. **Assistant, Baseball Operations:** Steve Martone. **Systems Architect:** Brian Nicosia. **Research Assistant:** Jim Logue, Alex Rubin, David Grabiner. **Administrative Assistant:** Mary Pellino.

Brian Cashman

Major League Staff

Manager: Joe Girardi.

Coaches: Bench—Tony Pena; **Pitching**—Larry Rothschild; **Batting**—Kevin Long; **First Base**—Mick Kelleher; **Third Base**—Rob Thomson; **Bullpen**—Mike Harkey.

Medical/Training

Team Physician, New York: Dr. Christopher Ahmad.

Head Athletic Trainer: Steve Donohue. **Assistant Athletic Trainer:** Mark Littlefield. **Strength/Conditioning Coordinator:** Dana Cavalea.

Player Development

Telephone: (813) 875-7569. **Fax:** (813) 873-2302.

Senior VP, Baseball Operations: Mark Newman. **VP, Player Personnel:** Billy Connors. **Director, Player Development:** Pat Roessler. **Assistant Director, Baseball Operations:** Eric Schmitt. **Administrative Assistant:** Jackie Williams. **Minor League Coordinators:** Nardi Contreras (pitching), Rick Down (hitting), Torre Tyson (defensive), Julio Mosquera (Catching).

Farm System

Class	Club	Manager	Hitting Coach	Pitching Coach(s)/Coach
Triple-A	Scranton/WB (IL)	Dave Miley	Butch Wynegar	S Aldred/F Menechino
Double-A	Trenton (EL)	Tony Franklin	Tom Slater	T Phelps/L Dorante
High A	Tampa (FSL)	Luis Sojo	Justin Turner	J Ware/M Garza
Low A	Charleston (SAL)	Carlos Mendoza	Gregg Colbrunn	D Borrell/B Baisley
Short-season	Staten Island (NYP)	Justin Pope	Ty Hawkins	C Chantres/D Valiente
Rookie	Tampa (GCL)	Tom Nieto	Edwar Gonzalez	J Rosado/PJ Pilittere
Rookie	Yankees I (DSL)	Raul Dominguez	Roy Gomez	J Duran/T Olivares
Rookie	Yankees II (DSL)	Carlos Mota	Caonabo Cosme	R Guillen/S Encarnacion

Scouting

Telephone: (813) 875-7569. **Fax:** (813) 873-2302.

VP, Amateur Scouting: Damon Oppenheimer. **Assistant Director, Amateur Scouting:** John Kremer.

Manager, Professional Scouting: Will Kuntz.

Professional Scouts: Ron Brand (Plano, TX), Joe Caro (Tampa, FL), Jay Darnell (San Diego, CA), Gary Denbo (Tampa, FL), Bill Emslie (Tampa, FL), Jalal Leach (Sacramento, CA), Bill Livesey (St Petersburg, FL), Bill Mele (Boston, MA), Tim Naehring (Cincinnati, OH), Greg Orr (Sacramento, CA), Josh Paul (Tampa, FL), Kevin Reese (Sterling, VA), Rick Williams (Tampa, FL), Tom Wilson (Lake Havasu, AZ), Bob Miske (part-time, Amherst, NY). **Amateur Scouting, National Crosscheckers:** Brian Barber, Kendall Carter, Tim Kelly.

Area Scouts: Mark Batchko (North Texas), Steve Boros (South Texas, KS), Denis Boucher (Canada), Andy Cannizaro, Jeff Deardorff (Cleremont, FL), Mike Gibbons (Liberty Township, OH), Matt Hyde (Canton, MA), David Keith (Anaheim, CA), Scott Lovekamp (Lynchburg, VA), Carlos Marti (Miramar, FL), Tim McIntosh (Stockton, CA), Darryl Monroe (Decatur, GA), Jeff Patterson (Yorba Linda, CA), Cesar Presbott (Bronx, NY), Lloyd Simmons, Dennis Twombley (Redondo Beach, CA), DJ Svihlik (Birmingham, AL), Mike Thurman (West Linn, OR), Dennis Woody.

Director, International Scouting: Donny Rowland. **Assistant Director, International Operations:** Alex Cotto. **International Crosschecker:** Dennis Woody. **Coordinator, International Player Development:** Pat McMahon. **Latin American Crosscheckers:** Victor Mata (Dominican Republic), Ricardo Final (Venezuela).

Scouting Development Coaches: Argenis Paulino, Jonnathan Saturria.

Dominican Republic Scouts: Esteban Castillo, Raymi Dicent, Arturo Pena, Juan Rosario, Jose Sabino, Raymond Sanchez. **Venezuela Scouts:** Alan Atacho, Darwin Bracho, Jose Gavidia, Borman Landaeta, Cesar Suarez. **International Scouts:** Carlos Levy (Panama), Edgar Rodriguez (Nicaragua), Luis Sierra (Colombia), Lee Sigman (Mexico), Doug Skiles (Europe), Ken Su (Taiwan), John Wadsworth (Australia).

Oakland Athletics

Office Address: 7000 Coliseum Way, Oakland, CA 94621.
Telephone: (510) 638-4900. **Fax:** (510) 562-1633. **Website:** www.oaklandathletics.com

Ownership
Owner/Managing Partner: Lewis Wolff.

BUSINESS OPERATIONS

Lew Wolff

President: Michael Crowley. **Executive Assistant to President:** Carolyn Jones. **General Counsel:** Neil Kraetsch. **Senior Counsel:** Ryan Horning.

Finance/Administration
Vice President, Finance: Paul Wong. **Senior Director, Finance:** Kasey Jarcik. **Senior Manager, Payroll:** Kathy Leviege. **Accounting Manager:** Ling Ding. **Senior Accountant, Accounts Payable:** Isabelle Mahaffey.
Director, Human Resources: Kim Kubo. **Human Resources Coordinator:** Michaele Smith. **Director, Information Technology:** Nathan Hayes. **Systems Administrator:** David Frieberg. **Office Services Coordinator:** Julie Vasconcellos. **Executive Offices Receptionist:** Maggie Baptist.

Sales/Marketing
VP, Sales/Marketing: Jim Leahey. **Assistant, Sales/Marketing Assistant:** Katie Burr.

Marketing/Advertising
Senior Director, Marketing: Troy Smith. **Senior Manager, Digital Marketing:** Travis LoDolce. **Manager, Advertising/ Marketing:** Amy MacEwen. **Creative Services Manager:** Mike Ono. **Senior Director, Corporate Partnerships:** Darrin Gross. **Director, Partnership Services:** Franklin Lowe. **Corporate Account Manager:** Jill Golden. **Coordinator, Corporate Sales/Services:** Tim Sommer. **Senior Manager, Promotion/Events:** Heather Rajeski. **Special Events Coordinator:** Caroline Griggs. **Special Events Assistant:** Sandy Karbel.

Public Relations/Communications
VP, Communications/Broadcasting: Ken Pries. **Director, Public Relations:** Bob Rose. **Senior Manager, Player/ Media Relations:** Kristy Fick. **Baseball Information Manager:** Mike Selleck. **Media Services Manager:** Debbie Gallas. **Coordinator, Media Relations/Broadcast:** Adam Loberstein. **Team Photographer:** Michael Zagaris.
Director, Community Relations: Detra Paige. **Community Relations Coordinator:** Erik Farrell. **Senior Director, Multimedia Services:** David Don. **Stadium Entertainment Production Manager:** Matt Shelton. **Multimedia Services Manager:** Jon Martin.

Stadium Operations
VP, Stadium Operations: David Rinetti. **Director, Stadium Operations:** Paul La Veau. **Senior Manager, Stadium Operations Events:** Kristy Ledbetter. **Stadium Services Manager:** Randy Duran. **Guest Services Manager:** Whitney Tool.

2012 SCHEDULE
Standard Game Times: 7:05 p.m.; Sat./Sun. 1:05.

MARCH		JULY	
28-29 vs. Seattle (in Tokyo)	14-15 . at Los Angeles (AL)	1 . . . . .at Texas	20-22 . . . . . . Minnesota
	16-17 . . . . .at Texas	2-4. . . . . Boston	23-25 . . . . . at Tampa Bay
APRIL	18-20 . . . at San Francisco	6-8. . . . . Seattle	27-30 . . . . . .at Cleveland
6-7. . . . . Seattle	21-23 . . . Los Angeles (AL)	13-15 . . . . . at Minnesota	31 . . . . Boston
9-11. . . . . . . Kansas City	25-27 . . . . .New York (AL)	17-18 . . . . Texas	
13-15 . . . . .at Seattle	28-30 . . . . . at Minnesota	19-22 . . . .New York (AL)	**SEPTEMBER**
16-19 . at Los Angeles (AL)		24-26 . . . . . at Toronto	1-2. . . . . Boston
20-22 . . . . . . Cleveland	**JUNE**	27-29 . . . . .at Baltimore	3-5. . . . . Los Angeles (AL)
23-25 . . . . . Chicago (AL)	1-3. . . . . .at Kansas City	30-31 . . . . . .Tampa Bay	7-9. . . . . .at Seattle
27-29 . . . .at Baltimore	4-7. . . . . Texas		10-13 . at Los Angeles (AL)
30 . . . . .at Boston	8-10 . . . . at Arizona	**AUGUST**	14-16 . . . . . . Baltimore
	12-14 . . . . . at Colorado	1 . . . . .Tampa Bay	18-20 . . . . .at Detroit
MAY	15-17 . . . . . . San Diego	2-5. . . . . .Toronto	21-23 . . at New York (AL)
1-2. . . . . .at Boston	19-21 . . Los Angeles (NL)	6-8. . . . . Los Angeles (AL)	24-27 . . . . .at Texas
4-6. . . . . . at Tampa Bay	22-24 . . . San Francisco	10-12 . . . .at Chicago (AL)	28-30 . . . . Seattle
8-9. . . . . .Toronto	25-27 . . . . . . .at Seattle	14-16 . . . . .at Kansas City	
10-13 . . . . Detroit	28-30 . . . . .at Texas	17-19 . . . . . . Cleveland	**OCTOBER**
			1-3. . . . . Texas

GENERAL INFORMATION
Stadium (year opened): The Coliseum (1968).
Team Colors: Kelly green and gold.

Player Representative: Unavailable.
Home Dugout: Third Base.
Playing Surface: Grass.

Ticket Sales/Operations/Services
Executive Director, Ticket Sales/Operations: Steve Fanelli. **Senior Director, Ticket Operations:** Josh Ziegenbusch. **Senior Manager, Ticket Operations:** David Adame. **Ticket Services Manager:** Catherine Glazier. **Premium Services Manager:** Moti Bycel. **Box Office Manager:** Anthony Blue. **Ticket Operations Coordinator:** Anuj Patel. **Ticket Services Coordinator:** Jason Hicks. **Director, Ticket Sales:** Brian DiTucci. **Sales/Ticket Operations Coordinator:** Judy Quinata.

Travel/Clubhouse
Director, Team Travel: Mickey Morabito. **Equipment Manager:** Steve Vucinich. **Visiting Clubhouse Manager:** Mike Thalblum. **Assistant Equipment Manager:** Brian Davis. **Umpire/Clubhouse Assistant:** Matt Weiss. **Clubhouse Assistant:** William Angel. **Arizona Clubhouse Supervisor:** Jesse Sotomayor. **Arizona Clubhouse Manager:** James Gibson. **Arizona Assistant Clubhouse Manager:** Chad Yaconetti.

BASEBALL OPERATIONS

VP/General Manager: Billy Beane.
Assistant GM: David Forst. **Director, Player Personnel:** Billy Owens. **Special Assistant to GM:** Grady Fuson. **Special Assistant to GM:** Chris Pittaro. **Executive Assistant:** Betty Shinoda. **Director, Baseball Administration:** Pamela Pitts. **Director, Baseball Operations:** Farhan Zaidi. **Video Coordinator:** Adam Rhoden. **Special Assistant to Baseball Operations:** Scott Hatteberg.

Billy Beane

Major League Staff
Manager: Bob Melvin.
Coaches: Bench—Chip Hale; **Pitching**—Curt Young; **Batting**—Chili Davis; **First Base**—Tye Waller; **Third Base**—Mike Gallego; **Bullpen**—Rick Rodriguez.

Medical, Training
Head Athletic Trainer: Nick Paparesta. **Assistant Athletic Trainer:** Walt Horn. **Assistant Athletic Trainer:** Brian Schulman. **Strength/Conditioning Coach:** Michael Henriques. **Major League Massage Therapist:** Ozzie Lyles. **Coordinator, Medical Services:** Larry Davis. **Team Physicians:** Dr. Allan Pont, Dr. Elliott Schwartz. **Team Orthopedist:** Dr. Jon Dickinson. **Associate Team Orthopedist:** Dr. Will Workman. **Consulting Orthopedist:** Dr. Lewis Yocum. **Arizona Team Physicians:** Dr. Fred Dicke, Dr. Doug Freedberg.

Player Development
Telephone: (510) 638-4900. **Fax:** (510) 563-2376.
Director, Player Development: Keith Lieppman. **Director, Minor League Operations:** Ted Polakowski. **Administrative Assistant, Player Development:** Valerie Vander Heyden. **Minor League Roving Instructors:** Juan Navarrete (infield), Ron Plaza (infield), Gil Patterson (pitching), Todd Steverson (hitting). **Minor League Instructor:** Ruben Escalera. **Minor League Video Coordinator:** Mark Smith. **Minor League Medical Coordinator:** Jeff Collins. **Minor League Strength/Conditioning Coordinator:** Josh Cuffe. **Minor League Strength/Conditioning Coach:** Thomas Shea. **Special Instructor, Pitching/Rehabilitation:** Garvin Alston.
Supervisor, Arizona Clubhouse: Jesse Sotomayor. **Manager, Arizona Clubhouse:** James Gibson. **Staff, Arizona Clubhouse:** Chad Yaconetti.

Farm System

Class	Club (League)	Manager	Coach	Pitching Coach
Triple-A	Sacramento (PCL)	Darren Bush	Greg Sparks	Scott Emerson
Double-A	Midland (TL)	Steve Scarsone	Tim Garland	Don Schulze
High A	Stockton (CAL)	Webster Garrison	Brian McArn	Craig Lefferts
Low A	Burlington (MWL)	Aaron Nieckula	Haas Pratt	John Wasdin
Short-season	Vermont (NYP)	Rick Magnante	Casey Myers	Ariel Prieto
Rookie	Athletics (AZL)	Marcus Jensen	Juan Dilone	Jimmy Escalante
Rookie	Athletics (DSL)	Ruben Escalera	Rahdames Perez	Gabriel Ozuna

Scouting
Telephone: (510) 638-4900. **Fax:** (510) 563-2376.
Director, Scouting: Eric Kubota (Rocklin, CA).
Assistant Director, Scouting: Michael Holmes (Winston Salem, NC). **Director, Pro Scouting/Baseball Development:** Dan Feinstein (Lafayette, CA). **National Crosschecker:** Ron Vaughn (Corona, CA). **West Coast Supervisor:** Scott Kidd (Folsom, CA). **Midwest Supervisor:** Ron Marigny (Houston, TX). **Special Assignment Scout:** Craig Weissmann (San Diego, CA). **Pro Scouts:** Jeff Bittiger (Saylorsburg, PA), Dan Freed (Lexington, IL), John McLaren (Peoria, AZ), Will Schock (Oakland, CA), Steve Sharpe (Kansas City, MO), Tom Thomas (Phoenix, AZ), Mike Ziegler (Orlando, FL).
Area Scouts: Neil Avent (Greensboro, NC), Yancy Ayres (Topeka, KS), Armann Brown (Houston, TX), Jermaine Clark (Discovery Bay, CA), Jim Coffman (Portland, OR), Matt Higginson (Burlington, ON), Rick Magnante (Sherman Oaks, CA), Eric Martins (Diamond Bar, CA), Kevin Mello (Chicago, IL), Kelcey Mucker (Baton Rouge, LA), Matt Ranson (Kennesaw, GA), Trevor Ryan (Tempe, AZ), Trevor Schaffer (Belleair, FL), Rich Sparks (Sterling Heights, MI), J.T. Stotts (Moorpark, CA).
Director, Latin American Operations: Raymond Abreu (Santo Domingo, DR). **Coordinator, International Scouting:** Sam Geaney (Oakland, CA). **Coordinator, Latin American Scouting:** Julio Franco (Caracas, VZ).
International Scouts: Ruben Barradas (Venezuela), Juan Carlos De La Cruz (Dominican Republic), Angel Eusebio (Dominican Republic), Andri Garcia (Venezuela), Adam Hislop (Taiwan), Lewis Kim (South Korea), Pablo Marmol (Dominican Republic), Juan Mosquera (Panama), Tito Quintero (Colombia), Amaury Reyes (Dominican Republic), Oswaldo Troconis (Venezuela), Juan Villanueva (Venezuela).

Philadelphia Phillies

Office Address: Citizens Bank Park, One Citizens Bank Way, Philadelphia, PA 19148.
Telephone: (215) 463-6000. **Website:** www.phillies.com.

Ownership
Operated By: The Phillies.
President/CEO: David Montgomery. **Chairman:** Bill Giles.

BUSINESS OPERATIONS

Vice President/General Counsel: Rick Strouse. **VP, Phillies Enterprises:** Richard Deats. **VP, Employee/Customer Services:** Kathy Killian. **Director, Ballpark Enterprises/Business Development:** Joe Giles. **Director, Information Systems:** Brian Lamoreaux. **Director, Employee Benefits/Services:** JoAnn Marano.

Ballpark Operations
Senior VP, Administration/Operations: Michael Stiles. **Director, Ballpark Operations:** Mike DiMuzio. **Director, Event Operations:** Eric Tobin. **Manager, Ballpark Operations/Security:** Sal DeAngelis. **Manager, Concessions Development:** Bruce Leith. **Head Groundskeeper:** Mike Boekholder. **PA Announcer:** Dan Baker. **Official Scorers:** Jay Dunn, Mike Maconi, Joseph Bellina.

David Montgomery

Communications
Telephone: (215) 463-6000. **Fax:** (215) 389-3050.
VP, Communications: Bonnie Clark. **Director, Baseball Communications:** Greg Casterioto. **Coordinator, Baseball Communications:** Kevin Gregg. **Baseball Communications Assistant:** Craig Hughner. **Communications Assistant:** Deanna Sabec.

Finance
VP/CFO: John Nickolas. **Director, Payroll Services:** Karen Wright.

Marketing/Promotions
Senior VP, Marketing/Sales: David Buck. **Manager, Client Services/Alumni Relations:** Debbie Nocito. **Director, Corporate Partnership:** Rob MacPherson. **Director, Advertising Sales:** Brian Mahoney. **Managers, Advertising Sales:** Scott Nickle, Tom Sullivan.
Director, Marketing Programs/Events: Kurt Funk. **Director, Entertainment:** Chris Long. **Manager, Broadcasting:** Rob Brooks. **Manager, Advertising/Internet Services:** Jo-Anne Levy-Lamoreaux.

Sales/Tickets
Telephone: (215) 463-1000. **Fax:** (215) 463-9878.
VP, Sales/Ticket Operations: John Weber. **Director, Ticket Department:** Dan Goroff. **Director, Ticket Technology/Development:** Chris Pohl. **Director, Season Ticket Sales:** Derek Schuster. **Manager, Suite Sales/Services:** Tom Mashek.

2012 SCHEDULE
Standard Game Times: 7:05 p.m.; Sun. 1:35

APRIL
5 . . . . at Pittsburgh
7-8 . . . . . . at Pittsburgh
9 . . . . Miami
11-12 . . . . Miami
13-15 . . . . New York (NL)
16-18 . . . at San Francisco
19-22 . . . . at San Diego
23-25 . . . . . . at Arizona
27-30 . . . . . Chicago (NL)

MAY
1-3 . . . . at Atlanta
4-6 . . . . . at Washington
7-9 . . . . . .New York (NL)
11-13 . . . . San Diego
14-15 . . . . Houston
16-17 . . . .at Chicago (NL)

18-20 . . . . Boston
21-23 . . . . . Washington
24-27 . . . . . .at St. Louis
28-30 . . . . . at New York

JUNE
1-3 . . . . Miami
4-7 . . . . Los Angeles (NL)
8-10 . . . . . . at Baltimore
12-14 . . . . at Minnesota
15-17 . . . . . . at Toronto
19-21 . . . . Colorado
22-24 . . . . . . Tampa Bay
25-28 . . . . . . Pittsburgh
29-30 . . . . at Miami

JULY
1 . . . . at Miami

3-5 . . . . at New York (NL)
6-8 . . . . Atlanta
13-15 . . . . . at Colorado
16-18 . at Los Angeles (NL)
20-22 . . . San Francisco
23-25 . . . . . Milwaukee
27-29 . . . . . . at Atlanta
31 . . . . . . at Washington

AUGUST
1-2 . . . . . at Washington
3-5 . . . . Arizona
6-8 . . . . Atlanta
10-12 . . . . St. Louis
13-15 . . . . at Miami
16-19 . . . . at Milwaukee
20-23 . . . . . Cincinnati
24-26 . . . . . Washington

28-30 . . . .New York (NL)
31 . . . . at Atlanta

SEPTEMBER
1-2 . . . . at Atlanta
3-5 . . . . . . .at Cincinnati
7-9 . . . . Colorado
10-12 . . . . Miami
13-16 . . . . . . .at Houston
17-19 . . at New York (NL)
21-23 . . . . Atlanta
25-27 . . . . . Washington
28-30 . . . . at Miami

OCTOBER
1-3 . . . . . . at Washington

GENERAL INFORMATION
Stadium (year opened): Citizens Bank Park (2004).
Team Colors: Red, white and blue.
Player Representative: Unavailable.
Home Dugout: First Base.
Playing Surface: Natural Grass.

Manager, Phone Center: Phil Feather. Manager, Season Ticket Services: Mike Holdren.

Travel/Clubhouse
Director, Team Travel/Clubhouse Services: Frank Coppenbarger.
Manager, Visiting Clubhouse: Kevin Steinhour. Manager, Home Clubhouse: Phil Sheridan. Manager, Equipment/ Umpire Services: Dan O'Rourke.

BASEBALL OPERATIONS
Senior VP/General Manager: Ruben Amaro Jr.
Assistant GM: Scott Proefrock. Assistant GM, Player Personnel: Benny Looper. Director, Baseball Administration: Susan Ingersoll Papaneri. Director, Professional Scouting: Mike Ondo. Baseball Information Analyst: Jay McLaughlin. Senior Advisor to GM: Dallas Green. Senior Advisor to the President/GM: Pat Gillick. Special Assistant to GM: Charley Kerfeld. Special Consultant, Baseball Operations: Ed Wade. Baseball Operations Representative: Chris Cashman. Administrative Assistant: Adele MacDonald.

Ruben Amaro Jr.

Major League Staff
Manager: Charlie Manuel.
Coaches: Bench—Pete Mackanin; Pitching—Rich Dubee; Batting—Greg Gross; First Base—Sam Perlozzo; Third Base—Juan Samuel; Bullpen Coach—Mick Billmeyer; Bullpen Catcher—Jesus Tiamo.

Medical/Training
Director, Medical Services: Dr. Michael Ciccotti. Head Athletic Trainer: Scott Sheridan. Assistant Athletic Trainer: Shawn Fcasni. Strength/Conditioning Coordinator: Dong Lien. Manual Therapy Specialist: Ichiro Kitano. Employee Assistance Professional: Dickie Noles.

Player Development
Telephone: (215) 463-6000. Fax: (215) 755-9324.
Assistant GM, Player Personnel: Benny Looper. Director, Player Development: Joe Jordan.
Assistant Directors, Minor League Operations: Steve Noworyta, Lee McDaniel. Administrative Assistant, Minor League Operations: Ray Robles. Director, Florida Operations: John Timberlake. Minor League Equipment Manager: Joe Cynar.
Field Coordinator: Mike Compton. Assistant Field Coordinator: Jorge Velandia. Coordinators: James Ready (trainer), Ernie Whitt (catching), Gorman Heimueller (pitching), Paul Fornier (conditioning), Steve Henderson (hitting), Andy Abad (outfield/baserunning), Doug Mansolino (infield).

Farm System

Class	Club(League)	Manager	Coach	Pitching Coach
Triple-A	Lehigh Valley (IL)	Ryne Sandberg	Sal Rende	Rod Nichols
Double-A	Reading (EL)	Dusty Wathan	Frank Cacciatore	Bob Milacki
High A	Clearwater (FSL)	Chris Truby	John Mizerock	Dave Lundquist
Low A	Lakewood (SAL)	Mickey Morandini	Greg Legg/Lino Connell	Les Lancaster
Short-season	Williamsport (NYP)	Andy Tracy	Rafael DeLima	Aaron Fultz
Rookie	Clearwater (GCL)	Roly DeArmas	Kevin Jordan	Steve Schrenk
Rookie	Phillies (DSL)	Manny Amador	L. Arzeno/ C. Henriquez	Alex Conception
Rookie	Phillies (VSL)	Trino Aguilar	S. Navas	Les Straker

Scouting
Director, Scouting: Marti Wolever (Papillion, NE).
Assistant Director, Scouting: Rob Holiday (Philadelphia, PA). Coordinators, Scouting: Mike Ledna (Arlington Heights, IL), Bill Moore (Alta Loma, CA).
Regional Supervisors: Gene Schall (East/Harleysville, PA), Brian Kohlscheen (Central/Norman, OK), Darrell Conner (West/Riverside, CA).
Area Scouts: Shane Bowers (La Verne, CA), Steve Cohen (Spring, TX), Joey Davis (Ranco Murrieta, CA), Nate Dion (West Chester, OH), Mike Garcia (Moreno Valley CA), Brad Holland (Gilbert AZ), Eric Jacques (Bellevue, WA), Aaron Jersild (Atlanta, GA), Alan Marr (Sarasota, FL), Paul Murphy (Wilmington, DE), Demerius Pittman (Corona CA), Paul Scott (Rockwall, TX), David Seifert (Paw Paw, IL), Mike Stauffer (Brandon, MS), Eric Valent (Wernersville PA).
International Supervisor: Sal Agostinelli (Kings Park (NY).
International Scouts: Alex Agostino (Canada), Norman Anciani (Panama), Nathan Davison (Australia), Arnold Elles (Colombia), Tomas Herrera (Mexico), Joe Ko (Korea), Eric Jacques (Europe), Allan Lewis (Panama, Central America), Jesus Mendez (Venezuela), Manabu Noto (Japan), Koby Perez (Dominican Republic), Darryn Smith (South Africa).
Director, Major League Scouting: Gordon Lakey (Barker, TX). Special Assignment Scouts: Howie Frieling (Apex, NC), Dave Hollins (Orchard Park, NY). Major League Scout: Advance Scout: Craig Colbert. Professional Scouts: Sonny Bowers (Hewitt, TX), Dean Jongewaard (Fountain Valley, CA), Jesse Levis (Fort Washington, PA), Jon Mercurio (Coraopolis, PA), Roy Tanner (North Charleston, SC), Del Unser (Scottsdale, AZ), Dan Wright (Cave Springs, AR).

Pittsburgh Pirates

Office Address: PNC Park at North Shore, 115 Federal St, Pittsburgh, PA 15212.
Mailing Address: P.O. Box 7000, Pittsburgh, PA 15212.
Telephone: (412) 323-5000. **Fax:** (412) 325-4412. **Website:** www.pirates.com

Ownership
Chairman of the Board: Robert Nutting.
Board of Directors: Donald Beaver, G. Ogden Nutting, Robert Nutting, William Nutting, Duane Wittman.

BUSINESS OPERATIONS

President: Frank Coonelly. **Executive Vice President/CFO:** Jim Plake. **Executive VP/General Manager, PNC Park:** Dennis DaPra.
Executive VP/Chief Marketing Officer: Lou DePaoli. **VP/General Counsel:** Bryan Stroh. **VP, Community/Public Affairs:** Patty Paytas.

Finance/Administration/Information Technology
Senior Director, Human Resources: Pam Nelson Minteer. **Senior Director, Information Technology:** Terry Zeigler. **Director, Employee Services:** Patti Mistick. **Manager, Payroll/Benefits:** Dineen Runkey. **Risk Manager:** Leila Smith. **Manager, Business Systems:** Sunnie Fenk. **Manager, IT Operations:** Jeff Hammond. **Accounting Manager:** Mark Oresic
Manager, Ticket Accounting/Reporting: Dave Wysocki.

Frank Coonelly

Communications
Fax: (412) 325-4413.
Senior Director, Communications: Brian Warecki. **Director, Media Relations:** Jim Trdinich. **Director, Broadcasting:** Marc Garda. **Manager, Media Relations:** Dan Hart.

Community Relations
Director, Community Relations: Michelle Mejia. **Manager, Diversity Initiatives:** Chaz Kellem.

Marketing
Senior Director, Marketing/Special Events: Brian Chiera. **Senior Director, Corporate Partnerships:** Mike Egan.
Senior Director, Business Analytics: Jim Alexander. **Director, Alumni Affairs/Promotions/Licensing:** Joe Billetdeaux. **Director, Advertising/Creative Services:** Kiley Cauvel. **Director, Special Events:** Christine Serkoch. **Manager, Promotions:** Dan Millar. **Manager, In-Game Entertainment:** Eric Wolff.

Stadium Operations
Senior Director, Ballpark Operations: Chris Hunter. **Senior Director, Security/Contract Services:** Jeff Podobnik.
Manager, Security/Service Operations: Mark Weaver. **Director, Field Operations:** Manny Lopez. **Operations Manager:** J.J. McGraw. **Guest Relations Manager:** Melissa Cushey.

2012 SCHEDULE
Standard Game Times: 7:05 p.m.; Sun. 1:35.

APRIL		
5 . . . . .Philadelphia	18-20 . . . . . . .at Detroit	2-5. . . . . Houston	24-26 . . . . . .Milwaukee
7-8. . . . . . . .Philadelphia	21-23 . . . .New York (NL)	6-8. . . . . . San Francisco	27-29 . . . . St. Louis
10-12 . at Los Angeles (NL)	25-27 . . . . Chicago (NL)	13-15 . . . . . at Milwaukee	31 . . . . at Milwaukee
13-15 . . . at San Francisco	28-30 . . . . Cincinnati	16-18 . . . . . at Colorado	
16-18 . . . . at Arizona		20-22 . . . . .Miami	**SEPTEMBER**
20-22 . . . . St. Louis	**JUNE**	23-25 . . . . Chicago (NL)	1-2. . . . . . . at Milwaukee
23-25 . . . . .Colorado	1-3. . . . . . . at Milwaukee	26-29 . . . . . .at Houston	3-5. . . . . Houston
27-30 . . . . . . at Atlanta	5-7. . . . . . . .at Cincinnati	30-31 . . . .at Chicago (NL)	7-9. . . . . . . Chicago (NL)
	8-10 . . . . . . Kansas City		10-12 . . . . .at Cincinnati
MAY	12-14 . . . . . .at Baltimore	**AUGUST**	14-17 . . . .at Chicago (NL)
	15-17 . . . . .at Cleveland	1 . . . . . . .at Chicago (NL)	18-20 . . . . . . .Milwaukee
1-3. . . . . . . .at St. Louis	19-21 . . . . . . Minnesota	3-5. . . . . . . .at Cincinnati	21-23 . . . . . .at Houston
4-6. . . . . Cincinnati	22-24 . . . . Detroit	6-9. . . . . Arizona	24-27 . . . at New York (NL)
8-10 . . . . . . .Washington	25-28 . . . . at Philadelphia	10-12 . . . . . . San Diego	28-30 . . . . Cincinnati
11-13 . . . . Houston	29-30 . . . . . . .at St. Louis	13-16 . . .Los Angeles (NL)	
14-15 . . . . . at Miami		17-19 . . . . . .at St. Louis	**OCTOBER**
16-17 . . . . at Washington	**JULY**	20-22 . . . . . at San Diego	1-3. . . . . Atlanta
	1 . . . . .at St. Louis		

GENERAL INFORMATION
Stadium (year opened): PNC Park (2001).
Team Colors: Black and gold.

Player Representative: Unavailable.
Home Dugout: Third Base.
Playing Surface: Grass.

Florida Operations
Senior Director, Florida Operations: Trevor Gooby. **Manager, Florida Operations:** A.J. Grant. **Manager, Sales/Marketing:** Rachelle Madrigal. **Manager, Concessions:** Terry Pajka.

Ticketing
Telephone: (800) 289-2827. **Fax:** (412) 325-4404.
Senior Director, Ticket Sales/Service: Christopher Zaber. **Director, Suite Sales/Service:** Terri Smith. **Director, New Business Development:** Jim Popovich..

BASEBALL OPERATIONS

Senior VP/General Manager: Neal Huntington.
Assistant GM, Scouting: Greg Smith. **Assistant GM, Development:** Kyle Stark. **Director, Player Personnel:** Tyrone Brooks. **Director, Baseball Operations:** Kevan Graves. **Director, Baseball Systems Development:** Dan Fox. **Special Assistants to GM:** Jim Benedict, Marc DelPiano, David Jauss, Jax Robertson, Doug Strange.
Major League Scouts: Mike Basso, Kurt Kemp, Bob Minor, Steve Williams. **Pro Scouts:** Jamie Brewington, Jim Dedrick, Rob Guzik, Phil Huttmann, Alvin Rittman, Gary Robinson, Lewis Shaw. **Coordinator, Baseball Operations:** Alex Langsam. **Baseball Operations Assistant:** Will Lawton. **Video Coordinator:** Kevin Roach. **Advance Scouting Coordinator:** Simon Ferrer.

Major League Staff

Neal Huntington

Manager: Clint Hurdle.
Coaches: Bench—Jeff Banister; **Pitching**—Ray Searage; **Hitting**—Gregg Ritchie; **First Base**—Luis Silverio; **Third Base**—Nick Leyva; **Bullpen**—Euclides Rojas; **Coach**—Mark Strittmatter.

Medical/Training
Medical Director: Dr. Patrick DeMeo. **Team Physician:** Dr. Edward Snell. **Head Major League Athletic Trainer:** Todd Tomczyk. **Assistant Major League Athletic Trainer:** Ben Potenziano. **Head Major League Strength/Conditioning Coach:** Brendon Huttmann. **Assistant Major League Strength/Conditioning Coach/Latin American Strength/Conditioning Coordinator:** Kiyoshi Momose. **Physical Therapist/Rehab Coordinator:** Erwin Valencia.

Minor Leagues
Director, Minor League Operations: Larry Broadway.
Special Assistant, Minor League Operations: Frank Kremblas. **Field Coordinator:** Brad Fischer. **Advisor, Minor League Operations:** Woody Huyke. **DSL Field Coordinator/Manager:** Larry Sutton. **Outfield/Baserunning Coordinator:** Kimera Bartee. **Pitching Coordinator:** Scott Mitchell. **Infield Coordinator:** Gary Green. **Hitting Coordinator:** Jeff Livesey. **Catching Coordinator:** Tom Prince. **Rehab/DSL Pitching Coach:** Miguel Bonilla.
Athletic Training Coordinator: Carl Randolph. **Strength/Conditioning Coordinator:** Mike Winkler. **Athletic Development Coordinator:** Joe Hughes. **Rehab Coordinator:** Jeremiah Randall. **Director, Mental Conditioning:** Bernie Holliday. **Mental Conditioning Coordinator:** Tyson Holt. **Coordinator, Minor League Operations:** Diane DePasquale.

Farm System

Class	Club (League)	Manager	Coach(es)	Pitching Coach
Triple-A	Indianapolis (IL)	Dean Treanor	Jeff Branson	Tom Filer
Double-A	Altoona (EL)	P.J. Forbes	Ryan Long	Jeff Johnson
High A	Bradenton (FSL)	Carlos Garcia	Kory DeHaan	Mike Steele
Low A	West Virginia (SAL)	Rick Sofield	Edgar Varela	Willie Glen
Short-season	State College (NYP)	Dave Turgeon	David Howard	Justin Meccage
Rookie	Bradenton (GCL)	Tom Prince	Mike Lum	Bobby St. Pierre
Rookie	Pirates (DSL1)	Larry Sutton	Ramon Zapata/Johe Acosta	Henry Corniel
Rookie	Pirates (DSL2)	Gera Alvarez	Jonathan Prieto/Cecilio Beltre	Dan Urbina

Scouting
Fax: (412) 325-4414.
Director, Scouting: Joe Delli Carri. **Coordinator:** Jim Asher. **National Supervisors:** Jack Bowen (Bethel Park, PA), Jimmy Lester (Columbus, GA), Matt Ruebel (Oklahoma City, OK). **Regional Supervisors:** Jesse Flores (Sacramento, CA), Rodney Henderson (Lexington, KY), Everett Russell (Thibodaux, LA), Greg Schilz (Alexandria, VA). **Area Supervisors:** Rick Allen (Agoura Hills, CA), Matt Bimeal (Baldwin City, KS), Jerome Cochran (Slidell, LA), Trevor Haley (Conroe, TX), Sean Heffernan (Florence, SC), Greg Hopkins (Beaverton, OR), Jerry Jordan (Kingsport, TN), Chris Kline (Northampton, MA), Mike Leuzinger (Canton, TX), Darren Mazeroski (Panama City Beach, FL), Nick Presto (Palm Beach Gardens, FL), Mike Sansoe (Walnut Creek, CA), Brian Selman (Scottsdale, AZ), Brian Tracy (Orange, CA), Matt Wondolowski (Washington D.C.), Anthony Wycklendt (Grafton, WI). **Part-Time Scouts:** Elmer Gray (Pittsburgh, PA), Enrique Hernandez (Puerto Rico).
Director, Latin American Scouting: Rene Gayo. **Full-Time Scouts:** Orlando Covo (Colombia), Nelson Llenas (Dominican Republic), Juan Mercado (Dominican Repuplic), Rodolfo Petit (Venezuela), Victor Santana (Dominican Republic), Jesus Chino Valdez (Mexico). **Part-Time Scouts:** Esteban Alvarez (Dominican Republic), Luis Campusano (Dominican Republic), Pablo Csorgi (Venezuela), Denny Diaz (Dominican Republic), Daniel Espitia Garcia (Colombia), Fernando Hernandez (Mexico), Jhoan Hidalgo (Venezuela), Jose Lavagnino (Mexico), Javier Magdaleno (Venezuela), Esau Medina (Dominican Republic), Ezequiel Mora (Mexico), Juan Morales (Venezuela), Robinson Ortega (Colombia), Jose Pineda (Panama), Juan Pinto (Mexico), Cristobal Santoya (Colombia), Ruben Tinoco (Mexico), Marc Van Zanten (Netherlands Antilles), Leon Taylor (Jamaica), Darryl Yrausquin (Aruba).
International Scouts: Fu-Chun Chiang (Taiwan), Tony Harris (Australia).

St. Louis Cardinals

Office Address: 700 Clark Street, St. Louis MO 63102.
Telephone: (314) 345-9600. **Fax:** (314) 345-9523. **Website:** www.cardinals.com.

Ownership
Operated By: St. Louis Cardinals, LLC.
Chairman/Chief Executive Officer: William DeWitt, Jr.
President: Bill DeWitt III. **Senior Administrative Assistant to Chairman:** Grace Pak. **Senior Administrative Assistant to President:** Julie Laningham.

BUSINESS OPERATIONS

Bill DeWitt III

Vice President, Event Services: Vicki Bryant. **Manager, Event Services:** Missy Tobey. **Director, Human Resources:** Christine Nelsondelete. **Manager Employee Benefits:** Karen Browndelete.

Finance
Fax: (314) 345-9520.
Senior VP/Chief Financial Officer: Brad Wood. **Director, Finance:** Rex Carter.

Marketing/Sales
Fax: (314) 345-9529.
Senior VP, Sales/Marketing: Dan Farrell. **Administrative Assistant, VP Sales/Marketing:** Gail Ruhling. **VP, Corporate Marketing/Stadium Entertainment:** Thane van Breusegen. **Director, Scoreboard Operations/Senior Account Executive:** Tony Simokaitis.

Media Relations/Community Relations
Fax: (314) 345-9530.
Director, Media Relations: Brian Bartow. **Manager, Media Relations/New Media:** Melody Yount. **Director, Public Relations/Government Affairs:** Ron Watermon. **Director, Publications:** Steve Zesch. **VP, Cardinals Care/Community Relations:** Michael Hall.
Administrative Assistant: Jama Fabry. **Director, Target Marketing:** Ted Savage. **Youth Baseball Commissioner, Cardinals Care:** Keith Brooks.

Stadium Operations
Fax: (314) 345-9535.
VP, Stadium Operations: Joe Abernathy. **Administrative Assistant:** Hope Baker. **Director, Security/Special Services:** Joe Walsh. **Director, Quality Assurance/Guest Services:** Mike Ball. **Manager, Stadium Operations:** Cindy Richards. **Head Groundskeeper:** Bill Findley. **Assistant Head Groundskeeper:** Chad Casella. **PA Announcer:** John Ulett. **Official Scorers:** Gary Muller, Jeff Durbin, Mike Smith.

2012 SCHEDULE

Standard Game Times: 7:15 p.m.; Sun. 1:15.

APRIL
4 . . . . at Miami
6-8 . . . . at Milwaukee
9-11 . . . . at Cincinnati
13-15 . . . . Chicago (NL)
17-19 . . . . Cincinnati
20-22 . . . . . at Pittsburgh
23-25 . . . .at Chicago (NL)
27-29 . . . . . . .Milwaukee

MAY
1-3 . . . . Pittsburgh
4-6 . . . . .at Houston
7-9 . . . . at Arizona
11-13 . . . . Atlanta
14-15 . . . Chicago (NL)
16-17 . . . at San Francisco

18-20 . at Los Angeles (NL)
21-23 . . . . San Diego
24-27 . . . . .Philadelphia
28-30 . . . . at Atlanta

JUNE
1-4 . . . . . at New York (NL)
5-7 . . . . .at Houston
8-10 . . . . Cleveland
12-14 . . . . . Chicago (AL)
15-17 . . . . . Kansas City
19-21 . . . . . . .at Detroit
22-24 . . . .at Kansas City
25-27 . . . . . . at Miami
29-30 . . . . . . Pittsburgh

JULY
1 . . . . Pittsburgh

2-5 . . . . Colorado
6-8 . . . . .Miami
13-15 . . . . .at Cincinnati
16-18 . . . . at Milwaukee
20-22 . . . . Chicago (NL)
23-26 . . .Los Angeles (NL)
27-29 . . . .at Chicago (NL)
31 . . . . at Colorado

AUGUST
1-2 . . . . at Colorado
3-5 . . . . .Milwaukee
6-9 . . . . . . San Francisco
10-12 . . . .at Philadelphia
14-16 . . . . .Arizona
17-19 . . . . Pittsburgh
21-23 . . . . Houston

24-26 . . . . .at Cincinnati
27-29 . . . . at Pittsburgh
30-31 . . . . at Washington

SEPTEMBER
1-2 . . . . . at Washington
3-5 . . . . . .New York (NL)
7-9 . . . . .Milwaukee
10-12 . . . . . at San Diego
13-16 . at Los Angeles (NL)
18-20 . . . . Houston
21-23 . . . .at Chicago (NL)
24-26 . . . . . . .at Houston
28-30 . . . . . Washington

OCTOBER
1-3 . . . . Cincinnati

GENERAL INFORMATION
Stadium (year opened): Busch Stadium (2006).
Team Colors: Red and white.

Player Representative: Kyle McClellan.
Home Dugout: First Base.
Playing Surface: Grass.

Ticketing
Fax: (314) 345-9522.
VP, Ticket Sales/Service: Joe Strohm. **Director, Ticket Sales/Services:** Rob Fasoldt. **Manager, Ticket Development:** Brady Bruhn. **Director, Ticket Development:** Derek Thornburg. **Director, Client Relations:** Delores Scanlon. **Manager, Ticket Technology:** Jennifer Needham. **Manager, Premium Tickets:** Mary Clare Bena. **Director, Ticket Sales/Marketing:** Martin Coco. **Receptionist:** Marilyn Mathews.

Travel/Clubhouse
Fax: (314) 345-9523.
Traveling Secretary: C.J. Cherre. **Equipment Manager:** Rip Rowan. **Assistant Equipment Manager:** Ernie Moore. **Visiting Clubhouse Manger:** Jerry Risch. **Video Coordinator:** Chad Blair.

BASEBALL OPERATIONS
Fax: (314) 345-9599.
VP, General Manager: John Mozeliak.
Assistant GM: Mike Girsch. **Executive Assistant:** Linda Brauer. **Senior Special Assistants to GM:** Gary LaRocque, Mike Jorgensen. **Director, Player Personnel:** Matt Slater. **Director, Major League Administration:** Judy Carpenter-Barada. **Director, International Operations:** Moises Rodriguez. **Director, Scouting:** Dan Kantrovitz. **Manager, Baseball Information:** Jeremy Cohen. **Quantitative Analyst:** Chris Correa. **Baseball Operations Assistants:** Tony Ferreira, Jared Odom.

John Mozeliak

Player Development
Fax: (314) 345-9519.
Farm Director: John Vuch.
Minor League Field Coordinator: Mark DeJohn. **Coordinators:** Brent Strom (pitching), Dann Bilardello (roving catching), Derrick May (hitting), Keith Joynt (minor league rehab), Rene Pena (minor league strength/conditioning).
Minor League Equipment Manager: Buddy Bates.

Major League Staff
Telephone: (314) 345-9600.
Manager: Mike Matheny.
Coaches: Bench—Mike Aldrete; **Pitching**—Derek Lilliquist; **Hitting**—Mark McGwire; **Hitting Instructor**—John Mabry; **First Base**—Chris Maloney; **Third Base**—Jose Oquendo; **Bullpen**—Dyar Miller.

Medical/Training
Medical Advisor: Dr. George Paletta. **Head Trainer:** Greg Hauck. **Assistant Trainer:** Chris Conroy. **Assistant Trainer/ Rehabilitation Coordinator:** Adam Olsen.

Farm System

Class	Club (League)	Manager	Hitting Coach	Pitching Coach
Triple-A	Memphis (PCL)	Ron Warner	Mark Budaska	Blaise Ilsley
Double-A	Springfield (TL)	Mike Shildt	Phillip Wellman	Bryan Eversgerd
High A	Palm Beach (FSL)	Johnny Rodriguez	Jeff Albert	Dennis Martinez
Low A	Quad Cities (MWL)	Luis Aguayo	Joe Kruzel	Arthur "Ace" Adams
Short-season	Batavia (NYP)	Dann Bilardello	Roger LaFrancois	Dernier Orozco
Rookie	Johnson City (APP)	Oliver Marmol	Ramon Ortiz	Doug White
Rookie	Cardinals (GCL)	Steve Turco	Oliver Marmol	Tim Leveque
Rookie	Cardinals (DSL)	Fray Peniche	Jobel Jimenez	Bill Villanueva

Scouting
Fax: (314) 345-9519.
Professional Scouts: Bruce Benedict (Atlanta, GA), Alan Benes (Town & Country, MO), Chuck Fick (Newbury Park, CA), Mike Jorgensen (Fenton, MO), Mike Juhl (Indian Trail, NC), Marty Keough (Scottsdale, AZ), Gary LaRocque (Greensboro, NC), Deric McKamey (Bluffton, OH), Joe Rigoli (Parsippany, NJ), Kerry Robinson (Ballwin, MO).
Crosscheckers: Joe Almaraz (San Antonio, TX), Mike Roberts (Hot Springs, AR), Jeremy Schied (Aliso Viejo, CA), Roger Smith (Eastman, GA).
Area Scouts: Matt Blood (Durham, NC), Nicholas Brannon (Baton Rouge, LA), Jay Catalano (Joelton, TN), Rob Fidler (Atlanta, GA), Ralph Garr, Jr. (Houston, TX), Charlie Gonzalez (Weston, FL), Kris Gross (Chicago, IL), Brian Hopkins (Brunswick, OH), Jeff Ishii (Chino, CA), Aaron Krawiec (Gilbert, AZ), Aaron Looper (Shawnee, OK), Sean Moran (Levittown, PA), Sam Pepper (San Diego, CA), Jamal Strong (Victorville, CA), Matt Swanson (Ripon, CA).
Part-Time Scouts: Alec Adame (Los Angeles, CA), Vince Bailey (Renton, WA), Manny Guerra (Las Vegas, NV), Jimmy Matthews (Athens, GA), Andy Miller (Santa Barbara, CA), Sam Pepper (So. Cal.), Juan Ramos (Carolina, Puerto Rico).
Director, International Operations: Moises Rodriguez. **Baseball Operations Assistant, International:** Luis Morales. **International Crosschecker:** Cesar Geronimo, Jr. **Administrator, Dominican Republic Operations:** Aaron Rodriguez.
International Scouts: Angel Oralles (Dominican Republic), Jose Gregorio Gonzalez (Venezuela), Crysthiam Blanco (Nicaragua), Henry Sandoval (VZ/Dutch Caribbean).

San Diego Padres

Office Address: Petco Park, 100 Park Blvd, San Diego, CA 92101.
Mailing Address: PO Box 122000, San Diego, CA 92112.
Telephone: (619) 795-5000.
E-mail address: comments@padres.com. **Website:** www.padres.com.
Twitter: @padres. **Facebook:** www.facebook.com/padres

Ownership
Operated By: Padres LP.
Chairman: John Moores. **Vice Chairmen/CEO:** Jeff Moorad.
President/COO: Tom Garfinkel.

BUSINESS OPERATIONS
Senior VP, Business Operations: Brent Stehlik. **Executive VP/Senior Advisor:** Dave Winfield. **VP, Strategy/Business Analysis:** John Abbamondi.
Special Assistant to President/COO: Trevor Hoffman. **Special Assistant to President/COO:** Tony Gwynn.

Finance/Administration/Information Technology
Executive VP/CFO: Fred Gerson. **Senior VP, Business Administration/General Counsel:** Erik Greupner. **VP, Information Technology:** Steve Reese. **Director, Accounting:** Todd Bollman.

Public Affairs/Communications/Community Relations/Military Affairs
Telephone: (619) 795-5265. **Fax:** (619) 795-5266.
Senior VP, Public Affairs: Sarah Farnsworth. **VP, Community Relations:** Sue Botos. **Director, Communications:** Warren Miller. **Director, Military Affairs:** Michael Berenston.
Editor, Publications: Bret Picciolo. **Manager, Communications:** Shana Wilson. **Coordinator, Media Relations:** Josh Ishoo.
Manager, Community Affairs/Padres Foundation: Nhu Tran. **Manager, Latino Affairs:** Alex Montoya. **Coordinator, Community Affairs/Padres Foundation:** Christina Papasedero.

Jeff Moorad

Entertainment/Partnerships/Marketing/Creative Services
VP, Corporate Partnerships: Tyler Epp. **Director, Entertainment/Production:** Erik Meyer. **Director, Brand Development:** Nicole Smith. **Director, Partnership Development:** Joe Mulford.
Manager, Promotions/Merchandising: Michael Babida. **Manager, In-Park Entertainment:** Mike Grace. **Manager, Entertainment/Production Engineer:** Hendrik Jaehn. **Manager, Game Presentation/Production:** Jennifer Cota. **Manager, Marketing Services:** Harrison Boyd. **Manager, Creative Services:** Oliver Yambao.

Ballpark Operations
VP, Ballpark Operations/GM, Petco Park: Mark Guglielmo. **VP, Petco Park Events:** Jeremy Horowitz.
Director, Security: John Leas. **Director, Event Operations:** Ken Kawachi. **Director, Field/Landscape Maintenance:**

2012 SCHEDULE
Standard Game Times: 7:05 p.m.; Sun. 1:05

APRIL
5-8 . . . . . Los Angeles (NL)
10-12 . . . . Arizona
13-15 . at Los Angeles (NL)
16-18 . . . . . . at Colorado
19-22 . . . . . .Philadelphia
24-26 . . . . . .Washington
27-29 . . . at San Francisco
30 . . . . .Milwaukee

MAY
1-2 . . . . .Milwaukee
4-6 . . . . .Miami
7-9 . . . . .Colorado
11-13 . . . at Philadelphia
14-15 . . . at Washington
16-17 . . . Los Angeles (NL)

18-20 . . . Los Angeles (AL)
21-23 . . . . . . .at St. Louis
24-27 . . . at New York (NL)
28-30 . . . .at Chicago (NL)

JUNE
1-3 . . . . Arizona
5-7 . . . . San Francisco
8-10 . . . . . at Milwaukee
12-14 . . . . .at Seattle
15-17 . . . . . .at Oakland
18-20 . . . . Texas
22-24 . . . . Seattle
25-28 . . . . . .at Houston
29-30 . . . . at Colorado

JULY
1 . . . . at Colorado

2-4 . . . . at Arizona
5-8 . . . . Cincinnati
13-15 . at Los Angeles (NL)
16-19 . . . . Houston
20-22 . . . . . . .Colorado
23-25 . . . at San Francisco
27-29 . . . . . . at Miami
30-31 . . . . .at Cincinnati

AUGUST
1-2 . . . . . . .at Cincinnati
3-5 . . . . . .New York (NL)
6-8 . . . . . . Chicago (NL)
10-12 . . . . at Pittsburgh
13-16 . . . . . . at Atlanta
17-19 . . . . San Francisco
20-22 . . . . . . Pittsburgh

24-26 . . . . . . at Arizona
27-29 . . . . Atlanta
31 . . . . at Colorado

SEPTEMBER
1-2 . . . . at Colorado
3-5 . . . at Los Angeles (NL)
7-9 . . . . Arizona
10-12 . . . . St. Louis
14-16 . . . . . . .Colorado
18-20 . . . . at Arizona
21-23 . . . at San Francisco
25-27 . . . Los Angeles (NL)
28-30 . . . . . San Francisco

OCTOBER
1-3 . . . . . . at Milwaukee

GENERAL INFORMATION
Stadium (year opened): Petco Park (2004).
Team Colors: Blue, white, tan and gray

Player Representative: Heath Bell
Home Dugout: First Base.
Playing Surface: Grass.

Luke Yoder. **Director, Guest Services:** Kameron Durham. **Official Scorers:** Jack Murray, Bill Zavestoski.

Ticketing
　　Telephone: (619) 795-5500. **Fax:** (619) 795-5034.
　　VP, Ticket Sales/Service: Jarrod Dillon.
　　Director, Ticket Operations: Jim Kiersnowski. **Director, Season Ticket Sales/Services:** Jonathan Tillman. **Director, Group Ticket Sales/Suite Rentals:** Amy Saxon. **Manager, Season Ticket Sales:** Robert Davis.

Travel, Clubhouse
　　Director, Team Travel/Equipment Manager: Brian Prilaman. **Assistant Equipment Manager/Umpire Room Attendant:** Tony Petricca. **Assistant to Equipment Manager:** Spencer Dallin. **Visiting Clubhouse Manager:** David Bacharach.

BASEBALL OPERATIONS
　　Telephone: (619) 795-5076. **Fax:** (619) 795-5361.
　　Executive VP/General Manager: Josh Byrnes.
　　Senior VP, Baseball Operations: Omar Minaya. **VP/Assistant GM:** AJ Hinch. **VP/Assistant GM:** Fred Uhlman Jr. **VP/Assistant GM, Player Personnel:** Chad MacDonald. **Special Assistant to GM:** Scott Bream. **Special Assistants, Baseball Operations:** Brad Ausmus, Mark Loretta.
　　Director, Baseball Operations: Josh Stein. **Director, Team Travel/Equipment Manager:** Brian Prilaman. **Assistant, Baseball Operations/Professional Scouting:** Alex Slater. **Assistant to the Director, Scouting:** Sam Ray. **Architect, Baseball Systems:** Wells Oliver. **Developer, Baseball Systems:** Brian McBurney. **Assistant, Amateur Scouting/Video:** Eddie Ciafardini. **Assistants, Baseball Operations:** Nick Ennis, Ben Sestanovich. **SR Quantitative Analyst:** Chris Long. **Video Coordinator, Clubhouse:** Mike Tompkins. **Executive Assistant:** Julie Myers.

Josh Byrnes

Medical/Training
　　Club Physician: Scripps Clinic Medical Staff. **Head Athletic Trainer:** Todd Hutcheson. **Assistant Athletic Trainer:** Paul Navarro. **Strength/Conditioning Coach:** Jim Malone.

Player Development
　　Telephone: (619) 795-5343. **Fax:** (619) 795-5036.
　　VP, Player Development/International Scouting: Randy Smith.
　　Manager, Player Development/International Operations: Juan Lara. **Administrator, Dominican Republic Operations:** Cesar Rizik. **Manager, Minor Leagues:** Ilana Miller. **Roving Instructors:** Randy Johnson (field coordinator), Mike Cather (pitching), Sean Berry (hitting), Glen Barker (outfield/baserunning), Gary Jones (infield), Evaristo Lantigua (Latin American instruction), Joseph Tarantino (trainer), Dan Morrison (strength/conditioning), Ryan Bitzel (rehab).

Farm System

Class	Farm Club (League)	Manager	Coach	Pitching Coach
Triple-A	Tucson (PCL)	Terry Kennedy	Bob Skube	Steve Webber
Double-A	San Antonio (TL)	John Gibbons	Tom Tornincasa	Jimmy Jones
High A	Lake Elsinore (CAL)	Shawn Wooten	David Newhan	Bronswell Patrick
Low A	Ft Wayne (MWL)	Jose Valentin	Jacque Jones	Willie Blair
Short-season	Eugene (NWL)	Pat Murphy	Chris Prieto	Nelson Cruz
Rookie	Padres (AZL)	Jim Gabella	I Cruz/D Easley	D Rajsich/T Worrell
Rookie	Padres (DSL)	Michael Collins	J Ramirez/J Guillen	M Rojas/J Quezada

Major League Staff
　　Manager: Bud Black.
　　Coaches: Bench—Rick Renteria; **Pitching**—Darren Balsley; **Hitting**—Phil Plantier; **Assistant Hitting**—Alonzo Powell; **First Base**—Dave Roberts; **Third Base**—Glenn Hoffman; **Bullpen**—Darrel Akerfelds.

Scouting
　　Telephone: (619) 795-5362. **Fax:** (619) 795-5036.
　　Director, Scouting: Jaron Madison. **Assistant to the Director, Scouting:** Sam Ray.
　　Major League Scout: Ray Crone (Waxahachie, TX). **Professional Scouts:** Joe Bochy (Plant City, FL), Chris Bourjos (Scottsdale, AZ), Scott Bream (Phoenix, AZ), Jim Elliot (Winston-Salem, NC), Al Hargesheimer (Arlington Heights, IL), Jeffrey Hammonds (Madison, AL), Kevin Jarvis (Franklin, TN), Jeff Pickler (Chandler, AZ), Van Smith (Belleville, IL), John Vander Wal (Grand Rapids, MI), Mike Venafro (Ft Myers, FL), Chris Young (Austin, TX). **Advance Scout:** Gregg Olson (Newport Beach, CA). **National Crosscheckers:** Bob Filotei (Mobile, AL), Billy Gasparino (Venice, CA). **Regional Supervisors:** Sean Campbell (Franlkin, TN), Pete DeYoung (La Jolla, CA), Tim Holt (Allen, TX), Chip Lawerence (Palmetto, FL).
　　Amateur Scouts: Justin Baughman (Portland, OR), Willie Bosque (Winter Garden, FL), Adam Bourassa (Winston-Salem, NC), Jim Bretz (South Windsor, CT), Mark Conner (Hendersonville, TN), Jeff Curtis (Arlington, TX), Lane Decker (Piedmont, OK), Kevin Ellis (Katy, TX), Josh Emmerick (Oceanside, CA), David Francia (Dickinson, AL), Noah Jackson (Mill Valley, CA), Chris Kelly (Atlanta, GA), Dave Lottsfeldt (Castle Rock, CO), Brent Mayne (Costa Mesa, CA), Andrew Salvo (Manassas, VA), Jeff Stewart (Normal, IL). **Part-Time Scouts:** Robert Gutierrez (Carol City, FL), Hank Krause (Akron, IA), Willie Ronda (Las Lomas Rio Piedras, Puerto Rico), Cam Walker (Centerville, IA), Murray Zuk (Souris, Manitoba).
　　Coordinator, Latin American Scouting: Felix Feliz. **Coordinator, Pacific Rim:** Trevor Schumm. **Supervisor, Venezuela:** Yfrain Linares. **Supervisor, Central America/Mexico:** Robert Rowley. **International Scouts:** Antonio Alejos (Venezuela), Milton Croes (Aruba), Marcial Del Valle (Colombia), Emenegildo Diaz (DR), Mayron Isenia (Curacao), Elvin Jarquin (Nicaragua), Martin Jose (DR), Victor Magdaleno (Venezuela), Ricardo Montenegro (Panama), Luis Prieto (Venezuela), Ysrael Rojas (DR), Jose Salado (DR).

San Francisco Giants

Office Address: AT&T Park, 24 Willie Mays Plaza, San Francisco, CA 94107.
Telephone: (415) 972-2000. **Fax:** (415) 947-2800. **Website:** sfgiants.com, sfgigantes.com.

OWNERSHIP

Operated by: San Francisco Baseball Associates L.P.

Administration

President/Chief Executive Officer: Laurence M. Baer. **Chairman Emeritus:** William H Neukom. **Special Assistant:** Willie Mays. **Senior Advisor:** Willie McCovey.

Finance

Senior VP/Chief Financial Officer: John F. Yee. **VP, Finance:** Lisa Pantages. **Senior VP/Chief Information Officer:** Bill Schlough. **Senior Director, Information Technology:** Ken Logan.

Human Resources/Legal

Chief People Officer: Leilani Gayles. **VP, Human Resources:** Joyce Thomas. **Senior VP/ General Counsel:** Jack F. Bair. **VP/Deputy General Counsel:** Elizabeth R. Murphy.

Laurence M. Baer

Communications

Telephone: (415) 972-2445. **Fax:** (415) 947-2800.
Senior Vice President, Communications: Staci Slaughter. **Senior Director, Broadcast Services:** Maria Jacinto. **Senior Director, Media Relations:** Jim Moorehead. **Media Relations Manager:** Matt Chisholm. **Hispanic Media Relations Coordinator/Spanish Language Broadcaster:** Erwin Higueros. **VP, Public Affairs/Community Relations:** Shana Daum. **VP, Creative Services:** Nancy Donati. **Director, Photography/Archives:** Missy Mikulecky.

Revenue

Senior VP, Revenue: Mario Alioto. **Managing VP, Sponsorship/New Business Development:** Jason Pearl. **VP, Strategic Revenue Services:** Jerry Drobny. **VP, Sponsor/Special Event Support:** Danny Dann. **Director, Special Events:** Valerie McGuire. **Director, Sponsorship Sales:** Bill Lawrence. **VP, Retail Operations:** Dave Martinez.

Ticketing

Telephone: (415) 972-2000. **Fax:** (415) 972-2500.
Managing VP, Ticket Sales/Services: Russ Stanley. **VP, Sales:** Jeff Tucker. **Director, Season Ticket Sales:** Craig Solomon. **Senior Director, Ticket Services:** Devin Lutes. **Senior Ticket Operations Manager:** Anita Sprinkles. **Senior Box Office Manager:** Todd Pierce. **VP, Client Relations:** Annemarie Hastings.

Marketing

Senior VP, Consumer Marketing: Tom McDonald. **Senior Director, Marketing/Entertainment:** Chris Gargano. **Director, Executive Producer:** Paul Hodges.

2012 SCHEDULE

Standard Game Times: 7:15 p.m.; Sun. 1:05

APRIL		
6-8 . . . . at Arizona	18-20 . . . . Oakland	3-5 . . . . . at Washington	23-26 . . . . Atlanta
9 . . . . at Colorado	21-23 . . . . at Milwaukee	6-8 . . . . at Pittsburgh	28-30 . . . . . . .at Houston
11-12 . . . . . at Colorado	24-27 . . . . . . at Miami	13-15 . . . . Houston	31 . . . . . .at Chicago (NL)
13-15 . . . . Pittsburgh	28-30 . . . . .Arizona	17-19 . . . . . . at Atlanta	
16-18 . . . . .Philadelphia		20-22 . . . . at Philadelphia	SEPTEMBER
20-23 . . . at New York (NL)	JUNE	23-25 . . . . San Diego	1-2 . . . . . .at Chicago (NL)
24-26 . . . . . .at Cincinnati	1-4 . . . . Chicago (NL)	27-29 . . .Los Angeles (NL)	3-5 . . . . .Arizona
27-29 . . . . . . San Diego	5-7 . . . . . at San Diego	30-31 . . . . .New York (NL)	7-9 . . . . Los Angeles (NL)
	8-10 . . . . Texas		10-12 . . . . . at Colorado
MAY	12-14 . . . . Houston	AUGUST	14-16 . . . . at Arizona
1-3 . . . . .Miami	15-17 . . . . . . .at Seattle	1-2 . . . . . .New York (NL)	17-20 . . . . .Colorado
4-6 . . . . .Milwaukee	18-20 . at Los Angeles (AL)	3-5 . . . . at Colorado	21-23 . . . . San Diego
7-9 . . at Los Angeles (NL)	22-24 . . . . . .at Oakland	6-9 . . . . .at St. Louis	25-27 . . . . .Arizona
11-13 . . . . . . at Arizona	25-27 . . .Los Angeles (NL)	10-12 . . . . . . .Colorado	28-30 . . . . . at San Diego
14-15 . . . . . . .Colorado	28-30 . . . . . . Cincinnati	13-15 . . . . .Washington	
16-17 . . . . St. Louis		17-19 . . . . at San Diego	OCTOBER
	JULY	20-22 . at Los Angeles (NL)	1-3 . . . at Los Angeles (NL)
	1 . . . . Cincinnati		

GENERAL INFORMATION

Stadium (year opened): AT&T Park (2000).
Team Colors: Black, orange and cream.

Player Representative: Matt Cain.
Home Dugout: Third Base.
Playing Surface: Grass.

Facilities

Senior VP, Facilities: Alfonso G Felder. **Senior VP, Ballpark Operations:** Jorge Costa. **Senior Director, Ballpark Operations:** Gene Telucci. **Senior Director, Security:** Tinie Roberson. **VP, Guest Services:** Rick Mears. **Head Groundskeeper:** Greg Elliott. **PA Announcer:** Renel Brooks-Moon. **Official Scorers:** Chuck Dybdal, Art Santo Domingo, Michael Duca, Dave Feldman

Clubhouse/Travel

Giants Equipment Manager: Miguel Murphy. **Home Clubhouse Assistants:** Brandon Evans, Ron Garcia, David Lowenstein. **Visitors Clubhouse Manager:** Harvey Hodgerney.

BASEBALL OPERATIONS

Brian Sabean

Telephone: (415) 972-1922. **Fax:** (415) 947-2929.
Senior VP/General Manager: Brian R Sabean.
VP, Player Personnel: Dick Tidrow. **VP, Baseball Operations:** Bobby Evans. **Special Assistant to GM:** Felipe Alou. **Special Assistant to GM, Scouting:** John Barr. **Senior Advisor, Baseball Operations:** Tony Siegle. **Senior Director, Baseball Operations/Pro Scouting:** Jeremy Shelley. **Director, Minor League Operations/Quantitative Analysis:** Yeshayah Goldfarb. **Executive Assistant to GM:** Karen Sweeney. **Coordinator, Video Operations:** Danny Martin.

Major League Staff

Manager: Bruce Bochy.
Coaches: Bench—Ron Wotus; **Pitching**—Dave Righetti; **Hitting**—Hensley Meulens/Joe Lefebvre; **First Base**—Roberto Kelly; **Third Base**—Tim Flannery; **Bullpen**—Mark Gardner/Bill Hayes.

Medical Training

Team Physicians: Dr. Robert Murray, Dr. Ken Akizuki, Dr. Anthony Saglimbeni. **Head Trainer:** Dave Groeschner. **Assistant Trainers:** Mark Gruesbeck, Anthony Reyes. **Strength/Conditioning Coach:** Carl Kochan. **Coordinator, Medical Administration:** Chrissy Yuen.

Player Development

Director, Player Development: Fred Stanley.
Senior Consultant, Player Personnel: Jack Hiatt. **Special Assistants:** Joe Amalfitano, Jim Davenport. **Director, Arizona Baseball Operations:** Alan Lee. **Coordinator, Minor League Instruction:** Shane Turner. **Coordinator, Minor League Pitching:** Bert Bradley. **Coordinator, Minor League Hitting:** Steve Decker. **Minor League Roving Instructors:** Lee Smith (pitching), Jose Alguacil (infield), Henry Cotto (baserunning/outfield), Kirt Manwaring (catching). **Manager, Player Personnel Administration:** Clara Ho. **Coordinator, Minor League Operations:** Eric Flemming. **Arizona Minor League Operations Assistant:** Gabriel Alvarez. **Baseball Operations Assistants:** Colin Sabean, Jose Bonilla.

Farm System

Class	Farm Club (League)	Manager	Coach(es)	Pitching Coach
Triple-A	Fresno (PCL)	Bob Mariano	Russ Morman	Pat Rice
Double-A	Richmond (EL)	Dave Machemer	Ken Joyce	Ross Grimsley
High A	San Jose (CAL)	Andy Skeels	Gary Davenport	Steve Kline
Low A	Augusta (SAL)	Lipso Nava	Nestor Rojas	Mike Caldwell
Short-season	Salem-Keizer (NWL)	Tom Trebelhorn	R. Ward/H. Borg	Jerry Cram
Rookie	Giants (AZL)	Derin McMains	V. Torres/B. Horton	M. Couchee/L. McCall
Rookie	Giants (DSL)	Jesus Tavarez	C. Valderrama/ J. Perra	Marcos Aguasvivas

Scouting

Telephone: (415) 972-2360. **Fax:** (415) 947-2929.
Special Assistant to GM, Scouting: John Barr (Haddonfield, NJ).
Senior Advisors, Scouting: Ed Creech (Moultrie, GA), Joe Lefebvre (Hookset, NH), Matt Nerland (Clayton, CA), Paul Turco Sr (Sarasota, FL). **Coordinator, Amateur Scouting:** Doug Mapson (Chandler, AZ). **Coordinator, Scouting Administration:** Adam Nieting. **Special Assignment Scouts:** Lee Elder (Evans, GA), Tom Korenek (Houston, TX), Darren Wittcke (Gresham, OR). **Advance Scouts:** Steve Balboni (Murray Hill, NJ), Keith Champion (Ballwin, MO). **Major League Scouts:** Brian Johnson (Detroit, MI), Michael Kendall (Rancho Palos Verde, CA), Stan Saleski (Dayton, OH), Paul Turco Jr. (Tampa, FL), Tom Zimmer (Seminole, FL). **Senior Consultants, Scouting:** Dick Cole (Costa Mesa, CA).
Supervisors: East—John Castleberry (High Point, NC); **Midwest**—Arnold Brathwaite (Grand Prairie, TX); **West**—Joe Strain (Englewood, CO). **Territorial Scouts: East Region**—Ray Callari (Cote St. Luc, Quebec), Kevin Christman (Noblesville, IN), John DiCarlo (Glenwood, NJ), Jeremy Cleveland (Morrisville, NC), Andrew Jefferson (Atlanta, GA), Ronnie Merrill (Tampa, FL), Mike Metcalf (Sarasota, FL), Glenn Tufts (Bridgewater, MA). **Midwest Region**—Lou Colletti (Elk Grove Village, IL), Daniel Murray (Prairie Village, KS), Todd Thomas (Dallas, TX), Hugh Walker (Jonesboro, AR). **West Region**—Brad Cameron (Los Alamitos, CA), Chuck Hensley (Erie, CO), Gil Kubski (Huntington Beach, CA), Keith Snider (Stockton, CA), Matt Woodward (Vancouver, WA). **Part-Time Scouts:** Bob Barth (Williamstown, NJ), Jim Chapman (Langley, BC), Felix Negron (Bayamon, PR), Tim Rock (Orlando, FL).
Director, Dominican Operations: Pablo Peguero. **Latin America Crosschecker:** Joe Salermo (Hallandale Beach, FL). **Venezuela Supervisor:** Ciro Villalobos. **Assistant Director, Dominican Operations:** Felix Peguero. **Coordinator, Pacific Rim Operations:** John Cox. **International Scouts:** Jonathan Arraiz (Venezuela), Jonathan Bautista (Dominican Republic), Phillip Elhage (Curacao/Bonaire/Aruba), Edgar Fernandez (Venezuela), Ricardo Heron (Panama), Juan Marquez (Venezuela), Sebastian Martinez (Venezuela), Daniel Mavarez (Colombia), Sandy Moreno (Nicaragua), Jim Patterson (Australia), Luis Pena (Mexico), Jesus Stephens (Dominican Republic).

Seattle Mariners

Office Address: 1250 First Avenue South, Seattle, WA 98134.
Mailing Address: P.O. Box 4100, Seattle, WA 98194.
Telephone: (206) 346-4000. **Fax:** (206) 346-4400. **Website:** www.mariners.com.

Ownership
Board of Directors: Minoru Arakawa, John Ellis, Chris Larson, Howard Lincoln, Wayne Perry, Frank Shrontz, Rob Glaser.
Chair/CEO: Howard Lincoln.
President/Chief Operating Officer: Chuck Armstrong.

BUSINESS OPERATIONS

Chuck Armstrong

Finance
Executive Vice President, Finance/Ballpark Operations: Kevin Mather. **VP, Finance:** Tim Kornegay. **Controller:** Greg Massey. **VP, Human Resources:** Marianne Short.

Corporate Business/Marketing
Executive VP, Business/Operations: Bob Aylward. **VP, Corporate Business/Community Relations:** Joe Chard. **Director, Corporate Business:** Ingrid Russell-Narcisse. **Director, Community Relations:** Gina Hasson. **Manager, Community Programs:** Sean Grindley. **VP, Marketing:** Kevin Martinez. **Director, Marketing:** Gregg Greene.

Sales
VP, Sales: Frances Traisman. **Director, Group Business Development:** Bob Hellinger. **Director, Ticket Sales:** Cory Carbary.

Baseball Information/Communications
Telephone: (206) 346-4000. **Fax:** (206) 346-4400.
VP, Communications: Randy Adamack.
Senior Director, Baseball Information: Tim Hevly. **Assistant Director, Baseball Information:** Jeff Evans. **Manager, Baseball Information:** Kelly Munro. **Manager, Baseball Information:** Fernando Alcala.
Director, Public Information: Rebecca Hale. **Director, Graphic Design:** Carl Morton. **Director, Community Relations:** Gina Hasson. **Manager, Community Programs:** Sean Grindley.

Ticketing
Telephone: (206) 346-4001. **Fax:** (206) 346-4100.
Director, Ticketing/Parking Operations: Malcolm Rogel. **Director, Ticket Services:** Jennifer Sweigert.

Stadium Operations
VP, Ballpark Operations: Scott Jenkins. **Senior Director, Safeco Field Operations:** Tony Pereira. **Director,**

2012 SCHEDULE
Standard Game Times: 7:10 p.m.; Sun. 1:10.

MARCH
28-29 vs. Oakland (in Tokyo)

APRIL
6-7 . . . . .at Oakland
9-12 . . . . .at Texas
13-15 . . . . Oakland
17-19 . . . . . Cleveland
20-22 . . . . . Chicago (AL)
24-26 . . . . .at Detroit
27-29 . . . . . at Toronto
30 . . . . . . at Tampa Bay

MAY
1-3 . . . . . . at Tampa Bay
4-6 . . . . Minnesota
7-9 . . . . Detroit
11-13 . . . at New York (AL)

14-15 . . . . . . .at Boston
16-17 . . . .at Cleveland
18-20 . . . . . at Colorado
21-23 . . . . Texas
24-27 . . Los Angeles (AL)
28-30 . . . . . . .at Texas

JUNE
1-3 . . . . . .at Chicago (AL)
4-6 . . . at Los Angeles (AL)
8-10 . . . . Los Angeles (NL)
12-14 . . . . . San Diego
15-17 . . . . . San Francisco
18-20 . . . . at Arizona
22-24 . . . . . at San Diego
25-27 . . . . . . Oakland
28-30 . . . . Boston

JULY
1 . . . . Boston
2-4 . . . . Baltimore
6-8 . . . . .at Oakland
13-15 . . . . Texas
16-19 . . . .at Kansas City
20-22 . . . . at Tampa Bay
23-25 . . . . .New York (AL)
26-29 . . . . . Kansas City
30-31 . . . . .Toronto

AUGUST
1 . . . . .Toronto
3-5 . . . . . at New York (AL)
6-8 . . . . . . .at Baltimore
10-12 . at Los Angeles (AL)
13-15 . . . . . .Tampa Bay
17-19 . . . . . .Minnesota

20-22 . . . . . . Cleveland
24-26 . . . .at Chicago (AL)
27-30 . . . . . at Minnesota
31 . . . . . Los Angeles (AL)

SEPTEMBER
1-2 . . . . Los Angeles (AL)
3-5 . . . . Boston
7-9 . . . . Oakland
11-13 . . . . at Toronto
14-16 . . . . .at Texas
17-19 . . . . . . Baltimore
21-23 . . . . Texas
25-27 .
 at Los Angeles (AL)
28-30 . . . . . . .at Oakland

OCTOBER
1-3 . . . . . Los Angeles (AL)

GENERAL INFORMATION
Stadium (year opened): Safeco Field (1999).
Team Colors: Northwest green, silver and navy blue.

Player Representative: Unavailable.
Home Dugout: First Base.
Playing Surface: Grass.

Engineering/Maintenance: Joe Myhra. **Security:** Sly Servance. **Director, Events:** Jill Hashimoto.
VP, Information Services: Dave Curry. **Director, PBX/Retail Systems:** Oliver Roy. **Director, Database/Applications:** Justin Stolmeier. **Director, Procurement:** Sandy Fielder. **Head Groundskeeper:** Bob Christofferson. **Assistant Head Groundskeepers:** Tim Wilson, Leo Liebert. **PA Announcer:** Tom Hutyler. **Official Scorer:** Eric Radovich.

Merchandising
Senior Director, Merchandise: Jim LaShell. **Director, Retail Merchandising:** Julie McGillivray. **Director, Retail Stores:** Doug Orwiler.

Travel/Clubhouse
Director, Team Travel: Ron Spellecy.
Clubhouse Manager: Ted Walsh. **Visiting Clubhouse Manager:** Henry Genzale. **Video Coordinator:** Jimmy Hartley. **Assistant Video Coordinator:** Craig Manning.

BASEBALL OPERATIONS
Executive VP/General Manager: Jack Zduriencik.
Assistant GM: Jeff Kingston. **Special Assistants:** Tony Blengino, Roger Hansen, Ken Madeja, Joe McIlvaine, Ted Simmons, Pete Vuckovich.
Administrator, Baseball Operations: Debbie Larsen.

Jack Zduriencik

Major League Staff
Manager: Eric Wedge.
Coaches: Bench—Robby Thompson; **Pitching**—Carl Willis; **Batting**—Chris Chambliss; **First Base**—Mike Brumley; **Third Base**—Jeff Datz; **Bullpen**—Jaime Navarro.

Medical/Training
Medical Director: Dr. Edward Khalfayan. **Club Physician:** Dr. Mitchel Storey. **Head Trainer:** Rick Griffin. **Assistant Trainers:** Rob Nodine, Takayoshi Morimoto. **Stength/Conditioning:** Allen Wirtala, James Clifford.

Player Development
Telephone: (206) 346-4316. **Fax:** (206) 346-4300.
Director, Player Development: Chris Gwynn. **Director, Minor League/International Administration:** Hide Sueyoshi. **Administrator, Minor League Operations:** Jan Plein. **Assistant, Minor League Operations:** Casey Brett. **Coordinator, Minor League Instruction:** Jack Howell. **Coordinator, Athletic Training:** Jimmy Southard. **Coordinator, Rehabilitation:** Chris Gorosics. **Roving Instructors:** Danny Garcia (strength/conditioning), Darrin Garner (infield/baserunning), John Stearns (catching), Jose Castro/Lee May Jr. (hitting), Rick Waits (pitching), Gary Wheelock (rehab pitching), Jesus Azuaje (Latin America field coordinator), Nasusel Cabrera (Latin America pitching coordinator).

Farm System

Class	Club (League)	Manager	Coach	Pitching Coach
Triple-A	Tacoma (PCL)	Daren Brown	Jeff Pentland	Dwight Bernard
Double-A	Jackson (SL)	Jim Pankovits	Cory Snyder	Lance Painter
High A	High Desert (CAL)	Pedro Grifol	Roy Howell	Tom Dettore
Low A	Clinton (MWL)	Eddie Menchaca	Tommy Cruz	Andrew Lorraine
Short-season	Everett (NWL)	Rob Mummau	Andy Bottin	Rich Dorman
Rookie	Pulaski (APP)	Jose Moreno	Rafael Santo Domingo	Nasusel Cabrera
Rookie	Peoria (AZL)	Mike Kinkade	Scott Steinmann/B.Johnson	Cibney Bello
Rookie	Mariners (DSL)	Claudio Almonte	M.Pimentel/F. Gerez	Danielin Acevedo
Rookie	Mariners (VSL)	Russell Vasquez	E. Ruiz/J. Umbria	Carlos Hernandez

Scouting
Telephone: (206) 346-4000. **Fax:** (206) 346-4300.
Director, Amateur Scouting: Tom McNamara. **Scouting Administrator:** Hallie Larson.
Major League Scouts: Roger Hansen (Stanwood, WA), Bob Harrison (Long Beach, CA), Greg Hunter (Seattle, WA), Steve Jongewaard (Napa, CA), Bill Kearns (Milton, MA), Joe McIlvaine (Newtown Square, PA), John McMichen (Treasure Island, FL), Ken Madeja (Novi, MI), Bill Masse (Manchester, CT), Frank Mattox (Peoria, AZ), Joe Nigro (Staten Island, NY), Duane Shaffer (Anaheim, CA), Ted Simmons (Chesterfield, MO), Pete Vuckovich (Johnstown, PA), Woody Woodward (Palm Coast, FL).
National Crosschecker: Mark Lummus (Cleburne, TX). **Territorial Supervisors: West**—Butch Baccala (Weimar, CA), **North East**—Alex Smith (Abingdon, MD), **Southeast**—Sean O'Connor (Treasure Island, FL), **Midwest**—Jeremy Booth (Houston, TX). **Area Supervisors:** Dave Alexander (Lafayette, IN), Garrett Ball (Atlanta, GA), Jesse Kapellusch (Emporia, KS), Steve Markovich (Highlands, NJ), Devitt Moore (Houston, TX), Mike Moriarty (Marlton, NJ), Rob Mummau (Palm Harbor, FL), Brian Nichols (Taunton, MA), Chris Pelekoudas (Goodyear, AZ), Stacey Pettis (Antioch, CA), John Ramey (Wildomar, CA), Joe Ross (Kirkland, WA), Tony Russo (Montgomery, IL), Noel Sevilla (Sunrise, FL), Bob Steinkamp (Beatrice, NE), Greg Whitworth (Los Angeles, CA), Brian Williams (Cincinnati, OH).
VP, International Operations: Bob Engle (Tampa, FL). **Coordinator, Special Projects International:** Ted Heid (Glendale, AZ). **Coordinator, Pacific Rim:** Pat Kelly; **Special Assignment International:** Eugene Grimaldi (Paris, France). **Coordinator, Canada/Europe:** Wayne Norton (Port Moody, British Columbia). **Coordinator, Latin America:** Patrick Guerrero (Dominican Republic). **Administrative Director, Dominican Operations:** Martin Valerio. **Coordinator, Venezuelan Operations:** Emilio Carrasquel (Barquisimeto, Venezuela). Jamey Storvick (Taiwan), Luis Molina (Panama), Franklin Taveras, Jr. (Dominican Republic), Yasushi Yamamoto (Japan).

Tampa Bay Rays

Office Address: Tropicana Field, One Tropicana Drive, St. Petersburg, FL 33705.
Telephone: (727) 825-3137. **Fax:** (727) 825-3111. **Website:** www.raysbaseball.com.

OWNERSHIP

Principal Owner: Stuart Sternberg. **President:** Matt Silverman.

Business Operations

Senior Vice President, Administration/General Counsel: John Higgins. **Senior VP, Business Operations:** Brian Auld. **Senior VP:** Mark Fernandez. **Senior VP, Development/Business Affairs:** Michael Kalt. **VP, Development:** Melanie Lenz. **Senior Director, Development:** William Walsh. **Senior Director, Procurement/Business Services:** Bill Wiener, Jr. **Senior Director, Information Technology:** Juan Ramirez. **Director, Human Resources:** Jennifer Tran. **Director, Partner/VIP Relations:** Cass Halpin.

Finance

VP, Finance: Rob Gagliardi. **Controller:** Patrick Smith.

Stuart Sternberg

Marketing/Community Relations

VP, Marketing: Tom Hoof. **Senior Director, Marketing:** Brian Killingsworth. **Senior Director, Community Relations:** Suzanne Murchland.

Communications/Broadcasting

Phone: (727) 825-3242.

VP, Communications: Rick Vaughn. **Director, Communications:** Dave Haller. **Senior Director, Broadcasting:** Larry McCabe.

Corporate Partnerships

Senior Director, Corporate Partnerships: Aaron Cohn. **Directors, Corporate Partnerships:** Josh Bullock, Richard Reeves. **Director, Corporate Partnership Services:** Devin O'Connell.

Ticket Sales

Phone: (888) FAN-RAYS.

VP, Sales/Service: Brian Richeson. **Senior Director, Season Ticket Sales/Service:** Jeff Tanzer. **Director, Ticket Operations:** Robert Bennett. **Assistant Director, Ticket Operations:** Ken Mallory.

Stadium Operations

VP, Operations/Facilities: Rick Nafe. **Senior Director, Building Operations:** Scott Kelyman. **Director, Event Operations:** Tom Karac. **Director, Building Operations:** Chris Raineri. **Director, Audio/Visual Services:** Ron Golick. **Head Groundskeeper:** Dan Moeller. **VP, Branding/Fan Experience:** Darcy Raymond. **Director, In-Game Entertainment:** Lou Costanza. **Director, Customer Service/Stadium Experience:** Eric Weisberg.

2012 SCHEDULE

Standard Game Times: 7:10 p.m.; Sun. 1:40.

APRIL		
6-8 . . . . . . New York (AL)	18-20 . . . . Atlanta	2-4 . . . . . . New York (AL)	23-25 . . . . Oakland
10-12 . . . . .at Detroit	21-23 . . . . .Toronto	5-8 . . . . . . .at Cleveland	27-29 . . . . .at Texas
13-16 . . . . . . .at Boston	25-27 . . . . . . .at Boston	13-15 . . . . Boston	30-31 . . . . at Toronto
17-19 . . . . . . at Toronto	28-30 . . . . . Chicago (AL)	16-19 . . . . . . Cleveland	
20-22 . . . . Minnesota		20-22 . . . . Seattle	**SEPTEMBER**
24-26 . . . Los Angeles (AL)	**JUNE**	24-26 . . . . . at Baltimore	1-2 . . . . at Toronto
27-29 . . . . .at Texas	1-3 . . . . Baltimore	27-29 . at Los Angeles (AL)	3-5 . . . . . . .New York (AL)
30 . . . . Seattle	5-7 . . . . at New York (AL)	30-31 . . . . . . .at Oakland	7-9 . . . . Texas
	8-10 . . . . at Miami		11-13 . . . . . .at Baltimore
MAY	12-14 . . . . .New York (NL)	**AUGUST**	14-16 . . . at New York (AL)
1-3 . . . . Seattle	15-17 . . . . .Miami	1 . . . . .at Oakland	17-20 . . . . Boston
4-6 . . . . Oakland	19-21 . . . . at Washington	3-5 . . . . Baltimore	21-23 . . . . .Toronto
8-10 . . . . at New York (AL)	22-24 . . . . at Philadelphia	7-9 . . . . .Toronto	25-26 . . . . .at Boston
11-13 . . . . . .at Baltimore	25-27 . . . . .at Kansas City	10-12 . . . . . at Minnesota	27-30 . . . . at Chicago (AL)
14-15 . . . . . . at Toronto	28-30 . . . . Detroit	13-15 . . . . . . at Seattle	**OCTOBER**
16-17 . . . . Boston	**JULY**	16-19 . at Los Angeles (AL)	1-3 . . . . Baltimore
	1 . . . . Detroit	20-22 . . . . . Kansas City	

GENERAL INFORMATION

Stadium (year opened): Tropicana Field (1998).
Team Colors: Dark blue, light blue, yellow.
Player Representative: Evan Longoria.

Home Dugout: First Base.
Playing Surface: AstroTurf
Game Day Grass 3D-60 H.

Travel/Clubhouse
Director, Team Travel: Jeff Ziegler. Equipment Manager, Home Clubhouse: Chris Westmoreland. Visitors Clubhouse Manager: Guy Gallagher. Video Coordinator: Chris Fernandez.

BASEBALL OPERATIONS

Executive VP, Baseball Operations: Andrew Friedman. Senior VP, Baseball Operations: Gerry Hunsicker.
Directors, Baseball Operations: Chaim Bloom, Erik Neander. Director, Major League Administration: Sandy Dengler. Senior Baseball Advisor: Don Zimmer. Special Assistant, Baseball Operations: Rocco Baldelli.
Architect, Baseball Systems: Brian Plexico. Director, Baseball Research/Development: James Click. Assistant, Baseball Operations Systems: Matt Hahn. Developer, Baseball Systems: Rob Naberhaus. Baseball Operations Analyst: Joshua Kalk. Analyst, Baseball Research/Development: Leland Chen. Assistants, Baseball Research/Development: Peter Bendix, Shawn Hoffman.

Andrew Friedman

Major League Staff
Manager: Joe Maddon.
Coaches: Bench—Dave Martinez; Pitching—Jim Hickey; Hitting—Derek Shelton; First Base—George Hendrick; Third Base—Tom Foley; Bullpen—Stan Boroski.

Medical/Training
Medical Director: Dr. James Andrews. Medical Team Physician: Dr. Michael Reilly. Orthopedic Team Physician: Dr. Koco Eaton. Head Athletic Trainer: Ron Porterfield. Assistant Athletic Trainers: Paul Harker, Mark Vinson. Strength/Conditioning Coach: Kevin Barr.

Player Development
Telephone: (727) 825-3267. Fax: (727) 825-3493.
Director, Minor League Operations: Mitch Lukevics. Assistant, Minor League Operations: Jeff McLerran. Administrator, Player Development: Giovanna Rodriguez.
Field Coordinators: Jim Hoff, Bill Evers. Minor League Coordinators: Skeeter Barnes (outfield/baserunning), Dick Bosman (pitching), Steve Livesey (hitting), Jamie Nelson (catching), Matt Quatraro (hitting), Dewey Robinson (pitching), Joe Benge (medical), Joel Smith (rehabilitation/athletic training), Trung Cao (strength/conditioning).
Equipment Manager: Tim McKechney. Assistant Equipment Manager: Shane Rossetti. Video Coordinator: Jeff Butler.

Farm System

Class	Club (League)	Manager	Coach	Pitching Coach
Triple-A	Durham (IL)	Charlie Montoyo	Dave Myers	Neil Allen
Double-A	Montgomery (SL)	Billy Gardner Jr.	Ozzie Timmons	R.C. Lichtenstein
High A	Charlotte (FSL)	Jim Morrison	Joe Szekely	Steve Watson
Low A	Bowling Green (MWL)	Brady Williams	Manny Castillo	Bill Moloney
Short-season	Hudson Valley (NYP)	Jared Sandberg	Dan DeMent	Kyle Snyder
Rookie	Princeton (APP)	Michael Johns	Reinaldo Ruiz	Darwin Peguero
Rookie	Rays (GCL)	Paul Hoover	W. Rincones/H. Torres	Marty DeMerritt
Rookie	Rays (DSL)	Julio Zorrilla	A. DeFreites/R. Guerrero	Jose Gonzalez/Roberto Gil
Rookie	Rays (VSL)	Esteban Gonzalez	A. Freire/G. Omaña	J. Moncada/G. Melendez

Scouting
Telephone: (727) 825-3241. Fax: (727) 825-3493.
Director, Scouting: R.J. Harrison (Phoenix, AZ). Assistant Director, Amateur Scouting: Rob Metzler.
Administrator, Scouting: Nancy Berry. Director, Pro Scouting: Matt Arnold. Coordinator, Advance Scouting: Mike Calitri. Special Assignment Scouts: Bart Braun (Vallejo, CA), Mike Cubbage (Keswick, VA), Larry Doughty (Leawood, KS). Major League Scouts: Bob Cluck (San Diego, CA), Jeff McAvoy (Palmer, MA).
Professional Scouts: Rico Brogna, (Woodbury, CT), Jason Grey (Mesa, AZ), Jason Karegeannes (Long Beach, CA), Brian Keegan (Matthews, NC), Jim Pransky (Davenport, IA).
Pro/International Scout: Carlos Rodriguez (Miami, FL).
National Crosschecker: Tim Huff (Cave Creek, AZ). East Coast Crosschecker: Kevin Elfering (Wesley Chapel, FL).
Midwest Crosschecker: Ken Stauffer (Katy, TX). North Midwest Crosschecker: Jeff Cornell (Lee's Summitt, MO). West Coast Crosschecker: Fred Repke (Carson City, NV). Scout Supervisors: Tim Alexander (Jamesville, NY), James Bonnici (Birmingham, MI), Evan Brannon (St. Petersburg, FL), Rickey Drexler (New Iberia, LA), Jayson Durocher (Phoenix, AZ), J.D. Elliby (OK), Brett Foley (Naperville, IL), Brian Hickman, (NC) Milt Hill (Cumming, GA), Paul Kirsch (Sherwood, OR), Robbie Moen (El Segundo, CA), Brian Morrison (Fairfield, CA), Pat Murphy (Marble Falls, TX), Lou Wieben (Little Ferry, NJ), Jake Wilson (Ramona, CA).
Part-Time Area Scouts: Tom Couston (Sarasota, FL), Jose Hernandez (Miami, FL), Jim Lief (Wellington, FL), Gil Martinez (San Juan, PR), Graig Merritt (Pitts Meadow, Canada), Casey Onaga (Aiea, HI), Jack Sharp (Dallas, TX), Donald Turley (Spring, TX), Peter Woodworth (St. Petersburg, FL).
Director, International Operations: Carlos Alfonso (Naples, FL). Director, Dominican Republic Operations: Eddy Toledo. Director, Venezuelan Operations: Ronnie Blanco. Pacific Rim Coordinator: Tim Ireland. Assistant, International/Minor League Operations: Patrick Walters. Consultant, International Operations: John Gilmore. International Scouts: Eddie Diaz (Mexico), Chairon Isenia (Curacao), Keith Hsu (Taiwan), Tateki Uchibori (Japan). Coordinator, Colombia: Manny Esquivia. Coordinator, Brazil: Adriano De Souza.

Texas Rangers

Office Address: 1000 Ballpark Way, Arlington, TX 76011.
Mailing Address: P.O. Box 90111, Arlington, TX 76011.
Telephone: (817) 273-5222. **Fax:** (817) 273-5110. **Website:** www.texasrangers.com.

Ownership

Co-Chairman: Ray C. Davis, Bob R. Simpson.
CEO/President: Nolan Ryan.

BUSINESS OPERATIONS

Chief Operating Officer: Rick George. **Senior Executive Vice President:** Jim Sundberg.
Executive VP/Chief Financial Officer: Kellie Fischer.

Executive VP, Communications: John Blake. **Executive VP, Business Partnerships/
Development:** Joe Januszewski. **Executive VP, Ballpark/Event Operations:** Rob Matwick.
Executive VP, Rangers Enterprises: Jay Miller. **Executive VP, In-Park Entertainment:** Chuck
Morgan. **Executive Assistant to CEO/President:** Courtney Krug. **Executive Assistant to
COO/Finance:** Gabrielle Stokes. **Executive Assistant:** Leslie Dempsey. **Manager, Ownership
Concierge Services:** Amy Beam.

Nolan Ryan

Finance/Accounting

Assistant VP/Controller: Starr Gulledge. **Payroll Manager:** Donna Ebersole.

Human Resources/Legal/Information Technology

VP, Human Resources/Risk Management: Terry Turner. **Associate Counsel:** Kate Cassidy. **Managers, Human
Resources:** Shannon Abbott, Shelby Carpenter, Mercedes Riley. **VP, Information Technology:** Mike Bullock. **Manager,
IT Systems/Customer Service:** Fred Phillips.

Business/Event Operations

VP, Rangers Enterprises: Grady Raskin. **Assistant VP, Customer Service:** Donnie Pordash. **Director, Event
Operations:** Danielle Cornwell. **Director, Parking/Security:** Mike Smith.

Communications/Community Relations

Assistant VP, Player Relations: Taunee Paur Taylor. **Senior Director, Media Relations:** Rich Rice. **Senior Director,
Broadcasting:** Angie Swint. **Assistant Director, Player Relations:** Ashleigh Greathouse. **Manager, Media Services:**
Brian SanFilippo. **Manager, Publications/Media Relations:** Rob Morse. **Coordinator, Communications:** Amber Sims.
Assistant, Player Relations: Becky Reed. **VP, Community Outreach/Executive Director, Foundation:** Karin Morris.
Assistant VP, Community Outreach: Breon Davis.

Facilities

VP, Ballpark Facilities Operations: Gib Searight. **Director, Grounds:** Dennis Klein. **Director, Ballpark Construction/
Development:** Andrew St. Julian.

2012 SCHEDULE

Standard Game Times: 7:05 p.m.; Sun. 2:05.

APRIL		
6-8 . . . . Chicago (AL)	18-20 . . . . . . .at Houston	3-5 . . . . . .at Chicago (AL)	23-26 . . . . Minnesota
9-12 . . . . Seattle	21-23 . . . . .at Seattle	6-8 . . . . Minnesota	27-29 . . . . . . .Tampa Bay
13-15 . . . . . at Minnesota	25-27 . . . . .Toronto	13-15 . . . . . . .at Seattle	31 . . . . .at Cleveland
17-18 . . . . .at Boston	28-30 . . . . Seattle	17-18 . . . . . .at Oakland	**SEPTEMBER**
19-22 . . . . .at Detroit	**JUNE**	20-22 . at Los Angeles (AL)	1-2 . . . . .at Cleveland
23-25 . . . .New York (AL)	1-3 . . . at Los Angeles (AL)	23-25 . . . . Boston	3-6 . . . . . .at Kansas City
27-29 . . . . . . .Tampa Bay	4-7 . . . . .at Oakland	27-29 . . . . Chicago (AL)	7-9 . . . . . at Tampa Bay
30 . . . . at Toronto	8-10 . . . at San Francisco	30-31 . . . Los Angeles (AL)	11-13 . . . . Cleveland
MAY	12-14 . . . . Arizona		14-16 . . . . Seattle
	15-17 . . . . Houston	**AUGUST**	18-20 . at Los Angeles (AL)
1-2 . . . . at Toronto	18-20 . . . . . at San Diego	1-2 . . . . Los Angeles (AL)	21-23 . . . . .at Seattle
4-6 . . . . .at Cleveland	22-24 . . . . .Colorado	3-5 . . . . .at Kansas City	24-27 . . . . Oakland
7-10 . . . . . . .at Baltimore	25-27 . . . . Detroit	6-8 . . . . .at Boston	28-30 . . . Los Angeles (AL)
11-13 . . . Los Angeles (AL)	28-30 . . . . Oakland	10-12 . . . . Detroit	**OCTOBER**
14-15 . . . . . . Kansas City	**JULY**	13-16 . . . at New York (AL)	1-3 . . . . .at Oakland
16-17 . . . . Oakland	1 . . . . Oakland	17-19 . . . . . . at Toronto	
		20-22 . . . . . . Baltimore	

GENERAL INFORMATION

Stadium (year opened): Rangers
Ballpark in Arlington (1994).
Team Colors: Royal blue and red.

Player Representative: Unavailable.
Home Dugout: First Base.
Playing Surface: Grass.

Marketing/Game Presentation
    Assistant VP, Marketing: Kelly Calvert. **Senior Director, Promotions/Special Events:** Sherry Flow. **Senior Creative Director, Graphic Design:** Rainer Uhlir. **Director, In-Game Entertainment:** Michael Cruz. **Creative Director, Media:** Rush Olson.

Merchandising
    Assistant VP, Merchandising: Diane Atkinson. **Director, Merchandising:** Stephen Moore.

Sponsorship/Ticket Sales/Ticket Operations
    VP, Corporate Sales: Jim Cochrane. **Director, Sponsorship Sales:** Guy Tomcheck. **VP, Ticket Sales/Services:** Paige Farragut. **Director, Ticket Services:** Mike Lentz. **Manager, Ticket Services:** Ben Rogers.

BASEBALL OPERATIONS

Jon Daniels

    Telephone: (817) 273-5222. **Fax:** (817) 273-5285.
    General Manager: Jon Daniels.
    Assistant GM: Thad Levine. **Senior Advisor to the GM:** John Hart. **Senior Special Assistant to the GM, Scouting:** Don Welke. **Senior Advisor to GM:** Tom Giordano. **Director, Baseball Operations:** Matt Vinnola. **Assistant, Baseball Operations:** Matt Klotsche. **Executive Assistant to GM:** Barbara Pappenfus.

Major League Staff
    Manager: Ron Washington.
    Coaches: Bench—Jackie Moore; **Pitching**—Mike Maddux; **Hitting**—Scott Coolbaugh; **First Base**—Gary Pettis; **Third Base**—Dave Anderson; **Bullpen**—Andy Hawkins.

Medical/Training
    Team Physician: Dr. Keith Meister. **Team Internist:** Dr. David Hunter. **Spine Consultant:** Dr. Andrew Dossett. **Head Trainer/Medical Director:** Jamie Reed. **Director, Strength/Conditioning:** Jose Vazquez.

Player Development
    Telephone: (817) 273-5224. **Fax:** (817) 273-5285.
    Senior Director, Player Development: Tim Purpura.
    Director, Minor League Operations: Jake Krug. **Special Assistants, Player Development:** Harry Spilman, Mark Conor. **Manager, Cultural Enhancement:** Bill McLaughlin. **Special Assistant:** Dave Oliver. **Assistant, Player Development:** Paul Kruger. **Field Coordinator:** Jayce Tingler. **Coordinators:** Danny Clark (pitching), Randy Ready (hitting), Luis Ortiz (assistant hitting), Hector Ortiz (catching), Keith Comstock (rehab pitching), Casey Candaele (infield/baserunning), Brian Dayette (special assignment coach), Napoleon Pichardo (strength/conditioning), Brian Bobier (medical), Dale Gilbert (rehab), Eduardo Tomas (DR strength/conditioning). **Manager, Minor League Complex Operations:** Chris Guth.

Farm System

Class	Club (League)	Manager	Coach	Pitching Coach
Triple-A	Round Rock (PCL)	Bobby Jones	Brant Brown/Spike Owen	Terry Clark
Double-A	Frisco (TL)	Steve Buechele	Jason Hart	Jeff Andrews
High A	Myrtle Beach (CL)	Jason Wood	Julio Garcia/Kenny Holmberg	Brad Holman
Low A	Hickory (SAL)	Bill Richardson	Josue Perez/Humberto Miranda	Storm Davis
Short-season	Spokane (NWL)	Tim Hulett	Oscar Bernard/Vinny Lopez	Ryan O'Malley
Rookie	Rangers (AZL)	Corey Ragsdale	Donzell McDonald/Justin Mashore	Oscar Marin
Rookie	Rangers (DSL)	Ryley Westman	A. Infante/G. Mercedes	Pablo Blanco/Jose Jaimes

Scouting
    Telephone: (817) 273-5277. **Fax:** (817) 273-5285.
    Senior Director, Player Personnel: A.J. Preller.
    Director, Amateur Scouting: Kip Fagg. **Director, Pro Scouting:** Josh Boyd. **Director, International Scouting:** Mike Daly. **Special Assistant, Scouting:** Scott Littlefield. **Special Assistant/Major League Scout:** Greg Smith (Davenport, WA). **Manager, Amateur Scouting:** Bobby Crook. **Pro Scouts:** Mike Anderson (Austin, TX), Russ Ardolina (Rockville, MD), Keith Boeck (Chandler, AZ), Chris Briones (Reno, NV), Scot Engler (Montgomery, IL), Ross Fenstermaker (Elk Grove, CA), Todd Walther (Dallas, TX), Mickey White (Sarasota, FL). **National Crosschecker:** Mike Grouse (Olathe, KS), Clarence Johns (Atlanta, GA). **Southeastern Crosschecker:** John Booher (Buda, TX). **Eastern Crosschecker:** Phil Geisler (Mount Horeb, WI). **Western Crosschecker:** Casey Harvie (Lake Stevens, WA). **Midwest Crosschecker:** Randy Taylor (Katy, TX).
    Area Scouts: Doug Banks (Scottsdale, AZ), Ryan Coe (Acworth, GA), Roger Coryell (Ypsilanti, MI), Jay Eddings (Sperry, OK), Steve Flores (Temecula, CA), Jonathan George (North Huntingdon, PA), Todd Guggiana (Long Beach, CA), Jay Heafner (Katy, TX), Chris Kemp (Charlotte, NC), Derek Lee (Frankfurt, IL), Gary McGraw (Gaston, OR), Butch Metzger (Sacramento, CA), Takeshi Sakurayama (Manchester, CT), Dustin Smith (Olathe, KS), Cliff Terracuso (Palm Beach Gardens, FL), Frankie Thon (Guaynabo, Puerto Rico), Jeff Wood (Birmingham, AL). **Part-Time Scouts:** Buzzie Keller (Seguin, TX), Mike McAbee (Euless, TX), James Vilade (Frisco, TX), Steve Watson (Austin, TX). **Video Scouts:** Nick English (Pasadena, CA), Ryan Lakey (Houston, TX), Bobby Houston (Wildomar, CA).
    Senior Advisor, Pacific Rim Operations: Jim Colborn. **Coordinator, Pacific Rim Operations:** Joe Furukawa (Japan). **Coordinator, International Scouting:** Gil Kim (Dominican Republic). **Dominican Program Coordinator:** Danilo Troncosco. **Manager, Korean Operations:** Curtis Jung. **Assistant, International Operations:** Stosh Hoover. **Latin America Crosschecker:** Roberto Aquino (Dominican Republic). **International Scouts:** Pedro Avila (Venezuela), Willy Espinal (Dominican Republic), Jose Fernandez (Florida), Daniel Floyd (West Australia), Chu Halabi (Aruba), Barry Holland (Australia), Bill McLaughlin (Mexico), Rodolfo Rosario (Dominican Republic), Joel Ronda (Puerto Rico), Rafic Saab (Venezuela), Hamilton Sarabia (Colombia), Eduardo Thomas (Panama), Hajime Watabe (Japan).

Toronto Blue Jays

Office/Mailing Address: 1 Blue Jays Way, Suite 3200, Toronto, Ontario M5V 1J1.
Telephone: (416) 341-1000. **Fax:** (416) 341-1250. **Website:** www.bluejays.com.

Ownership

Operated by: Toronto Blue Jays Baseball Club. **Principal Owner:** Rogers Communications Inc.

BUSINESS OPERATIONS

Paul Beeston

Vice Chairman, Rogers Communications: Phil Lind. **President, Rogers Media:** Keith Pelley. **President/CEO, Toronto Blue Jays/Rogers Centre:** Paul Beeston.

VP, Special Projects: Howard Starkman. **Special Assistants to the Organization:** Roberto Alomar, Pat Hentgen. **Executive Assistant to the President/CEO:** Sue Cannell.

Finance/Administration

Senior VP, Business Operations: Stephen R Brooks. **Executive Assistant:** Donna Kuzoff. **Senior Director/Controller:** Lynda Kolody. **Director, Payroll/Benefits:** Brenda Dimmer. **Director, Risk Management:** Suzanne Joncas. **Financial Business Managers:** Leslie Galant-Gardiner, Tanya Proctor. **Senior Manager/Assistant Controller:** Ciaran Keegan. **Manager, Stadium Payroll:** Sharon Dykstra. **Manager, Ticket Receipts/Vault Services:** Joseph Roach.

Director, Human Resources: Claudia Livadas. **Senior Manager, Human Resources:** Fiona Nugent. **Advisor, Human Resources:** Reena Patel. **Director, Information Technology:** Mike Maybee. **Manager, Information Technology:** Anthony Miranda. **VP, Business Affairs/Legal Counsel:** Matthew Shuber. **Executive Assistant, Business Affairs:** Liza Daniel.

Marketing/Community Relations

VP, Marketing/Merchandising: Anthony Partipilo. **VP, Corporate Partnerships:** Mark Ditmars. **Executive Assistant, Marketing:** Maria Cresswell. **Director, Marketing Services:** Natalie Agro. **Director, Game Entertainment/Promotions:** Marnie Starkman. **Executive Director, Jays Care Foundation:** Danielle Bedasse. **Directors, Corporate Partnership/Business Development:** John Griffin, Rob Swann. **Director, Partnership Marketing Services:** Krista Semotiuk. **Senior Managers, Partnership Sales/Business Development:** Honsing Leung, Mark Palmer. **Manager, Corporate Partnership Marketing:** Kelly Haley. **Executive Assistant Darla McKeen.**

Communications

Telephone: (416) 341-1301/1302/1303. **Fax:** (416) 341-1250.

VP, Communications: Jay Stenhouse. **Manager, Baseball Information:** Mal Romanin. **Coordinator, Baseball Information:** Erik Grosman. **Coordinator, Communications:** Sue Mallabon.

Stadium Operations

VP, Stadium Operations/Security: Mario Coutinho. **Executive Assistant:** June Sym. **Director, Guest Experience:** Carmen Day. **Manager, Event Services:** Julie Minott. **Manager, Game Operations:** Karyn Gottschalk.

2012 SCHEDULE

Standard Game Times: 7:07 p.m.; Sat/Sun: 1:07

APRIL			
5 . . . . .at Cleveland	18-20 . . . . .New York (NL)	2-5. . . . . . . Kansas City	27-29 . . . at New York (AL)
7-8. . . . . . . .at Cleveland	21-23 . . . . . at Tampa Bay	6-8. . . . . .at Chicago (AL)	30-31 . . . . . . .Tampa Bay
9-11 . . . . Boston	25-27 . . . . .at Texas	13-15 . . . . Cleveland	
13-15 . . . . Baltimore	28-30 . . . . . . Baltimore	16-18 . . . at New York (AL)	SEPTEMBER
17-19 . . . . . . .Tampa Bay		20-22 . . . . .at Boston	1-2. . . . . .Tampa Bay
20-23 . . . . .at Kansas City	JUNE	24-26 . . . . Oakland	3-5. . . . . Baltimore
24-26 . . . . .at Baltimore	1-3. . . . . Boston	27-29 . . . . Detroit	7-9. . . . . .at Boston
27-29 . . . . Seattle	5-7. . . . .at Chicago (AL)	30-31 . . . . . .at Seattle	11-13 . . . . Seattle
30 . . . . Texas	8-10 . . . . at Atlanta		14-16 . . . . Boston
	11-13 . . . . . Washington	AUGUST	18-20 . . at New York (AL)
MAY	15-17 . . . . .Philadelphia	1 . . . . .at Seattle	21-23 . . . . at Tampa Bay
1-2. . . . . Texas	18-20 . . . . at Milwaukee	2-5. . . . . . . .at Oakland	24-26 . . . . . .at Baltimore
3-6. . . at Los Angeles (AL)	22-24 . . . . . . at Miami	7-9. . . . . . at Tampa Bay	27-30 . . . . .New York (AL)
8-9. . . . . . . .at Oakland	25-27 . . . . . . .at Boston	10-12 . . . .New York (AL)	
10-13 . . . . . at Minnesota	28-30 . . . Los Angeles (AL)	13-16 . . . . Chicago (AL)	OCTOBER
14-15 . . . . . .Tampa Bay		17-19 . . . . Texas	1-3. . . . . Minnesota
16-17 . . . . .New York (AL)	JULY	21-23 . . . . . . .at Detroit	
	1 . . . . . . Los Angeles (AL)	24-26 . . . . . .at Baltimore	

GENERAL INFORMATION

Stadium (year opened): Rogers Centre (1989).
Team Colors: Blue and white.

Player Representative: Unavailable.
Home Dugout: Third Base.
Playing Surface: Artificial.

Ticket Operations
Director, Ticket Operations: Justin Hay. Director, Ticket Services: Sheila Stella. Manager, Box Office: Christina Dodge. Manager, Ticket Operations: Scott Hext.

Ticket Sales/Service
VP, Ticket Sales/Service: Jason Diplock. Executive Assistant: Stacey Jackson. Director, Premium Sales: Mike Hook. Director, Ticket Sales/Service: Franc Rota. Manager, Group Development: Ryan Gustavel. Manager, Premier Client Services: Erik Bobson. Manager, Ticket Sales: John Santana.

Travel/Clubhouse
Director, Team Travel/Clubhouse Operations: Mike Shaw. Equipment Manager: Jeff Ross. Clubhouse Manager: Kevin Malloy. Visiting Clubhouse Manager: Len Frejlich. Video Operations: Robert Baumander. Coordinator, Advance Scouting/Video: Brian Abraham. Team Employee Assistance Program: Brian Shaw.

BASEBALL OPERATIONS

Senior VP, Baseball Operations/General Manager: Alex Anthopoulos.
VP, Baseball Operations/Assistant GM: Tony LaCava. Assistant GM: Jay Sartori. Special Assistant to GM: Dana Brown. Consultant: Cito Gaston. Administrator, Baseball Operations: Heather Connolly. Baseball Information Analyst: Joe Sheehan. Executive Assistant to GM: Anna Coppola.

Major League Staff
Manager: John Farrell.
Coaches: Bench—Don Wakamatsu; Pitching—Bruce Walton; Hitting—Dwayne Murphy; First Base—Torey Lovullo; Third Base—Brian Butterfield; Bullpen—Pete Walker. Coach: Luis Rivera.

Alex Anthopoulos

Medical/Training
Medical Advisor: Dr. Bernie Gosevitz. Consulting Physician: Dr. Ron Taylor. Consulting Team Physicians: Irv Feferman, Noah Forman. Head Trainer: George Poulis. Assistant Trainer: Hap Hudson. Strength/Conditioning Coordinator: Bryan King. Director, Team Safety: Ron Sandelli.

Player Development
Telephone: (727) 734-8007. Fax: (727) 734-8162.
Director, Minor League Operations: Charlie Wilson. Director, Employee Assistance Program: Ray Karesky. Minor League Field Coordinator: Doug Davis. Senior Advisor: John Mallee. Assistant, Latin American Administration: Blake Bentley. Coordinator, Minor League Administration: Joanna Nelson. Assistant, Player Development: Mike Nielsen. Administrative Assistant: Kim Marsh. Roving Instructors: Anthony Iapoce (hitting), Mike Mordecai (infield), Rich Miller (outfield/baserunning), Dane Johnson (pitching), Rick Langford (rehab pitching coach). Minor League Coordinators: Mike Frostad (athletic training), Billy Wardlow (equipment), Donovan Santas (strength/conditioning), Chris Joyner (assistant strength/conditioning), Jeff Stevenson (rehab).

Farm System

Class	Club (League)	Manager	Hitting Coach	Pitching Coach
Triple-A	Las Vegas (PCL)	Marty Brown	Chad Mottola	Bob Stanley
Double-A	New Hampshire (EL)	Sal Fasano	Joe Nunnally	Tom Signore
High A	Dunedin (FSL)	Mike Redmond	Ralph Dickenson	Darold Knowles
Low A	Lansing (MWL)	John Tamargo Jr	Kenny Graham	Vince Horsman
Short-season	Vancouver (NWL)	Clayton McCullough	Dave Pano	Jim Czajkowski
Rookie	Bluefield (APP)	Dennis Holmberg	Paul Elliott	Antonio Caceres
Rookie	Blue Jays (GCL)	Omar Malave	John Schneider	Unavailable
Rookie	Blue Jays (DSL)	Cesar Martin	Guadalupe Javalera	Hector Eduardo/Oswald Peraza

Scouting
Director, Amateur Scouting: Andrew Tinnish. Director, Pro Scouting: Perry Minasian. Special Assistant, Amateur Scouting: Chuck LaMar. Senior Advisor/Pro Scout: Mel Didier.
Major League Scouts: Jim Beattie, Russ Bove, Sal Butera, Kevin Cash, Ed Lynch. Professional Crosscheckers: Kevin Briand, Jon Lalonde, Brian Parker. Pro Scouts: Mike Alberts, Matt Anderson, Steve Connelly, Dan Cox, Kimball Crossley, CJ Ebarb, Bob Fontaine, Nick Manno, David May Jr, Brad Matthews, Ryan Mittleman, Wayne Morgan, Jim Skaalen, Steve Springer, Doug Witt. National Crosscheckers: Dean Decillis, Mike Mangan, Marc Tramuta. Regional Crosscheckers: Tom Burns, Dan Cholowsky, Steve Miller, Tim Rooney, Rob St Julien. Area Scouts: Joey Aversa (Fountain Valley, CA), Coulson Barbiche (Columbus, OH), Darold Brown (Elk Grove, CA), Jon Bunnell (Overland Park, KS), Mike Burns (Houston, TX), Blake Crosby (Gilbert, AZ), Kevin Fox (La Mirada, CA), Ryan Fox (Yakima, WA), Bobby Gandolfo (Lansdale, PA), Joel Grampietro (Tampa, FL), John Hendricks (Mocksville, NC), Brian Johnston (Baton Rouge, LA), Randy Kramer (Aptos, CA), Jim Lentine (San Clementine, CA), Eric McQueen (Acworth, GA), Mike Medici (Naperville, IL), Nate Murrie (Bowling Green, KY), Matt O'Brien (Clermont, FL), Cliff Pastornicky (Birmingham, AL), Wes Penick (Clive, IA), Michael Pesce (New Hyde Park, NY), Jorge Rivera (Puerto Nuevo, PR), Darin Vaughan (Tulsa, OK), Michael Wagner (Addison, TX).
Canada Scouts: Don Cowan (Delta, BC), Jamie Lehman (Brampton, ON). Special Assistant, Latin American Operations: Ismael Cruz. Director, Dominican Republic: Jose Rosario. Director, Venezuela: Luis Marquez. International Scouts: Jean Carlos Alvarez (Santo Domingo, DR), Jose Contreras (Oriente, VZ), Luciano del Rosario (San Pedro, DR), Ramses Lara (Barquesimeto, VZ), Erick Medina (Cartagena, Columbia), Rafael Moncada (San Diego Valencia, VZ), Lorenzo Perez (Manoguayabo, DR), Daniel Sotelo (Managua, Nicaragua), Marino Tejeda (Santo Domingo, DR).

Washington Nationals

Office Address: 1500 South Capitol St. SE, Washington, DC 20003.
Telephone: (202) 640-7000. **Fax:** (202) 547-0025.
Website: www.nationals.com.

Ownership
Managing Principal Owner: Theodore Lerner.
Principal Owners: Annette Lerner, Mark Lerner, Marla Lerner Tanenbaum, Debra Lerner Cohen, Robert Tanenbaum, Edward Cohen, Judy Lenkin Lerner.

BUSINESS OPERATIONS
Chief Operating Officer, Lerner Sports: Alan Gottlieb. **COO:** Andrew Feffer. **Senior Advisor to Ownership:** Bob Wolfe. **Senior Vice President, Administration:** Elise Holman. **Vice President, Government/Municipal Affairs:** Gregory McCarthy. **Executive Assistant:** Cheryl Rampy. **Director, Client Services/Special Projects:** Britton Stackhouse Miller.

Ted Lerner

Business Affairs/Legal
VP, Ballpark Enterprises/Guest Services: Catherine Silver. **Director, Ballpark Enterprises:** Maggie Gessner. **Director, Guest Services/Hospitality Operations:** Jonathan Stahl. **Manager, Customer Service/Training:** Robert Asperheim. **Coordinator, Guest Services:** Billy Langenstein. **VP/Managing Director, Corporate Partnerships/Business Development:** John Knebel. **Director, Corporate Partnerships:** Allen Hermeling. **Senior Manager, Corporate Partnerships:** Samuel Cole.
VP/General Counsel: Damon Jones. **Deputy General Counsel:** Amy Inlander Minniti. **Executive Assistant:** Helena Wise.

Finance/Human Resources
Chief Financial Officer: Lori Creasy. **VP, Finance:** Ted Towne. **Director, Accounting:** Kelly Pitchford. **Senior Accountants:** Ross Hollander, Michael Page, Rachel Proctor. **VP, Human Resources:** Sonya Jenkins. **Director, Benefits:** Stephanie Giroux. **Coordinator, Human Resources:** Alan Gromest. **Assistant, Human Resources:** Ricardo Aponte Jr.

Media Relations/Communications
Senior Director, Baseball Information: John Dever. **Director, Baseball Media Relations:** Mike Gazda. **Manager, Baseball Media Relations:** Bill Gluvna. **VP/Managing Director, Communications/Brand Development:** Lara Potter. **Director, Creative Services/New Media:** Chad Kurz. **Senior Manager, Communications:** Joanna Comfort. **Manager, Communications:** Alexandra Schauffler.

Community Relations
Senior Director, Community Relations: Israel Negron. **Manager, Community Relations:** Nicole Murray. **Coordinator, Community Relations:** Kyle Mann.

2012 SCHEDULE
Standard Game Times: 7:05 p.m.; Sun. 1:35

APRIL		
5 . . . . .at Chicago (NL)	18-20 . . . . . . Baltimore	3-5 . . . . . . San Francisco
7-8 . . . . . .at Chicago (NL)	21-23 . . . at Philadelphia	6-8 . . . . Colorado
9-11 . . . . at New York (NL)	25-27 . . . . . . at Atlanta	13-16 . . . . . . at Miami
12-15 . . . . Cincinnati	28-30 . . . . at Miami	17-19 . . . .New York (NL)
16-19 . . . . Houston		20-22 . . . . Atlanta
20-22 . . . . .Miami	**JUNE**	23-25 . . at New York (NL)
24-26 . . . . . at San Diego	1-3 . . . . Atlanta	26-29 . . . . at Milwaukee
27-29 . at Los Angeles (NL)	5-7 . . . . . .New York (NL)	31 . . . . . . .Philadelphia
	8-10 . . . . . . .at Boston	
MAY	11-13 . . . . . . at Toronto	**AUGUST**
1-3 . . . . .Arizona	15-17 . . . .New York (AL)	1-2 . . . . . . .Philadelphia
4-6 . . . . . . .Philadelphia	19-21 . . . . . .Tampa Bay	3-5 . . . . Miami
8-10 . . . . . . at Pittsburgh	22-24 . . . at Baltimore	6-9 . . . . .at Houston
11-13 . . . . . .at Cincinnati	25-28 . . . . . at Colorado	10-12 . . . . at Arizona
14-15 . . . . . . San Diego	29-30 . . . . . . at Atlanta	13-15 . . . at San Francisco
16-17 . . . . Pittsburgh		17-19 . . . .New York (NL)
	JULY	20-22 . . . . Atlanta
	1 . . . . at Atlanta	

24-26 . . . . at Philadelphia	
28-29 . . . . at Miami	
30-31 . . . . St. Louis	
SEPTEMBER	
1-2 . . . . St. Louis	
3-6 . . . . . . Chicago (NL)	
7-9 . . . . .Miami	
10-12 . . at New York (NL)	
14-16 . . . . at Atlanta	
18-20 . . . Los Angeles (NL)	
21-24 . . . . . . .Milwaukee	
25-27 . . . . at Philadelphia	
28-30 . . . . . . .at St. Louis	
OCTOBER	
1-3 . . . . .Philadelphia	

GENERAL INFORMATION
Stadium (year opened): Nationals Park (2008).
Team Colors: Red, white and blue.

Player Representative: Unavailable.
Home Dugout: First Base.
Playing Surface: Grass.

Marketing/Broadcasting

VP, Marketing/Broadcasting: John Guagliano. **Executive Director, Production/Entertainment/Promotions:** Jacqueline Coleman. **Director, Consumer Marketing:** Scott Lewis. **Manager, Promotions/Events:** Amanda Hauge. **Manager, Production/Operations:** Dave Lundin. **Producer:** Benjamin Smith. **Editor:** Mark Jackson. **Senior Designer:** Lisa Grondines. **Copy Editor/New Media Manager:** Noah Frank.

Ticketing/Sales

VP/Managing Director, Sales/Client Services: Chris Gargani. **Director, Ticket Sales:** David McElwee. **Senior Director, Ticket Operations:** Tom Jackson. **Director, Ticket Operations:** Derek Younger. **Manager, Box Office:** Tyler Hubbard.

Senior Account Executive, Group Sales: Brian Beck. **Senior Account Executive, Ticket Sales:** Katherine Mitchell, Kevin Nawrocki. **Manager, Sales Development:** Rob Erwin. **Manager, Premium Sales:** Michael Shane. **Senior Manager, Ticket Services:** Andy Burns. **Manager, Client Services:** Richard Medina.

Ballpark Operations

VP, Facilities: Frank Gambino. **Senior Manager, Ballpark Operations:** Adam Lasky. **Head Groundskeeper:** John Turnour. **Assistant Head Groundskeeper:** Mike Hrivnak. **Assistant Groundskeeper:** Matt Coates. **Director, Security:** Stewart Branam. **Manager, Security:** Reemberto Rodriguez. **Director, Engineering Operations:** James Pantazis. **Director, Florida Operations:** Thomas Bell. **Manager, Florida Operations:** Jonathan Tosches.

BASEBALL OPERATIONS

Executive VP/General Manager: Mike Rizzo.

Assistant GM: Bryan Minniti. **Special Assistant to GM, Major League Administration:** Harolyn Cardozo. **Senior Advisor to GM:** Phillip Rizzo. **VP, Clubhouse Operations/Team Travel:** Rob McDonald. **Director, Baseball Operations:** Adam Cromie. **Analyst, Baseball Operations:** Sam Mondry-Cohen. **Assistant, Baseball Operations:** Aron Weston. **Coordinator, Advance Scouting:** Erick Dalton. **Assistant, Advance Scouting:** Christopher Rosenbaum.

Mike Rizzo

Major League Staff

Manager: Davey Johnson.

Coaches: Bench—Randy Knorr; **Pitching**—Steve McCatty; **Hitting**—Rick Eckstein; **First Base**—Trent Jewett; **Third Base**—Bo Porter; **Bullpen**—Jim Lett.

Medical, Training

Team Medical Director: Dr. Wiemi Duoghui. **Head Trainer:** Lee Kuntz. **Assistant Trainer:** Mike McGowen. **Strength/Conditioning Coach:** John Philbin.

Player Development

Assistant GM/VP, Player Development: Bob Boone.

Senior Assistant, Player Development: Pat Corrales. **Director, Player Development:** Doug Harris. **Director, Minor League Operations:** Mark Scialabba. **Assistant Director, Minor League Operations:** Ryan Thomas. **Director, Florida Operations:** Thomas Bell. **Manager, Florida Operations:** Jonathan Tosches. **Administrative Assistant, Florida Operations:** Dianne Wiebe. **Dominican Republic Academy Administrator:** Fausto Severino.

Coordinators: Bobby Henley (field), Spin Williams (pitching), Rick Schu (hitting), Jeff Garber (infield), Tony Tarasco (outfield/base running), Gary Cathcart (instruction), Mark Grater (rehab pitching), Steve Gober (medical/rehab), Landon Brandes (strength/conditioning). **Manager, Minor League Equipment/Clubhouse:** Calvin Minasian.

Farm System

Class	Club	Manager	Coach(es)	Pitching Coach
Triple-A	Syracuse (IL)	Tony Beasley	Troy Gingrich	Greg Booker
Double-A	Harrisburg (EL)	Matt LeCroy	Eric Fox	Paul Menhart
High A	Potomac (CL)	Brian Rupp	Marlon Anderson	Chris Michalak
Low A	Hagerstown (SAL)	Brian Daubach	Mark Harris	Franklin Bravo
Short-season	Auburn (NYP)	Gary Cathcart	Luis Ordaz	Sam Narron
Rookie	Nationals (GCL)	Tripp Keister	Amaury Garcia	Michael Tejera

Scouting

Assistant GM/VP, Player Personnel: Roy Clark.

Director, Scouting: Kris Kline. **Director, Pro Scouting:** Bill Singer. **Director, Player Procurement:** Kasey McKeon. **Special Assistants to GM:** Chuck Cottier, Deric Ladnier, Ron Rizzi, Jay Robertson, Bob Schaefer. **Assistant, Scouting:** Eddie Longosz. **Professional Scout:** Mike Daughtry. **Crosscheckers:** Mark Baca (National/West), Jimmy Gonzales (National/Mid West), Jeff Zona (National/East).

Area Supervisors: Steve Arnieri (Barrington, IL), Fred Costello (Livermore, CA), Reed Dunn (Nashville, TN), Paul Faulk (Little River, SC), Ed Gustafson (Lubbock, TX), Craig Kornfeld (Santa Margarita, CA), John Malzone (Needham, MA), Alex Morales (Wellington, FL), Tim Reynolds (Irvine, CA), Eric Robinson (Acworth, GA), Mitch Sokol (Phoenix, AZ), Paul Tinnell (Bradenton, FL), Tyler Wilt (Willis, TX). **Part-Time Area Scout:** Bobby Myrick (Colonial Heights, VA).

Director, Latin American Operations: Johnny DiPuglia. **Dominican Republic Scouting Supervisor:** Moises De La Mota. **Venezuela Scouting Supervisor:** German Robles.

International Scouts: Modesto Ulloa (Dominican Republic). **Part-Time Scouts:** Pablo Arias (Dominican Republic), Carlos Ulloa (Dominican Republic), Juan Garcia (Venezuela), Salvador Donadelli (Venezuela), Rafael Hernandez (Colombia), Caryl Van Zanten (Curacao), Miguel Ruiz (Panama).

MEDIA INFORMATION

LOCAL MEDIA INFORMATION

AMERICAN LEAGUE

BALTIMORE ORIOLES
Radio Announcers: Joe Angel, Fred Manfra. **Flagship Station:** WBAL Radio 1090 AM.
TV Announcers: Mike Bordick, Jim Hunter, Jim Palmer, Gary Thorne. **Flagship Station:** Mid-Atlantic Sports Network (MASN).

BOSTON RED SOX
Radio Announcers: Joe Castiglione, Dave O'Brien. **Flagship Station:** WEEI (850 AM).
TV Announcers: Don Orsillo, Jerry Remy. **Flagship Station:** New England Sports Network (regional cable).
Spanish Radio Announcers: Oscar Baez, Uri Berenguer. **Flagship Station:** WWZN (1510 AM).

CHICAGO WHITE SOX
Radio Announcers: Ed Farmer, Darrin Jackson, Chris Rongey. **Flagship Station:** WSCR The Score 670-AM.
TV Announcers: Ken Harrelson, Steve Stone. **Flagship Stations:** WGN TV-9, WCIU-TV, Comcast SportsNet Chicago (regional cable).

CLEVELAND INDIANS
Radio Announcers: Tom Hamilton, Mike Hegan, Jim Rosenhaus. **Flagship Station:** WTAM 1100-AM.
TV Announcers: Rick Manning, Matt Underwood. **Flagship Station:** SportsTime Ohio.

DETROIT TIGERS
Radio Announcers: Dan Dickerson, Jim Price. **Flagship Station:** WXYT 97.1 FM and AM 1270.
TV Announcers: Rod Allen, Mario Impemba. **Flagship Station:** FOX Sports Detroit (regional cable).

KANSAS CITY ROYALS
Radio Announcers: Denny Matthews, Bob Davis, Steve Stewart. **Kansas City affiliate:** KCSP 610-AM.
TV Announcers: Ryan Lefebvre, Joel Goldberg. **Flagship Station:** FOX Sports Kansas City.

LOS ANGELES ANGELS
Radio Announcers: Terry Smith, Jose Mota. **Spanish:** Rolando Nichols, Jose Tolentino, Amaury Pi-Gonzalez. **Flagship Station:** AM 830, ESPN Radio 710-AM, 1330 KWKW (Spanish).
TV Announcers: Victor Rojas, Mark Gubicza. **Flagship Stations:** FSN West (regional cable).

MINNESOTA TWINS
Radio Announcers: Cory Provus, Dan Gladden, Jack Morris. **Radio Network Studio Host:** Kris Atteberry. **Radio Engineer:** Kyle Hammer. **Spanish Radio Play-by-Play:** Alfonso Fernandez.
Flagship Station: 1500 ESPN.
TV Announcers: Bert Blyleven, Dick Bremer. **Flagship Station:** Fox Sports North.

NEW YORK YANKEES
Radio Announcers: John Sterling, Suzyn Waldman.
Flagship Station: WCBS 880-AM.
Spanish Radio Announcers: Beto Villa, Francisco Rivera.
TV Announcers: John Flaherty, Michael Kay, Al Leiter, Paul O'Neill, Ken Singleton.
Flagship Station: YES Network (Yankees Entertainment & Sports).

OAKLAND ATHLETICS
Radio Announcers: Vince Cotroneo, Ken Korach. **Flagship Station:** KGMZ 95.7 The Game, FM. **TV Announcers:** Ray Fosse, Glen Kuiper. **Flagship Stations:** Comcast Sports Net California.

SEATTLE MARINERS
Radio Announcers: Ron Fairly, Dave Henderson, Ken Levine, Ken Wilson. **Flagship Station:** KOMO 1000-AM.
TV Announcers: Mike Blowers, Rick Rizzs, Dave Simms. **Flagship Station:** FOX Sports Net Northwest.

TAMPA BAY RAYS
Radio Announcers: Andy Freed, Dave Wills. **Flagship Station:** Sports Animal WDAE 620 AM.
TV Announcers: Brian Anderson, Dewayne Staats, Todd Kalas. **Flagship Station:** Sun Sports.

TEXAS RANGERS
Radio Announcers: Eric Nadel, Steve Busby; Spanish—Eleno Ornelas. **Flagship Station:** KES 103.3 FM, KZMP 1540 AM (Spanish).
TV Announcers: Dave Barnett, Tom Grieve. **Flagship Stations:** Fox Sports Southwest (regional cable), TXA 21 (Fridays).

TORONTO BLUE JAYS
Radio Announcers: Jerry Howarth, Alan Ashby, Mike Wilner. **Flagship Station:** SportsNet Radio Fan 590-AM.
TV Announcers: Buck Martinez, Pat Tabler. **Flagship Station:** Rogers Sportsnet.

NATIONAL LEAGUE

ARIZONA DIAMONDBACKS
Radio Announcers: Greg Schulte, Tom Candiotti, Jeff Munn, Mike Fetters. **Spanish:** Miguel Quintana, Oscar Soria,

Richard Saenz. **Flagship Stations:** KTAR 620-AM, ESPN DEPORTES 710-AM (Spanish).
TV Announcers: Daron Sutton, Mark Grace, Luis Gonzalez, Joe Garagiola Sr. **Flagship Stations:** FOX Sports Arizona (regional cable).

ATLANTA BRAVES
Radio Announcers: Jim Powell, Don Sutton. **Flagship Station:** WCNN-AM 680 The Fan and WNNX-FM (100.5).
TV Announcers: FS South, SportSouth and Peachtree TV—Chip Caray, Joe Simpson. **Flagship Stations:** FS South and SportSouth (regional cable) and Peachtree TV (OTA).

CHICAGO CUBS
Radio Announcers: Pat Hughes, Keith Moreland. **Flagship Station:** WGN 720-AM.
TV Announcers: Len Kasper, Bob Brenly. **Flagship Stations:** WGN Channel 9 (national cable), Comcast Sports Net Chicago (regional cable), WCIU-TV Channel 26.

CINCINNATI REDS
Radio Announcers: Marty Brennaman, Thom Brennaman, Jeff Brantley, Jim Kelch. **Flagship Station:** WLW 700-AM.
TV Announcers: Chris Welsh, Thom Brennaman, Jeff Brantley. **Flagship Station:** Fox Sports Ohio (regional cable).

COLORADO ROCKIES
Radio Announcers: Jack Corrigan, Jerry Schemmel. **Flagship Station:** KOA 850-AM.
TV Announcers: Drew Goodman, George Frazier, Jeff Huson.

HOUSTON ASTROS
Radio Announcers: Brett Dolan, Milo Hamilton, Dave Raymond. **Spanish:** Alex Trevino, Francisco Romero. **Flagship Stations:** KTRH 740-AM, KLAT 1010-AM (Spanish).
TV Announcers: Bill Brown, Jim Deshaies. **Flagship Station:** Fox Sports Net.

LOS ANGELES DODGERS
Radio Announcers: Vin Scully, Rick Monday, Charley Steine. **Spanish:** Jaime Jarrín, Fernando Valenzuela, Pepe Yñiguez.
Flagship Stations: AM570 Fox Sports LA, KTNQ 1020-AM (Spanish).
TV Announcers: Vin Scully, Steve Lyons, Eric Collins.
Flagship Stations: KCAL 9, PRIME TICKET (regional cable).

MIAMI MARLINS
Radio Announcers: Dave Van Horne, Glenn Geffner. **Flagship Stations:** WAXY 790-AM, WAQI 710-AM (Spanish).
Spanish Radio Announcers: Felo Ramirez, Yiky Quintana.
TV Announcers: Tommy Hutton, Rich Waltz Frank Forte, Craig Minervini, Allison Williams, Preston Wilson, Cliff Floyd.
Spanish TV Announcers: Cookie Rojas, Raul Striker Jr. **Flagship Stations:** FSN Florida (regional cable).

MILWAUKEE BREWERS
Radio Announcers: Bob Uecker. **Flagship Station:** WTMJ 620-AM.
TV Announcers: Bill Schroeder, Brian Anderson. **Flagship Station:** Fox Sports Net North.

NEW YORK METS
Radio Announcers: Howie Rose, Wayne Hagin, Ed Coleman. **Flagship Station:** WFAN 660-AM. **TV Announcers:** Gary Cohen, Keith Hernandez, Ron Darling, Ralph Kiner, Kevin Burkhardt. **Flagship Stations:** PIX11-TV, Sports Net New York (regional cable).

PHILADELPHIA PHILLIES
Radio Announcers: Larry Andersen, Scott Franzke, Jim Jackson. **Flagship Stations:** WPHT 1210-AM.
TV Announcers: Tom McCarthy, Gary Matthews, Chris Wheeler. **Flagship Stations:** WPHL phl17, Comcast SportsNet (regional cable).

PITTSBURGH PIRATES
Radio Announcers: Steve Blass, Greg Brown, Bob Walk, John Wehner. **Flagship Station:** Sports Radio 93.7 FM The Fan.
TV Announcers: Tim Neverett, Steve Blass, Greg Brown, Bob Walk, John Wehner. **Flagship Station:** ROOT SPORTS (regional cable).

ST. LOUIS CARDINALS
Radio Announcers: Mike Shannon, John Rooney. **Flagship Station:** KMOX 1120 AM.
TV Announcers: Rick Horton, Al Hrabosky, Dan McLaughlin. **Flagship Stations:** Fox Sports Midwest.

SAN DIEGO PADRES
Radio Announcers: Jerry Coleman, Ted Leitner, Andy Masur, Bob Scanlan. **Flagship Station:** XX Sports Radio 1090-AM/ESPN 1700-AM.
TV Announcers: Dick Enberg, Mark Grant, Tony Gwynn. **Flagship Station:** Unavailable.

SAN FRANCISCO GIANTS
Radio Announcers: Mike Krukow, Duane Kuiper, Jon Miller, Dave Flemming. **Spanish:** Tito Fuentes, Erwin Higueros. **Flagship Station:** KNBR 680-AM (English); ESPN Deportes-860AM (Spanish).
TV Announcers: CSN Bay Area—Mike Krukow, Duane Kuiper; KNTV-NBC 11—Jon Miller, Mike Krukow, Duane Kuiper. **Flagship Stations:** KNTV-NBC 11, CSN Bay Area (regional cable).

WASHINGTON NATIONALS
Radio Announcers: Charlie Slowes, Dave Jageler. **Flagship Station:** WJFK 106.7 FM.
TV Announcers: Bob Carpenter, FP Santangelo. **Flagship Station:** Mid-Atlantic Sports Network (MASN).

NATIONAL MEDIA INFORMATION

BASEBALL STATISTICS

ELIAS SPORTS BUREAU INC.
Official Major League Statistician
Mailing Address: 500 Fifth Ave, Suite 2140, New York, NY 10110. **Telephone:** (212) 869-1530. **Fax:** (212) 354-0980.
Website: www.esb.com.
President: Seymour Siwoff.
Executive Vice President: Steve Hirdt. **Vice President:** Peter Hirdt. **Data Processing Manager:** Chris Thorn.

MAJOR LEAGUE BASEBALL ADVANCED MEDIA
Official Minor League Statistician
Mailing Address: 75 Ninth Ave, New York, NY 10011. **Telephone:** (212) 485-3444. **Fax:** (212) 485-3456. **Website:** MiLB.com.
Assistant Director, Stats Operation: Chris Lentine. **Managers of Stats:** Shawn Geraghty, Ian Schwartz. **Stats Supervisors:** Nicole Burdett, Jason Rigatti.

MiLB.COM
Official Website of Minor League Baseball
Mailing Address: 75 Ninth Ave, New York, NY 10011. **Telephone:** (212) 485-3444. **Fax:** (212) 485-3456. **Website:** MiLB.com.
Senior Editorial Manager, MiLB.com: Brendon Desrochers. **Director, Minor League Club Initiatives:** Nathan Blackmon. **Club Producers:** Dan Marinis, Danny Wild. **Columnist:** Ben Hill.

STATS Inc.
Mailing Address: 2775 Shermer Road, Northbrook, IL 60062. **Telephone:** (847) 583-2100. **Fax:** (847) 470-9140. **Website:** www.stats.com. **Email:** sales@stats.com. **Twitter:** twitter.com/STATSBiznews, twitter.com/STATS_MLB. **CEO:** Gary Walrath. **Executive Vice Presidents:** Steve Byrd, Robert Schur. **Senior Vice President, Sales:** Greg Kirkorsky. **Director, Sports Operations:** Allan Spear. **Manager, Baseball Operations:** Jeff Chernow.

TELEVISION NETWORKS

ESPN/ESPN2
Mailing Address, ESPN Connecticut: ESPN Plaza, Bristol, CT 06010. **Telephone:** (860) 766-2000. **Fax:** (860) 766-2213.
Mailing Address, ESPN New York Executive Offices: 77 W 66th St, New York, NY, 10023. **Telephone:** (212) 456-7777. **Fax:** (212) 456-2930.
Executive Chairman, ESPN, Inc.: George Bodenheimer.
President: John Skipper. **Executive VP, Administration:** Ed Durso. **Executive VP, Content:** Vinnie Malhorta. **Executive VP, Production:** Norby Williamson. **Executive VP, News/Talent/Content Operations:** Steve Anderson. **Senior VP, Programming/Acquisitions:** Carol Stiff. **Senior VP, Production:** Mark Gross. **Senior VP/Executive Producer, Production:** Jed Drake. **Coordinating Producer, Event Production:** Matt Sandulli. **Senior Coordinating Producer, Baseball Tonight:** Jay Levy. **Senior VP, Operations:** Jodi Markley.

ESPN CLASSIC, ESPNEWS
VP, Strategic Program Planning: John Papa.

ESPN INTERNATIONAL, ESPN DEPORTES
Executive VP/Managing Director, ESPN International: Russell Wolff.
Senior VP, ESPN Deportes: Traug Keller. **General Manager, ESPN Deportes:** Lino Garcia. **VP, ESPN Deportes, Programming:** Freddy Rolon.

FOX SPORTS
Mailing Address, Los Angeles: Fox Network Center, Building 101, Fifth floor, 10201 West Pico Blvd, Los Angeles, CA 90035. **Telephone:** (310) 369-6000. **Fax:** (310) 969-6700.
Mailing Address, New York: 1211 Avenue of the Americas, 20th Floor, New York, NY 10036. **Telephone:** (212) 556-2500. **Fax:** (212) 354-6902. **Website:** www.foxsports.com.
Chairman/CEO, Fox Sports Media Group: David Hill. **Vice Chairman, Fox Sports Media Group:** Ed Goren. **Co-Presidents/Co-COOs:** Randy Freer, Eric Shanks. **Executive VP, Production/Coordinating Studio Producer:** Scott Ackerson. **Executive VP, Production/Field Operations:** Bill Brown. **Executive VP, Programming/Production:** George Greenberg. **Executive VP/Creative Director:** Gary Hartley. **Senior VP, Production:** John Entz. **Senior VP, Prodution:** Jack Simmons. **Senior VP, Field/Technical Opearations, MLB on Fox:** Jerry Steinberg. **Coordinating Producer, MLB on Fox:** Pete Macheska. **Director, Game Production, MLB on Fox:** Bill Webb. **Senior VP, Media Relations:** Lou D'Ermilio. **VP, Communications:** Dan Bell. **Director, Communications:** Ileana Pena. **Publicist:** Eddie Motl.

MLB NETWORK
Mailing Address: 40 Hartz Way, Suite 10, Secaucus, NJ 07094. **Telephone:** (201) 520-6400.
President/CEO: Tony Petitti. **Executive VP, Advertising/Sales:** Bill Morningstar. **Senior VP, Marketing/Promotion:** Mary Beck. **Senior VP, Distribution/Affiliate Sales/Marketing:** Art Marquez. **Senior VP, Programming/Business Affairs:** Rob McGlarry. **Senior VP, Finance/Administration:** Tony Santomauro. **VP, Programming:** Andy Butters. **VP, Engineering/I.T.:** Mark Haden. **VP, Operations/Engineering:** Susan Stone. **Director, Remote Operations:** Tom Guidice. **Director, Studio Operations:** Karen Whritner. **VP, Business Public Relations, Major League Baseball:** Matt Bourne.

Manager, Business Public Relations/Entertainment/Major League Baseball: Lauren Verrusio.

TURNER SPORTS
Mailing Address: 1015 Techwood Drive, Atlanta, GA 30318. **Telephone:** (404) 827-1700. **Fax:** (404) 827-1339. **Website:** www.tbs.com/sports/mlb.
President: David Levy. **Senior VP, Executive Producer:** Jeff Behnke. **Executive VP, Chief Operating Officer:** Lenny Daniels. **Senior VP, Turner Sports Strategy/Marketing/Programming:** Christina Miller. **Senior VP, Creative/Content:** Craig Barry. **VP, Sports Program Planning:** John Vandegrift. **Executive VP, Turner Sports Ad Sales/Marketing:** Jon Diament. **VP, Production:** Howard Zalkowitz. **Coordinating Producer, MLB:** Glenn Diamond. **Senior VP, Public Relations:** Sal Petruzzi. **Publicist:** Eric Welch.

FOX SPORTS NET
Mailing Address: 10201 W Pico Blvd, Building 103, Los Angeles, CA 90035. **Telephone:** (310) 369-1000. **Fax:** (310) 969-6049.
Chairman/CEO, Fox Sports Media Group: David Hill. **President, Fox National Cable Networks:** Bob Thompson. **President, Fox Regional Cable Sports Networks:** Randy Freer. **Senior VP, Media Relations:** Lou D'Ermilio. **Senior VP, Fox Sports Net/Editor-in-Chief, Fox Sports Interactive Media:** Rick Jaffe.

OTHER TELEVISION NETWORKS

CBS SPORTS
Mailing Address: 51 W 52nd St, New York, NY 10019. **Telephone:** (212) 975-5230. **Fax:** (212) 975-4063.
Chairman: Sean McManus. **Executive VP:** David Berson. **Executive VPs, Programming:** Mike Aresco, Rob Correa. **Executive Producer/VP, Production:** Harold Bryant. **Senior VP, Communications:** LeslieAnne Wade.

CNN SPORTS
Mailing Address: One CNN Center, Atlanta, GA 30303. **Telephone:** (404) 878-1600. **Fax:** (404) 878-0011.
Vice President, Production: Jeffrey Green.

HBO SPORTS
Mailing Address: 1100 Avenue of the Americas, New York, NY 10036. **Telephone:** (212) 512-1000. **Fax:** (212) 512-1751. **President, HBO Sports:** Ken Hershman.

NBC SPORTS
Mailing Address: 30 Rockefeller Plaza, Suite 1558, New York, NY 10112. **Telephone:** (212) 664-2014. **Fax:** (212) 664-6365.
Chairman: Mark Lazarus. **President:** Jon Litner. **President, Programing:** Jonathan Miller. **Executive Producer:** Sam Flood. **Senior VP, Communications:** Greg Hughes.

ROGERS SPORTSNET (Canada)
Mailing Address: 9 Channel Nine Court, Toronto, ON M1S 4B5. **Telephone:** (416) 332-5600. **Fax:** (416) 332-5629. **Website:** www.sportsnet.ca.
President, Rogers Media: Keith Pelley. **President, Rogers Sportsnet:** Scott Moore. **Director, Communications/Promotions:** Dave Rashford.

THE SPORTS NETWORK (Canada)
Mailing Address: 9 Channel Nine Court, Toronto, ON M1S 4B5. **Telephone:** (416) 384-5000. **Fax:** (416) 332-4337. **Website:** www.tsn.ca.

RADIO NETWORKS

ESPN RADIO
Address: ESPN Plaza, 935 Middle St, Bristol, CT 06010. **Telephone:** (860) 766-2000, (800) 999-9985. **Fax:** (860) 589-5523. **Website:** espnradio.espn.go.com/espnradio/index.
GM, ESPN Radio Network: Mo Davenport. **Senior Director, Content:** Scott Masteller. **Senior Director, Operations/Events:** Keith Goralski. **Senior Director, Radio Content/Operations:** Peter Gianesini. **Senior Director, ESPN Deportes Radio:** Freddy Rolon. **Executive Producer:** John Martin. **Senior Director, Engineering:** Kevin Plumb. **Executive Director, Affiliate Relations:** Jim Roberts.

SIRIUS XM SATELLITE RADIO
Mailing Address: 1500 Eckington Place NE, Washington, DC 20002. **Telephone:** (202) 380-4000. **Fax:** 202-380-4500. **Hotline:** (866) 652-6696. **E-Mail Address:** mlb@siriusxm.com. **Website:** www.siriusxm.com.
President/Chief Content Officer: Scott Greenstein. **Senior VP, Sports:** Steve Cohen. **VP, Sports:** Brian Hamilton. **Executive Producers, MLB Network Radio:** Chris Eno, Brent Gambill. **Senior Director, Communications/Sports Programming:** Andrew Fitzpatrick,

SPORTS BYLINE USA
Mailing Address: 300 Broadway, Suite 8, San Francisco, CA 94133. **Telephone:** (415) 434-8300. **Guest Line:** (800) 358-4457. **Studio Line:** (800) 878-7529. **Fax:** (415) 391-2569. **E-Mail Address:** editor@sportsbyline.com. **Website:** www.sportsbyline.com. **President:** Darren Peck. **Executive Producer:** Ira Hankin.

YAHOO SPORTS RADIO
Mailing Address: 5353 West Alabama Street, Suite 415, Houston, TX 77056. **Telephone:** (800) 224-2004. **Fax:** (713) 479-5333 . **E-Mail Address formula:** first initial, last name@yahoosportsradio.com. **Website:** www.yahoosportsradio.com.
CEO: David Gow. **CMO:** Graham McKernan. **Senior Programming Director:** Craig Larson.

GENERAL INFORMATION

MAJOR LEAGUE BASEBALL PLAYERS ASSOCIATION

Mailing Address: 12 E. 49th St., 24th Floor, New York, NY 10017. **Telephone:** (212) 826-0808. **Fax:** (212) 752-4378. **E-Mail Address:** feedback@mlbpa.org. **Website:** www.mlbplayers.com.

Year Founded: 1966. **Twitter:** @MLB_Players.

Executive Director/General Counsel: Michael Weiner.

Chief Labor Counsel: David Prouty. **Senior Advisor:** Rick Shapiro. **Assistant General Counsels:** Doyle Pryor, Robert Lenaghan, Ian Penny, Matt Nussbaum, Robert Guerra. **Special Counsel:** Steve Fehr.

Director, Player Relations: Tony Clark. **Chief Administrative Officer:** Martha Child. **Chief Financial Officer:** Marietta DiCamillo. **Special Assistants to the Executive Director:** Bobby Bonilla, Phil Bradley, Rick Helling, Stan Javier, Mike Myers, Steve Rogers. **Player Relations:** Allyne Price, Virginia Carballo, Leonor Barua. **Contract Administrator:** Cindy Abercrombie. **Director, Communications:** Greg Bouris. **Director, Player Trust:** Melissa Persaud. **Accounting Assistants:** Jennifer Cooney, Terri Hinkley, Yolanda Largo. **Program Coordinator:** Hillary Falk. **Administrative Assistants:** Aisha Hope, Melba Markowitz, Sharon O'Donnell, Lisa Pepin, Deirdre Sweeney. **Receptionist:** Rebecca Rivera.

Director, Business Affairs/Licensing/Senior Counsel, Business: Timothy Slavin. **General Manager, Business Affairs/Media/International:** Richard White. **Director, Licensing/Business Development:** Evan Kaplan. **Senior Category Director, Retail Development/Apparel/Events Director:** Nancy Willis. **Category Director, Interactive Media:** Michael Amin. **New Media Content Director:** Chris Dahl. **Licensing Manager, Hard Goods/Collectibles:** Tom Cerabino. **Manager, Player Marketing/Business Development:** Ed Cerulo. **Business Services Manager:** Heather Gould. **Licensing Manager, Apparel/Retail Development:** Paul McNeill. **Licensing Assistant, Interactive Media:** Eric Rivera. **Office Services Clerk:** Victor Lugo.

Executive Board: Player representatives of the 30 major league clubs.

MLBPA Association Representatives: Curtis Granderson, Jeremy Guthrie. **Alternate Association Representatives:** Dave Bush, Carlos Villanueva. **MLBPA Pension Representatives:** Chris Capuano, Aaron Heilman. **Alternate Pension Representatives:** Ross Ohlendorf, Kevin Slowey.

SCOUTING

MAJOR LEAGUE BASEBALL SCOUTING BUREAU

Mailing Address: 3500 Porsche Way, Suite 100, Ontario, CA 91764. **Telephone:** (909) 980-1881. **Fax:** (909) 980-7794.

Year Founded: 1974.

Director: Frank Marcos. **Assistant Director:** Rick Oliver. **Office Coordinator:** Debbie Keedy. **Administrative Assistant:** Adam Cali.

Scouts: Rick Arnold (Spring Mills, PA), Andy Campbell (Gilbert, AZ), Mike Childers (Lexington, KY), Craig Conklin (Morro Bay, CA), Dan Dixon (Temecula, CA), Rusty Gerhardt (Overton, TX), Dennis Haren (San Diego, CA), Chris Heidt (Rockford, IL), Don Kohler (Asbury, NJ), Mike Larson (Waseca, MN), Johnny Martinez (St Louis, MO), Paul Mirocke (Wesley Chapel, FL), Carl Moesche (Gresham, OR), Tim Osborne (Woodstock, GA), Charles Peterson (Pembina, ND), Gary Randall (Rock Hill, SC), Willie Romay (Miami Springs, FL), Kevin Saucier (Pensacola, FL), Harry Shelton (Ocoee, FL), Pat Shortt (South Hempstead, NY), Craig Smajstrla (Pearland, TX), Ed Sukla (Irvine, CA), Jim Walton (Shattuck, OK).

Supervisor, Canada: Walt Burrows (Brentwood Bay, B.C.). **Canadian Scouts:** Curtis Bailey (Red Deer, Alberta), Jason Chee-Aloy (Toronto, Ontario), Bill Green (Vancouver, B.C.), Andrew Halpenny (Winnipeg, Manitoba), Ian Jordan (Kirkland, Quebec), Ken Lenihan (Bedford, Nova Scotia), Chris Kemlo (Oshawa, Ontario), Ken Lenihan (Beford Nova Scotia), Todd Plaxton (Saskatoon, Saskatchewan), Jasmin Roy (Longueuil, Quebec), Bob Smyth (Ladysmith, B.C.), Tony Wylie (Anchorage, AK).

Supervisor, Puerto Rico: Pepito Centeno (Cidra, PR).

Video Technicians: Matt Barnicle (Long Beach, CA), Ty Boyles (Phoenix, AZ), Wayne Mathis (Cuero, TX), Christie Wood (Raleigh, N.C.).

PROFESSIONAL BASEBALL SCOUTS FOUNDATION

Mailing Address: 5010 North Parkway Calabasas, Suite 201, Calabasas, CA 91302.

Telephone: (818) 224-3906. **Fax:** (818) 267-5516.

Website: www.probaseballscouts.com.

SCOUT OF THE YEAR FOUNDATION

Mailing Address: P.O. Box 211585, West Palm Beach, FL 33421. **Telephone:** (561) 798-5897, (561) 818-4329. **E-mail Address:** bertmazur@aol.com.

President: Roberta Mazur. **Vice President:** Tracy Ringolsby. **Treasurer:** Ron Mazur II.

Board of Advisers: Pat Gillick, Roland Hemond, Gary Hughes, Tommy Lasorda.

Scout of the Year Program Advisory Board: Tony DeMacio, Joe Klein, Roland Hemond, Gary Hughes, Dan Jennings, Linda Pereira.

UMPIRES

JIM EVANS ACADEMY OF PROFESSIONAL UMPIRING

Mailing Address: 200 South Wilcox St., #508, Castle Rock, CO 80104. **Telephone:** (303) 290-7411. **E-mail Address:** jeapu@umpireacademy.com. **Website:** www.umpireacademy.com.

Operator: Jim Evans.

MAJOR LEAGUES

PROFESSIONAL BASEBALL UMPIRE CORP

Street Address: 9550 16th Street North, St. Petersburg, FL 33716.
Mailing Address: P.O. Box A, St. Petersburg, FL 33731-1950.
Telephone: (727) 822-6937. **Fax:** (727) 821-5819.
President: Pat O'Conner. **Secretary/VP, Legal Affairs/General Counsel:** D. Scott Poley. **Executive Director, PBUC:** Justin Klemm. **Chief of Instruction/PBUC Evaluator:** Mike Felt. **Field Evaluators/Instructors:** Jorge Bauza, Dusty Dellinger, Matt Hollowell, Larry Reveal, Darren Spagnardi. **Medical Coordinator:** Mark Stubblefield. **Special Assistant, PBUC:** Lillian Patterson.

THE UMPIRE SCHOOL

Mailing Address: P.O. Box A, St. Petersburg, FL, 33731.
Telephone: (877) 799-UMPS. **Fax:** (727) 821-5819.
Email: info@therightcall.net. **Website:** www.therightcall.net.
Executive Director: Justin Klemm. **Chief of Instruction:** Mike Felt. **Curriculum Coordinator:** Larry Reveal. **Lead Rules Instructor:** Jorge Bauza. **Field Leaders:** Dusty Dellinger, Matt Hollowell, Darren Spagnardi. **Medical Coordinator:** Mark Stubblefield. **Administrator:** Andy Shultz.

WENDELSTEDT UMPIRE SCHOOL

Mailing Address: 100 Minges Creek Place, Suite A205, Battle Creek, MI, 49015.
Telephone: 800-818-1690. **Fax:** 888-881-9801. **E-mail Address:** admin@umpireschool.com. **Website:** www.umpire-school.com.

WORLD UMPIRES ASSOCIATION

Mailing Address: P.O. Box 394, Neenah, WI 54957. **Telephone:** (920) 969-1580. **Fax:** (920) 969-1892. **E-mail Address:** worldumpiresassn@aol.com. **Website:** www.worldumpires.com.
Year Founded: 2000.
President: Joe West. **Vice President:** Fielden Culbreth. **Secretary/Treasurer:** Jerry Layne. **Labor Counsel:** Brian Lam. **Administrator:** Phil Janssen.

TRAINERS

PROFESSIONAL BASEBALL ATHLETIC TRAINERS SOCIETY

Mailing Address: 1201 Peachtree St., 400 Colony Square, Suite 1750, Atlanta, GA 30361. **Telephone:** (404) 875-4000, ext. **1. Fax:** (404) 892-8560. **E-mail Address:** rmallernee@mallernee-branch.com. **Website:** www.pbats.com.
Year Founded: 1983.
President: Richie Bancells (Baltimore Orioles). **Secretary:** Mark O'Neal (Chicago Cubs). **Treasurer:** Jeff Porter (Atlanta Braves). **American League Head Athletic Trainer Representative:** Ron Porterfield (Tampa Bay Rays). **American League Assistant Athletic Trainer Representative:** Rob Nodine (Seattle Mariners). **National League Head Athletic Trainer Representative:** Roger Caplinger (Milwaukee Brewers). **National League Assistant Athletic Trainer Representative:** Mike Kozak (Florida Marlins). **Immediate Past President:** Jamie Reed (Texas Rangers).
General Counsel: Rollin Mallernee II.

MUSEUMS

BABE RUTH BIRTHPLACE

Office Address: 216 Emory St., Baltimore, MD 21230. **Telephone:** (410) 727-1539. **Fax:** (410) 727-1652. **E-mail Address:** info@baberuthmuseum.com. **Website:** www.baberuthmuseum.com.
Year Founded: 1973.
Executive Director: Mike Gibbons. **Deputy Director:** John Ziemann. **Chief Curator:** Shawn Herne. **Communications:** Tim Richardson.
Hours: Museum open Tuesday-Sunday: 10 a.m. to 5 p.m. Gift shop open daily, 10 a.m. to 5 p.m. Closed New Year's Day, Thanksgiving and Christmas.

CANADIAN BASEBALL HALL OF FAME AND MUSEUM

Museum Address: 386 Church St., St. Marys, Ontario N4X 1C2. **Mailing Address:** P.O. Box 1838, St. Marys, Ontario N4X 1C2. **Telephone:** (519) 284-1838. **Fax:** (519) 284-1234. **E-mail Address:** baseball@baseballhalloffame.ca.
Website: www.baseballhalloffame.ca.
Year Founded: 1983.
President/CEO: Tom Valcke. **Director, Operations:** Scott Crawford.
Museum Hours: May—weekends only; June 1-Oct. 8—Monday-Saturday, 10:30-4 p.m.; Sunday, noon-4 p.m.

FIELD OF DREAMS MOVIE SITE

Address: 28995 Lansing Rd., Dyersville, IA 52040. **Telephone:** (563) 875-8404; (888) 875-8404. **Fax:** (563) 875-7253. **E-mail Address:** info@fodmoviesite.com. **Website:** www.fieldofdreamsmoviesite.com. **Year Founded:** 1989. **Office/Business Manager:** Betty Boeckenstedt. **Hours:** April-November, 9 a.m.-6 p.m.

LITTLE LEAGUE BASEBALL MUSEUM

Office Address: 525 Route 15 South, Williamsport, PA 17701. **Mailing Address:** P.O. Box 3485, Williamsport, PA 17701. **Telephone:** (570) 326-3607. **Fax:** (570) 326-2267. **E-mail Address:** museum@littleleague.org.
Website: www.littleleague.org/museum.
Year Founded: 1982.
Director: Janice Ogurcak. **Administrative Assistant:** Adam Thompson.
Museum Hours: Labor Day-Memorial Day, Friday and Saturday, 10 a.m.-5 p.m. June, Monday, Thursday, Friday,

Saturday, 10 a.m.-5 p.m.; Sunday, noon-5 p.m. July-August, Monday through Saturday, 10 a.m.-5 p.m.; Sunday, noon-5 p.m.

LOUISVILLE SLUGGER MUSEUM AND FACTORY

Office Address: 800 W. Main St., Louisville, KY 40202. **Telephone:** (502) 588-7228, (877) 775-8443. **Fax:** (502) 585-1179.

Website: www.sluggermuseum.org.

Year Founded: 1996.

Executive Director: Anne Jewell.

Museum Hours: Mon-Sat, Jan. 2-Dec. 23 except Thanksgiving, 9 a.m.-5 p.m. Sun, noon-5 p.m.

NATIONAL BASEBALL HALL OF FAME AND MUSEUM

Address: 25 Main St., Cooperstown, NY 13326. **Telephone:** (888) 425-5633, (607) 547-7200. **FAX:** (607) 547-2044. **E-mail Address:** info@baseballhalloffame.org. **Website:** www.baseballhall.org.

Year Founded: 1939.

Chairman: Jane Forbes Clark. **Vice Chairman:** Joe Morgan. **President:** Jeff Idelson.

Museum Hours: Memorial Day Weekend-The Day Before Labor Day, 9 a.m.-9 p.m.; remainder of year, 9 a.m.-5 p.m. Open daily except Thanksgiving, Christmas, New Year's Day.

2012 Hall of Fame Induction Ceremony: July 22, 1:30 p.m. ET, Cooperstown, NY.

NEGRO LEAGUES BASEBALL MUSEUM

Mailing Address: 1616 E. 18th St., Kansas City, MO 64108. **Telephone:** (816) 221-1920. **Fax:** (816) 221-8424. **E-mail Address:** nlmuseum@hotmail.com. **Website:** www.nlbm.com.

Year Founded: 1990.

President: Bob Kendrick. **Executive Director Emeritus:** Don Motley.

Museum Hours: Tues.-Sat. 9 a.m.-6 p.m.; Sun. noon-6 p.m.

NOLAN RYAN FOUNDATION AND EXHIBIT CENTER

Mailing Address: 2925 South Bypass 35, Alvin, TX 77511. **Telephone:** (281) 388-1134. **FAX:** (281) 388-1135. **Website:** www.nolanryanfoundation.org.

Hours: Mon.-Sat. 9 a.m.-4 p.m.

RESEARCH

SOCIETY FOR AMERICAN BASEBALL RESEARCH

Mailing Address: 4455 East Camelback Rd., Suite D-140, Phoenix, AZ 85018. **Telephone:** (800) 969-7227. **Fax:** (602) 595-5690. **Website:** www.sabr.org.

Year Founded: 1971.

President: Vince Gennaro. **Vice President:** Bill Nowlin. **Secretary:** Todd Lebowitz. **Treasurer:** F.X. **Flinn. Directors:** Gary Gillette, Tom Hufford, Paul Hirsch, Leslie Heaphy. **Executive Director:** Marc Appleman. **Web Content Editor/Producer:** Jacob Pomrenke.

ALUMNI ASSOCIATION

MAJOR LEAGUE BASEBALL PLAYERS ALUMNI ASSOCIATION

Mailing Address: 1631 Mesa Ave., Copper Building, Suite D, Colorado Springs, CO 80906. **Telephone:** (719) 477-1870. **Fax:** (719) 477-1875.

E-mail Address: postoffice@mlbpaa.com. **Website:** www.baseballalumni.com.

Facebook: facebook.com/majorleaguebaseballplayersalumniassociation. **Twitter:** @MLBPAA.

Chief Executive Officer: Dan Foster (dan@mlbpaa.com). **Chief Operating Officer:** Geoffrey Hixson (geoff@mlbpaa.com). **Vice President, Legends Entertainment Group:** Chris Torgusen (chris@mlbpaa.com). **Director, Special Events:** Mike Groll (mikeg@mlbpaa.com). **Director, Administration:** Mary Russell Baucom (maryrussell@mlbpaa.com). **Special Events Coordinators:** Tyler Kourajian (tyler@mlbpaa.com), Michael Obyc (michael@mlbpaa.com). **Public Relations Coordinator:** Nikki Warner (nikki@mlbpaa.com). **Director, Memorabilia:** Matthew Hazzard (matt@mlbpaa.com). **Memorabilia Coordinators:** Billy Horn (bhorn@mlbpaa.com), Matt Tissi (mtissi@mlbpaa.com), Greg Thomas (greg@mlbpaa.com).

President: Brooks Robinson.

Chairman: Jim Hannan. **Vice President, Secretary:** Fred Valentine. **Board of Directors:** Sandy Alderson, John Doherty, Denny Doyle, Brian Fisher, Joseph Garagiola Jr., Doug Glanville, Jim "Mudcat" Grant, Rich Hand, Steve Rogers, Will Royster, Jim Sadowski, Jose Valdivielso. **Legal Counsel:** Sam Moore.

MINOR LEAGUE BASEBALL ALUMNI ASSOCIATION

Mailing Address: P.O. Box A, St. Petersburg, FL 33731. **Telephone:** (727) 822-6937. **Fax:** (727) 821-5819. **E-Mail Address:** alumni@minorleaguebaseball.com. **Website:** www.milb.com.

ASSOCIATION OF PROFESSIONAL BALL PLAYERS OF AMERICA

Mailing Address: 101 S. Kraemer Ave., Suite 112, Placentia, CA 92870. **Telephone:** (714) 528-2012. **Fax:** (714) 528-2037.

E-mail Address: ballplayersassn@aol.com. **Website:** www.apbpa.org.

Year Founded: 1924.

President: Roland Hemond. **First Vice President:** Tal Smith. **Second VP:** Stephen Cobb. **Third VP:** Tony Siegle. **Secretary/Treasurer:** Dick Beverage. **Membership Services Administrator:** Jennifer Joost-Van Sant. **Membership Services Manager:** Patty Joost.

Directors: Tony Gwynn, Whitey Herzog, Tony La Russa, Tom Lasorda, Brooks Robinson, Nolan Ryan, Tom Seaver, James Leyland, Mike Scioscia.

BASEBALL ASSISTANCE TEAM (BAT)

Mailing Address: 245 Park Ave., 34th Floor, New York, NY 10167.
Telephone: (212) 931-7822, Fax: (212) 949-5433.
Website: www.baseballassistanceteam.com.
Year Founded: 1986.
To Make a Donation: (866) 605-4594.
President: Ted Sizemore.
Vice Presidents: Bob Gibson (HOF), Frank Torre, Greg Wilcox.
Board of Directors: Ruben Amaro Sr., Steve Garvey, Luis Gonzalez, Joe Morgan (HOF), Jim Pongracz, Robin Roberts (HOF), Octavio "Cookie" Rojas, Gary Thorne, Randy Winn.
Executive Director: Joseph Grippo. **Secretary:** Thomas Ostertag. **Treasurer:** Scott Stamp. **Consultant:** Sam McDowell. **Operations:** Dominique Correa, Erik Nilsen.

MINISTRY

BASEBALL CHAPEL

Mailing Address: P.O. Box 302, Springfield, PA 19064. **Telephone:** (610) 690-2477.
E-mail Address: office@baseballchapel.org. **Website:** www.baseballchapel.org.
Year Founded: 1973.
President: Vince Nauss.
Hispanic Ministry: Cali Magallanes, Gio Llerena. **Director, Ministry Operations:** Rob Crose.
Board of Directors: Don Christensen, Greg Groh, Dave Howard, Vince Nauss, Bill Sampen, Walt Wiley.

TRADE/EMPLOYMENT

BASEBALL WINTER MEETINGS

Mailing Address: P.O. Box A, St. Petersburg, FL 33731. **Telephone:** (727) 822-6937. **Fax:** (727) 821-5819. **E-Mail Address:** BaseballWinterMeetings@milb.com. **Website:** www.baseballwintermeetings.com.
2012 Convention: Dec. 3-6, Gaylord Opryland Resort, Nashville, TN.

BASEBALL TRADE SHOW

Mailing Address: P.O. Box A, St. Petersburg, FL 33731. **Telephone:** (866) 926-6452. **Fax:** (727) 683-9865. **E-Mail Address:** tradeshow@milb.com. **Website:** www.baseballtradeshow.com.
Contact: Noreen Brantner, Sr. Asst. Director, Exhibition Services & Sponsorships.
2012 Show: Dec. 3-5, Gaylord Opryland Resort, Nashville, TN.

PROFESSIONAL BASEBALL EMPLOYMENT OPPORTUNITIES

Mailing Address: P.O. Box A, St. Petersburg, FL 33731-1950. **Telephone:** 866-WE-R-PBEO. **Fax:** 727-821-5819. **Website:** www.PBEO.com. **Email:** info@pbeo.com. **Contact:** Mark Labban, Manager, Business Development.

BASEBALL CARD MANUFACTURERS

PANINI AMERICA INC.

Mailing Address: Panini America, 5325 FAA Blvd., Suite 100, Irving TX 75061. **Telephone:** (817) 662-5300, (800) 852-8833.
Website: www.donruss.com.
Marketing Manager: Scott Prusha.

GRANDSTAND CARDS

Mailing Address: 22647 Ventura Blvd., #192, Woodland Hills, CA 91364. **Telephone:** (818) 992-5642. **Fax:** (818) 348-9122. **E-mail Address:** gscards1@pacbell.net. **Website:** www.grandstandcards.com.

MULTIAD SPORTS

Mailing Address: 1720 West Detweiller Dr., Peoria, IL 61615. **Telephone:** (800) 348-6485, ext. 5111. **Fax:** (309) 692-8378. **E-mail Address:** bjeske@multiad.com. **Website:** www.multiad.com/sports.

TOPPS

Mailing Address: One Whitehall St., New York, NY 10004. **Telephone:** (212) 376-0300. **Fax:** (212) 376-0573.
Website: www.topps.com.

UPPER DECK

Mailing Address: 2251 Rutherford Rd., Carlsbad, CA 92008. **Telephone:** (800) 873-7332. **Fax:** (760) 929-6548.
E-mail Address: customer_service@upperdeck.com. **Website:** www.upperdeck.com.

SPRING TRAINING

CACTUS LEAGUE

For spring training schedules, see page 244

ARIZONA DIAMONDBACKS

Major League Clubs
Complex Address: Salt River Fields at Talking Stick, 7555 N Pima Road, Scottsdale, AZ 85256. **Telephone:** (480) 270-5000. **Seating Capacity:** 11,000 (7,000 fixed seats, 4,000 lawn seats). **Location:** From Loop-101, use exit 44 (Indian Bend Road) and proceed west for approximately one-half mile; turn right at Pima Road to travel north and proceed one-quarter mile; three entrances to Salt River Fields will be available on the righthand side.

Minor League Clubs
Complex Address: Same as major league club.

CHICAGO CUBS

Major League Complex Address: HoHoKam Stadium, 1235 N Center St, Mesa, AZ 85201. **Telephone:** (480) 668-0500. **Seating Capacity:** 13,100. **Location:** Main Street (US Highway 60) to Center Street, north 1 1/2 miles on Center Street.
Hotel Address: Best Western Dobson Ranch Inn, 1666 S Dobson Rd, Mesa, AZ 85202. **Telephone:** (480) 831-7000.

Minor League Clubs
Complex Address: Fitch Park, 160 E Sixth Place, Mesa, AZ 85201. **Telephone:** (480) 668-0500. **Fax:** (480) 668-4501. **Hotel Address:** Best Western Mezona, 250 W Main St, Mesa, AZ 85201. **Telephone:** (480) 834-9233.

CHICAGO WHITE SOX

Major League Complex Address: Camelback Ranch—Glendale, 10710 West Camelback Road, Glendale, AZ 85037. **Telephone:** (623) 302-5200. **Seating Capacity:** 13,000.
Hotel Address: Comfort Suites Glendale, 9824 W Camelback Rd, Glendale, AZ 85305. **Telephone:** (623) 271-9005. **Hotel Address:** Renaissance Glendale Hotel & Spa, 9495 W Coyotes Blvd, Glendale, AZ 85305. **Telephone:** 629-937-3700.
Minor League Complex Address: Same as major league club.

CINCINNATI REDS

Complex Address: Cincinnati Reds Player Development Complex, 3125 S Wood Blvd, Goodyear, AZ 85338. **Telephone:** (623) 932-6590. **Ballpark Address:** Goodyear Ballpark, 1933 S Ballpark Way, Goodyear, AZ 85338. **Telephone:** (623) 882-3120.
Hotel Address: Marriott Residence Inn, 7350 N Zanjero Blvd, Glendale, AZ 85305. **Telephone:** (623) 772-8900. **Fax:** (623) 772-8905.

Minor League Clubs
Complex Address: Same as major league club.

CLEVELAND INDIANS

Major League
Complex Address: Cleveland Indians Player Development Complex, 2601 S Wood Blvd, Goodyear, AZ 85338. **Telephone:** (623) 302-5678. **Fax:** (623) 302-5670. **Seating Capacity:** 8,000.
Hotel Address: Quality Inn, 950 North Dysart Road, Goodyear, AZ 85338. **Telephone:** (623) 932-9191. **Telephone:** (863) 294-4451.

Minor League
Complex Address/Hotel: Same as major league club.

COLORADO ROCKIES

Major League
Complex Address: Salt River Fields at Talking Stick, 7555 N Pima Rd, Scottsdale, AZ 85258. **Telephone:** (480) 270-5800. **Seating Capacity:** 11,000. **Location:** From Loop 101 northbound, Take exit 44 (Indian Bend Rd) and turn left, proceeding west for approximately a half mile, turn right at Pima and the ballpark will be located on the right; From Loop 101 southbound, take exit 43 (Via De Ventura) and turn right, proceeding west for a half mile, turn left at the Via De Ventura entrance into the ballpark parking lot. **Hotel Address:** The Scottsdale Plaza Resort, 7200 North Scottsdale Road, Scottsdale, AZ 85253. **Telephone:** (480) 948-5000. **Fax:** (480) 951-5100.

Minor League
Complex/Hotel Address: Same as major league club.

KANSAS CITY ROYALS

Major League
Complex Address: Surprise Stadium, 15946 N Bullard Ave, Surprise, AZ 85374. **Telephone:** (623) 222-2222. **Seating Capacity:** 10,700. **Location:** I-10 West to Route 101 North, 101 North to Bell Road, left on Bell for five miles, stadium on left.
Hotel Address: Wigwam Resort, 300 East Wigwam Blvd, Litchfield Park, Arizona 85340. **Telephone:** (623)-935-3811

Minor League
Complex: Same as major league club. **Hotel Address:** Comfort Hotel and Suites, 13337 W Grand Ave, Surprise, AZ 85374. **Telephone:** (623) 583-3500.

LOS ANGELES ANGELS

Complex Address: Tempe Diablo Stadium, 2200 W Alameda, Tempe, AZ 85282. **Telephone:** (480) 858-7500. **Fax:** (480) 438-7583. **Seating Capacity:** 9,558. **Location:** I-10 to exit 153B (48th Street), south one mile on 48th Street to Alameda Drive, left on Alameda.

Minor League Clubs
Complex Address: Tempe Diablo Minor League Complex, 2225 W Westcourt Way, Tempe, AZ 85282. **Telephone:** (480) 858-7558.
Hotel Address: Sheraton Phoenix Airport, 1600 South 52nd Street, Tempe, AZ 85281. **Telephone:** (480) 967-6600.

LOS ANGELES DODGERS

Complex Address: Camelback Ranch, 10710 West Camelback Rd, Phoenix, AZ 85037. **Seating Capacity:** 13,000 plus standing room.
   Location: I-10 or I-17 to Loop 101 West or North, Take Exit 5, Camelback Road West to ballpark. **Telephone:** (623) 302-5000. **Hotel:** Unavailable.

Minor League
   Complex/Hotel Address: Same as major league club.

MILWAUKEE BREWERS

Major League
   Complex Address: Maryvale Baseball Park, 3600 N 51st Ave, Phoenix, AZ 85031. **Telephone:** (623) 245-5555. **Seating Capacity:** 9,000. **Location:** I-10 to 51st Ave, north on 51st Ave.
   Hotel Address: Staybridge Suites, 9340 West Cabella Drive, Glendale, AZ 85305. **Telephone:** (623) 842-0000

Minor League
   Complex Address: Maryvale Baseball Complex, 3805 N 53rd Ave, Phoenix, AZ 85031. **Telephone:** (623) 245-5600. **Hotel Address:** Same as major league club.

OAKLAND ATHLETICS

Major League
   Complex Address: Phoenix Municipal Stadium, 5999 E Van Buren, Phoenix, AZ 85008. **Telephone:** (602) 225-9400. **Seating Capacity:** 8,500. **Location:** I-10 to exit 153 (48th Street), HoHoKam Expressway to Van Buren Street (US Highway 60), right on Van Buren. **Hotel Address:** Doubletree Suites Hotel, 320 N 44th St, Phoenix, AZ 85008. **Telephone:** (602) 225-0500.

Minor League
   Complex Address: Papago Park Baseball Complex, 1802 N 64th St, Phoenix, AZ 85008. **Telephone:** (480) 949-5951. **Hotel Address:** Crowne Plaza, 4300 E Washington, Phoenix, AZ 85034. **Telephone:** (602) 273-7778.

SAN DIEGO PADRES

Major League
   Complex Address: Peoria Sports Complex, 8131 W Paradise Lane, Peoria, AZ 85382. **Telephone:** (623) 486-7000. **Fax:** (623) 486-7154. **Seating Capacity:** 11,333. **Location:** I-17 to Bell Road exit, west on Bell to 83rd Ave.
   Hotel Address: Country Inn and Suites (623) 879-9000, 20221 N 29th Avenue, Phoenix, AZ 85027.

Minor League
   Complex/Hotel: Same as major league club.

SAN FRANCISCO GIANTS

Complex Address: Scottsdale Stadium, 7408 E Osborn Rd, Scottsdale, AZ 85251. **Telephone:** (480) 990-7972. **Fax:** (480) 990-2643. **Seating Capacity:** 11,500. **Location:** Scottsdale Road to Osborne Road, east on Osborne 1/2 mile.
   Hotel Address: Hilton Garden Inn Scottsdale Old Town, 7324 East Indian School Rd, Scottsdale, AZ 85251. **Telephone:** (480) 481-0400.

Minor League Clubs
   Complex Address: Giants Minor League Complex 8045 E Camelback Road, Scottsdale, AZ 85251. **Telephone:** (480) 990-0052. **Fax:** (480) 990-2349.

SEATTLE MARINERS

Major League
   Complex Address: Peoria Sports Complex, 15707 N 83rd Ave, Peoria, AZ 85382. **Telephone:** (623) 776-4800. **Fax:** (623) 776-4829. **Seating Capacity:** 11,000. **Location:** I-17 to Bell Road exit, west on Bell to 83rd Ave.
   Hotel Address: LaQuinta Inn & Suites, 16321 N 83rd Ave, Peoria, AZ 85382. **Telephone:** (623) 487-1900.

Minor League
   Complex Address: Peoria Sports Complex (1993), 15707 N 83rd Ave, Peoria, AZ 85382. **Telephone:** (623) 776-4800. **Fax:** (623) 776-4828. **Hotel Address:** Hampton Inn, 8408 W Paradise Lane, Peoria, AZ 85382. **Telephone:** (623) 486-9918.

TEXAS RANGERS

Major League
   Complex Address: Surprise Stadium, 15754 N Bullard Ave, Surprise, AZ 85374. **Telephone:** (623) 266-8100. **Seating Capacity:** 10,714. **Location:** I-10 West to Route 101 North, 101 North to Bell Road, left at Bell for seven miles, stadium on left. **Hotel Address:** Windmill Suites at Sun City West, 12545 W Bell Rd, Surprise, AZ 85374. **Telephone:** (623) 583-0133.

Minor League
   Complex Address: Same as major league club.
   Hotel Address: Hampton Inn, 2000 N Litchfield Rd, Goodyear, AZ 85338. **Telephone:** (623) 536-1313; Holiday Inn Express, 1313 N Litchfield Rd, Goodyear, AZ 85338.

GRAPEFRUIT LEAGUE

For spring training schedules, see page 246

ATLANTA BRAVES

Major League
Stadium Address: Champion Stadium at ESPN Wide World of Sports Complex, 700 S Victory Way, Kissimmee, FL 34747. **Telephone:** (407) 939-1500. **Seating Capacity:** 9,500. **Location:** I-4 to exit 25B (Highway 192 West), follow signs to Magic Kingdom/Wide World of Sports Complex, right on Victory Way.
Hotel Address: World Center Marriott, World Center Drive, Orlando, FL 32821. **Telephone:** (407) 239-4200.

Minor League
Complex Address: Same as major league club. **Telephone:** (407) 939-2232. **Fax:** (407) 939-2225. **Hotel Address:** Marriot Village at Lake Buena Vista, 8623 Vineland Ave, Orlando, FL 32821. **Telephone:** (407) 938-9001.

BALTIMORE ORIOLES

Major League
Complex Address: Ed Smith Stadium, 2700 12th Street, Sarasota, FL 34237. **Telephone:** (941) 893-6300. **Fax:** (941) 893-6377. **Seating Capacity:** 7,500. **Location:** I-75 to exit 210, West on Fruitville Road, right on Tuttle Avenue. **Hotel Address:** Homewood Suites by Hilton, 3470 Fruitville Road, Sarasota, FL 34237. **Telephone:** (941) 365-7300.

Minor League
Complex Address: Buck O'Neil Baseball Complex at Twin Lakes Park, 6700 Clark Rd, Sarasota, FL 34241. **Telephone:** (941) 923-1996. **Hotel Address:** Days Inn, 5774 Clark Rd, Sarasota, FL 34233. **Telephone:** (941) 921-7812. **Hotel Address:** AmericInn, 5931 Fruitville Rd, Sarasota, FL 34232. **Telephone:** (941) 342-8778.

BOSTON RED SOX

Major League
Complex Address: JetBlue Park at Fenway South, Fort Myers, FL 33913. **Telephone:** (239) 334-4799.
Directions: From the North:Take I-75 South to Exit 131 (Daniels Parkway); Make a left off the exit and go east for approximately two miles; JetBlue Park will be on your left.
From the South: Take I-75 North to Exit 131 (Daniels Parkway); Make a right off exit and go east for approximately two miles; JetBlue Park will be on your left.

Minor League
Complex Address: Fenway South, Fort Myers, FL 33913.

DETROIT TIGERS

Major League
Complex Address: Joker Marchant Stadium, 2301 Lakeland Hills Blvd, Lakeland, FL 33805. **Telephone:** (863) 686-8075. **Seating Capacity:** 9,000. **Location:** I-4 to exit 33 (Lakeland Hills Boulevard).

Minor League
Complex: Tigertown, 2125 N Lake Ave, Lakeland, FL 33805. **Telephone:** (863) 686-8075.

HOUSTON ASTROS

Major League
Complex Address: Osceola County Stadium, 631 Heritage Park Way, Kissimmee, FL 34744. **Telephone:** (321) 697-3200. **Fax:** (321) 697-3197.
Seating Capacity: 5,300. **Location:** From Florida Turnpike South, take exit 244, west on US 192, right on Bill Beck Blvd
Hotel Address: Hilton Grand Vacations Club, 8122 Arrezzo Way, Orlando, FL 32811. **Telephone:** (407) 465-2600. **Fax:** (407) 465-2612.

Minor League
Complex Address/Hotel: Same as major league club.

MIAMI MARLINS

Major League
Complex Address: Roger Dean Stadium, 4751 Main St, Jupiter, FL 33458. **Telephone:** (561) 775-1818. **Telephone:** (561) 799-1346. **Seating Capacity:** 7,000.
Location: I-95 to exit 83, east on Donald Ross Road for one mile to Central Blvd, left at light, follow Central Boulevard to circle and take Main Street to Roger Dean Stadium. **Hotel Address:** Hilton Garden Inn, 3505 Kyoto Gardens Dr, Palm Beach Gardens, FL 33410. **Telephone:** (561) 694-5833. **Fax:** (561) 694-5829.

Minor League
Complex Address: Same as major league club. **Hotel Address:** Same as major league club.

MINNESOTA TWINS

Major League
Complex Address: Lee County Sports Complex/ Hammond Stadium, 14100 Six Mile Cypress Pkwy, Fort Myers, FL 33912. **Telephone:** (239) 533-7610. **Seating Capacity:** 8,100. **Location:** Exit 21 off I-75, west on Daniels Parkway, left on Six Mile Cypress Parkway.
Hotel Address: Hilton Garden Inn, 12600 University Drive, Fort Myers, FL 33907. **Telephone:** (239) 790-3500.

Minor League
Complex Address/Hotel: Same as major league club.

NEW YORK METS

Major League
Complex Address: Digital Domain Park, 525 NW Peacock Blvd, Port St Lucie, FL 34986. **Telephone:** (772) 871-2100. **Seating Capacity:** 7,000. **Location:** Exit 121C (St Lucie West Blvd) off I-95, east 1/4 mile, left onto NW Peacock. **Hotel Address:** Hilton Hotel, 8542 Commerce Centre Drive, Port St Lucie, FL 34986. **Telephone:** (772) 871-6850.

Minor League
Complex Address: Same as major league club. **Hotel Address:** Main Stay Suites, 8501 Champions Way, Port St Lucie, FL 34986. **Telephone:** (772) 460-8882.

NEW YORK YANKEES

Major League

Complex Address: George M Steinbrenner Field, One Steinbrenner Dr, Tampa, FL 33614. **Telephone:** (813) 879-2244. **Seating Capacity:** 11,076. **Hotel:** Unavailable.

Minor League

Complex Address: Yankees Player Development/ Scouting Complex, 3102 N Himes Ave, Tampa, FL 33607. **Telephone:** (813) 875-7569. **Hotel:** Unavailable.

PHILADELPHIA PHILLIES

Major League

Complex Address: Bright House Networks Field, 601 N Old Coachman Rd, Clearwater, FL 33765. **Telephone:** (727) 467-4457. **Fax:** (727) 712-4498. **Seating Capacity:** 8,500. **Location:** Route 60 West, right on Old Coachman Road, ballpark on right after Drew Street.

Hotel: Holiday Inn Express, 2580 Gulf to Bay Blvd, Clearwater, FL 33765. **Telephone:** (727) 797-6300. **Hotel:** La Quinta Inn, 21338 US 19 North, Clearwater, FL 33765. **Telephone:** (727) 799-1565.

Minor League

Complex Address: Carpenter Complex, 651 N Old Coachman Rd, Clearwater, FL 33765. **Telephone:** (727) 799-0503. **Fax:** (727) 726-1793. **Hotel Addresses:** Hampton Inn, 21030 US Highway 19 North, Clearwater, FL 34625. **Telephone:** (727) 797-8173. **Hotel Address:** Econolodge, 21252 US Hwy 19, Clearwater, FL 34625. **Telephone:** (727) 799-1569.

PITTSBURGH PIRATES

Major League

Stadium Address (March 2-31): McKechnie Field, 17th Ave West and Ninth Street West, Bradenton, FL 34205. **Seating Capacity:** 6,562. **Location:** US 41 to 17th Ave, west to 9th Street. (Workouts from Feb 19-29 held at): Pirate City, 1701 27th St E, Bradenton, FL 34208. **Telephone:** (941) 747-3031. **Fax:** (941) 747-9549.

Minor League

Complex/Hotel Address: Pirate City, 1701 27th St E, Bradenton, FL 34208.

ST LOUIS CARDINALS

Major League

Complex Address: Roger Dean Stadium, 4795 University Dr, Jupiter, FL 33458. **Telephone:** (561) 775-1818. **Fax:** (561) 799-1380. **Seating Capacity:** 6,864. **Location:** I-95 to exit 58, east on Donald Ross Road for 1/4 mile.

Hotel Address: Embassy Suites, 4350 PGA Blvd, Palm Beach Gardens, FL 33410. **Telephone:** (561) 622-1000.

Minor League

Complex: Same as major league club. **Hotel:** Double Tree Palm Beach Gardens.

TAMPA BAY RAYS

Major League

Stadium Address: Charlotte Sports Park, 2300 El Jobean Road, Port Charlotte, FL 33948. **Telephone:** (941) 235-5025. **Seating Capacity:** 6,823 (5,028 fixed seats). **Location:** I-75 to US-17 to US-41, turn left onto El Jobean Rd Hotel Address: The Rays do not retain a club hotel.

Minor League

Complex/Hotel Address: Same as major league club.

TORONTO BLUE JAYS

Major League

Stadium Address: Florida Auto Exchange Stadium, 373 Douglas Ave, Dunedin, FL 34698. **Telephone:** (727) 733-0429. **Seating Capacity:** 5,509. **Location:** US 19 North to Sunset Point; west on Sunset Point to Douglas Avenue; north on Douglas to Stadium; ballpark is on the southeast corner of Douglas and Beltrees.

Minor League

Complex Address: Bobby Mattick Training Center at Englebert Complex, 1700 Solon Ave, Dunedin, FL 34698. **Telephone:** (727) 743-8007. **Hotel Address:** Baymont Inn & Suites 26508 US 19 North, Clearwater, FL 33761. **Telephone:** (727) 796-1234.

WASHINGTON NATIONALS

Major League

Complex Address: Space Coast Stadium, 5800 Stadium Pkwy, Viera, FL 32940. **Telephone:** (321) 633-9200. **Seating Capacity:** 8,100. **Location:** I-95 southbound to Fiske Blvd (exit 74), south on Fiske/Stadium Parkway to stadium; I-95 northbound to State Road #509/Wickham Road (exit 73), left off exit, right on Lake Andrew Drive; turn right on Stadium Parkway, stadium is 1/2 mile on left.

Hotel Address: Hampton Inn, 130 Sheriff Drive, Viera, FL. **Telephone:** (321) 255-6868.

Minor League

Complex Address: Carl Barger Complex, 5600 Stadium Pkwy, Viera, FL 32940. **Telephone:** (321) 633-8119. **Hotel Address:** Hampton Inn, 130 Sheriff Drive, Viera, FL (321) 255-6868.

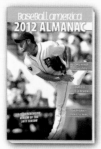

MINOR LEAGUES

MINOR LEAGUE BASEBALL

NATIONAL ASSOCIATION OF PROFESSIONAL BASEBALL LEAGUES

MINOR LEAGUE BASEBALL

™

Street Address: 9550 16th Street North, St Petersburg, FL 33716.
Mailing Address: PO Box A, St Petersburg, FL 33731-1950.
Telephone: (727) 822-6937. **Fax:** (727) 821-5819. **Fax (marketing):** (727) 894-4227. **Fax (licensing):** (727) 825-3785.
President: Pat O'Conner.
Vice President: Stan Brand. **Senior VP, Finance:** David Nunes. **Senior VP, Legal Affairs/General Counsel:** D Scott Poley. **VP, Baseball/Business Operations:** Tim Brunswick. **VP, Business Development:** Tina Gust. **Special Counsel:** George Yund. **Executive Director, Communications:** Steve Densa. **Managing Director, Security/Facility Operations:** John Skinner. **Assistant Director, Legal Affairs:** Louis Brown. **Manager, Baseball Operations/Executive Assistant to the President:** Mary Wooters.

Pat O'Conner

AFFILIATED MEMBERS/COUNCIL OF LEAGUE PRESIDENTS

Triple-A

League	President	Telephone	Fax Number
International	Randy Mobley	(614) 791-9300	(614) 791-9009
Mexican	Plinio Escalante	011-52-555-557-1007	011-52-555-395-2454
Pacific Coast	Branch Rickey	(512) 310-2900	(512) 310-8300

Double-A

League	President	Telephone	Fax Number
Eastern	Joe McEacharn	(207) 761-2700	(207) 761-7064
Southern	Unavailable	(770) 321-0400	(770) 321-0037
Texas	Tom Kayser	(210) 545-5297	(210) 545-5298

High Class A

League	President	Telephone	Fax Number
California	Charlie Blaney	(805) 985-8585	(805) 985-8580
Carolina	John Hopkins	(336) 691-9030	(336) 464-2737
Florida State	Chuck Murphy	(386) 252-7479	(386) 252-7495

Low Class A

League	President	Telephone	Fax Number
Midwest	George Spelius	(608) 364-1188	(608) 364-1913
South Atlantic	Eric Krupa	(727) 456-1240	(727) 499-6853

Short-Season

League	President	Telephone	Fax Number
New York-Penn	Ben Hayes	(727) 289-7112	(727) 683-9691
Northwest	Bob Richmond	(208) 429-1511	(208) 429-1525

Rookie Advanced

League	President	Telephone	Fax Number
Appalachian	Lee Landers	(704) 252-2656	Unavailable
Pioneer	Jim McCurdy	(509) 456-7615	(509) 456-0136

Rookie

League	President	Telephone	Fax Number
Arizona	Bob Richmond	(208) 429-1511	(208) 429-1525
Dominican Summer	Orlando Diaz	(809) 532-3619	(809) 532-3619
Gulf Coast	Operated by MILB	(727) 456-1734	(727) 821-5819
Venezuela Summer	Saul Gonzalez	011-58-241-823-8101	011-58-241-823-8101

NATIONAL ASSOCIATION BOARD OF TRUSTEES

TRIPLE-A
At-large: Ken Young (Norfolk). **International League:** Mike Tamburro (Pawtucket). **Pacific Coast League:** Sam Bernabe, Chairman (Iowa). **Mexican League:** Cuauhtemoc Rodriguez (Quintana Roo).

DOUBLE-A
Eastern League: Joe Finley, (Trenton). **Southern League:** Stan Logan (Birmingham). **Texas League:** Reid Ryan (Corpus Christi).

CLASS A
California League: Tom Volpe (Stockton). **Carolina League:** Chuck Greenberg (Myrtle Beach). **Florida State League:** Ken Carson, Secretary (Dunedin). **Midwest League:** Dave Walker (Burlington). **South Atlantic League:** Chip Moore (Rome).

SHORT-SEASON
New York-Penn League: Bill Gladstone (Tri-City). **Northwest League:** Bobby Brett (Spokane).

ROOKIE
Appalachian League: Mitch Lukevics (Princeton). **Pioneer League:** Dave Baggott, vice chairman (Ogden). **Gulf Coast League:** Bill Smith (Twins).

PROFESSIONAL BASEBALL PROMOTION CORP
Street Address: 9550 16th Street North, St Petersburg, FL 33716.
Mailing Address: PO Box A, St Petersburg, FL 33731-1950.
Telephone: (727) 822-6937. **Fax:** (727) 821-5819. **Fax/Marketing:** (727) 894-4227. **Fax/Licensing:** (727) 825-3785.
President: Pat O'Conner.
Senior VP, Finance: David Nunes. **Senior VP, Legal Affairs/General Counsel:** D Scott Poley. **VP, Baseball/Business Operations:** Tim Brunswick. **VP, BIRCO/Business Services:** Brian Earle. **VP, Business Development:** Tina Gust. **VP, Sales/Marketing:** Rod Meadows. **Executive Director, Communications:** Steve Densa. **Director, Information Technology:** Rob Colamarino. **Director, Licensing:** Sandie Hebert. **Director, Business Development:** Scott Kravchuk. **Managing Director, Security/Facility Operations:** John Skinner.
Senior Assistant Director, Exhibition Services/Sponsorships: Noreen Brantner. **Senior Assistant Director, Event Services:** Kelly Butler. **Assistant Director, Licensing:** Carrie Adams. **Assistant Director, Sales/Marketing:** Melissa Agee. **Assistant Director, Legal Affairs:** Louis Brown. **Assistant Director, Business Development:** Jill Dedene. **Assistant Director, Accounting:** James Dispanet. **Senior Account Manager:** Heather Raburn. **Manager, Office Operations:** Jeff Carrier. **Manager, Sponsor Relations:** Nicole Ferro. **Manager, Business Development:** Mark Labban. **Contract Manager:** Jeannette Machicote. **Manager, Team Relations/Sponsorship Development:** Mary Marandi. **Manager, Creative Services:** Rusty Morris. **Trademark Manager:** Bryan Sayre. **Manager, Baseball Operations/Executive Assistant to President:** Mary Wooters. **Staff Accountant:** Michelle Heystek. **Coordinator, Business Services:** Jessica Watts. **Special Assistant to the President:** Robert Fountain.

PROFESSIONAL BASEBALL UMPIRE CORP
Street Address: 9550 16th Street North, St Petersburg, FL 33716.
Mailing Address: PO Box A, St Petersburg, FL 33731-1950.
Telephone: (727) 822-6937. **Fax:** (727) 821-5819.
President: Pat O'Conner. **Secretary/VP, Legal Affairs/General Counsel:** D Scott Poley. **Executive Director, PBUC:** Justin Klemm. **Chief, Instruction/PBUC Evaluator:** Mike Felt. **Field Evaluators/Instructors:** Jorge Bauza, Dusty Dellinger, Matt Hollowell, Larry Reveal, Darren Spagnardi. **Medical Coordinator:** Mark Stubblefield.

GENERAL INFORMATION

Regular Season	Teams	Games	Opening Day	Closing Day	All-Star Games Date	Host
International	14	144	April 5	Sept. 3	*July 11	Buffalo
Pacific Coast	16	144	April 5	Sept. 3	*July 11	Buffalo
Eastern	12	142	April 5	Sept. 3	July 11	Reading
Southern	10	140	April 5	Sept. 3	June 19	Tennessee
Texas	8	140	April 5	Sept. 3	June 28	Tulsa
California	10	140	April 5	Sept. 3	#June 19	Winston-Salem
Carolina	8	140	April 6	Sept. 3	#June 19	Winston-Salem
Florida State	12	140	April 5	Sept. 2	June 16	Charlotte
Midwest	16	140	April 5	Sept. 3	June 19	Kane County
South Atlantic	14	140	April 5	Sept. 3	June 19	Charleston
New York-Penn	14	76	June 18	Sept. 5	Aug. 14	Mahoning Valley
Northwest	8	76	June 15	Sept. 1	None	
Appalachian	10	68	June 19	Aug. 28	None	
Pioneer	8	76	June 18	Sept. 6	None	
Arizona	13	56	June 20	Aug. 29	None	
Gulf Coast	14	60	June 18	Aug. 25	None	

*Triple-A All-Star Game. #California League vs. Carolina League

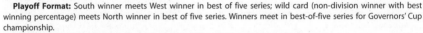

Office Address: 55 South High St, Suite 202, Dublin, Ohio 43017.
Telephone: (614) 791-9300. Fax: (614) 791-9009.
E-Mail Address: office@ilbaseball.com. Website: www.ilbaseball.com.
Years League Active: 1884-

President/Treasurer: Randy Mobley.
Vice Presidents: Dave Rosenfield, Tex Simone. Assistant to the President: Chris Sprague.
Corporate Secretary: Max Schumacher.
Directors: North Johnson (Gwinnett), Don Beaver (Charlotte), Joe Finley (Lehigh Valley), George Habel (Durham), Joe Napoli (Toledo), Bob Rich Jr (Buffalo), Dave Rosenfield (Norfolk), James Timlin (Scranton/Wilkes-Barre), Ken Schnacke (Columbus), Max Schumacher (Indianapolis), Naomi Silver (Rochester), John Simone (Syracuse), Mike Tamburro (Pawtucket), Gary Ulmer (Louisville).
Office Manager: Gretchen Addison.
Division Structure: North—Buffalo, Lehigh Valley, Pawtucket, Rochester, Scranton/Wilkes-Barre, Syracuse. West—Columbus, Indianapolis, Louisville, Toledo. South—Charlotte, Durham, Gwinnett, Norfolk.
Regular Season: 144 games. 2012 Opening Date: April 5. Closing Date: Sept 3. All-Star Game: July 11 at Buffalo (IL vs Pacific Coast League).

Randy Mobley

Playoff Format: South winner meets West winner in best of five series; wild card (non-division winner with best winning percentage) meets North winner in best of five series. Winners meet in best-of-five series for Governors' Cup championship.
Triple-A Championship Game: Sept 18 at Durham (IL vs Pacific Coast League).
Roster Limit: 24. Player Eligibility: No restrictions.
Official Baseball: Rawlings ROM-INT.
Umpires: Gerard Ascani (Tampa, FL), Sean Barber (Lakeland, FL), Lance Barrett (Burleson, TX), Craig Barron (Fayetteville, GA), Toby Basner (Snellville, GA), Kelvin Bultron (Canovanas, Puerto Rico), Jon Byrne (Thornlie, WA), Vic Carapazza (Palm Harbor, FL), Travis Carlson (Lakeland, FL), John Conrad (Meriden, CT), Chris Conroy (North Adams, MA), Mike Estabrook (Boynton Beach, FL), Manny Gonzalez (Valenica, Venezuela), Jeff Gosney (Lakeland, FL), Adam Hamari (Marquette, MI), Will Little (Fall Branch, TN), Mark Lollo (New Lexington, OH), Brad Myers (Holland, OH), Alan Porter (Warminster, PA), David Rackley (League City, TX), DJ Reyburn (Franklin, TX), Jonathan Saphire (Centerville, OH), David Soucy (Bluffton, SC), Chris Ward (Ashland, KY), Chad Whitson (Dublin, OH).

STADIUM INFORMATION

Club	Stadium	Opened	Dimensions			Capacity	2011 Att.
			LF	CF	RF		
Buffalo	Coca-Cola Field	1988	325	404	325	18,025	521,530
Charlotte	Knights Stadium	1990	335	400	335	10,002	279,107
Columbus	Huntington Park	2009	325	400	318	10,100	608,165
Durham	Durham Bulls Athletic Park	1995	305	400	327	10,000	467,646
Gwinnett	Coolray Field	2009	335	400	335	10,427	351,565
Indianapolis	Victory Field	1996	320	402	320	14,500	580,082
Lehigh Valley	Coca-Cola Park	2008	336	400	325	10,000	661,045
Louisville	Louisville Slugger Field	2000	325	400	340	13,131	601,372
Norfolk	Harbor Park	1993	333	410	318	12,067	397,889
Pawtucket	McCoy Stadium	1946	325	400	325	10,031	583,947
Rochester	Frontier Field	1997	335	402	325	10,840	448,024
* Scranton/WB	PNC Field	1989	330	408	330	10,310	298,098
Syracuse	Alliance Bank Stadium	1997	330	400	330	11,671	374,680
Toledo	Fifth Third Field	2002	320	408	315	10,300	549,438

* Scranton will play home schedule on the road at the following teams' ballparks: Buffalo, Lehigh Valley, Pawtucket, Rochester, Syracuse and short-season Batavia.

BUFFALO BISONS

Office Address: Coca-Cola Field, One James D Griffin Plaza, Buffalo, NY 14203.
Telephone: (716) 846-2000. Fax: (716) 852-6530.
E-Mail address: info@bisons.com. Website: www.bisons.com.
Affiliation (first year): New York Mets (2009). Years in League: 1886-90, 1912-70, 1998-

Ownership/Management

Operated By: Rich Products Corp.
Principal Owner/President: Robert Rich Jr. President, Rich Entertainment Group: Melinda Rich. President, Rich Baseball Operations: Jon Dandes. Vice President/Treasurer: David Rich. VP/Secretary: William Gisel.

VP/General Manager: Mike Buczkowski. **VP, Finance:** Joseph Segarra. **Corporate Counsel:** Jill Bond, William Grieshober. **Director, Sales:** Anthony Sprague. **Director, Stadium Operations:** Tom Sciarrino. **Controller:** Kevin Parkinson. **Senior Accountants:** Rita Clark, Nicole Hill. **Accountant:** Amy Delaney. **Director, Ticket Operations:** Mike Poreda. **Director, Public Relations:** Brad Bisbing. **Director, Game Day Entertainment/Promotions Coordinator:** Matt La Sota. **Sales Coordinators:** Rachel Osucha, Mike Simoncelli. **Account Executives:** Lindsay Carucci, Jeffrey Erbes, Mark Gordon, Jim Harrington, Robert Kates, Geoff Lundquist, Burt Mirti, Frank Mooney.
Manager, Merchandise: Sara Bukas. **Manager, Office Services:** Margaret Russo. **Executive Assistant:** Tina Lesher. **Community Relations:** Gail Hodges. **Director, Food Services:** Robert Free. **Assistant Concessions Manager:** Roger Buczek. **Head Groundskeeper:** Chad Laurie. **Chief Engineer:** Pat Chella. **Home Clubhouse/Baseball Operations Coordinator:** Scott Lesher. **Visiting Clubhouse Manager:** Dan Brick.

FIELD STAFF
Manager: Wally Backman. **Coach:** Unavailable. **Pitching Coach:** Mark Brewer.

GAME INFORMATION
Radio Announcers: Ben Wagner, Duke McGuire. **No of Games Broadcast:** Home-72, Road-72. **Flagship Station:** WWKB-1520.
PA Announcer: Jason Mollica. **Official Scorers:** Kevin Lester, Jon Dare.
Stadium Name: Coca-Cola Field. **Location:** From north, take I-190 to Elm Street exit, left onto Swan Street; From east, take I-190 West to exit 51 (Route 33) to end, exit at Oak Street, right onto Swan Street; From west, take I-190 East, exit 53 to I-90 North, exit at Elm Street, left onto Swan Street. **Standard Game Times:** 7:05 pm, Sun 1:05. **Ticket Price Range:** $5-18.
Visiting Club Hotels: Adams Mark Hotel, 120 Church St, Buffalo, NY 14202. **Telephone:** (716) 845-5100. Hyatt Hotel, 2 Fountain Plaza, Buffalo, NY 14202. **Telephone:** (716) 856-1234.

CHARLOTTE KNIGHTS

Office Address: 2280 Deerfield Dr, Fort Mill, SC 29715.
Telephone: (704) 357-8071. **Fax:** (704) 329-2155.
E-Mail address: knights@charlotteknights.com. **Website:** www.charlotteknights.com.
Affiliation (first year): Chicago White Sox (1999). **Years in League:** 1993-

Ownership/Management
Operated by: Knights Baseball, LLC.
Principal Owners: Don Beaver, Bill Allen.
Vice President/General Manager: Dan Rajkowski. **Director, Broadcast Communications:** Matt Swierad. **VP, Sales:** Chris Semmens. **Director, Stadium Operations:** Tom Gorter. **Director, Merchandising:** Becka Leveille. **Business Manager:** Michael Sanger. **Ticket Sales Coordinators:** Tony Furr, Dave LaCroix, Mac Simmons. **Ticket Office Manager:** Matt Millward. **Coordinator, Community/Team Relations:** Lindsey Roycraft. **Marketing/Development:** Bill Walker. **Head Groundskeeper:** Eddie Busque. **Clubhouse Manager:** Dan Morphis. **Corporate Sales Account Executive:** Brett Butler. **Executive Assistant to VP/GM:** Julie Clark.

FIELD STAFF
Manager: Joel Skinner. **Coach:** Andy Tomberlin. **Pitching Coach:** Richard Dotson.

GAME INFORMATION
Radio Announcer: Mike Pacheco, Matt Swierad. **No. of Games Broadcast:** Home-72 Road-72. **Flagship Station:** WRHI 1340-AM/94.3-FM.
PA Announcer: Ken Conrad. **Official Scorers:** Sam Copeland, Bill Walker.
Stadium Name: Knights Stadium. **Location:** Exit 88 off I-77, east on Gold Hill Road. **Ticket Price Range:** $8-13.
Visiting Club Hotel: Comfort Suites, 10415 Centrum Parkway, Pineville, NC 28134. **Telephone:** 704-540-0559.

COLUMBUS CLIPPERS

Office Address: 330 Huntington Park Lane, Columbus, OH 43215.
Telephone: (614) 462-5250. **Fax:** (614) 462-3271. **Tickets:** (614) 462-2757.
E-Mail address: info@clippersbaseball.com. **Website:** www.clippersbaseball.com.
Affiliation (fourth year): Cleveland Indians (2009). **Years in League:** 1955-70, 1977-

Ownership/Management
Operated By: Columbus Baseball Team Inc.
Principal Owner: CBT Inc. **Board of Directors:** Steven Francis, Tom Fries, Wayne Harer, Thomas Katzenmeyer, David Leland, Cathy Lyttle, Robert Milbourne, Richard Smith, McCullough Williams.
President/General Manager: Ken Schnacke. **Assistant GM:** Mark Warren. **Director, Ballpark Operations:** Steve Dalin. **Assistant Director, Ballpark Operations:** Phil Colilla. **Director, Ticket Operations:** Scott Ziegler. **Assistant Director, Ticket Operations:** Eddie Langhenry. **Director:** Marketing/Sales: Mark Galuska. **Assistant Director, Marketing:** Patrick Thompson. **Assistant Director, Sales:** Brittany McKittrick. **Assistant Directors, Promotions:** Seth Rhodes, Shannon O'Boyle. **Director, Communications/Media/Team Historian:** Joe Santry. **Assistant Director, Media Relations:** Anthony Slosser. **Assistant Director, Communications:** Ben Leland. **Directors, Broadcasting:** Ryan Mitchell, Scott Leo. **Director,**

MINOR LEAGUES

Merchandising: Krista Oberlander. **Assistant Director, Merchandising:** David Beckel. **Director, Group Sales:** Ben Keller. **Assistant Directors, Group Sales:** Brett Patton, Barry Keck, Steve Kuilder. **Director, Multimedia:** Josh Glenn. **Assistant Director, Multimedia:** Yoshi Ando.

Director, Social Media: Stefanie Altman Olejniczak. **Director, Finance:** Bonnie Badgley. **Executive Assistant to the President/GM:** Ashley Held. **Office Manager:** Kelly Ryther. **Director, Sponsor Relationships:** Joyce Martin. **Director, Event Planning:** Micki Shier. **Director, Clubhouse Operations:** George Robinson. **Clubhouse Manager:** Matt Pruzinsky. **Ballpark Superintendent:** Gary Delozier. **Head Groundskeeper:** Wes Ganobcik. **Assistant Groundskeeper:** Cliff Biegler, Nick Roe.

FIELD STAFF

Manager: Mike Sarbaugh. **Coach:** Phil Clark. **Pitching Coach:** Ruben Niebla. **Trainer:** James Quinlan. **Strength/Conditioning Coach:** Todd Kubacki.

GAME INFORMATION

Radio Announcers: Ryan Mitchell, Scott Leo. **No of Games Broadcast:** Home-72, Road-72. **Flagship Station:** WMNI 920AM.

PA Announcer: Matt Leininger. **Official Scorers:** Jim Habermehl, Ray Thomas.

Stadium Name: Huntington Park. **Location:** From north: South on I-71 to I-670 west, exit at Neil Avenue, turn left at intersection onto Neil Avenue. From south: North on I-71. Exit at Front St. (#100A). Turn left at intersection onto Front Street. Turn left onto Nationwide Blvd From east: West on I-70. Exit at Fourth Street. Continue on Fulton Street to Front Street. Turn right onto Front Street. Turn left onto Nationwide Blvd From west: East on I-70. Exit at Fourth Street. Continue on Fulton Street to Front Street. Turn right onto Front Street. Turn left onto Nationwide Blvd **Ticket Price Range:** $6-20.

Visiting Club Hotels: Crowne Plaza, 33 E Nationwide Blvd, Columbus, OH 43215. **Telephone:** (877) 348-2424. Drury Hotels Columbus Convention Center, 88 E. Nationwide Blvd, Columbus, OH 43215. **Telephone:** (614) 221-7008. Hyatt Regency Downtown, 350 N High St., Columbus, OH 43215. **Telephone:** (614) 463-1234.

DURHAM BULLS

Office Address: 409 Blackwell St, Durham, NC 27701.
Mailing Address: PO Box 507, Durham, NC 27702.
Telephone: (919) 687-6500. **Fax:** (919) 687-6560.
Website: www.durhambulls.com.
Affiliation (first year): Tampa Bay Rays (1998). **Years in League:** 1998-2011.

Ownership/Management

Operated By: Capitol Broadcasting Company, Inc.

President, CEO: Jim Goodmon. **Vice President:** George Habel.

General Manager: Mike Birling. **Director, Corporate Partnerships:** Chris Overby. **Account Executives, Sponsorship:** Dustin Bass, Elizabeth Pritchett, Patrick Kinas. **Manager, Sponsorship Services:** Molly Boyce. **Sponsorship Services Assistant:** Faith Inman. **Director, Marketing:** Scott Carter. **Director, Promotions:** Krista Boyd. **Coordinator, Mascot/Community Relations:** Nicholas Tennant. **Coordinator, Media Relations:** Zach Weber. **Director, Ticket Operations:** Tim Seaton. **Manager, Premium Ticket Sales:** Mike Miller. **Ticket Sales Associates:** Alexis Howard, Cody Harrison, Eli Starkey. **Manager, Group Ticket Sales:** Brian Simorka. **Group Sales Associates:** Kevin Kelly, Tyler Churchill, Jessica Kennedy, Andrew Bryda. **Account Executives, Tickets:** Dennis Fryer, Lauren Powell, Evan Watchempino.

Director, Special Events: Mary Beth Warfford. **Director, Merchandise:** Bryan Wilson. **Box Office Sales:** Jerry Mach. **Director, Stadium Operations:** Josh Nance. **GM, Concessions:** Tammy Scott. **Assistant GM, Concessions:** Ralph Orona. **Head Groundskeeper:** Scott Strickland. **Manager, Business:** Rhonda Carlile. **Supervisor, Accounting:** Theresa Stocking. **Manager, Home Clubhouse:** Colin Saunders. **Manager, Visiting/Umpires Clubhouses:** Aaron Kuehner. **Executive Assistant:** Nick Lind. **Team Ambassador:** Bill Law.

FIELD STAFF

Manager: Charlie Montoyo. **Coach:** Dave Myers. **Pitching Coach:** Neil Allen. **Trainer:** Mike Sandoval.

GAME INFORMATION

Radio Announcers: Patrick Kinas, Ken Tanner. **No. of Games Broadcast:** Home-72, Road-72. **Flagship Stations:** 620-AM The Buzz, 99.9 FM the Fan.

PA Announcer: Tony Riggsbee. **Official Scorer:** Brent Belvin.

Stadium Name: Durham Bulls Athletic Park. **Location:** From Raleigh, I-40 West to Highway 147 North, exit 12B to Willard, two blocks on Willard to stadium. From I-85, Gregson Street exit to downtown, left on Chapel Hill Street, right on Mangum Street. **Standard Game Times:** 7:05 pm, Sunday 5:05 pm Ticket Price Range: $6-14.

Visiting Club Hotel: Durham Marriot at the Civic Center, 201 Foster St, Durham, NC 27701. **Telephone:** (919) 768-6000.

GWINNETT BRAVES

Office Address: One Braves Ave, Lawrenceville, GA 30043.
Mailing Address: PO Box 490310, Lawrenceville, GA 30049.

Telephone: (678) 277-0300. **Fax:** (678) 277-0338.
E-Mail Address: gwinnettinfo@braves.com. **Website:** www.gwinnettbraves.com.
Affiliation (first year): Atlanta Braves (1966). **Years in League:** 1884, 1915-17, 1954-64, 1966-

Ownership/Management
General Manager: North Johnson.
Assistant GM: Shari Massengill. **Office Manager:** Tyra Williams. **Receptionist:** Sheena Trimiar. **Ticket Sales Manager:** Ryan Moore. **Ticket Operations Manager:** Josh Holley. **Account Executives:** Jerry Pennington, Paige Fleckenstein, Hunter Brown. **Corporate Sales Manager:** Samantha Dunn. **Client Services Representative:** Jordan Buck. **Marketing/Promotions Manager:** Maggie Neil. **Game Production Manager:** Mitch Rood. **Community Relations Manager:** Lindsay Harmon. **Media Relations Manager:** Dave Lezotte. **Sports Turf Manager:** Chris Ball. **Stadium Operations Manager:** Ryan Stoltenberg. **Stadium Operations Coordinator:** Jonathan Blair. **Facilities Maintenance Manager:** Gary Hoopaugh. **Clubhouse Manager:** Nick Dixon. **ARAMARK General Manager:** Bobby Dicicco.

FIELD STAFF
Manager: Dave Brundage. **Coach:** Jamie Dismuke. **Pitching Coach:** Marty Reed. **Trainer:** Mike Graus.

GAME INFORMATION
Radio Announcers: Tony Schiavone, Judd Hickinbotham. **No of Games Broadcast:** Home-72 Road-72. **Flagship Station:** WDUN 550-AM.
PA Announcer: Jeff Bergmann. **Official Scorer:** Guy Curtright.
Stadium Name: Coolray Field.
Location: I-85 (at Exit 115, SR 20 West) and I-985 (at Exit 4), follow signs to park. **Ticket Price Range:** $5-30.
Visiting Club Hotel: Courtyard by Marriott Buford/Mall of Georgia, 1405 Mall of Georgia Boulevard, Buford, GA 30519. **Telephone:** (678) 215-8007.

INDIANAPOLIS INDIANS

Office Address: 501 W Maryland Street, Indianapolis, IN 46225.
Telephone: (317) 269-3542. **Fax:** (317) 269-3541.
E-Mail address: indians@indyindians.com. **Website:** www.IndyIndians.com.
Affiliation (first year): Pittsburgh Pirates (2005). **Years in League:** 1963, 1998-

Ownership/Management
Operated By: Indians Inc.
President/Chairman of the Board: Max Schumacher.
Vice President/General Manager: Cal Burleson.
Assistant GM: Randy Lewandowski. **Director, Special Projects:** Bruce Schumacher. **Director, Marketing/Communications:** Chris Herndon. **Director, Facilities:** Tim Hughes. **Director, Business Operations:** Brad Morris. **Director, Tickets/Operations:** Matt Guay. **Director, Corporate Partnerships:** Joel Zawacki. **Director, Merchandising:** Mark Schumacher. **Director, Broadcasting:** Howard Kellman. **Office Manager:** Julie Rumschlag. **Administrative Assistant:** Angela Kendall. **Assistant Director, Facilities:** Bill Sampson. **Stadium Maintenance Manager:** Allan Danehy. **Head Groundskeeper:** Joey Stevenson. **Media Relations Manager:** Brian Bosma. **Community Relations/Promotions Manager:** Ryan Bowman. **Radio Broadcaster:** Scott McCauley. **Game Entertainment/Promotions Manager:** Brian McLaughlin. **Marketing Manager:** Diana Nolting. **Telecast/Production Manager:** Scott Templin.
Merchandise Manager: Missy Weaver. **Sponsorship Services Coordinator:** Drew Donovan. **Sponsorship Sales Account Executives:** Amanda Murray, Christina Toler. **Sponsorship Services Manager:** Keri Oberting. **Senior Ticket/Premium Services Manager:** Kerry Vick. **Ticket Sales Manager:** Chad Bohm. **Ticket Services Manager:** Bryan Spisak. **Ticket Sales Executives:** Ryan Barrett, Lauren Davis, Ty Eaton, Jonathan Howard, Chris Inderstrodt. **Operations Manager:** Steve Bray. **Operations Support:** Ricky Floyd, Jeri Naessens. **Marketing Communications Assistant:** Kelsey Adams. **Community Relations/Promotions Assistant:** Morgan Barbour. **Stadium Operations Assistant:** Tom Chapman. **Business Operations Assistant:** Matt Fleck. **Web Design Assistant:** Jaclyn Kitch. **Game Entertainment/Production Assistant:** Seth Tanner. **Ticket Services Representatives:** Austin Antisdel, Nathan Butler, Kris Morrow, Kasey Samson, Matthew Toohey. **IT Consultant:** Sean Couse. **Home Clubhouse Manager:** Bob Martin. **Visiting Clubhouse Manager:** Jeremy Martin.

FIELD STAFF
Manager: Dean Treanor. **Coach:** Jeff Branson. **Pitching Coach:** Tom Filer. **Trainer:** Bryan Housand.

GAME INFORMATION
Radio Announcers: Howard Kellman, Scott McCauley. **No. of Games Broadcast:** Home-72, Road-72. **Flagship Station:** WNDE 1260-AM. **PA Announcer:** David Pygman. **Official Scorers:** Bill McAfee, Gary Johnson, Bill Potter, Kim Rogers. **Stadium Name:** Victory Field. **Location:** I-70 to West Street exit, north on West Street to ballpark; I-65 to Martin Luther King and West Street exit, south on West Street to ballpark.
Standard Game Times: 7:05 pm; Wed 1:05; Fri 7:15; Sun 1:15.
Ticket Price Range: $9-14.
Visiting Club Hotels: Courtyard by Marriott, 601 West Washington, Indianapolis, IN 46204. **Telephone:** (317) 822-

9054.

LEHIGH VALLEY IRONPIGS

Office Address: 1050 IronPigs Way, Allentown, PA 18109.
Telephone: (610) 841-7447. **Fax:** (610) 841-1509.
E-Mail address: info@ironpigsbaseball.com. **Website:** www.ironpigsbaseball.com.
Affiliation (first year): Philadelphia Phillies (2008). **Years in League:** 2008-

OWNERSHIP/MANAGEMENT

Ownership: LV Baseball LP.
President: Chuck Domino.
General Manager: Kurt Landes. **Assistant GM:** Howard Scharf. **Director, Media Relations:** Matt Provence. **Manager, Media Relations:** Jon Schaeffer. **Director, Community Relations:** Sarah Marten. **Director, Merchandise:** Adam Fondl. **Director, Ticket Sales:** Scott Hodge. **Director, Ticket Operations:** Amy Schoch. **Director, Group Sales:** Don Wilson. **Director, Marketing:** Ron Rushe. **Marketing Services Managers:** Erin Holt, Alicia Marinelli. **Director, Creative Services:** Matt Zidik. **Manager, Creative Services:** Tyler DeRouen. **Director, Promotions:** Lindsey Knupp. **Director, Special Events/Catering:** Mary Nixon. **Manager, Special Events/Catering:** Nick Wootsick. **Director, Concessions:** Alex Rivera. **Manager, Concessions:** Brock Hartranft. **Executive Chef:** Jan Giejda. **Controller:** Deb Landes. **Manager, Finance:** Michelle Perl.
Director, Stadium Operations: Garrett Fahrmann. **Stadium Operations Managers:** Paul Cashin, Jason Kiesel. **Marketing Managers:** Scott Evans, Brandon Greene, Rick Polster. **Managers, Ticket Operations:** Katie Leonick, Erin Owens. **Tickets/Group Representatives:** Mark Anderson, Ryan Hines, Brad Ludwig, Ben Muell, Holly Pinkerton, Alicia Rohrbach, Justin Scariato, Katie Ward. **Director, Field Operations:** Bill Butler. **Receptionist:** Pat Golden.

FIELD STAFF

Manager: Ryne Sandberg. **Hitting Coach:** Sal Rende. **Pitching Coach:** Rod Nichols. **Trainers:** Chris Mudd, Jason Kirkman. **Strength/Conditioning:** Jason Meredith.

GAME INFORMATION

Radio Announcers: Matt Provence, Jon Schaeffer. **No. Games Broadcast:** 144 (72 Home; 72 Away). **Flagship Radio Station:** ESPN 1240/1320 AM. **Television Station:** TV2. **Television Announcers:** Mike Zambelli, Steve Degler, Matt Provence, Doug Heater. **No. Games Televised:** 72 Home. **PA Announcer:** Tim Chorones. **Official Scorers:** Mike Falk, Jack Logic, David Sheriff. **Stadium Name:** Coca-Cola Park. **Location:** Take US 22 to exit for Airport Road South. Head south, make right on American Parkway. Left into stadium. **Standard Game Times:** 7:05 pm; Sat 6:35; Sun 1:35 (April-June), 5:35 (July-August).

LOUISVILLE BATS

Office Address: 401 E Main St, Louisville, KY 40202.
Telephone: (502) 212-2287. **Fax:** (502) 515-2255.
E-Mail address: info@batsbaseball.com. **Website:** www.batsbaseball.com.
Affiliation (first year): Cincinnati Reds (2000). **Years in League:** 1998-

OWNERSHIP/MANAGEMENT

Chariman: Dan Ulmer Jr. **Board of Directors:** Edward Glasscock, Gary Ulmer, Kenny Huber, Steve Trager, J Michael Brown.
President/CEO: Gary Ulmer. **Vice President, Business Operations:** James Breeding. **Senior VP, Marketing:** Greg Galiette. **Senior VP, Corporate Sales:** Dale Owens. **VP, Operations/Technology:** Scott Shoemaker. **Director, Baseball Operations:** Josh Hargreaves. **Controller:** Michele Anderson. **Director, Ticket Operations:** Kyle Reh. **Director, Media/Public Relations:** Nick Evans. **Director, Group Sales:** Bryan McBride. **Director, Broadcasting:** Matt Andrews. **Director, Corporate Suites:** Sarah Nordman. **Assistant Director, Stadium Operations:** Randy Williams. **Graphic Designer:** Tony Brown. **Assistant Director, Marketing:** Kerri Ferrell. **Senior Account Executives:** Hal Norwood, Evan Patrick, Curtis Cunningham. **Account Executives:** Brad Wagner, Michael Harmon. **Assistant Director, Ticket Operations:** Brian Knight. **Groundskeeper:** Tom Nielsen. **Assistant Groundskeeper:** Jason Boston.

FIELD STAFF

Manager: David Bell. **Hitting Coach:** Ryan Jackson. **Pitching Coach:** Ted Power. **Trainer:** Jimmy Mattocks.

GAME INFORMATION

Radio Announcers: Matt Andrews. **No. of Games Broadcast:** Home-72, Road-72. **Flagship Station:** WKRD 790-AM. **PA Announcer:** Shane Duvall. **Official Scorer:** Dave Arnold. **Organist:** Bob Ramsey.
Stadium Name: Louisville Slugger Field. **Location:** I-64 and I-71 to I-65 South/North to Brook Street exit, right on Market Street, left on Jackson Street; stadium on Main Street between Jackson and Preston. **Ticket Price Range:** $6-11.

Visiting Club Hotel: Galt House Hotel, 140 North Fourth Street, Louisville, KY 40202. Telephone: (502) 589-5200.

NORFOLK TIDES

Office Address: 150 Park Ave, Norfolk, VA 23510.
Telephone: (757) 622-2222. Fax: (757) 624-9090.
E-Mail Address: receptionist@norfolktides.com. Website: www.norfolktides.com.
Affiliation (first year): Baltimore Orioles (2007). Years in League: 1969-

Ownership/Management
Operated By: Tides Baseball Club Inc.
President: Ken Young.
General Manager: Joe Gregory.
Executive Vice President/Senior Advisor to the President: Dave Rosenfield. Assistant GM: Ben Giancola. Director, Media Relations: Ian Locke. Director, Community Relations: Heather McKeating. Director, Ticket Operations: Gretchen Todd. Director, Group Sales: Stephanie Hierstein. Director, Stadium Operations: Mike Zeman. Business Manager: Andrew Garrelts. Manager, Merchandising: Ann Marie Piddisi. Corporate Sponsorships/Promotions: Jonathan Mensink. Group/Corporate Sales: Christina Dewey. Military Liaison: Chris Hoffpauir. Assistant Director, Stadium Operations: Mike Cardwell. Box Office Manager: Linda Waisanen. Assistant to the Director, Tickets: Sze Fong. Event Staff Manager: Matt Moyer. Group Sales Representatives: Amanda Goodman, Corry Gross. Media Relations Assistant: JD Rhamstine. Administrative Assistant: Lisa Cox.
Head Groundskeeper: Kenny Magner. Assistant Groundskeeper: Keith Collins. Home Clubhouse Manager: Kevin Casey. Visiting Clubhouse Manager: Mark Bunge.

FIELD STAFF
Manager: Ron Johnson. Hitting Coach: Denny Walling. Pitching Coach: Mike Griffin.

GAME INFORMATION
Radio Announcers: Pete Michaud, Tony Mercurio. No. of Games Broadcast: Home-72, Road-72. Flagship Station: ESPN 94.1 FM.
PA Announcer: Jack Ankerson. Official Scorers: Mike Holtzclaw, Dave Lewis.
Stadium Name: Harbor Park. Location: Exit 9, 11A or 11B off I-264, adjacent to the Elizabeth River in downtown Norfolk. Standard Game Times: 7:15 pm, Sun. 1:15. Ticket Price Range: $11-14.
Visiting Club Hotel: Sheraton Waterside, 777 Waterside Dr, Norfolk, VA 23510. Telephone: (757) 622-6664.

PAWTUCKET RED SOX

Office Address: One Ben Mondor Way, Pawtucket, RI 02860.
Mailing Address: PO Box 2365, Pawtucket, RI 02861.
Telephone: (401) 724-7300. Fax: (401) 724-2140.
E-Mail Address: info@pawsox.com. Website: www.pawsox.com.
Affiliation (first year): Boston Red Sox (1973). Years in League: 1973-

Ownership/Management
Operated by: Pawtucket Red Sox Baseball Club, Inc.
President: Mike Tamburro.
Vice President/General Manager: Lou Schwechheimer. VP, Chief Financial Officer: Matt White. VP, Sales/ Marketing: Michael Gwynn. VP, Stadium Operations: Mick Tedesco. VP, Public Relations: Bill Wanless. Director, Community Relations: Jeff Bradley. Manager, Sales: Augusto Rojas. Director, Merchandising: Eric Petterson. Director, Media Creation: Kevin Galligan. Director, Concession Services: Jim Hogan. Director, Corporate Sales: Mike Abramson. Director, Warehouse Operations: Dave Johnson. Administrative Assistant: Lauren Dincecco. Ticket Operations: Adam Perri. Account Executives: Tom Linehan, Peter Sachs, Whitney Goulish. Field Superintendant: Matt McKinnon. Assistant Groundskeeper: Kyle Carney. Director, Security: Rick Medeiros. Director, Clubhouse Operations: Carl Goodreau. Executive Chef: Ken Bowdish.

FIELD STAFF
Manager: Arnie Beyeler. Hitting Coach: Gerald Perry. Pitching Coach: Rich Sauveur. Trainer: Jon Jochim.

GAME INFORMATION
Radio Announcers: Aaron Goldsmith, Steve Hyder. No. of Games Broadcast: Home-72, Away-72. Flagship Station: WHJJ 920-AM.
PA Announcer: Scott Fraser. Official Scorer: Bruce Guindon.
Stadium Name: McCoy Stadium. Location: From north, 95 South to exit 2A in Massachusetts (Newport Ave), follow Newport Ave for 2 miles, right on Columbus Ave, follow one mile, stadium on right. From south, 95 North to exit 28 (School Street), right at bottom of exit ramp, through two sets of lights, left onto Pond Street, right on Columbus Ave, stadium entrance on left. From west (Worcester), 295 North to 95 South and follow directions from north. From east (Fall River), 195 West to 95 North and follow directions from south. Standard Game Times: 7 pm; Sat 6, Sun 1. Ticket Price Range: $5-11.

Visiting Club Hotel: Marriott Courtyard Providence Downtown, 32 Exchange Terrace at Memorial Blvd, Providence, RI 02903, (401) 272-1191.

ROCHESTER RED WINGS

Office Address: One Morrie Silver Way, Rochester, NY 14608.
Telephone: (585) 454-1001. Fax: (585) 454-1056, (585) 454-1057.
E-Mail Address: info@redwingsbaseball.com. Website: www.redwingsbaseball.com.
Affiliation (first year): Minnesota Twins (2003). Years in League: 1885-89, 1891-92, 1895-

Ownership/Management
Operated by: Rochester Community Baseball.
COO/CEO/President: Naomi Silver. Chairman: Gary Larder.
General Manager: Dan Mason. Assistant GM: Will Rumbold. Controller: Darlene Giardina. Head Groundskeeper: Gene Buonomo. Director, Media/Public Relations: Chuck Hinkel. Director, Corporate Development: Nick Sciarratta. Director, Group/Picnic: Parker Allen. Director, Marketing: Matt Cipro. Director, Ticket Operations: Rob Dermody. Director, Production: John Blotzer. Director, Merchandising: Barbara Moore. Director, Human Resources: Paula LoVerde. Assistant Director, Group Sales: Bob Craig. Account Executives: Danielle Barone, Eric Friedman, Derek Swanson. Executive Secretary: Ginny Colbert. General Manager, Food Services: Jeff Dodge. Director/Catering: Courtney Trawitz. Manager, Concessions: Jeff DeSantis. Executive Chef: Mark Feiock. Warehouse Manager: Rob Burgett. Business Manager, Concessions: Dave Bills.

FIELD STAFF
Manager: Gene Glynn. Coach: Tom Brunansky. Pitching Coach: Bobby Cuellar. Trainer: Chad Jackson.

GAME INFORMATION
Radio Announcers: Josh Whetzel. No. of Games Broadcast: Home-72, Away-72. Flagship Stations: WHTK 1280-AM, WYSL 1040-AM.
PA Announcer: Kevin Spears. Official Scorer: Warren Kozereski.
Stadium Name: Frontier Field. Location: I-490 East to exit 12 (Brown/Broad Street) and follow signs; I-490 West to exit 14 (Plymouth Ave) and follow signs. Standard Game Times: 7:05 pm, Sun 1:35. Ticket Price Range: $6.50-10.50
Visiting Club Hotel: Rochester Plaza, 70 State St, Rochester, NY 14608. Telephone: (585) 546-3450.

SCRANTON/WILKES-BARRE
YANKEES

Office Address: 50 Glenmaura National Blvd Suite 101, Moosic, PA 18507.
Telephone: (570) 969-2255. Fax: (570) 963-6564.
E-Mail address: info@swbyankees.com. Website: www.swbyankees.com.
Affiliation (first year): New York Yankees (2007). Years in League: 1989-

Ownership/Management
Owned By: The Multi-Purpose Stadium Authority of Lackawanna County.
Operated By: SWB Yankees, LLC.
President: Kristen Rose. VP, Ticket Sales: Doug Augis. VP, Marketing/Corporate Services: Katie Beekman. VP, Stadium Operations: Curt Camoni. VP, Accounting/Finance: Paul Chilek. Director, Corporate Partnerships: Mike Trudnak. Director, Field Operations: Steve Horn. Director, Facility Operations: Joe Villano. Director, Media Relations/Broadcasting: Mike Vander Woude. Senior Sponsor Service Manager: Kristina Knight. Manager, Community Relations/Play Ball: Ryan Beardsley. Group Sales Manager: Bob McLane. Customer Service/Inside Sales Representative: Kelly Cusick. Operations Manager: Rob Galdieri. Staff Accountant: William Steiner.

FIELD STAFF
Manager: Dave Miley. Hitting Coach: Butch Wynegar. Pitching Coach: Scott Aldred. Coach: Frank Menechino. Trainer: Darren London. Strength/Conditioning Coach: Lee Tressel.

GAME INFORMATION
Radio Announcer: Mike Vander Woude. No of Games Broadcast: Home-72 Road-72. Flagship Stations: WICK 1400 AM/WYCK 1340 AM.
 * Scranton will play all home games on the road in 2012.

SYRACUSE CHIEFS

Office Address: One Tex Simone Dr, Syracuse, NY 13208.
Telephone: (315) 474-7833. **Fax:** (315) 474-2658.
E-Mail Address: baseball@syracusechiefs.com. **Website:** www.syracusechiefs.com.
Affiliation (third year): Washington Nationals (2009). **Years in League:** 1885-89, 1891-92, 1894-1901, 1918, 1920-27, 1934-55, 1961-

Ownership/Management

Operated by: Community Owned Baseball Club of Central New York, Inc.
Chairman: Charles Rich. **President:** William Dutch. **Executive Vice President/COO:** Anthony "Tex" Simone. **General Manager:** John Simone. **Assistant GM/Director, Marketing/Promotions:** Mike Voutsinas. **Assistant GM, Business:** Don Lehtonen. **Director, Sales:** Paul Fairbanks. **Director, Group Sales:** Victor Gallucci. **Director, Broadcasting/Public Relations:** Jason Benetti. **Assistant Director, Broadcasting/Public Relations:** Kevin Brown. **Director, Merchandising:** Wendy Shoen. **Director, Ticket Office:** Josh Jones. **Coordinator, Group Sales:** Erin Shappell. **Coordinator, Diversity:** R Otis Jennings. **Administrative Assistant:** Priscilla Venditti. **Turf Manager:** Jon Stewart. **Team Historian:** Ron Gersbacher.

FIELD STAFF

Manager: Tony Beasley. **Coach:** Jerry Browne. **Pitching Coach:** Greg Booker. **Trainer:** Atushi Toriida. **Strength Coordinator:** Mike Warren.

GAME INFORMATION

Radio Announcers: Jason Benetti/Kevin Brown. **No. of Games Broadcast:** Home-72, Away-72. **Flagship Station:** The Score 1260 AM. **PA Announcer:** Brent Axe. **Official Scorer:** Tom Leo.
Stadium Name: Alliance Bank Stadium. **Location:** New York State Thruway to exit 36 (I-81 South), to 7th North Street exit, left on 7th North, right on Hiawatha Boulevard. **Standard Game Times:** 7 pm, Sun 2, 6. **Ticket Price Range:** $6-10.
Visiting Club Hotel: Ramada Inn, 1305 Buckley Rd, Syracuse, NY 13212. **Telephone:** (315) 457-8670.

TOLEDO MUD HENS

Office Address: 406 Washington St, Toledo, OH 43604.
Telephone: (419) 725-4367. **Fax:** (419) 725-4368.
E-Mail address: mudhens@mudhens.com. **Website:** www.mudhens.com.
Affiliation (first year): Detroit Tigers (1987). **Years in League:** 1889, 1965-

Ownership/Management

Operated By: Toledo Mud Hens Baseball Club, Inc.
Chairman of the Board: Michael Miller.
Vice President: David Huey. **Secretary/Treasurer:** Charles Bracken.
President/General Manager: Joseph Napoli.
Chief Marketing Officer: Kim McBroom. **Assistant GM/Director, Corporate Partnerships:** Neil Neukam. **Assistant GM, Ticket Sales/Operations:** Erik Ibsen. **Assistant GM, Food/Beverage:** Craig Nelson. **CFO:** Pam Alspach. **Manager, Promotions:** Michael Keedy. **Director, Media/Public Relations:** Jason Griffin. **Director, Ticket Sales/Services:** Thomas Townley. **Accounting:** Sheri Kelly, Brian Leverenz. **Manager, Gameday Operations:** Greg Setola. **Manager, Community Relations:** Cheri Pastula. **Corporate Sales Associate:** Ed Sintic. **Season Ticket/Group Sales Associates:** Frank Kristie, Kyle Moll, John Mulka. **Manager, Online Marketing:** Nathan Steinmetz. **Season Ticket Service Coordinator:** Jessica Morelli. **Special Events Coordinator:** Emily Croll. **Media Services Coordinator:** Becky Walker.
Graphic Designer: Dan Royer. **Manager, Souvenir Sales:** Craig Katz. **Manager, Swamp Shop:** Stephanie Miller. **Manager, Ballpark Operations:** Ken Westenkirchner. **Office Manager:** Carol Hamilton. **Executive Assistant:** Tracy Evans. **Turf Manager:** Jake Tyler. **Clubhouse Manager:** Joe Sarkisian. **Team Historian:** John Husman.

FIELD STAFF

Manager: Phil Nevin. **Coach:** Leon Durham. **Pitching Coach:** AJ Sager. **Trainer:** Matt Rankin.

GAME INFORMATION

Radio Announcers: Jim Weber, Jason Griffin. **No of Games Broadcast:** Home-72 Road-72. **Flagship Station:** WCWA 1230 AM.
PA Announcer: Unavailable. **Official Scorers:** Jeff Businger, Ron Kleinfelter, Guy Lammers.
Stadium Name: Fifth Third Field. **Location:** From Ohio Turnpike 80/90, exit 54 (4A) to I-75 North, follow I-75 North to exit 201-B, left onto Erie Street, right onto Washington Street; From Detroit, I-75 South to exit 202-A, right onto Washington Street; From Dayton, I-75 North to exit 201-B, left onto Erie Street, right on Washington Street; From Ann Arbor, Route 23 South to I-475 East, I-475 east to I-75 South, I-75 South to exit 202-A, right onto Washington Street. **Ticket Price Range:** $9.
Visiting Club Hotel: Park Inn, 101 North Summit, Toledo, OH 43604. **Telephone:** (419) 241-3000.

PACIFIC COAST LEAGUE

Address: One Chisholm Trail, Suite 4200, Round Rock, Texas 78681.
Telephone: (512) 310-2900. **Fax:** (512) 310-8300.
E-Mail Address: office@pclbaseball.com. **Website:** www.pclbaseball.com.
President: Branch B Rickey.

Vice President: Don Logan (Las Vegas).

Directors: Don Beaver (New Orleans), Sam Bernabe (Iowa), John Pontius (Memphis), Chris Cummings (Fresno), Dave Elmore (Colorado Springs), Aaron Artman (Tacoma), Chuck Johnson (Las Vegas), George King (Round Rock), Greg Miller (Salt Lake), Bill Shea (Omaha), Art Matin (Oklahoma), Jeff Moorad (Tucson), Jeff Savage (Sacramento), John Traub (Albuquerque), Frank Ward (Nashville), Stuart Katzoff (Reno).

Director, Business: Melanie Fiore. **Director, Baseball Operations:** Dwight Hall. **Media/ Operations Assistant:** Patrick Kurish.

Division Structure: American Conference—Northern: Iowa, Memphis, Nashville, Omaha. **Southern:** Albuquerque, New Orleans, Oklahoma, Round Rock. Pacific Conference—Northern: Colorado Springs, Reno, Salt Lake, Tacoma. Southern: Fresno, Las Vegas, Sacramento, Tucson.

Regular Season: 144 games. **2012 Opening Date:** April 5. **Closing Date:** Sept 3.

All-Star Game: July 11 at Buffalo Bisons, Buffalo, New York (PCL vs International League).

Branch Rickey

Playoff Format: Pacific Conference/Northern winner meets Southern winner, and American Conference/Northern winner meets Southern winner in best-of-five semifinal series. Winners meet in best-of-five series for league championship.

Triple-A Championship Game: Sept 18 (PCL vs International League).

Roster Limit: 24. **Player Eligibility Rule:** No restrictions.

Brand of Baseball: Rawlings ROM.

Umpires: Jordan Baker (Shawnee, OK), Steve Barga (Castle Rock, CO), Cory Blaser (Westminster, CO), Angel Campos (San Bernadino, CA), Clint Fagan (Tomball, TX), Shaun Francis (Cohoes, NY), Tyler Funneman (Wildwood, IL), Hal Gibson (Scottsdale, AZ), Joel Hospodka (Omaha, NE), Mike Jarboe (La Crescenta, CA), Barry Larson (Hayden, ID), Kellen Levy (Mesa, AZ), Eric Loveless (Layton, UT), Mike Lusky (Baldwin Park, CA), Patrick Mahoney (Pittsburg, CA), Benjamin May (Racine, WI), Michael Muchlinski (Ephrata, WA), Mark Ripperger (Carlsbad, CA), Brett Robson (Cannington Western Australia), Matt Schaufert (St Louis, MO), Stuart Scheurwater (Regina, Saskatchewan, Canada), Chris Segal (Burke, VA), Brian Sinclair (San Antonio, TX), John Tumpane (Oak Lawn, IL), Quinn Wolcott (Puyallup, WA)

STADIUM INFORMATION

Club	Stadium	Opened	LF	CF	RF	Capacity	2011 Att.
Albuquerque	Isotopes Park	2003	340	400	340	13,279	578,328
Colorado Springs	Security Service Field	1988	350	410	350	8,400	339,009
Fresno	Chukchansi Park	2002	324	402	335	12,500	494,051
Iowa	Principal Park	1992	335	400	335	11,000	500,675
Las Vegas	Cashman Field	1983	328	433	328	9,334	314,032
Memphis	AutoZone Park	2000	319	400	322	14,300	493,528
Nashville	Herschel Greer Stadium	1978	327	400	327	10,700	335,143
New Orleans	Zephyr Field	1997	333	405	332	10,000	372,017
Oklahoma City	RedHawks Field	1998	325	400	325	11,455	378,877
Omaha	Werner Park	2011	310	402	315	9,023	410,326
Reno	Aces Ballpark	2009	339	410	340	9,100	432,314
Round Rock	The Dell Diamond	2000	330	400	325	10,000	618,261
Sacramento	Raley Field	2000	330	405	325	14,014	600,306
Salt Lake	Spring Mobile Ballpark	1994	345	420	315	15,500	437,769
Tacoma	Cheney Stadium	1960	325	425	325	8000	378,518
Tucson	Kino Stadium	1998	340	405	340	11,500	242,136

ALBUQUERQUE ISOTOPES

Office Address: 1601 Avenida Cesar Chavez SE, Albuquerque, NM 87106.
Telephone: (505) 924-2255. **Fax:** (505) 242-8899.
E-Mail address: info@abqisotopes.com. **Website:** www.abqisotopes.com.
Affiliation (first year): Los Angeles Dodgers (2009). **Years in League:** 1972-2000, 2003-

Ownership/Management

President: Ken Young. **Secretary/Treasurer:** Emmett Hammond. **General Manager:** John Traub. **Assistant GM, Sales/Marketing:** Nick LoBue. **Director, Box Office/Retail Operations:** Chrissy Baines. **Director, Sales/Promotions:** Adam Beggs. **Director, Media Relations:** Steve Hurlbert. **Director, Stadium Operations:** Bobby Atencio. **Manager, Promotions/Marketing:** Chris Holland. **Manager, Suite Relations:** Paul Hartenberger. **Manager, Creative Services:** Kris Shepard. **Season Ticket/Group Sales Representatives:** Quentin Andes, Jason Buchta, Alex Tainsh, David Wenigmann.

Director, Accounting: Cynthia DiFrancesco. Assistant Director, Retail Operations: Patrick Westrick. Assistant Director, Box Office Operations: Andréa Blann.

Stadium Operations Assistant: Joe Fara. Coordinator, Community Relations: Kim Stoebick. Director, Field Operations: Shawn Moore. Assistant Director, Field Operations: Casey Griffin. Home Clubhouse Manager: Tony Iliano. Visiting Clubhouse Manager: Rick Pollack. Front Office Assistant: Mark Otero. GM, Ovations Foodservices: Jay Satenspiel. Assistant GM/Office Manager, Ovations Foodservices: Kyle Bruin. Catering Manager, Ovations Foodservices: Karla Lewis. Purchasing/Warehouse Director, Ovations Foodservices: Matt Butler. Head Chef: Scott Eastburn.

FIELD STAFF
Manager: Lorenzo Bundy. Coach: John Valentin. Pitching Coach: Glenn Dishman. Trainer: Yosuke Nakajima. Strength/Conditioning Coach: Brandon McDaniel.

GAME INFORMATION
Radio Announcer: Robert Portnoy. No. of Games Broadcast: Home-72 Road-72. Flagship Station: KNML 610-AM. PA Announcer: Stu Walker. Official Scorers: Gary Herron, James Hilchen.

Stadium Name: Isotopes Park. Location: From 1-25, exit east on Avenida Cesar Chavez SE to University Boulevard; From I-40, exit south on University Boulevard SE to Avenida Cesar Chavez. Standard Game Times: 7:05 pm, Sun 6:05. Ticket Price Range: $7-$25.

Visiting Club Hotel: MCM Elegante, 2020 Menaul NE, Albuquerque, NM 87107. Telephone: (505) 884-2511.

COLORADO SPRINGS SKY SOX

Office Address: 4385 Tutt Blvd, Colorado Springs, CO 80922. Telephone: (719) 597-1449. Fax: (719) 597-2491. E-Mail address: info@skysox.com. Website: www.skysox.com. Affiliation (first year): Colorado Rockies (1993). Years in League: 1988-

Ownership/Management
Operated By: Colorado Springs Sky Sox Inc.
Principal Owner: David Elmore.
President/General Manager: Tony Ensor. Assistant GM/Director, Public Relations: Mike Hobson. Director, Corporate Sales: Chris Phillips. Director, Broadcast Operations: Dan Karcher. Director, Accounting: Kelly Hanlon. Director, Ticket Sales: Whitney Shellem. Director, Group Sales: Keith Hodges. Director, Community Relations: Jon Eddy. Graphics Manager: Erin Eads. Director, Promotions: Wes Sharp. Manager, Stadium Operations: Eric Martin. Manager, Corporate Sales: Alec Shepherd. Assistant Director, Group Sales: Jim Rice. Groups Sales Manager: Geri Woessner. Special Event Manager: Brien Smith. GM, Diamond Creations: Don Giuliano. Director, Catering: Chris Evans. Head Groundskeeper: Steve DeLeon. Administrative Assistant: Marianne Paine. Home Clubhouse Manager: Ricky Grima. Visiting Clubhouse Manager: Steve Martin.

FIELD STAFF
Manager: Stu Cole. Coach: Rene Lachemann. Pitching Coach: Bo McLaughlin. Trainer: Heath Townsend.

GAME INFORMATION
Radio Announcer: Dan Karcher. No. of Games Broadcast: Home-72 Road-72. Flagship Station: AM 1300 "The Sports Animal."
PA Announcer: Josh Howe. Official Scorer: Marty Grantz, Rich Wastler, Ken Jones.
Stadium Name: Security Service Field. Location: I-25 South to Woodmen Road exit, east on Woodmen to Powers Boulevard, right on Powers to Barnes Road. Standard Game Times: 7:05 pm, Sat 6:05, Sun 1:05. Ticket Price Range: $5-13.
Visiting Club Hotel: Hilton Garden Inn, 1810 Briargate Parkway, Colorado Springs, CO 80920. Telephone: (719) 598-6866.

FRESNO GRIZZLIES

Office Address: 1800 Tulare St, Fresno, CA 93721. Telephone: (559) 320-4487. Fax: (559) 264-0795. E-Mail address: info@fresnogrizzlies.com. Website: www.fresnogrizzlies.com. Affiliation (first year): San Francisco Giants (1998). Years in League: 1998-

Ownership/Management
Operated By: Fresno Baseball Club, LLC.
President: Chris Cummings. Executive Vice President: Brian Glover. Chief Financial Officer: SuSin Correa. VP, Sales: Derek Franks. VP, Marketing/Stadium Events: Drew Vertiz. Director, Client Services: Andrew Melrose. Director, Corporate Sales: Jerry James. Director, Stadium Operations: Harvey Kawasaki. Director, Event Operations: Matt Studwell. Director, Human Resources: Ashley Tennell. Manager, Marketing/Promotions: Cody Turner. Coordinator, Community Relations: Ryan Moran. Coordinator, Media Relations: Chris Kutz. Coordinator, Stadium/Baseball Operations: Joe Castillo. Coordinators, Entertainment/Mascot: Troy Simeon, Nick Haas. Graphic Designers: Zack Alvarez, Sam Hansen.

Inside Sales Manager: Andrew Milios. Group Sales Manager: Freddie Dominguez, Jr. Ticket Office Manager: Pat Wallach. Senior Group Sales Account Executive: Adam Gleich. Corporate Sponsorship Account Executive: Matt Ruiz. Ticket Account Executives: Chris Curry, Jon Stockton. Assistant Ticket Sales Manager: Cody Holden. Ticket Sales Assistant: Andrea Renfro. Corporate Sponsorship Assistant: Matt Hagopian. Manager, Operations: Ira Calvin. Head Groundskeeper: David Jacinto. Finance Managers: Monica Delacerda, Brian Mehlman. Manager, Team Store: Lalonnie Calderon. Manager, Guest Services: Steve Sodini. Receptionist: DeeAnn Hernandez. GM, Ovations Concessions: Tim Dickert.

FIELD STAFF

Manager: Bob Mariano. Hitting Coach: Russ Morman. Pitching Coach: Pat Rice. Athletic Trainer: Eric Ortega. Strength/Conditioning Coach: Yousef Zamat.

GAME INFORMATION

Radio Announcer: Doug Greenwald. No. of Games Broadcast: Home-72 Road-72. Flagship Station: 105.5 FM The Truth (Wilks Broadcasting).

Official Scorer: Unavailable.

Stadium Name: Chukchansi Park. Location: 1800 Tulare St, Fresno, CA 93721. Directions: From 99 North, take Fresno Street exit, left on Fresno Street, left on Inyo or Tulare to stadium; From 99 South, take Fresno Street exit, left on Fresno Street, right on Broadway to H Street; From 41 North, take Van Ness exit toward Fresno, left on Van Ness, left on Inyo or Tulare, stadium is straight ahead; From 41 South, take Tulare exit, stadium is located at Tulare and H Streets, or take Van Ness exit, right on Van Ness, left on Inyo or Tulare, stadium is straight ahead. Ticket Price Range: $8-18.

Visiting Club Hotel: Holiday Inn Downtown Fresno, 1055 Van Ness, Fresno, CA 93721. Telephone: (888) 465-4329.

IOWA CUBS

Office Address: One Line Drive, Des Moines IA 50309.
Telephone: (515) 243-6111. Fax: (515) 243-5152.
E-mail address: info@iowacubs.com. Website: www.iowacubs.com
Affiliation (first year): Chicago Cubs (1981). Years in League: 1969-

Ownership/Management

Operated By: Raccoon Baseball Inc.

Chairman/Principal Owner: Michael Gartner. Executive Vice President: Michael Giudicessi.

President/General Manager: Sam Bernabe. Shareholder: Mike Gartner. VP/Assistant GM: Jim Nahas. VP/CFO: Sue Tollefson. VP/Director, Broadcast Operations: Deene Ehlis. Director, Media Relations: Randy Wehofer. Director, Communications: Scott Sailor. Director, Marketing/Video Presentation: Blake Havard. Director, Ticket Operations: Kenny Houser. Director, Luxury Suites: Brent Conkel. Assistant Ticket Manager: Eric Hammes. Director, Group Sales: Aaron Roland. Director, Stadium Operations: Jeff Tilley. Manager, Stadium Operations: Jake Samo. Corporate Sales Executive: Nate Teut. Corporate Relations: Red Hollis. Head Groundskeeper: Chris Schlosser.

Director, Merchandise: Rick Giudicessi. Accountant: Lori Auten. Manager, Cub Club: John Gordon. Director, Information Technology: Ryan Clutter. Landscape Coordinator: Shari Kramer.

FIELD STAFF

Manager: Dave Bialas. Hitting Coach: Dave Keller. Pitching Coach: Mike Mason. Trainer: Nick Frangella.

GAME INFORMATION

Radio Announcers: Deene Ehlis, Randy Wehofer. No. of Games Broadcast: Home-72 Road-72. Flagship Station: AM 940 KPSZ.

PA Announcers: Aaron Johnson, Mark Pierce, Corey Coon. Official Scorers: Unavailable. Stadium Name: Principal Park. Location: I-80 or I-35 to I-235, to Third Street exit, south on Third Street, left on Line Drive. Standard Game Times: 7:05 pm; Sun 1:05. Ticket Price Range: $6-11.

Visiting Club Hotel: Embassy Suites, 101 East Locust St, Des Moines IA 50309. Telephone: (515) 244-1700.

LAS VEGAS 51S

Office Address: 850 Las Vegas Blvd North, Las Vegas, NV 89101. Telephone: (702) 943-7200. Fax: (702) 943-7214.
E-Mail address: info@lv51.com. Website: www.lv51.com/.
Affiliation (fourth year): Toronto Blue Jays (2009). Years in League: 1983-.

Ownership/Management

Operated By: Stevens Baseball Group.

Executive Director: Don Logan. General Manager/VP, Marketing: Chuck Johnson. VP, Sales/Marketing: Mike Hollister. VP, Ticket Operations: Mike Rodriguez. VP, Operations/Security: Nick Fitzenreider. Director, Finance: Drew Dondero. Special Assistant to GM: Bob Blum. Controller: Araxi Demirjian. Director, Broadcasting: Russ Langer. Director, Group Ticket Sales: Melissa Harkavy. Director, Season Ticket Sales: Erik Eisenberg. Manager, Community Relations: Larry Brown. Manager, Baseball Administration: Denise Korach. Media Relations Director: Jim Gemma. Ticket Operations Assistant: Michelle Taggart. Administrative Assistants: Jan Dillard, Pat Dressel. Account Executives: Justin Dunbar, Bryan Frey, Josh Rusnak. Merchandise Coordinator: Jason Weber. Sponsorship Services Manager:

William Graham. **Operations Manager:** Chip Vespe.

FIELD STAFF

Manager: Marty Brown. **Hitting Coach:** Chad Mottola. **Coach:** Danny Solano. **Pitching Coach:** Bob Stanley. **Trainer:** Voon Chong. **Strength/Conditioning Coach:** Rob Helmick.

GAME INFORMATION

Radio Announcer: Russ Langer. **No. of Games Broadcast:** Home-72 Road-72. **Flagship Station:** Fox Sports Radio 920-AM.

PA Announcer: Dan Bickmore. **Official Scorers:** Gary Arlitz, Mark Wasik.

Stadium Name: Cashman Field. **Location:** I-15 to US 95 exit (downtown), east to Las Vegas Boulevard North exit, one-half mile north to stadium. **Standard Game Time:** 7:05 pm. **Ticket Price Range:** $10-14.

Visiting Club Hotel: Golden Nugget Hotel & Casino, 129 Fremont Street, Las Vegas, NV 89101. **Telephone:** (702) 385-7111.

MEMPHIS REDBIRDS

Office Address: 175 Toyota Plaza, Suite 300, Memphis, TN 38103.
Telephone: (901) 721-6000. **Fax:** (901) 842-1222.
Website: www.memphisredbirds.com.
Affiliation (first year): St. Louis Cardinals (1998). **Years in League:** 1998-

Ownership/Management

Ownership: Memphis Redbirds Baseball Foundation, Inc.
Managed by: Global Spectrum.
General Manager: Ben Weiss. **Assistant GM/Director, Sales:** Derek Goldfarb. **Director, Operations:** Mark Anderson. **Coordinator, Operations:** Kevin Rooney. **Director, Finance:** Art Davis. **Director, Marketing:** Adam Goldberg. **Ticket Operations Manager:** Travis Trumitch. **Ticket Sales Manager:** Jason Mott. **Marketing Manager:** Erin O'Donnell. **Media Relations Manager:** Jordan Marie Johnson. **Graphic Designer/Photographer:** Allison Rhoades. **Special Event Coordinator:** Kellie Grabert. **Corporate Sales Executives:** Corey Bush, Valerie Hight, Brendan Kelly. **Corporate Sales Coordinator:** Leigh Eisenberg. **Sales Coordinator:** Jonathan Leshner. **Ticket Sales Executives:** Jacob Boggs, Travis Gortman, Keith Moore, Nolan Yoder. **Staff Accountant:** Cindy Neal. **Office Coordinator:** Linda Smith. **Head Groundskeeper:** Ed Collins. **Chief Engineer:** Danny Abbott. Maintenance: Spencer Shields.

FIELD STAFF

Manager: Ron Warner. **Coach:** Mark Budaska. **Pitching Coach:** Blaise Ilsley. **Trainer:** Jeremy Clipperton.

GAME INFORMATION

Radio Announcer: Steve Selby. **No. of Games Broadcast:** Home-72 Road-72. **Flagship Station:** WHBQ 560-AM.

PA Announcer: Unavailable. **Official Scorer:** JJ Guinozzo. **Stadium Name:** AutoZone Park. **Location:** North on I-240, exit at Union Avenue West, one and half mile to park. **Standard Game Times:** 7:05 pm, Sat 6:05, Sun 1:35. **Ticket Price Range:** $5-17.

Visiting Club Hotel: Sleep Inn at Court Square, 40 N Front, Memphis, TN 38103. **Telephone:** (901) 522-9700.

NASHVILLE SOUNDS

Office Address: 534 Chestnut Street, Nashville, TN 37203.
Telephone: (615) 690-HITS. **Fax:** (615) 256-5684.
E-Mail address: info@nashvillesounds.com. **Website:** www.nashvillesounds.com
Affiliation (first year): Milwaukee Brewers (2005). **Years in League:** 1998-

Ownership/Management

Operated By: MFP Baseball.
Owners: Frank Ward, Masahiro Honzawa.
Vice President/General Manager: Brad Tammen. **Assistant GM:** Doug Scopel. **Director, Accounting:** Barb Walker. **Director, Community Relations:** Michael Bigley. **Director, Corporate Sales:** Jason Franke. **Manager, Sales/Sports Marketing:** Drew Himsworth. **Manager, Stadium Operations:** Mike Simonson. **Manager, Community Relations:** Buddy Yelton. **Manager, Ticketing:** Eric Laue. **Manager, Media Relations:** Michael Whitty. **Manager, Advertising/Marketing:** Cliff McCardle. **Manager, Merchandise:** Janell Bullock. **Manager, Sales:** AJ Rockwell. **Account Executives:** Walt Clark, Kevin Samborski, Amanda Zuzik. **Coordinator, Accounts:** Brandon Yerger. **Office Manager:** Sharon Ridley. **Head Groundskeeper:** Thomas Trotter. **Assistant Groundskeeper:** Alex Norman. **Clubhouse Managers:** J.R. **Rinaldi, Thomas Miller.**

FIELD STAFF

Manager: Mike Guerrero. **Coach:** Al LaBoeuf. **Pitching Coach:** Fred Dabney. **Trainer:** Greg Barajas. **Strength/Conditioning Coach:** Andrew Emmick.

GAME INFORMATION

Radio Announcer: Jeff Hem. **No of Games Broadcast:** Home-72 Road-72. **Flagship Station:** Unavailable.

PA Announcers: Eric Berner, Jim Kiser. **Official Scorers:** Eric Jones, Trevor Garrett, Robert Hernberger.

Stadium Name: Herschel Greer Stadium. Location: I-65 to Wedgewood exit, west to Eighth Avenue, right on Eighth to Chestnut Street, right on Chestnut. Standard Game Times: 7:05 pm, Sat 6:35, Sun 2:05 (April-June), 6:35 (July-Sept). Ticket Price Range: $8-14.

Visiting Club Hotel: Holiday Inn Vanderbilt, 2613 West End Ave, Nashville, TN 37203. Telephone: (615) 327-4707.

NEW ORLEANS ZEPHYRS

Office Address: 6000 Airline Dr, Metairie, LA 70003.
Telephone: (504) 734-5155. Fax: (504) 734-5118.
E-Mail address: zephyrs@zephyrsbaseball.com. Website: www.zephyrsbaseball.com.
Affiliation (first year): Miami Marlins (2009). Years in League: 1998-

Ownership/Management

Managing Partner/President: Don Beaver.
Executive Director/COO: Ron Maestri.
Minority Owner/Vice President/General Counsel: Walter Leger.
General Manager: Mike Schline. VP, Sales/Marketing/Community Relations: Jeff Booker. Director, Finance/Accounting: Donna Light. Director, Broadcasting/Team Travel: Tim Grubbs. Color Analyst/Speakers Bureau: Ron Swoboda. Director, Media Relations: Dave Sachs. Director, Promotions/Merchandise: Brandon Puls. Director, Ticket Operations: Kathy Kaleta. Director, Community Relations: Chris Carlock. Director, Stadium Operations: Nathan McNair. Assistant, Stadium Operations: Jose Avila. Director, Clubhouse: Brett Herbert. Director, Group Sales: Trey Shields. Group Outings Coordinators: Katie Bonaccorso, Angela Campiere, Kurt Cavataio. Coordinator, Marketing: Leigh Pechon. Head Groundskeeper: Thomas Marks. Assistant Groundskeeper: Corey Cazaubon.
Maintenance Coordinator: Craig Shaffer. Receptionist: Susan Radkovich. Director, Operations, Messina's Inc.: George Messina. Administrative Assistant, Messina's Inc.: Priscilla Arbello. Catering Manager, Messina's Inc.: Darin Yuratich.

FIELD STAFF

Manager: Ron Hassey. Hitting Coach: Damon Minor. Pitching Coach: Charlie Corbell. Trainer: Dustin Luepker. Strength/Conditioning: Unavailable.

GAME INFORMATION

Radio Announcers: Tim Grubbs, Ron Swoboda. No. of Games Broadcast: Home-72 Road-72. Flagship Station: WMTI 106.1 FM.

PA Announcer: Doug Moreau. Official Scorer: JL Vangilder.
Stadium Name: Zephyr Field. Location: I-10 West toward Baton Rouge, exit at Clearview Pkwy (exit 226) and continues south, right on Airline Drive (US 61 North) for 1 mile, stadium on left; From airport, take Airline Drive (US 61) east for 4 miles, stadium on right. Standard Game Times: 7 pm, Sat 6, Sun 2 (April-May), 6 (June-Sept). Ticket Price Range: $6-10.

Visiting Club Hotel: Sheraton Four Points, 6401 Veterans Memorial Blvd., Metairie, LA 70003. Telephone: (504) 885-5700.

OKLAHOMA CITY REDHAWKS

Office Address: 2 S Mickey Mantle Dr, Oklahoma City, OK 73104.
Telephone: (405) 218-1000. Fax: (405) 218-1001.
E-Mail address: info@okcredhawks.com. Website: www.okcredhawks.com.
Affiliation (first year): Houston Astros (2011). Years in League: 1963-1968, 1998-

Ownership/Management

Operated By: Oklahoma Baseball Club LLC.
Principal Owner: Mandalay Baseball Properties.
President/General Manager: Michael Byrnes. CFO: Steve McEwen. VP, Ticketing: Jenna Byrnes. Director, Ticket Sales: Matt Hernandez. Director, Facility Operations: Harlan Budde. Director, Operations: Mike Prange. Director, Corporate Partnerships: Melissa Bird. Director, Sponsor Services: Chris Hart. Director, Media Relations/Broadcasting: JP Shadrick. Director, Entertainment: Megan Fitzgerald. Manager, Merchandise: Nancy Simmons. Manager, Baseball Operations: John Brammer. Ticket Office Manager: Armando Reyes. Office Manager: Travis Hunter. Head Groundskeeper: Monte McCoy.

FIELD STAFF

Manager: Tony DeFrancesco. Coach: Leon Roberts. Pitching Coach: Burt Hooton. Strength/Conditioning Coach: Gary McCoy. Trainer: Mike Freer.

GAME INFORMATION

No. of Games Broadcast: Home-72 Road-72. Station: KGHM-AM 1340 Website: www.1340thegame.com
Ballpark location: Bricktown area in downtown Oklahoma City, near interchange of I-235 and I-40; Off I-240 take Sheridan exit to Bricktown; off I-40 take Shields exit, north to Bricktown. Standard Game Times: 7:05 pm, Sun 2:05 (April-May), 6:05 (June-August). Ticket Price Range: $5-15.

OMAHA STORM CHASERS

Office Address: Werner Park, 12356 Ballpark Way, Papillion, NE 68046.
Administrative Office Phone: (402) 734-2550. **Ticket Office Phone:** (402) 738-5100. **Fax:** (402) 734-7166. **E-mail Address:** info@omahastormchasers.com. **Website:** www.omahastormchasers.com.
Affiliation (first year): Kansas City Royals (1969). **Years in League:** 1998-

Ownership/Management

Operated by: Omaha Royals Limited Partnership and Omaha Storm Chasers Baseball Club.
Principal Owners: William Shea, Warren Buffett, Walter Scott.
President/General Manager: Martie J Cordaro.
Assistant GM: Rob Crain. **Assistant GM, Business Operations:** Laurie Schlender. **Director, Broadcasting:** Mark Nasser. **Director, Business Development:** Dave Endress. **Director, Community Relations:** Andrea Stava. **Director, Group Sales:** Danny Dunbar. **Director, Merchandise:** Jason Kinney. **Baseball Operations/Broadcasting:** Brett Pollock. **Creative Services Manager:** Ben Tupman. **Media Relations Manager:** Mike Feigen. **Promotions Manager:** Ben Hemmen.
Ballpark Operations Manager: Brett Myers. **Senior Ticket Sales Executive:** Rustin Buysse. **Corporate Partnerships Executive:** Ben Kratz. **Ticket Operations Manager:** Kaci Long. **Ticket Operations Assistant:** Ryan Worthen. **Ticket Package Executive:** Mark Wilhelm. **Ticket Sales Executive:** Andrew Madden. **Finance Assistant:** Drew Stauder. **Head Groundskeeper:** Mitch McClary. **Assistant Groundskeeper:** Noah Diercks. **Administrative Assistant:** Dana Becker.

FIELD STAFF

Manager: Mike Jirschele. **Hitting Coach:** Tommy Gregg. **Pitching Coach:** Doug Henry. **Athletic Trainer:** Dave Iannicca. **Strength Coach:** Joey Greany.

GAME INFORMATION

Radio Announcer: Mark Nasser. **No. of Games Broadcast:** Home-72, Away-72. **Flagship Station:** KOIL-AM 1180. **PA Announcers:** Bill Jensen, Craig Evans, Jake Ryan. **Official Scorers:** Frank Adkisson, Steve Pivovar, Ryan White.
Stadium Name (year opened): Werner Park (2011). **Location:** Hwy 370, just east of I-80 (exit 439).
Standard Game Times: 6:35 pm (April-May); 7:05 (June-Sept); Fri/Sat 7:05; Sun 2:05
Visiting Club Hotel: Courtyard Omaha La Vista, 12560 Westport Parkway, La Vista, NE 68128. **Telephone:** (402) 339-4900. **Fax:** (402) 339-4901.

RENO ACES

Office Address: 250 Evans Ave, Reno, NV 89501.
Telephone: (775) 334-4700. **Fax:** (775) 334-4701. **Website:** www.renoaces.com
Affiliation (fourth year): Arizona Diamondbacks (2009). **Years in League:** 2009-present

Ownership/Management

President/Managing Partner: Stuart Katzoff.
Partners: Jerry Katzoff, Herb Simon, Steve Simon.
Chief Financial Officer: Kevin Bower. **General Counsel:** Brett Beecham.
Executive Vice President, Business Operations: Justin Piper.
General Manager: Rick Parr.
VP, Baseball Operations/Communications: TJ Lasita. **Director, Broadcasting:** Ryan Radtke. **Manager, Communications:** Zak Basch. **Director, Marketing Partnerships:** Brady Raggio. **Director, Partnership Services/Events:** Andrei Losche. **Account Executive, Marketing Partnerships:** JonPaul Ryan. **Director, Ticketing:** Brian Moss. **Account Executive, Group Tickets:** Ashley Belka. **Account Executives:** Heather Bennett, Jeff Anderson. **Manager, Client Services:** Adam Kincaid. **Director, Ticket Operations:** Charles Lucas. **Manager, Ticket Operations:** Sarah Bliss. **Director, Marketing:** Brett McGinness. **Manager, Promotions:** Amanda Alling. **VP, Ballpark Operations:** David Avila. **Director, Ballpark Operations:** Tara O'Connor. **Manager, Grounds:** Eric Blanton. **Assistant, Grounds:** Dan Kastens. **Director, Merchandise:** Jessica Berry. **Assistant Director, Merchandise:** Linda Hanson. **Controller:** Jerry Meyer. **Staff Accountant:** Sarah Montes.

FIELD STAFF

Manager: Brett Butler. **Hitting Coach:** Rick Burleson. **Pitching Coach:** Mike Parrott. **Trainer:** Joe Metz. **Strength/Conditioning Coordinator:** Vaughn Robinson.

GAME INFORMATION

Radio Announcer: Ryan Radtke. **No. of Games Broadcast:** Home-72, Away-72. **Flagship Station:** Fox Sports 630 AM. **PA Announcer:** Mike Hagerty.
Official Scorers: Chad Hartley, Jack Kuestermeyer. **Stadium Name:** Aces Ballpark.
Location: From Carson City (south of Reno): 395 North to I-80 West, Exit 14 (Wells Ave), left on Wells, right at Kuenzli Street, ballpark on right; From East, I-80 West to exit 14 (Wells Avenue), left on Wells, right on Kuenzli, right at East 2nd Street; From West, I-80 East to Exit 13 (Virginia St), right on Virginia, left on Second, ballpark on left; From North, 395 South to I-80 West, Exit 14 (Wells Ave), left on Wells, right on Kuenzli.
Standard Game Times: 7:05 pm, 6:35, 1:05. **Ticket Price Range:** $7-30.
Visiting Club Hotel: Silver Legacy Resort Casino. **Telephone:** 775-325-7401.

ROUND ROCK EXPRESS

Office Address: 3400 East Palm Valley Blvd, Round Rock, TX 78665.
Telephone: (512) 255-2255. **Fax:** (512) 255-1558.
E-Mail Address: info@rrexpress.com. **Website:** www.roundrockexpress.com.
Affiliation (first year): Texas Rangers (2011). **Year in League:** 2005-

Ownership/Management

Operated By: Ryan Sanders Baseball, LP.
Principal Owners: Nolan Ryan, Don Sanders.
Owners: Reid Ryan (CEO), Reese Ryan (CFO), Brad Sanders, Bret Sanders, Jay Miller, Eddie Maloney.
Executive VP, Ryan Sanders Baseball: JJ Gottsch.
Executive Assistants, Ryan Sanders Baseball: Debbie Bowman, Kelly Looman.
President: Dave Fendrick. **Executive VP/General Manager:** George King. **VP, Corporate Sales:** Henry Green.
VP, Ticket Sales: Gary Franke. **VP, Marketing:** Laura Fragoso. **VP, Business Development:** Gregg Miller. **Director, Communications/Baseball Operations:** Larry Little. **Director, Stadium Operations:** David Powers. **Controller:** Debbie Coughlin. **Director, United Heritage Center:** Scott Allen. **Director, Broadcasting:** Mike Capps. **Director, Merchandising:** Brooke Milam. **Director, Entertainment/Promotions:** Clint Musslewhite. **Director, Ticket Operations:** Ross Scott. **Director, Baseball Outreach:** Chris Almendarez. **Director, Stadium Maintenance:** Aurelio Martinez.
  Account Executives: David Allen, Luke Crum. **Client Services Manager:** Rob Runnels. **Communications/Baseball Operations Manager:** Tim Jackson. **Retail Manager:** Debbie Goodman. **Corporate Sales Manager:** Brian Spieles. **Head Groundskeeper:** Garrett Reddehase. **Clubhouse Manager:** Kenny Bufton. **Communications Intern:** Wade Hilligoss. **Maintenance Staff:** Raymond Alemon, Ofelia Gonzalez. **Event Staff Coordinator:** Randy Patterson. **Office Manager:** Wendy Abrahamsen.

FIELD STAFF

Manager: Bobby Jones. **Hitting Coach:** Brant Brown. **Pitching Coach:** Terry Clark. **Coach:** Spike Owen. **Trainer:** Jason Roberts. **Strength Coach:** Ric Mabie.

GAME INFORMATION

Radio Announcers: Mike Capps, Jerry Grote. **No. of Games Broadcast:** Home—72, Road—72. **Flagship Station:** The Horn 104.9 FM ESPN Radio Austin. **PA Announcer:** Clint Musslewhite. **Official Scorer:** Tommy Tate. **Stadium Name:** The Dell Diamond.
  Location: US Highway 79, 3.5 miles east of Interstate 35 (exit 253) or 1.5 miles west of Texas Tollway 130.
  Standard Game Times: 7:05 pm, 6:05, 1:05. **Ticket Price Range:** $7-$14
  Visiting Club Hotel: Hilton Garden Inn, 2310 North IH-35, Round Rock, TX 78681. **Telephone:** (512) 341-8200.

SACRAMENTO RIVER CATS

Office Address: 400 Ballpark Dr, West Sacramento, CA 95691.
Telephone: (916) 376-4700. **Fax:** (916) 376-4710.
E-Mail address: reception@rivercats.com. **Website:** www.rivercats.com.
Affiliation (first year): Oakland Athletics (2000).
Years in League: 1903, 1909-11, 1918-60, 1974-76, 2000-Present

Ownership/Management

Operated By: Sacramento River Cats Baseball Club, LLC.
Owner/CEO: Susan Savage.
General Manager: Jeff Savage. **Executive VP/CFO:** Dan Vistica. **Director, Finance, IT/Accounting Services:** Jess Olivares. **Human Resources Manager:** Grace Bailey. **Accounting Clerk:** Madeline Strika. **Head Groundskeeper:** Chris Ralston. **Coordinator, Grounds:** Marcelo Clamar. **Coordinator, Employee Services:** Angela Kroeker. **Building Superintendent:** Danny Reilly. **Manager, Event Service/Building Operations:** Grady Wooden. **Manager, Corporate Partnerships:** Greg Coletti. **Account Executive, Corporate Partnerships:** Ryan Von Sossan. **Account Executive, Corporate Partnerships:** Stacy Knight. **Coordinators, Partnership Activation:** Andrew Shipp, Stephen Caselli. **Manager, Merchandise:** Rose Holland. **Coordinator, Website/Research:** Brent Savage. **Coordinator, Online Merchandise Sales:** Megan Osgood. **Director, Ticket Sales:** Alex Zamansky. **Director, Ticket Operations:** John Krivacic.
  Manager, Inside Sales: Chris Dreesman. **Senior Corporate Account Executive:** Steve Gracio. **Corporate Account Executives:** Stuart Scally, Dave Matolo, Tyler Axelrod. **Group Events Account Executives:** Samantha Bottari, Ashley Hansen, Emily Higginson. **Group Events Account Executive:** Jessica Wilson. **Ticket Operations Assistant:** Elyse Cusack. **Senior Director, Marketing/Events/Entertainment:** Jennifer Castleberry. **Community Relations:** Tony Asaro. **Manager, Advertising:** Genene Chacon. **Coordinator, Public Relations/ Baseball Ops:** Zak Basch. **Coordinator, Media Relations/Interactive Media:** Nick Lozito. **Coordinator, Multimedia/Graphics:** Mike Villarreal. **Graphic Designer:** Sara Molina. **Coordinators, Events/Entertainment:** Sara Wendt, Samantha Klasing. **Coordinator, Day of Game Events:** Leslie Lindsey. **Mascot Coordinator:** Rhett Holland.

FIELD STAFF

Manager: Darren Bush. **Hitting Coach:** Greg Sparks. **Pitching Coach:** Scott Emerson. **Trainer:** Brad LaRosa. **Strength Coach:** Sean Doran.

GAME INFORMATION
Radio Announcer: Johnny Doskow. **No. of Games Broadcast:** Home-72 Road-72. **Flagship Station:** Talk 650 KSTE. **PA Announcer:** Greg Lawson. **Official Scorers:** Brian Berger, Ryan Bjork, Mark Honbo. **Stadium Name:** Raley Field. **Location:** I-5 to Business-80 West, exit at Jefferson Boulevard. **Standard Game Time:** 7:05 pm. **Ticket Price Range:** $8-60.
Visiting Club Hotel: Holiday Inn.

SALT LAKE BEES

Office Address: 77 W 1300 South, Salt Lake City, UT 84115.
Telephone: (801) 325-6900. **Fax:** (801) 485-6818.
E-Mail Address: info@slbees.com. **Website:** www.slbees.com.
Affiliation (first year): Los Angeles Angels of Anaheim (2001). **Years in League:** 1915-25, 1958-65, 1970-84, 1994-.

Ownership/Management
Operated by: Larry H Miller Baseball Inc.
Principal Owner: Gail Miller.
CEO, Larry H Miller Group of Companies: Greg Miller.
President: Randy Rigby. **Executive Vice President/CFO:** Robert Hyde. **Senior VP:** Jim Olson. **VP/General Manager:** Marc Amicone. **Senior VP, Broadcasting:** Chris Baum. **General Counsel:** Robert Tingey. **Director, Corporate Travel:** Judy Adams. **Senior VP, Communications:** Linda Luchetti. **Director, Broadcasting:** Steve Klauke. **Communications Manager:** Hannah Lee. **Senior VP, Strategic Partnerships:** Mike Snarr. **VP, Corporate Partnerships:** Greg Tanner. **VP, Marketing:** Craig Sanders. **VP, Ticket Sales:** Clay Jensen.
Director, Game Operations: Chance Fessler. **Director, Ticket Sales/Services:** Casey Patterson. **Director, Corporate Partnerships:** Brian Prutch. **Box Office Manager:** Laura Russell. **Ticket/Group Sales Manager:** Brad Jacoway. **VP, Public Safety:** Jim Bell. **Director, Public Safety:** Al Higham. **VP, Food Services:** Mark Stedman. **Director, Food Services:** Dave Dalton. **Youth Programs Coordinator:** Nate Martinez. **Clubhouse Manager:** Eli Rice.

FIELD STAFF
Manager: Keith Johnson. **Coach:** Jim Eppard. **Pitching Coach:** Erik Bennett. **Trainer:** Brian Reinker.

GAME INFORMATION
Radio Announcer: Steve Klauke. **No. of Games Broadcast:** Home-72, Away-72. **Flagship Station:** ESPN 1230-AM.
PA Announcer: Jeff Reeves. **Official Scorers:** Howard Nakagama, Terry Harward.
Stadium Name: Spring Mobile Ballpark. **Location:** I-15 North/South to 1300 South exit, east to ballpark at West Temple.
Standard Game Times: 6:35 (April-May), 7:05 (June-Sept); Sun 1:05.
Ticket Price Range: $8-24.
Visiting Club Hotel: Sheraton City Centre, 150 W 500 South, Salt Lake City, UT 84101. **Telephone:** (801) 401-2000.

TACOMA RAINIERS

Stadium/Office Address: 2502 South Tyler St, Tacoma, WA 98405.
Telephone: (253) 752-7707. **Fax:** (253) 752-7135.
Website: www.tacomarainiers.com.
Affiliation: Seattle Mariners (1995). **Years in League:** 1904-1905, 1960-

Ownership/Management
Owners: The Baseball Club of Tacoma.
President: Aaron Artman.
Director, Administration/Assistant to the President: Patti Stacy. **Vice President, Corporate Partnerships:** Kevin Tiemann. **VP, Ticket Sales:** Chip Maxson. **Creative Director:** Tony Canepa. **Director, Corporate Partner Services:** Audrey Berglund. **Director, Media Development/Events:** Alyson Jones. **Director, Game Entertainment:** Jessica McDaniel. **Director, Facilities/Head Groundskeeper:** Ryan Schutt. **Director, Ticket Sales:** Shane Santman. **Director, Operations:** Ashley Roth. **Director, Corporate Partnerships:** Jim Flavin. **Ticket Operations Manager:** Cameron Badgett. **Manager, Guest Services/Community Development:** Mallory Beckingham. **Media Development Manager:** Ben Spradling. **Event Manager:** Brooke Bourn. **Event Coordinator:** Bijou Felder. **Coordinator, Publications/Marketing:** Rebekka Rizzo. **Suite Services Manager:** Nicole Strunks. **Controller:** Brian Coombe. **Accounting:** Elise Schorr. **Corporate Sales Managers:** Joe Corona, Stephen Corbin, Stephen Molnar. **Nightly Suite Coordinator:** Thomas Knowlton. **Group Event Coordinator:** Ryan Latham, Graham Stream, Jessica Blengino, Ainsley O'Keefe, Alexandra Snyder. **Home Clubhouse Manager:** Eddie Romprey.

FIELD STAFF
Manager: Daren Brown. **Coach:** Alonzo Powell. **Pitching Coach:** Dwight Bernard. **Trainer:** Tom Newberg. **Assistant Trainer:** Jeremy Clipperton.

GAME INFORMATION
Radio Broadcaster: Mike Curto. **No. of Games Broadcast:** Home-72, Away-72. **Flagship Station:** KHHO 850-AM.
PA Announcer: Unavailable. **Official Scorers:** Gary Brooks, Michael Jessee.

Stadium Name: Cheney Stadium. Location: From I-5, take exit 132 (Highway 16 West) for 1.2 miles to 19th Street East exit, right on Tyler St for 1/3 mile. Standard Game Times: 7 pm, Sun, 1:35. Ticket Price Range: $9-$25.

Visiting Club Hotel: Hotel Murano, 1320 Broadway Plaza Tacoma, WA 98402. Telephone: (253) 238-8000.

TUCSON PADRES

Office Address: 2500 E Ajo Way, Tucson, AZ 85713.

Telephone: (520) 434-1367. Fax: (520) 434-1361.

Email address: info@tucsonpadres.com. Website: www.tucsonpadres.com.

Affiliation (first year): San Diego Padres (2011). Years in League: 1969-2008, 2011-

Ownership/Management

Operated By: Tucson Triple-A Baseball, LLC.

Vice President/General Manager: Mike Feder. Senior Advisor: Jack Donovan. Business Manager/Director, Merchandising: Pattie Feder. Director, Operations: Eric May. Director, Game Day Operations: Debbie Clark. Director, Sales: James Jensen. Executive Assistant: Taylor Bonatus. Director, Inside Sales: Sandy Davis. Director, Community Relations: Crissy Ahmann-Perham. Manager, Community Relations: Tanner Popish. Director, Broadcasting/Media Relations: Tim Hagerty. Home Clubhouse Manager: TJ Laidlaw. Visiting Clubhouse Manager: Cory McClelland.

FIELD STAFF

Manager: Terry Kennedy. Hitting Coach: Bob Skube. Pitching Coach: Steve Webber. Trainer: Wade Yamasaki.

GAME INFORMATION

Radio Announcer: Tim Hagerty. No. of Games Broadcast: Home-72 Road-72. Flagship Station: Unavailable.

PA Announcer: Jonas Hunter. Official Scorer: Michael Guymon.

Stadium Name: Kino Stadium. Location: 2500 E Ajo Way Tucson, AZ 85713.

Standard Game Times: 7:05 pm Sun 2:05. Ticket Price Range: $5:50-$10.50.

Visiting Club Hotel: DoubleTree at Reid Park, 445 South Alvernon Way Tucson, AZ 85711-4198. Telephone: (520) 881-4200.

EASTERN LEAGUE

Office Address: 30 Danforth St, Suite 208, Portland, ME 04101.
Telephone: (207) 761-2700. **Fax:** (207) 761-7064.
E-Mail Address: elpb@easternleague.com. **Website:** www.easternleague.com.
Years League Active: 1923-.

President/Treasurer: Joe McEacharn.

Vice President/Secretary: Charles Eshbach. **VP:** Chuck Domino. **Assistant to President:** Bill Rosario.

Joe McEacharn

Directors: Greg Agganis (Akron), Rick Brenner (New Hampshire), Lou DiBella (Richmond), Bill Dowling (New Britain), Charles Eshbach (Portland), Joe Finley (Trenton), Bob Lozinak (Altoona), Art Matin (Erie), Michael Reinsdorf (Harrisburg), Brian Shallcross (Bowie), Craig Stein (Reading), Mike Urda (Binghamton).

Division Structure: Eastern—Binghamton, New Britain, New Hampshire, Portland, Reading, Trenton. Western—Akron, Altoona, Bowie, Erie, Harrisburg, Richmond.

Regular Season: 142 games. **2012 Opening Date:** April 5. **Closing Date:** Sept 3.

All-Star Game: July 11 at Reading.

Playoff Format: Top two teams in each division meet in best-of-five series. Winners meet in best-of-five series for league championship.

Roster Limit: 24. **Player Eligibility Rule:** No restrictions. **Brand of Baseball:** Rawlings.

Umpires: Joey Amaral (Columbia, MD), Joseph Born (Lafayette, IN), Brian De Brauwere (Hummelstown, PA), Ramon De Jesus (Santo Domingo, Dominican Republic), Andrew Dudones (Uniontown, OH), James Guyll (Fort Wayne, IN), Luke Hamilton (Goshen, IN), Joseph Hannigan (Westmont, IL), Travis Hatch (Ravenswood, Australia), Thomas Honec (Harrisonburg, VA), Kiff Kinkead (Wilmington, NC), Shaun Lampe (Scottsdale, AZ), Nicolas Lentz (Holland, MI), Nicholas Mahrley (Bartlett, IL), Jeffrey Morrow (Fenton, MO), Timothy Rosso (Saddle Brook, NJ), Christopher Vines (Kennesaw, GA), Thomas Woodring (Boulder, NV).

STADIUM INFORMATION

			Dimensions				
Club	**Stadium**	**Opened**	**LF**	**CF**	**RF**	**Capacity**	**2011 Att.**
Akron	Canal Park	1997	331	400	337	9,097	266,265
Altoona	Blair County Ballpark	1999	325	405	325	7,210	285,906
Binghamton	NYSEG Stadium	1992	330	400	330	6,012	209,044
Bowie	Prince George's Stadium	1994	309	405	309	10,000	255,832
Erie	Jerry Uht Park	1995	312	400	328	6,000	224,443
Harrisburg	Metro Bank Park	1987	325	400	325	6,300	291,248
New Britain	New Britain Stadium	1996	330	400	330	6,146	363,759
New Hampshire	Northeast Delta Dental Stadium	2005	326	400	306	6,500	373,482
Portland	Hadlock Field	1994	315	400	330	7,368	369,424
Reading	FirstEnergy Stadium	1951	330	400	330	9,000	456,957
Richmond	The Diamond	1985	330	402	330	9,560	447,520
Trenton	Mercer County Waterfront Park	1994	330	407	330	6,150	379,501

AKRON AEROS

Office Address: 300 S Main St, Akron, OH 44308.
Telephone: (330) 253-5151. **Fax:** (330) 253-3300.
E-Mail address: info@akronaeros.com. **Website:** www.akronaeros.com.
Affiliation (first year): Cleveland Indians (1989). **Years in League:** 1989-

OWNERSHIP, MANAGEMENT

Operated By: Akron Professional Baseball, Inc.

Principal Owners: Mike Agganis, Greg Agganis.

Executive VP/General Manager: Jeff Auman. **CFO:** Ken Fogel. **Director, Corporate Sales:** Calvin Funkhouser. **VP, Ticketing:** Gary Thomas. **Director, Ticketing:** Joel Leroy. **Assistant Director, Ticketing:** Ross Swaldo. **Group Sales Representatives:** Mitch Cromes, Jeremy Heit. **Director, Merchandise/Promotions:** Scott Riley. **IT Specialist:** Arlene Spahn. **Director, Food/Beverage:** Nate Michel. **Assistant Director, Food/Beverage:** Matt Vanderhoff. **Coordinator, Suites/Picnics:** Sierra Sawtelle. **Head Groundskeeper:** Chris Walsh. **Director, Stadium Operations:** Adam Horner. **Office Manager:** Emily Myers.

FIELD STAFF

Manager: Chris Tremie. **Coach:** Rouglas Odor. **Pitching Coach:** Tony Arnold. **Trainer:** Chad Wolfe.

GAME INFORMATION

Radio Announcer: Jim Clark. **No of Games Broadcast:** Home-71 Road-71. **Flagship Station:** Fox Sports Radio 1350-AM. **PA Announcer:** Leonard Grabowski. **Official Scorer:** Unavailable.

Stadium Name: Canal Park. **Location:** From I-76 East or I-77 South, exit onto Route 59 East, exit at Exchange/Cedar,

right onto Cedar, left at Main Street; From I-76 West or I-77 North, exit at Main Street/Downtown, follow exit onto Broadway Street, left onto Exchange Street, right at Main Street. **Standard Game Time:** 7:05 pm, Sun 1:05.

Ticket Price Range: $5-10.

Visiting Club Hotel: Akron Ramada Plaza Hotel, 20 W Mill St, Akron, OH 44308. **Telephone:** (330) 384-1500.

ALTOONA CURVE

Office Address: Blair County Ballpark, 1000 Park Avenue, Altoona, PA 16602.
Telephone: (814) 943-5400. **Fax:** (814) 942-9132.
E-Mail Address: frontoffice@altoonacurve.com. **Website:** www.altoonacurve.com.
Affiliation (first year): Pittsburgh Pirates (1999). **Years in League:** 1999-present.

OWNERSHIP, MANAGEMENT

Operated By: Lozinak Professional Baseball.
Managing Members: Bob & Joan Lozinak. **COO:** David Lozinak. **CFO:** Mike Lozinak. **Chief Administrative Officer:** Steve Lozinak. **General Manager:** Rob Egan. **Senior Advisor:** Sal Baglieri. **Assistant GM, Marketing/Promotions:** Matt Hoover. **Director, Finance:** Mary Lamb. **Director, Ticketing:** Mike Pence. **Director, Creative Services:** John Foreman. **Director, Mascot/Brand Development:** Bill Bettwy. **Director, Communications:** Mike Passanisi. **Director, Community Relations:** Elsie Gibney. **Director, Merchandising:** Claire Hoover. **Director, Ballpark Operations:** Kirk Stiffler. **Assistant Operations Manager:** Doug Mattern. **Head Groundskeeper:** Brian Soukup.
Box Office Manager: Chris Keefer. **Sponsorship Sales Account Executive:** Chuck Griswold. **Ticket Sales Associates:** Mollie Shoemaker, Cody Clifton, Steffan Langguth. **Administrative Assistant:** Carol Schmittle. **Manager, Concessions:** Glenn McComas. **Assistant Manager, Concessions:** Michelle Anna.

FIELD STAFF

Manager: PJ Forbes. **Hitting Coach:** Ryan Long. **Pitching Coach:** Jeff Johnson. **Trainer:** Mike Zalno.

GAME INFORMATION

Radio Announcer: Mike Passanisi. **No. of Games Broadcast:** Home-71 Road-71. **Flagship Station:** ESPN Radio 1430 (WVAM-AM).
PA Announcer: Rich DeLeo. **Official Scorers:** Ted Beam, Dick Wagner.
Stadium Name: Blair County Ballpark. **Location:** Located just off the Frankstown Road Exit of I-99. **Standard Game Times:** 7 pm, 6:30 (April-May); Sun 6, 2 (April-May). **Ticket Price Range:** $5-12. **Visiting Club Hotel:** Ramada Altoona, Route 220 and Plank Road, Altoona, PA 16602. **Telephone:** (814) 946-1631.

BINGHAMTON METS

Office Address: 211 Henry St, Binghamton, NY 13901.
Mailing Address: PO Box 598, Binghamton, NY 13902.
Telephone: (607) 723-6387. **Fax:** (607) 723-7779.
E-Mail address: bmets@bmets.com. **Website:** www.bmets.com.
Affiliation (first year): New York Mets (1992). **Years in League:** 1923-37, 1940-63, 1966-68, 1992-

OWNERSHIP, MANAGEMENT

Principal Owners: Bill Maines, David Maines, George Scherer, Michael Urda.
General Manager: Jim Weed. **Director, Stadium Operations:** Richard Tylicki. **Director, Ticket Operations:** Casey Both. **Director, Video Production:** Rob Sternberg. **Director, Marketing:** Heith Tracy. **Corporate Sales Executive:** Josh Patton. **Special Event Coordinators:** Connor Gates, Erica Mincher, Bob Urda. **Scholastic Programs Coordinator:** Lou Ferraro. **Office Manager:** Amy Fancher. **Merchandising Manager:** Lisa Shattuck. **Director, Broadcast/Media Relations:** Tim Heiman. **Sports Turf Manager:** EJ Folli. **Home Clubhouse Manager:** Zaq Bell.

FIELD STAFF

Manager: Pedro Lopez. **Coach:** Luis Natera. **Pitching Coach:** Glenn Abbott.

GAME INFORMATION

Radio Announcer: Tim Heiman. **No. of Games Broadcast:** Home-71 Road-71. **Flagship Station:** WNBF 1290-AM.
PA Announcer: Unavailable. **Official Scorer:** Steve Kraly.
Stadium Name: NYSEG Stadium. **Location:** I-81 to exit 4S (Binghamton), Route 11 exit to Henry Street. **Standard Game Times:** 6:35, Fri-Sat 7:05, Day Games 1:05. **Ticket Price Range:** $9-11.
Visiting Club Hotel: Best Western, 569 Harry L Drive, Johnson City, NY 13790. **Telephone:** (607) 729-9194.

BOWIE BAYSOX

Office Address: Prince George's Stadium, 4101 NE Crain Hwy, Bowie, MD 20716.
Telephone: (301) 805-6000. **Fax:** (301) 464-4911.
E-Mail address: info@baysox.com. **Website:** www.baysox.com.
Affiliation (first year): Baltimore Orioles (1993). **Years in League:** 1993-

OWNERSHIP, MANAGEMENT

Owned By: Bowie Baysox Baseball Club LLC.
President: Ken Young.
General Manager: Brian Shallcross. **Assistant GM:** Phil Wrye. **Director, Marketing:** Brandan Kaiser. **Director, Field/Facility Operations:** Matt Parrott. **Director, Ticket Operations:** Charlene Fewer. **Assistant Director, Ticket Operations:** Vince Riggs. **Director, Sponsorships:** Matt McLaughlin. **Promotions Manager:** Chris Rogers. **Communications Manager:** Matt Wilson. **Community Programs Manager:** Kate Milstead. **Account Executive:** Megan Holloway. **Group Events Managers:** Jerran Leber, Jeff Gibbons. **Box Office Manager:** Adam Hornish. **Stadium Operations Manager:** Brian Cipcic. **Assistant Groundskeeper:** Jason Green. **Director, Gameday Personnel:** Darlene Mingioli. **Clubhouse Manager:** Andy Maalouf. **Bookkeeper:** Carol Terwilliger.

FIELD STAFF

Manager: Gary Kendall. **Coach:** Denny Hocking. **Pitching Coach:** Kennie Steenstra.

GAME INFORMATION

Radio Announcer: Ben Gordon-Goldstein. **No. of Games Broadcast:** 72. **Flagship Station:** www.baysox.com.
PA Announcer: Adrienne Roberson. **Official Scorers:** Bill Hay, Carl Smith, Peter O'Reilly.
Stadium Name: Prince George's Stadium. **Location:** 1/4 mile south of US 50/Route 301 Interchange in Bowie.
Standard Game Times: 7:05 p.m; Sun 2:05 (April-June), 6:05 (July-Sept.). **Ticket Price Range:** $7-17.
Visiting Club Hotel: Best Western Annapolis, 2520 Riva Rd, Annapolis, MD 21401. **Telephone:** (410) 224-2800.

ERIE SEAWOLVES

Office Address: 110 E 10th St, Erie, PA 16501.
Telephone: (814) 456-1300. **Fax:** (814) 456-7520.
E-Mail address: seawolves@seawolves.com. **Website:** www.seawolves.com.
Affiliation (first year): Detroit Tigers (2001). **Years in League:** 1999-

OWNERSHIP, MANAGEMENT

Principal Owners: Mandalay Baseball Properties, LLC. **President:** Greg Coleman. **Assistant GM, Sales:** Mike Uden. **Director, Media Relations/Broadcaster:** Greg Gania. **Director, Accounting/Finance:** Amy McArdle. **Director, Corporate Marketing:** Mark Pirrello. **Director, Operations:** Ryan Stephenson. **Ticket Operations Manager:** Cody Herrick. **Director, Business Development:** Darryl Murphy. **Director, Entertainment:** Courtney Buchna. **Ticket Office Assistant:** Rachel O'Connor. **Director, Food/Beverage (Pro Sports Catering):** Deanna Mierzwa.

FIELD STAFF

Manager: Chris Cron. **Coach:** Jerry Martin. **Pitching Coach:** Ray Burris. **Trainer:** Chris McDonald.

GAME INFORMATION

Radio Announcer: Greg Gania. **No. of Games Broadcast:** Home-71 Road-71. **Flagship Station:** Fox Sports Radio WFNN 1330-AM.
PA Announcer: Bob Shreve. **Official Scorer:** Les Caldwell.
Stadium Name: Jerry Uht Park. **Location:** US 79 North to East 12th Street exit, left on State Street, right on 10th Street. **Standard Game Times:** 7:05 pm, 6:35 (April-May), Sun 1:35. **Ticket Prices:** $8-12.
Visiting Club Hotel: Bel Aire Clarion Hotel, 2800 West 8th St Erie, PA 16505.

HARRISBURG SENATORS

Office Address: Metro Bank Park, City Island, Harrisburg, PA 17101.
Mailing Address: PO Box 15757, Harrisburg, PA 17105.
Telephone: (717) 231-4444. **Fax:** (717) 231-4445.
E-Mail address: information@senatorsbaseball.com. **Website:** www.senatorsbaseball.com.
Affiliation (first year): Washington Nationals (2005). **Years in League:** 1924-35, 1987-

OWNERSHIP, MANAGEMENT

Operated By: Senators Partners, LLC.
Chairman: Michael Reinsdorf. **CEO:** Bill Davidson.
President: Kevin Kulp. **General Manager:** Randy Whitaker.
Assistant GM: Aaron Margolis. **Accounting Manager:** Donna Demczak. **Senior Corporate Sales Executive:** Todd Matthews. **Director, Ticket Sales:** Nate DeFazio. **Senior Account Executives:** Jonathan Boles, Jessica Kauffman. **Ticket Sales Executive:** Daniel Haubert. **Director, Ticket Operations:** Dave Simpson. **Director, Merchandise:** Ann Marie Naumes. **Director, Stadium Operations:** Tim Foreman. **Head Groundskeeper:** Brandon Forsburg. **Stadium Operations Coordinator:** Ben Moyer. **Director, Broadcasting/Media Relations:** Terry Byrom. **Broadcaster/Media Relations Intern:** Matt Dudas. **Director, Community Relations:** Emily Winslow. **Community Relations Intern:** Mary Kate Holder. **Director, Digital/New Media:** Ashley Grotte. **Digital/New Media Intern:** Dani Wexelman. **Game Entertainment Coordinator:** Sean Purcell. **Ticket Sales Interns:** Lindsay Behrenhausen, Kevin Dougherty, Tom Kronenberger.

FIELD STAFF

Manager: Matt LeCroy. **Coach:** Eric Fox. **Pitching Coach:** Paul Menhart. **Trainer:** Jeff Allred.

GAME INFORMATION

Radio Announcers: Terry Byrom, Matt Dudas. **No. of Games Broadcast:** Home-71 Road-71. **Flagship Station:** 1460-AM. **PA Announcer:** Chris Andre.

Official Scorers: Terry Walters, Bruce Bashore. **Stadium Name:** Metro Bank Park. **Location:** I-83, exit 23 (Second Street) to Market Street, bridge to City Island.

Ticket Price Range: $5-12.50.

Visiting Club Hotel: Park Inn Harrisburg West, 5401 Carlisle Pike, Mechanicsburg, PA 17050. **Telephone:** (800) 772-7829. **Visiting Team Workout Facility:** Gold's Gym, 3401 Hartzdale Dr, Camp Hill, PA 17011. **Telephone:** (717) 303-2070.

NEW BRITAIN ROCK CATS

Office Address: 230 John Karbonic Way, New Britain, CT 06051.
Mailing Address: PO Box 1718, New Britain, CT 06050.
Telephone: (860) 224-8383. **Fax:** (860) 225-6267.
E-Mail address: rockcats@rockcats.com. **Website:** www.rockcats.com.
Affiliation (first year): Minnesota Twins (1995). **Years in League:** 1983-

OWNERSHIP, MANAGEMENT (UPDATE)

Operated By: Greater Hartford Sports Management, LLC.
Directors: William F Dowling, Coleman B Levy Esq.
President/CEO: William F Dowling. **Vice President:** Evan Levy. **Assistant GM:** Ricky Ferrell. **Director, Broadcasting:** Jeff Dooley. **Director, Ticket Operations:** Brendan O'Donnell. **Director, Group Sales:** Jonathan Lissitchuck. **Director, Promotions:** Kim Pizighelli. **Director, Media Relations:** Robert Dowling. **Corporate Sales/Hospitality:** Andres Levy. **Group Sales Manager:** Evan Paradis. **Marketing Coordinator:** Lori Soltis. **Corporate Sponsorship Manager:** Kate Baumann. **Director, Community Relations:** Amy Helbling. **Manager, Corporate Developement:** Steve Kunsey. **Controller:** Jim Bonfiglio. **Director, Stadium Operations:** Eric Fritz. **Client Service Coordinator:** Amanda Goldsmith. **Box Office Manager:** Josh Montinieri. **On-Site Manager, Concessionaire Centerplate:** Sheila Fagan.

FIELD STAFF

Manager: Jeff Smith. **Coach:** Rudy Hernandez. **Pitching Coach:** Stu Cliburn. **Trainer:** Larry Bennese.

GAME INFORMATION

Radio Announcer: Jeff Dooley, Joe D'Ambrosio. **No. of Games Broadcast:** Home-71 Road-71. **Flagship Station:** WTIC 1080-AM/96.5-FM, WMRD 1150-AM.

PA Announcer: Don Steele. **Official Scorer:** Ed Smith.

Stadium Name: New Britain Stadium. **Location:** From I-84, take Route 72 East (exit 35 of Route 9 South (exit 39A), left at Ellis Street (exit 25), left at South Main Street, stadium one mile on right; From Route 91 or Route 5, take Route 9 North to Route 71 (exit 24), first exit. **Ticket Price Range:** $5-18.

Visiting Club Hotel: Holiday Inn Express, 120 Laning St, Southington, CT 06489. **Telephone:** (860) 276-0736.

NEW HAMPSHIRE
FISHER CATS

Office Address: 1 Line Dr, Manchester, NH 03101.
Telephone: (603) 641-2005. **Fax:** (603) 641-2055.
E-Mail address: info@nhfishercats.com. **Website:** www.nhfishercats.com.
Affiliation (first year): Toronto Blue Jays (2004). **Years in League:** 2004-

OWNERSHIP

Operated By: DSF Sports
Owner: Art Solomon. **President:** Rick Brenner.

MANAGEMENT

President/General Manager: Rick Brenner. **Vice President, Sales:** Mike Ramshaw. **VP, Business Operations:** Matt Person. **Corporate Controller:** Cindy Garron. **Director, Box Office Operations:** Tim Hough. **Director, Group Sales:** Josh Hubbard. **Director, Facilities/Turf:** Shawn Meredith. **Director, Promotions:** Matt Kowallis. **Director, Broadcast/Media Relations:** Tom Gauthier. **Creative Services/Corporate Sales Manager:** Jake Dodge. **Stadium Operations Manager:** DJ White. **Merchandise Manager:** Justin Stecz. **Community Relations Manager:** Kim Blanchard. **Senior Ticket Sales Manager:** Dan Ferguson. **Senior Public Affairs Manager:** Jenna Raizes.

Ticket Sales Account Executives: Mike Coziahr, Chris Aubertin, Billy Ferris. **Ticket Sales Assistant:** Chris Fontana. **Executive Assistant/Office Manager:** Kayla Hines. **Box Office Assistant:** Matt Generali. **President, Advantage Food/Beverage:** Tim Restall. **Director, Food/Beverage Operations:** Chris Carlisle. **Executive Chef:** Alan Foley

FIELD STAFF

Manager: Sal Fasano. **Hitting Coach:** Jon Nunnally. **Pitching Coach:** Tom Signore. **Trainer:** Bob Tarpey.

GAME INFORMATION

Radio Announcers: Tom Gauthier, Bob Lipman, Dick Lutsk. **No. of Games Broadcast:** Home-71 Road-71. **Flagship Station:** WGIR 610-AM.

PA Announcer: Alex James. **Official Scorers:** Chick Smith, Lenny Parker, Greg Royce, Pete Dupuis, Chris Foley.

Stadium Name: Northeast Delta Dental Stadium. **Location:** From I-93 North, take I-293 North to exit 5 (Granite Street), right on Granite Street, right on South Commercial Street, right on Line Drive. **Ticket Price Range:** $6-12.

Visiting Club Hotel: Comfort Inn, 298 Queen City Ave, Manchester, NH 03102. **Telephone:** (603) 668-2600.

PORTLAND SEA DOGS

Office Address: 271 Park Ave, Portland, ME 04102.
Mailing Address: PO Box 636, Portland, ME 04104.
Telephone: (207) 874-9300. **Fax:** (207) 780-0317.
E-Mail address: seadogs@seadogs.com. **Website:** www.seadogs.com.
Affiliation (first year): Boston Red Sox (2003). **Years in League:** 1994-

OWNERSHIP, MANAGEMENT

Operated By: Portland, Maine Baseball, Inc.
Chairman: Bill Burke.
Treasurer: Sally McNamara. **President:** Charles Eshbach. **Executive Vice President/General Manager:** Geoff Iacuessa. **Senior VP:** John Kameisha. **VP, Financial Affairs/Operations:** Jim Heffley. **Assistant GM, Media Relations:** Chris Cameron. **Director, Sales/Marketing/Promotions:** Liz Riley. **Director, Ticketing:** Dave Strong. **Director, Group Sales/Video Operations Manager:** Brian Murphy. **Sales Director, Ticketing:** Courtney Rague. **Group Sales Manager:** Brayton Chase. **Director, Broadcasting:** Mike Antonellis. **Director, Food Services:** Mike Scorza. **Assistant Director, Food Services:** Greg Moyes. **Clubhouse Managers:** Craig Candage Sr, Nick Fox. **Head Groundskeeper:** Rick Anderson.

FIELD STAFF

Manager: Kevin Boles. **Coach:** Dave Joppie. **Pitching Coach:** Bob Kipper. **Trainer:** Brandon Henry.

GAME INFORMATION

Radio Announcer: Mike Antonellis. **No. of Games Broadcast:** Home-71 Road-71. **Flagship Station:** WPEI 95.9 FM.

PA Announcer: Dean Rogers. **Official Scorer:** Thom Hinton.

Stadium Name: Hadlock Field. **Location:** From South, I-295 to exit 5, merge onto Congress Street, left at St John Street, merge right onto Park Ave; From North, I-295 to exit 6A, right onto Park Ave. **Ticket Price Range:** $4-9.

Visiting Club Hotel: DoubleTree by Hilton Portland Maine, 363 Maine Mall Rd, South Portland, ME 04106. **Telephone:** (207) 775-6161.

READING PHILLIES

Office Address: Route 61 South/1900 Centre Ave, Reading, PA 19605.
Mailing Address: PO Box 15050, Reading, PA 19612.
Telephone: (610) 375-8469. **Fax:** (610) 373-5868.
E-Mail Address: info@readingphillies.com. **Website:** www.readingphillies.com.
Affiliation (first year): Philadelphia Phillies (1967). **Years in League:** 1933-35, 1952-61, 1963-65, 1967-.

OWNERSHIP, MANAGEMENT

Operated By: E&J Baseball Club, Inc.
Principal Owner: Reading Baseball LP.
Managing Partner: Craig Stein.
General Manager: Scott Hunsicker. **Assistant GM:** Ashley Peterson. **Director, Stadium Operations/Concessions:** Andy Bortz. **Director, Sales:** Joe Bialek. **Director, Baseball Operations/Merchandise:** Kevin Sklenarik. **Director, PR/Media Relations:** Eric Scarcelli. **Director, Ticket Operations:** Mike Becker. **Director, Group Sales:** Mike Robinson. **Director, Communications:** Chris McConney. **Controller:** Kristyne Haver. **Corporate Sales/Graphic Artist/Game Entertainment:** Matt Jackson. **Assistant Director, Tickets:** Tim McGee. **Assistant Director, Groups:** Holly Frymyer. **Director, Community Relations:** Matt Hoffmaster. **Video Director:** Andy Kauffman. **Client Relationship Managers:** Curtis Burns, Jon Muldowney, Anthony Pignetti. **Head Groundskeeper:** Dan Douglas. **Office Manager:** Deneen Giesen. **Educational Programs/Youth Coordinator:** Todd Hunsicker. **Merchandising Manager:** Jason Yonkovitch.

FIELD STAFF

Manager: Dusty Wathan. **Coach:** Frank Cacciatore. **Pitching Coach:** Bob Milacki.

GAME INFORMATION

Radio Announcer: Brian Seltzer. **No. of Games Broadcast:** Home-71, Away-71. **Flagship Station:** ESPN 1240-AM.

PA Announcer: Dave Bauman. **Official Scorers:** Paul Jones, Brian Kopetsky, Josh Leiboff, Dick Shute.

Stadium Name: FirstEnergy Stadium. **Location:** From east, take Pennsylvania Turnpike West to Morgantown exit, to 176 North, to 422 West, to Route 12 East, to Route 61 South exit; From west, take 422 East to Route 12 East, to Route 61 South exit; From north, take 222 South to Route 12 exit, to Route 61 South exit; From south, take 222 North to 422

West, to Route 12 East exit at Route 61 South. **Standard Game Times:** 7:05 pm, 6:35 (April-May), Sun 1:05. **Ticket Price Range:** $6-11.

Visiting Club: Crowne Plaza Reading Hotel 1741 Papermill Road, Wyomissing, PA 19610. **Telephone:** (610) 376-3811.

RICHMOND FLYING SQUIRRELS

Office Address: 3001 N Boulevard, Richmond, VA 23230.
Telephone: (804) 359-3866. **Fax:** (804) 359-1373.
E-Mail address: info@squirrelsbaseball.com. **Website:** www.squirrelsbaseball.com.
Affiliation (first year): San Francisco Giants (2009). **Years in League:** 2009-

OWNERSHIP, MANAGEMENT

Operated By: Navigators Baseball LP.
President/Managing Partner: Lou DiBella.
CEM: Chuck Domino. **Vice President/COO:** Todd "Parney" Parnell.
General Manager: Bill Papierniak. **Assistant GM:** Tom Denlinger. **Controller:** Faith Casey. **Assistant Controller:** Gail Olberg. **Director, Corporate Sales:** Ben Terry. **Corporate Sales Executives:** Mike Murphy, Jerrine Lee. **Director, Tickets:** Brendon Porter. **Box Office Manager:** Patrick Flower. **Ticket/Group Sales Specialist:** Chris Joyner. **Director, Broadcasting:** Jon Laaser. **Director, Media Relations:** Anthony Oppermann. **Director, Community Relations/Promotions:** Christina Shisler. **Coordinator, In-Game Entertainment:** Kellye Semonich. **Director, Group Sales:** Randy Atkinson. **Group Sales Executives:** Megan Angstadt, Renée Blessington, Amanda Schuman. **Suites/Group Sales Executive:** Elyse Holben. **Executive Director, Food/Beverage/Merchandise:** Ben Rothrock. **Assistant Directors, Food/Beverage:** Eric Freeman, Clint Chamberlain. **Director, Field Operations:** Steve Ruckman. **Director, Stadium Operations:** Tom White.

FIELD STAFF

Manager: Dave Machemer. **Coach:** Ken Joyce. **Pitching Coach:** Ross Grimsley.

GAME INFORMATION

Radio Announcers: Jon Laaser, Anthony Oppermann. **No. of Games Broadcast:** Home-71 Road-71. **Flagship Station:** Sports Radio 910 WRNL-AM. **PA Announcer:** Jimmy Barrett. **Official Scorer:** Scott Day. **Stadium Name:** The Diamond. **Capacity:** 9,560.

Location: Right off I-64 at the Boulevard exit. **Standard Game Times:** 7:05 pm, Sat 6:35, Sun 5:05. **Ticket Price Range:** $7-11.

Visiting Club Hotel: Unavailable.

TRENTON THUNDER

Office Address: One Thunder Road, Trenton, NJ 08611.
Telephone: (609) 394-3300. **Fax:** (609) 394-9666.
E-Mail address: fun@trentonthunder.com. **Website:** www.trentonthunder.com.
Affiliation (first year): New York Yankees (2003). **Years in League:** 1994-

OWNERSHIP, MANAGEMENT

Operated By: Garden State Baseball, LLP.
General Manager/COO: Will Smith.
Senior Vice President, Corporate Sales/Sponsorships: Eric Lipsman. **Director, Ticket Operations:** Matt Pentima. **Director, Public Relations:** Bill Cook. **Director, Merchandising:** Joe Pappalardo. **VP, Operations:** Ryan Crammer. **Director, Food/Beverage:** Kevin O'Byrne. **Assistant Director, Food/Beverage:** Chris Champion. **Director, Community Relations:** Patience Purdy. **VP, Business Development:** CJ Johnson. **Office Manager:** Susanna Hall. **Production Manager:** Greg Lavin. **Manager, Baseball Operations/Accounting:** Jeff Hurley. **Director, Broadcasting:** Jay Burnham. **Director, Corporate Partnerships/Business Development:** Patrick McMaster. **Stadium Operations Manager:** Steve Brokowsky. **Ticket Sales Manager:** Bobby Picardo. **Group Sales Account Executives:** TJ Jahn, Nate Schneider.
Business Development Executive: Jennifer Murphy. **Ticket Sales Account Executives:** Caitlin Reardon, Jeremy Sanders. **Group Sales Account Representative:** Chris Kiernan. **Building Superintendent:** Scott Ribsam. **Home Clubhouse Manager:** Tom Kackley. **Visiting Clubhouse Manager:** Jim Billington. **Head Groundskeeper:** Ryan Hills.

FIELD STAFF

Manager: Tony Franklin. **Hitting Coach:** Tom Slater. **Pitching Coach:** Tommy Phelps. **Coach:** Luis Dorante. **Trainer:** Scott DiFrancesco. **Strength/Conditioning Coach:** Kaz Manabe.

GAME INFORMATION

Radio Announcer: Jay Burnham. **No. of Games Broadcast:** Home-71 Road 71. **Flagship Station:** WTSR 91.3 FM.
Official Scorers: Jay Dunn, Greg Zak.
Stadium Name: Samuel L Plumeri Sr Field at Mercer County Waterfront Park.
Location: From I-95, take Route 1 North to Route 29 South, stadium entrance just before tunnel; From NJ Turnpike, take Exit 7A and follow I-195 West, Road will become Rte 29, Follow through tunnel and ballpark is on left.
Standard Game Times: 7:05 pm, Sun 1:05.
Ticket Price Range: $9-13. **Visiting Club Hotel:** Trenton Marriott at Lafayette Yard. **Telephone:** (609) 421-4000.

SOUTHERN LEAGUE

Mailing Address: 2551 Roswell Rd, Suite 330, Marietta, GA 30062.
Telephone: (770) 321-0400. **Fax:** (770) 321-0037.
E-Mail Address: loriwebb@southernleague.com.
Website: www.southernleague.com. **Years League Active:** 1964-.

Interim President: Steve DeSalvo.
Directors: Bruce Baldwin (Pensacola), Peter Bragan, Jr (Jacksonville), Steve DeSalvo (Mississippi), Tom Dickson (Montgomery), Doug Kirchhofer (Tennessee), Rich Mozingo(Chattanooga), Jonathan Nelson (Birmingham), Miles Prentice (Huntsville), Bill Shanahan (Mobile), Reese Smith (Jackson).
VP, Operations: Lori Webb. **Media Relations Director:** Peter Webb.
Division Structure: North: Birmingham, Chattanooga, Huntsville, Jackson, Tennessee. **South:** Jacksonville, Mississippi, Mobile, Montgomery, Pensacola.
Regular Season: 140 games (split schedule). **2012 Opening Date:** April 5. **Closing Date:** Sept 3.
All-Star Game: June 19, Tennessee Smokies
Playoff Format: First-half division winners meet second-half division winners in best-of-five series. Winners meet in best-of-five series for league championship.
Roster Limit: 24. **Player Eligibility Rule:** No restrictions.
Brand of Baseball: Rawlings.
Umpires: Unavailable

STADIUM INFORMATION

Club	Stadium	Opened	Dimensions LF	CF	RF	Capacity	2011 Att.
Birmingham	Regions Park	1988	340	405	340	10,800	261,623
Chattanooga	AT&T Field	2000	325	400	330	6,362	224,974
Huntsville	Joe W. Davis Municipal Stadium	1985	345	405	330	10,488	93,340
Jackson	Pringles Park	1998	310	395	320	6,000	106,689
Jacksonville	Baseball Grounds of Jacksonville	2003	321	420	317	11,000	309,310
Mississippi	Trustmark Park	2005	335	402	332	7,416	191,653
Mobile	Hank Aaron Stadium	1997	325	400	310	6,000	210,956
Montgomery	Montgomery Riverwalk Stadium	2004	314	380	332	7,000	256,403
*Pensacola	Maritime Park	2012	325	400	335	Unavailable	N/A
Tennessee	Smokies Park	2000	330	400	330	6,000	265,341

*Expansion team replaces Carolina

BIRMINGHAM BARONS

Office Address: 100 Ben Chapman Dr, Hoover, AL 35244.
Mailing Address: PO Box 360007, Birmingham, AL 35236.
Telephone: (205) 988-3200. **Fax:** (205) 988-9698.
E-Mail Address: barons@barons.com. **Website:** www.barons.com.
Affiliation (first year): Chicago White Sox (1986). **Years in League:** 1964-65, 1967-75, 1981-

OWNERSHIP, MANAGEMENT

Principal Owners: Don Logan, Jeff Logan, Stan Logan.
General Manager: Jonathan Nelson. **Director, Stadium Operations:** James Young. **Director, Broadcasting:** Curt Bloom. **Director, Media Relations:** Nick Dobreff. **Director, Sales:** John Cook. **Director, Tickets:** Brandon Harms. **Director, Production:** Zane Davitz. **Manager, Operations:** David Madison. **Assistant, Sales/Marketing:** David Krakower. **Corporate Event Planner:** Charlie Santiago. **General Manager, Grand Slam Catering:** Eric Crook. **Director, Concessions:** Taylor Youngson. **Office Manager:** Jennifer Dillard. **Accountant:** Jo Ann Bragan. **Head Groundskeeper:** Daniel Ruggiero.

FIELD STAFF

Manager: Bobby Magallanes. **Hitting Coach:** Brandon Moore. **Pitching Coach:** Bobby Thigpen. **Trainer:** Josh Fallin. **Strength/Conditioning:** Raymond Smith.

GAME INFORMATION

Radio Announcer: Curt Bloom. **No of Games Broadcast:** Home-70 Road-70. **Flagship Station:** Unavailable.
PA Announcers: Eddie Layne, Derek Scudder. **Official Scorer:** Unavailable. **Stadium Name:** Regions Park. **Location:** I-459 to Highway 150 (exit 10) in Hoover. **Standard Game Times:** 7:05 pm, Sat 6:30, Sun 2:05 (first half), 5:05 (second half). **Ticket Price Range:** $7-12.
Visiting Club Hotel: Hoover Microtel Inn & Suites, 500 Jackson Dr, Birmingham, AL 35244. **Telephone:** (205) 444-3033.

CHATTANOOGA LOOKOUTS

Office Address: 201 Power Alley, Chattanooga, TN 37402.
Mailing Address: PO Box 11002, Chattanooga, TN 37401.
Telephone: (423) 267-2208. **Fax:** (423) 267-4258.
E-Mail Address: lookouts@lookouts.com. **Website:** www.lookouts.com.
Affiliation (first year): Los Angeles Dodgers (2009). **Years in League:** 1964-65, 1976-

OWNERSHIP, MANAGEMENT

Operated By: Scenic City Baseball LLC.
Principal Owners: Frank Burke, Charles Eshbach.
President/General Manager: Rich Mozingo. **Vice President/Assistant GM:** John Maedel. **Co-Directors, Group Sales:** John Quirk, Gavin Cox. **Director, Merchandising/Marketing:** Chrysta Jorgensen. **Director, Media Relations:** Peter Intza. **Director, Concessions:** Steve Sullivan. **Director, Broadcasting:** Larry Ward. **Head Groundskeeper:** Joe Fitzgerald. **Director, Stadium Operations/Assistant Director, Broadcasting:** Will Poindexter. **Director, Business Administration/Accounting:** Amy Leffew. **Stadium Operations Associate:** Josh Weeks. **Concessions Associate:** Andrew Zito. **Group Sales Associate:** Morgan Billups. **Marketing Associate:** James Lee. **Ticketing Associate:** Bryan Soulard.

FIELD STAFF

Manager: Carlos Subero. **Coach:** Franklin Stubbs. **Pitching Coach:** Chuck Crim.

GAME INFORMATION

Radio Announcers: Larry Ward, Will Poindexter. **No. of Games Broadcast:** Home-70 Road-70. **Flagship Station:** 106.9 FM (WPLZ-HD2).
PA Announcer: John Maedel. **Official Scorers:** Wirt Gammon, Andy Paul.
Stadium Name: AT&T Field. **Location:** From I-24, take US 27 North to exit 1C (4th Street), first left onto Chestnut Street, left onto Third Street. **Ticket Price Range:** $5-9.
Visiting Club Hotel: Holiday Inn, 2232 Center Street, Chattanooga, TN 37421. **Telephone:** (423) 485-1185.

HUNTSVILLE STARS

Office Address: 3125 Leeman Ferry Rd, Huntsville, AL 35801.
Telephone: (256) 882-2562. **Fax:** (256) 880-0801.
E-Mail Address: info@huntsvillestars.com. **Website:** www.huntsvillestars.com.
Affiliation (first year): Milwaukee Brewers (1999). **Years in League:** 1985-

OWNERSHIP, MANAGEMENT

Operated By: Huntsville Stars LLC.
President: Miles Prentice.
General Manager: Buck Rogers. **Assistant GM:** Babs Rogers. **Director, Media Relations:** Jill Cacic. **Director, Corporate Sales:** Ryan Edwards. **Manager, Tickets:** Sydney Marcelain. **Office Manager:** Earl Grilliot. **Head Groundskeeper:** Kelly Rensel.

FIELD STAFF

Manager: Darnell Coles. **Coach:** Dwayne Hosey. **Pitching Coach:** John Curtis. **Athletic Trainer:** Aaron Hoback. **Strength/Conditioning Coach:** Tim Giffords.

GAME INFORMATION

PA Announcer: Matt Mitchell. **Official Scorer:** Don Rizzardi.
Stadium Name: Joe W Davis Municipal Stadium. **Location:** I-65 to I-565 East, south on Memorial Parkway to Drake Avenue exit, right on Don Mincher Drive. **Ticket Price Range:** $5-$20. **Visiting Club Hotel:** Holiday Inn, 401 Williams Avenue, Huntsville, AL, 35801. **Telephone:** 256-533-1400.

JACKSON GENERALS

Office Address: 4 Fun Place, Jackson, TN 38305.
Telephone: (731) 988-5299. **Fax:** (731) 988-5246.
E-Mail Address: fun@diamondjaxx.com. **Website:** www.diamondjaxx.com.
Affiliation (third year): Seattle Mariners (2007). **Years in League:** 1998-

OWNERSHIP, MANAGEMENT

Operated by: Jackson Baseball Club LP.
Chairman: David Freeman. **President:** Reese Smith.
General Manager: Jason Compton. **Vice President, Sales/Marketing:** Mike Peasley. **Director, Security/Stadium Operations:** Robert Jones. **Manager, Media Relations/Broadcasting:** Chris Harris. **Manager, Tickets/Merchandise:** Hunter Ellington. **Turf Manager:** Tyler Brewer. **Manager, Catering/Concessions:** Kurt Brown. **Manager, Home Clubhouse:** CJ Fedewa. **Manager, Visiting Clubhouse:** Dustin Smith. **Sales Executives:** Xan Stewart, Nick Hall. **Sales

Executive/Promotions: Justin Bernhard. **Administrative Assistant:** Laura Hassall. **Community Relations/Ticketing Assistant:** Hannah Betler. **Media Relations Assistant:** Bradley Field.

FIELD STAFF

Manager: Jim Pankovits. **Coach:** Cory Snyder. **Pitching Coach:** Lance Painter. **Trainer:** Matt Toth .

GAME INFORMATION

Radio Announcer: Chris Harris. **No. of Games Broadcast:** Home-70, Away-70. **Flagship Station:** WNWS 101.5 FM. **PA Announcer:** Dan Reeves. **Official Scorer:** Mike Henson. **Stadium Name:** Pringles Park. **Location:** From I-40, take exit 85 South on FE Wright Drive, left onto Ridgecrest Road. **Standard Game Times:** 7:05 pm, Sat 6:05, Sun 2:05 or 6:05. **Ticket Price Range:** $6-10. **Visiting Club Hotel:** Doubletree Hotel, 1770 Hwy 45 Bypass, Jackson, TN 38305. **Telephone:** (731) 664-6900.

JACKSONVILLE SUNS

Office Address: 301 A Philip Randolph Blvd, Jacksonville, FL 32202.
Mailing Address: PO Box 4756, Jacksonville, FL 32201.
Telephone: (904) 358-2846. **Fax:** (904) 358-2845.
E-Mail Address: info@jaxsuns.com. **Website:** www.jaxsuns.com.
Affiliation (first year): Miami Marlins (2009). **Years In League:** 1970-Present

OWNERSHIP, MANAGEMENT

Operated by: Baseball Jax Inc.
Principal Owner/Chairman of the Board: Peter Bragan. **Senior Madame Chairman:** Mary Frances Bragan.
President: Peter Bragan Jr. **General Manager:** Chris Peters. **Director, Field Operations:** Ed Attalla. **Director, Merchandise:** Lindsey Weeks. **Assistant GM:** Casey Nichols. **Director, Business Administration:** Barbara O'Berry. **Director, Video Services:** David Scheldorf. **Director, Group Sales:** January Putt Squyres. **Manager, Group Sales:** Trevor Johnson. **Director, Ticket Operations:** Amy Delettre. **Director, Stadium Operations:** JD Metrie. **Director, Community Relations:** Sarah Foster. **Manager, Media Relations/Website:** Wesley Mitchell. **Manager, Box Office:** Theresa Viets. **General Manager, Ballpark Foods:** Jamie Davis. **Assistant GM, Ballpark Foods/Finance:** Mitch Buska. **Manager, Stadium Operations:** Jarrod Simmons. **Account Executives:** Chris Clark, Coyle Self.

FIELD STAFF

Manager: Andy Barkett. **Hitting Coach:** Kevin Randel. **Pitching Coach:** John Duffy. **Trainer:** Julio Hernandez.

GAME INFORMATION

Radio Announcer: Unavailable. **No. of Games Broadcast:** Home-70, Away-70. **Flagship Station:** WFXJ 930-AM. **PA Announcer:** Wesley Mitchell. **Official Scorer:** Jason Eliopulos. **Datacaster:** Brian Delettre. **Press Box Assistant:** Tom Stallings. **Stadium Name:** The Baseball Grounds of Jacksonville. **Location:** I-95 South to Martin Luther King Parkway exit, follow Gator Bowl Blvd around Alltel Stadium; I-95 North to Exit 347 (Emerson Street), go right to Hart Bridge Expressway, take Sports Complex exit, left at light to stop sign, take left and follow around Alltel Stadium; From Mathews Bridge, take A Philip Randolph exit, right on A Philip Randolph, straight to stadium. **Standard Game Times:** 7:05 pm, Wed 1:05/7:05, Thur 7:35, Sat 6:05, Sun 3:05/6:05. **Ticket Price Range:** $7.50-22.50. **Visiting Club Hotel:** Hyatt Regency Jacksonville Riverfront, 225 Coastline Dr, Jacksonville, FL 32202. **Telephone:** (904) 633-9095.

MISSISSIPPI BRAVES

Office Address: Trustmark Park, 1 Braves Way, Pearl, MS 39208.
Mailing Address: PO Box 97389, Pearl, MS 39288.
Telephone: (601) 932-8788. **Fax:** (601) 936-3567.
E-Mail Address: mississippi.braves@braves.com. **Website:** www.mississippibraves.com.
Affiliation (first year): Atlanta Braves (2005). **Years in League:** 2005-

OWNERSHIP, MANAGEMENT

Operated By: Atlanta National League Baseball Club Inc.
General Manager: Steve DeSalvo. **Assistant GM:** Jim Bishop. **Ticket Manager:** Nick Anderson. **Merchandise Manager:** Sarah Banta. **Manager, Public Relations/Advertising/Design:** Brian Byrd. **Sales Associate:** Miranda Black, Jacob Newton, Jeff Van, Jamie Myrick, Sean Guillotte. **Head Chef:** Tina Funches. **Suites/Catering Manager:** Debbie Herrington. **Stadium Operations Manager:** Matt McCoy. **Promotions/Entertainment Manager:** Brian Prochilo. **Concessions Manager:** Felicia Thompson. **Office Administrator:** Christy Shaw. **Restaurant Manager:** Gene Slaughter. **Commissary Manager:** James Davis. **Director, Field/Facility Operations:** Matt Taylor. **Receptionist:** Shelia Tolleson.

FIELD STAFF

Manager: Aaron Holbert. **Coach:** Garey Ingram. **Pitching Coach:** Mike Alvarez. **Trainer:** Ricky Alcantara.

GAME INFORMATION

Radio Announcer: Kyle Tate. **No. of Games Broadcast:** Home-70 Road-70. **Flagship Station:** WYAB 103.9 FM. **PA Announcer:** Derrel Palmer. **Official Scorer:** Mark Beason. **Stadium Name:** Trustmark Park. **Location:** I-20 to exit

48/Pearl (Pearson Road). **Ticket Price Range:** $6-$20.
Visiting Club Hotel: Holiday Inn Trustmark Park, 110 Bass Pro Drive, Pearl, MS 39208. **Telephone:** (601) 939-5238.

MOBILE BAYBEARS

Office Address: Hank Aaron Stadium, 755 Bolling Bros Blvd, Mobile, AL 36606.
Telephone: (251) 479-2327. **Fax:** (251) 476-1147.
E-Mail Address: baybears@mobilebaybears.com. **Website:** www.mobilebaybears.com
Affiliation (first year): Arizona Diamondbacks (2007). **Years in League:** 1966, 1970, 1997-

OWNERSHIP, MANAGEMENT
Operated by: HWS Baseball Group.
Principal Owner: Mike Savit.
President/COO: Bill Shanahan. **General Sales Manager:** Jeff Long. **Assistant General Manager, Finance:** Betty Adams. **Assistant GM, Promotions/Corporate Sales:** Mike Callahan. **Assistant GM, Stadium Operations:** John Hilliard. **Director, Community Relations/Director, Audio/Visual:** Ari Rosenbaum. **Director, Media Relations (team related):** Wayne Randazzo. **Director, Youth Programs/Media Relations (non-team related):** JR Wittner. **Sales Manager:** John Golz. **Concessions Manager:** Tara Crawford. **Box Office Manager:** Adam Mettler. **Head Groundskeeper:** Caleb Adams. **Clubhouse Manager:** Hank Copley. **Stadium Operations Assistant:** Wade Vadakin. **Internet Liaison/Team Chaplain:** Lorin Barr.

FIELD STAFF
Manager: Turner Ward. **Hitting Coach:** Jay Bell. **Pitching Coach:** Dan Carlson. **Trainer:** Joe Metz.

GAME INFORMATION
Radio Announcer: Wayne Randazzo. **No. of Games Broadcast:** Home-70, Away-70.
Flagship Station: 107.3 FMhd2, www.baybearsradio.com.
PA Announcer: Mike Callahan. **Official Scorers:** Unavailable.
Stadium Name: Hank Aaron Stadium. **Location:** I-65 to exit 1 (Government Blvd East), right at Satchel Paige Drive, right at Bolling Bros Blvd.
Standard Game Times: 7:05 pm, Sun 2:05. **Ticket Price Range:** $5-15.
Visiting Club Hotel: Riverview Plaza, 64 S Water St, Mobile, AL 36602. **Telephone:** (251) 438-4000.

MONTGOMERY BISCUITS

Office Address: 200 Coosa St, Montgomery, AL 36104.
Telephone: (334) 323-2255. **Fax:** (334) 323-2225.
E-Mail address: info@biscuitsbaseball.com. **Website:** www.biscuitsbaseball.com.
Affiliation (first year): Tampa Bay Rays (2004). **Years in League:** 1965-1980, 2004-

OWNERSHIP, MANAGEMENT
Operated By: Montgomery Professional Baseball LLC.
Principal Owners: Tom Dickson, Sherrie Myers.
President: Greg Rauch. **General Manager:** Marla Terranova Vickers. **Sales Director:** Scott Trible. **Corporate Account Executive:** Ross Winkler. **Director, Marketing:** Jordan Mandelkorn. **Media Relations:** Joe Davis. **Marketing Assistant:** Jordan Mandelkorn. **Box Office Manager:** Devon Hasting. **Sponsorship Service Representatives:** Jonathan Vega, Lauren Baggett. **Director, Retail Operations:** Monte Meyers. **Director, Stadium Operations:** Steve Blackwell. **Head Groundskeeper:** Drew Ellis. **Catering Managers:** Mike Smith, Marissa Gordon. **Concessions Managers:** Andrew Minnich, Geoff Siddons. **Director, Business Operations:** Linda Fast. **Assistant Business Manager:** Dewanna Croy. **Administrative Assistant:** Bill Sisk. **Season Ticket Concierge:** Bob Rabon. **Inside Sales Representative:** Alicia Ingram.

FIELD STAFF
Manager: Billy Gardner Jr. **Coach:** Ozzie Timmons. **Pitching Coach:** RC Lichtenstein.

GAME INFORMATION
Radio Announcer: Joe Davis. **No of Games Broadcast:** Home-70 Road-70. **Flagship Station:** WLWI 1440-AM. **PA Announcer:** Rick Hendrick. **Official Scorer:** Kyle Kreutzer. **Stadium Name:** Montgomery Riverwalk Stadium.
Location: I-65 to exit 172, east on Herron Street, left on Coosa Street.
Ticket Price Range: $8-12. **Visiting Club Hotel:** Candlewood Suites.

PENSACOLA BLUE WAHOOS

Office Address: 41 N Jefferson St, Pensacola, FL 32502.
Mailing Address: PO 12587, Pensacola, FL 32591.
Telephone: (850) 934-8444. **Fax:** (850) 791-6256.
E-Mail Address: info@bluewahoos.com. **Website:** www.bluewahoos.com.
Affiliation (first year): Cincinnati Reds (2012). **Years in League:** 2012-Present

OWNERSHIP, MANAGEMENT

Operated by: Northwest Florida Professional Baseball LLC.
Principal Owner: Quint and Rishy Studer.
President: Bruce Baldwin. **Executive Vice President:** Jonathan Griffith. **Receptionist:** Linda Aguado. **VP, Sales:** Van Leventhal. **VP, Community Relations:** Julia Borshak. **Stadium Operations Manager:** Rylan Brody. **Creative Services Manager:** Andrew Demsky. **Director, Sports Turf Management:** Ray Sayre. **Special Events Manager:** Shelley Yates. **Sales Manager:** Travis Painter. **Media Relations Coordinator/Broadcaster:** Tommy Thrall. **Director, Food/Beverage:** Mark Micallef.

FIELD STAFF

Manager: Jim Riggleman. **Coach:** Tony Jaramillo. **Pitching Coach:** Tom Brown. **Trainer:** Charles Leddon. **Strength Coach:** Jon Berdanier

GAME INFORMATION

Radio Announcers: Tommy Thrall. **No. of Games Broadcast:** Home-70, Away-70. **Flagship Stations:** WBSR ESPN Radio Pensacola 1450 AM & 101.1 FM. **PA Announcer:** Unavailable. **Official Scorer:** Unavailable.
Stadium Name: Blue Wahoos Ballpark. **Standard Game Times:** 7 pm, Sat 6:30, Sun 2. **Ticket Price Range:** $15-$5.
Visiting Club Hotel: Hilton Garden Inn, Hampton Inn, Homewood Suites by Hilton.

TENNESSEE SMOKIES

Office Address: 3540 Line Drive, Kodak, TN 37764.
Telephone: (865) 286-2300. **Fax:** (865) 523-9913.
E-Mail Address: info@smokiesbaseball.com. **Website:** www.smokiesbaseball.com.
Affiliation (first year): Chicago Cubs (2007). **Years in League:** 1964-67, 1972-

OWNERSHIP, MANAGEMENT

Operated By: SPBC, LLC.
President: Doug Kirchhofer.
General Manager: Brian Cox. **Assistant GM:** Jeff Shoaf. **Director, Stadium Operations:** Bryan Webster. **Director, Community Relations:** Lauren Chesney. **Director, Food/Beverage:** Tony DaSilveira. **Director, Media Relations:** Adam Kline. **Director, Entertainment/Client Services:** Ryan Cox. **Director, Video Production/Graphic Design:** Tim Avery. **Director, Ticket/Retail Operations:** Robby Scheuermann. **Director, Field Operations:** Stuart Morris. **Director, Corporate Ticket Development:** Matt Strutner. **Senior Corporate Sales Executive:** Ken Franz. **Senior Corporate Sales Executive:** Dan Blue. **Group Sales Manager:** Rey Regenstreif-Harms. **Group Sales Representatives:** Baylor Love, Jeff Martin, Casey McDannald, Will Thompson. **Business Manager:** Suzanne French. **Administrative Assistant:** Tolena Trout.

FIELD STAFF

Manager: Buddy Bailey. **Hitting Coach:** Mariano Duncan. **Pitching Coach:** Jeff Fassero. **Trainer:** AJ Larson.

GAME INFORMATION

Radio Announcer: Mick Gillispie. **No. of Games Broadcast:** Home-70 Road-70. **Flagship Station:** WNML 99.1-FM/990-AM. **PA Announcer:** Unavailable. **Official Scorers:** Jack Tate, Jared Smith, Bernie Reimer.
Stadium Name: Smokies Park. **Location:** I-40 to exit 407, Highway 66 North. **Standard Game Times:** 7:15 pm, Sat 6:15, Sun 2/5. **Ticket Price Range:** $5-10.
Visiting Club Hotel: Days Inn-Exit 407, 3402 Winfield Dunn Pkwy, Kodak, TN 37764. **Telephone:** (865) 933-4500.

TEXAS LEAGUE

Mailing Address: 2442 Facet Oak, San Antonio, TX 78232.
Telephone: (210) 545-5297. **Fax:** (210) 545-5298.
E-Mail Address: texasleague@sbcglobal.net. **Website:** www.texas-league.com.
Years League Active: 1888-1890, 1892, 1895-1899, 1902-1942, 1946-.
President/Treasurer: Tom Kayser.
Vice Presidents: Mike Melega, Bill Valentine. **Corporate Secretary:** Eric Edelstein. **Assistant to the President:** Rich Weimert.
Directors: Jon Dandes (Northwest Arkansas), Ken Schrom (Corpus Christi), William DeWitt III (Springfield), Dale Hubbard (Tulsa), Scott Sonju (Frisco), Miles Prentice (Midland), Russ Meeks (Arkansas), Burl Yarbrough (San Antonio).
Division Structure: North—Arkansas, Northwest Arkansas, Springfield, Tulsa. South—Corpus Christi, Frisco, Midland, San Antonio.
Regular Season: 140 games (split schedule). **2012 Opening Date:** April 5. **Closing Date:** Sept 3. **All-Star Game:** June 28 at Tulsa.
Playoff Format: First-half division winners play second-half division winners in best-of-five series. Winners meet in best-of-five series for league championship.
Roster Limit: 24. **Player Eligibility Rule:** No restrictions.
Brand of Baseball: Rawlings.

Tom Kayser

Umpires: Nick Bailey (Big Spring, TX), Matt Benham (Spokane, WA), Ryan Blakney (Wenatchee, WA), Seth Buckminster (Fort Worth, TX), Ian Fazio (Tavenier, FL), Brian Hertzog (Lake Stevens, WA), Brandon Misun (Oklahoma City, OK), Gabe Morales (Livermore, CA), Alex Ortiz (Los Angeles, CA), Justin Sassman (Lewisville, TX), Adam Schwarz (Riverside, CA), Greg Stanzak (Surprise, AZ),

STADIUM INFORMATION

| Club | Stadium | Opened | Dimensions | | | Capacity | 2011 Att. |
			LF	CF	RF		
Arkansas	Dickey-Stephens Park	2007	332	413	330	5,842	300,594
Corpus Christi	Whataburger Field	2005	325	400	315	5,362	395,128
Frisco	Dr Pepper Ballpark	2003	335	409	335	10,216	509,331
Midland	Citibank Ballpark	2002	330	410	322	4,669	308,810
NW Arkansas	Arvest Ballpark	2008	325	400	325	6,500	310,613
San Antonio	Nelson Wolff Municipal Stadium	1994	310	402	340	6,200	294,176
Springfield	John Q. Hammons Field	2003	315	400	330	6,750	337,166
Tulsa	ONEOK Field	2010	330	400	307	7,833	366,291

ARKANSAS TRAVELERS

Office Address: Dickey-Stephens Park, 400 West Broadway, North Little Rock, AR 72114.
Mailing Address: PO Box 55066, Little Rock, AR 72215.
Telephone: (501) 664-1555. **Fax:** (501) 664-1834.
E-Mail address: travs@travs.com. **Website:** www.travs.com.
Affiliation (first year): Los Angeles Angels (2001). **Years in League:** 1966-

OWNERSHIP, MANAGEMENT

Ownership: Arkansas Travelers Baseball Club, Inc.
President: Russ Meeks.
General Manager: Pete Laven. **Assistant GM, Sales:** Paul Allen. **Assistant GM, Tickets:** David Kay. **Director, Broadcasting/Media Relations:** Phil Elson. **Director, Finance:** Ann McClure. **Director, In-Game Entertainment:** Tommy Adam. **Director, Merchandise:** Debra Wingfield. **Park Superintendent:** Greg Johnston. **Assistant Park Superintendent:** Reggie Temple. **Account Executive/Suite Manager:** Brian Lyter. **Director, Office Manager:** Jared Schein. **Account Executive:** Shane Johnson.

FIELD STAFF

Manager: Mike Micucci. **Coach:** Francisco Matos. **Pitching Coach:** Trevor Wilson. **Trainer:** Mike Metcalfe.

GAME INFORMATION

Radio Announcers: Phil Elson, RJ Hawk. **No. of Games Broadcast:** Home-70 Road-70. **Flagship Station:** KARN 920 AM.
PA Announcer: Russ McKinney. **Official Scorers:** Tim Cooper, Mike Garrity, Todd Traub.
Stadium Name: Dickey-Stephens Park. **Location:** I-30 to Broadway exit, proceed west to ballpark, located at Broadway Avenue and the Broadway Bridge. **Standard Game Time:** 7:10 pm Ticket Price Range: $3-12.
Visiting Club Hotel: Hilton Little Rock, 925 S University Avenue, Little Rock, AR 72204. **Telephone:** (501) 664-5020. **Fax:** (501) 614-3803.

CORPUS CHRISTI HOOKS

Office Address: 734 East Port Ave, Corpus Christi, TX 78401.
Telephone: (361) 561-4665. **Fax:** (361) 561-4666.
E-Mail Address: info@cchooks.com. **Website:** www.cchooks.com.
Affiliation (first year): Houston Astros (2005). **Years in League:** 1958-59, 2005-

OWNERSHIP, MANAGEMENT

Operated By: Ryan-Sanders Baseball.
Principal Owners: Eddie Maloney, Reese Ryan, Reid Ryan, Nolan Ryan, Brad Sanders, Bret Sanders, Don Sanders. **CEO:** Reid Ryan. **CFO:** Reese Ryan. **Executive Vice President:** JJ Gottsch.
President: Ken Schrom. **VP/General Manager:** Michael Wood. **VP, Sales:** Adam Nuse. **Director, Sponsor Services:** Elisa Macias. **Director, Retail:** Brooke Milam. **Controller:** Christy Lockard. **Director, Communications:** Matt Rogers. **Director, Broadcasting:** Matt Hicks. **Director, Stadium Operations:** Tina Athans. **Director, Group Sales:** Andy Steavens. **Director, Ballpark Entertainment:** Steve Richards. **Director, Ticket Services:** Bryan Mayhood. **Account Executives:** Jeff Mackor, Justin Sommer, Craig Wendel. **Field Superintendent:** Izzy Hinojosa. **Assistant Groundskeeper:** Josh Brewer.

Field Staff

Manager: Keith Bodie. **Hitting Coach:** Joel Chimelis. **Pitching Coach:** Gary Ruby. **Athletic Trainer:** Eric Montague.

GAME INFORMATION

Radio Announcers: Matt Hicks, Michael Coffin, Gene Kasprzyk. **No. of Games Broadcast:** Home-70 Road-70. **Flagship Station:** KKTX-AM 1360. **PA Announcer:** Lon Gonzalez. **Stadium Name:** Whataburger Field. **Location:** I-37 to end of interstate, left at Chaparral, left at Hirsh Ave. **Ticket Price Range:** $5-12.
Visiting Club Hotel: Omni Hotel, 900 N Shoreline Dr, Corpus Christi, TX 78401. **Telephone:** (361) 886-3553.

FRISCO ROUGHRIDERS

Office Address: 7300 RoughRiders Trail, Frisco, TX 75034.
Telephone: (972) 731-9200. **Fax:** (972) 731-5355.
E-Mail Address: info@ridersbaseball.com. **Website:** www.ridersbaseball.com.
Affiliation (first year): Texas Rangers (2003). **Years in League:** 2003-

OWNERSHIP, MANAGEMENT

Operated by: Mandalay Baseball Properties.
President/General Manager: Scott Sonju. **Senior Vice President:** Billy Widner. **VP, Finance/HR:** Dustin Alban. **VP, Partnerships/Communications:** Scott Burchett. **Director, Corporate Partnerships:** Steven Nelson. **Manager, Corporate Partnerships:** Mark Playko. **Manager, Partner/Event Services:** Kristin Russell. **Manager, Partner Services:** Matt Ratliff. **Partner Services Coordinator:** David Kosydar. **Director, Community Development:** Michael Davidow. **Director, Ticket Sales:** Justin Ramquist. **Director, Ticket Operations:** Mac Amin. **Manager, Ticket Operations:** Jason Brayman. **Manager, Marketing/Special Events:** Gabrielle Ganz. **Senior Corporate Marketing Manager:** Adam Krouse. **Director, Game Entertainment:** Gabriel Wilhelm. **VP, Operations:** Michael Poole. **Director, Operations:** Scott Arnold. **Directors, Maintenance:** Alfonso Bailon, Gustavo Bailon. **Head Groundskeeper:** David Bicknell.

FIELD STAFF

Manager: Steve Buechele. **Coach:** Brant Brown. **Pitching Coach:** Jeff Andrews. **Trainer:** Carlos Olivas. **Strength/ Conditioning:** Eric McMahon.

GAME INFORMATION

Broadcaster: Unavailable. **No. of Games Broadcast:** Home-70, Away-70. **Flagship Station:** 1630 KKGM.
PA Announcer: John Clemens. **Official Scorer:** Larry Bump. **Stadium Name:** Dr Pepper Ballpark. **Location:** Dallas North Tollway to State Highway 121. **Standard Game Times:** 7 pm, Sun 6. **Visiting Club Hotel:** Unavailable.

MIDLAND ROCKHOUNDS

Office Address: 5514 Champions Dr, Midland, TX 79706.
Telephone: (432) 520-2255. **Fax:** (432) 520-8326.
Website: www.midlandrockhounds.org.
Affiliation (first year): Oakland Athletics (1999). **Years in League:** 1972-

OWNERSHIP, MANAGEMENT

Operated By: Midland Sports, Inc.
Principal Owners: Miles Prentice, Bob Richmond. **President:** Miles Prentice. **Executive Vice President:** Bob Richmond. **General Manager:** Monty Hoppel. **Assistant GM:** Jeff VonHolle. **Assistant GM, Marketing/Tickets:** Jamie Richardson. **Assistant GM, Merchandise/Facilities:** Ray Fieldhouse. **Assistant GM, Media Relations:** Greg Bergman. **Director, Broadcasting/Publications:** Bob Hards. **Director, Business Operations:** Eloisa Galvan. **Director, Ticket Operations:** Michael Richardson. **Executive Director, Group Events:** Jeremy Lukas. **Head Groundskeeper:** Eric

Campbell. **Office Manager:** Frances Warner.

Assistant Groundskeeper: Jason Smith. **Assistant Concessions Manager:** Reggie Donald. **Home Clubhouse Manager:** Joseph Slye. **Director, Stadium Operations/Promotions/Events:** Manabu Beppu. **Director, Public Relations:** Brian Smith. **Director, Video Board Operations/Sales Associate:** Sean Clement. **Promotions/Marketing Executive:** Kasey Decker. **Assistant Director, Operations/Sales Associate:** Chris Freeman.

FIELD STAFF

Manager: Steve Scarsone. **Coach:** Tim Garland. **Pitching Coach:** Don Schulze. **Trainer:** Justin Whitehouse.

GAME INFORMATION

Radio Announcer: Bob Hards. **No. of Games Broadcast:** Home-70, Away-70. **Flagship Station:** MyCountry 96.1-FM. **PA Announcer:** Wes Coles. **Official Scorer:** Steve Marcum.
Stadium Name: Citibank Ballpark. **Location:** From I-20, exit Loop 250 North to Highway 191 intersection. **Standard Game Times:** 7 pm, 6:30 (Mon-Wed), Sun 2 (April–May), 6 (June-Aug). **Ticket Price Range:** $6-10.
Visiting Club Hotel: Sleep Inn and Suites, 5612 Deauville Blvd, Midland, TX 79706. **Telephone:** (432) 694-4200.

NORTHWEST ARKANSAS
NATURALS

Office Address: 3000 S 56th Street, Springdale, AR 72762.
Telephone: (479) 927-4900. **Fax:** (479) 756-8088.
E-Mail Address: info@nwanaturals.com. **Website:** www.nwanaturals.com.
Affiliation (first year): Kansas City Royals (1995). **Years in League:** 1987-

OWNERSHIP, MANAGEMENT

Principal Owner: Rich Products Corp.
Chairman: Robert Rich Jr. **President, Rich Entertainment:** Melinda Rich.
President, Rich Baseball: Jon Dandes. **General Manager:** Eric Edelstein.
Assistant GM: Justin Cole. **Business Manager:** Morgan Helmer.
Marketing/PR Manager: Frank Novak. **Stadium Operations Director:** George Sisson. **Head Groundskeeper:** Monty Sowell. **Ticket Office Coordinator:** Shea Tedford. **Group Sales Manager:** Mark Zaiger. **Broadcaster/Baseball Operations Coordinator:** Steven Davis. **Sponsorship/Community Relations Coordinator:** Katie Hiegel. **Entertainment Coordinator:** Douglas Webb. **Senior Account Executives:** Dustin Dethlefs, Andrew Thaxton Account Executives: Brad Ziegler, Sam Haugen, Lexi Levang. **Head Groundskeeper:** Monty Sowell.
Assistant Groundskeeper: Justin Sherley. **Equipment Manager:** Danny Helmer

FIELD STAFF

Manager: Brian Poldberg. **Coach:** Terry Bradshaw. **Pitching Coach:** Larry Carter. **Trainer:** Unavailable.

GAME INFORMATION

Radio Announcers: Steven Davis. **No. of Games Broadcast:** Home-70, Away-70. **Flagship:** ESPN 92.1 The Ticket (KQSM-FM). **PA Announcer:** Bill Rogers. **Official Scorer:** Chris Ledeker.
Stadium Name: Arvest Ballpark. **Location:** I-540 to US 412 West (Sunset Ave); Left on 56th St. **Ticket Price Range:** $6-12. **Standard Game Times:** 7 pm; Sun 2 (April/May), 6 (May 27-Sept 2).
Visiting Club Hotel: Holiday Inn Springdale; 1500 S 48th St, Springdale, AR 72762. **Telephone:** (479) 751-8300.

SAN ANTONIO MISSIONS

Office/Mailing Address: 5757 Highway 90 West, San Antonio, TX 78227.
Telephone: (210) 675-7275. **Fax:** (210) 670-0001. **E-Mail Address:** sainfo@samissions.com. **Website:** www.samissions.com.
Affiliation (first year): San Diego Padres (2007).
Years In Texas League: 1888, 1892, 1895-99, 1907-42, 1946-64, 1968-

OWNERSHIP, MANAGEMENT

Operated by: Elmore Sports Group.
Principal Owner: David Elmore.
President: Burl Yarbrough. **General Manager:** Dave Gasaway.
Assistant GMs: Mickey Holt, Jeff Long, Bill Gerlt. **GM, Diamond Concessions:** Mike Lindal. **Controller:** Ivan Molina. **Director, Broadcasting:** Mike Saeger. **Office Manager:** Delia Rodriguez. **Box Office Manager:** Rob Gusick. **Director, Operations:** John Hernandez. **Director, Group Sales:** George Levandoski. **Director, Public Relations:** Jim White. **Field Superintendent:** Karsten Blackwelder. **Assistant Field Superintendent:** Dan Looney.

Field Staff

Manager: John Gibbons. **Coach:** Tom Tornicasa. **Pitching Coach:** Jimmy Jones. **Trainer:** Nathan Stewart.

Game Information

Radio Announcers: Roy Acuff, Mike Saeger. **No. of Games Broadcast:** Home-70, Away-70. **Flagship Station:** KKYX

680-AM. **PA Announcer:** Stan Kelly. **Official Scorer:** David Humphrey.
    Stadium Name: Nelson W Wolff Stadium. **Location:** From I-10, I-35 or I-37, take US Hwy 90 West to Callaghan Road exit. **Standard Game Times:** 7:05 pm, Sun 4:05/6:05.
    Visiting Club Hotel: Holiday Inn Northwest/Sea World. **Telephone:** (210) 520-2508.

SPRINGFIELD CARDINALS

    Office Address: 955 East Trafficway, Springfield, MO 65802.
    Telephone: (417) 863-0395. **Fax:** (417) 863-0388.
    E-Mail address: springfield@cardinals.com. **Website:** www.springfieldcardinals.com.
    Affiliation (first year): St. Louis Cardinals (2005). **Years in League:** 2005-

OWNERSHIP, MANAGEMENT

    Operated By: St. Louis Cardinals.
    Vice President/General Manager: Matt Gifford. **VP, Baseball/Business Operations:** Scott Smulczenski. **VP, Sales:** Kim Inman. **VP, Facility Operations:** Bill Fischer. **Director, Ticket Operations:** Angela Deke. **Director, Sales/Marketing:** Dan Reiter. **Manager, Promotions/Productions:** Kent Shelton. **Manager, Market Development:** Scott Bailes. **Manager, Stadium/Game Day Operations:** Aaron Lowrey. **Manager, Public Relations/Broadcaster:** Jeff Levering. **Senior Account Executive:** Matt Collier. **Account Executives:** Tim Clubb, David Douglass, Niki Lodholz, Zack Pemberton. **Account Representative:** Brandon Mahler. **Coordinator, Sales Services; Lindsay Bone. Box Office Supervisor/Office Assistant:** Ayrica Batson. **Head Groundskeeper:** Brock Phipps. **Assistant Groundskeeper:** Derek Edwards.

FIELD STAFF

    Manager: Mike Shildt. **Coach:** Phillip Wellman. **Pitching Coach:** Bryan Eversgerd. **Trainer:** Jason Hall.

GAME INFORMATION

    Radio Announcer: Jeff Levering. **No. of Games Broadcast:** Home-70 Road-70. **Flagship Station:** 98.7 FM.
    PA Announcer: Kevin Howard, Chris Cannon. **Official Scorers:** Mark Stillwell, Tim Tourville.
    Stadium Name: Hammons Field. **Location:** Highway 65 to Chestnut Expressway exit, west to National, south on National, west on Trafficway. **Standard Game Time:** 7:10 pm. **Ticket Price Range:** $6-25.
    Visiting Club Hotel: University Plaza Hotel, 333 John Q Hammons Parkway, Springfield, MO 65806. **Telephone:** (417) 864-7333.

TULSA DRILLERS

    Office Address: 201 N Elgin, Tulsa, OK 74120.
    Telephone: (918) 744-5998. **Fax:** (918) 747-3267.
    E-Mail Address: mail@tulsadrillers.com. **Website:** www.tulsadrillers.com.
    Affiliation (first year): Colorado Rockies (2003). **Years in League:** 1933-42, 1946-65, 1977-

OWNERSHIP, MANAGEMENT

    Operated By: Tulsa Baseball Inc.
    Co-Chairmen: Dale Hubbard, Jeff Hubbard.
    General Manager: Mike Melega. **Assistant GM:** Jason George. **Bookkeeper:** Cheryll Couey. **Executive Assistant:** Kara Biden. **Director, Stadium Operations:** Mark Hilliard. **Director, Media/Public Relations:** Brian Carroll. **Director, Ticket Operations:** Brandon Shiers. **Director, Marketing/Business Development:** Rob Gardenhire. **Director, Merchandise:** Tom Jones. **Director, Group Ticket Sales:** Geoff Beaty. **Manager, Promotions:** Michael Taranto. **Manager, Video Productions:** David Ruckman. **Head Groundskeeper:** Gary Shepherd. **Manager, Group Sales:** Matt Larson. **Manager, Business Development:** Kevin Butcher. **Manager, Game Entertainment:** Justin Gorski. **Assistant Bookkeeper:** Jenna Higgins. **Mascot Coordinator:** Vincent Pace. **Marketing Assistant:** Drew LaFollette.
    Ticket Office Assistant: Dustin Davis. **Merchandise Assistant:** Ashley Norfleet. **Media Assistant:** Sean Murphy. **Assistant Director, Food Service:** Shantel Lawson-Johnson. **Manager, Food Service:** Deanna Mierzwa. **Manager, Catering:** Carter Witt, Cody Malone. **Team Photographer:** Rich Crimi. **Director, Food Service:** Jason L Wilson. **Director, Concessions:** Wayne Campbell. **Director, Catering:** Carter Witt. **Executive Chef:** Cody Malone.

FIELD STAFF

    Manager: Duane Espy. **Coach:** Kevin Riggs. **Pitching Coach:** Dave Schuler. **Trainer:** Austin O'Shea.

GAME INFORMATION

    Radio Announcer: Dennis Higgins. **No. of Games Broadcast:** Home-70 Road-70. **Flagship Station:** KTBZ 1430-AM.
    PA Announcer: Kirk McAnany. **Official Scorers:** Bruce Howard, Duane DaPron, Larry Lewis, Barry Lewis.
    Stadium Name: ONEOK Field. **Location:** Take I-244 to the Cincinnati/Detroit Exit (#6A); Go north on Detroit Ave, take a right onto John Hope Franklin Blvd, take a right on Elgin Ave. **Standard Game Times:** 7:05 pm, Sun 2:05 (first half), 7:05 (second half.
    Visiting Club Hotel: Southern Hills Marriott, 1902 E 71st St, Tulsa, OK 74136. **Telephone:** (918) 493-7000.

CALIFORNIA LEAGUE

Office Address: 3600 South Harbor Blvd, Suite 122, Oxnard, CA 93035.
Telephone: (805) 985-8585. **Fax:** (805) 985-8580.
Website: www.californialeague.com. **E-Mail:** info@californialeague.com.
Years League Active: 1941-1942, 1946-
President: Charlie Blaney.

Vice President: Tom Volpe.
Directors: Bobby Brett (Rancho Cucamonga), Pete Carfagna (Lancaster), Dave Elmore (Inland Empire), DG Elmore (Bakersfield), Dave Heller (High Desert), Gary Jacobs (Lake Elsinore), Mike Savit (Modesto), Tom Seidler (Visalia), Tom Volpe (Stockton), Bill Schlough (San Jose).
Director, Operations: Matt Blaney. **Director, Marketing:** Pete Thuresson. **Historian:** Chris Lampe. **Legal Counsel:** Jonathan Light. **CPA:** Jeff Hass.
Regular Season: 140 games (split schedule).
2012 Opening Date: April 5. **Closing Date:** Sept 3.
Playoff Format: Six teams. First-half winners in each division earn first-round bye; second-half winners meet wild cards with next best overall records in best-of-three quarterfinals. Winners meet first-half champions in best-of-five semifinals. Winners meet in best-of-five series for league championship.
All-Star Game: at Carolina League, June 19 at Winston-Salem, NC.
Roster Limit: 25 active (35 under control).
Player Eligibility: No more than two players and one player/coach on active list may have more than six years experience.
Brand of Baseball: Rawlings.
Umpires: Mike Cascioppo, Johnathan Bostwick, Roger Craig, Eric Gillam, Ryan Goodman, Matt Heersema, Ryan Karle, Aaron Roberts, Mike Terry, Nathan White.

Charlie Blaney

Club	Stadium	Opened	Dimensions			Capacity	2011 Att.
			LF	CF	RF		
Bakersfield	Sam Lynn Ballpark	1941	328	354	328	2,700	40,056
High Desert	Mavericks Stadium	1991	340	401	340	3,808	119,028
Inland Empire	San Manuel Stadium	1996	330	410	330	5,000	185,411
Lake Elsinore	The Diamond	1994	330	400	310	7,866	225,769
Lancaster	Clear Channel Stadium	1996	350	410	350	4,500	147,129
Modesto	John Thurman Field	1952	312	400	319	4,000	180,785
R. Cucamonga	The Epicenter	1993	335	400	335	6,615	155,903
San Jose	Municipal Stadium	1942	320	390	320	5,208	222,547
Stockton	Banner Island Ballpark	2005	300	399	326	5,200	198,705
Visalia	Recreation Ballpark	1946	320	405	320	2,468	118,065

BAKERSFIELD BLAZE

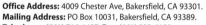

Office Address: 4009 Chester Ave, Bakersfield, CA 93301.
Mailing Address: PO Box 10031, Bakersfield, CA 93389.
Telephone: (661) 716-4487. **Fax:** (661) 322-6199.
E-Mail Address: blaze@bakersfieldblaze.com. **Website:** www.bakersfieldblaze.com.
Affiliation: Cincinnati Reds (2011). **Years In League:** 1941-42, 1946-75, 1978-79, 1982-

OWNERSHIP, MANAGEMENT
Principal Owner: Bakersfield Baseball Club LLC.
President: DG Elmore.
General Manager: Elizabeth Martin. **Assistant GM:** Philip Guiry. **Director, Broadcasting/Media Relations:** Dan Besbris. **Director, Marketing/Community Relations:** Megan Murphy. **Office Manager:** Erin Rojas.

FIELD STAFF
Manager: Ken Griffey. **Coach:** Eli Marrero. **Pitching Coach:** Rigo Beltran. **Trainer:** Clete Sigwart.

GAME INFORMATION
Radio: Dan Besbris 1230AM.
PA Announcer: Mike Cushine. **Official Scorer:** Tim Wheeler.
Stadium Name: Sam Lynn Ballpark. **Location:** Highway 99 to California Avenue, east three miles to Chester Avenue, north two miles to stadium. **Standard Game Time:** 7:30 pm. **Ticket Price Range:** $7-10.
Visiting Club Hotel: Double Tree, 3100 Camino Del Rio Court Bakersfield, CA 93308. **Telephone:** (661) 323-7111.

HIGH DESERT MAVERICKS

Stadium/Office Address: 12000 Stadium Way, Adelanto, CA 92301.
Telephone: (760) 246-6287. **Fax:** (760) 246-3197.
E-Mail address: ejensen@hdmavs.com. **Website:** www.hdmavs.com.
Affiliation (first year): Seattle Mariners (2007). **Years in League:** 1991-

OWNERSHIP, MANAGEMENT
Operated By: Main Street California.
Vice President: Stefanie Brown. **General Manager:** Eric Jensen. **Assistant GM:** Jesse Zumbro. **Director, Ticket Sales:** Ryan Kirkendoll. **Account Executive:** Michelle Alipio. **Sponsorship Coordinator:** Stacey Sharp. **Director, Food/Beverage:** Daniel Gonzalez. **Controller:** Robin Buckles. **Head Groundskeeper:** Rafael Roberto Ramirez. **Clubhouse Manager:** Antonio Gutierrez.

FIELD STAFF
Manager: Pedro Grifol. **Coach:** Roy Howell. **Pitching Coach:** Tom Dettore. **Athletic Trainer:** BJ Downie.

GAME INFORMATION
Radio Announcer: None.
PA Announcer: Ernie Escajeda. **Official Scorer:** Julie Diza.
Stadium Name: Stater Bros Stadium. **Location:** I-15 North to Highway 395 to Adelanto Road. **Standard Game Times:** 7:05 pm; Sun 3:05. **Ticket Price Range:** $6-7.50
Visiting Club Hotel: Motel 6, 9757 Cataba Rd, Hesperia, CA 92395. **Telephone:** (760) 947-0094.

INLAND EMPIRE 66ERS

Office Address: 280 South E St, San Bernardino, CA 92401.
Telephone: (909) 888-9922. **Fax:** (909) 888-5251.
Website: www.ie66ers.com.
Affiliation (second year): Los Angeles Angels of Anaheim (2011). **Years in League:** 1941, 1987-

OWNERSHIP, MANAGEMENT
Operated by: Inland Empire 66ers Baseball Club of San Bernardino.
Principal Owners: David Elmore, Donna Tuttle.
Owner/President: Dave Elmore. **Owner/Chairman:** Donna Tuttle. **Assistant General Managers:** Ryan English, Joe Hudson. **Vice President, Marketing:** Kevin Shaw. **CFO:** John Fonseca. **Director, Broadcasting/Media Relations:** Sam Farber. **Director, Group Sales:** Steve Pelle. **Corporate Groups Executive:** Adam Franey. **Community Groups Sales Manager:** Kelsey Beckenbach. **Groups Sales Manager:** Emma Moore. **Stadium Operations Manager:** Jordan Smith. **Director, Ticketing:** Joey Seymour. **Manager, Graphics/Website:** Robert Peters. **Administrative Assistant:** Angie Rodriguez. **Head Groundskeeper:** Jason Hilderbrand.

FIELD STAFF
Manager: Bill Haselman. **Hitting Coach:** Paul Sorrento. **Pitching Coach:** Brandon Emanuel. **Trainer:** Greg Spence. **Strength/Conditioning Coach:** Ben Gaal.

GAME INFORMATION
Radio Announcer: Sam Farber. **Flagship Station:** KCAA 1050-AM.
PA Announcer: JJ Gould. **Official Scorer:** Bill Maury-Holmes.
Stadium Name: 66ers Stadium. **Location:** From south, I-215 to 2nd Street exit, east on 2nd, right on G Street; from north, I-215 to 3rd Street exit, left on Rialto, right on G Street. **Standard Game Times:** 7:05 pm; Sun 1:05 (April-June), 6:05 (July-Aug). **Ticket Price Range:** $5-10.
Visiting Club Hotel: Hilton San Bernardino, 285 East Hospitality Lane, San Bernardino, CA 92408. **Telephone:** (909) 889-0133.

LAKE ELSINORE STORM

Office Address: 500 Diamond Dr, Lake Elsinore, CA 92530.
Mailing Address: PO Box 535, Lake Elsinore, CA 92531.
Telephone: (951) 245-4487. **Fax:** (951) 245-0305.
E-Mail Address: info@stormbaseball.com. **Website:** www.stormbaseball.com.
Affiliation (first year): San Diego Padres (2001). **Years in League:** 1994-

OWNERSHIP, MANAGEMENT
Owners: Gary Jacobs, Len Simon.
President: Dave Oster. **Vice President/General Manager:** Chris Jones. **VP/GM, Events:** Bruce Kessman. **Assistant GM:** Tracy Kessman. **Director, Stadium Operations:** Matt Schaffner. **Director, Broadcasting:** Sean McCall. **Assistant**

Director, Media Relations: Eric Theiss. **Director, Group Sales:** Raj Narayanan. **Group Sales Executive/Director, Game Operations :** Robert Gillett. **Senior Graphics/Animation Designer:** Mark Beskid. **Director, Ticketing:** JT Onyett. **Account Executive, Ticketing:** Colt Riley. **Director, Corporate Partnerships:** Paul Stiritz. **Director, Mascot Operations:** Patrick Gardenier. **Director, Administration:** Rick Riegler. **Director, Finance:** Marcy Sattelmaier. **Director, Merchandise:** Donna Grunow. **Assistant Director, Merchandise:** Kasey Rawitzer. **Director, Marketing:** Courtney Kessler.

GM, Catering: Arjun Suresh. **Executive Chef:** Steve Bearse. **Director, Concessions:** Toby Sattler. **Director, Grounds/Maintenance:** Peter Hayes. **Assistant Director, Grounds/Maintenance:** Rob Gladwell. **Maintenance Supervisor:** Jassiel Reza. **Office Manager:** Peggy Mitchell. **Clubhouse Manager:** Terrance Tucker.

FIELD STAFF

Manager: Shawn Wooten. **Hitting Coach:** David Newhan. **Pitching Coach:** Bronswell Patrick. **Trainer:** Will Sinon.

GAME INFORMATION

Radio Announcer: Sean McCall. **No. of Games Broadcast:** Home-70 Road-70. **Flagship Station:** Unavailable. **PA Announcer:** Joe Martinez. **Official Scorer:** Lloyd Nixon. **Stadium Name:** The Diamond. **Location:** From I-15, exit at Diamond Drive, west one mile to stadium. **Standard Game Times:** 7:05 pm, Saturday 6:05, Sun 2:05 (first half), 6:05 (second half). **Ticket Price Range:** $8-11. **Visiting Club Hotel:** Lake Elsinore Hotel and Casino, 20930 Malaga St, Lake Elsinore, CA 92530. **Telephone:** (951) 674-3101.

LANCASTER JETHAWKS

Office Address: 45116 Valley Central Way, Lancaster, CA 93536.
Telephone: (661) 726-5400. **Fax:** (661) 726-5406.
E-Mail Address: info@jethawks.com. **Website:** www.jethawks.com.
Affiliation (first year): Houston Astros (2009). **Years in League:** 1996-

OWNERSHIP, MANAGEMENT

Operated By: Hawks Nest LLC.
President: Pete Carfagna. **Vice President:** Brad Seymour.
General Manager: Derek Sharp. **Director, Stadium Operations:** John Laferney. **Director, Sales/Marketing:** Will Thornhill. **Promotions Manager:** Jeremy Castillo. **Director, Community Relations/Ticket Operations:** Will Murphy. **Director, Food/Beverage:** Adam Fillenworth. **Senior Ticket Sales Account Executives:** Dale Billodeaux, Jenn Adamczyk. **Ticket Sales Assistant:** Emilee Hess. **Graphic Design/Merchandise Assistant:** Ralph Agtrap. **Media Relations Assistant:** Jason Schwartz. **Concessions Assistant:** Curtis Kalleward.

FIELD STAFF

Manager: Rodney Linares. **Coach:** Darryl Robinson. **Pitching Coach:** Don Alexander. **Trainer:** Bryan Baca.

GAME INFORMATION

Radio Announcer: Jason Schwartz. **No. of Games Broadcast:** Home-70, Away-70. **Flagship Station:** www.jethawks.com .
PA Announcer: John Tyler. **Official Scorer:** David Guenther.
Stadium Name: Clear Channel Stadium. **Location:** Highway 14 in Lancaster to Avenue I exit, west one block to stadium. **Standard Game Times:** 7 pm, Sun 2 (April–June), 5 (July-Sept). **Ticket Price Range:** $6-12.
Visiting Club Hotel: Palmdale Hotel, 300 West Palmdale Blvd, Palmdale, CA 93551. **Telephone:** (661) 947-9593.

MODESTO NUTS

Office Address: 601 Neece Dr, Modesto, CA 95351.
Mailing Address: PO Box 883, Modesto, CA 95353.
Telephone: (209) 572-4487. **Fax:** (209) 572-4490.
E-Mail Address: fun@modestonuts.com. **Website:** www.modestonuts.com.
Affiliation (first year): Colorado Rockies (2005). **Years in League:** 1946-64, 1966-

OWNERSHIP, MANAGEMENT

Operated by: HWS Group IV.
Principal Owner: Mike Savit.
President: Bill Shanahan. **Vice President/GM:** Michael Gorrasi. **Assistant GM, Corporate Sponsorship/Sales:** Tyler Richardson. **Assistant GM, Operations:** Ed Mack. **Director, Group Sales:** Eric Rauber. **Director, Stadium Operations:** Ryan Thomas. **In-Game Production Entertainment:** Steven Almanza, Kyle Eckerfield. **Manager, Promotions:** Otoma Agnew. **Manager, Ticket Sales:** John Engelbrecht. **Manager, Ticket Sales:** Bradley Reynolds. **Manager, Operations:** Wayne Loeblein, Jr.

FIELD STAFF

Manager: Lenn Sakata. **Coach:** Jon Stone. **Pitching Coach:** Darryl Scott. **Trainer:** Chris Dovey.

GAME INFORMATION

Radio Announcer: Unavailable.
PA Announcer: Unavailable. **Official Scorer:** Unavailable.

Stadium Name: John Thurman Field. Location: Highway 99 in southwest Modesto to Tuolomne Boulevard exit, west on Tuolomne for one block to Neece Drive, left for 1/4 mile to stadium. Standard Game Times: 7:05 pm, Sun 1:05. Ticket Price Range: $6-12.

Visiting Club Hotel: Clarion Inn, 1612 Sisk Rd, Modesto, CA 95350. Telephone: (209) 521-1612.

RANCHO CUCAMONGA
QUAKES

Office Address: 8408 Rochester Ave, Rancho Cucamonga, CA 91730.
Mailing Address: PO Box 4139, Rancho Cucamonga, CA 91729.
Telephone: (909) 481-5000. Fax: (909) 481-5005.
E-Mail Address: info@rcquakes.com. Website: www.rcquakes.com.
Affiliation (first year): Los Angeles Dodgers (2011). Years in League: 1993-

OWNERSHIP, MANAGEMENT

Operated By: Brett Sports & Entertainment.
Principal Owner: Bobby Brett.
President: Brent Miles. Vice President/General Manager: Grant Riddle. VP, Tickets: Monica Ortega. Director, Group Sales: Linda Rathfon. Group Sales Coordinator: Kyle Burleson. Group Sales Account Executive: Matt Sirios. Director, Season Tickets/Operations: Dirk Manley. Account Executives: Melinda Balandra, Arturo Torres. Director, Sponsorships: Andrew Zamarripa. Sponsorship Account Executives: Matt Franco, Chris Pope. Accounting Manager: Amara McClellan. Public Relations Manager/Voice of the Quakes: Mike Lindskog. Office Manager: Shelley Scebbi. Director, Food/Beverage: Peter Neubert.

FIELD STAFF

Manager: Juan Bustabad. Coach: Michael Boughton. Pitching Coach: Matt Herges. Trainer: TBA.

GAME INFORMATION

Radio Announcer: Mike Lindskog. No of Games: Home-70, Road-70. Flagship Station: KSPA AM 1510.
PA Announcer: Chris Albaugh. Official Scorer: Ryan Wilson.
Stadium Name: The Epicenter. Location: I-10 to I-15 North, exit at Foothill Boulevard, left on Foothill, left on Rochester to Stadium Way. Standard Game Times: 7:05 pm, Sun 2:05 (April-July), 5:05 (July-Sept). Ticket Price Range: $8-12.
Visiting Club Hotel: Best Western Heritage Inn, 8179 Spruce Ave, Rancho Cucamonga, CA 91730. Telephone: (909) 466-1111.

SAN JOSE GIANTS

Office Address: 588 E Alma Ave, San Jose, CA 95112.
Mailing Address: PO Box 21727, San Jose, CA 95151.
Telephone: (408) 297-1435. Fax: (408) 297-1453.
E-Mail Address: info@sjgiants.com. Website: www.sjgiants.com.
Affiliation (first year): San Francisco Giants (1988). Years in League: 1942, 1947-58, 1962-76, 1979-

OWNERSHIP, MANAGEMENT

Operated by: Progress Sports Management.
Principal Owners: San Francisco Giants, Heidi Stamas, Richard Beahrs.
President/CEO: Daniel Orum.
Chief Operating Officer/General Manager: Mark Wilson. Chief Marketing Officer: Juliana Paoli. VP, Operations/Assistant GM: Zach Walter. VP, Sales: Ainslie Walter. VP, Baseball Operations: Lance Motch. Director, Player Personnel: Linda Pereira. Director, Marketing: Mandy Stone. Director, Sales: Taylor Haynes. Director, Broadcasting: Joe Ritzo. Director, Finance/Human Resources: Tyler Adair. Ticket Services Manager: Kellen Minteer. Ticket Sales Account Executive: Taylor Wilding. Marketing Coordinator: Sarah Carpenter. Assistant, Marketing/Merchandise: Brad Brown. Finance Assistant: Mike Butera.

FIELD STAFF

Manager: Andy Skeels. Coach: Gary Davenport. Pitching Coach: Brian Cooper. Trainer: David Getsoff. Strength/Conditioning Coach: Dustin Brooks.

GAME INFORMATION

Radio Announcers: Joe Ritzo, Rocky Koplik. No. of Games Broadcast: Home-70, Away-70. Flagship: www.sjgiants.com.
Television Announcers: Joe Ritzo, Dan Dibley, Rocky Koplik. No. of Games Broadcast: Home-20, Away-Unavailable.
Flagship Station: Comcast Hometown Network Channel 104.

PA Announcer: Russ Call. **Official Scorers:** Brian Burkett, Mike Hohler, Michael Melligan, Michael Duca. **Stadium Name:** Municipal Stadium. **Location:** South on I-280, Take 10th/11th Street Exit, Turn right on 10th Street, Turn left on Alma Ave; North on I-280: Take the 10th/11th Street Exit, Turn left on 10th Street, Turn Left on Alma Ave. **Standard Game Times:** 7 pm, Sat 5, Sun 1 (5 after July 8). **Ticket Price Range:** $7-16. **Visiting Club Hotel:** Pruneyard Plaza Hotel, 1995 S Bascom Ave, Campbell, CA 95008. **Telephone:** (408) 559-4300.

STOCKTON PORTS

Office Address: 404 W Fremont St, Stockton, CA 95203.
Telephone: (209) 644-1900. **Fax:** (209) 644-1931.
E-Mail Address: info@stocktonports.com. **Website:** www.stocktonports.com.
Affiliation (first year): Oakland Athletics (2005). **Years in League:** 1941, 1946-72, 1978-

OWNERSHIP, MANAGEMENT
Operated By: 7th Inning Stretch LLC.
President: Pat Filippone. **General Manager:** Luke Reiff. **Director, Marketing:** Jeremy Neisser. **Director, Corporate Sales:** Zach Sharkey. **Director, Business Development:** Tim Pasisz. **Director, Ticket Sales:** Jeff Kaminski. **Community Relations Manager:** Margaret Sacchet. **Stadium Operations Manager:** Bryan Meadows. **Ticket Office Manager:** Tim Pollack. **Account Executive:** Peter Lopez. **Bookkeeper:** Lia Her. **Manager, Group Sales:** Griffin Shibley. **Office Manager:** Deborah Auditor. **Food/Beverage Service Provider:** Ovations.

FIELD STAFF
Manager: Webster Garrison. **Hitting Coach:** Brian McArn. **Pitching Coach:** Craig Lefferts. **Trainer:** Nathan Brooks.

GAME INFORMATION
Radio Announcer: Zack Bayrouty. **No of Games Broadcast:** Home-70, Away-70. **Flagship Station:** KWSX 1280 AM. **TV:** Comcast Hometown Network, Channel 104, Regional Telecast.
PA Announcer: Mike Conway. **Official Scorer:** Paul Muyskens.
Stadium Name: Banner Island Ballpark. **Location:** From I-5/99, take Crosstown Freeway (Highway 4) exit El Dorado Street, north on El Dorado to Fremont Street, left on Fremont.
Standard Game Times: 7:05 pm, Sun 2:09 first half, 6:05 second half. **Ticket Price Range:** $6-$12.
Visiting Club Hotel: Hampton Inn Stockton, 5045 South State Route 99 East, Stockton, CA 95215. **Telephone:** (209) 946-1234.

VISALIA RAWHIDE

Office Address: 300 N Giddings St, Visalia, CA 93291.
Telephone: (559) 732-4433. **Fax:** (559) 739-7732.
E-Mail Address: info@rawhidebaseball.com. **Website:** www.rawhide-baseball.com.
Affiliation (first year): Arizona Diamondbacks (2007). **Years in League:** 1946-62, 1968-75, 1977-

OWNERSHIP, MANAGEMENT
Operated By: Top of the Third Inc.
Principal Owners: Tom Seidler, Kevin O'Malley.
President/General Manager: Tom Seidler. **Assistant GM:** Jennifer Pendergraft. **Executive Assistant:** Kacey Conley. **Director, Food/Beverage Operations:** Chris Henstra.
Director, Ticketing: Mike Candela. **Assistant, Ticketing:** Dan Makela. **Director, Broadcasting:** Donny Baarns. **Manager, Media Relations:** Josh Jackson. **Manager, Hispanic Marketing:** Jesus Romero.
Ballpark Operations Manager/Head Groundskeeper: Dan Hargey. **Ballpark Operations Assistants:** Cody Gray, Charlie Bennett. **Group/Event Coordinators:** Charlie Saponara, Jesus Romero. **Community Relations Coordinator:** Laura Brinkman. **Clubhouse Manager:** Ty Pendergraft. **Ballpark Operations:** Les Kissick.

FIELD STAFF
Manager: Jason Hardtke. **Hitting Coach:** Jacob Cruz. **Pitching Coach:** Doug Drabek. **Trainer:** Ben Fraser.

GAME INFORMATION
Radio Announcers: Donny Baarns, Josh Jackson. **No. of Games Broadcast:** Home-70, Away-70. **Flagship Station:** KJUG 1270-AM.
PA Announcer: Brian Anthony. **Official Scorer:** Harry Kargenian.
Stadium Name: Recreation Ballpark. **Location:** From Highway 99, take 198 East to Mooney Boulevard exit, left at second signal on Giddings; four blocks to ballpark. **Standard Game Times:** 7 pm, Sun 2 (first half), 6 (second half). **Ticket Price Range:** $5-20.
Visiting Club Hotel: Lamp Liter Inn, 3300 W Mineral King Ave, Visalia, CA 93291. **Telephone:** (559) 732-4511.

CAROLINA LEAGUE

Office Address: 1806 Pembroke Rd, Suite 2-B, Greensboro, NC 27408.
Mailing Address: same as street address.
Telephone: (336) 691-9030. **Fax:** (336) 464-2737.
E-Mail Address: office@carolinaleague.com. **Website:** www.carolinaleague.com.
Years League Active: 1945-.

President/Treasurer: John Hopkins.
Vice President: Art Silber (Potomac). **Corporate Secretary:** Ken Young (Frederick).
Directors: Tim Zue (Salem), Rex Angel (Lynchburg), Chuck Greenberg (Myrtle Beach), Dave Ziedelis (Frederick), Steve Bryant (Carolina), Jack Minker (Wilmington), Billy Prim (Winston-Salem), Art Silber (Potomac).
Administrative Assistant: Marnee Larkins.
Division Structure: North—Frederick, Lynchburg, Potomac, Wilmington. South—Carolina, Myrtle Beach, Salem, Winston-Salem.
Regular Season: 140 games (split schedule). **2012 Opening Date:** April 6. **Closing Date:** Sept 3.
All-Star Game: June 19 at Winston-Salem (Carolina League vs California League).
Playoff Format: First-half division winners play second-half division winners in best-of-three series; if a team wins both halves, it plays a wild card (team in that division with next-best second-half record). Division series winners meet in best-of-five series for Mills Cup.
Roster Limit: 25 active. **Player Eligibility Rule:** No age limit. No more than two players and one player/coach on active list may have six or more years of prior minor league service.
Brand of Baseball: Rawlings.
Umpires: John Bacon (Sherrodsville, OH), Garrett Corl (Port Matilda, PA), Richard Gonzalez (Maryland Heights, MO), Matthew Jones (Newtown, PA), Aaron Larsen (Tomah, WI), Benjamin Leake (Roswell, GA), Thomas Newsom III (King, NC), Lawrence Reeves (Gastonia, NC).

John Hopkins

STADIUM INFORMATION

| Club | Stadium | Opened | Dimensions | | | Capacity | 2011 Att. |
			LF	CF	RF		
* Carolina	Five County Stadium	1991	330	400	309	6,500	112,181
Frederick	Harry Grove Stadium	1990	325	400	325	5,400	296,296
Lynchburg	City Stadium	1939	325	390	325	4,000	169,367
Myrtle Beach	BB&T Coastal Field	1999	325	405	328	5,200	213,200
Potomac	Pfitzner Stadium	1984	315	400	315	6,000	171,096
Salem	Salem Memorial Stadium	1995	325	401	325	53,053	226,337
Wilmington	Frawley Stadium	1993	325	400	325	6,532	288,738
Winston-Salem	BB&T Ballpark	2010	315	399	323	5,500	312,416

* Replaces Kinston in league

CAROLINA MUDCATS

CAROLINA
MUDCATS

Office Address: 1501 NC Hwy 39, Zebulon, NC 27597.
Mailing Address: PO Drawer 1218, Zebulon, NC 27597.
Telephone: (919) 269-2287. **Fax:** (919) 269-4910.
E-Mail Address: muddy@carolinamudcats.com. **Website:** www.carolinamudcats.com.
Affiliation (first year): Cleveland Indians (2012). **Years in League:** 2012-

OWNERSHIP, MANAGEMENT
Operated by: Carolina Mudcats Professional Baseball Club Inc.
Majority Owner/President: Steve Bryant.
General Manager: Joe Kremer. **Assistant GM:** Eric Gardner. **Office Manager:** Jackie DiPrimo. **Director, Stadium Operations:** Daniel Spence. **Stadium Operations:** Vinny Jones. **Director, Promotions/Marketing:** Sean Nickelsen. **Director, Food/Beverage:** Dwayne Lucas. **Director, Merchandise:** Anne Allen. **Director, Video Operations/Multimedia Productions/Website:** Aaron Bayles. **Director, Tickets:** Stephen Boham. **Director, External Affairs/Corporate Development:** Ricky Ray. **Director, Group Sales:** Chris Signorelli. **Associate, Group Sales/Luxury Suites:** Everette Blackman. **Director, Field Operations:** John Packer. **Social Networking/Promotions:** Matt Poloni.

FIELD STAFF
Manager: Edwin Rodriguez. **Hitting Coach:** Scooter Tucker. **Pitching Coach:** Scott Erickson. **Trainer:** Jeremy Heller.

GAME INFORMATION
Radio Announcer: Darren Headrick. **No. of Games Broadcast:** Home-70, Away-70. **Flagship Station:** Unavailable. **PA Announcer:** Ricky Ray. **Official Scorer:** John Hobgood.
Stadium Name: Five County Stadium. **Location:** From Raleigh, US 64 East to 264 East, exit at Highway 39 in Zebulon.
Standard Game Times: 7:15 pm, Sat 6:15, Sun 2. **Ticket Price Range:** $6-11.

Visiting Club Hotel: Hampton Inn Wake Forest NC, 12318 Wake Union Church Road, Wake Forest, NC 27587. **Telephone:** (919) 554-0222. **Fax:** (919) 554-1499.

FREDERICK KEYS

Office Address: 21 Stadium Dr, Frederick, MD 21703.
Telephone: (301) 662-0013. **Fax:** (301) 662-0018.
E-Mail address: info@frederickkeys.com. **Website:** www.frederickkeys.com.
Affiliation (first year): Baltimore Orioles (1989). **Years in League:** 1989-

OWNERSHIP, MANAGEMENT
Ownership: Maryland Baseball Holding LLC.
President: Ken Young. **General Manager:** Dave Ziedelis. **Assistant GM:** Branden McGee. **Director, Marketing/Public Relations:** Adam Pohl. **Director, Ticket Sales:** Jeff Wiggins. **Creative Production Manager:** Matt Houston. **Promotion Manager:** Brandon Apter. **Marketing Assistant:** Bridget McCabe. **Public Relations Assistant:** Derek LeComte. **Account Managers:** Maggie Dignan, Alyssa Moore, Matt Miller. **Box Office Manager:** Felicia Adamus. **Ticket Sales Assistant:** Joe Welch. **Box Office Assistant:** Catherine Larkin. **Stadium Operations Manager:** Travis Watts. **Head Groundskeeper:** Brannon Burks. **Office Manager:** Barb Freund. **Finance Manager:** Tami Hetrick. **General Manager, Ovations:** Anita Clarke.

FIELD STAFF
Manager: Orlando Gomez. **Coach:** Jose Hernandez. **Pitching Coach:** Blaine Beatty.

GAME INFORMATION
Radio Announcers: Adam Pohl, Derek LeComte.
PA Announcer: Andy Redmond. **Official Scorers:** Bob Roberson, Dennis Hetrick, Dave Musil.
Stadium Name: Harry Grove Stadium. **Location:** From I-70, take exit 54 (Market Street), left at light; From I-270, take exit 32 (I-70 Baltimore/Hagerstown) towards Baltimore (I-70), to exit 54 at Market Street. **Ticket Price Range:** $9-12.
Visiting Club Hotel: Best Western, 420 Prospect Blvd Frederick, MD 21701. **Telephone:** (301) 695-6200.

LYNCHBURG HILLCATS

Office Address: Lynchburg City Stadium, 3180 Fort Ave, Lynchburg, VA 24501.
Mailing Address: PO Box 10213, Lynchburg, VA 24506.
Telephone: (434) 528-1144. **Fax:** (434) 846-0768.
E-Mail address: info@lynchburg-hillcats.com. **Website:** www.lynchburg-hillcats.com.
Affiliation (first year): Atlanta Braves (2011). **Years in League:** 1966-

OWNERSHIP, MANAGEMENT
Operated By: Lynchburg Baseball Corp.
President: C Rex Angel.
General Manager: Paul Sunwall. **Assistant GM:** Ronnie Roberts. **Head Groundskeeper/Sales:** Darren Johnson. **Director, Broadcasting:** Erik Wilson. **Director, Food/Beverage:** Zach Willis. **Director, Promotions:** Ashley Stephenson. **Director, Group Sales:** Brad Goodale. **Ticket Manager:** John Hutt. **Office Manager:** Diane Tucker.

FIELD STAFF
Manager: Luis Salazar. **Coach:** Bobby Moore. **Pitching Coach:** Derek Botelho. **Trainer:** Ty Cobbs. **Strength/Conditioning Coach:** Unavailable.

GAME INFORMATION
Radio Announcer: Erik Wilson. **No. of Games Broadcast:** Home-70 Road-70. **Flagship Station:** WKDE 105.5-FM.
PA Announcer: Chuck Young. **Official Scorers:** Malcolm Haley, Chuck Young.
Stadium Name: Calvin Falwell Field at Lynchburg City Stadium. **Location:** US 29 Business South to Lynchburg City Stadium (exit 6); US 29 Business North to Lynchburg City Stadium (exit 4). **Ticket Price Range:** $5-9.
Visiting Club Hotel: Best Western, 2815 Candlers Mountain Rd, Lynchburg, VA 24502. **Telephone:** (434) 237-2986.

MYRTLE BEACH PELICANS

Office Address: 1251 21st Ave N, Myrtle Beach, SC 29577.
Telephone: (843) 918-6002. **Fax:** (843) 918-6001.
E-Mail Address: info@myrtlebeachpelicans.com. **Website:** www.myrtlebeachpelicans.com.
Affiliation (Second year): Texas Rangers (2011). **Years in League:** 1999-

OWNERSHIP, MANAGEMENT
Operated By: Myrtle Beach Pelicans LP. **Managing Partner:** Chuck Greenberg.
General Manager: Scott Brown. **Senior Director, Business Development:** Guy Schuman. **Senior Director, Finance:**

Anne Frost. **Sports Turf Manager:** Corey Russell. **Director, Ticket Sales:** Zach Brockman. **Ticket Account Managers:** Glen Goodwin, Katelyn Guild, Emily Luchansky, Justin Shively. **Director, Broadcasting/Media Relations:** Joel Godett. **Director, Marketing/Promotions:** Jen Borowski. **Community Relations Manager:** Tyler Alewine. **Executive Producer, In-Game Entertainment:** Jake White. **Facility Operations Manager:** Mike Snow. **Director, Merchandising:** Dan Bailey. **Director, Food/Beverage:** Brad Leininger. **Clubhouse Manager:** Stan Hunter. **Visiting Clubhouse Manager:** Bob Leber. **Administrative Assistant:** Beth Freitas. **Accounting Assistant:** Karen Ulyicsni.

FIELD STAFF

Manager: Jason Wood. **Coach:** Julio Garcia. **Pitching Coach:** Brad Holman. **Athletic Trainer:** Jeff Bodenhamer. **Strength/Conditioning:** Ryan McNeal.

GAME INFORMATION

Radio Announcer: Joel Godett **No. of Games Broadcast:** Home-70, Road-70. **Flagship Station:** ESPN Radio The Team 93.9-FM/93.7-FM/1050-AM.
PA Announcer: Mike Browne. **Official Scorer:** Steve Walsh.
Stadium Name: BB&T Coastal Federal Field. **Location:** US Highway 17 Bypass to 21st Avenue North, 1/2 mile to stadium. **Standard Game Times:** 7:05 pm; Sun 3:05/6:05. **Ticket Price Range:** $7-13.
Visiting Club Hotel: Hampton Inn-Broadway at the Beach, 1140 Celebrity Circle, Myrtle Beach, SC 29577. **Telephone:** (843) 916-0600.

POTOMAC NATIONALS

Office Address: 7 County Complex Ct, Woodbridge, VA 22192.
Mailing Address: PO Box 2148, Woodbridge, VA 22195.
Telephone: (703) 590-2311. **Fax:** (703) 590-5716.
E-Mail Address: info@potomacnationals.com.
Website: www.potomacnationals.com.
Affiliation (first year): Washington Nationals (2005). **Years in League:** 1978-

OWNERSHIP, MANAGEMENT

Operated By: Potomac Baseball LLC.
Principal Owner: Art Silber. **President:** Lani Silber Weiss.
General Manager: Josh Olerud. **Assistant GM, Stadium Operations:** Carter Buschman. **Director, Ticket Operations:** Michelle Metzgar. **Director, Food Services:** Jim Johnson. **Director, Media Relations:** Will Flemming.

FIELD STAFF

Manager: Brian Rupp. **Hitting Coach:** Marlon Anderson. **Pitching Coach:** Chris Michalak.

GAME INFORMATION

Radio Announcer: Will Flemming. **No. of Games Broadcast:** Home-70 Road-70.
Flagship: www.potomacnationals.com.
Official Scorer: David Vincent, Ben Trittipoe.
Stadium Name: G Richard Pfitzner Stadium. **Location:** From I-95, take exit 158B and continue on Prince William Parkway for five miles, right into County Complex Court. **Standard Game Times:** 7:05 pm; Sat 6:35, Sun 1:05. **Ticket Price Range:** $8-15.
Visiting Club Hotel: Country Inn and Suites Woodbridge, VA, 2621 Prince William Parkway Woodbridge, VA 22192. **Telephone:** (703) 492-6868.

SALEM RED SOX

Office Address: 1004 Texas St, Salem, VA 24153.
Mailing Address: PO Box 842, Salem, VA 24153.
Telephone: (540) 389-3333. **Fax:** (540) 389-9710.
E-Mail Address: info@salemsox.com. **Website:** www.salemsox.com.
Affiliation (first year): Boston Red Sox (2009). **Years in League:** 1968-

OWNERSHIP, MANAGEMENT

Operated By: Carolina Baseball LLC/Fenway Sports Group.
President: Sam Kennedy. **Vice President/General Manager:** Todd Stephenson. **Senior Assistant GM:** Allen Lawrence. **Director, Ticketing:** Steven Elovich. **Director, Media Relations:** Dave Cawley. **Director, Food/Beverage:** Tim Anderson. **Assistant GM/Director, Stadium Operations:** Tracy Schneweis. **Head Groundskeeper:** Josh Marden. **Operations:** Pete Morrison. **Sales Coordinators:** Shea Maple, Todd Handy. **Merchandise Manager:** Jon Ainlay. **Clubhouse Manager:** Tom Wagner.

FIELD STAFF

Manager: Billy McMillon. **Hitting Coach:** Rick Gedman. **Pitching Coach:** Kevin Walker. **Trainer:** David Herrara.

GAME INFORMATION

Radio Announcer: Evan Lepler. **No. of Games Broadcast:** Home-70 Road-70. **Flagship Station:** WFIR 960-AM.
PA Announcer: Travis Jenkins. **Official Scorer:** Billy Wells.

Stadium Name: Lewis-Gale Field at Salem Memorial Ballpark. **Location:** I-81 to exit 141 (Route 419), follow signs to Salem Civic Center Complex. **Standard Game Times:** 7:05 pm; Sat 6:05, Sun 4:05. **Ticket Price Range:** $8-11. **Visiting Club Hotel:** Comfort Inn Airport, 5070 Valley View Blvd, Roanoke, VA 24012. **Telephone:** (540) 527-2020.

WILMINGTON BLUE ROCKS

Office Address: 801 Shipyard Dr, Wilmington, DE 19801.
Telephone: (302) 888-2015. **Fax:** (302) 888-2032.
E-Mail Address: info@bluerocks.com. **Website:** www.bluerocks.com.
Affiliation (first year): Kansas City Royals (2007). **Years in League:** 1993-

OWNERSHIP, MANAGEMENT

Operated by: Wilmington Blue Rocks LP.
Honorary President: Matt Minker. **President:** Tom Palmer. **Vice President:** Jack Minker. **Secretary/Treasurer:** Bob Stewart. **General Manager:** Chris Kemple. **Assistant GM:** Andrew Layman. **Director, Broadcasting/Media Relations:** John Sadak. **Assistant Director, Broadcasting/Media Relations:** Jeff O'Connor. **Director, Merchandise:** Jim Beck. **Merchandise Assistant:** Josh Argo. **Director, Game Entertainment:** Kyle Love. **Production Assistant:** Mike Diodati. **Director, Marketing:** Dave Arthur. **Marketing Assistant:** Edwin Wagner. **New Media, Manager/Account Executive:** Matt Janus. **Director, Community Affairs:** Kevin Linton. **Community Affairs, Assistant:** Dan Trimble.
Director, Sales/Ticket Operations: Jared Forma. **Group Sales, Manager:** Stefani Dichiara-Rash. **Group Sales Associates:** Joe Fargnoli, Pat McVey, Greg Mathews. **Ticket Office Assistants:** David Herman, Reginald Hinson. **Director, Field Operations:** Steve Gold. **Director, Finance:** Joe Valenti. **Office Manager:** Elizabeth Kolodziej.

FIELD STAFF

Manager: Vance Wilson. **Coach:** Damon Hollins. **Pitching Coach:** Steve Luebber. **Athletic Trainer:** James Stone. **Strength/Conditioning Coach:** Adam Vish.

GAME INFORMATION

Radio Announcers: John Sadak, Jeff O'Connor. **No. of Games Broadcast:** Home-70, Away-70. **Flagship Station:** 89.7 WGLS-FM.
PA Announcer: Kevin Linton. **Official Scorers:** Dick Shute, Adam Kamras.
Stadium Name: Judy Johnson Field at Daniel S Frawley Stadium. **Location:** I-95 North to Maryland Ave (exit 6), right on Maryland Ave, and through traffic light onto Martin Luther King Blvd, right at traffic light on Justison St, follow to Shipyard Dr; I-95 South to Maryland Ave (exit 6), left at fourth light on Martin Luther King Blvd, right at fourth light on Justison St, follow to Shipyard Dr. **Standard Game Times:** 7:05 pm, 6:35 (April-May), Sat 6:05, Sun 1:35. **Ticket Price Range:** $4-10.
Visiting Club Hotel: Clarion Belle, 1612 N DuPont Hwy, New Castle, DE 19720. **Telephone:** (302) 299-1408.

WINSTON-SALEM DASH

Office Address: 926 Brookstown Ave, Winston-Salem, NC 27101.
Stadium Address: 951 Ballpark Way, Winston-Salem, NC 27101.
Telephone: (336) 714-2287. **Fax:** (336) 714-2288.
Website: www.wsdash.com. **E-Mail Address:** info@wsdash.com.
Affiliation (first year): Chicago White Sox (1997). **Years in League:** 1945-present

OWNERSHIP/MANAGEMENT

Operated by: Sports Menagerie LLC. **Principal Owner:** Billy Prim. **President:** Geoff Lassiter. **VP/CFO:** Kurt Gehsmann. **VP, Baseball Operations:** Ryan Manuel. **VP, Ticket Sales:** Mike Thompson. **VP, Corporate Partnerships:** Josh Neelon. **VP, Sponsorship Services:** Gerri Brommer. **Director, Entertainment:** Trey Kalny. **Staff Accountant:** Yimeng Huo. **Director, Marketing/Communications:** Brandon Cathey. **Sponsor Services Manager:** Tom Baxter. **Sponsor Services Manager/ MVP Coordinator:** Emily Faircloth. **Associate Director, Creative Services:** Caleb Pardick. **Graphic Design Assistant:** Will Redding. **Associate Director, Events/Marketing:** Nikki Caldwell. **Box Office Manager:** Zach Matthews. **Season Ticket Sales Manager:** Chris Wood.
Outside Sales Representatives: Darren Hill, Hudson Callaway, Brandon Stump. **Group Sales Manager:** Russell Parmele. **Group Sales Representatives:** Sarah Baumann, Jamie Curtis, Rebecca Phelps. **Inside Sales Representatives:** Jay Andrews, Cameron Harris. **Sales Coordinator:** Caire Six. **Head Groundskeeper:** Doug Tanis. **Director, Stadium Operations:** Corey Bugno. **Director, Facility Management:** Frank DeBerry. **Director, Media Relations:** Alex Vispoli.

FIELD STAFF

Manager: Tommy Thompson. **Coach:** Gary Ward. **Pitching Coach:** JR Perdew. **Athletic Trainer:** Corey Barton. **Strength Coach:** Robert S Powell.

GAME INFORMATION

Radio Announcer: Alex Vispoli. **No. of Games Broadcast:** Home-70, Away-70. **Flagship Station:** www.wsdash.com. **PA Announcer:** Cabell Philpott. **Official Scorers:** Bill Grainger, Steve Vrabel.
Stadium Name: BB&T Ballpark. **Stadium Location:** I-40 Business to Peters Creek Parkway exit (exit 5A). **Standard Game Times:** 7 pm, Sun 2 (first half) 5 (second half). **Visiting Club Hotel:** Unavailable.

FLORIDA STATE LEAGUE

Office Address: 115 E Orange Ave Daytona Beach, FL 32114.
Mailing Address: PO Box 349, Daytona Beach, FL 32115.
Telephone: (386) 252-7479. **Fax:** (386) 252-7495.
E-Mail Address: fslbaseball@cfl.rr.com. **Website:** www.floridastateleague.com.
Years League Active: 1919-1927, 1936-1941, 1946-.

President/Treasurer: Chuck Murphy.
Executive Vice President: Ken Carson. **Vice Presidents:** North Division—Ken Carson. South Division—Paul Taglieri. **Corporate Secretary:** C David Hood. **Special Advisor:** Ben J Hayes.
Directors: Mike Bauer (Jupiter/Palm Beach), Ken Carson (Dunedin), Jeff Eiseman (Port Charlotte), Marvin Goldklang (Fort Myers), Trevor Gooby (Bradenton), Ron Myers (Lakeland), Brady Ballard (Daytona), Kyle Smith (Brevard County), Vance Smith (Tampa), Paul Taglieri (St Lucie), John Timberlake (Clearwater).
Office Manager: Laura LeCras.
Division Structure: North—Brevard County, Clearwater, Daytona, Dunedin, Lakeland, Tampa. South—Fort Myers, Jupiter, Palm Beach, Port Charlotte, St. Lucie, Bradenton.
Regular Season: 140 games (split schedule).
2012 Opening Date: April 5. **Closing Date:** Sept 2.
All-Star Game: June 16 at Charlotte.

Chuck Murphy

Playoff Format: First-half division winners meet second-half winners in best-of-three series. Winners meet in best-of-five series for league championship.
Roster Limit: 25. **Player Eligibility Rule:** No age limit. No more than two players and one player-coach on active list may have six or more years of prior minor league service.
Brand of Baseball: Rawlings.
Umpires: Bryan Fields (Dallas, TX), Ramon Hernandez (Columbia, MO), Patrick Hoberg (Urbandale, IA), Brett Houseman (Dayton, OH), Matthew McCoy (Tallahassee, FL), Roberto Ortiz (Caguas, PR), Alex Ransom (Winfield, MO), Jose Rivera (San Juan, PR), Matthew Springer (Albany, OR), Brett Terry (Portland, OR), Christopher Tipton (Flint, MI), Jeffrey Woods (St Louis, MO).

STADIUM INFORMATION

Club	Stadium	Opened	Dimensions LF	CF	RF	Capacity	2011 Att.
Bradenton	McKechnie Field	1923	335	400	335	6,602	103,978
Brevard County	Space Coast Stadium	1994	340	404	340	7,500	93,903
Charlotte	Charlotte Sports Park	2009	343	413	343	5,028	166,552
Clearwater	Bright House Field	2004	330	400	330	8,500	177,117
Daytona	Jackie Robinson Ballpark	1930	317	400	325	4,200	154,557
Dunedin	Florida Auto Exchange Stadium	1977	335	400	327	5,509	43,148
Fort Myers	Hammond Stadium	1991	330	405	330	7,900	122,328
Jupiter	Roger Dean Stadium	1998	330	400	325	6,871	82,071
Lakeland	Joker Marchant Stadium	1966	340	420	340	7,828	62,324
Palm Beach	Roger Dean Stadium	1998	330	400	325	6,871	69,210
St. Lucie	Digital Domain Park	1988	338	410	338	7,000	105,379
Tampa	Steinbrenner Field	1996	318	408	314	11,026	117,162

BRADENTON MARAUDERS

Mailing Address: 1701 27th Street East, Bradenton, FL 34208.
Telephone: (941) 747-3031. **Fax:** (941) 747-9442.
E-Mail Address: MaraudersInfo@pirates.com. **Website:** www.BradentonMarauders.com.
Affiliation (first year): Pittsburgh Pirates (2010). **Years in League (Bradenton):** 1919-20, 1923-24, 1926.

OWNERSHIP/MANAGEMENT
Operated By: Pittsburgh Associates.
Director, Florida Operations: Trevor Gooby. **Manager, Florida Operations:** AJ Grant. **Concessions Manager:** Terry Pajka. **Manager, Sales/Marketing:** Rachelle Madrigal. **Coordinator, Sales/Marketing:** Stacy Morgan. **Coordinator, Stadium Operations:** Kris Koch. **Coordinator, Ticket Operations:** Justin Kristich. **Head Groundskeeper:** Victor Madrigal.

FIELD STAFF
Manager: Carlos Garcia. **Coach:** Kory DeHaan. **Pitching Coach:** Mike Steele. **Athletic Trainer:** Dru Scott. **Strength/Conditioning Coach:** Unavailable.

GAME INFORMATION
Radio: Unavailable.

PA Announcer: Art Ross. **Official Scorer:** Unavailable.
Stadium Name: McKechnie Field. **Location:** I-75 to exit 220 (220B from I-75N) to SR 64 West/Manatee Ave, Left onto 9th St West, McKechnie Field on the left. **Standard Game Times:** 7 pm, Tues 6, Sun 5. **Ticket Price Range:** $5-7.
Visiting Club Hotel: Courtyard by Marriott Bradenton Sarasota Waterfront, 100 Riverfront Drive West, Bradenton, FL 34205. **Telephone:** (941) 747-3727.

BREVARD COUNTY MANATEES

Office Address: 5800 Stadium Pkwy, Suite 101, Viera, FL 32940.
Telephone: (321) 633-9200. **Fax:** (321) 633-4418.
E-Mail Address: info@spacecoaststadium.com. **Website:** www.manateesbaseball.com.
Affiliation (first year): Milwaukee Brewers (2005). **Years in League:** 1994-

OWNERSHIP/MANAGEMENT
Operated By: Central Florida Baseball Group LLC.
Chairman: Dr Tom Winters. **Vice Chairman:** Dewight Titus. **President:** Charlie Baumann.
General Manager: Kyle Smith. **Business Operations Manager:** Kelley Wheeler. **Director, Ticketing:** Chad Lovitt. **Box Office Manager:** Frank Longobardo. **Clubhouse Manager:** Ryan McDonald. **Head Groundskeeper:** Doug Lopas. **Team Chaplains:** Donnie Legg, Abraham Medina.

FIELD STAFF
Manager: Joe Ayrault. **Coach:** Ned Yost IV. **Pitching Coach:** Mark Dewey. **Trainer:** Tommy Craig. **Strength/Conditioning Coordinator:** Jonah Mergen

GAME INFORMATION
PA Announcer: JC Meyerholz. **Radio:** None.
Official Scorer: Brandon Revels.
Stadium Name: Space Coast Stadium. **Location:** I-95 North to Wickham Rd (exit 191), left onto Wickham, right at traffic circle onto Lake Andrew Drive for 1 1/2 miles through the Brevard County government office complex to the four-way stop, right on Stadium Parkway, Space Coast Stadium 1/2 mile on the left; I-95 South to Rockledge exit (exit 195), left onto Stadium Parkway, Space Coast Stadium is 3 miles on right. **Standard Game Times:** 6:35 pm, Sun 5:05. **Tickets:** $7.
Visiting Club Hotel: Holiday Inn Hotel & Conference Center, 8928 N Wickham Rd, Viera, FL 32940. **Telephone:** (321) 255-0077.

CHARLOTTE STONE CRABS

Office Address: 2300 El Jobean Rd, Port Charlotte, FL 33948.
Mailing Address: 2300 El Jobean Rd, Building A, Port Charlotte, FL 33948.
Telephone: (941) 206-4487. **Fax:** (941) 206-3599.
E-Mail Address: info@stonecrabsbaseball.com.
Website: www.stonecrabsbaseball.com.
Affiliation (first year): Tampa Bay Rays (2009). **Years in League:** 2009-

OWNERSHIP/MANAGEMENT
Operated By: Ripken Baseball.
General Manager: Jim Pfander. **Director, Food/Beverage Operations:** Corey Brandt. **Marketing Manager:** Regina Van Henkelum. **Box Office Manager:** Chris Sprunger. **Director, Sales:** Michael Warren. **Account Representatives:** Lee Pace, Colby Miller, Jen Burns, Josh Murray. **Full Charge Bookkeeper:** Tamera Figueroa. **Accounting Clerk:** Sue Denny.

FIELD STAFF
Manager: Jim Morrison. **Coach:** Joe Szekely. **Pitching Coach:** Steve Watson.

GAME INFORMATION
PA Announcer: Josh Grant. **Official Scorer:** Unavailable.
Stadium Name: Charlotte Sports Park. **Location:** I-75 to Exit 179, turn left onto Toldeo Blade Blvd then right on El Jobean Rd. **Ticket Price Range:** $7-11.
Visiting Club Hotel: Days Inn, 1941 Tamiami Trail, Port Charlotte, FL 33948. **Telephone:** 941-627-8900.

CLEARWATER THRESHERS

Office Address: 601 N Old Coachman Rd, Clearwater, FL 33765.
Telephone: (727) 712-4300. **Fax:** (727) 712-4498.
Website: www.threshersbaseball.com.
Affiliation (first year): Philadelphia Phillies (1985). **Years in League:** 1985-

OWNERSHIP/MANAGEMENT
Operated by: Philadelphia Phillies.

Chairman: Bill Giles. **President:** David Montgomery.

Director, Florida Operations/General Manager: John Timberlake. **Assistant Director, Minor League Operations:** Lee McDaniel. **Business Manager:** Dianne Gonzalez. **Assistant GM/Director, Sales:** Dan McDonough. **Assistant GM/Ticketing:** Jason Adams. **Office Administration:** DeDe Angelillis. **Manager, Group Sales:** Dan Madden. **Assistant Manager, Group Sales:** Bobby Mitchell. **Manager, Ballpark Operations:** Jerry Warren. **Operations Assistant:** Sean McCarthy. **Coordinator, Facility Maintenance:** Cory Sipe. **Manager, Special Events:** Doug Kemp. **Manager, Community Relations/Promotions:** Amanda Koch. **Clubhouse Manager:** Mark Meschede. **Manager, Food/Beverage:** Brad Dudash. **Assistant, Food/Beverage:** John Kerstetter. **Ticket Office Managers:** Pat Privelege, Kyle Webb.

Group Sales Assistant: Michelle Finley. **Media/Public Relations Assistant:** Joe Charlton. **Operations Assistant:** Sean McCarthy. **Coordinator, Audio/Video:** Nic Repper. **Interns:** John Kerstetter.

FIELD STAFF

Manager: Chris Truby. **Coach:** John Mizerock. **Pitching Coach:** Dave Lundquist.

GAME INFORMATION

Radio: None.
PA Announcer: Don Guckian. **Official Scorer:** Larry Wiederecht.
Stadium Name: Bright House Field. **Location:** US 19 North and Drew Street in Clearwater.
Standard Game Times: 7 pm, Fri/Sat 6:30. **Ticket Price Range:** $5-9.50.
Visiting Club Hotel: La Quinta Inn, 3301 Ulmerton Road, Clearwater, FL, 33762. **Telephone:** (800) 753-3757.

DAYTONA CUBS

Office Address: 105 E Orange Ave, Daytona Beach, FL 32114.
Telephone: (386) 257-3172. **Fax:** (386) 257-3382.
E-Mail Address: info@daytonacubs.com. **Website:** www.daytonacubs.com.
Affiliation (first year): Chicago Cubs (1993). **Years in League:** 1920-24, 1928, 1936-41, 1946-73, 1977-87, 1993-

OWNERSHIP/MANAGEMENT

Operated By: Big Game Florida LLC.
Principal Owner/President: Andrew Rayburn.
General Manager: Brady Ballard. **Assistant GM:** Josh Lawther. **Director, Broadcasting/Media Relations:** Robbie Aaron. **Director, Stadium Operations:** JR Laub. **Director, Tickets:** Amanda Earnest. **Director, Sales:** Clint Cure. **Director, Corporate Accounts:** Michael Morse. **Manager, Special Events/Community Relations:** Janelle Yonkovitch. **Director, Groups/Merchandise:** Jim Jaworski. **Manager, Group Sales:** Zach Palmer. **Office Manager:** Tammy Devine.

FIELD STAFF

Manager: Brian Harper. **Hitting Coach:** Desi Wilson. **Pitching Coach:** Marty Mason. **Trainer:** Peter Fagan.

GAME INFORMATION

Radio Announcer: Robbie Aaron. **No. of Games Broadcast:** Home-70, Road-70. **Flagship Station:** AM-1230 WSBB.
PA Announcer: Tim Lecras. **Official Scorer:** Don Roberts.
Stadium Name: Jackie Robinson Ballpark. **Location:** I-95 to International Speedway Blvd Exit (Route 92), east to Beach Street, south to Magnolia Ave east to ballpark; A1A North/South to Orange Ave west to ballpark. **Standard Game Time:** 7:05 pm. **Ticket Price Range:** $6-12.
Visiting Club Hotel: Acapulco Hotel & Resort, 2505 S Atlantic Ave Daytona Beach Shores, FL 32218. **Telephone:** (386) 761-2210.

DUNEDIN BLUE JAYS

Office Address: 373 Douglas Ave Dunedin, FL 34698.
Telephone: (727) 733-9302. **Fax:** (727) 734-7661.
E-Mail Address: dunedin@bluejays.com. **Website:** www.dunedinbluejays.com.
Affiliation (first year): Toronto Blue Jays (1987). **Years in League:** 1978-79, 1987- present

OWNERSHIP/MANAGEMENT

Director/General Manager, Florida Operations: Shelby Nelson. **Assistant GM:** Janette Donoghue. **Accounting Manager:** Gayle Gentry. **Manager, Group Sales/Retail/Community Relations:** Kathi Wiegand. **Manager, Sales/Service:** Mike Liberatore. **Communications Coordinator:** Craig Durham. **Community Relations Coordinator:** Vince Caffiero. **Supervisor, Ticket Sales/Operations Supervisor:** Jonathon Valdez. **Ticket Operations Coordinator:** Alan Aldwell. **Administrative Assistant/Receptionist:** Michelle Smith. **Senior Consultant:** Ken Carson. **Stadium Operations Supervisors:** Zac Phelps, Leon Harrell. **Head Superintendent:** Patrick Skunda. **Grounds Crew Supervisor:** Matt Johnson.

FIELD STAFF

Manager: Mike Redman. **Hitting Coach:** Ralph Dickenson. **Pitching Coach:** Darold Knowles. **Trainer:** Dan McIntosh.

GAME INFORMATION

Radio: None. **PA Announcer:** Alan Wilcox. **Official Scorer:** Josh Huff.

Stadium Name: Florida Auto Exchange Stadium. Location: From I-275, north on Highway 19, left on Sunset Point Rd for 4 1/2 miles, right on Douglas Ave stadium is 1/2 mile on right. Standard Game Times: 7 pm, Sun 1. Ticket Price Range: $6.

Visiting Club Hotel: Comfort Inn Countryside, 26508 US 19 N, Clearwater, FL 33761. Telephone: (727) 796-1234.

FORT MYERS MIRACLE

Office Address: 14400 Six Mile Cypress Pkwy, Fort Myers, FL 33912.
Telephone: (239) 768-4210. Fax: (239) 768-4211.
E-Mail Address: miracle@miraclebaseball.com.
Website: www.miraclebaseball.com.
Affiliation (first year): Minnesota Twins (1993). Years in League: 1926, 1978-87, 1991-

OWNERSHIP/MANAGEMENT

Operated By: Greater Miami Baseball Club LP.
Principal Owner/Chairman: Marvin Goldklang. Executive Advisor To The Chairman: Mike Veeck. President: Steve Gliner. VP/General Manager: Andrew Seymour. Senior Director, Corporate Sales/Marketing: Terry Simon. Senior Director, Business Operations: Suzanne Reaves. Director, Media Relations/Promotions: Gary Sharp. Director, Food/Beverage: Phillip Busch. Manager, Tickets: Adam Rielly. Account Executive: Sean Kelly. Director, Broadcasting/Account Executive: Alex Margulies. Broadcasting/Multimedia Assistant: Brice Zimmerman. Food/Beverage Assistant: BJ Potter. Community Relations Manager: Savannah Martin. Customer Relations Associate: Nicole Greer. Administrative Assistant/Operations: Kyle Amann. Head Groundskeeper: Keith Blasingim. Clubhouse Manager: Brock Rasmussen.

FIELD STAFF

Manager: Jake Mauer. Coach: Jim Dwyer. Pitching Coach: Steve Mintz. Trainer: Chris Johnson.

GAME INFORMATION

Radio Announcers: Alex Margulies, Brice Zimmerman. No. of Games Broadcast: Home-70, Road-70. Internet Broadcasts: www.miraclebaseball.com.
PA Announcer: Gary Sharp. Official Scorer: Scott Pedersen.
Stadium Name: William H Hammond Stadium. Location: Exit 131 off I-75, west on Daniels Parkway, left on Six Mile Cypress Parkway. Standard Game Times: 7:05 pm, Sat 6:05; Sun 1:05. Ticket Price Range: $5-9.50.
Visiting Club Hotel: Fairfield Inn by Marriot, 7090 Cypress Terrace, Fort Myers, FL 33907. Telephone: (239) 437-5600.

JUPITER HAMMERHEADS

Office Address: 4751 Main Street, Jupiter, FL 33458.
Telephone: (561) 775-1818. Fax: (561) 691-6886.
E-Mail Address: f.desk@rogerdeanstadium.com
Website: www.jupiterhammerheads.com.
Affiliation (first year): Miami Marlins (2002). Years in League: 1998-

OWNERSHIP/MANAGEMENT

Owned By: Miami Marlins.
Operated By: Jupiter Stadium, LTD.
General Manager, Jupiter Stadium, LTD: Mike Bauer. Executive Assistant: Carol McAteer. Assistant GM, Jupiter Stadium LTD/GM Jupiter Hammerheads: Melissa Kuper. Assistant GM, Jupiter Stadium: Lisa Fegley. Director, Accounting: John McCahan. Corporate Partnership/Business Development: Chris Snyder. Group Sales Coordinator: Gary Lohmann. Minor League Assistant: Kristen Cummins. Manager, Stadium/Event Operations: Bryan Knapp. Director, Grounds: Jordan Treadway. Assistant Directors, Grounds: Matt Eggerman, Matt Dierdorff. Stadium Building Manager: Walter Herrera. Merchandise Manager: Lauren Gurley. Ticket Manager: Jason Cantone. Press Box Manager: Dave Albrecht. Office Manager: David Vago.

FIELD STAFF

Manager: Andy Haines. Coach: Corey Hart. Pitching Coach: Joe Coleman.

GAME INFORMATION

Radio: None. PA Announcers: John Frost, Dick Sanford, Lou Palmer. Official Scorer: Brennan McDonald.
Stadium Name: Roger Dean Stadium. Location: I-95 to exit 83, east on Donald Ross Road for 1/4 mile.
Standard Game Times: 6:30 pm, Sun 5. Ticket Price Range: $6.50-8.50.
Visiting Club Hotel: Comfort Inn & Suites Jupiter, 6752 West Indiantown Rd, Jupiter, FL 33458. Telephone: (561) 745-7997.

LAKELAND FLYING TIGERS

Office Address: 2125 N Lake Ave, Lakeland, FL 33805.
Mailing Address: 2125 N Lake Ave, Lakeland, FL 33805.
Telephone: (863) 686-8075. **Fax:** (863) 688-9589.
Website: www.lakelandflyingtigers.com.
Affiliation (first year): Detroit Tigers (1967). **Years in League:** 1919-26, 1953-55, 1960, 1962-64, 1967-.

OWNERSHIP/MANAGEMENT

Owned By: Detroit Tigers, Inc.
Principal Owner: Mike Ilitch. **President:** David Dombrowski. **Director, Florida Operations:** Ron Myers.
General Manager: Zach Burek. **Manager, Administration/Operations:** Shannon Follett. **Ticket Manager:** Ryan Eason. **Group Sales Manager:** Dan Lauer. **Receptionist:** Maria Walls.

FIELD STAFF

Manager: Dave Huppert. **Coach:** Larry Herndon. **Pitching Coach:** Mike Maroth.

GAME INFORMATION

Radio: None.
PA Announcers: Shari Szabo, Kevin Davis. **Official Scorer:** Ed Luteran.
Stadium Name: Joker Marchant Stadium. **Location:** Exit 33 on I-4 to 33 South, 1.5 miles on left. **Standard Game Times:** 6:30 pm, Fri 7:11, Sat 6, Sun 1. **Ticket Price Range:** $4-7.
Visiting Club Hotel: Imperial Swan Hotel & Suites, 4141 South Florida Ave Lakeland, FL 33813. **Telephone:** (863) 647-3000.

PALM BEACH CARDINALS

Office Address: 4751 Main Street, Jupiter, FL 33458.
Telephone: (561) 775-1818. **Fax:** (561) 691-6886.
E-Mail address: f.desk@rogerdeanstadium.com.
Website: www.palmbeachcardinals.com.
Affiliation (first year): St. Louis Cardinals (2003). **Years in League:** 2003-

OWNERSHIP/MANAGEMENT

Owned By: St. Louis Cardinals.
Operated By: Jupiter Stadium LTD.
General Manager, Jupiter Stadium, LTD: Joe Pinto. **Executive Assistant:** Carol McAteer. **Assistant GM:** Mike Bauer. **Director, Accounting:** John McCahan. **Director, Marketing:** Jonathan Yates. **Director, Ticket Sales/Promotions:** Lisa Fegley. **Minor League Assistant:** Kristen Cummins, Cody Pavlock. **Group Sales Assistant:** Zachary Nicholson. **Corporate Partnership Sales Representative:** Judie Gibson. **Corporate Partnership Assistants:** Steve Kelly, Caleb Mette. **Manager, Stadium/Event Operations:** Bryan Knapp. **Stadium Operations Assistants:** Jared Larson, Dustin Lewis. **Director, Grounds:** Jordan Treadway. **Assistant Director, Grounds:** Matt Eggerman. **Grounds Crew Assistant:** Tyler Potter. **Merchandise Manager:** Lauren Gurley.
Merchandise Assistant: Jeff Jackson. **Ticket Manager:** Amanda Avila. **Assistant Ticket Manager:** Jason Cantone. **Ticket Office Assistant:** Gary Lohmann. **Press Box Manager:** Tyler Krochmal. **Office Manager:** David Vago.

FIELD STAFF

Manager: Johnny Rodriguez. **Coach:** Jeff Albert. **Pitching Coach:** Dennis Martinez.

GAME INFORMATION

Radio: None. **PA Announcers:** John Frost, Dick Sanford, Lou Palmer.
Official Scorer: Lou Villano.
Stadium Name: Roger Dean Stadium. **Location:** I-95 to exit 83, east on Donald Ross Road for 1/4 mile.
Standard Game Times: 6:30 pm; Sun 5. **Ticket Price Range:** $6.50-8.50.
Visiting Club Hotel: Comfort Inn & Suites Jupiter, 6752 West Indiantown Rd, Jupiter, FL 33458. **Telephone:** (561) 745-7997.

ST. LUCIE METS

Office Address: 525 NW Peacock Blvd, Port St Lucie, FL 34986.
Telephone: (772) 871-2100. **Fax:** (772) 878-9802.
Website: www.DigitalDomainPark.com
Affiliation (first year): New York Mets (1988). **Years in League:** 1988-

OWNERSHIP/MANAGEMENT

Operated by: Sterling Mets LP.
Chairman/CEO: Fred Wilpon. **President:** Saul Katz. **Senior Executive Vice President/COO:** Jeff Wilpon.
Director, Florida Operations/General Manager: Paul Taglieri. **Assistant Director, Florida Operations/Assistant GM:** Traer Van Allen. **Manager, Sales/Ballpark Operations:** Ryan Strickland. **Manager, Food/Beverage Operations:** Brian Paupeck. **Manager, Group Sales/Community Relations:** Katie Hatch. **Manager, Ticketing/Merchandise:** Clinton Van Allen. **Manager, Media Relations:** Matt Gagnon. **Executive Assistant:** Cynthia Malaspino. **Accountant:** Paula Andreozzi.

FIELD STAFF

Manager: Ryan Ellis. **Coach:** Benny Distefano/Jose Carreno. **Pitching Coach:** Phil Regan.

GAME INFORMATION

Radio: None.
PA Announcer: Matt Gagnon. **Official Scorer:** Bob Adams.
Stadium Name: Digital Domain Park. **Location:** Exit 121 (St Lucie West Blvd) off I-95, east 1/2 mile, left on NW Peacock Blvd. **Standard Game Times:** 6:30 pm, Sun 1. **Ticket Price Range:** $4-8.
Visiting Club Hotel: SpringHill Suites, 2000 NW Courtyard Circle, Port St Lucie, FL 34986. **Telephone:** (772) 871-2929.

TAMPA YANKEES

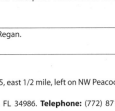

Office Address: One Steinbrenner Dr, Tampa, FL 33614.
Telephone: (813) 875-7753. **Fax:** (813) 673-3174.
E-Mail Address: vsmith@yankees.com. **Website:** tybaseball.com.
Affiliation (first year): New York Yankees (1994). **Years in League:** 1919-27, 1957-1988, 1994-

OWNERSHIP, MANAGEMENT

Operated by: New York Yankees LP.
Principal Owner: Harold Z Steinbrenner.
General Manager: Vance Smith. **Assistant GM, Sales/Marketing:** Matt Gess. **Business Operations:** Julie Kremer.
Director, Ticket Operations: Jennifer Magliochetti. **Head Groundskeeper:** Ritchie Anderson.

FIELD STAFF

Manager: Luis Sojo. **Hitting Coach:** Justin Turner. **Pitching Coach:** Jeff Ware. **Coach:** Mario Garza. **Trainer:** Lee Myer. **Strength/Conditioning:** Jay Signorelli.

GAME INFORMATION

Radio: None.
PA Announcer: Unavailable. **Official Scorer:** Unavailable.
Stadium Name: George M Steinbrenner Field. **Location:** I-275 to Dale Mabry Hwy, North on Dale Mabry Hwy (Facility is at corner of West Dr Martin Luther King Blvd & Dale Mabry Hwy). **Standard Game Times:** 7 pm, Sat 6, Sun 1, 5. **Ticket Price Range:** $4-6.

MIDWEST LEAGUE

Office Address: 1118 Cranston Rd, Beloit, WI 53511.
Mailing Address: PO Box 936, Beloit, WI 53512.
Telephone: (608) 364-1188. **Fax:** (608) 364-1913.
E-Mail Address: mwl@midwestleague.com. **Website:** www.midwestleague.com.

Years League Active: 1947-.

President/Treasurer: George H Spelius.

George Spelius

Vice President/Legal Counsel/Secretary: Richard A Nussbaum II.

Directors: Rick Brenner (Bowling Green), Peter Carfagna (Lake County), Lew Chamberlin (West Michigan), Dennis Conerton (Beloit), Tom Dickson (Lansing), Jason Freier (Fort Wayne), David Heller (Quad Cities), Gary Keoppel (Cedar Rapids), Joe Kernan (South Bend), Gary Mayse (Dayton), Paul Schnack (Clinton), William Stavropoulos (Great Lakes), Rocky Vonachen (Peoria), Dave Walker (Burlington), Mike Woleben (Kane County), Rob Zerjav (Wisconsin).

League Administrator: Holly Voss.

Division Structure: East—Bowling Green, Dayton, Fort Wayne, Lake County, Lansing, South Bend, Great Lakes, West Michigan. West—Beloit, Burlington, Cedar Rapids, Clinton, Kane County, Peoria, Quad Cities, Wisconsin.

Regular Season: 140 games (split schedule). **2012 Opening Date:** April 5. **Closing Date:** Sept 3.

All-Star Game: June 19 at Kane County (Geneva, Ill.).

Playoff Format: Eight teams qualify. First-half and second-half division winners and wild-card teams meet in best-of-three quarterfinal series. Winners meet in best-of-three series for division championships. Division champions meet in best-of-five final for league championship.

Roster Limit: 25 active. **Player Eligibility Rule:** No age limit. No more than two players and one player-coach on active list may have more than five years experience.

Brand of Baseball: Rawlings ROM-MID.

Umpires: Unavailable.

STADIUM INFORMATION

			Dimensions				
Club	**Stadium**	**Opened**	**LF**	**CF**	**RF**	**Capacity**	**2011 Att.**
Beloit	Pohlman Field	1982	325	380	325	3,500	66,982
Bowling Green	Bowling Green Ballpark	2009	312	401	325	4,559	237,070
Burlington	Community Field	1947	338	403	318	3,200	54,284
Cedar Rapids	Veterans Memorial Stadium	2000	315	400	325	5,300	169,000
Clinton	Ashford University Field	1937	335	390	325	4,000	115,253
Dayton	Fifth Third Field	2000	338	402	338	7,230	571,886
Fort Wayne	Parkview Field	2009	336	400	318	8,100	376,022
Great Lakes	Dow Diamond	2007	332	400	325	5,200	264,249
Kane County	Fifth Third Bank Ballpark	1991	335	400	335	7,400	410,262
Lake County	Classic Park	2003	320	400	320	7,273	235,897
Lansing	Cooley Law School Stadium	1996	305	412	305	11,000	345,089
Peoria	Peoria Chiefs Stadium	2002	310	400	310	7,500	187,915
Quad Cities	Modern Woodmen Park	1931	343	400	318	4,024	223,025
South Bend	Coveleski Regional Stadium	1987	336	405	336	5,000	112,795
West Michigan	Fifth Third Ballpark	1994	317	402	327	10,051	372,555
Wisconsin	Fox Cities Stadium	1995	325	400	325	5,500	240,998

BELOIT SNAPPERS

Office Address: 2301 Skyline Dr, Beloit, WI 53511.
Mailing Address: PO Box 855, Beloit, WI 53512.
Telephone: (608) 362-2272. **Fax:** (608) 362-0418.
E-Mail Address: snappy@snappersbaseball.com.
Website: www.snappersbaseball.com.
Affiliation (first year): Minnesota Twins (2005). **Years in League:** 1982-

OWNERSHIP/MANAGEMENT

Operated by: Beloit Professional Baseball Association Inc.

Chairman: Dennis Conerton. **President:** Perry Folts.

General Manager: Matthew Bosen. **Corporate Sales/Promotions:** Matt Glocke. **Director, Media/Community Relations/Marketing:** Justin Waters. **Director, Tickets/Merchandise:** Katie Pietrowiak. **Food/Beverage:** Andrew Davis. **Head Groundskeeper:** Kevin Dvorak.

FIELD STAFF

Manager: Nelson Prada. **Hitting Coach:** Tommy Watkins. **Pitching Coach:** Gary Lucas. **Trainer:** Alan Rail.

GAME INFORMATION

Radio Announcer: Andrew Liebetrau. **No. of Games Broadcast:** 25. **Flagship Station:** 1380-AM ESPN.
PA Announcer: Justin Waters. **Official Scorer:** Unavailable.
Stadium Name: Pohlman Field. **Location:** I-90 to exit 185-A, right at Cranston Road for 1 1/2 miles; I-43 to Wisconsin 81 to Cranston Road, right at Cranston for 1 1/2 miles.
Standard Game Times: 7 pm, 6:30 (April-May), Sun 2. **Ticket Price Range:** $6-8.
Visiting Club Hotel: Rodeway Inn, 2956 Milwaukee Rd, Beloit, WI 53511. **Telephone:** (608) 364-4000.

BOWLING GREEN HOT RODS

Office Address: Bowling Green Ballpark, 300 8th Avenue, Bowling Green, KY 42101.
Telephone: (270) 901-2121. **Fax:** (270) 901-2165.
E-Mail address: fun@bghotrods.com. **Website:** www.bghotrods.com.
Affiliation (first year): Tampa Bay Rays (2009). **Years in League:** 2010-

OWNERSHIP/MANAGEMENT

Operated By: DSF Sports.
Owner: Art Solomon. **President:** Brad Taylor. **General Manager:** Ryan Gates. **Assistant GM, Operations:** Ken Clary. **Controller:** Sally Lancaster. **Senior Sales Manager:** Keith Hetzer. **Director, Ticket Sales:** Bill Robinson. **Senior Manager, Community/Merchandising:** Kyle Hanrahan. **Creative Services Manager:** Atlee McHeffey. **Broadcast/ Media Relations Manager:** Hank Fuerst. **Promotions Manager:** Jennifer Johnson. **Account Executive:** Adam Smedberg. **Account Executive:** Greg Heroy.

FIELD STAFF

Manager: Brady Williams. **Coach:** Manny Castillo. **Pitching Coach:** Bill Moloney. **Trainer:** Jeremy Spencer.

GAME INFORMATION

Radio Announcer: Hank Fuerst. **No. of Games Broadcast:** Home-70 Road-70. **Flagship Station:** WBGN 1340-AM.
PA Announcer: Chris Kelly. **Official Scorer:** Unavailable.
Stadium Name: Bowling Green Ballpark. **Location:** From I-65, take Exit 26 (KY-234/ Cemetery Road) into Bowling Green for 3 miles, left onto College Street for 0.2 miles, right onto 8th Avenue. **Standard Game Times:** 6:35 pm, 7:05 (May-July); Fri 7:05, Sat 7:05, Sun 5:05/2:05. **Ticket Price Range:** $7-12.
Visiting Club Hotel: Candlewood Suites, 540 Wall Street, Bowling Green, KY 42104. **Telephone:** (270) 843-5505.

BURLINGTON BEES

Office Address: 2712 Mt Pleasant St, Burlington, IA 52601.
Mailing Address: PO Box 824, Burlington, IA 52601.
Telephone: (319) 754-5705. **Fax:** (319) 754-5882. **E-Mail Address:** staff@gobees.com. **Website:** www.gobees.com.
Affiliation (first year): Oakland Athletics (2011). **Years in League:** 1962-

OWNERSHIP/MANAGEMENT

Operated By: Burlington Baseball Association Inc.
President: Dave Walker.
General Manager: Chuck Brockett. **Assistant GM:** Jared Schjei. **Director, Group Outings:** Kim Brockett. **Director, Sales:** John Rodgers. **Groundskeeper:** TJ Brewer.

FIELD STAFF

Manager: Aaron Nieckula. **Coach:** Haas Pratt. **Pitching Coach:** John Wasdin. **Athletic Trainer:** Travis Tims.

GAME INFORMATION

Radio Announcer: John Rodgers. **No. of Games Broadcast:** Home-70, Away-70. **Flagship Station:** NewsRadio KBUR 1490-AM. **PA Announcer:** Nathan McCoy. **Official Scorer:** Ted Gutman.
Stadium Name: Community Field. **Location:** From US 34, take US 61 North to Mt Pleasant Street, east 1/8 mile. **Standard Game Times:** 6:30 pm, Sun 2. **Ticket Price Range:** $4-8.
Visiting Club Hotel: Pzazz Best Western FunCity, 3001 Winegard Dr, Burlington, IA 52601. **Telephone:** (319) 753-2223.

CEDAR RAPIDS KERNELS

Office Address: 950 Rockford Rd SW, Cedar Rapids, IA 52404.
Mailing Address: PO Box 2001, Cedar Rapids, IA 52406.
Telephone: (319) 363-3887. Fax: (319) 363-5631. E-Mail Address: kernels@kernels.com. Website: www.kernels.com.
Affiliation (first year): Los Angeles Angels (1993). Years in League: 1962-

OWNERSHIP/MANAGEMENT
Operated by: Cedar Rapids Ball Club Inc.
President: Gary Keoppel.
General Manager: Doug Nelson. Assistant GM: Scott Wilson. Sales: Morgan Hawk. IT/Communications Manager: Andrew Pantini. Sports Turf Manager: Jesse Roeder. Director, Ticket/Group Sales: Andrea Murphy. Director, Finance: Charlie Patrick. Entertainment/Community Relations Manager: Brandon Clemens. Stadium Operations Manager: Seth Dohrn. Director, Corporate Sales/Marketing: Jessica Fergesen. Corporate Sales Executive: Wes Cooling. Director, Food/Beverage: Debra Maier. Receptionist: Marcia Moran.

FIELD STAFF
Manager: Jamie Burke. Hitting Coach: Mike Eylward. Pitching Coach: Chris Gissell. Athletic Trainer: Omar Uribe. Strength Coach: Joe Griffin.

GAME INFORMATION
Radio Announcer: Morgan Hawk. No. of Games Broadcast: Home-70, Away-70. Flagship Station: KMRY 1450-AM. PA Announcers: Scott Beatty, Josh Paulson. Official Scorers: Steve Meyer, Josh Schroeder.
Stadium Name: Veterans Memorial Stadium. Location: From I-380 North, take the Wilson Ave exit, turn left on Wilson Ave. After the railroad tracks, turn right on Rockford Road. Proceed .8 miles, stadium is on left. From I-380 South, exit at First Avenue. Proceed to Eighth Avenue (first stop sign) and turn left. Stadium entrance is .1 miles on right (before tennis courts). Standard Game Times: 6:35 pm, Sun 2:05. Ticket Price Range: $7-11.
Visiting Club Hotel: Best Western Cooper's Mill, 100 F Ave NW, Cedar Rapids, IA 52405. Telephone: (319) 366-5323.

CLINTON LUMBERKINGS

Office Address: Ashford University Field, 537 Ball Park Drive, Clinton, IA 52732.
Mailing Address: PO Box 1295, Clinton, IA 52733.
Telephone: (563) 242-0727. Fax: (563) 242-1433.
E-Mail Address: lumberkings@lumberkings.com. Website: www.lumberkings.com.
Affiliation (first year): Seattle Mariners (2009). Years in League: 1956-

OWNERSHIP/MANAGEMENT
Operated By: Clinton Baseball Club Inc.
President: Paul Schnack.
General Manager: Ted Tornow. Assistant GM: Nate Kreinbrink. Director, Broadcasting/Media Relations: Chad Seely. Director, Operations: Mitch Butz. Manager, Stadium/Sportsturf: Dustin Krogman. Accountant: Ryan Marcum. Assistant Director, Operations: Morty Kriner. Director, Facility Compliance: Tom Whaley. Office Procurement Manager: Les Moore. Clubhouse Manager: Kirby Rock.

FIELD STAFF
Manager: Eddie Menchaca. Coach: Tommy Cruz. Pitching Coach: Andrew Lorraine. Trainer: Jacob Naas. Strength/Conditioning: Will Lindholm.

GAME INFORMATION
Radio Announcer: Chad Seely. No. of Games Broadcast: Home-70, Away-70. Flagship Station: KCLN 1390-AM. PA Announcer: Brad Seward. Official Scorers: Jared Lueders, J Robert Willey.
Stadium Name: Ashford University Field. Location: Highway 67 North to Sixth Avenue North, right on Sixth, cross railroad tracks, stadium on right.
Standard Game Times: 6:30 pm (April-May 21, Aug 20-Sept), 7 (June-Aug 10); Sat 6, Sun 2. Ticket Price Range: $5-8.
Visiting Club Hotel: Super 8, 1711 Lincoln Way, Clinton IA 52732. Telephone: 563-242-8870.

DAYTON DRAGONS

Office Address: Fifth Third Field, 220 N Patterson Blvd, Dayton, OH 45402.
Mailing Address: PO 2107, Dayton, OH 45401.
Telephone: (937) 228-2287. Fax: (937) 228-2284.
E-Mail Address: dragons@daytondragons.com. Website: www.daytondragons.com.
Affiliation (first year): Cincinnati Reds (2000). Years in League: 2000-

OWNERSHIP/MANAGEMENT

Operated By: Dayton Professional Baseball Club LLC/Mandalay Baseball Properties, LLC. **Owners:** Mandalay Baseball Properties LLC, Earvin "Magic" Johnson, Archie Griffin.

President: Robert Murphy.

Executive Vice President: Eric Deutsch. **Executive VP/General Manager:** Gary Mayse. **VP, Accounting/Finance:** Mark Schlein. **VP, Corporate Partnerships:** Jeff Webb. **VP, Sponsor Services:** Brad Eaton.

Director, Media Relations: Tom Nichols. **Director, Operations:** Andrew Ottmar. **Director, Entertainment:** Kaitlin Rohrer. **Director, Sponsor Services:** Brandy Abney. **Senior Marketing Manager:** Clint Taylor. **Marketing Managers:** Erin Beadle, Amanda Fawcett, Lindsey Huerter, Samantha Weaver. **Director, Ticket Sales:** Andrew Aldenderfer. **Director, Group Sales:** Mike Vujea. **Assistant Box Office Manager:** Stefanie Mitchell. **Ticketing Assistant:** Brendan Fowler. **Corporate Marketing Managers:** Chad Adams, Sean Allen, Trafton Eutsler, Dean Freson, Viterio Jones, Nick Kuchey, Katie Streck. **Senior Operations Director:** Joe Eaglowski. **Facilities Operations Manager:** Joe Elking. **Baseball Operations Manager:** John Wallace. **Entertainment Assistant:** Caitlin Bernard. **Director, Merchandising:** Shari Sharkins. **Office Manager/Executive Assistant to the President:** Leslie Stuck. **Staff Accountant:** Dorothy Day. **Administrative Secretary:** Barbara Van Schaik. **Head Groundskeeper:** Dan Jennings.

FIELD STAFF

Manager: Delino Deshields. **Coach:** Alex Pelaez. **Pitching Coach:** Tom Browning. **Trainer:** Tyler Steele.

GAME INFORMATION

Radio Announcer: Tom Nichols. **No. of Games Broadcast:** Home-70, Away-70. **Flagship Station:** WONE 980 AM. **PA Announcers:** Ben Oburn, Kim Parker. **Official Scorers:** Matt Lindsay, Tom Harner, Mike Lucas. **Stadium Name:** Fifth Third Field. **Location:** I-75 South to downtown Dayton, left at First Street; I-75 North, right at First Street exit. **Ticket Price Range:** $7.00-$15.00.

Visiting Club Hotel: Comfort Inn, 7125 Miller Lane, Dayton, OH 45414. **Phone:** (937) 890-9995. **Fax:** (937) 890-9995.

FORT WAYNE TINCAPS

Office Address: 1301 Ewing St Fort Wayne, IN 46802.
Telephone: (260) 482-6400. **Fax:** (260) 471-4678.
E-Mail Address: info@tincaps.com. **Website:** www.tincaps.com.
Affiliation (first year): San Diego Padres (1999). **Years in League:** 1993-.

OWNERSHIP/MANAGEMENT

Operated By: Hardball Capital.

Owners: Jason Freier, Chris Schoen.

President/General Manager: Mike Nutter. **Vice President/Assistant GM, Sales/Finance:** Brian Schackow. **VP/Senior Assistant GM, Corporate Partnerships:** David Lorenz. **VP/Assistant GM, Marketing/Entertainment/Promotions:** Michael Limmer. **Director, Group Sales:** Brad Shank. **Assistant Director, Group Sales:** Jared Parcell. **Director, Ticketing:** Pat Ventura. **Assistant Director, Ticketing/Reading Program Director:** Paige Salway. **Director, Food/Beverage:** Bill Lehn. **Culinary Director:** Scott Kammerer. **Manager, Catering:** Brandon Tinkle. **Food/Beverage Operations Manager:** Dan Krleski. **Coordinators, Special Events:** Holly Raney, Jen Walters.

Director, Facilities: Tim Burkhart. **Assistant Director, Maintenance:** Donald Miller. **Head Groundskeeper:** Keith Winter. **Assistant, Head Groundskeeper:** Andrew Burnette. **Creative Director:** Tony DesPlaines. **Manager, Video Production:** Melissa Darby. **Managers, Ticket Sales:** Tyler Baker, Brent Harring, Austin Allen, Justin Shurley, Erik Lose. **Manager, Corporate Partnerships:** Evan Ashton. **Director, Broadcasting:** Mike Couzens. **Office Manager:** Cathy Tinney. **Manager, Merchandise:** Karen Schieber. **Assistant Director, Marketing/Community Relations:** Abby Naas.

FIELD STAFF

Manager: Jose Valentin. **Hitting Coach:** Jacque Jones. **Pitching Coach:** Willie Blair. **Trainer:** Dan Turner.

GAME INFORMATION

Radio Announcers: Mike Couzens, Mike Maahs. **No. of Games Broadcast:** Home-70, Away-70. **Flagship Station:** WKJG 1380-AM. **PA Announcers:** Jared Parcell, Jim Shovlin. **Official Scorers:** Rich Tavierne, Bill Salyer, Bill Scott. **Stadium Name:** Parkview Field. **Location:** Downtown Fort Wayne off of Jefferson Blvd. **Ticket Price Range:** $5-12.50.

Visiting Club Hotel: Downtown Courtyard by Marriott, 1150 S Harrison Street, Fort Wayne, IN 46802. **Telephone:** (260) 490-3629.

GREAT LAKES LOONS

Office Address: 825 East Main St, Midland, MI 48640.
Mailing Address: 825 East Main St, Midland, MI 48640.
Telephone: (989) 837-2255. **Fax:** (989) 837-8780.
E-Mail Address: info@loons.com. **Website:** www.loons.com.
Affiliation (first year): Los Angeles Dodgers (2007). **Years in League:** 2007-.

OWNERSHIP/MANAGEMENT

Operated By: Michigan Baseball Operations.

Stadium Ownership: Michigan Baseball Foundation.
Founder/Foundation President: William Stavropoulos.
President/General Manager: Paul Barbeau. VP, Corporate Partnerships/Event Operations: Scott Litle. VP, Facilities/Operations: Matt McQuaid. VP, Finance: Tammy Brinkman. VP, Marketing/Entertainment: Chris Mundhenk. GM, ESPN 100.9-FM: Jerry O'Donnell. GM, Dow Diamond Events: Dave Gomola. Assistant GM, Business Operations (Loons)/Director, Programs/Fund Development (MBF): Patti Tuma. Assistant GM, Production/Entertainment: Chris Lones. Assistant GM, Retail Operations/Guest Services: Ann Craig. Assistant GM, Ticket Sales: Lance LeFevre. Director, Accounting: Jamie Start. Director, Corporate Partnerships: Emily Schafer. Director, Food/Beverage: Jenny Coleman. Director, Ticket Sales: Tiffany Seward. Team Broadcaster (ESPN 100.9-FM): Brad Golder. Director, Programming (ESPN 100.9-FM): Jared Sandler. Director, Promotions: Linda Lones.
Director, Sales (ESPN 100.9-FM): Jay Arons. Director, Ticket Services: Kevin Schunk. Assistant to MBF President: Marge Parker. Communications Manager: Alex Wassel. Traffic Manager (ESPN 100.9-FM): Robin Gover. Accounting Manager: Kyle McIntyre. Corporate Account Executive: Kevin Rathbun. Group Sales Coordinator: Eric Ramseyer. Group Sales Coordinator: Matt Hoffman. Executive Chef: Eric Brewster. Concessions Manager: Matt Stevens. Retail Manager: Jenean Clarkson. Stadium Operations Manager: Dan Straley. Head, Grounds: Matt Ellis.

FIELD STAFF
Manager: John Shoemaker. Coach: Razor Shines. Pitching Coach: Hector Berrios.

GAME INFORMATION
Radio Announcer: Brad Golder. No. of Games Broadcast: Home-70, Away-70. Flagship Station: ESPN 100.9-FM WLUN. PA Announcer: Jerry O'Donnell. Official Scorers: Terry Wilczek, Larry Loiselle.
Stadium Name: Dow Diamond. Location: I-75 to US-10 W, Take the M-20/US-10 Business exit on the left toward downtown Midland, Merge onto US-10 W/MI-20 W (also known as Indian Street), Turn left onto State Street, The entrance to the stadium is at the intersection of Ellsworth and State Streets.
Standard Game Times: 6:05 pm (April), 7:05 (May-Sept), Sun 2:05. Ticket Price Range: $6-9.
Visiting Club Hotel: Holiday Inn, 810 Cinema Dr, Midland, MI 48642. Telephone: (989) 794-8500.

KANE COUNTY COUGARS

Office Address: One Cougar Trail, Geneva, IL 60134.
Telephone: (630) 232-8811. Fax: (630) 232-8815.
E-Mail Address: info@kanecountycougars.com. Website: www.kccougars.com.
Affiliation (first year): Kansas City Royals (2011). Years in League: 1991-

OWNERSHIP/MANAGEMENT
Operated By: Cougars Baseball Partnership/American Sports Enterprises, Inc.
Managing Partners: Mike Woleben, Mike Murtaugh.
General Manager: Curtis Haug. Director, Stadium Operations: Mike Klafehn. Senior Director, Finance/Administration: Doug Czurylo. Finance/Accounting Manager: Lance Buhmann. Senior Director, Ticketing: R Michael Patterson. Senior Ticket Sales Representative: Alex Miller. Sales Representatives: Joe Golota, Derek Weber. Director, Ticket Services/Community Relations: Amy Mason. Senior Ticket Operations Representative: Paul Quillia. Ticket Operations/Sales Representative: Jenni Brechtel. Ticket Operations Representative: Lisa Carrillo. Media Placement Coordinator: Bill Baker. Director, Public Relations: Shawn Touney. Promotions Coordinator: Heather Mills. Promotions Assistant: Derek Harrigan.
Design/Graphics: Emmet Broderick. Webmaster: Kevin Sullivan. Director, Security: Dan Klinkhamer. Stadium Maintenance Supervisor: Jeff Snyder. Director, Food/Beverage: Mike Koski. Kitchen Manager: Jon Williams. Business Manager: Robin Hull.

FIELD STAFF
Manager: Brian Buchanan. Hitting Coach: Julio Bruno. Pitching Coach: Jim Brower. Trainer: Mark Keiser. Strength Coach: David Kathmann.

GAME INFORMATION
Radio Announcer: Unavailable. No. of Games Broadcast: Home-70, Away-70. Flagship Station: WBIG 1280-AM. PA Announcer: Kevin Sullivan. Official Scorer: Unavailable.
Stadium Name: Fifth Third Bank Ballpark. Location: From east or west, I-88 (Ronald Reagan Memorial Tollway) to Farnsworth Avenue North exit, north five miles to Cherry Lane, left into stadium complex; from northwest, I-90 (Jane Addams Memorial Tollway) to Randall Road South exit, south to Fabyan Parkway, east to Kirk Road, north to Cherry Lane, left into stadium complex. Standard Game Times: 6:30 pm, Sun 1. Ticket Price Range: $8-14.
Visiting Club Hotel: Unavailable.

LAKE COUNTY CAPTAINS

Office Address: Classic Park, 35300 Vine Street, Eastlake, OH 44095-3142.
Telephone: (440) 975-8085. Fax: (440) 975-8958.
E-Mail Address: bseymour@captainsbaseball.com. Website: www.captainsbase-ball.com.

Affiliation (first year): Cleveland Indians (2003). **Years in League:** 2010-

OWNERSHIP/MANAGEMENT

Operated By: Cascia, LLC.
Owners: Peter and Rita Carfagna, Ray and Katie Murphy.
Chairman/Secretary/Treasurer: Peter Carfagna. **Vice Chairman:** Rita Carfagna. **Vice President:** Ray Murphy. **Senior VP:** Pete E Carfagna. **VP, General Manager:** Brad Seymour. **Assistant GM, Sales:** Neil Stein. **Senior Director, Media/Community Relations:** Craig Deas. **Director, Promotions:** Jake Schrum. **Director, Captains Concessions:** John Klein. **Manager, Stadium Operations:** Josh Porter. **Director, Turf Management/Stadium Operations:** Dan Stricko. **Director, Finance:** Rob Demko. **Manager, Ticket Operations/Merchandise:** Jen Yorko. **Manager, Group Sales:** Amy Gladieux. **Director, Special Projects:** Bill Levy. **Senior Ticket Sales Account Excutive:** Andrew Grover. **Ticket Sales Account Executives:** David Kodish, Dan Torf. **Office Assistant:** Jim Carfagna.

FIELD STAFF

Manager: David Wallace. **Coach:** Jim Rickon. **Pitching Coach:** Jeff Harris.

GAME INFORMATION

Radio Announcer: Craig Deas. **No. of Games Broadcast:** Home-70, Away-70. **Flagship Station:** WELW 1330-AM.
PA Announcer: Ray Milavec. **Official Scorer:** Glen Blabolil.
Stadium Name: Classic Park. **Location:** From Ohio State Route 2 East, exit at Ohio 91, go left and the stadium is 1/4 mile north on your right. From Ohio State Route 90 East, exit at Ohio 91, go right and the stadium in approximately five miles north on your right. **Standard Game Times:** 6:30 pm (April-May), 7 (May-Sept.); Sat 1 (April-May), 7 (May-Sept.); Sun 1.
Visiting Club Hotel: Comfort Inn & Suites, 7701 Reynolds Road, Mentor, OH 44060. **Telephone:** (440) 951-7333.

LANSING LUGNUTS

Office Address: 505 E Michigan Ave, Lansing, MI 48912.
Telephone: (517) 485-4500. **Fax:** (517) 485-4518.
E-Mail Address: info@lansinglugnuts.com. **Website:** www.lansinglug-nuts.com.
Affiliation (first year): Toronto Blue Jays (2005). **Years in League:** 1996-

OWNERSHIP/MANAGEMENT

Operated By: Take Me Out to the Ballgame LLC.
Principal Owners: Tom Dickson, Sherrie Myers.
General Manager: Pat Day. **Assistant GM:** Nick Grueser. **Director, Business Operations:** Heather Viele. **Director, Sales:** Nick Brzezinski. **Corporate Account Executives:** Scott Tenney, Kohl Tyrrell. **Group Sales Representatives:** Chris Arth, Adam Wood. **Box Office Manager:** Josh Calver. **Season Ticket Concierge:** David Link. **Retail Manager:** Matt Hicks. **Stadium Operations Manager:** Dennis Busse. **Director, Food/Beverage:** Brett Telder. **Concessions Manager:** Gregg Kraly. **Director, Marketing:** Julia Janssen. **Marketing Assistant:** Lauren Truax. **Sponsorship Service Representatives:** Michaela McAnany, Sara Walker. **Administrative Assistant:** Angela Sees. **Head Groundskeeper:** Mike Kacsor.

FIELD STAFF

Manager: John Tamargo, Jr. **Hitting Coach:** Kenny Graham. **Pitching Coach:** Vince Horsman. **Trainer:** James Gardiner.

GAME INFORMATION

Radio Announcer: Jesse Goldberg-Strassler. **No of Games Broadcast:** Home-70, Away-70. **Flagship Station:** WQTX 92.1-FM.
PA Announcer: Unavailable. **Official Scorer:** Unavailable.
Stadium Name: Cooley Law School Stadium. **Location:** I-96 East/West to US 496, exit at Larch Street, north of Larch, stadium on left. **Ticket Price Range:** $8-10.
Visiting Club Hotel: Unavailable.

PEORIA CHIEFS

Office Address: 730 SW Jefferson, Peoria, IL 61605.
Telephone: (309) 680-4000. **Fax:** (309) 680-4080.
E-Mail Address: feedback@chiefsnet.com. **Website:** www.peoriachiefs.com.
Affiliation (first year): Chicago Cubs (2005). **Years in League:** 1983-

OWNERSHIP/MANAGEMENT

Operated By: Peoria Chiefs Community Baseball Club LLC.
President: Rocky Vonachen. **Vice President/General Manager:** Ralph Converse. **VP, Ticket Sales:** Eric Oballi. **Broadcast/Media Manager:** Nathan Baliva. **Manager, Box Office:** Ryan Sivori. **Entertainment/Events Manager:** Russ Leonard. **Account Executives:** Mike Schulte, Kevin Hall, Kevin McBain, Sam Annable. **Merchandise Manager:** Paige Peugh. **Head Groundskeeper:** Mike Reno. **Director, Food/Beverage:** Keith Thompson. **Executive Chef:** Chad Ramenda.

FIELD STAFF
  Manager: Casey Kopitzke. **Coach:** Barbaro Garbey. **Pitching Coach:** Tom Pratt. **Trainer:** Shane Nelson.

GAME INFORMATION
  Radio Announcer: Nathan Baliva. **No. of Games Broadcast:** Home-70, Away-70. **Flagship Station:** Unavailable. **PA Announcer:** Unavailable. **Official Scorer:** Bryan Moore
  Stadium Name: Peoria Chiefs Stadium. **Location:** From South/East, I-74 to exit 93 (Jefferson Street), continue one mile, stadium is one block on left; From North/West, I-74 to Glen Oak Exit, Turn right on Glendale which turns into Kumpf Blvd, Turn right on Jefferson, stadium on left. **Standard Game Times:** 7 pm, 6:30 (April-May, after Aug 24), Sat 6:30, Sun 1.
  Ticket Price Range: $7-11.
  Visiting Club Hotel: Jameson Inn & Suites, 4112 N Brandywine Drive, Peoria, IL 61614. **Telephone:** 309-685-5226.

QUAD CITIES RIVER BANDITS

  Office Address: 209 S Gaines St, Davenport, IA 52802.
  Telephone: (563) 322-6348. **Fax:** (563) 324-3109.
  E-Mail Address: bandit@riverbandits.com. **Website:** www.riverbandits.com.
  Affiliation (first year): St Louis Cardinals (2005). **Years in League:** 1960-

OWNERSHIP/MANAGEMENT
  Operated by: Main Street Iowa LLC, David Heller, Bob Herrfeldt.
  General Manager: Stefanie Brown.
  Assistant GM: Andrew Chesser. **VP, Sales:** Shawn Brown. **Director, Media Relations:** Unavailable. **Director, Group Sales:** Matt Tangen. **Director, Baseball Operations:** Bob Evans. **Director, Stadium Operations/Head Groundskeeper:** Kyle Brudos. **Director, Community Relations, Merchandise:** Whitney Campbell. **Director, Special Events:** Andrea Nolan. **Director, Marketing/Promotions:** Shane Huff Manager, Production: JD Davis. **Manager, Stadium Operations:** Elliott Sweitzer. **Manager, Special Events:** Kayla Steffensmeier. **Manager, Box Office:** Ciara Breese. **Account Executive:** Elizabeth Shirley. **Director, Food/Beverage:** Patrick Glackin. **Executive Chef:** Kirk Hansen.

FIELD STAFF
  Manager: Luis Aguayo. **Coach:** Joe Kruzel. **Pitching Coach:** Ace Adams. **Trainer:** Scott Ensell.

GAME INFORMATION
  Radio: None.
  PA Announcer: Scott Werling. **Official Scorer:** Jim Tappa.
  Stadium Name: Modern Woodmen Park. **Location:** From I-74, take Grant Street exit left, west onto River Drive, left on South Gaines Street; from I-80, take Brady Street exit south, right on River Drive, left on South Gaines Street. **Standard Game Times:** 7 pm, Sat: 7, Sun: 2 (April-May), 5 (June, July, August). **Ticket Price Range:** $5-13.
  Visiting Club Hotel: Clarion Hotel, 5202 Brady St, Davenport, IA 52806. **Telephone:** (563) 391-1230.

SOUTH BEND
SILVER HAWKS

  Office Address: 501 W South St, South Bend, IN 46601.
  Mailing Address: PO Box 4218, South Bend, IN 46634.
  Telephone: (574) 235-9988. **Fax:** (574) 235-9950.
  E-Mail Address: hawks@silverhawks.com. **Website:** www.silverhawks.com.
  Affiliation (first year): Arizona Diamondbacks (1997). **Years in League:** 1988-.

OWNERSHIP/MANAGEMENT
  Owner: Swing-Batter-Swing LLC.
  President: Joe Hart.
  Director, Finance/Administration: Cheryl Carlson. **Assistant GM, Operations:** Peter Argueta. **Director, Production:** Todd Edwards. **Director, Corporate Sponsors:** John Shaver. **Director, Ticket Sales:** Robbie Lightfoot. **Assistant Director, Group Sales:** Dan Loding. **Director, Promotions/Community Relations:** Mollie Radzinski. **Director, Merchandise/Design:** Andrew Bowen. **Box Office Manager:** Jason Dreier. **Group Partnership Executives:** Adam Jacobsen, Erin Kostos. **Director, Broadcasting:** Travis Lucian. **Director, Food/Beverage:** Cory Nichols. **Head Groundskeeper:** Joel Reinebold.

FIELD STAFF
  Manager: Mark Haley. **Hitting Coach:** Bobby Smith. **Pitching Coach:** Wellington Cepeda. **Trainer:** Kevin Burroughs. **Strength Coach:** Andrew Slorp.

GAME INFORMATION
  Radio Announcer: Unavailable. **Flagship Station:** www.silverhawks.com.
  Stadium Name: Stanley Coveleski Regional Stadium. **Location:** I-80/90 toll road to exit 77, take US 31/33 south to

South Bend to downtown (Main Street), to Western Avenue, right on Western, left on Taylor. **Ticket Price Range:** $6-32.
   Visiting Club Hotel: Double Tree by Hilton 123 N St Joseph Street, South Bend, IN 46601. **Telephone:** (574) 234-2000.

WEST MICHIGAN WHITECAPS

Office Address: 4500 West River Dr, Comstock Park, MI 49321.
Mailing Address: PO Box 428, Comstock Park, MI 49321.
Telephone: (616) 784-4131. **Fax:** (616) 784-4911.
E-Mail Address: playball@whitecaps-baseball.com. **Website:** www.whitecapsbaseball.com.
Affiliation (first year): Detroit Tigers (1997). **Years in League:** 1994-

OWNERSHIP/MANAGEMENT
Operated By: Whitecaps Professional Baseball Corp.
Principal Owners: Denny Baxter, Lew Chamberlin.
President: Scott Lane. **Vice President, Whitecaps Professional Baseball:** Jim Jarecki. **VP, Sales:** Steve McCarthy.
Manager, Facility Events: Dan Glowinski. **Manager, Operations:** Craig Yust. **Director, Food/Beverage:** Matt Timon.
Community Relations Coordinator: Courtney Galat. **Director, Marketing/Media:** Mickey Graham. **Promotions/Multi-Media Manager:** Brian Oropallo. **Box Office Manager:** Meghan Brennan. **Groundskeeper:** Adam Farrell. **Manager, Facility Maintenance:** John Passarelli. **Director, Ticket Sales:** Chad Sayen.

FIELD STAFF
Manager: Ernie Young. **Coach:** Scott Dwyer:. **Pitching Coach:** Mark Johnson. **Trainer:** TJ Saunders

GAME INFORMATION
Radio Announcers: Ben Chiswick, Dan Elve. **No. of Games Broadcast:** Home-70, Away-70. **Flagship Station:** WBBL 107.3-FM.
PA Announcers: Mike Newell, Bob Wells. **Official Scorers:** Mike Dean, Don Thomas.
Stadium Name: Fifth Third Ballpark. **Location:** US 131 North from Grand Rapids to exit 91 (West River Drive). **Ticket Price Range:** $6-13.
Visiting Club Hotel: Holiday Inn Express-GR North, 358 River Ridge Dr NW, Walker, MI 49544. **Telephone:** (616) 647-4100.

WISCONSIN TIMBER RATTLERS

Office Address: 2400 N Casaloma Dr, Appleton, WI 54913.
Mailing Address: PO Box 7464, Appleton, WI 54912.
Telephone: (920) 733-4152. **Fax:** (920) 733-8032.
E-Mail Address: info@timberrattlers.com. **Website:** www.timberrattlers.com.
Affiliation (first year): Milwaukee Brewers (2009). **Years in League:** 1962-

OWNERSHIP/MANAGEMENT
Operated By: Appleton Baseball Club, Inc.
Chairman: Marc Snyder
President/General Manager: Rob Zerjav. **Assistant GM/Director, Ticket Sales:** Aaron Hahn. **Controller:** Cathy Spanbauer. **Vice President, Marketing:** Angie Ceranski. **Director, Media Relations:** Chris Mehring. **Director, Food/Beverage:** Ryan Grossman. **Director, Stadium Operations:** Ron Kaiser. **Director, Community Relations:** Dayna Baitinger. **Corporate Partnerships:** Ryan Cunniff, Jerrad Radocay. **Merchandise Manager:** Jay Grusz, ski. **Box Office Manager:** Ryan Moede. **Group Sales:** Chumley Hodgson, Seth Merrill, Jim Meulendyke, Liz Wockenfus. **Graphic Designer/Marketing Assistant:** Ann Mollica. **Production Manager/Marketing Assistant:** Cameron Wengrzyn. **Clubhouse Manager:** Travis Voss. **Office Manager:** Mary Robinson. **Groundskeeper:** Eddie Warczak.

FIELD STAFF
Manager: Matt Erickson. **Coach:** Dusty Rhodes. **Pitching Coach:** Chris Hook. **Trainer:** Jeff Paxson.

GAME INFORMATION
Radio Announcer: Chris Mehring. **No. of Games Broadcast:** Home-70, Away-70. **Flagship Station:** WNAM 1280-AM.
PA Announcer: Joe Dotterweich. **Official Scorer:** Jay Gruszynski.
Stadium Name: Time Warner Cable Field at Fox Cities Stadium. **Location:** Highway 41 to Highway 15 (00) exit, west to Casaloma Drive, left to stadium. **Standard Game Times:** 7:05 pm, 6:35 (April-May), Sat 6:35, Sun 1:05. **Ticket Price Range:** $5-25.
Visiting Club Hotel: Microtel Inn & Suites, 321 Metro Dr, Appleton, WI 54913. **Telephone:** (920) 997-3121.

SOUTH ATLANTIC LEAGUE

Office Address: 111 Second Avenue NE, Suite 335, St Petersburg, FL 33701-3464.
Telephone: (727) 456-1240. **Fax:** (727) 499-6853.
E-Mail Address: office@saloffice.com. **Website:** www.southatlanticleague.com.

Years League Active: 1904-1964, 1979-.
President/Secretary/Treasurer: Eric Krupa.
First Vice President: Chip Moore (Rome). **Second Vice President:** Craig Brown (Greenville).
Directors: Don Beaver (Hickory), Cooper Brantley (Greensboro), Craig Brown (Greenville), Brian DeWine (Asheville), Jeff Eiseman (Augusta), Joseph Finley (Lakewood), Jason Freier (Savannah), Marvin Goldklang (Charleston), Alan Levin (West Virginia), Chip Moore (Rome), Bruce Quinn (Hagerstown), Brad Smith (Kannapolis), Bill Shea (Lexington), Tom Volpe (Delmarva).
Division Structure: North—Delmarva, Greensboro, Hagerstown, Hickory, Kannapolis, Lakewood, West Virginia. South—Asheville, Augusta, Charleston, Greenville, Lexington, Rome, Savannah.
Regular Season: 140 games (split schedule). **2012 Opening Date:** April 5. **Closing Date:** Sept 3.
All-Star Game: June 19 at Charleston.
Playoff Format: First-half and second-half division winners meet in best-of-three semifinal series. Winners meet in best-of-five series for league championship.
Roster Limit: 25 active. **Player Eligibility Rule:** No age limit. No more than two players and one player-coach on active list may have more than five years of experience.
Brand of Baseball: Rawlings.
Umpires: Ryan Bealo (Conklin, NY), Joshuah Clark (McDonough, GA), Andrew Draper (Lowville, NY), Jose Esteras (Hialeah, FL), Blake Felix (Fort Worth, TX), Shane Livensparger (Ponte Vedra Beach, FL), Ivan Mercado (Levittown Toa Baja, PR), Robert Moreno (Cumana, Suacre, VZ), Michael Patterson II (New Windsor, MD), Dane Ratajski (Woodstock, MD), Jeremy Riggs (Suffolk, VA), Charles Tierney (Louisville, KY), Junior Valentine (Maryville, TN), Jansen Visconti (Latrobe, PA).

Eric Krupa

STADIUM INFORMATION

Club	Stadium	Opened	LF	CF	RF	Capacity	2011 Att.
Asheville	McCormick Field	1992	326	373	297	4,000	157,199
Augusta	Lake Olmstead Stadium	1995	330	400	330	4,322	200,115
Charleston	Joseph P. Riley Jr. Ballpark	1997	306	386	336	5,800	265,465
Delmarva	Arthur W. Perdue Stadium	1996	309	402	309	5,200	211,993
Greensboro	NewBridge Bank Park	2005	322	400	320	7,599	388,218
Greenville	Fluor Field	2006	310	400	302	5,000	327,558
Hagerstown	Municipal Stadium	1931	335	400	330	4,600	123,593
Hickory	L.P. Frans Stadium	1993	330	401	330	5,062	131,131
Kannapolis	Fieldcrest Cannon Stadium	1995	330	400	310	4,700	138,487
Lakewood	FirstEnergy Park	2001	325	400	325	6,588	382,070
Lexington	Whitaker Bank Ballpark	2001	320	401	318	6,033	312,349
Rome	State Mutual Stadium	2003	335	400	330	5,100	186,345
Savannah	Historic Grayson Stadium	1941	290	410	310	8,000	135,415
West Virginia	Appalachian Power Park	2005	330	400	320	4,300	165,996

Dimensions (header spanning LF, CF, RF)

ASHEVILLE TOURISTS

Office Address: McCormick Field, 30 Buchanan Place, Asheville, NC 28801.
Telephone: (828) 258-0428. **Fax:** (828) 258-0320.
E-Mail Address: info@theashevilletourists.com.
Website: www.theashevilletourists.com.
Affiliation (first year): Colorado Rockies (1994). **Years in League:** 1976-

Ownership/Management
Operated By: DeWine Seeds Silver Dollar Baseball, LLC.
President: Brian DeWine.
General Manager: Larry Hawkins. **Assistant GM:** Chris Smith. **Box Office Manager:** Neil Teitelbaum. **Office Manager:** Ryan Straney. **Merchandise/Promotions Manager:** Jon Clemmons. **Broadcasting Manager:** Doug Maurer. **Group Sales Manager:** Matt Riley. **Group Sales Representatives:** Lauren Stewart, Natalie Tobey. **Outside Sales Representative:** Bob Jones. **Stadium Operations Director:** Patrick Spence. **Director, Food/Beverage:** Craig Phillips (Pro Sports Catering). **Publications/Website:** Bill Ballew.

FIELD STAFF
Manager: Joe Mikulik. **Hitting Coach:** Mike Devereaux. **Pitching Coach:** Joey Eischen. **Trainer:** Billy Whitehead.

GAME INFORMATION

Radio Announcer: Doug Maurer. **No. of Games Broadcast:** Home-70, Away-70. **Flagship Station:** WRES 100.7-FM. **PA Announcer:** Rick Rice. **Official Scorer:** Jim Baker.
Stadium Name: McCormick Field. **Location:** I-240 to Charlotte Street South exit, south one mile on Charlotte, left on McCormick Place. **Ticket Price Range:** $6-11.
Visiting Club Hotel: Quality Inn, 1 Skyline Drive, Arden, NC 28704. **Telephone:** (828) 684-6688.

AUGUSTA GREENJACKETS

Office Address: 78 Milledge Rd, Augusta, GA 30904.
Mailing Address: PO Box 3746 Hill Station, Augusta, GA 30914.
Telephone: (706) 736-7889. **Fax:** (706) 736-1122.
E-Mail Address: info@greenjacketsbaseball.com.
Website: www.greenjacketsbaseball.com.
Affiliation (first year): San Francisco Giants (2005). **Years in League:** 1988-.

Ownership/Management

Owners: Baseball Enterprises, LCC.
Operated By: Ripken Professional Baseball.
General Manager: Nick Brown. **Assistant GM:** Bob Flannery. **Director, Stadium Operations:** Kevin Waller. **Director, Game Entertainment/Marketing:** Lauren Christie. **Ticket Sales Manager:** Andy Beuster. **Box Office Manager:** Brian Marshall. **Account Executives:** Dan Szatkowski, Zach Lecker, Marissa Ponzi, Gabe Gadson. **Bookkeeper:** Debbie Brown. **Events Coordinator:** Renee Ducote.

FIELD STAFF

Manager: Lipso Nava. **Hitting Coach:** Nestor Rojas. **Pitching Coach:** Mike Caldwell. **Trainer:** Garret Havig.

GAME INFORMATION

Radio Announcer: Eric Little. **No. of Games Broadcast:** Home-70, Away-70. **Flagship Station:** WRDW 1630-AM. **PA Announcer:** Scott Skadan. **Official Scorer:** Ted Miller.
Stadium Name: Lake Olmstead Stadium. **Location:** I-20 to Washington Road exit, east to Broad Street exit, left on Milledge Road. **Standard Game Times:** 7:05 pm; Sun 5:35 (April-June), 2:05 (July-Sept). **Ticket Price Range:** $7-12.
Visiting Club Hotel: Microtel 2909 Riverwest Drive, Augusta, GA. **Telephone:** (706) 481-8010.

CHARLESTON RIVERDOGS

Office Address: 360 Fishburne St, Charleston, SC 29403.
Mailing Address: PO Box 20849, Charleston, SC 29413.
Telephone: (843) 723-7241. **Fax:** (843) 723-2641.
E-Mail Address: admin@riverdogs.com. **Website:** www.riverdogs.com.
Affiliation (first year): New York Yankees (2005). **Years in League:** 1973-78, 1980-.

Ownership/Management

Operated by: The Goldklang Group/South Carolina Baseball Club LP.
Chairman: Marv Goldklang. **President:** Mike Veeck. **Director of Fun:** Bill Murray. **Co-Owners:** Dr Gene Budig, Al Phillips, Peter Freund.
Executive Vice President/General Manager: Dave Echols. **Assistant GMs:** Andy Lange, Harold Craw. **Director, Promotions:** Noel Blaha. **Director, Special Events:** Melissa Azevedo. **Director, Merchandise:** Mike DeAntonio. **Director, Community Relations:** Lauren Allio. **Director, Broadcasting/Media Relations:** Sean Houston. **Box Office Manager:** David Cullins. **Sales Managers:** Jake Terrell, Annie Fuller. **Business Manager:** Dale Stickney. **Office Manager:** Kristal Lessington. **Head Groundskeeper:** Mike Williams. **Clubhouse Manager:** Kenneth Bassett.

FIELD STAFF

Manager: Carlos Mendoza. **Coach:** Greg Colbrunn. **Pitching Coach:** Danny Borrell. **First-Base Coach:** Brian Baisley. **Trainer:** Jorge Vargas. **Strength/Conditioning Coach:** Mike Kicia.

GAME INFORMATION

Radio Announcer: Sean Houston. **No. of Games Broadcast:** Home-70, Away-70. **Flagship Station:** WTMZ 910-AM. **PA Announcer:** Ken Carrington. **Official Scorer:** Jeremy Helms.
Stadium Name: Joseph P Riley Jr Ballpark. **Location:** From US 17, take Lockwood Drive North, right on Fishburne Street. **Standard Game Times:** 7:05 pm, Sun 5:05. **Ticket Price Range:** $5-18.
Visiting Club Hotel: Crowne Plaza Charleston, 4381 Tanger Outlet Blvd, N Charleston, SC 29418. **Telephone:** (843) 744-4422.

DELMARVA SHOREBIRDS

Office Address: 6400 Hobbs Rd, Salisbury, MD 21804.
Mailing Address: PO Box 1557, Salisbury, MD 21802.
Telephone: (410) 219-3112. **Fax:** (410) 219-9164.
E-Mail Address: info@theshorebirds.com. **Website:** www.theshorebirds.com.
Affiliation (first year): Baltimore Orioles (1997). **Years in League:** 1996-

Ownership/Management

Operated By: 7th Inning Stretch, LLP.
Directors: Tom Volpe, Pat Filippone.
General Manager: Chris Bitters.
Assistant GM: Jimmy Sweet. **Director, Community Relations/Marketing:** Shawn Schoolcraft. **Director, Ticket Sales:** David Bledsoe. **Group Sales Manager:** Sam Ward. **Ticket Sales Account Executive:** Mike Steinhice. **Ticket Sales Account Executive:** Zac Penman. **Director, Stadium Operations:** Aaron Becker. **Head Groundskeeper:** Dave Super. **Director, Broadcasting/Graphic Design:** Bret Lasky. **Box Office Manager:** Fred Schnarrs. **Accounting Manager:** Gail Potts. **Office Manager:** Audrey Vane.

FIELD STAFF

Manager: Ryan Minor. **Coach:** Einar Diaz. **Pitching Coach:** Troy Mattes.

GAME INFORMATION

Radio Announcer: Bret Lasky. **No of Games Broadcast:** Home-70, Away-70. **Flagship Station:** 960 WTGM.
PA Announcer: Unavailable. **Official Scorer:** Gary Hicks.
Stadium Name: Arthur W Perdue Stadium. **Location:** From US 50 East, right on Hobbs Road; From US 50 West, left on Hobbs Road. **Standard Game Times:** 7:05 pm Ticket Price Range: $4-12.
Visiting Club Hotel: Unavailable.

GREENSBORO GRASSHOPPERS

Office Address: 408 Bellemeade St, Greensboro, NC 27401.
Telephone: (336) 268-2255. **Fax:** (336) 273-7350.
E-Mail Address: info@gsohoppers.com. **Website:** www.gsohoppers.com.
Affiliation (first year): Miami Marlins (2003). **Years in League:** 1979-.

Ownership/Management

Operated By: Greensboro Baseball LLC.
Principal Owners: Cooper Brantley, Wes Elingburg, Len White.
President/General Manager: Donald Moore.
Vice President, Baseball Operations: Katie Dannemiller. **CFO:** Jimmy Kesler. **Assistant GM/Head Groundskeeper:** Jake Holloway. **Assistant GM, Sales/Marketing:** Tim Vangel. **Director, Ticket Sales:** Erich Dietz. **Coordinator, Ticket Services:** Kyle Smith. **Director, Promotions/Community Relations:** Joey Burridge. **Director, Production/Entertainment:** Shawn Russell. **Director, Creative Services:** Amanda Williams. **Director, Merchandise:** Yunhui Bradshaw. **Executive Director, Business Development:** John Redhead. **Group Sales Associates:** Todd Olson, Murray White. **Sales Associate:** Rosalee Brewer. **Assistant Director, Stadium Operations:** Chad Green. **Assistant Groundskeeper:** Kaid Musgrave.

FIELD STAFF

Manager: Dave Berg. **Coach:** Frankie Moore. **Pitching Coach:** Blake McGinley. **Trainer:** Patrick Amorelli.

GAME INFORMATION

Radio Announcer: Andy Durham. **No. of Games Broadcast:** Home-70, Away-0. **Flagship Station:** WPET 950-AM.
PA Announcer: Jim Scott. **Official Scorer:** Unavailable.
Stadium Name: NewBridge Bank Park. **Location:** From I-85, take Highway 220 South (exit 36) to Coliseum Blvd, continue on Edgeworth Street, ballpark at corner of Edgeworth and Bellemeade Streets. **Standard Game Times:** 7 pm, Sun 4. **Ticket Price Range:** pre-sale $6-9 gameday $7-10
Visiting Club Hotel: Continental Inn & Suites 6102 Landmark Center Boulevard, Greensboro, NC 27407. **Telephone:** (336) 553-2763.

GREENVILLE DRIVE

Office Address: 945 South Main St, Greenville, SC 29601.
Telephone: (864) 240-4500. **Fax:** (864) 240-4501.
E-Mail Address: info@greenvilledrive.com. **Website:** www.greenvilledrive.com.
Affiliation (first year): Boston Red Sox (2005). **Years in League:** 2005-

Ownership/Management
Operated By: Greenville Drive, LLC.
Co-Owner/President: Craig Brown.
Co-Owners: Roy Bostock, Paul Raether.
General Manager: Mike deMaine. **Senior Vice President:** Nate Lipscomb. **VP, Finance:** Eric Blagg. **VP, Ticket Sales:** Eric Rowley. **VP, Ballpark Experience:** Eric Jarinko. **Director, Food/Beverage:** Larry Mattson. **Director, Game Entertainment:** Sam LoBosco. **Special Events/Suite Services Manager:** Jennifer Brown. **Production Manager:** Josh Cozzini. **Box Office Manager:** Ryan Miller. **Community Relations/Special Projects Manager:** Samantha Bauer. **Concessions Manager:** Michael Rennison. **Senior Account Executives:** Jeff Chiappini, Brendan Jones. **Account Executives:** Amanda LaVecchia, Ryan Nowland, Leah White. **Head Groundskeeper:** Greg Burgess. **Assistant Groundskeeper:** Ross Groenevelt. **General Accountant:** Connie Pynne.

FIELD STAFF
Manager: Carlos Febles. **Hitting Coach:** Darren Fenster. **Pitching Coach:** Dick Such. **Head Trainer:** Mauricio Elizondo.

GAME INFORMATION
Radio Announcer: Ed Jenson. **No. of Games Broadcast:** Home-70, Away-0. **Flagship Station:** www.greenvilledrive. com. **PA Announcer:** John Oliver. **Official Scorer:** Sanford Rogers.
Stadium Name: Fluor Field. **Location:** From south, I-85N to exit 42 toward downtown Greenville, turn left onto Augusta Road, stadium is two miles on the left; From north, I-85S to I-385 toward Greenville, turn left onto Church Street, turn right onto University Ridge. **Standard Game Times:** 7 pm, Sun 4. **Ticket Price Range:** $5-8.
Visiting Club Hotel: Hampton Inn Greenville-Haywood, 246 Congaree Road, Greenville, SC 29607. **Telephone:** (864) 288-1200.

HAGERSTOWN SUNS

Office Address: 274 E Memorial Blvd, Hagerstown, MD 21740.
Telephone: (301) 791-6266. **Fax:** (301) 791-6066.
E-Mail Address: info@hagerstownsuns.com. **Website:** www.hagerstownsuns.com.
Affiliation (first year): Washington Nationals (2007). **Years in League:** 1993-

Ownership/Management
Principal Owner/Operated by: Hagerstown Baseball LLC.
President: Bruce Quinn. **General Manager:** Bill Farley.
Director, Marketing/Community Relations: Sara Grasmon. **Director, Media Relations:** Matt Leite. **Director, Group Sales:** Josh Mastin. **Stadium Operations/Account Executive:** Charles Warhurst. **Director, Human Resources/Account Executive:** Lori Kendall. **Director, Promotions/Entertainment:** Christy Buchar. **Director, Ticket Operations:** Paul Krenzler. **Assistant, Stadium Operations/Food/Beverage:** Terry Sines.

FIELD STAFF
Manager: Brian Daubach. **Coach:** Mark Harris. **Pitching Coach:** Franklin Bravo. **Trainer:** Jon Kotredes.

GAME INFORMATION
Radio Announcer: Matt Leite. **No. of Games Broadcast:** Home-70, Away-70. **Flagship Station:** WJEJ 1240-AM. **PA Announcer:** Unavailable. **Official Scorer:** Will Kauffman.
Stadium Name: Municipal Stadium. **Location:** Exit 32B (US 40 West) on I-70 West, left at Eastern Boulevard; Exit 6A (US 40 East) on I-81, right at Eastern Boulevard. **Standard Game Times:** 7:05 pm (April-Sept), Sun 1:05 (April-Sept).
Ticket Price Range: $9-12.
Visiting Club Hotel: Clarion Hotel, 901 Dual Highway, Hagerstown, MD, 21740.

HICKORY CRAWDADS

Office Address: 2500 Clement Blvd NW, Hickory, NC 28601.
Mailing Address: PO Box 1268, Hickory, NC 28603.
Telephone: (828) 322-3000. **Fax:** (828) 322-6137.
E-Mail Address: crawdad@hickorycrawdads.com.
Website: www.hickorycrawdads.com.
Affiliation (first year): Texas Rangers (2009). **Years in League:** 1952, 1960, 1993-

Ownership/Management

Operated by: Hickory Baseball Inc.
Principal Owners: Don Beaver, Luther Beaver, Charles Young.
President: Don Beaver.
General Manager: Mark Seaman. **Assistant GM:** Charlie Downs. **Director, Promotions:** Jared Weymier. **Director, Broadcasting/Media Relations:** Andrew Buchbinder. **Business Manager:** Donna White. **Director, Special Events:** Matt Moes. **Community Relations Coordinator:** Megan Meade. **Clubhouse Manager:** Billy Watkins. **Director, Group Sales:** Kathryn Bobel. **Director, Ticket Operations/Merchandising:** Douglas Locascio. **Group Sales Assistants:** Brad Dworin, Alex Neitzel. **Media Relations Assistant:** Jeff Dunlap. **Concessions Assistant:** Luke Addison. **Promotions Assistant:** Ashley Fernandez. **Head Groundskeeper:** Andrew Tallent. **Stadium Operations Assistant:** Jullian Bernard.

FIELD STAFF

Manager: Bill Richardson. **Hitting Coach:** Josue Perez. **Pitching Coach:** Storm Davis. **Coach:** Humberto Miranda. **Trainer:** Jacob Newburn. **Strength/Conditioning:** Anthony Miller.

GAME INFORMATION

Radio Announcer: Andrew Buchbinder. **No. of Games Broadcast:** Home-70, Away-70. **Flagship Station:** WMNC 92.1-FM.
PA Announcers: Ralph Mangum, Jason Savage. **Official Scorer:** Mark Parker.
Stadium Name: L.P Frans Stadium. **Location:** I-40 to exit 123 (Lenoir North), 321 North to Clement Blvd, left for 1/2 mile. **Standard Game Times:** 7 pm, Sun 5.
Visiting Club Hotel: Crowne Plaza, 1385 Lenior-Rhyne Boulevard SE, Hickory, NC 28602. **Telephone:** (828) 323-1000.

KANNAPOLIS INTIMIDATORS

Office Address: 2888 Moose Rd, Kannapolis, NC 28083.
Mailing Address: PO Box 64, Kannapolis, NC 28082.
Telephone: (704) 932-3267. **Fax:** (704) 938-7040.
E-Mail Address: info@intimidatorsbaseball.com.
Website: www.intimidatorsbaseball.com.
Affiliation (first year): Chicago White Sox (2001). **Years in League:** 1995-

Ownership/Management

Operated by: Smith Family Baseball Inc.
President: Brad Smith.
General Manager: Randy Long. **Head Groundskeeper/Director, Stadium Operations:** Billy Ball. **Assistant GM, Sales/Marketing:** Jason Bright. **Assistant GM:** Greg Pizzuto. **Assistant Groundskeeper:** Kevin Madgenic. **Director, Broadcasting/Media Relations/Sales Executive:** Josh Feldman. **Interns:** Darren Cozart, Adam Sproles.

FIELD STAFF

Manager: Julio Vinas. **Coach:** Rob Sasser. **Pitching Coach:** Jose Bautista. **Trainer:** Scott Johnson. **Strength/Conditioning Coach:** Tim Rodmaker.

GAME INFORMATION

Radio Announcer: Josh Feldman. **No. of Games Broadcast:** Home-70, Away-0. **Flagship Station:** www.intimidatorsbaseball.com.
PA Announcer: Sean Fox. **Official Scorer:** Unavailable.
Stadium Name: Fieldcrest Cannon Stadium. **Location:** Exit 63 on I-85, west on Lane Street to Stadium Drive. **Standard Game Times:** 7:05 pm, Sun 5:05. **Ticket Price Range:** $5-$9.
Visiting Club Hotel: Fairfield Inn by Marriott, 3033 Cloverleaf Pkwy, Kannapolis, NC 28083. **Telephone:** (704) 795-4888.

LAKEWOOD BLUECLAWS

Office Address: 2 Stadium Way, Lakewood, NJ 08701.
Telephone: (732) 901-7000. **Fax:** (732) 901-3967.
Email Address: info@blueclaws.com. **Website:** www.blueclaws.com.
Affiliation (first year): Philadelphia Phillies (2001). **Years in League:** 2001-

Ownership/Management

Operated By: American Baseball Company, LLC.
President: Joseph Finley. **Partners:** Joseph Caruso, Lewis Eisenberg, Joseph Plumeri, Craig Stein.
General Manager: Geoff Brown. **Assistant GM, Operations:** Brandon Marano. **Assistant GM, Tickets:** Joe Harrington. **Controller:** Bob Halsey. **Director, Marketing:** Mike Ryan. **Director, Promotions:** Hal Hansen. **Director, Community Relations:** Jim DeAngelis. **Director, Sponsorship:** Zack Rosenberg. **Director, Business Development:** Dan DeYoung. **Director, Group Sales:** Jim McNamara. **Director, New Client Development:** Mike Van Hise. **Director, Ticket Operations:** Rebecca Ramos. **Director, Special Events:** Steve Farago. **Director, Inside Sales:** Lisa Carone. **Director, Corporate Sponsorship:** Chris Tafrow. **Director, Premium Seating:** Ross Pibal. **Director, Regional Sales, John Fierko. Executive Chef:** Sandy Cohen. **Front Office Manager:** Jaimie Smith. **Media/Public Relations Manager:** Greg Giombarrese.
Ticket Sales Managers: Rob Vota, Pete Walsifer. **Corporate Sales Manager:** Dave Ricci. **Regional Sales Managers:** Casey Coppinger, Kevin Fenstermacher, Andrew Granozio. **Merchandise Manager:** Garret Streisel. **Marketing Manager:** Amy DeMichele. **Ticket Sales Coordinator:** Libby Rowe. **Food/Beverage Manager:** Mike Barry. **Clubhouse Manager:** Russ Schaffer. **Head Groundskeeper:** Ryan Radcliffe.

FIELD STAFF

Manager: Mickey Morandini. **Hitting Coach:** Greg Legg. **Pitching Coach:** Les Lancaster. **Trainer:** Mickey Kozack.

GAME INFORMATION

Radio Announcers: Adam Giardino, Greg Giombarrese. **No. of Games Broadcast:** Home-70, Away-70. **Flagship Station:** WOBM 1160-AM.
PA Announcers: Kevin Clark, Mike Stoughton. **Official Scorers:** Joe Bellina, Jared Weiss.
Stadium Name: FirstEnergy Park. **Location:** Route 70 to New Hampshire Ave, north on New Hampshire for 2 1/2 miles to ballpark. **Standard Game Times:** 7:05 pm, 6:35 (April-May), Sun 1:05, 5:05 (July-Aug). **Ticket Prices:** $7-12.
Visiting Team Hotel: Quality Inn of Toms River, 815 Route 37 West, Toms River, NJ 08755. **Telephone:** (732) 341-3400.

LEXINGTON LEGENDS

Office Address: 207 Legends Lane, Lexington, KY 40505.
Telephone: (859) 252-4487. **Fax:** (859) 252-0747.
E-Mail Address: webmaster@lexingtonlegends.com. **Website:** www.lexington-legends.com.
Affiliation (first year): Houston Astros (2001). **Years in League:** 2001-

Ownership/Management

Operated By: Ivy Walls Management Co.
Principal Owner: Bill Shea. **President/COO:** Andy Shea
General Manager: Seth Poteat. **Vice President, Facilities:** Gary Durbin. **Director, Stadium Operations/Human Resource Manager:** Shannon Kidd. **Staff Accountant:** Tina Wright. **Director, Corporate Sales:** Jake Thayer. **Box Office Manager:** David Barry. **Director, Ticket Operations:** Adam English. **Director, Creative Services/Graphic Designer:** Ty Cobb. **Director, Broadcasting/Media Relations:** Keith Elkins. **Account Executive:** Ron Borkowski. **Senior Sales Executive:** Kyle Krebs. **Director, Community Relations/Special Events:** Sarah Piester. **Promotions Coordinator:** Lauren Shrader. **Head Groundskeeper:** Blake Anderson. **Facility Specialist:** Steve Moore.

FIELD STAFF

Manager: Ivan DeJesus Sr. **Hitting Coach:** Josh Bonifay. **Pitching Coach:** Dave Borkowski. **Trainer:** Grant Hufford.

GAME INFORMATION

Radio Announcer: Keith Elkins. **No. of Games Broadcast:** Home-70, Away-70. **Flagship Station:** WLXG 1300-AM.
PA Announcer: Unavailable. **Official Scorer:** Unavailable.
Stadium Name: Whitaker Bank Ballpark. **Location:** From I-64/75, take exit 113, right onto North Broadway toward downtown Lexington for 1.2 miles, past New Circle Road (Highway 4), right into stadium, located adjacent to Northland Shopping Center. **Standard Game Times:** 7:05 pm, Sun 1:35. **Ticket Price Range:** $4-$23.
Visiting Club Hotel: Ramada Inn and Conference Center, 2143 N Broadway, Lexington, KY 40505. **Telephone:** (859) 299-1261.

ROME BRAVES

Office Address: State Mutual Stadium, 755 Braves Blvd, Rome, GA 30161.
Mailing Address: PO Box 1915, Rome, GA 30162-1915.
Telephone: (706) 368-9388. **Fax:** (706) 368-6525.
E-Mail Address: rome.braves@braves.com. **Website:** www.romebraves.com.
Affiliation (first year): Atlanta Braves (2003). **Years in League:** 2003-

Ownership/Management

Operated By: Atlanta National League Baseball Club Inc.
General Manager: Michael Dunn. **Assistant GM:** Jim Jones. **Director, Stadium Operations:** Eric Allman. **Director, Ticket Manager:** Doug Bryller. **Director, Culinary Services:** Dave Atwood. **Director, Food/Beverage:** Brad Smith. **Special Projects Manager:** Erin White. **Administrative Manager:** Christina Shaw. **Account Representatives:** John Layng, Kyle Allen. **Head Groundskeeper:** Bryant Powers. **Retail Manager:** Starla Roden. **Warehouse Operations Manager:** Terry Morgan. **Neighborhood Outreach Coordinator:** Laura Harrison.

FIELD STAFF

Manager: Randy Ingle. **Coach:** Carlos Mendez. **Pitching Coach:** Derrick Lewis. **Trainer:** Brandon Harris.

GAME INFORMATION

Radio Announcer: JB Smith. **No. of Games Broadcast:** Home-70, Away-70. **Flagship Station:** WATG 95.7 FM.
PA Announcer: Tony McIntosh. **Official Scorers:** Jim O'Hara, Lyndon Huckaby.
Stadium Name: State Mutual Stadium. **Location:** I-75 North to exit 190 (Rome/Canton), left off exit and follow Highway 411/Highway 20 to Rome, right at intersection on Highway 411 and Highway 1 (Veterans Memorial Highway), stadium is at intersection of Veterans Memorial Highway and Riverside Parkway. **Ticket Price Range:** $4-10.
Visiting Club Hotel: Days Inn, 840 Turner McCall Blvd, Rome, GA 30161. **Telephone:** (706) 295-0400.

SAVANNAH SAND GNATS

Office Address: 1401 E Victory Dr, Savannah, GA 31404.
Mailing Address: PO Box 3783, Savannah, GA 31414.
Telephone: (912) 351-9150. **Fax:** (912) 352-9722.
E-Mail Address: info@sandgnats.com. **Website:** www.sandgnats.com.
Affiliation (first year): New York Mets (2007). **Years in League:** 1904-1915, 1936-1960, 1962, 1984-

Ownership/Management

Operated By: Savannah Professional Baseball, LLC.
President: John Katz.
Vice President, Business Operations: Jeremy Auker. **VP, Food/Beverage:** Scott Burton. **VP, Public Affairs:** Ryan Kirwan. **Stadium Operations Manager:** Evan Christian. **Ticketing/Accounting Manager:** Darryl Aldridge. **Coordinator, Media/Community Affairs:** Ariel Wagner. **Head Groundskeeper:** Andy Rock.

FIELD STAFF

Manager: Luis Rojas. **Coach:** George Greer/Joel Fuentes. **Pitching Coach:** Frank Viola.

GAME INFORMATION

Radio Announcer: Unavailable. **No. of Games Broadcast:** Home-70, Away-0. **Flagship Station:** WBMQ 960-AM.
PA Announcer: Unavailable. **Official Scorer:** Unavailable.
Stadium Name: Historic Grayson Stadium. **Location:** I-16 to 37th Street exit, left on 37th, right on Abercorn Street, left on Victory Drive; From I-95 to exit 16, east on 204, right on Victory Drive, Stadium is on right in Daffin Park. **Standard Game Times:** 7:05 pm, Sun 2:05. **Ticket Price Range:** $7-10.
Visiting Club Hotel: Fairfield Inn & Suites, 2 Lee Blvd, Savannah, GA 31405. **Telephone:** (912) 353-7100.

WEST VIRGINIA POWER

Office Address: 601 Morris St, Suite 201, Charleston, WV 25301.
Telephone: (304) 344-2287. **Fax:** (304) 344-0083.
E-Mail Address: info@wvpower.com. **Website:** www.wvpower.com.
Affiliation (first year): Pittsburgh Pirates (2009). **Years in League:** 1987-

Ownership/Management

Operated By: West Virginia Baseball, LLC.
Principal Owner: Alan Levin.
Executive Vice President: Andy Milovich. **General Manager:** Tim Mueller. **Assistant GM, Operations:** Jeremy Taylor. **Assistant GM, Marketing:** Kristin Call. **Accountant:** Diane Hill. **Director, Food/Beverage:** Jeff Meehan. **Director, Media Relations:** Adam Marco. **Event Planners:** Kevin Buffalino, Will Bell. **Event Planner:** Amanda Colebank. **Box Office Manager:** Nikki Mirth. **Groundskeeper:** Brent Szarka. **Receptionist:** Jessica McCullough.

FIELD STAFF

Manager: Rick Sofield. **Coach:** Edgar Varela. **Pitching Coach:** Willie Glen. **Trainer:** Phillip Mastro.

GAME INFORMATION

Radio Announcer: Adam Marco. **No. of Games Broadcast:** Home-70, Away-70. **Flagship Station:** ESPN 104.5 FM and 1490-AM (WSWW).
PA Announcer: Unavailable. **Official Scorer:** Unavailable.
Stadium Name: Appalachian Power Park. **Location:** I-77 South to Capitol Street exit, left on Lee Street, left on Brooks Street. **Standard Game Times:** 7:05 pm, Sun 2:05. **Ticket Price Range:** $6-8.
Visiting Club Hotel: Charleston Conference Center, 400 Second Avenue SW, South Charleston, WV 25303. **Telephone:** (304) 744-4641.

NEW YORK-PENN LEAGUE

Mailing Address: 6161 MLK Street North, Suite 205, St Petersburg, FL 33703.
Telephone: (727) 289-7112. **Fax:** (727) 683-9691.
Website: www.newyork-pennleague.com.
Years League Active: 1939–

President: Ben J Hayes.

President Emeritus: Robert F Julian. **Treasurer:** Jon Dandes (Jamestown). **Secretary:** Doug Estes.

Directors: Tim Bawmann (Lowell), Steve Cohen (Brooklyn), Jon Dandes (Jamestown), Jeff Eiseman (Aberdeen), Tom Ganey (Auburn), Bill Gladstone (Tri-City), Jeff Goldklang (Hudson Valley), Chuck Greenberg (State College), Kyle Bostick (Vermont), Michael Savit (Mahoning Valley), E Miles Prentice (Connecticut), Naomi Silver (Batavia), Art Matin (Staten Island), Paul Velte (Williamsport).

League Historian: Charles Wride.

Division Structure: McNamara—Aberdeen, Brooklyn, Hudson Valley, Staten Island. Pinckney—Auburn, Batavia, Jamestown, Mahoning Valley, State College, Williamsport. Stedler—Lowell, Connecticut, Tri-City, Vermont.

Regular Season: 76 games. **2012 Opening Date:** June 17. **Closing Date:** Sept 4. **All-Star Game:** Aug 16 at Lowell. **Playoff Format:** Division winners and wild-card team meet in best-of-three semifinals. Winners meet in best-of-three series for league championship.

Roster Limit: 30 active, but only 25 may be in uniform and eligible to play in any given game.
Player Eligibility Rule: No more than four players 23 or older; no more than three players on active list may have four or more years of prior service. **Brand of Baseball:** Rawlings. **Umpires:** Unavailable.

Ben Hayes

STADIUM INFORMATION

Club	Stadium	Opened	Dimensions LF	CF	RF	Capacity	2011 Att.
Aberdeen	Ripken Stadium	2002	310	400	310	6,000	242,723
Auburn	Falcon Park	1995	330	400	330	2,800	48,429
Batavia	Dwyer Stadium	1996	325	400	325	2,600	37,029
Brooklyn	KeySpan Park	2001	315	412	325	7,500	245,087
Connecticut	Dodd Stadium	1995	309	401	309	6,270	62,317
Hudson Valley	Dutchess Stadium	1994	325	400	325	4,494	149,243
Jamestown	Russell E. Diethrick Jr. Park	1941	335	410	353	3,324	42,086
Lowell	Edward LeLacheur Park	1998	337	400	301	4,842	167,222
Mahoning Valley	Eastwood Field	1999	335	405	335	6,000	111,048
State College	Medlar Field at Lubrano Park	2006	325	399	320	5,412	139,007
Staten Island	Richmond County Bank Ballpark	2001	325	400	325	6,500	192,568
Tri-City	Joseph L. Bruno Stadium	2002	325	400	325	5,000	156,297
Vermont	Centennial Field	1922	323	405	330	4,000	88,711
Williamsport	Bowman Field	1923	345	405	350	4,200	68,124

ABERDEEN IRONBIRDS

Office Address: 873 Long Drive, Aberdeen, MD 21001.
Telephone: (410) 297-9292. **Fax:** (410) 297-6653.
E-Mail Address: info@ironbirdsbaseball.com.
Website: www.ironbirdsbaseball.com.
Affiliation (first year): Baltimore Orioles (2002). **Years in League:** 2002-

OWNERSHIP, MANAGEMENT

Operated By: Ripken Professional Baseball LLC.

Principal Owner: Cal Ripken Jr. **Co-Owner/Executive Vice President:** Bill Ripken. **VP:** Jeff Eiseman.

General Manager: Aaron Moszer. **Assistant GM:** Kari Rumfield. **Director, Ticket Operations:** Brad Cox. **Director, Retail Merchandising:** Don Eney. **Video Production Manager:** Jason Vaughn. **Manager, Facilities:** Steve Fairbaugh. **Head Groundskeeper:** Patrick Coakley.

FIELD STAFF

Manager: Gary Allenson. **Coach:** Brad Komminsk. **Pitching Coach:** Alan Mills.

GAME INFORMATION
Radio Announcer: Towney Godfrey. **No. of Games Broadcast:** Home-38, Away-38. **Flagship Station:** MiLB.com.
PA Announcer: Jay Szech. **Official Scorer:** Joe Stetka.
Stadium Name: Ripken Stadium. **Location:** I-95 to exit 85 (Route 22), west on 22 West, right onto Long Drive.
Ticket Price Range: $7-16.

AUBURN DOUBLEDAYS

Office Address: 130 N Division St, Auburn, NY 13021.
Telephone: (315) 255-2489. **Fax:** (315) 255-2675.
E-Mail Address: ddays@auburndoubledays.com.
Website: www.auburndoubledays.com.
Affiliation (first year): Washington Nationals (2011). **Years in League:** 1958-80, 1982-

OWNERSHIP, MANAGEMENT
Operated by: Auburn Community Non-Profit Baseball Association Inc.
President: David Daum. **General Manager:** Adam Winslow

FIELD STAFF
Manager: Gary Cathcart. **Coach:** Luis Ordaz. **Pitching Coach:** Sam Narron.

GAME INFORMATION
Radio Announcer: Unavailable. **No of Games Broadcast:** Home-38 Away-38. **Flagship Station:** Unavailable.

BATAVIA MUCKDOGS

Office Address: Dwyer Stadium, 299 Bank St, Batavia, NY 14020.
Telephone: (585) 343-5454. **Fax:** (585) 343-5620.
E-Mail Address: tsick@muckdogs.com. **Website:** www.muckdogs.com.
Affiliation (first year): St. Louis Cardinals (2007). **Years in League:** 1939-53, 1957-59, 1961-

OWNERSHIP, MANAGEMENT
Operated By: Red Wings Management, LLC.
General Manager: Travis Sick. **Assistant GM:** Mike Ewing. **Director, Stadium Operations:** Don Rock. **Director, Merchandise:** Barbara Moore. **Clubhouse Manager:** Tony Pecora.

FIELD STAFF
Manager: Dann Bilardelo. **Coach:** Roger LaFrancois. **Pitching Coach:** Dernier Orozco. **Trainer:** Mike Petrarca.

GAME INFORMATION
Radio Announcer: Matthew Coller. **No. of Games Broadcast:** Home-38 Away-20.
Flagship Station: WBTA 1490-AM. **PA Announcer:** Unavailable. **Official Scorer:** Greg Parks.
Stadium Name: Dwyer Stadium.
Location: I-90 to exit 48, left on Route 98 South, left on Richmond Avenue, left on Bank Street.
Standard Game Times: 7:05 pm, Sun 1:05, 5:05. **Ticket Price Range:** $5.50-7.50.
Visiting Club Hotel: Days Inn of Batavia, 200 Oak St, Batavia, NY 14020. **Telephone:** (585) 343-1440.

BROOKLYN CYCLONES

Office Address: 1904 Surf Ave, Brooklyn, NY 11224.
Telephone: (718) 449-8497. **Fax:** (718) 449-6368.
E-Mail Address: info@brooklyncyclones.com. **Website:** www.brooklyncyclones.com.
Affiliation (first year): New York Mets (2001). **Years in League:** 2001-

OWNERSHIP, MANAGEMENT
Chairman, CEO: Fred Wilpon.
President: Saul Katz. **COO:** Jeff Wilpon.
General Manager: Steve Cohen. **Assistant GM:** Kevin Mahoney. **Director, Communications:** Billy Harner. **Director, New Business Development:** Gary J Perone. **Graphics Manager:** Kevin Jimenez. **Operations Manager:** Vladimir Lipsman.. **Head Groundskeeper:** Kevin Ponte. **Account Executives:** Greg Conway, Danny Diaz, Randy Lauwasser, Jake McCalister, Ricky Viola. **Staff Accountant:** Tatiana Isdith. **Administrative Assistant, Community Relations:** Sharon Lundy-Ross.

FIELD STAFF
Manager: Rich Donnelly. **Coach:** Bobby Malek. **Pitching Coach:** Frank Viola.

GAME INFORMATION

Radio Announcer: Warner Fusselle. **No. of Games Broadcast:** Home-38, Away-38. **Flagship Station:** WKRB 90.3-FM. **PA Announcer:** Unavailable. **Official Scorer:** Unavailable. **Stadium Name:** MCU Park. **Location:** Belt Parkway to Cropsey Ave South, continue on Cropsey until it becomes West 17th St, continue to Surf Ave, stadium on south side of Surf Ave; By subway, west/south to Stillwell Ave./Coney Island station. **Ticket Price Range:** $8-17. **Visiting Club Hotel:** Holiday Inn Express, 279 Butler Street, Brooklyn, NY 11217. **Telephone:** (718) 855-9600.

CONNECTICUT TIGERS

Office Address: 14 Stott Avenue, Norwich, CT 06360.
Mailing Address: 14 Stott Avenue, Norwich, CT 06360.
Telephone: (860) 887-7962. **Fax:** (860) 886-5996.
E-Mail Address: info@cttigers.com. **Website:** www.cttigers.com.
Affiliation (first year): Detroit Tigers (1999). **Years in League:** 1966-

OWNERSHIP, MANAGEMENT

Operated By: Oneonta Athletic Corp.
President: Miles Prentice. **Vice President/General Manager:** CJ Knudsen. **VP/Assistant GM:** Eric Knighton. **Director, Community Relations/Promotions:** Dave Schermerhorn. **Director, Concessions/Merchandise:** Heather Bartlett. **Director, Facilities/Turf Management:** Bryan Barkley. **Box Office Manager:** Bobby DeVito. **Group Sales Account Executive:** Josh Postler.

FIELD STAFF

Manager: Andrew Graham. **Coach:** Mike Rabelo. **Pitching Coach:** Jorge Cordova. **Trainer:** TJ Obergefell.

GAME INFORMATION

Radio: Eric Knighton.
PA Announcer: Ed Weyant. **Official Scorer:** Chris Cote.
Stadium Name: Dodd Stadium. **Location:** Exit 82 off I-395. **Standard Game Times:** 7:05 p.m., **Sun** 4:05 pm. **Ticket Price Range:** $7-20.

HUDSON VALLEY RENEGADES

Office Address: Dutchess Stadium, 1500 Route 9D, Wappingers Falls, NY 12590.
Mailing Address: PO Box 661, Fishkill, NY 12524.
Telephone: (845) 838-0094. **Fax:** (845) 838-0014.
E-Mail Address: info@hvrenegades.com. **Website:** www.hvrenegades.com.
Affiliation (first year): Tampa Bay Rays (1996). **Years in League:** 1994-.

OWNERSHIP, MANAGEMENT

Operated by: Keystone Professional Baseball Club Inc.
Principal Owner: Marv Goldklang. **President:** Jeff Goldklang
General Manager: Eben Yager. **Assistant GM:** Corey Whitted. **Director, Special Events:** Rick Zolzer. **Director, Stadium Operations:** Tom Hubmaster. **Director, Baseball Communications:** Joe Ausanio. **Director, Business Operations:** Vicky DeFreese. **Director, Ticket Sales/Operations:** Kristen Huss. **Director, Corporate Partnerships:** Andy Willmert. **Director, Group Sales:** Sean Kammerer. **Manager, Community Marketing/Communications:** Corinne Adams. **Manager, New Business Development:** Dave Neff. **Manager, Game Day Entertainment:** Kevin McGuire. **Manager, Stadium Operations:** Kyle Mondschein. **Ticket Sales Coordinator:** Chris Yager. **Head Groundskeeper:** Time Merante. **Community Relations Specialist:** Bob Outer.

FIELD STAFF

Manager: Jared Sandberg. **Pitching Coach:** Kyle Snyder. **Bench Coach:** Dan DeMent. **Trainer:** Brian Newman.

GAME INFORMATION

Radio Announcer: Ben Gellman-Chomsky. **No. of Games Broadcast:** Home-38, Away-38.
Flagship Stations: WBNR 1260-AM/WLNA 1420-AM.
PA Announcer: Rick Zolzer. **Official Scorers:** Unavailable.
Stadium Name: Dutchess Stadium. **Location:** I-84 to exit 11 (Route 9D North), north one mile to stadium.
Standard Game Times: 7:05 pm, Sun 5:05.
Visiting Club Hotel: Days Inn, 20 Schuyler Blvd and Route 9, Fishkill, NY 12524. **Telephone:** (845) 896-4995.

JAMESTOWN JAMMERS

Office Address: 485 Falconer St, Jamestown, NY 14701.
Mailing Address: PO Box 638, Jamestown, NY 14702.
Telephone: (716) 664-0915. **Fax:** (716) 664-4175.
E-Mail Address: email@jamestownjammers.com.
Website: www.jamestownjammers.com.
Affiliation (first year): Miami Marlins (2002). **Years in League:** 1939-57, 1961-73, 1977-.

OWNERSHIP, MANAGEMENT
Operated By: Rich Baseball Operations.
President: Robert Rich Jr. **Chief Operating Officer:** Jonathon Dandes.
General Manager: Matthew Drayer. **Sales/Operations Manager:** John Pogorzelski. **Head Groundskeeper:** Josh Waid.

FIELD STAFF
Manager: Angel Espada. **Coach:** Unavailable. **Pitching Coach:** Brendan Sagara.

GAME INFORMATION
Radio: Unavailable.
PA Announcer: Unavailable. **Official Scorers:** Jim Riggs, Scott Eddy.
Stadium Name: Russell E Diethrick Jr Park. **Location:** From I-90, south on Route 60, left on Buffalo Street, left on Falconer Street. **Standard Game Times:** 7:05 pm, Sun 6:05. **Ticket Price Range:** $5-7.
Visiting Club Hotel: Red Roof Inn, 1980 Main St, Falconer, NY 14733. **Telephone:** (716) 665-3670.

LOWELL SPINNERS

Office Address: 450 Aiken St, Lowell, MA 01854.
Telephone: (978) 459-2255. **Fax:** (978) 459-1674.
E-Mail Address: info@lowellspinners.com. **Website:** www.lowellspinners.com.
Affiliation (first year): Boston Red Sox (1996). **Years in League:** 1996-

OWNERSHIP, MANAGEMENT
Operated By: Diamond Action Inc.
Owner/CEO: Drew Weber.
President/General Manager: Tim Bawmann. **VP, Business Operations:** Brian Lindsay. **VP/Controller:** Patricia Harbour. **VP, Corporate Communications:** Jon Goode. **VP, Stadium Operations:** Dan Beaulieu. **Director, Facility Management:** Gareth Markey. **Director, Media Relations:** Jon Boswell. **Director, Merchandising:** Jeff Cohen. **VP, Group Ticketing:** Jon Healy. **Director, Ticket Operations:** Justin Williams. **Director, Game Day Entertainment:** Matt Steinberg. **Administrative Assistant:** Christine Roy. **Head Groundskeeper:** Jeff Paolino. **Director, Creative Services:** Jarrod FitzGerald. **Clubhouse Manager:** Del Christman.

FIELD STAFF
Manager: Bruce Crabbe. **Hitting Coach:** Nelson Paulino. **Pitching Coach:** Paul Abbott.

GAME INFORMATION
Radio Announcer: Ken Cail. **No. of Games Broadcast:** Home-38 Away-38. **Flagship Station:** WCAP 980-AM.
PA Announcer: George Brown. **Official Scorer:** David Rourke.
Stadium Name: Edward A LeLacheur Park. **Location:** From Route 495 and 3, take exit 35C (Lowell Connector), follow connector to exit 5B (Thorndike Street) onto Dutton Street, left onto Father Morrissette Boulevard, right on Aiken Street. **Standard Game Times:** 7:05 p.m., **Sun 5:**05 p.m. **6/24, 8/19 1:**05. **Ticket Price Range:** $5-10.
Visiting Club Hotel: Radisson of Chelmsford, 10 Independence Dr, Chelmsford, MA 01879. **Telephone:** (978) 356-0800.

MAHONING VALLEY
SCRAPPERS

Office Address: 111 Eastwood Mall Blvd, Niles, OH 44446.
Mailing Address: 111 Eastwood Mall Blvd, Niles, OH 44446.
Telephone: (330) 505-0000. **Fax:** (303) 505-9696.
E-Mail Address: info@mvscrappers.com. **Website:** www.mvscrappers.com.
Affiliation (first year): Cleveland Indians (1999). **Years in League:** 1999-

OWNERSHIP, MANAGEMENT
Operated By: HWS Baseball Group.
Managing General Partner: Michael Savit.

General Manager: Jordan Taylor. **Assistant GM, Business Operations:** Debbie Primmer. **Director, Sales:** Matt Thompson. **Box Office Manager/Merchandise Manager:** Stephanie Fife. **Director, Stadium Operations:** Brad Hooser. **Director, Marketing/Promotions:** Heather Sahli. **Director, Group Sales:** Mark Libs. **Account Executive:** Chris Sumner. **Head Groundskeeper:** Matt Rollins.

FIELD STAFF
Manager: Ted Kubiak. **Coach:** Unavailable. **Pitching Coach:** Greg Hibbard.

GAME INFORMATION
Radio Announcer: Unavailable. **No. of Games Broadcast:** Home-38, Away-38. **Flagship Station:** 1570 WHTX. **PA Announcer:** Unavailable. **Official Scorer:** Craig Antush.
Stadium Name: Eastwood Field. **Location:** I-80 to 11 North to 82 West to 46 South; stadium located behind Eastwood Mall. **Ticket Price Range:** $5-11.
Visiting Club Hotel: Days Inn & Suites, 1615 Liberty St, Girard, OH 44429. **Telephone:** (330) 759-9820.

STATE COLLEGE SPIKES

Office Address: 112 Medlar Field, Lubrano Park, University Park, PA 16802.
Telephone: (814) 272-1711. **Fax:** (814) 272-1718.
Website: www.statecollegespikes.com.
Affiliation (first year): Pittsburgh Pirates (2007). **Years in League:** 2006-.

OWNERSHIP, MANAGEMENT
Operated By: Spikes Baseball LP.
Chairman/Managing Partner: Chuck Greenberg.
Vice President/General Manager: Jason Dambach.
Director, Corporate Sales: Scott Walker. **Director, Promotions/Community Relations:** David Wells. **Director, Ballpark Operations:** Dan Petrazzolo. **Accounting Manager:** Karen Mahon. **Accounting/Box Office Assistant:** Ashley Davidson. **Ticket Account Executives:** Kris McDonough, Will West. **Sports Turf Manager:** Matt Neri.

FIELD STAFF
Manager: Dave Turgeon. **Hitting Coach:** Dave Howard. **Pitching Coach:** Justin Meccage. **Trainer:** Justin Ahrens.

GAME INFORMATION
Radio Announcers: Steve Jones. **No of Games Broadcast:** Home-38 Road-38. **Flagship Station:** WZWW 95.3-FM.
PA Announcer: Jeff Brown. **Official Scorer:** Dave Baker, John Dixon, Justin Fraker.
Stadium Name: Medlar Field at Lubrano Park. **Location:** From west, US 322 to Mount Nittany Expressway, I-80 to exit 158 (old exit 23/Milesburg), follow Route 150 South to Route 26 South; From east, I-80 to exit 161 (old exit 24/Bellefonte) to Route 26 South or US 220/I-99 South. **Standard Game Times:** 7:05 pm, Sun 6:05. **Ticket Price Range:** $6-14.
Visiting Club Hotel: Ramada Conference Center State College, 1450 Atherton St, State College, PA 16801. **Telephone:** (814) 238-3001.

STATEN ISLAND YANKEES

Stadium Address: 75 Richmond Terrace, Staten Island, NY 10301.
Telephone: (718) 720-9265. **Fax:** (718) 273-5763.
Website: www.siyanks.com.
Affiliation (first year): New York Yankees (1999). **Years in League:** 1999-

OWNERSHIP, MANAGEMENT
Operated by: Nostalgic Partners
Principal Owners: Staten Island Minor League Holdings LLC.
Executive Vice President/General Manager: Jane Rogers.
Finance Manager: Tom Phillips. **Assistant General Manager:** John McCutchan. **VP, Ticket Sales:** Jason Cohen. **Director, Ticket Sales/Operations:** Matt Gulino. **Director, Entertainment:** Mike d'Amboise. **Assistant Director, Entertainment:** Mike Katz. **Director, Sponsor Services:** Tak Mihara. **Manager, Sponsor Services:** Kerry Haley, Jill Wright. **Manager, Ticket Operations:** Jason Donders. **Coordinator, Sales/Marketing:** Melissa Loughran. **Manager, Corporate Marketing:** Rob Saarinen. **Group Sales Coordinators:** Andrew Wall, Evan Doyle, John DeLuca, Ken Greco, Matt Magnani, Mike Kitlas, Tim Holder, Zach Johnston. **Customer Account Managers:** Dwayne Douglas, Steve McCann. **Groundskeeper:** Ryan Woodley.

FIELD STAFF
Manager: Justin Pope. **Hitting Coach:** Ty Hawkins. **Pitching Coach:** Carlos Chantres. **Coach:** Danilo Valiente.

GAME INFORMATION
Radio Announcer: Unavailable. **No. of Games Broadcast:** Home-38, Away-38. **Flagship Station:** Unavailable.
PA Announcer: Unavailable. **Official Scorer:** Unavailable.

Stadium Name: Richmond County Bank Ballpark at St George. **Location:** From I-95, take exit 13E (1-278 and Staten Island), cross Goethals Bridge, stay on I-278 East and take last exit before Verrazano Narrows Bridge, north on Father Cappodanno Boulevard, which turns into Bay Street, which goes to ferry terminal; ballpark next to Staten Island Ferry Terminal. **Standard Game Times:** 7pm, Sun 4.
Visiting Club Hotel: Unavailable.

TRI-CITY VALLEYCATS

Office Address: Joseph L Bruno Stadium, 80 Vandenburg Ave, Troy, NY 12180.
Mailing Address: PO Box 694, Troy, NY 12181.
Telephone: (518) 629-2287. **Fax:** (518) 629-2299.
E-Mail Address: info@tcvalleycats.com. **Website:** www.tcvalleycats.com.
Affiliation (first year): Houston Astros (2001). **Years in League:** 2002-

OWNERSHIP, MANAGEMENT
Operated By: Tri-City ValleyCats Inc.
Principal Owners: Martin Barr, John Burton, William Gladstone, Rick Murphy, Alfred Roberts, Stephen Siegel.
President: William Gladstone.
Vice President/General Manager: Rick Murphy. **Assistant GM:** Matt Callahan. **Fan Development Manager:** Michelle Skinner. **Stadium Operations Manager:** Keith Sweeney. **Community Relations Manager:** Ryan Burke. **Media Relations Manager:** Chris Chenes. **Business Development Manager:** Joel Pagliaro. **Account Executives:** Chris Dawson, Kyle Wheeler, Michael Johnson. **Food/Beverage Coordinator:** Gian Rafaniello. **Box Office Manager:** Jessica Kaszeta. **Bookkeeper:** Gene Gleason.

FIELD STAFF
Manager: Stubby Clapp. **Coach:** Mark Bailey. **Pitching Coach:** Rick Aponte. **Trainer:** Michael Rendon.

GAME INFORMATION
Radio Announcer: Unavailable . **No. of Games Broadcast:** Home-38. **Flagship Station:** MiLB.com.
PA Announcer: Anthony Pettograsso. **Official Scorer:** Kevin Whitaker.
Stadium Name: Joseph L Bruno Stadium. **Location:** From north, I-87 to exit 7 (Route 7), go east 1 1/2 miles to I-787 South, to Route 378 East, go over bridge to Route 4, right to Route 4 South, one mile to Hudson Valley Community College campus on left; From south, I-87 to exit 23 (I-787), I-787 north six miles to exit for Route 378 east, over bridge to Route 4, right to Route 4 South, one mile to campus on left; From east, Massachusetts Turnpike to exit B-1 (I-90), nine miles to Exit 8 (Defreestville), left off ramp to Route 4 North, five miles to campus on right; From west, I-90 to exit 24 (I-90 East), I-90 East for six miles to I-787 North (Troy), 2.2 miles to exit for Route 378 East, over bridge to Route 4, right to Route 4 south for one mile to campus on left. **Standard Game Times:** 7 pm, Sun 5. **Ticket Price Range:** $5-10.
Visiting Club Hotel: Holiday Inn Express, 8 Empire Drive, Rensselaer, NY 12144.

VERMONT LAKE MONSTERS

Office Address: 1 King Street Ferry Dock, Burlington, VT 05401.
Telephone: (802) 655-4200. **Fax:** (802) 655-5660.
E-Mail Address: info@vermontlakemonsters.com. **Website:** www.vermontlakemonsters.com.
Affiliation (first year): Oakland Athletics (2011). **Years in League:** 1994-

OWNERSHIP, MANAGEMENT
Operated by: Vermont Expos Inc.
Principal Owner/President: Ray Pecor.
General Manager: Nate Cloutier. **Assistant GM:** Joe Doud. **Accounts Manager/Merchandise Director:** Kate Echo. **Director, Media Relations:** Paul Stanfield. **Clubhouse Operations:** Phil Schelzo.

FIELD STAFF
Manager: Rick Magnante. **Coach:** Casey Myers. **Pitching Coach:** Ariel Prieto.

GAME INFORMATION
Radio Announcers: Chris Villani. **No. of Games Broadcast:** Home-38, Away-12. **Flagship Station:** 101.3 ESPN.

WILLIAMSPORT CROSSCUTTERS

Office Address: Bowman Field, 1700 W Fourth St, Williamsport, PA 17701.
Mailing Address: PO Box 3173, Williamsport, PA 17701.
Telephone: (570) 326-3389. **Fax:** (570) 326-3494.
E-Mail Address: mail@crosscutters.com. **Website:** www.crosscutters.com.
Affiliation (first year): Philadelphia Phillies (2007). **Years in League:** 1968-72, 1994-

OWNERSHIP, MANAGEMENT

Operated By: Geneva Cubs Baseball Inc.
Principal Owners: Paul Velte, John Schreyer.
President: Paul Velte. **Executive Vice President:** John Schreyer.
VP/General Manager: Doug Estes. **VP, Marketing/Public Relations:** Gabe Sinicropi. **Director, Concessions:** Bill Gehron. **Director, Ticket Operations/Community Relations:** Sarah Budd. **Director, Partner Services:** Jennifer Hoover. **Head Groundskeeper:** Unavailable.

FIELD STAFF

Manager: Andy Tracy. **Coach:** Rafael DeLima. **Pitching Coach:** Aaron Fultz.

GAME INFORMATION

Radio Announcer: Todd Bartley. **No. of Games Broadcast:** Home-38, Away-38. **Flagship Station:** WLYC 1050-AM, 104.1-FM.
PA Announcer: Rob Thomas. **Official Scorer:** Ken Myers.
Stadium Name: Bowman Field. **Location:** From south, Route 15 to Maynard Street, right on Maynard, left on Fourth Street for one mile; From north, Route 15 to Fourth Street, left on Fourth. **Ticket Price Range:** $5-$8.
Visiting Club Hotel: Best Western, 1840 E Third St, Williamsport, PA 17701. **Telephone:** (570) 326-1981.

NORTHWEST LEAGUE

Office Address: 620 W Franklin St, Boise, ID 83702.
Mailing Address: PO Box 1645, Boise, ID 83701.
Telephone: (208) 429-1511. **Fax:** (208) 429-1525.
E-Mail Address: bobrichmond@qwestoffice.net. **Website:** www.northwestleague.com.
Years League Active: 1954-.
President/Treasurer: Bob Richmond.
Vice President: Dave Elmore (Eugene). **Corporate Secretary:** Jerry Walker (Salem-Keizer).
Directors: Dave Elmore (Eugene), Bobby Brett (Spokane), Tom Volpe (Everett), Jake Kerr (Vancouver), Mike McMurray (Yakima), Brent Miles (Tri-City), Jerry Walker (Salem-Keizer), Neil Leibman (Boise). **Administrative Assistant:** Rob Richmond.
Division Structure: East—Boise, Spokane, Tri-City, Yakima. West—Eugene, Everett, Salem-Keizer, Vancouver.
Regular Season: 76 games (split schedule). **2012 Opening Date:** June 15. **Closing Date:** Sept 1.
Playoff Format: First-half division winners meet second-half division winners in best-of-three series. Winners meet in best-of-three series for league championship.
All-Star Game: None.
Roster Limit: 30 active, 35 under control. **Player Eligibility Rule:** No more than three players on active list may have four or more years of prior service.
Brand of Baseball: Rawlings.
Umpires: Unavailable.

Bob Richmond

STADIUM INFORMATION

			Dimensions				
Club	Stadium	Opened	LF	CF	RF	Capacity	2011 Att.
Boise	Memorial Stadium	1989	335	400	335	3,426	98,860
Eugene	PK Park	2010	335	400	325	4,000	114,690
Everett	Everett Memorial Stadium	1984	324	380	330	3,682	96,345
Salem-Keizer	Volcanoes Stadium	1997	325	400	325	4,100	105,973
Spokane	Avista Stadium	1958	335	398	335	7,162	183,458
Tri-City	Dust Devils Stadium	1995	335	400	335	3,700	85,953
Vancouver	Nat Bailey Stadium	1951	335	395	335	6,500	162,162
Yakima	Yakima County Stadium	1993	295	406	295	3,000	66,545

BOISE HAWKS

Office Address: 5600 N Glenwood St Boise, ID 83714.
Telephone: (208) 322-5000. **Fax:** (208) 322-6846.
Website: www.boisehawks.com.
Affiliation (first year): Chicago Cubs (2001). **Years in League:** 1975-76, 1978, 1987-

Ownership/Management
Operated by: Boise Baseball LLC.
CEO: Neil Leibman.
President/General Manager: Todd Rahr. **Vice President/Business Operations:** Dina Duncan. **VP/Sales/Marketing:** Jinny Giery. **Client Services Manager:** Greg Marconi. **Sponsorship Sales Manager:** Jesse Robinson. **Ticket Sales Assistant:** Thomas Wolff. **Ticket Sales Assistant:** JD Bowers. **Event/Community Outreach Manager:** Lauren Hamm. **Merchandise/Creative Services Coordinator:** Kelly Kerkvliet. **Digital Content Manager:** Ken Hyde. **Media/Broadcast Manager:** Mike Safford. **Head Groundskeeper:** Chuck Barto. **Media Relations Coordinator:** Courtney Garner. **Box Office Coordinator:** Nicholas Black. **Event Operations Coordinator:** Jake Abbott. **Director, Food/Beverage/Home Plate Food Services:** Geno George. **Manager, Food/Beverage Operations:** Jake Lusk.

FIELD STAFF
Manager: Mark Johnson. **Coach:** Bill Buckner. **Pitching Coach:** David Rosario. **Trainer:** Bob Grimes.

GAME INFORMATION
Radio Announcer: Mike Safford. **No. of Games Broadcast:** Home-38, Away-38. **Flagship Station:** KTIK 1350-AM.
PA Announcer: Unavailable. **Official Scorer:** Unavailable.
Stadium Name: Memorial Stadium. **Location:** I-84 to Cole Road, north to Western Idaho Fairgrounds at 5600 North Glenwood Street. **Standard Game Time:** 7:15 pm. **Ticket Price Range:** $6-$14.
Visiting Club Hotel: Owyhee Plaza Hotel, 1109 Main St, Boise, ID 83702. **Telephone:** (208) 343-4611.

EUGENE EMERALDS

Office Address: 2760 Martin Luther King Jr Blvd, Eugene, OR 97401.
Mailing Address: PO Box 5566, Eugene, OR 97405.
Telephone: (541) 342-5367. **Fax:** (541) 342-6089. **E-Mail Address:** info@go-ems.com.
Website: www.emeraldsbaseball.com.
Affiliation (first year): San Diego Padres (2001). **Years in League:** 1955-68, 1974-

Ownership/Management
Operated By: Elmore Sports Group Ltd.
Principal Owner: David Elmore.
General Manager: Allan Benavides. **Assistant GM:** Sarah Heth. **Director, Corporate Sales:** Matt Dompe. **Director, Food/Beverage:** Kelly Hallquest. **Director, Mascot Operations:** Teigh Bowen. **Director, Finance:** Andy Hoedt. **Director, Corporate Events:** Tyler Tostenson.

FIELD STAFF
Manager: Pat Murphy. **Coach:** Chris Prieto. **Pitching Coach:** Nelson Cruz.

GAME INFORMATION
Radio Announcer: Chris Fisher. **No. of Games Broadcast:** Home-38, Away-38. **Flagship Station:** 95.3 "The Score".
PA Announcer: Matt Dompe. **Official Scorer:** George McPherson.
Stadium Name: PK Park, 2760 Martin Luther King Jr Blvd. **Standard Game Time:** 7:05 pm, Sun 1:05. **Ticket Price Range:** $6-12.
Visiting Club Hotel: Valley River Inn, 1000 Valley River Way, Eugene, OR 97401. **Telephone:** (541) 743-1000.

EVERETT AQUASOX

Mailing Address: 3802 Broadway, Everett, WA 98201.
Telephone: (425) 258-3673. **Fax:** (425) 258-3675.
E-Mail Address: aquasox@aquasox.com. **Website:** www.aquasox.com.
Affiliation (first year): Seattle Mariners (1995). **Years in League:** 1984-

Ownership/Management
Operated by: 7th Inning Stretch, LLC
Directors: Tom Volpe, Pat Filippone.
Executive Vice President: Tom Backemeyer. **VP, Corporate Sponsorships:** Brian Sloan. **Director, Corporate Partnerships/Broadcasting:** Pat Dillon. **Director, Food/Beverage:** Todd Holterhoff. **Director, Community Relations:** Katie Crawford. **Director, Tickets:** Ryan Pearman. **Account Executives:** Alex Dadisman, Joe Haller, Erica Fensterbush. **Head Groundskeeper:** Brian Burroughs.

FIELD STAFF
Manager: Rob Mummau. **Pitching Coach:** Rich Dorman. **Hitting Coach:** Andy Bottin. **Trainer:** Spyder Webb

GAME INFORMATION
Radio Announcer: Pat Dillon. **No. of Games Broadcast:** Home-38, Away-38. **Flagship Station:** KRKO 1380-AM.
PA Announcer: Tom Lafferty. **Official Scorer:** Pat Castro.
Stadium Name: Everett Memorial Stadium. **Location:** I-5, exit 192. **Standard Game Times:** 7:05 pm, Sun 1:05/4:05.
Ticket Price Range: $7-17.
Visiting Club Hotel: Holiday Inn, Downtown Everett, 3105 Pine St, Everett, WA 98201. **Telephone:** (425) 339-2000.

SALEM-KEIZER VOLCANOES

Street Address: 6700 Field of Dreams Way, Keizer, OR 97303.
Mailing Address: PO Box 20936, Keizer, OR 97307.
Telephone: (503) 390-2225. **Fax:** (503) 390-2227.
E-Mail Address: ticket_office@volcanoesbaseball.com. **Website:** www.volcanoesbaseball.com.
Affiliation (first year): San Francisco Giants (1997). **Years in League:** 1997-

Ownership/Management
Operated By: Sports Enterprises Inc.
Principal Owners: Jerry Walker, Bill Tucker.
General Manager: Jerry Walker. **Vice President, Operations:** Rick Nelson. **Senior Account Executive:** Jerry Howard. **Director, Ticket Office Operations:** Bea Howard. **Assistant Ticket Office Manager/Webmaster:** Michael Trevino. **Outside Sales Executives:** Marc Kaufman, Drew Pryse. **Director, Business Development:** Justin Lacche.

FIELD STAFF
Manager: Tom Trebelhorn. **Coach:** Ricky Ward. **Pitching Coach:** Jerry Cram. **Coach:** Hector Borg.

GAME INFORMATION
Radio Announcer: Matt Pedersen. **No. of Games Broadcast:** Home-38, Away-38. **Flagship Station:** KBZY AM-1490.
PA Announcer: Michael Trevino. **Official Scorer:** Scott Sepich.
Stadium Name: Volcanoes Stadium. **Location:** I-5 to exit 260 (Chemawa Road), west one block to Stadium Way NE, north six blocks to stadium. **Standard Game Times:** 6:35 pm, 7:05 (Fri-Sat), Sun 5:05. **Ticket Price Range:** $7-11.
Visiting Club Hotel: Comfort Suites, 630 Hawthorne Ave SE, Salem, OR 97301. **Telephone:** (503) 585-9705.

SPOKANE INDIANS

Office Address: Avista Stadium, 602 N Havana, Spokane, WA 99202.
Mailing Address: PO Box 4758, Spokane, WA 99220.
Telephone: (509) 535-2922. **Fax:** (509) 534-5368.
E-Mail Address: mail@spokaneindiansbaseball.com.
Website: www.spokaneindiansbaseball.com.
Affiliation (first year): Texas Rangers (2003). **Years in League:** 1972, 1983-

Ownership/Management
Operated By: Longball Inc.
Principal Owner: Bobby Brett. **Senior Advisor:** Andrew Billig.
Vice President/General Manager: Chris Duff. **Senior VP:** Otto Klein. **VP, Tickets:** Josh Roys. **Director, Business Operations:** Lesley DeHart. **Director, Sponsorships:** Jon Luke. **Promotions Coordinators:** Kyle Day, Alex Capeloto. **Group Sales Coordinators:** Nick Gaebe, Amy Custer. **Director, Concessions/Operations:** Justin Stottlemyre. **Director, Public Relations:** Bud Bareither. **CFO:** Greg Sloan. **Accounting:** Dawnelle Shaw. **Head Groundskeeper:** Tony Lee. **Assistant Director, Stadium Operations:** Larry Blumer.

FIELD STAFF
Manager: Tim Hulett. **Coaches:** Oscar Bernard, Vinny Lopez. **Pitching Coach:** Ryan O'Malley.

GAME INFORMATION
Radio Announcer: Mike Boyle. **No. of Games Broadcast:** Home-38, Away-38. **Flagship Station:** 1510 KGA.
PA Announcer: Unavailable. **Official Scorer:** Peter Legner.
Stadium Name: Avista Stadium at the Spokane Fair and Expo Center. **Location:** From west, I-90 to exit 283B (Thor/Freya), east on Third Avenue, left onto Havana; From east, I-90 to Broadway exit, right onto Broadway, left onto Havana. **Standard Game Time:** 6:30 pm. **Ticket Price Range:** $5-11.
Visiting Club Hotel: Mirabeau Park Hotel & Convention Center, N 1100 Sullivan Rd, Spokane, WA 99037. **Telephone:** (509) 924-9000.

TRI-CITY DUST DEVILS

Office Address: 6200 Burden Blvd, Pasco, WA 99301.
Telephone: (509) 544-8789. **Fax:** (509) 547-9570.
E-Mail Address: info@dustdevilsbaseball.com. **Website:** www.dustdevilsbaseball.com.
Affiliation (first year): Colorado Rockies (2001). **Years in League:** 1955-1974, 1983-1986, 2001-.

Ownership/Management
Operated by: Northwest Baseball Ventures.
Principal Owners: George Brett, Hoshino Dreams Corp, Brent Miles.
President: Brent Miles. **Vice President/General Manager:** Derrel Ebert. **VP, Business Operations:** Tim Gittel. **Assistant GM, Sponsorships:** Kelli Foos. **Director, Ticket Sales:** Dan O'Neill. **Director, Sponsorships:** Lauren Coombs. **Director, Group Sales:** Anne Brenner. **Sponsorships Coordinator:** Erik Mertens. **Account Executives:** Andrew Klein, Austin Redman. **Group Sales Coordinator:** Sam Spuhler. **Media Relations Coordinator:** Heath Harshman. **Head Groundskeeper:** Michael Angel.

FIELD STAFF
Manager: Freddie Ocasio. **Coach:** Anthony Sanders. **Pitching Coach:** Dave Burba. **Trainer:** Andy Stover.

GAME INFORMATION
Radio Announcer: Unavailable. **No. of Games Broadcast:** Home-38, Away-38. **Flagship Station:** Newstalk 870 AM KFLD.
PA Announcer: Patrick Harvey. **Official Scorers:** Tony Wise, Scott Tylinski.
Stadium Name: Gesa Stadium. **Location:** I-182 to exit 9 (Road 68), north to Burden Blvd, right to stadium. **Standard

Game Time: 7:15 pm **Ticket Price Range:** $6-9.
   Visiting Club Hotel: Red Lion Hotel-Columbia Center, 1101 N Columbia Center Blvd, Kennewick, WA 99336. **Telephone:** (509) 783-0611

VANCOUVER CANADIANS

Office Address: Scotiabank Field at Nat Bailey Stadium, 4601 Ontario St, Vancouver, British Columbia V5V 3H4.
   Telephone: (604) 872-5232. **Fax:** (604) 872-1714.
   E-Mail Address: staff@canadiansbaseball.com. **Website:** www.canadiansbaseball.com.
   Affiliation (first year): Toronto Blue Jays (2011). **Years in League:** 2000-

Ownership/Management
   Operated by: Vancouver Canadians Professional Baseball LLP.
   Principal Owners: Jake Kerr, Jeff Mooney. **President:** Andy Dunn.
   General Manager: Jason Takefman. **Assistant GMs:** Rob Fai, JC Fraser, Allan Bailey. **VP, Sales/Marketing:** Graham Wall. **Manager, Sales/Marketing Services:** Angela de Ruiter. **Manager, Sales/Promotions:** Grace Kim. **Coordinator, Sales/Community Relations:** Vanessa Williams. **Manager, Community Relations:** Jeff Holloway. **Head Groundskeeper:** Tom Archibald. **Groundskeeper:** Trevor Sheffield.

FIELD STAFF
   Manager: Clayton McCullough. **Hitting Coach:** Dave Pano. **Pitching Coach:** Jim Czajkowski. **Trainer:** Shawn McDermott.

GAME INFORMATION
   Radio Announcer: Rob Fai. **No. of Games Broadcast:** Home-38, Away-38. **Flagship Station:** The Team 1040-AM.
   PA Announcer: Don Andrews. **Official Scorer:** Unavailable.
   Stadium Name: Nat Bailey Stadium. **Location:** From downtown, take Cambie Street Bridge, left on East 25th Ave./King Edward Ave, right on Main Street, right on 33rd Ave, right on Ontario St to stadium; From south, take Highway 99 to Oak Street, right on 41st Ave, left on Main Street to 33rd Ave, right on Ontario St to stadium. **Standard Game Times:** 7:05 pm, Sun 1:05. **Ticket Price Range:** $9-20.
   Visiting Club Hotel: Accent Inns, 10551 Edwards Dr, Richmond, BC V6X 3L8. **Telephone:** (604) 273-3311.

YAKIMA BEARS

Office Address: 17 N 3rd Street, Suite 101, Yakima, WA 98901.
   Mailing Address: PO Box 483, Yakima, WA 98907.
   Telephone: (509) 457-5151. **Fax:** (509) 457-9909.
   E-Mail Address: info@yakimabears.com. **Website:** www.yakimabears.com.
   Affiliation (first year): Arizona Diamondbacks (2001). **Years in League:** 1955-66, 1990-
   Ownership/Management
   Operated by: Short Season LLC.
   Managing Partners: Mike McMurray, Mike Ellis, Josh Weinman, Myron Levin, Mike Ormsby.
   President: Mike McMurray.
   General Manager: KL Wombacher. **Assistant GM:** Aaron Arndt. **Chief Financial Officer:** Laura McMurray. **Director, Ballpark Operations:** Jared Jacobs. **Director, Merchandise:** Lauren Wombacher. **Director, Media Relations/ Broadcasting:** John Hadden.

FIELD STAFF
   Manager: Audo Vicente. **Hitting Coach:** Jason Camilli. **Pitching Coach:** Doug Bochtler. **Trainer:** Unavailable.

GAME INFORMATION
   Radio Announcer: John Hadden. **No. of Games Broadcast:** Home-38, Away-38. **Flagship Station:** KUTI 1460-AM.
   PA Announcer: Todd Lyons. **Official Scorer:** Unavailable.
   Stadium Name: Yakima County Stadium. **Location:** I-82 to exit 34 (Nob Hill Boulevard), west to Fair Avenue, right on Fair, right on Pacific Avenue. **Standard Game Times:** 7:05 pm, Sun 5:35. **Ticket Price Range:** $4.50-$9.50.
   Visiting Club Hotel: Best Western Ahtanum Inn, 2408 Rudkin Rd, Union Gap, WA 98903. **Telephone:** (509) 248-9700.

APPALACHIAN LEAGUE

APPALACHIAN LEAGUE
of professional baseball clubs

ROOKIE ADVANCED

Mailing Address: 759 182nd Avenue E, Redington Shores, FL 33708.
Telephone: 727-954-4876. **Fax:** None.
E-Mail Address: office@appyleague.net. **Website:** www.appyleague.com.
Years League Active: 1921-25, 1937-55, 1957-.
President/Treasurer: Lee Landers. **Corporate Secretary:** Jim Holland (Princeton).
Directors: Charlie Wilson (Bluefield), Nick Capra (Bristol), Scott Sharp (Burlington), Ronnie Richardson (Danville), Jim Rantz (Elizabethton), Fred Nelson (Greeneville), Jon Vuch (Johnson City), Adam Wogan (Kingsport), Mitch Lukevics (Princeton), Chris Gwynn (Pulaski).
Executive Committee: Wayne Carpenter (Pulaski), Kurt Kemp (Danville), David Lane (Greeneville), Dan Moushon (Burlington), Jon Vuch (Johnson City), Charlie Wilson (Bluefield)
Board of Trustee: Mitch Lukevics (Princeton).
League Administrator: Bobbi Landers.
Division Structure: East—Bluefield, Burlington, Danville, Princeton, Pulaski. **West**—Bristol, Elizabethton, Greeneville, Johnson City, Kingsport.
Regular Season: 68 games. **2012 Opening Date:** June 19. **Closing Date:** Aug. 28.
All-Star Game: None.
Playoff Format: First round (best of three): East winner versus West 2nd place; West winner versus East 2nd place. Winners meet in best-of-three series for league championship.
Roster Limit: 30 active, 35 under control. **Player Eligibility Rule:** No more than three players on the active roster may have three or more years of prior minor league service.
Brand of Baseball: Rawlings.
Umpires: Unavailable

Lee Landers

STADIUM INFORMATION

			Dimensions				
Club	**Stadium**	**Opened**	**LF**	**CF**	**RF**	**Capacity**	**2011 Att.**
Bluefield	Bowen Field	1939	335	400	335	2,250	26,395
Bristol	DeVault Memorial Stadium	1969	325	400	310	2,000	22,433
Burlington	Burlington Athletic Stadium	1960	335	410	335	3,000	28,427
Danville	Dan Daniel Memorial Park	1993	330	400	330	2,588	28,523
Elizabethton	Joe O'Brien Field	1974	335	414	326	1,500	28,900
Greeneville	Pioneer Park	2004	331	400	331	2,400	45,015
Johnson City	Howard Johnson Field	1956	320	410	320	2,500	25,961
Kingsport	Hunter Wright Stadium	1995	330	410	330	2,500	31,988
Princeton	Hunnicutt Field	1988	330	396	330	1,950	27,685
Pulaski	Calfee Park	1935	335	405	310	2,500	30,236

BLUEFIELD BLUE JAYS

Office Address: Stadium Drive, Bluefield, WV 24701.
Mailing Address: PO Box 356, Bluefield, WV 24701.
Telephone: (276) 326-1326. **Fax:** (276) 326-1318.
E-Mail Address: babybirds1@comcast.net. **Website:** www.minorleaguebaseball.com.
Affiliation (second year): Toronto Blue Jays (2011). **Years in League:** 1946-55, 1957-

OWNERSHIP, MANAGEMENT
Director: Charlie Wilson (Toronto Blue Jays).
Vice President: Bill Looney. **Secretary:** MK Burton. **Counsel:** David Kersey.
President: George McGonagle. **General Manager:** Chris Maxwell. **Director, Field Operations/Grounds:** Mike White.

FIELD STAFF
Manager: Dennis Holmberg. **Coach:** Paul Elliott. **Pitching Coach:** Antonio Caceres.

GAME INFORMATION
Stadium Name: Bowen Field. **Location:** I-77 to Bluefield exit 1, Route 290 to Route 460 West, fourth light right onto Leatherwood Lane, left at first light, past Chevron station and turn right, stadium 1/4 mile on left. **Ticket Price Range:** $4.
Visiting Club Hotel: Quality Inn Bluefield, 3350 Big Laurel Highway, Bluefield, WV 24701. **Telephone:** (304) 325-6170.

BRISTOL WHITE SOX

Ballpark Location: 1501 Euclid Ave, Bristol, VA 24201.
Mailing Address: PO Box 1434, Bristol, VA 24203.
Telephone: (276) 206-9946. **Fax:** (276) 669-7686.
E-Mail Address: brisox@btes.tv. **Website:** www.bristolsox.com.
Affiliation (first year): Chicago White Sox (1995). **Years in League:** 1921-25, 1940-55, 1969-

OWNERSHIP, MANAGEMENT

Owned by: Chicago White Sox.
Operated by: Bristol Baseball Inc.
Director: Buddy Bell (Chicago White Sox).
President: Mahlon Luttrell. **Vice Presidents:** Lynn Armstrong, Perry Hustad.
General Manager: Mahlon Luttrell. **Treasurer:** Dorothy Cox. **Secretary:** Tim Johnston.

FIELD STAFF

Manager: Pete Rose Jr. **Coach:** Greg Briley. **Pitching Coach:** Larry Owens. **Trainer:** Kevin Pillifant. **Conditioning Coach:** Ibrahim Rivera.

GAME INFORMATION

Radio: Internet broadcast through milb.com.
PA Announcer: Chuck Necessary. **Official Scorer:** Perry Hustad.
Stadium Name: DeVault Memorial Stadium. **Location:** I-81 to exit 3 onto Commonwealth Ave, right on Euclid Ave for 1/2 mile. **Standard Game Time:** 7 p.m. **Ticket Price Range:** $3-6.
Visiting Club Hotel: Holiday Inn, 3005 Linden Drive Bristol VA 24202. **Telephone:** (276) 466-4100.

BURLINGTON ROYALS

Office Address: 1450 Graham St, Burlington, NC 27217.
Mailing Address: PO Box 1143, Burlington, NC 27216.
Telephone: (336) 222-0223. **Fax:** (336) 226-2498.
E-Mail Address: info@burlingtonroyals.com. **Website:** www.burlingtonroyals.com
Affiliation (first year): Kansas City Royals (2007). **Years in League:** 1986-

OWNERSHIP, MANAGEMENT

Operated by: Burlington Baseball Club Inc.
Director: Scott Sharp (Kansas City Royals).
President: Miles Wolff. **Vice President:** Dan Moushon.
General Manager: Ben Abzug. **Director, Stadium Operations:** Mike Thompson.

FIELD STAFF

Manager: Tommy Shields. **Coach:** Jon Williams. **Pitching Coach:** Carlos Martinez.

GAME INFORMATION

Radio Announcer: Unavailable. **No. of Games Broadcast:** Home-34, Away-7.
Flagship: www.burlingtonroyals.com.
PA Announcer: Tyler Williams. **Official Scorer:** Dale Hunt.
Stadium Name: Burlington Athletic Stadium. **Location:** I-40/85 to exit 145, north on Route 100 (Maple Avenue) for 1 1/2 miles, right on Mebane Street for 1 1/2 miles, right on Beaumont, left on Graham. **Standard Game Time:** 7 p.m. **Ticket Price Range:** $4-8.

DANVILLE BRAVES

Office Address: Dan Daniel Memorial Park, 302 River Park Dr, Danville, VA 24540.
Mailing Address: PO Box 378, Danville, VA 24543.
Telephone: (434) 797-3792. **Fax:** (434) 797-3799.
E-Mail Address: info@dbraves.com. **Website:** www.dbraves.com.
Affiliation (first year): Atlanta Braves (1993). **Years in League:** 1993-

OWNERSHIP, MANAGEMENT

Operated by: Atlanta National League Baseball Club Inc. **Director:** Ronnie Richardson (Atlanta Braves). **General Manager:** David Cross. **Assistant GM:** Bob Kitzmiller. **Operations Manager:** Brandon Bennett. **Head Groundskeeper:** Jon Hall.

FIELD STAFF

Manager: Jonathan Schuerholz. **Coach:** Rick Albert. **Pitching Coach:** Gabe Luckert. **Athletic Trainer:** Kyle Damschroder.

GAME INFORMATION
Radio Announcer: Nick Pierce. **No. of Games Broadcast:** Home-34 (internet only), Away-None. **Flagship Station:** None. **PA Announcer:** Jay Stephens. **Official Scorer:** Mark Bowman.
Stadium Name: American Legion Field Post 325 Field at Dan Daniel Memorial Park. **Location:** US 29 Bypass to River Park Drive/Dan Daniel Memorial Park exit; follow signs to park. **Standard Game Times:** 7 pm, Sun 4. **Ticket Price Range:** $4-7. **Visiting Club Hotel:** Unavailable.

ELIZABETHTON TWINS

Office Address: 300 West Mill Street, Elizabethton, TN 37643.
Stadium Address: 208 N Holly Lane, Elizabethton, TN 37643.
Mailing Address: 136 S Sycamore St, Elizabethton, TN 37643.
Telephone: (423) 547-6441. **Fax:** (423) 547-6442.
E-Mail Address: etwins@cityofelizabethton.org.
Website: www.elizabethtontwins.com.
Affiliation (first year): Minnesota Twins (1974). **Years in League:** 1937-42, 1945-51, 1974-

OWNERSHIP, MANAGEMENT
Operator: City of Elizabethton.
Director: Jim Rantz (Minnesota Twins).
President: Harold Mains.
General Manager: Mike Mains. **Clubhouse Operations/Head Groundskeeper:** David McQueen.

FIELD STAFF
Manager: Ray Smith. **Coach:** Jeff Reed. **Pitching Coach:** Ivan Arteaga. **Trainer:** Ryan Headwall.

GAME INFORMATION
Radio Announcer: Unavailable. **No. of Games Broadcast:** Home-34, Away-6. **Flagship Station:** WBEJ 1240-AM. **PA Announcer:** Tom Banks. **Official Scorer:** Unavailable. **Stadium Name:** Joe O'Brien Field. **Location:** I-81 to Highway I-26, exit at Highway 321/67, left on Holly Lane. **Standard Game Time:** 7 p.m. **Ticket Price Range:** $3-5. **Visiting Club Hotel:** Holiday Inn, 101 W. Springbrook Dr, Johnson City, TN 37601. **Telephone:** (423) 282-4611.

GREENEVILLE ASTROS

Office Address: 135 Shiloh Road, Greeneville, TN 37743.
Mailing Address: PO Box 5192, Greeneville, TN 37743.
Telephone: (423) 638-0411. **Fax:** (423) 638-9450.
E-Mail Address: greeneville@astros.com. **Website:** www.greenevilleastros.com.
Affiliation (first year): Houston Astros (2004). **Years in League:** 2004-

OWNERSHIP, MANAGEMENT
Operated by: Houston Astros Baseball Club.
Director: Fred Nelson (Houston Astros).
General Manager: David Lane. **Assistant GM:** Hunter Reed. **Head Groundskeeper:** Tyler Mittesteadt. **Clubhouse Operations:** Unavailable.

FIELD STAFF
Manager: Omar Lopez. **Pitching Coach:** Hector Mercado. **Hitting Coach:** Cesar Cedeno. **Trainer:** Corey O'Brien.

GAME INFORMATION
Internet Radio: Steve Wilhoit
PA Announcer: Bobby Rader. **Officil Scorer:** Johnny Painter.
Stadium Name: Pioneer Park. **Location:** On the campus of Tusculum College, 135 Shiloh Rd Greeneville, TN 37743.
Standard Game Time: 7 p.m, 6 (Sat/Sun). **Ticket Price Range:** $5-7.
Visiting Club Hotel: Jameson Inn.

JOHNSON CITY CARDINALS

Office Address: 111 Legion St, Johnson City, TN 37601.
Mailing Address: PO Box 179, Johnson City, TN 37605.
Telephone: (423) 461-4866. **Fax:** (423) 461-4864.
E-Mail Address: contact@jccardinals.com. **Website:** www.jccardinals.com.
Affiliation (first year): St. Louis Cardinals (1975). **Years in League:** 1911-13, 1921-24, 1937-55, 1957-61, 1964-

OWNERSHIP, MANAGEMENT

Owned by: St. Louis Cardinals
Operated by: Johnson City Sports Foundation Inc.
President: Lee Sowers (JCSF).
Director: John Vuch (St. Louis Cardinals). **General Manager:** Chuck Arnold.
Assistant GM: Sean Salemme.

FIELD STAFF

Manager: Oliver Marmol. **Coach:** Ramon Ortiz. **Pitching Coach:** Doug White.

GAME INFORMATION

Radio: None.
PA Announcer: Unavailable. **Official Scorer:** Gene Renfro.
Stadium Name: Howard Johnson Field at Cardinal Park. **Location:** I-26 to exit 23, left on East Main, through light onto Legion Street. **Standard Game Time:** 7 p.m. **Ticket Price Range:** $4-$6.
Visiting Club Hotel: Holiday Inn, 101 W Springbrook Dr, Johnson City, TN 37601. **Telephone:** (423) 282-4611.

KINGSPORT METS

Office Address: 800 Granby Rd, Kingsport, TN 37660.
Mailing Address: PO Box 1128, Kingsport, TN 37662.
Telephone: (423) 378-3744. **Fax:** (423) 392-8538.
E-Mail Address: info@kmets.com. **Website:** www.kmets.com.
Affiliation (first year): New York Mets (1980). **Years in League:** 1921-25, 1938-52,
1957, 1960-63, 1969-82, 1984-

OWNERSHIP, MANAGEMENT

Operated By: S&H Baseball LLC.
Director: Adam Wogan (New York Mets).
President: Rick Spivey. **Vice President:** Steve Harville. **VP/General Manager:** Roman Stout. **Accountant:** Bob Dingus.
Director, Concessions: Teresa Haywood. **Head Groundskeeper:** Josh Warner. **Clubhouse Manager:** Travis Baker.
Interns: Mookie Jeter, JT Chadwell.

Field Staff

Manager: Jon Debus. **Coach:** Yunir Garcia. **Pitching Coach:** Jonathan Hurst.

GAME INFORMATION

Radio: None.
PA Announcer: Don Spivey. **Official Scorer:** Eddie Durham.
Stadium Name: Hunter Wright Stadium. **Location:** I-81 to I-181 North, exit 1 (Stone Drive), left on West Stone Drive (U.S. 11W), right on Granby Road. Standard Game Time: 6 pm, 7 (doubleheaders). **Ticket Price Range:** $2-5.
Visiting Club Hotel: The Jameson Inn, 3004 Bays Mountain Plaza, Kingsport, TN 37660. **Telephone:** (423) 282-4611.

PRINCETON RAYS

Office Address: 205 Old Bluefield Rd, Princeton, WV 24740.
Mailing Address: PO Box 5646, Princeton, WV 24740.
Telephone: (304) 487-2000. **Fax:** (304) 487-8762.
E-Mail Address: princetonrays@frontier.com . **Website:** www.princetonrays.net .
Affiliation (first year): Tampa Bay Rays (1997). **Years in League:** 1988-

OWNERSHIP, MANAGEMENT
Operated By: Princeton Baseball Association Inc.
Director: Mitch Lukevics (Tampa Bay Rays). **President:** Mori Williams.
General Manager: Jim Holland. **Director, Stadium Operations:** Mick Bayle. **Official Scorer:** Bob Redd. **Head, Security/Ticket Sales:** Ken Wallace. **Graphic Designer:** Warren Hypes. **Clubhouse Manager:** Anthony Dunagan. **Administrative Assistant:** Tommy Thomason. **Chaplain:** Craig Stout.

FIELD STAFF
Manager: Michael Johns. **Coach:** Reinaldo Ruiz. **Pitching Coach:** Darwin Peguero. **Athletic Trainer:** Nick Flynn

GAME INFORMATION
Radio Announcer: Kyle Cooper. **No. of Games Broadcast:** Home-34, Away-34. **Flagship Station:** WMTD 102.3-FM.
Official Scorer: Bob Redd.
Stadium Name: Hunnicutt Field. **Location:** Exit 9 off I-77, US 460 West to downtown exit, left on Stafford Drive, stadium located behind Mercer County Technical Education Center. **Standard Game Times:** 7:05 pm, Sun 3.
Ticket Price Range: $4-6.
Visiting Club Hotel: Days Inn, I-77 and Ambrose Lane, Princeton, WV 24740. **Telephone:** (304) 425-8100.

PULASKI MARINERS

Shipping Address: 700 South Washington Ave, Pulaski VA 24301.
Mailing Address: PO Box 676, Pulaski, VA 24301.
Telephone: (540) 980-1070. **Fax:** (540) 980-1850.
E-Mail Address: info@pulaskimariners.net
Affiliation (first year): Seattle Mariners (2008). **Years in League:** 1946-50, 1952-55, 1957-58, 1969-77, 1982-92, 1997-2006, 2008-

OWNERSHIP, MANAGEMENT
Operated By: Pulaski Baseball Inc.
Director: Pedro Grifol (Seattle Mariners).
President/General Manager: Tom Compton.

FIELD STAFF
Manager: Jose Moreno. **Hitting Coach:** Rafael Santo Domingo. **Pitching Coach:** Nasusel Cabrera.

GAME INFORMATION
Radio: None.
PA Announcer: Unavailable. **Official Scorer:** Charles Altizer.
Stadium Name: Calfee Park. **Location:** Interstate 81 to Exit 89-B (Route 11), north to Pulaski, right on Pierce Avenue.
Standard Game Times: 7 p.m.
Ticket Price Range: $4-6.
Visiting Club Hotel: Comfort Inn, 4424 Cleburne Blvd, Dublin, Virginia. **Telephone:** (540) 674-1100.

PIONEER LEAGUE

Office Address: 2607 S Southeast Blvd, Building B, Suite 115, Spokane, WA 99223.
Mailing Address: PO Box 2564, Spokane, WA 99220.
Telephone: (509) 456-7615. **Fax:** (509) 456-0136.
E-Mail Address: fanmail@pioneerleague.com. **Website:** www.pioneerleague.com.
Years League Active: 1939-42, 1946-.
President/Secretary/Treasurer: Jim McCurdy.
Vice President: Mike Ellis (Missoula).
Directors: Dave Baggott (Ogden), Mike Ellis (Missoula), DG Elmore (Helena), Kevin Greene (Idaho Falls), Michael Baker (Grand Junction), Jeff Katofsky (Orem), Vinny Purpura (Great Falls), Jim Iverson (Billings).
League Administrator: Teryl MacDonald. **Executive Assistant:** Mary Ann McCurdy.
Division Structure: North—Billings, Great Falls, Helena, Missoula. South—Grand Junction, Idaho Falls, Ogden, Orem.
Regular Season: 76 games (split schedule). **2012 Opening Date:** June 20. **Closing Date:** Sept 8.
Playoff Format: First-half division winners meet second-half division winners in best-of-three series. Winners meet in best-of-three series for league championship.
All-Star Game: None.
Roster Limit: 35 active, 30 dressed for each game. **Player Eligibility Rule:** No more than 17 players 21 and older, provided that no more than two are 23 or older (age limits waived). No player on active list may have three or more years of prior minor league service.
Brand of Baseball: Rawlings.
Umpires: Unavailable.

Jim McCurdy

STADIUM INFORMATION

Club	Stadium	Opened	Dimensions			Capacity	2011 Att.
			LF	CF	RF		
Billings	Dehler Park	2008	329	410	350	3,071	101,516
Casper	Mike Lansing Field	2002	355	400	345	2,500	57,120
Great Falls	Centene Stadium at Legion Park	1956	335	414	335	3,800	66,106
Helena	Kindrick Field	1939	335	400	325	1,700	31,962
Idaho Falls	Melaleuca Field	1976	340	400	350	3,400	91,551
Missoula	Ogren Park at Allegiance Field	2004	309	398	287	3,500	87,345
Ogden	Lindquist Field	1997	335	396	334	5,000	132,799
Orem	Home of the Owlz	2005	305	408	312	4,500	81,229

BILLINGS MUSTANGS

Office Address: Dehler Park, 2611 9th Avenue North, Billings, MT 59101.
Mailing Address: PO Box 1553, Billings, MT 59103.
Telephone: (406) 252-1241. **Fax:** (406) 252-2968.
E-Mail Address: mustangs@billingsmustangs.com. **Website:** www.billingsmustangs.com .
Affiliation (first year): Cincinnati Reds (1974). **Years in League:** 1948-63, 1969-

OWNERSHIP, MANAGEMENT
Operated By: Billings Pioneer Baseball Club
President: Woody Hahn.
General Manager: Gary Roller. **Senior Director, Corporate Sales/Partnerships:** Chris Marshall. **Senior Director, Broadcasting/Media Relations:** Ryan Schuiling. **Senior Director, Food/Beverage Services:** Curt Prchal. **Senior Director, Field Maintenance/Facilities:** John Barta.

FIELD STAFF
Manager: Pat Kelly. **Hitting Coach:** Ray Martinez. **Pitching Coach:** Tony Fossas. **Strength/Conditioning Coach:** Zach Gjestvang. **Athletic Trainer:** Clete Sigwart.

GAME INFORMATION
Radio Broadcaster: Ryan Schuiling. **No. of Games Broadcast:** Home-38, Away-38. **Flagship Station:** KYSX 105.1 FM.
PA Announcer: Kyle Riley. **Official Scorer:** Matt Schoonover.
Stadium Name: Dehler Park. **Location:** I-90 to Exit 450, north on 27th Street North to 9th Avenue North. **Standard Game Times:** 7:05 pm, Sun 2:05. **Ticket Price Range:** $3-9. **Visiting Club Hotel:** Unavailable.

GRAND JUNCTION ROCKIES

Office Address: 1315 North Ave, Grand Junction, CO 81501.
Telephone: (970) 255-7625. **Fax:** (970) 241-2374.
E-Mail Address: timray@gjrockies.com.
Website: www.gjrockies.com.
Affiliation (first year): Colorado Rockies (2001). **Years in League:** 2001-

OWNERSHIP, MANAGEMENT
Principal Owners/Operated by: GJR LLC.
General Manager: Tim Ray. **Assistant GM:** Mike Ruvolo. **Operations Manger:** Paula Brown.

FIELD STAFF
Manager: Tony Diaz. **Hitting Coach:** Drew Saylor. **Pitching Coach:** Unavailable. **Trainer:** Josh Guperman.

GAME INFORMATION
Radio Announcer: Unavailable. **No. of Games Broadcast:** Home-38, Away-38. **Flagship Station:** KNAM 92.3 FM..
Official Scorer: Dan Kenyon.
Stadium Name: Mike Lansing Field. **Location:** 1315 North Ave, Grand Junction, CO 81501. **Standard Game Times:**
7:05 pm, Sun 2:05. **Ticket Price Range:** $7-10.
Visiting Club Hotel: Unavailable.

GREAT FALLS VOYAGERS

Office Address: 1015 25th St N, Great Falls, MT 59401.
Mailing Address: 1015 25th St N, Great Falls, MT 59401.
Telephone: (406) 452-5311. **Fax:** (406) 454-0811.
E-Mail Address: voyagers@gfvoyagers.com. **Website:** www.gfvoyagers.com.
Affiliation (first year): Chicago White Sox (2003). **Years in League:** 1948-1963, 1969-

OWNERSHIP/MANAGEMENT
Operated By: Great Falls Baseball Club, Inc.
President: Vinney Purpura. **General Manager:** Kattie Swartz. **Assistant GM:** Scott Reasoner. **Sales Manager:** Erik
Wolf. **Head Groundskeeper:** Billy Chafin.

FIELD STAFF
Manager: Ryan Newman. **Coach:** Charlie Poe. **Pitching Coach:** Brian Drahman.

GAME INFORMATION
Radio Announcer: Adam Seidel. **No. of Games Broadcast:** Home-38, Away-38. **Flagship Station:** ESPN Montana
99.9.
PA Announcer: Lance DeHaan. **Official Scorer:** Mike Lewis.
Stadium Name: Centene Stadium located at Legion Park. **Location:** From I-15 to exit 281 (10th Ave S), left on 26th, left
on Eighth Ave North, right on 25th, ballpark on right, past railroad tracks. **Ticket Price Range:** $6-9.
Visiting Club Hotel: Quality Inn, 220 Central Ave N Great Falls, MT 59401. **Telephone:** (406) 761-3410.

HELENA BREWERS

Office Address: 1300 N Ewing, Helena, MT 59601.
Mailing Address: PO Box 6756, Helena, MT 59604.
Telephone: (406) 495-0500. **Fax:** (406) 495-0900.
E-Mail Address: info@helenabrewers.net. **Website:** www.helenabrewers.net.
Affiliation (first year): Milwaukee Brewers (2003). **Years in League:** 1978-2000, 2003-

OWNERSHIP, MANAGEMENT
Operated by: Helena Baseball Club LLC.
Principal Owner: DG Elmore.
General Manager: Paul Fetz. **Director, Operations/Ticketing:** Morgan Halpert. **Director, Group Sales/Marketing:**
Nick Allen. **Radio Announcer/Director, Broadcasting/Media Relations:** Steve Wendt.

FIELD STAFF
Manager: Jeff Isom. **Hitting Coach:** Don Money. **Pitching Coach:** Elvin Nina. **Trainer:** Jimmy Gentry.

GAME INFORMATION
Radio Announcer: Unavailable. **No. of Games Broadcast:** Home-38, Away-38. **Flagship Station:** KCAP 1340-AM.
PA Announcer: Randy Bowsher. **Official Scorers:** Kevin Higgens, Craig Struble, Jim Shope, Andrew Gideon.
Stadium Name: Kindrick Field. **Location:** Cedar Street exit off I-15, west to Last Chance Gulch, left at Memorial Park.
Standard Game Time: 7:05 pm, Sun 1:05. **Ticket Price Range:** $6-9.

Visiting Club Hotel: Red Lion Colonial. Telephone: 406-443-2100.

IDAHO FALLS CHUKARS

Office Address: 568 W Elva, Idaho Falls, ID 83402.
Mailing Address: PO 2183, Idaho, ID 83403.
Telephone: (208) 522-8363. Fax: (208) 522-9858.
E-Mail Address: chukars@ifchukars.com. Website: www.ifchukars.com.
Affiliation (first year): Kansas City Royals (2004). Years in League: 1940-42, 1946-

OWNERSHIP/MANAGEMENT
Operated By: The Elmore Sports Group.
Principal Owner: David Elmore.
President/General Manager: Kevin Greene. Assistant GM, Merchandise: Andrew Daugherty. Account Manager/
Food Service Specialist: Paul Henderson. Director, Corporate Sales: Jack Mosimann. Clubhouse Manager: Jared
Troescher.

FIELD STAFF
Manager: Omar Ramirez. Hitting Coach: Justin Gemoll. Pitching Coach: Jerry Nyman.

GAME INFORMATION
Radio Announcers: John Balginy, Aaron Cox. No. of Games Broadcast: Home-38 Road-38. Flagship Station: KUPI
980-AM.
Official Scorer: John Balginy.
Stadium Name: Melaleuca Field. Location: I-15 to West Broadway exit, left onto Memorial Drive, right on Mound
Avenue, 1/4 mile to stadium. Standard Game Times: 7:15 pm, Sun 4. Ticket Price Range: $6-9.
Visiting Club Hotel: Guesthouse Inn & Suites, 850 Lindsay Blvd, Idaho Falls, ID 83402. Telephone: (208) 522-6260.

MISSOULA OSPREY

Office Address: 140 N Higgins, Suite 201, Missoula, MT 59802.
Telephone: (406) 543-3300. Fax: (406) 543-9463.
E-Mail Address: info@missoulaosprey.com. Website: www.missoulaosprey.com.
Affiliation (first year): Arizona Diamondbacks (1999). Years in League: 1956-60, 1999-

OWNERSHIP/MANAGEMENT
Operated By: Mountain Baseball LLC.
President: Mike Ellis. Vice President: Judy Ellis.
Executive VP: Matt Ellis. VP, Finance/Merchandising: Shelly Ellis. GM/Operations: Jared Amoss. GM/Sales/
Marketing: Jeff Griffin. Director, Stadium Operations: Byron Dike. Box Office Manager: Andrew Brown. Office
Manager: Nola Hunter.

FIELD STAFF
Manager: Andy Green. Pitching Coach: Gil Heredia. Hitting Coach: JR Bradley. Strength/Conditioning: Andrew
Slorp. Trainer: Scott Barringer.

GAME INFORMATION
Radio Announcer: Ben Catley. No. of Games Broadcast: Home-38, Away-38. Flagship Station: KMPT 930-AM.
PA Announcer: Dan Stromme. Official Scorer: Dan Hunter, David Kinsey.
Stadium Name: Ogren Park at Allegiance Field. Location: 700 Cregg Lane. Directions: Take Orange Street to Cregg
Lane, west on Cregg Lane, stadium west of McCormick Park. Standard Game Times: 7:05 pm, Sun 5:05. Ticket Price
Range: $6-12.
Visiting Club Hotel: Mountain Valley Inn, 420 W Broadway, Missoula, Mt 59802. Telephone: (406) 728-4500

OGDEN RAPTORS

Office Address: 2330 Lincoln Ave, Ogden, UT 84401.
Telephone: (801) 393-2400. Fax: (801) 393-2473.
E-Mail Address: homerun@ogden-raptors.com. Website: www.ogden-raptors.com.
Affiliation (first year): Los Angeles Dodgers (2003). Years in League: 1939-42,
1946-55, 1966-74, 1994-

OWNERSHIP/MANAGEMENT
Operated By: Ogden Professional Baseball, Inc.
Principal Owners: Dave Baggott, John Lindquist. Chairman/President: Dave
Baggott.
General Manager: Joey Stein. VP/Director, Marketing: John Stein. Broadcaster/Media Relations: Eric Knighton.

Director, Merchandise: Gerri Kopinski. **Public Relations:** Pete Diamond. **Groundskeeper:** Kenny Kopinski. **Assistant Groundkeeper:** Bob Richardson. **Assistant Food Director:** Louise Hillard. **Clubhouse Manager:** Kirby Hoover. **Director, Press Box:** Brandon Kunimura.

FIELD STAFF

Manager: Damon Berryhill. **Coach:** Juhnny Washington. **Pitching Coach:** Chuck Crim. **Trainer:** Robert Dyson. **Strength/Conditioning:** Adam Wagner.

GAME INFORMATION

Radio Announcer: Jake Kelman. **No. of Games Broadcast:** Home-38, Away-38. **Flagship Station:** 1490 AM KOGN. **PA Announcer:** Pete Diamond. **Official Scorer:** Dennis Kunimura.

Stadium Name: Lindquist Field. **Location:** I-15 North to 21th Street exit, east to Lincoln Avenue, south three blocks to park. **Standard Game Times:** 7 pm, Sun 1. **Ticket Price Range:** $6-9.

Visiting Club Hotel: Hotel Ben Lomond, 2510 Washington Blvd, Ogden, UT 84401. **Telephone:** (801) 627-1900.

OREM OWLZ

Office Address: 970 W University Parkway, Orem, UT 84058.
Telephone: (801) 377-2255. **Fax:** (801) 377-2345.
E-Mail Address: fan@oremowlz.com. **Website:** www.oremowlz.com.
Affiliation (first year): Los Angeles Angels (2001). **Years in League:** 2001-

OWNERSHIP, MANAGEMENT

Operated By: Bery Bery Gud To Me LLC.
Principal Owner: Jeff Katofsky.
General Manager: Brett Crane. **Director, Promotions/Community Relations:** Jillian Dingee. **IT Manager:** Julie Hatch. **Director, Sales/Marketing:** Jed Chrisman. **Ticket Office Manager/Group Sales:** Barry Winterton. **Director, Broadcasting/Media Relations:** Brandon Marcus.

FIELD STAFF

Manager: Tom Kotchman. **Coach:** Tom Evans. **Pitching Coach:** Zeke Zimmerman. **Trainer:** Chris Wells.

GAME INFORMATION

Radio Announcer: Brandon Marcus. **No. of Games Broadcast:** Home-38, Away-38. **Flagship Station:** Unavailable. **PA Announcer:** Lincoln Fillmore. **Official Scorer:** Unavailable.

Stadium Name: Home of the Owlz. **Location:** Exit 269 (University Parkway) off I-15 at Utah Valley University campus. **Ticket Price Range:** $4-10.

Visiting Club Hotel: Courtyard Marriott 1600 N Freedom Blvd, Provo, UT 84604, (801)-373-2222

ARIZONA LEAGUE

Office Address: 620 W Franklin St, Boise, ID 83702.
Mailing Address: PO Box 1645, Boise, ID 83701.
Telephone: (208) 429-1511. **Fax:** (208) 429-1525. **E-Mail Address:** bobrichmond@qwestoffice.net
Years League Active: 1988-.
President/Treasurer: Bob Richmond.
Vice President: Oneri Fleita (Cubs). **Corporate Secretary:** Ted Polakowski (Athletics).
Administrative Assistant: Rob Richmond.
Division Structure: East/Central/West divisions.
Regular Season: 56 games. Aug 30 semifinal games; Aug 31 championship. **2012 Opening Date:** June 20. **Closing Date:** Aug 29.
Standard Game Times: 7 pm.
Playoff Format: Team with best record plays wildcard in one-game playoff on Aug 30; other two divisions play one-game playoff. Winners play for League championship on Aug 31.
All-Star Game: None.
Roster Limit: 35 active. **Player Eligibility Rule:** No player may have three or more years of prior minor league service.
Brand of Baseball: Rawlings.

Clubs	Playing Site	Manager	Coach	Pitching Coach
Angels	Angels complex, Tempe	Brenton Del Chiaro	Nathan Haynes	Jim Gott/Matt Wise
Athletics	Papago Park Baseball Complex, Phoenix	Marcus Jensen	Juan Dilone	Jimmy Escalante
Brewers	Maryvale Baseball Complex, Phoenix	Tony Diggs	Kenny Dominguez	Steve Cline
Cubs	Fitch Park, Mesa	Juan Cabreja	Jason Dubois	R. Tronerud/F. Castillo
D-backs	Salt River Fields at Talking Stick	Hector de la Cruz	Robby Hammock	Jeff Bajenaru
Dodgers	Camelback Ranch, Glendale	Matt Martin	Leo Garcia	Kremlin Martinez
Giants	Giants complex, Scottsdale	Derin McMains	Victor Torres	Michael Couchee
Indians	Goodyear Ballpark	Anthony Medrano	J. Betances/D. Malave	Steve Karsay
Mariners	Peoria Sports Complex	Mike Kinkade	S. Steinmann/B.Johnson	Cibney Bello
Padres	Peoria Sports Complex	Jim Gabella	I. Cruz/D Easley	D Rajsich/T Worrell
Rangers	Surprise Recreation Campus	Corey Ragsdale	D. McDonald/J. Mashore	Oscar Marin
Reds	Goodyear Ballpark	Jose Miguel Nieves	Jorge Orta	Derrin Ebert
Royals	Surprise Recreation Campus	Darryl Kennedy	A. David/N. Liriano	M. Davis/C. Reyes

GULF COAST LEAGUE

Operated By: Minor League Baseball.
Office Address: 9550 16th Street North, St. Petersburg, FL 33716.
Telephone: 727-456-1734. **Fax:** 727-821-5819.
Website: www.milb.com. **E-mail Address:** gcl@milb.com.
Vice President, Baseball/Business Operations: Tim Brunswick. **Assistant, Baseball Operations:** Andy Shultz.
2012 Opening Date: June 18. **Closing Date:** Aug. 25. **Regular Season:** 60 games.
Divisional Alignment: East—Astros, Cardinals, Marlins, Nationals. **North**—Blue Jays, Braves, Phillies, Pirates, Tigers, Yankees. **South**—Orioles, Rays, Red Sox, Twins.
Playoff Format: The division winner with the best record plays the wild card; the other two division winners meet in a one-game playoff. The winners meet in a best-of-three series.
All-Star Game: None. **Roster Limit:** 35 active, only 30 of whom may be in uniform and eligible to play in any given game. At least 10 must be pitchers as of July 1.
Player Eligibility Rule: No player may have three or more years of prior minor league service.
Brand of Baseball: Rawlings. **Statistician:** Major League Baseball Advanced Media.

Clubs	Playing Site	Manager	Coach(es)	Pitching Coach
Astros	Astros complex, Kissimmee	Ed Romero	E Alfonzo/G. MacKenzie	J. Garcia/C. Taylor
Blue Jays	Mattick Training Center, Dunedin	Omar Malave	J. Schneider/J. Lopez	David Williams
Braves	Disney's Wide World of Sports, Orlando	Rocket Wheeler	D.J. Boston	Vladimir Nunez
Cardinals	Cardinals complex, Jupiter	Steve Turco	Oliver Marmol	Tim Leveque
Marlins	Roger Dean complex, Jupiter	Jorge Hernandez	Bobby Bell	Jeremy Powell
Nationals	Carl Barger Baseball Complex, Melbourne	Tripp Keister	Amaury Garcia	Michael Tejera
Orioles	Twin Lakes Park, Sarasota	Ramon Sambo	Milt May	Larry Jaster
Phillies	Carpenter Complex, Clearwater	Roly DeArmas	Kevin Jordan	S. Schrenk/C. Arroyo
Pirates	Pirate City Complex, Bradenton	Tom Prince	Mike Lum	Bobby St. Pierre
Rays	Charlotte County Complex, Port Charlotte	Paul Hoover	W. Rincones/H. Torres	Marty DeMerritt
Red Sox	Jet Blue Park, Fort Myers	George Lombard	U. Washington/D. Tomlin	Walter Miranda
Tigers	Tigertown, Lakeland	Basilio Cabrera	Nelson Santovenia	Greg Sabat
Twins	Lee County Complex, Fort Myers	Ramon Borrego	Milt Cuyler	Henry Bonilla
Yankees	Himes complex, Tampa	Tom Nieto	E. Gonzalez, P.J. Pilettere	Jose Rosado

INDEPENDENT LEAGUES

AMERICAN ASSOCIATION

Office Address: 1415 Hwy 54 West, Suite 210, Durham, NC 27707.
Telephone: (919) 401-8150. **Fax:** (919) 401-8152. **Website:** www.americanassociationbaseball.com.
Year Founded: 2005.
Commissioner: Miles Wolff. **President:** Dan Moushon.
Administrative Assistant: Jason Deans. **Director, Umpires:** Kevin Winn.
Division Structure: North Division—Fargo-Moorhead RedHawks, St. Paul Saints, Sioux Falls Pheasants, Winnipeg Goldeyes.
Central Division—Gary SouthShore RailCats, Kansas City T-Bones, Lincoln Saltdogs, Sioux City Explorers, Wichita Wingnuts.
South Division—Amarillo Sox, El Paso Diablos, Grand Prairie AirHogs, Laredo Lemurs.
Regular Season: 100 games.
2012 Opening Date: May 17. **2012 Closing Date:** September 3.
Playoff Format: Three division winners and one wild card play in best-of-five series. Winners play for best-of-five American Association Championship.
Roster Limit: 22.
Eligibility Rule: Minimum of four first-year players; maximum of four veterans (at least six or more years of professional service).
Brand of Baseball: Rawlings.
Statistician: Pointstreak.com, 602-1595 16th Avenue, Richmond Hill, ON Canada L4B 3N9.

STADIUM INFORMATION

			Dimensions				
Club	Stadium	Opened	LF	CF	RF	Capacity	2011 Att.
Amarillo	Amarillo National Bank Sox Stadium	1949	355	429	355	7,500	138,865
El Paso	Cohen Stadium	1990	340	410	340	9,725	172,742
Fargo-Moorhead	Newman Outdoor Field	1996	314	408	318	4,513	175,918
Gary SouthShore	U.S. Steel Yard	2002	320	400	335	6,139	157,676
Grand Prairie	QuikTrip Park at Grand Prairie	2008	330	400	330	5,445	117,861
Kansas City	CommunityAmerica Ballpark	2003	300	396	328	6,537	261,115
Laredo	Uni-Trade Stadium	2012	335	405	335	6,000	N/A
Lincoln	Haymarket Park	2001	335	395	325	4,500	157,647
St. Paul	Midway Stadium	1982	320	400	320	6,069	240,206
Sioux City	Lewis and Clark Park	1993	330	400	330	3,630	64,000
Sioux Falls	Sioux Falls Stadium	1964	312	410	312	4,029	76,549
Wichita	Lawrence-Dumont Stadium	1934	344	401	312	6,055	159,239
Winnipeg	Shaw Park	1999	325	400	325	7,481	275,521

AMARILLO SOX

Office Address: 801 S Polk St, Amarillo, TX 79106.
Telephone: (806) 242-4653. **Fax:** (806) 322-1839.
E-Mail Address: mark.lee@amarillosox.com. **Website:** www.amarillosox.com.
VP/General Manager: Mark Lee. **Assistant General Manager:** Jaylin Henderson. **Director, Publications/Corporate Sales:** Ben Miller. **Director, Business Operations:** Dave Kost.
Field Manager: John Harris. **Coaches:** Cory Domel, Kevin Griffin.

GAME INFORMATION

Stadium Name: Amarillo National Bank Sox Stadium. **Location:** Take Grand St.†exit and proceed north on Grand St; Turn left onto SE 3rd Ave
Standard Game Times: 7:05 pm; Sun 6:05.
Visiting Club Hotel: Ashmore Inn & Suites, 2301 East I-40, Exit 72-A (Nelson St) Amarillo, TX 79104. **Telephone:** 806-374-0033

EL PASO DIABLOS

Office Address: 9700 Gateway North Blvd, El Paso, TX 79924.
Telephone: (915) 755-2000. **Fax:** (915) 757-0671.
E-Mail Address: info@diablos.com. **Website:** www.diablos.com.
Managing Partner/President: Matt LaBranche. **Business Manager:** Pat Hofman. **Director, Corporate Sponsorships:** Bernie Ricono. **Public Relations Director:** Lizette Espinosa. **Box Office Manager:** Steve Martinez. **Manager, Marketing/Events Manager:** Henry Quintana III. **Senior Account Executive:** Donna Blair. **Promotions Manager:** Victor Reta. **Account Executive/Military Liaison:**

Kelsey Golackson.
Manager: Jorge Alvarez. **Coach:** Jerry Verastegui.

Radio Announcer: Alex Morales. **No. of Games Broadcast:** 100. **Flagship Station:** 1380-AM. **Webcast Address:** www.diablos.com.
Stadium Name: Cohen Stadium. **Location:** I-10 to U.S.54, Diana exit to Gateway North Boulevard.
Standard Game Times: 7:05 pm, Sun 6:05 pm.
Visiting Club Hotel: Holiday Inn Airport, 6655 Gateway West, El Paso, TX 79925. **Telephone:** (915) 778-6411.

FARGO-MOORHEAD
REDHAWKS

Office Address: 1515 15th Ave N, Fargo, ND 58102.
Telephone: (701) 235-6161. **Fax:** (701) 297-9247.
E-Mail Address: redhawks@fmredhawks.com. **Website:** www.fmredhawks.com.
Operated by: Fargo Baseball LLC.
President: Bruce Thom. **Chief Executive Officer:** Brad Thom.
General Manager: Josh Buchholz. **Senior Accountant:** Rick Larson. **Director, Promotions:** Eric Jorgenson. **Director, Ticket Sales/Assistant Director, Marketing:** Michael Larson. **Director, Community Relations/Group Events:** Karl Hoium. **Director, Food/Beverage:** Sean Kiernan. **Head Groundskeeper:** Sam Petersen.
Manager/Director, Player Procurement: Doug Simunic. **Player Procurement Consultant:** Jeff Bittiger. **Pitching Coach:** Steve Montgomery. **Coaches:** Bucky Burgau, Kole Zimmerman. **Trainer:** Craig Brandenburger. **Home Clubhouse Manager:** Unavailable. **Visiting Clubhouse Manager:** Chris Krick

Radio Announcer: Scott Miller. **No. of Games Broadcast:** 100. **Flagship Station:** 740-AM The FAN.
Stadium Name: Newman Outdoor Field. **Location:** I-29 North to exit 67, east on 19th Ave North, right on Albrecht Boulevard.
Standard Game Times: 7:02 pm, Sat 6, Sun 1.
Visiting Club Hotel: Howard Johnson Inn, 301 3rd Ave N, Fargo, ND 58102. **Telephone:** (701) 232-8850.

GARY SOUTHSHORE RAILCATS

Office Address: One Stadium Plaza, Gary, IN 46402.
Telephone: (219) 882-2255. **Fax:** (219) 882-2259.
E-Mail Address: info@railcatsbaseball.com. **Website:** www.railcatsbaseball.com.
Operated by: PLS Holdings.
Owner/CEO: Pat Salvi. **Owner:** Lindy Salvi.
President/General Manager: Kevin Spudic. **Assistant GM:** Becky Kremer. **Box Office Manager:** Adam Harris. **Director, Stadium Operations:** Nick Lampasona. **Director, Marketing/Promotions:** Natalie Kirby. **Manager,Merchandise:** Laura Blakeley. **Manager, Community Relations:** Radley Robinson. **Manager, Box Office:** Adam Harris. **Manager, Group Sales:** Aaron Pineda. **Account Executive:** Nikki Kimbrough. **Corporate Account Executive:** Percy Thornbor.
Manager, Media Relations/Broadcasting: Matt Friedman. **Graphic Designer:** Domonic Edwards. **Executive Assistant:** Arcella Moxley. **Stadium Maintenance:** Jim Kerr.
Manager: Greg Tagert.

No. of Games Broadcast: 100. **Flagship Station:** WLPR 89.1-FM.
Stadium Name: US Steel Yard. **Location:** I-80/94 to Broadway Exit (Exit 10), north on Broadway to Fifth Avenue, east one block to stadium.
Standard Game Times: 7:10 pm, Sat 6:10, Sun 2:10.
Visiting Club Hotel: Radisson Hotel at Star Plaza, 800 East 81st Avenue, Merrillville, IN 46410. **Telephone:** (219) 769-6311.

GRAND PRAIRIE AIRHOGS

Office Address: 1600 Lone Star Parkway, Grand Prairie, TX 75050.
Telephone: (972) 504-9383. **Fax:** (972) 504-2288.
Websites: www.airhogsbaseball.com/www.quiktrippark.com.†
Operated By: Southern Independent Baseball, LLC.
Owner: Gary Elliston. **President:** Scott Berry. **Vice President/General Manager:** Craig Brasfield. **Assistant GM, Operations:** J Willms. **Assistant GM, Broadcasting/New Media:** Josh Hirsch. **Business Development:** Karen Lucchesi.

Communications: David Hatchett. **Finance/Merchandise Manager:** Trista Earlston. **Box Office Manager:** Jeff Carman. **Corporate Sales:** Mark Vakos. **Outside Events Coordinator:** Matt Raffaele. **Director, Food/Beverage:**†Chris Moriarty.†
   Groundskeeper: Buddy Craig. **Receptionist:** Donna White.
   Manager: Ricky VanAsselberg. **Coaches:** Eric Champion, Barrett Weaver.

GAME INFORMATION

   Webcast Announcer: Josh Hirsch. **No. of Games Broadcast:** 100. **Webcast:** www.airhogsbaseball.com.
   Stadium Name: QuikTrip Park at Grand Prairie. **Location:** From I-30, take Beltline Road exit going north, take Lone Star Park entrance towards the stadium.
   Standard Game Times: 7:05 pm, Sun 6:05.
   Visiting Club Hotel: Crowne Plaza Suites Arlington, 700 Avenue H East, Arlington, TX 76011. **Telephone:** (817) 394-5000.

KANSAS CITY T-BONES

Office Address: 1800 Village West Parkway, Kansas City, KS 66111.
Telephone: (913) 328-2255. **Fax:** (913) 328-5674.
E-Mail Address: batterup@tbonesbaseball.com.
Website: www.tbonesbaseball.com.
Operated By: T-Bones Baseball Club, LLC; Ehlert Development.
Owner: John Ehlert. **President:** Adam Ehlert.
   VP/General Manager: Chris Browne. **Senior Director, Corporate Sales:** Seth Alberg. **Assistant GM, Group Sales:** Kurt Sieker. **Director, Media Relations/Press Box:** Stan Duitsman. **Director, Promotions:** Emily Hoskins. **Director, Ticket Operations/Box Office Manager:** Jason Young. **Assistant Director, Group Sales:** Ryan Thayer. **Operations Manager:** Jimmy Carrington. **Bookkeeper:** Sherrie Stover. **Account Executive:** Ryan Stos. **Director, Broadcasting:** Brian Bruce.
   Manager: Tim Doherty. **Coaches:** Caleb Balbuena, Kenny Hook. **Trainer:** Josh Adams.

GAME INFORMATION

   Radio Announcer: Brian Bruce. **No. of Games Broadcast:** 100. **Flagship Station:** KUDL 1660-AM.
   Stadium Name: CommunityAmerica Ballpark. **Location:** State Avenue West off I-435 and State Avenue. **Standard Game Times:** 7:05 pm, Sun 5:05 pm.
   Visiting Club Hotel: Unavailable.

LAREDO LEMURS

Office Address: 6320 Sinatra Drive, Laredo, TX 78045.
Telephone: (956) 753-6877. **Fax:** (956) 791-0672.
Website: www.laredolemurs.com.
Managing Partner: Mark Schuster.
President: Ruben Navas. **Marketing Assistant:** Norma Molina.
Manager: Pete Incaviglia. **Coaches:** Bill Bryk Jr., **Ricardo Cuevas.**

GAME INFORMATION

   Announcer: Unavailable. **No. of Games Broadcast:** 100. **Webcast:** www.laredolemurs.com.
   Stadium Name: Uni-Trade Stadium. **Location:** From North: I-35 to Exit 9 turn left onto Loop 20/Bob Bullock Blvd, south on Loop 20 for 3 miles, make right onto Sinatra Blvd, stadium on left; From South: I-35 to Exit 2 turn right onto Hwy 59 for 4 miles, turn left onto Loop 20 North for 2 miles, turn left onto Sinatra Drive, stadium on left.
   Standard Game Times: 7:30 pm.
   Visiting Club Hotel: La Posada Inn, 1000 Zaragoza Street, Laredo, TX 78040. **Telephone:** (956) 722-1701.

LINCOLN SALTDOGS

Office Address: 403 Line Drive Circle, Suite A, Lincoln, NE 68508.
Telephone: (402) 474-2255. **Fax:** (402) 474-2254.
E-Mail Address: info@saltdogs.com. **Website:** www.saltdogs.com.
Owner: Jim Abel. **President:** Charlie Meyer.
   Vice President/General Manager: Tim Utrup. **Assistant GM/Director, Sales/Marketing:** Bret Beer. **Director, Broadcasting/Communications:** Drew Bontadelli. **Director, Merchandising/Promotions:** Anne Duchek. **Director, Season Tickets/Ticket Packages:** Toby Antonson. **Director, Stadium Operations:** Dave Aschwege. **Assistant Director, Stadium Operations:** Jeff Koncaba. **Office Manager:** Alicia Oakeson. **Athletic Turf Manager:** Josh Klute. **Assistant Turf Managers:** JJ Borecky, Jen Roeber.
   Manager: Chris Miyake. **Coaches:** Jarrett Gardner, Beau Torbert.

GAME INFORMATION

Radio Announcer: Drew Bontadelli. **No. of Games Broadcast:** 100. **Flagship Station:** KFOR 1240-AM. **Webcast Address:** www.kfor1240.com.

Stadium Name: Haymarket Park. **Location:** I-80 to Cornhusker Highway West, left on First Street, right on Sun Valley Boulevard, left on Line Drive.

Standard Game Times: 7:05 pm (Mon-Sat), 5:05 pm (Sun).

Visiting Club Hotel: Country Inn & Suites, 5353 N 27th, Lincoln, NE 68521. **Telephone:** (402) 476-5353.

ST. PAUL SAINTS

Office Address: 1771 Energy Park Dr, St Paul, MN 55108.

Telephone: (651) 644-3517. **Fax:** (651) 644-1627.

E-Mail Address: funisgood@saintsbaseball.com. **Website:** www.saintsbaseball.com.

Principal Owners: Marv Goldklang, Bill Murray, Mike Veeck. **Chairman:** Marv Goldklang. **President:** Mike Veeck. **Executive Vice President/General Manager:** Derek Sharrer. **Executive VP:** Tom Whaley. **Assistant GMs:** Scott Bush, Chris Schwab. **VP, Customer Service/Community Partnerships:** Annie Huidekoper. **Director, Broadcast/Media Relations:** Sean Aronson. **Director, Ticket Sales:** Chuck Richards. **Coordinator Director, Special Events:** Max Huber. **Director, Ticket Services:** Adam Lowler.

Director, New Media/Technology Services: Chelsey Wentz. **Director, Promotions:** Brian Kaufenberg. **Director of Food/Beverage:** Curtis Nachtsheim. **Business Manager:** Leesa Anderson. **Office Manager:** Gina Kray. **Stadium Operations:** Bob Klepperich. **Groundskeeper:** Connie Rudolph.

Manager: George Tsamis. **Coaches:** Lamarr Rogers, Jason Verdugo, TJ Wiesner.

GAME INFORMATION

Radio Announcer: Sean Aronson. **No. of Games Broadcast:** 100. **Flagship Station:** Unavailable. **Webcast Address:** www.saintsbaseball.com.

Stadium Name: Midway Stadium. **Location:** From I-94, take Snelling Avenue North exit, west onto Energy Park Drive.

Standard Game Times: 7:05 p.m, Sun 1:05 pm.

Visiting Club Hotel: Crowne Plaza St Paul Riverfront, 11 Kellogg Blvd, St Paul MN 55101. **Telephone:** (651)292-1900.

SIOUX CITY EXPLORERS

Office Address: 3400 Line Drive, Sioux City, IA 51106.

Telephone: (712) 277-9467. **Fax:** (712) 277-9406.

E-Mail Address: promotions@xsbaseball.com. **Website:** www.xsbaseball.com.

President: Matt Adamski.

General Manager: Shane M Tritz. **Assistant GM:** Ashley Schoenrock. **Office Manager:** Julie Stinger.

Field Manager: Stan Cliburn.

GAME INFORMATION

Radio Announcer: Dave Nitz. **No. of Games Broadcast:** 100. **Flagship Station:** KSCJ 1360-AM. **Webcast Address:** www.xsbaseball.com.

Stadium Name: Lewis and Clark Park. **Location:** I-29 to Singing Hills Blvd, North, right on Line Drive.

Standard Game Times: 7:05 pm, Sun 6:05.

Visiting Club Hotel: Sioux City Hotel & Conference Center, 707 Fourth Street, Sioux City, IA 51101. **Telephone:** (712) 277-4101.

SIOUX FALLS PHEASANTS

Office Address: 1001 N West Ave, Sioux Falls, SD 57104.

Telephone: (605) 333-0179. **Fax:** (605) 333-0139.

E-Mail Address: info@sfpheasants.com. **Website:** www.sfpheasants.com.

Operated by: Sioux Falls Sports, LLC.

CEO/Managing Partner: Gary Weckwerth.

President: Jim Loria.

Director, Baseball Operations: Adam Peterman. **Director, Stadium Operations:** Larry McKenney. **Office/Ticketing Manager:** Kim Hipple. **VP, Media/Public Relations:** Jim Olander.

Manager: Steve Shirley.

GAME INFORMATION

Radio Announcer: Scott Beatty. **No. of Games Broadcast:** 100. **Flagship Station:** KWSN 1230-AM. **Webcast Address:** www.kwsn.com.

Stadium Name: Sioux Falls Stadium. **Location:** I-29 to Russell Street, east one mile, right on West Avenue.

Standard Game Times: 7:05 pm Sat, 6:05, Sun 2:05/5:05.

Visiting Club Hotel: Days Inn Sioux Falls, 3401 S Gateway Blvd, Sioux Falls, SD 57106. **Telephone:** (605) 361-9240.

WICHITA WINGNUTS

Office Address: 300 South Sycamore, Wichita, KS 67213.

Telephone: (316) 264-6887. **Fax:** (316) 264-2129.

Website: www.wichitawingnuts.com.

Owners: Steve Ruud, Dan Waller, Gary Austerman, Nick Easter, Nate Robertson.

President/General Manager: Josh Robertson. **Assistant GM/Director, Corporate Sales:** Ben Keiter. **Assistant GM/Director, Ticket Sales:** Jeremy Mock. **Special Assistant to GM:** Brian Holman. **Director, Broadcast:** Steve Schuster. **Director, Finance:** Kay Brown. **Director, Stadium Operations:** Jeff Kline. **Director, Operations/NBC World Series:** Casey Walkup. **Group Sales Manager:** Brian Turner. **Community Relations/Merchandise Manager:** Scott Johnson. **Clubhouse Manager:** Casey Stewart. **Assistant Clubhouse Manager:** Caleb Beeson.

Manager: Kevin Hooper. **Coaches:** Jose Amado, Brian Rose, Luke Robertson.

GAME INFORMATION

Radio Announcer: Steve Schuster. **No. of Games Broadcast:** 100. **Games Broadcast:** KWME 92.7-FM. **Webcast Address:** www.wichitawingnuts.com.

Stadium Name: Lawrence-Dumont Stadium. **Location:** 135 North to Kellogg (54) West, Take Seneca Street exit North to Maple, Go East on Maple to Sycamore, Stadium is located on corner of Maple and Sycamore.

Standard Game Times: 7:05 pm, Sun 2:05 pm.

Visiting Club Hotel: North Rock Suites, 7856 E 36th St, N, Wichita, KS, 67226. **Telephone:** (316) 634-2303.

WINNIPEG GOLDEYES

Office Address: One Portage Ave E, Winnipeg, Manitoba R3B 3N3.

Telephone: (204) 982-2273. **Fax:** (204) 982-2274.

E-Mail Address: goldeyes@goldeyes.com. **Website:** www.goldeyes.com.

Operated by: Winnipeg Goldeyes Baseball Club, Inc.

Principal Owner/President: Sam Katz.

General Manager: Andrew Collier. **Assistant GM:** Regan Katz. **Media Relations Manager:** Scott Unger. **Administrative Assistant:** Bonnie Benson. **Chief Financial Officer:** Jason McRae-King. **Controller:** Judy Jones. **Director, Sales/Marketing:** Dan Chase. **Sales/Marketing Coordinator:** Angela Sanche. **Account Representatives:** Paul Edmonds, Dennis McLean, Blake Schultz, Scott Taylor. **Promotions Coordinator:** Sarah Wallace. **Box Office Manager:** Kevin Arnst. **Retail Manager:** Megan Tucker. **Facility Manager/Head Groundskeeper:** Don Ferguson.

Manager/Director, Player Procurement: Rick Forney. **Coach:** Tom Vaeth. **Trainer:** Shane Zdebiak.

Clubhouse Manager: Jamie Samson.

GAME INFORMATION

Radio Announcer: Paul Edmonds. **No. of Games Broadcast:** 100. **Flagship Station:** TSN Radio 1290-AM.

Television Announcers: Scott Taylor, Ken Wiebe. **No. of Games Telecast:** Home-20. **Station:** Shaw TV Channel 9.

Stadium Name: Shaw Park. **Location:** North on Pembina Highway to Broadway, East on Broadway to Main Street, North on Main Street to Water Avenue, East on Water Avenue to Westbrook Street, North on Westbrook Street to Lombard Avenue, East on Lombard Avenue to Mill Street, South on Mill Street to ballpark.

Standard Game Times: 7 pm, Sat 6, Sun 1:30.

Visiting Club Hotel: The Radisson Hotel Winnipeg Downtown, 288 Portage Ave, Winnipeg, Manitoba R3C 0B8. **Telephone:** (204) 956-0410.

ATLANTIC LEAGUE

Mailing Address: 401 N Delaware Ave Camden, NJ 08102.
Telephone: (856) 541-9400. **Fax:** (856) 541-9410.
E-Mail Address: info@atlanticleague.com. **Website:** www.atlanticleague.com.
Year Founded: 1998.
Chief Executive Officer/Founder: Frank Boulton. **Vice Presidents:** Peter Kirk, Steven Kalafer.
Executive Director: Joe Klein.
Directors: Frank Boulton (Long Island, Bridgeport), Steve Kalafer (Somerset), Peter Kirk (Lancaster, York, Southern Maryland, Sugar Land), Frank Boulton/Peter Kirk (Camden).
League Operations Latin Coordinator: Ellie Rodriguez. **Director, Baseball Administration:** Patty MacLuckie.
Division Structure: Liberty—Bridgeport, Camden, Long Island, Southern Maryland. Freedom—Lancaster, Sugar Land, Somerset, York.
Regular Season: 140 games (split-schedule).
2012 Opening Date: April 26. **Closing Date:** Sept 23.
All-Star Game: July 11 at Camden
Playoff Format: First-half division winners meet second-half winners in best of five series. Winners meet in best-of-five final for league championship.
Roster Limit: 25. Teams may keep 27 players from start of season until May 31, 2012.
Eligibility Rule: No restrictions.
Brand of Baseball: Rawlings.
Statistician: Statistician: Pointstreak.com, 602-1595 16th Avenue, Richmond Hill, ON, Canada L4B 3N9.

STADIUM INFORMATION

Club	Stadium	Opened	LF	CF	RF	Capacity	2011 Att.
Bridgeport	The Ballpark at Harbor Yard	1998	325	405	325	5,300	160,653
Camden	Campbellis Field	2001	325	405	325	6,425	246,039
Lancaster	Clipper Magazine Stadium	2005	372	400	300	6,000	327,467
Long Island	Citibank Park	2000	325	400	325	6,002	410,619
Somerset	Commerce Bank Ballpark	1999	317	402	315	6,100	369,466
So. Maryland	Regency Stadium	2008	305	400	320	6,000	240,777
Sugar Land	Constellation Field	2012	325	400	343	7,500	------
York	Sovereign Bank Stadium	2007	300	400	325	5,000	278,410

BRIDGEPORT BLUEFISH

Office Address: 500 Main St, Bridgeport, CT 06604. **Telephone:** (203) 345-4800. **Fax:** (203) 345-4830. **Website:** www.bridgeportbluefish.com.
Operated by: Past Time Partners, LLC.
Principal Owner/CEO, Past Time Partners: Frank Boulton. **Senior VP, Past Time Partners:** Mike Pfaff. **Partners, Past Time Partners:** Tony Rosenthal, Fred Heyman, Jeffrey Serkes.
General Manager: Robert Goughan. **Business Manager:** Mary Jayne Wells. **Public Relations Director:** Paul Herrmann. **Community Relations Coordinator:** Marilyn Guarino. **Facilities Coordinator:** Tom Yario. **Promotions Coordinator:** Tim Carr. **Head Groundskeeper:** Ben Baker. **Broadcast Coordinator:** Perry Miles. **Merchandise Coordinator:** Bobby Aanonsen. **Ticket Sales Coordinator:** Dan Cunningham. **Ticket Sales Coordinator:** Nicole Salcito. **Account Executive/Operation Assistant:** Alex Magliocco.
Manager: Willie Upshaw. **Coach:** Terry McGriff. **Pitching Coach:** Unavailable. **Trainer:** Ericka Ventura.

GAME INFORMATION
Radio Announcer: Perry Miles. **No. of Games Broadcast:** 140 (webcast). **Flagship Station:** Unavailable. **PA Announcer:** Bill Jensen. **Official Scorer:** Chuck Sadowski.
Stadium Name: The Ballpark at Harbor Yard. **Location:** I-95 to exit 27, Route 8/25 to exit 1. **Standard Game Times:** 7:05 pm; Sat 6:05, Sun 2:05.
Visiting Club Hotel: Holiday Inn Bridgeport, 1070 Main St, Bridgeport, CT 06604. **Telephone:** (203) 334-1234.

CAMDEN RIVERSHARKS

Office Address: 401 N Delaware Ave, Camden, NJ 08102.
Telephone: (856) 963-2600. **Fax:** (856) 963-8534.
E-Mail Address: riversharks@riversharks.com. **Website:** www.riversharks.com.
Operated by: Camden Baseball, LLC
Principal Owners: Frank Boulton, Peter Kirk. **President:** Jon Danos. **Controller:** Emily Merrill. **General Manager:** Adam Lorber. **Director, Group Events:** Bob Nehring.
Director, Group Sales: Mark Schieber. **Director, Group Sales:** Lindsay Rosenberg. **Director, Finance/Ticketing:** Sean Maher. **Director, Corporate Partnerships:** Drew Nelson. **Corporate Partnerships Coordinator:** Curt Phair. **Marketing**

Manager: Kristin Segers. **Marketing Coordinator:** Lisa Verish. **Theme Night Manager:** Megan McLaughlin.
Creative Services Manager: Meaghan Rhoades. **Group Sales Managers:** Kimberly Perno, Ross Anderson. **Event Marketing Assitant:** Mike Barone. **Box Office Manager:** Dana Rommel. **Stadium Operations Manager:** Frank Slavinski. **Stadium Operations Assistant:** Nick Razler. **Office Manager:** Dolores Rozier.
Director, Baseball Operations/Manager: Jeff Scott. **Bench Coach:** Ron Karkovice. **Bench Coach:** Brett Bonvechio.

GAME INFORMATION
Radio: www.riversharks.com. **Riversharks Broadcaster:** Tim Saunders
PA Announcer: Kevin Casey. **Official Scorer:** Dick Shute. **Stadium Name:** Campbell's Field.
Location: From Philadelphia, right on Sixth Street, right after Ben Franklin Bridge toll booth, right on Cooper Street until it ends at Delaware Ave From Camden, I-676 to exit 5B, follow signs to field. **Standard Game Times:** 7:05 pm, Sat 5:35, Sun 1:05. Gates open one hour prior to game time.
Visiting Club Hotel: Holiday Inn, Route 70 and Sayer Avenue, Cherry Hill, NJ 08002. **Telephone:** (856) 663-5300.

LANCASTER BARNSTORMERS

Office Address: 650 North Prince St, Lancaster, PA 17603.
Telephone: (717) 509-4487. **Fax:** (717) 509-4486.
E-Mail Address: info@lancasterbarnstormers.com. **Website:** www.lancasterbarnstormers.com.
Operated by: Lancaster Barnstormers Baseball Club, LLC.
Principal Owners: Opening Day Partners.
President: Jon Danos.
Vice President, Business Development: Vince Bulik. **Controller:** Emily Merrill. **Assistant GM:** Kristen Simon. **Senior Director, Marketing:** Anthony DeMarco. **Director, Stadium Operations:** Don Pryer. **Finance Manager:** Brandi Garrraffa. **Creative Services Manager:** Shaun Kreider. **Ticket Services Manager:** Maureen Wheeler. **Stadium Operations Manager:** Ed Snyder. **Marketing Manager:** Bryan Shaffer. **Director, Business Development:** Bob Ford. **Group Events Coordinators:** Christopher Burton, Henry Holland, Dea Murray and John Warnick. **Client Services Representative:** Liz Welch.
Manager: Butch Hobson. **Pitching Coach:** Marty Janzen. **Hitting Coach:** Lance Burkhart. **Trainer:** Mia Del Hierro.

GAME INFORMATION
Radio Announcer: Dave Collins. **No. of Games Broadcast:** Home-70, Away-70. **Flagship Station:** WLPA 1490-AM. **PA Announcer:** John Witwer. **Official Scorer:** Joel Schreiner.
Stadium Name: Clipper Magazine Stadium. **Location:** From Route 30, take Fruitville Pike or Harrisburg Pike toward downtown Lancaster, stadium on North Prince between Clay Street and Frederick Street. **Standard Game Times:** 7 pm; Sun 1:30 pm. **Visiting Team Hotel:** Unavailable.

LONG ISLAND DUCKS

Mailing Address: 3 Court House Dr, Central Islip, NY 11722.
Telephone: (631) 940-3825. **Fax:** (631) 940-3800.
E-Mail Address: info@liducks.com. **Website:** www.liducks.com.
Operated by: Long Island Ducks Professional Baseball, LLC.
Owner/CEO: Frank Boulton. **Owner, Chairman:** Seth Waugh. **Owner/Senior VP, Baseball Operations:** Bud Harrelson.
President/General Manager: Michael Pfaff. **Assistant GMs:** Doug Cohen, Alex Scannella. **Director, Group Sales:** John Wolff. **Director, Administration:** Gerry Anderson. **Director, Season Sales:** Brad Kallman. **Manager, Merchandise/Client Services:** Jay Randall. **Manager, Box Office:** Ben Harper.. **Manager, Media Relations/Broadcasting:** Michael Polak. **Coordinator, Promotions:** Jordan Schiff. **Facilities Maintenance Coordinator:** Scott Marshall. **Coordinator, Administration:** Megan Gordon.
Account Executives: Mike Kennedy, Brian Leavy. **Ticket Assistant:** Steve Cohen. **Group Sales Assistant:** Frank Grande.
Manager: Kevin Baez. **Coaches:** Jay Loviglio, Steve Foucault, Bud Harrelson. **Trainers:** Tony Amin, Adam Lewis, Dorothy Pitchford.

GAME INFORMATION
Radio Announcers: Chris King, Michael Polak, David Weiss. **No. of Games Broadcast:** 140 on www.liducks.com. **Flagship Station:** WJVC, 96.1-FM. **PA Announcer:** Bob Ottone.

SOMERSET PATRIOTS

Office Address: One Patriots Park, Bridgewater, NJ 08807.
Telephone: (908) 252-0700. **Fax:** (908) 252-0776.
Website: www.somersetpatriots.com
Operated by: Somerset Baseball Partners, LLC.
Principal Owners: Steve Kalafer, Jack Cust, Josh Kalafer, Jonathan Kalafer, Byron Brisby, Don Miller. **Chairman:** Steve Kalafer.
President/General Manager: Patrick McVerry. **Senior Vice President, Marketing:** Dave Marek. **VP/Assistant GM:** Rob Lukachyk. **VP, Public Relations:** Marc Russinoff. **VP, Ticketing:** Bryan Iwicki. **Head Groundskeeper:** Dan Purner. **Senior Director, Group Sales:** Matt Kopas. **Director, Promotions/Events :** Kevin Forrester. **Director, Merchandise:** Rob Crossman. **Corporate Sales Manager:** Kevin Fleming. **Senior Account Executive/Community Relations Manager:** Brian Cahill.
Group Sales Manager: Tom McCartney. **Account Executive:** Deanna Liotard. **Executive Assistant to GM:** Michele DaCosta. **Controller:** Ron Schulz. **Accountant:** Stephanie Diez. **Receptionist:** Lorraine Ott. **GM, Centerplate:** Mike McDermott.
Manager: Sparky Lyle. **Director, Player Personnel/Pitching Coach:** Brett Jodie. **Hitting Coach:** Travis Anderson. **Trainer:** Katie Reynolds.

GAME INFORMATION
Radio Announcer: Justin Antweil. **No. of Games Broadcast:** Home-70, Away-70. **Flagship Station:** WCTC 1450-AM. **PA Announcer:** Paul Spychala. **Official Scorer:** John Nolan.
Stadium Name: TD Bank Ballpark. **Location:** Route 287 North to exit 13B/Route 287 South to exit 13 (Somerville Route 28 West); follow signs to ballpark. **Standard Game Times:** 7:05 pm; Sunday, 1:35, 5:05.
Visiting Club Hotel: Unavailable.

SOUTHERN MARYLAND
BLUE CRABS

Office Address: 11765 St Linus Dr, Waldorf, MD 20602.
Telephone: 301-638-9788. **Fax:** 301-638-9788.
E-Mail address: info@somdbluecrabs.com. **Website:** www.somdbluecrabs.com.
Principal Owners: Opening Day Partners LLC, Brooks Robinson.
Chairman: Peter Kirk. **President:** Jon Danos. **Controller:** Emily Merrill.
President: Keith Lupton. **General Manager:** Joel Seiden. **Assistant GM:** Brian Radle. **Director, Finance:** Sheree Ebron. **Sales Account Executives:** Sara Naar, Matthew Ammerman, Tori Wilkins, Dan Wilson. **Director, Corporate Sales:** Candace Gick. **Creative Services:** Kevin Kreigh. **Marketing Manager:** Courtney Freeland. **Director,Ticketing:** Josh Cockerham. **Community Relations:** Amanda McComas. **Stadium Operations:** Steve Bowden.
GM, Centerplate Concessions/Merchandise: Thomas Gergley. **Centerplate Chef:** Scott Fowler. **Head Groundskeeper:** Peter Lockwood. **Clubhouse Manager:** Sam Hunter
Manager: Patrick Osborn. **Hitting Coach:** Jeremy Owens (player/coach).

GAME INFORMATION
Radio: All Home and Away Games, www.somdbluecrabs.com. **Stadium:** Regency Furniture Stadium. **Standard Game Times:** 7:05 pm, Sat 6:35, Sun 2:05.

SUGAR LAND SKEETERS

Office Address: 16160 City Walk, Sugar Land Town Square, Sugar Land, TX 77479
Telephone: (281) 240.4487. **Fax:** (281) 240-4550.
E-Mail address: ask@sugarlandskeeters.com. **Website:** www.sugarlandskeeters.com.
Principal Owners: Opening Day Partners LLC.
Chairman: Peter Kirk. **President:** Jon Danos. **Controller:** Emily Merrill.
General Manager: Matt OiBrien. **VP/Business Development:** Christopher Hill. **Special Assistant to the President:** Deacon Jones. **Director, Baseball Operations:** Michael Kirk. **Director, Tickets:** Adam Tabakin. **Finance Manager:** Ginger Garza. **Event Marketing Director:** Lindsay Kirk. **Event Marketing Manager:** Ira Liebman. **Event Marketing Coordinator:** Paige Phillips. **Community Relations Coordinator:** Taylor McFarland. **Premium Services Manager:** Kelly Dunnbier. **Marketing Communications Manager:** Bryan Hodge.
Operations Manager: Chris Parsons. **Corporate Sales Manager:** Anthony Druilhet. **Corporate Sales Manager:** Alysse Day. **Sponsorship Service Manager:** Jeff Huebel. **Executive Producer:** Tom Gorman. **Sales Assistant:** Dianna Urrego. **Administrative Assistant:** Jennifer Schwarz. **Legends Concessions/Merchandise:** Matt Coonrad. **Head Groundskeeper:** Brad Detmore
Manager: Gary Gaetti. **Pitching Coach:** Britt Burns. **Coach:** Victor Gutierrez.

Constellation Field. **Standard Game Times:** 7:05 pm, Sun 6:05.

YORK REVOLUTION

Office Address: 5 Brooks Robinson Way, York, PA 17401.
Telephone: (717) 801-4487. **Fax:** (717) 801-4499.
E-mail Address: info@yorkrevolution.com. **Website:** www.yorkrevolution. com.

Operated by: York Professional Baseball Club, LLC.
Principal Owners: Opening Day Partners
President/General Manager: Eric Menzer. **Vice President/Business Development:** Neil Fortier. **Assistant GM, Business Operations:** John Gibson. **Finance Manager:** Lori Brunson. **Director, Ticketing:** Cindy Burkholder. **Box Office Manager:** Michael Foster. **Promotions/Communications Manager:** Paul Braverman. **Director, Marketing:** Staci Wilkenson. **Corporate Partnerships Associates:** Mike Chatburn, Reed Gunderson, Yari Marte Natal, Amanda Seimer. **Client Services Coordinator:** Karen Luciano. **Stadium Operations Manager:** Ryan Long.

Legends Hospitality General Manager Concessions/Merchandise/Catering: Rob Wilson. **Legends Hospitality Catering Manager:** Adam Baumbach. **Legends Hospitality Chef:** Tiffany Eger/

Manager: Andy Etchebarren. **Pitching Coach:** Mark Mason. **Infield Coach:** Enohel Polanco. **Baseball Operations Manager:** Andrew Ball.

Radio Announcer: Darrell Henry. **No. of Games Broadcast:** 140. **Flagship Station:** WOYK 1350 AM. **PA Announcer:** Chris DePatto and Ron Ruman. **Official Scorer:** Brian Wisler.

Stadium Name: Sovereign Bank Stadium. **Location:** Take Route 30 West to North George Street. **Directions:** Turn left onto North George Street. Follow that straight for four lights, Sovereign Bank Stadium is on left.

Standard Game Times: 6:30 pm, Sun 5. **Visiting Club Hotel:** The Yorktowne Hotel, 48 E Market St York, PA 17401. **Telephone:** (717) 848-1111.

CAN-AM LEAGUE

Office Address: 1415 Hwy 54 West, Suite 210, Durham, NC 27707.
Telephone: (919) 401-8150. **Fax:** (919) 401-8152. **Website:** www.canamleague.com.
Year Founded: 2004.
Commissioner: Miles Wolff. **President:** Dan Moushon.
Administrative Assistant: Jason Deans. **Director, Umpires:** Kevin Winn.
Division Structure: None.
Regular Season: 100 games.
2012 Opening Date: May 17. **2012 Closing Date:** September 3.
Playoff Format: Two teams with the best winning percentage meet in championship series.
Roster Limit: 22.
Eligibility Rule: Minimum of five first-year players; maximum of four veterans (at least six or more years of professional service).
Brand of Baseball: Rawlings.
Statistician: Pointstreak.com. **Address:** 602-1595 16th Avenue, Richmond Hill, ON, Canada L4B 3N9.

STADIUM INFORMAT ION

			Dimensions				
Club	Stadium	Opened	LF	CF	RF	Capacity	2011 Att.
Newark	Bears & Eagles Riverfront Stadium	1999	302	394	323	6,200	51,854
New Jersey	Yogi Berra Stadium	1998	308	398	308	3,784	84,865
Quebec	Stade Municipal	1938	315	385	315	4,800	149,330
Rockland	Provident Bank Park	2011	323	403	313	4,750	123,518
Worcester	Hanover Insurance Park-Fitton Field	1905	361	417	307	3,000	83,745

NEWARK BEARS

Office Address: 450 Broad St, Newark, NJ 07102.
Telephone: (973) 848-1000. **Fax:** (973) 621-0095.
Website: www.newarkbears.com.
Operated by: Danielle Dronet, Owner, CEO.
Owner/ Partner: Douglas Spiel.
Assistant General Manager: Alex Krohn. **Director, Stadium Operations:** Will Colavito. **Concessions Manager:** Buddy Caruso.
Manager: Tim Raines.

GAME INFORMATION

No. of Games Broadcast: 100. **Webcast:** All-In Internet Broadcasting.
Stadium Name: Bears & Eagles Riverfront Stadium. **Location:** Garden State Parkway North/South to exit 145 (280 East), to exit 15; New Jersey Turnpike North/South to 280 West, to exit 15A.
Standard Game Times: 6:35 pm, Wed 11:05 am, Sun 1:05.
Visiting Club Hotel: Unavailable.

NEW JERSEY JACKALS

Office Address: One Hall Dr, Little Falls, NJ 07424.
Telephone: (973) 746-7434. **Fax:** (973) 655-8006.
E-Mail Address: info@jackals.com. **Website:** www.jackals.com.
Operated by: Floyd Hall Enterprises, LLC.
Chairman: Floyd Hall.
President: Greg Lockard.
General Manager: Larry Hall. **Business Manager:** Jennifer Fertig. **Ticket Operations Manager:** Jeff Manahan. **Director, Group Sales:** Jordan Cascino. **Group Sales Representatives:** Michael Berhang, Shannon Koop. **Facilities Manager:** Aldo Licitra. **Concessions Manager:** Michelle Guarino.
Clubhouse Manager: Wally Brackett.
Manager: Joe Calfapietra. **Coaches:** Ed Ott, Ani Ramos.

GAME INFORMATION

Webcast Announcer: Cody Chrusciel. **No. of Games Broadcast:** 100. **Webcast Address:** www.jackals.com.
Stadium Name: Yogi Berra Stadium. **Location:** On the campus of Montclair State University; Route 80 or Garden State Parkway to Route 46, take Valley Road exit to Montclair State University.
Standard Game Times: 7:05 pm, Sat 6:35, Sun 2:05.
Visiting Club Hotel: Ramada Inn, 130 Rte 10 West, East Hanover, NJ 07936. **Telephone:** (973) 386-5622.

QUEBEC CAPITALES

Office Address: 100 Rue du Cardinal Maurice-Roy, Quebec City, QC G1K8Z1.
Telephone: (418) 521-2255. **Fax:** (418) 521-2266.
E-Mail Address: info@capitalesdequebec.com. **Website:** www.capitalesdequebec.com.
Owner: Jean Tremblay.
President: Michel Laplante.
General Manager: Alex Harvey. **Assistant GM:** Pier-Luc Nappert. **Director, Media/Marketing:** Marc-Antoine GariÈpy.
Assistant, Media/Marketing: Jonathan Roy.
Manager: Patrick Scalabrini.

GAME INFORMATION

Radio Announcer: Francois Paquet. **No. of Games Broadcast:** 100. **Flagship Station:** Quebec 800
AM. **Webcast Address:** www.quebec800.com.
Stadium Name: Stade Municipal de Quebec. **Location:** Highway 40 to Highway 173 (Centre-Ville) exit 2 to Parc
Victoria.
Standard Game Times: 7:05 pm, Sun 1:05 pm.
Visiting Club Hotel: Le Clarendon, 57 rue Sainte-Anne, Quebec, QC, G1R 3X4. **Telephone:** (418) 692-2480.

ROCKLAND BOULDERS

Office Address: 1 Provident Bank Park Drive, Pomona, NY 10970.
Telephone: (845) 364-0009. **Fax:** (845) 364-0001.
E-Mail Address: info@rocklandboulders.com. **Website:** www.rocklandboulders.com.
President: Ken Lehner. **Executive Vice President:** Shawn Reilly. **Counsel:** Jonathan Fine.
Director, First Impressions: Dana Fjermestad. **Ticket Manager:** Bret Kaufman. **Corporate
Partnership Manager:** Seth Cantor.
Manager: Dave LaPoint. **Coaches:** Damian Rolls. **Trainer:** Lori Rahim.

GAME INFORMATION

Radio Announcer: Seth Cantor.
Stadium Name: Provident Bank Park. **Location:** Take Exit 12 towards Route 45, make left at stop sign on Conklin
Road,make left on Route 45, turn right on Pomona Road, take 1st right on Fireman's Memorial Drive.
Standard Game Times: 7:05 pm, Sun 2:05/5:05.
Visiting Club Hotel: Unavailable.

WORCESTER TORNADOES

Office Address: 303 Main St, Worcester, MA 01613.
Telephone: (508) 792-2288. **Fax:** (506) 926-3662.
E-Mail Address: info@worcestertornadoes.com. **Website:** www.worcestertornadoes.com.
General Manager: Jorg Bassiacos. **Director, Communications:** Nick Gagalis. **Senior Account
Executive:** Sarah Farley. **Account Executives:** Gianna Cangello, Matt Cornaro, Patrick Flaherty.
Special Advisor to General Manager: Ed Riley.
Manager: Chip Plante. **Director, Player Personnel:** Brad Michals.

GAME INFORMATION

Webcast Announcer: Nick Gagalis. **No. of Games Broadcast:** 100. **Webcast Address:** www.worcestertornadoes.
com.
Stadium Name: Hanover Insurance Park at Fitton Field. **Location:** I-290 to exit 11 College Square, right on College
Street, left on Fitton Avenue.
Standard Game Times: 7:05 pm, Sun 4:05.
Visiting Club Hotel: Quality Inn & Suites, 50 Oriol Drive, Worcester, MA 01605. **Telephone:** (508) 852-2800.

FRONTIER LEAGUE

Office Address: 2041 Goose Lake Rd Suite 2A, Sauget, IL 62206.
Mailing Address: Same as above.
Telephone: (618) 215-4134. **Fax:** (618) 332-2115.
E-Mail Address: office@frontierleague.com. **Website:** www.frontierleague.com.
Year Founded: 1993.
Commissioner: Bill Lee.
Deputy Commissioner: Steve Tahsler.
President: Rich Sauget (Gateway). **Executive Committee:** Clint Brown (Florence), Steven Edelson (Lake Erie), Erik Haag (Southern Illinois), Stu Williams (Washington).
Board of Directors: Bill Bussing (Evansville), Steve Malliet (Normal/River City), David Martin (London), Alan Oremus (Joliet), Pat Salvi (Schaumburg), Mike Stranczek (Windy City), Bryan Wickline (Rockford), Leslye Wuerfel (Traverse City).
Division Structure: East—Evansville, Florence, Lake Erie, London, Southern Illinois, Traverse City, Washington. West—Gateway, Joliet, Normal, River City, Rockford, Schaumburg, Windy City.
Regular Season: 96 games. **2012 Opening Date:** May 17. **Closing Date:** Sept 2.
All-Star Game: July 11 at Normal.
Playoff Format: Division winners and 2 wild card teams meet in best-of-five Divisional Series. Winners meet in best-of-five series for league championship.
Roster Limit: 24. **Eligibility Rule:** Minimum of eleven Rookie 1/Rookie 2 players. No player may be 27 prior to Jan. 1 of current season with the exception of one player that may not be 30 years of age prior to Jan. 1 of the current season.
Brand of Baseball: Wilson.
Statistician: Pointstreak, 602-1595 16th Avenue, Richmond Hill, ONT L4B 3N9

STADIUM INFORMATION

Club	Stadium	Opened	LF	CF	RF	Capacity	2011 Att.
Evansville	Bosse Field	1915	315	415	315	5,110	97,937
Florence	Home of the Freedom	2004	325	395	325	4,200	83,436
Gateway	GCS Ballpark	2002	318	395	325	5,500	166,072
Joliet	Silver Cross Field	2002	330	400	327	6,229	108,610
Lake Erie	All-Pro Freight	2009	325	400	325	5,000	128,628
London	Labatt Park	1877	328	403	328	4,000	------
Normal	The Corn Crib	2010	356	400	344	7,000	114,917
River City	T.R. Hughes Ballpark	1999	320	382	299	4,989	71,958
Rockford	RiverHawks Stadium	2006	315	393	312	3,279	97,678
Schaumburg	Schaumburg Stadium	1999	355	400	353	8,107	------
So. Illinois	Rent One Park	2007	325	400	330	4,500	181,576
Traverse City	Wuerfel Park	2006	320	400	320	4,600	169,739
Washington	CONSOL Energy Park	2002	325	400	325	3,200	104,635
Windy City	Standard Bank Stadium	1999	335	390	335	2,598	86,727

EVANSVILLE OTTERS

Mailing Address: 1701 N Main St, Evansville, IN 47711.
Telephone: (812) 435-8686.
Operated by: Evansville Baseball, LLC.
President: Bill Bussing.
Senior Vice President: Bix Branson. **General Manager:** Joel Padfield. **Accounting Manager:** Casie Williams. **Account Executive/Director, Media Relations/Broadcasting:** Mike Radomski. **Director, Operations:** Jake Riffert. **Sports Turf Manager:** Lance Adler.
Manager, Baseball Operations: Andy McCauley. **Director, Player Personnel:** Kevin Cope.

GAME INFORMATION

Radio Announcer: Unavailable. **No. of Games Broadcast:** Home-48, Away-48. **Flagship Station:** WUEV 91.5-FM. **PA Announcer:** Zane Clodfelter. **Official Scorer:** Unknown.
Stadium Name: Bosse Field. **Location:** US 41 to Lloyd Expressway West (IN-62), Main St Exit, Right on Main St, ahead 1 mile to Bosse Field. **Standard Game Times:** 6:35 pm; Sun 6:05 pm.
Visiting Club Hotel: Unavailable.

FLORENCE FREEDOM

Office Address: 7950 Freedom Way, Florence, KY 41042.
Telephone: (859) 594-4487. **Fax:** (859) 594-3194.
E-Mail Address: info@florencefreedom.com
Website: www.florencefreedom.com.

Operated by: Canterbury Baseball, LLC.
President: Clint Brown. **Assistant GM:** Josh Anderson. **Director, Operations:** Matt Resar. **Director, Food/Beverage:** Kim Brown. **Director, Promotions:** Kevin Schwab.
Baseball Operations/Manager: Fran Riordan. **Pitching Coach:** Unavailable. **Trainer:** Chris Unkraut.

GAME INFORMATION

Flagship Station: 1160 AM. **Radio Broadcaster:** Unavailable. **PA Announcer:** Kevin Schwab. **Official Scorer:** Unavailable.
Stadium: Freedom Park. **Location:** I-71/75 South to exit 180, left onto US 42, right on Freedom Way; I-71/75 North to exit 180.
Standard Game Times: 7:05 pm; 6:05 (Sat/Sun).
Visiting Club Hotel: Wildwood Inn.

GATEWAY GRIZZLIES

Mailing Address: 2301 Grizzlie Bear Blvd, Sauget, IL 62206
Telephone: (618) 337-3000. **Fax:** (618) 332-3625
E-Mail Address: info@gatewaygrizzlies.com **Website:** www.gatewaygrizzlies.com
Operated by: Gateway Baseball, LLC
Managing Officer: Richard Sauget. **General Manager:** Steven Gomric. **Director, Stadium Operations:** Brent Pownall. **Director, Corporate Sales:** CJ Hendrickson. **Events Manager/Director, Player Procurement:** Jeff OíNeill. **Radio Broadcaster/Media Relations Director:** Adam Young. **Director, Group Sales:** Zach Prehn. **Director, Sales:** Craig Dohm. **Assistant Director, Stadium Operations:** Travis Holtkamp. **Director, Marketing:** Monica Rodriguez. **Sales Associate:** Michael Genetti. **Director, Promotions:** Katie Patton.
Manager: Phil Warren. **Pitching Coach:** Randy Martz. **Hitting Coach:** Darin Kinsolving. **Bench Coach:** Zach Borowiak. **Trainer:** Geof Manzo.

GAME INFORMATION

Radio Announcer: Adam Young. **No of Games Broadcast:** Home-48, Away-48. **Flagship Station:** 590-AM KFNS. **Affiliate Station:** 1400-AM KJFF. **PA Announcer:** Tom Calhoun.
Stadium Name: GCS Ballpark. **Location:** I-255 at exit 15 (Mousette Lane). **Standard Game Times:** 7:05 pm; 6:05/3:05 (Sun).
Visiting Club Hotel: Ramada Inn, 6900 N Illinois St, Fairview Heights, IL 62208. **Telephone:** (618) 632-4747.

JOLIET SLAMMERS

Office Address: 1 Mayor Art Schultz Dr, Joliet, IL 60432
Telephone: (815)722-2287. **Fax:** (815) 726-4304.
E-Mail Address: info@jolietslammers.com . **Website:** www.jolietslammers.com .
Operated by: Steel City Baseball, LLC.
Owner: J Alan Oremus.
President/General Manager: Bill Waliewski. **Vice President/Baseball Operations:** Ron Biga. **VP/Stadium Operations:** Paul Rathje. **Office/Business Manager:** Lois Dittrich. **Director, Corporate Sales:** Dan DeCaprio. **Director, Community Relations/Promotions:** Kelli Drechsel. **Director, Special Projects:** Ken Miller. **Stadium Operations:** Guy Massaro.
Manager: Bart Zeller. **Coach:** Ron Biga. **Pitching Coach:** Carmen Pignatiello. **Clubhouse Manager:** Unavailable. **Trainer:** ATI Physical Therapy

GAME INFORMATION

Radio Announcer: Aaron Morse. **No. of Games Broadcast:** Home-48, Away-48. **Flagship Station:** WJOL (AM 1340). **PA. Announcer:** Mike Slodki. **Official Scorer:** Dave Laketa.
Stadium Name: Silver Cross Field. **Location:** Corner of Mayor Art Schultz Drive and Jefferson Street in downtown Joliet. **Standard Game Times:** 7:05 pm, Sat 6:05, Sun 2:05.
Visiting Club Hotel: Fairfield Inn, 3239 Norman Ave Joliet, IL 60431.

LAKE ERIE CRUSHERS

Mailing Address: 2009 Baseball Blvd, Avon, OH, 44011.
Telephone: (440) 934-3636. **Fax:** (440) 934-2458.
E-Mail Address: info@lakeeriecrushers.com. **Website:** www.lakeeriecrushers.com.
Operated by: Avon Pro Baseball LLC.
Managing Officer: Steven Edelson.
Vice President, Business Operations: Daniel Helm. **VP, Corporate Sales:** Kevin Rooney. **Assistant GM, Operations:** Paul Siegwarth. **Accountant:** Lisa Rueber. **Box Office Manager:** Kelly Dolan. **Director, Group Sales:** Michael Link. **Director, Concessions/Catering:** Kevin Dailey. **Account Executives:** Michael Keefe, Matt Kendeigh.

Manager: John Massarelli. **Pitching Coach:** Chris Steinborn. **Hitting Coach:** Dave Schaub.

GAME INFORMATION

Stadium Name: All Pro Freight Stadium. **Location:** Intersection of I-90 and Colorado Ave in Avon, OH. **Standard Game Times:** 7:05 pm; Sun 5:05.

LONDON RIPPERS

Office Address: 277 Summit Dr, Waterford, MI 48328.
Stadium Address: 25 Wilson Avenue, London, ON N6H 1X2, Canada.
Telephone: (519) 800-3289.
Website: www.londonrippers.com. **E-Mail Address:** info@londonrippers.com.
Operated by: Summit Professional Baseball LLC. **Managing Partner/President/GM:** David H Martin. **VP Operations:** Alison Stier. **Assistant GM, Baseball Ops:** Matt Dillard. **Assistant GM, Business Ops:** David Hollerbach. **Director, Marketing/Creative Services:** Mark Callebs. **Director, Baseball Operations:** Shawn King.
Manager: David H Martin. **Pitching Coach:** Matt Dillard. **Hitting Coach:** Shawn King.

GAME INFORMATION

Stadium Name: Labatt Park
Stadium Location: Corner of Wison and Queens Ave in the heart of downtown London.
Standard Game Times: 6:30 pm; Fri-Sat 7; Sun 1
Mascot: Fungo. **Visiting Club Hotel:** Delta London Armouries, 325 Dundas Street, London, Ontario, N6B 1T9. **Telephone:** 519-679-6111.

NORMAL CORNBELTERS

Mailing Address:1000 West Raab Road, Normal, IL 61761. **Telephone:** 309-454-2255(BALL). **Fax:** 309- 454-2287(BATS). **Ownership:** Normal Baseball Group. **President:** Steve Malliet. **General Manager:** Kyle Kreger. **Corporate Partnerships Manager:** Lori Johnson. **Vice President, Fan Experiences:** Zach Ziler, Joe Rejc. **Public/Media Relations Manager:** Ashlynne Solvie. **Business Manager:** Heather Manint.
Manager: Chad Parker.

GAME INFORMATION

Radio Announcer: Unavailable. **Flagship Station:** WJBC 1230 AM, WHOW 95.9 FM. **No. of Games Broadcast:** Home-48, Away-48.
Stadium Name: The Corn Crib. **Location:** From I-55 North, Go south on I-55 and take the 165 exit (Heartland College). Turn left at light. Turn right on Raab Road to ballpark on right. From south, go north on I-55 and take the 165 exit (Heartland). Merge onto Route 51 (Main street). Turn right on Raab Road to ballpark on right.
Standard Game Times: 6:30 pm, Sun 5.

RIVER CITY RASCALS

Office Address: 900 TR Hughes Blvd, O'Fallon, MO 63366.
Telephone: (636) 240-2287. **Fax:** (636) 240-7313.
E-Mail Address: info@rivercityrascals.com. **Website:** www.rivercityrascals.com.
Operated by: PS and J Professional Baseball Club LLC. **Owners:** Tim Hoeksema, Jan Hoeksema, Fred Stratton, Anne Stratton, Pam Malliet, Steve Malliet, Michael Veeck, Greg Wendt.
Vice President/General Manager: Chris Franklin. **Director, Group/Ticket Sales:** Gina Perschbacher. **Director, Ticket Operations:** Courtney Oakley. **Ticket Sales Representative:** Ashley Phillips. **Ticket Sales Representative:** Jeremy Cowen.
Team Manager: Steve Brook. **Assistant Coach:** Mike Breyman. **Bench Coach:** Dave Garcia.

GAME INFORMATION

No. of Games Broadcast: Home-48, Away-48. **PA Announcer:** Randy Moehlman.
Stadium Name: T.R. Hughes Ballpark. **Location:** I-70 to exit 219, north on T.R. Hughes Road, follow signs to ballpark. **Standard Game Times:** 7:05 pm, Sun 6:05.
Visiting Club Hotel: America's Best Value Inn 1310 Bass Pro Drive St. Charles, MO (636) 947-5900.

ROCKFORD RIVERHAWKS

Office Address: 4503 Interstate Blvd Loves Park, IL 61111.
Telephone: (815) 885-2255. **Fax:** (815) 885-2204.
Website: www.rockfordriverhawks.com

Owned by: Rock River Valley Baseball. President: Bryan Wickline.

General Manager: Brad Sholes. Director, Broadcasting/Sales/Media Relations: Bill Czaja. Director, Operations: Chris Daleo. Head Groundskeeper: Tyler Clay.

Field Manager: Rich Austin. Hitting Coach: Patrick O'Sullivan. Pitching Coach: Scott Roehl.

GAME INFORMATION

Radio Announcer: Bill Czaja. No. of Games Broadcast: 96. Flagship Station: ESPN 1380. PA Announcer: Brett Myhres. Official Scorer: Josh Keener.

Stadium Name: RiverHawks Stadium. Location: I-90 (Jane Addams Tollway) to Riverside Blvd exit (automatic toll booth), east to Interstate Dr, north on Interstate Dr to dead end. Standard Game Times: 7:05 pm, Sat 6:05, Sun 3:05.

Visiting Club Hotel: Unavailable.

SCHAUMBURG BOOMERS

Office Address: 1999 S Springinsguth Road, Schaumburg, IL 60193

Telephone: (847) 461-3695 Fax (630) 439-3501

E-Mail Address: info@boomersbaseball.com Website: www.boomersbaseball.com

Owned by: Pat and Lindy Salvi

President/General Manager: Andy Viano. VP, Corporate Sales: Jeff Ney. VP, Marketing/Promotions: Dave Salvi. Director, Media Relations: Ed McCaskey. Manager, Stadium Operations: Jack Mikel. Box Office/Business Manager: Todd Fulk. Senior Account Executive: Meghan O'Brien. Fan Relations Coordinator: Saralyn Locke. Head Groundskeeper: Mike Tlusty. Creative Marketing Specialist: Dan Tomaszewski. Account Executive: Carly Salczynski. Community Relations Intern: Sara Romano.

Manager: Jamie Bennett. Hitting Coach: C.J. Thieleke. Bench Coach: Mike Kashirsky. Pitching Coach: Dusty Baker.

GAME INFORMATION

Broadcaster: Tim Calderwood. No. of Games Broadcast: Home-48, Away-48. Flagship Station: WRMN 1410 AM Elgin. Official Scorer: Unavailable

Stadium: Schaumburg Boomers Stadium. Location: I-290 to Thorndale Ave Exit, head West on Elgin-O'Hare Expressway until Springinsguth Road Exit. Second Left at Springinsguth Road (Shared parking lot with Schaumburg Metra Station).

Visiting Club Hotel: Unavailable

SOUTHERN ILLINOIS MINERS

Office Address: Rent One Park, 1000 Miners Drive, Marion, IL 62959.

Telephone: (618) 998-8499. Fax: (618) 969-8550.

E-Mail Address: info@southernillinoisminers.com. Website: www.southernillinoisminers.com.

Operated by: Southern Illinois Baseball Group. Owner: Jayne Simmons,

Vice President: Erik Haag. General Manager: Tim Arseneau. Assistant GM: Billy Richards. Director, Ticket Operations: Billy Leitner. Manager, Sales/Marketing Coordinator: Terra Brenner. Director, Video Production/Creative Services: Jeff Holtke. Director, Finance: Cathy Perry. Account Executives: Cory Lee, Eric Pionk.

Manager: Mike Pinto. Pitching Coach: Justin Lord. Hitting Coach: Ralph Santana. Coach/Advance Scout: John Lakin.

GAME INFORMATION

No. of Games Broadcast: 96. Flagship Station: 97.7 WHET-FM.

Stadium Name: Rent One Park. Location: US 57 to Route 13 East, right at Halfway Road to Fairmont Dr Standard Game Times: 7:05 pm; Sunday, 5:05 pm

Visiting Club Hotel: Days Inn 1802 Bittle Place, Marion, IL 62959.

TRAVERSE CITY BEACH BUMS

Office Address: 333 Stadium Dr, Traverse City, MI 49685.

Telephone: (231) 943-0100. Fax: (231) 943-0900.

E-Mail Address: info@tcbeachbums.com. Website: www.tcbeachbums.com.

Operated by: Traverse City Beach Bums, LLC.

Managing Partners: John Wuerfel, Leslye Wuerfel, Jason Wuerfel.

President/CEO: John Wuerfel.. Member/CFO: Leslye Wuerfel. Vice President/Director, Baseball Operations: Jason Wuerfel.

Manager: Gregg Langbehn. Hitting Coach: Shannon Hunt. Infield Coach: Matt Pulley. Trainer: Jennifer Scamehorn.

GAME INFORMATION

No. of Games Broadcast: Home-48, Away-48. Flagship Stations: WLDR 101.9-FM. PA Announcer: Tim Moeggenberg.

Stadium Name: Wuerfel Park. **Location:** 3 miles south of the Grand Traverse Mall just off US-31 and M-37 in Chums Village. Stadium is visible from the highway (Or north of US 31 and M-37 Chums Corner intersection). Turn-west on Chums Village Drive, north on Village Park Drive, right on Stadium Drive. **Standard Game Times:** 7:05 pm; Sun 5:05.

Visiting Club Hotel: Baymont Inn & Suites of Traverse City.

WASHINGTON WILD THINGS

Office Address: One Washington Federal Way, Washington, PA 15301.

Telephone: (724) 250-9555. **Fax:** (724) 250-2333.

E-Mail Address: info@washingtonwildthings.com . **Website:** www.washingtonwildthings.com.

Owned by: Sports Facility, LLC. **Operated by:** Washington Frontier League Baseball, LLC.

President/Chief Executive Officer: Stuart Williams. **General Manager:** Francine Williams. **Director, Marketing/Communications/Corporate Relations:** Christine Blaine. **Director. Assistant GM:** Steve Zavacky. **Corporate Partnership Manager:** Jim Gibson/Rick Minetti. **Ticket Operations/Merchandise/Community Relations:** Kate Billings. **Ticket Account Executives:** Andrew Gottlieb, Nick Halfhill, Kelly Williams. **Special Events:** Andrea Biedny, Wayne Herrod. **Controller:** Carrie Ammons.

Manager: Chris Bando. **Coach:** Lenny Randle.

GAME INFORMATION

Radio Announcer: Randy Gore. **No. of Games Broadcast:** Home-48, Away-48. **Flagship Station:** WJPA 95.3-FM. **Official Scorer:** Unavailable.

Stadium Name: CONSOL Energy Park. **Location:** I-70 to exit 15 (Chestnut Street), right on Chestnut Street to Washington Crown Center Mall, right at mall entrance, right on to Mall Drive to stadium. **Standard Game Times:** 7:05 pm

Visiting Club Hotel: Unavailable.

WINDY CITY THUNDERBOLTS

Office Address: 14011 South Kenton Ave, Crestwood, IL 60445-2252.

Telephone: (708) 489-2255. **Fax:** (708) 489-2999.

E-Mail Address: info@wcthunderbolts.com. **Website:** www.wcthunderbolts.com.

Owned by: Crestwood Professional Baseball, LLC.

General Manager: Mike Lucas. **Director, Operations:** Mike VerSchAve. **Director, Food/Beverage:** Adam Schwarzenpraub. **Director, Community Relations:** Zac Charbonneau.

Field Manager: Morgan Burkhart. **Pitching Coach:** Bobby Post.

GAME INFORMATION

Radio Announcer: Terry Bonadonna. **No. of Games Broadcast:** 96. **Flagship Station:** WXAV, 88.3 FM. **Official Scorer:** Steve Trotto.

Stadium Name: Standard Bank Stadium. **Location:** I-294 to S Cicero Ave, exit (Route 50), south for 1 1/2 miles, left at Midlothian Turnpike, right on Kenton Ave; I-57 to 147th Street, west on 147th to Cicero, north on Cicero, right on Midlothian Turnpike, right on Kenton. **Standard Game Times:** 7:05 pm; Sat 6:05, Sun 5:05.

Visiting Club Hotel: Georgioís Comfort Inn, 8800 W 159th St, Orland Park, IL 60462. **Telephone:** (708) 403-1100. **Fax:** (708) 403-1105.

NORTH AMERICAN LEAGUE

Office Address: 6111 Bollinger Canyon Road, Suite 580, San Ramon, CA 94583.

Telephone: (925) 302-7360. **Fax:** (925) 302-7375.

E-Mail Address: info@northamericanleague.com. **Website:** www.northamericanleague.com.

Founded: 2011.

CEO: Brian MacInnes. **Commissioner:** Kevin Outcalt. **Director, Operations:** Stephen Bedford. **Manager, Marketing/Media:** Justin Reschke. **Manager, Sales/Business Development:** Keith Barnard.

Division Structure: North: Edmonton, San Rafael, Chico, Maui, Yuma. South: Edinburg, San Angelo, McAllen, Forth Worth, Rio Grande Valley.

Regular Season: 96 games.

2012 Opening Date: May 24. **Closing Date:** Sept 3.

Playoff Format: Top six teams to meet in a double-elimination tournament.

Roster Limit: 23, expands to 25 after Sept 3.

Eligibility Rules: No minimum number of rookies, age limit of 31 as of Jan 1 unless player has Triple-A or above experience, or has top foreign league experience.

All-Star Game: Unavailable.

Statistician: Unavailable.

INTERNATIONAL

AMERICAS

MEXICO

MEXICAN LEAGUE

Member, National Association

NOTE: The Mexican League is a member of the National Association of Professional Baseball Leagues and has a Triple-A classification. However, its member clubs operate largely independent of the 30 major league teams, and for that reason the league is listed in the international section.

Address: Av Insurgentes Sur #797 3er. piso. Col. Napoles. C.P. 03810, Benito Juarez, Mexico, D.F. **Telephone:** 52-55-5557-1007. **Fax:** 52-55-5395-2454. **E-Mail Address:** oficina@lmb.com.mx. **Website:** www.lmb.com.mx.

Years League Active: 1955-.

President: Plinio Escalante Bolio. **Operations Manager:** Nestor Alba Brito.

Division Structure: Madero—Chihuahua, Laguna, Mexico, Monclova, Monterrey, Nuevo Laredo, Reynosa, Saltillo. Hidalgo—Campeche, Minatitlan, Oaxaca, Puebla, Quintana Roo, Tabasco, Veracruz, Yucatan.

Regular Season: 110 games (split-schedule). **2012 Opening Date:** March 20. **Closing Date:** July 29.

All-Star Game: May 18-20, Monterrey, Nuevo León.

Playoff Format: Eight teams qualify, including first- and second-half division winners plus wild-card teams with best overall records. Quarterfinals, semifinals and finals are all best of seven series.

Roster Limit: 28. **Roster Limit, Imports:** 6.

CAMPECHE PIRATES

Office Address: Calle Filiberto Qui Farfan No. 2, Col. Camino Real, CP 24020, Campeche, Campeche. **Telephone:** (52) 981-827-4759. **Fax:** (52) 981-8274767. **E-Mail Address:** piratas@prodigy.net.mx.

Website: www.piratasdecampeche.com.mx.

President: Gabriel Escalante Castillo. **General Manager:** Maria del Socorro Morales.

Manager: Hector Estrada.

CHIHUAHUA GOLDENS

Office Address: Blvd Juan Pablo II No 4506, Col Aeropuerto CP 31380. **Telephone:** (52) 614-459-0317. **Fax:** (52) 614-459-0336. **E-Mail Address:** icampos@doradoslmb.com. **Website:** www.doradoslmb.com.

President: Mario Rodriguez. **General Manager:** Iram Campos Lara.

Manager: Arturo de Freitas.

LAGUNA COWBOYS

Office Address: Juan Gutenberg s/n, Col Centro, CP 27000, Torreon, Coahuila. **Telephone:** (52) 871-718-5515. **Fax:** (52) 871-717-4335. **E-Mail Address:** unionlag@prodigy.net.mx. **Website:** www.clubvaquaroslaguna.com.

President: Carlos Gomez del Campo. **General Manager:** Carlos de la Garza.

Manager: Derek Bryant.

MEXICO CITY RED DEVILS

Office Address: Av Cuauhtemoc #451-101, Col Narvarte, CP 03020, Mexico DF. **Telephone:** (52) 555-639-8722. **Fax:** (52) 555-639-9722. **E-Mail Address:** diablos@sportsya.com. **Website:** www.diablos.com.mx.

President: Roberto Mansur Galán. **General Manager:** Eduardo de la Cerda.

Manager: Daniel Fernandez.

MONCLOVA STEELERS

Office Address: Cuauhtemoc #299, Col Ciudad Deportiva, CP 25750, Monclova, Coahuila. **Telephone:** (52) 866-636-2650. **Fax:** (52) 866-636-2688. **E-Mail Address:** acererosdelnorte@prodigy.net.mx. **Website:** www.acereros.com.mx.

President: Donaciano Garza Gutierrez. **General Manager:** Victor Favela Lopez.

Manager: Francisco Rodriguez.

MONTERREY SULTANS

Office Address: Av Manuel Barragan s/n, Estadio Monterrey, Apartado Postal 870, Monterrey, Nuevo Leon, CP 66460. **Telephone:** (52) 81-8351-0209. **Fax:** (52) 81-8351-8022. **E-Mail Address:** sultanes@sultanes.com.mx. **Website:** www.sultanes.com.mx.

President: José Maiz García. **General Manager:** Roberto Magdaleno Ramírez.

Manager: Felix Fermin.

NUEVO LAREDO OWLS

Office Address: Av Santos Degollado 235-G, Col Independencia, CP 88020, Nuevo Laredo, Tamaulipas. **Telephone:** (52) 867-712-2299. **Fax:** (52) 867-712-0736. **E-Mail Address:** tecolotes@globalpc.net. **Website:** www.tecolotesdenuevolaredo.com.

President: Victor Lozano Rendon. **General Manager:** Ruben Estrada Ordonez.

Manager: Gerardo Sanchez.

OAXACA WARRIORS

Office Address: M Bravo 417 Col Centro 68000, Oaxaca, Oaxaca. **Telephone:** (52) 951-515-5522. **Fax:** (52) 951-515-4966. **E-Mail Address:** oaxacaguerreros@gmail.com. **Website:** www.guerrerosdeoaxaca.com.mx.

President: Avellá Villa Vicente Pérez. **General Manager:** Lic Spindola Guillermo Morales.

Manager: Eddy Diaz.

MINATITLAN OILERS

Office Address: Av Avila Camacho esquina con H Colegio Militar, Estadio 18 de Marzo de 1938, Col De los Maestros, CP 96848, Minatitlan, Veracruz. **Telephone:** (52) 951-515-5522. **Fax:** (52) 951-515-4966. **E-Mail Address:** webmaster@petrolerosdeminatitlan.com.mx. **Website:** www.petrolerosdeminatitlan.com.mx.

Manager: Andres Mora.

PUEBLA PARROTS

Office Address: Calz Zaragoza S/N, Unidad Deportiva 5 de Mayo, Col Maravillas, CP 72220, Puebla, Puebla. **Telephone:** (52) 222-222-2116. **Fax:** (52) 222-222-2117. **E-Mail Address:** oficina@pericosdepuebla.com.mx. **Website:** www.pericosdepuebla.com.mx.

President: Rafael Moreno Valle Sanchez. **General Manager:** Edgar Ramirez.

Manager: Alfonso Jimenez.

QUINTANA ROO TIGERS

Office Address: Av Mayapan Mz 4 Lt 1 Super Mz 21, CP 77500, Cancun, Quintana Roo. **Telephone:** (52) 998-887-3108. **Fax:** (52) 998-887-1313. **E-Mail Address:** tigres@tigrescapitalinos.com.mx. **Website:** www.tigresqr.com.

President: Cuauhtémoc Rodriguez. **General Manager:** Francisco Minjarez.

Manager: Matias Carrillo.

SALTILLO SARAPE MAKERS

Office Address: Blvd Nazario Ortiz Esquina con Blvd Jesus Sanchez, CP 25280, Saltillo, Coahuila. **Telephone:** (52) 844-416-9455. **Fax:** (52) 844-439-1330. **E-Mail**

Address: aley@grupoley.com. **Website:** www.saraperos. com.mx.

President: Alvaro Ley Lopez. **General Manager:** Eduardo Valenzuela Guajardo.

Manager: Orlando Sanchez.

TABASCO OLMECS

Office Address: Explanada de la Ciudad Deportiva, Parque de Beisbol Centenario del 27 de Febrero, Col Atasta de Serra, CP 86100, Villahermosa, Tabasco. **Telephone:** (52) 993-352-2787. **Fax:** (52) 993-352-2788. **E-Mail Address:** olmecastab@prodigy.net.mx. **Website:** www. olmecasdetabasco.com.mx.

President: Raul Gonzalez Rodriguez. **General Manager:** Luis Guzman Ramos.

Manager: Luis de los Santos.

REYNOSA BRONCOS

Office Address: Paris 511, Esq c/ Tiburcio Garza Zamora Altos, Locales 6 y 7, Col Beatty, Reynosa, Tamps. **Telephone:** (52) 922-3462. **Fax:** (52) 925-7118. **E-Mail Address:** broncosdereynosa@gmail.com.

Website: www.broncosreynosa.com.

Manager: Homar Rojas.

VERACRUZ RED EAGLES

Office Address: Av Jacarandas S/N, Esquina España, Fraccionamiento Virginia, CP 94294, Boca del Rio, Veracruz. **Telephone:** (52) 229-935-5004. **Fax:** (229) 935-5008. **E-Mail Address:** rojosdelaguila@terra.com.mx. **Website:** www.aguiladeveracruz.com.

President: Jose Antonio Mansur Beltran. **General Manager:** Carlos Nahun Hernandez.

Manager: Enrique Reyes.

YUCATAN LIONS

Office Address: Calle 50 #406-B, Entre 35 y 37, Col Jesus Carranza, CP 97109, Merida, Yucatán. **Telephone:** (52) 999-926-3022. **Fax:** (52) 999-926-3631. **E-Mail Addresses:** leones@prodigy.net.mx. **Website:** www.leonesdeyucatan. com.mx.

President: Ricalde Gustavo Durán. **General Manager:** Jose Rivero.

Manager: Lino Rivera.

MEXICAN ACADEMY

Rookie Classification

Mailing Address: Angel Pola No 16, Col Periodista, CP 11220, Mexico, DF Telephone: (52) 555-557-1007. **Fax:** (52) 555-395-2454. **E-Mail Address:** mbl@prodigy.net.mx. **Website:** www.academialmb.com.

Member Clubs: Celaya, Guanajuato, Queretaro, Salamanca.

Director General: Raul Martinez. Administration: Pela Villalobos.

Regular Season: 50 games. 2008 Opening Date: Oct. 9. Closing Date: Dec. 21.

DOMINICAN REPUBLIC
DOMINICAN SUMMER LEAGUE

Member, National Association
Rookie Classification
Mailing Address: Calle Segunda No 64, Reparto Antilla, Santo Domingo, Dominican Republic. **Telephone/Fax:** (809) 532-3619. **Website:** www.dominicansummerleague. com. **E-Mail Address:** ligadeverano@codetel.net.do.

Years League Active: 1985-.

President: Orlando Diaz.

Member Clubs/Division Structure: Boca Chica North—Blue Jays, Brewers/Orioles (shared team), Cubs 2, Dodgers, Giants, Marlins, Mets, Pirates, Rays, Red Sox, Royals, Yankees 1. Santo Domingo North—Athletics, Cardinals, Mariners, Phillies. Boca Chica Baseball City—Cubs 1, Diamondbacks, Indians, Nationals, Orioles, Padres, Reds, Rockies, Tigers, Twins, White Sox, Yankees 2. San Pedro de Macoris—Angels, Astros, Braves, Rangers 1, Rangers 2.

Regular Season: 72 games. **2012 Opening Date:** June 3. **Closing Date:** Aug 20.

Playoff Format: Six teams qualify for playoffs, including four division winners and two wild-card teams. Teams with two best records receive a bye to the semifinals; four other playoff teams play best-of-three series. Winners advance to best-of-three semifinals. Winners advance to best-of-five championship series.

Roster Limit: 35 active. **Player Eligibility Rule:** No player may have four or more years of prior minor league service. Draft-eligible players may not participate in the DSL or VSL, with the exception of two players from Puerto Rico. No age limits apply.

VENEZUELA
VENEZUELAN SUMMER LEAGUE

Member, National Association
Rookie Classification
Mailing Address: Torre Movilnet, Oficina 10, Piso 9, Valencia, Carabobo, Venezuela. **Telephone:** (58) 241-823-8101. **Fax:** (58) 241-824-3340. **Website:** www.vsl.com.ve.

Years League Active: 1997-.

Administrator: Saul Gonzalez. **Coordinator:** Ramon Feriera.

Participating Organizations: Cardinals, Mariners, Mets, Phillies, Pirates, Rays, Tigers.

Regular Season: 70 games. **2012 Opening Date:** May 17. **Closing Date:** Aug 27.

Playoffs: Best-of-three series between top two teams in regular season.

Roster Limit: 35 active. **Player Eligibility Rule:** No player may have four or more years of prior minor league service. Draft-eligible players may not participate in the DSL or VSL, with the exception of two players from Puerto Rico. No age limits apply.

ASIA

CHINA
CHINA BASEBALL LEAGUE

Mailing Address: 5, Tiyuguan Road, Beijing 100763, China. **Telephone:** (86) 10-6716-9082. **Fax:** (86) 10-6716-2993. **E-Mail Address:** cga_cra@263.net.

Years League Active: 2002-.

Chairman: Hu Jian Guo. **Vice Chairmen:** Tom McCarthy, Shen Wei. **Executive Director:** Yang Jie. **General Manager, Marketing/Promotion:** Lin Xiao Wu.

Member Clubs: Beijing Tigers, Guangdong Leopards, Henan Elephants, Jiangsu Hopestars, Shanghai Golden Eagles, Sichuan Dragons, Tianjin Lions.

Regular Season: 28 games.

Playoff Format: Top two teams meet in one-game championship.

JAPAN

NIPPON PROFESSIONAL BASEBALL

Mailing Address: Imperial Tower, 14F, 1-1-1 Uchisaiwai-cho, Chiyoda-ku, Tokyo 100-0011. **Telephone:** 03-3502-0022. **Fax:** 03-3502-0140.

Website: www.npb.or.jp, www.npb.or.jp/eng

Commissioner: Ryozo Kato.

Executive Secretary: Kunio Shimoda. **Secretaries:** Atsushi Ihara, Shoji Numazawa. **Director, Baseball Operations:** Nobby Ito. **Director, Public Relations:** Katsuhisa Matsuzaki.

Director, Central League Operations: Kazunori Ogaki. **Director, Pacific League Operations:** Kazuo Nakano.

Japan Series: Best-of-seven series between Central and Pacific League champions, begins Oct 27 at home of Central League club.

All-Star Series: July 20 at Kyocera Dome (Osaka); July 21 at Matsuyama; July 23 at QVC Morioka.

Roster Limit: 70 per organization (one major league club, one minor league club). Major league club is permitted to register 28 players at a time, though just 25 may be available for each game.

Roster Limit, Imports: Four in majors (no more than three position players or pitchers); unlimited in minors.

CENTRAL LEAGUE

Regular Season: 144 games.

2012 Opening Date: March 30. **Closing Date:** Sept 27, with makeup games played until Oct 10.

Playoff Format: Second-place team meets third-place team in best-of-three series. Winner meets first-place team in best-of-seven series to determine representative in Japan Series (first-place team has one-game advantage to begin series).

CHUNICHI DRAGONS

Mailing Address: Chunichi Bldg 6F, 4-1-1 Sakae, Naka-ku, Nagoya 460-0008. **Telephone:** 052-261-8811. **Fax:** 052-263-7696.

Chairman: Bungo Shirai. **President:** Katsuhiko Sakai. **General Manager:** Ryohei Sato. **Field Manager:** Morimichi Takagi.

2012 Foreign Players: Tony Blanco, Maximo Nelson, Enyelbert Soto.

HANSHIN TIGERS

Mailing Address: 2-33 Koshien-cho, Nishinomiya-shi, Hyogo-ken 663-8152. **Telephone:** 0798-46-1515. **Fax:** 0798-46-3555.

Chairman: Shinya Sakai. **President:** Nobuo Minami. **General Manager:** Eiichi Takano. **Field Manager:** Yutaka Wada.

2012 Foreign Players: Craig Brazell, Cheng Kai Un, Randy Messenger, Matt Murton, Jason Standridge.

HIROSHIMA TOYO CARP

Mailing Address: 2-3-1 Minami Kaniya, Minami-ku, Hiroshima 732-8501. **Telephone:** 082-554-1000. **Fax:** 082-568-1190.

President: Hajime Matsuda. **General Manager:** Kiyoaki Suzuki. **Field Manager:** Kenjiro Nomura.

2012 Foreign Players: Brian Barden, Bryan Bullington, Kam Mickolio, Dennis Sarfate, Nick Stavinoha.

TOKYO YAKULT SWALLOWS

Mailing Address: Seizan Bldg, 4F, 2-12-28 Kita Aoyama, Minato-ku, Tokyo 107-0061. **Telephone:** 03-3405-8960. **Fax:** 03-3405-8961.

Chairman: Sumiya Hori. **President:** Tsuyoshi Klnugasa. **General Manager:** Junsei Atarashi. **Field Manager:** Junji Ogawa.

2012 Foreign Players: Wladimir Balentien, Tony Barnette, Rafael Fernandes, Lim Chang Yong, Lastings Milledge, Orlando Roman.

YOKOHAMA DeNA BAYSTARS

Mailing Address: Kannai Arai Bldg, 7F, 1-8 Onoe-cho, Naka-ku, Yokohama 231-0015. **Telephone:** 045-681-0811. **Fax:** 045-661-2500.

Chairman: Makoto Haruta. **President:** Jun Ikeda. **General Manager:** Shigeru Takada. **Field Manager:** Kiyoshi Nakahata.

2012 Foreign Players: Giancarlo Alvarado, Clayton Hamilton, Brandon Mann, Alex Ramirez, Wang Yi Cheng.

YOMIURI GIANTS

Mailing Address: Otemachi Nomura Bldg, 7F, 2-1-1 Otemachi, Chiyoda-ku, Tokyo 100-8151. **Telephone:** 03-3246-7733. **Fax:** 03-3246-2726.

Chairman: Kojiro Shiraishi. **President:** Tsunekazu Momoi. **General Manager:** Atsushi Harasawa. **Field Manager:** Tatsunori Hara.

2012 Foreign Players: John Bowker, Dicky Gonzalez, DJ Houlton, Lin Yi Hao, Scott Mathieson, Levi Romero.

PACIFIC LEAGUE

Regular Season: 144 games.

2012 Opening Date: March 30. **Closing Date:** Oct 5, with makeup games played until Oct 10.

Playoff Format: Second-place team meets third-place team in best-of-three series. Winner meets first-place team in best-of-seven series to determine league's representative in Japan Series (first-place team has one-game advantage to begin series).

CHIBA LOTTE MARINES

Mailing Address: 1 Mihama, Mihama-ku, Chiba-shi, Chiba-ken 261-8587. **Telephone:** 03-5682-6341.

Chairman: Takeo Shigemitsu. **President:** Iekuni Nakamura. **Field Manager:** Norifumi Nishimura.

2012 Foreign Players: Seth Greisinger, Hayden Penn, Carlos Rosa, Josh Whitesell.

FUKUOKA SOFTBANK HAWKS

Mailing Address: Fukuoka Yahoo! Japan Dome, Hawks Town, Chuo-ku, Fukuoka 810-0065. **Telephone:** 092-847-1006. **Fax:** 092-844-4600.

Owner: Masayoshi Son. **Chairman:** Sadaharu Oh. **President:** Kazuhiko Kasai. **Field Manager:** Koji Akiyama.

2012 Foreign Players: Alex Cabrera, Angel Castro, Brian Falkenborg, Wily Mo Pena, Renyel Pinto, Yang Yao-hsun.

HOKKAIDO NIPPON-HAM FIGHTERS

Mailing Address: 1 Hitsujigaoka, Toyohira-ku, Sapporo 062-8655. **Telephone:** 011-857-3939. **Fax:** 011-857-3900.

Chairman: Hiroji Okoso. **President:** Junichi Fujii. **General Manager:** Masao Yamada. **Field Manager:** Hideki Kuriyama.

2012 Foreign Players: Micah Hoffpauir, Bobby Keppel, Terrmel Sledge, Brian Wolfe.

ORIX BUFFALOES

Mailing Address: 3-Kita-2-30 Chiyozaki, Nishi-ku, Osaka 550-0023. **Telephone:** 06-6586-0221. **Fax:** 06-6586-0240.

Chairman: Yoshihiko Miyauchi. **President:** Hiroaki Nishina. **General Manager:** Yoshio Murayama. **Field Manager:** Akinobu Okada.

2012 Foreign Players: Aarom Baldiris, Freddy Ballestas, Alfredo Figaro, Hsu Ming Chieh, Lee Dae Ho, Evan McLane.

SAITAMA SEIBU LIONS

Mailing Address: 2135 Kami-Yamaguchi, Tokorozawa-shi, Saitama-ken 359-1189. **Telephone:** 04-2924-1155. **Fax:** 04-2928-1919.

President: Hajime Igo. **Field Manager:** Hisanobu Watanabe.

2012 Foreign Players: Chris Carter, Esteban German, Enrique Gonzalez, Randy Williams.

TOHOKU RAKUTEN GOLDEN EAGLES

Mailing Address: 2-11-6 Miyagino, Miyagino-ku, Sendai-shi, Miyagi-ken 983-0045. **Telephone:** 022-298-5300. **Fax:** 022-298-5360.

Chairman: Hiroshi Mikitani. **President:** Toru Shimada. **Field Manager:** Senichi Hoshino.

2012 Foreign Players: Jose Fernandez, Luis Garcia, Kelvin Jimenez, Darrell Rasner, Luis Terrero.

KOREA

KOREA BASEBALL ORGANIZATION

Mailing Address: 946-16 Dokokdong, Kangnam-gu, Seoul, Korea. **Telephone:** (02) 3460-4600. **Fax:** (02) 3460-4639.

Years League Active: 1982-.

Website: www.koreabaseball.com.

Commissioner: Shin Sang-woo. **Secretary General:** Ha Il-sung. **Deputy Secretary General:** Lee Sang-il.

Member Clubs: Doosan Bears, Hanwha Eagles, Kia Tigers, LG Twins, Lotte Giants, Samsung Lions, Seoul Heroes, SK Wyverns.

Regular Season: 133 games. **2010 Opening Date:** April 4.

Playoffs: Third- and fourth-place teams meet in best-of-three series; winner advances to meet second-place team in best-of-five series; winner meets first-place team in best-of-seven Korean Series for league championship.

Roster Limit: 26 active through Sept. **1, when rosters expand to 31. Imports:** Two active.

TAIWAN

CHINESE PROFESSIONAL BASEBALL LEAGUE

Mailing Address: 2F, No 32, Pateh Road, Sec 3, Taipei, Taiwan 10559. **Telephone:** 886-2-2577-6992. **Fax:** 886-2-2577-2606. **Website:** www.cpbl.com.tw.

Years League Active: 1990-.

Commissioner: Shou-Po Chao. **Secretary General:** Wen-pin Lee. **International Affairs:** Richard Wang. **E-Mail Address:** richard.wang@cpbl.com.tw.

Member Clubs: Brother Elephants, Uni Lions, Sinon Bulls, La New Bears.

Regular Season: 100 games. **2012 Opening Date:** March 28. **Playoffs:** Second- and third-place teams meet in best-of-five series; winner advances to meet first-place team in best-of-seven championship series.

Import Rule: Only three import players may be active, and only two may be on the field at the same time.

EUROPE

NETHERLANDS

DUTCH MAJOR LEAGUE

Mailing Address: Koninklijke Nederlandse Baseball en Softball Bond (Royal Dutch Baseball and Softball Association), Postbus 2650, 3430 GB Nieuwegein, Holland. **Telephone:** 31-30-751-3650. **Fax:** 31-30-751-3651. **Website:** www.knbsb.nl.

Member Clubs: ADO, Amsterdam Pirates, HCAW, Hoofddorp Pioniers, Kinheim, Neptunus, Sparta/Feyenoord, UVV.

President: Bob Bergkamp.

ITALY

SERIE A

Mailing Address: Federazione Italiana Baseball Softball, Viale Tiziano 74, 00196 Roma, Italy. **Telephone:** 39-06-32297201. **Fax:** 39-06-36858201. **Website:** www.fibs.it.

Member Clubs: Bologna, Godo, Grosseto, Nettuno, Parma, Paterno, Rimini, San Marino.

President: Riccardo Fraccari.

WINTER BASEBALL

CARIBBEAN BASEBALL CONFEDERATION

Mailing Address: Frank Feliz Miranda No 1 Naco, Santo Domingo, Dominican Republic. **Telephone:** (809) 381-2643. **Fax:** (809) 565-4654. **Website:** www.ebeisbol.com.

Commissioner: Juan Francisco Puello. **Secretary:** Benny Agosto.

Member Countries: Colombia, Dominican Republic, Mexico, Nicaragua, Puerto Rico, Venezuela (Colombia and Nicaragua do not play in the Caribbean Series).

2012 Caribbean Series: Dominican Republic, February.

DOMINICAN LEAGUE

Office Address: Estadio Quisqueya, 2da Planta, Ens La Fe, Santo Domingo, Dominican Republic. **Telephone:** (809) 567-6371. **Fax:** (809) 567-5720. **E-Mail Address:** ligadom@hotmail.com. **Website:** www.lidom.com.

Years League Active: 1951-.

President: Leonardo Matos Berrido. **Vice President:** Jose Rafael Alvarez Sanchez. **Administrator:** Marcos Rodríguez. **Public Relations Director:** Jorge Torres.

Member Clubs: Aguilas Cibaenas, Estrellas de Oriente, Gigantes del Cibao, Leones del Escogido, Tigres del Licey, Toros del Este.

Regular Season: 50 games. **2012 Opening Date:** Oct 16.

Playoff Format: Top four teams meet in 18-game round-robin. Top two teams advance to best-of-nine series for league championship. Winner advances to Caribbean Series.

Roster Limit: 30. **Imports:** 7.

MEXICAN PACIFIC LEAGUE

Mailing Address: Blvd Solidaridad No 335, Plaza las Palmas, Edificio A, Nivel 1, Local 4, Hermosillo, Sonora, Mexico CP 83246. **Telephone:** (52) 662-310-9714. **Fax:**

(52) 662-310-9715. **E-Mail Address:** ligadelpacifico@liga-delpacifico.com.mx. **Website:** www.ligadelpacifico.com.mx.

Years League Active: 1958-.
President: Omar Canizales. **Administration:** Vanessa Palacios. **Sports Manager:** Dennis Gonzalez Oviel.

Member Clubs: Culiacan Tomateros, Guasave Algodoneros, Hermosillo Naranjeros, Los Mochis Caneros, Mazatlan Venados, Mexicali Aguilas, Navojoa Mayos, Obregon Yaquis.

Regular Season: 68 games. **2010 Opening Date:** Oct. **16.**

Playoff Format: Six teams advance to best-of-seven quarterfinals. Three winners and losing team with best record advance to best-of-seven semifinals. Winners meet in best-of-seven series for league championship. Winner advances to Caribbean Series.

Roster Limit: 30. **Imports:** 5.

PUERTO RICAN LEAGUE

Office Address: Avenida Munoz Rivera 1056, Edificio First Federal, Suite 501, Rio Piedras, PR 00925. **Mailing Address:** PO Box 191852, San Juan, PR 00019. **Telephone:** (787) 765-6285, 765-7285. **Fax:** (787) 767-3028. **Website:** www.puertoricobaseballleague.com.

Years League Active: 1938-2011; 2008-
President: Joaquin Monserrate Matienzo. **Executive Director:** Benny Agosto.

Member Clubs: Arecibo Lobos, Caguas Criollos, Carolina Gigantes, Mayaguez Indios, Ponce Leones.

Regular Season: 42 games. **2012 Opening Date:** Nov 11.

Playoff Format: Top four teams meet in best-of-seven semifinal series. Winners meet in best-of-nine series for league championship. Winner advances to Caribbean Series.

Roster Limit: 30. **Imports:** 5.

VENEZUELAN LEAGUE

Mailing Address: Avenida Casanova, Centro Comercial "El Recreo", Torre Sur, Piso 3, Oficinas 6 y 7, Sabana Grande, Caracas, Venezuela. **Telephone:** (58) 212-761-6408. **Fax:** (58) 212-761-7661. **Website:** www.lvbp.com.

Years League Active: 1946-.
President: Jose Grasso Vecchio. **Vice Presidents:** Rafael Chaverogazdik, Gustavo Massiani. **General Manager:** Domingo Alvarez.

Member Clubs: Anzoategui Caribes, Aragua Tigres, Caracas Leones, La Guaira Tiburones, Lara Cardenales, Magallanes Navegantes, Margarita Bravos, Zulia Aguilas.

Regular Season: 64 games. **2012 Opening Date:** Oct 18.

Playoff Format: Top two teams in each division, plus a wild-card team, meet in 16-game round-robin series. Top two finishers meet in best-of-seven series for league championship. Winner advances to Caribbean Series.

Roster Limit: 26. **Imports:** 7.

COLOMBIAN LEAGUE

Office/Mailing Address: Unavailable. **Telephone:** Unavailable. **Website:** www.teamrenteria.com.

Member Clubs: Barranquilla, Cartagena, Monteria, Sincelejo.

Regular season: 65 games. **2010 Opening Date:** Oct. **28.**

Playoff Format: Top two teams meet in best-of-seven finals for league championship.

NICARAGUAN LEAGUE

Office Address/Mailing Address: Canal 2 TV, Casa #26, Managua, Nicaragua. **Telephone:** 505-2266-3645. **Website:** www.lnbp.com.ni.

Commissioner: Noel Urcuyo Baez. **General Manager:** Azalea Salmeron. **Marketing Director:** Jessica Market.

Member Clubs: Chinandega, Granada, Leon, Managua.

Regular Season: 40 games. **2012 Opening Date:** Dec 1.

Playoff Format: Top two teams meet in best-of-seven finals for league championship.

AUSTRALIA
AUSTRALIAN BASEBALL LEAGUE

Mailing Address: 1 Palm Meadows Drive, Carrara, QLD, 4211, Australia. **Telephone:** 61-7-5510-6819. **Fax:** 61-7-5510-6855. **E-Mail Address:** admin@ableague.com.au. **Website:** www.theabl.com.

CEO: Peter Wermuth. **Operations Manager:** Ben Foster.

Teams: Adelaide, Brisbane, Canberra, Melbourne, Perth, Sydney.

Playoff Format: First-place team plays second-place team in major semifinal; third-place team plays fourth-place team in minor semifinal, both best of three series. Loser of major semifinal plays winner of minor semifinal in best of three series. Winner of that series plays winner of major semifinal in best of three series for league championship.

DOMESTIC LEAGUE
ARIZONA FALL LEAGUE

Mailing Address: 2415 E. **Camelback Road, Suite 850, Phoenix, AZ** 85016. **Telephone:** (602) 281-7250. **Fax:** (602) 281-7313. **E-Mail Address:** afl@mlb.com. **Website:** www.mlb.com.

Years League Active: 1992-.
Operated by: Major League Baseball.
Executive Director: Steve Cobb. **Seasonal Assistant:** Joan McGrath.

Teams: Mesa Solar Sox, Peoria Javelinas, Peoria Saguaros, Phoenix Desert Dogs, Scottsdale Scorpions, Surprise Rafters.

2012 Opening Date: Unavailable. **Play usually opens in mid-October. Playoff Format:** Division champions meet in one-game championship.

Roster Limit: 30. Players with less than one year of major league service are eligible, with one foreign player and one player below the Double-A level allowed per team.

MINOR
LEAGUE
SCHEDULES

TRIPLE-A

INTERNATIONAL LEAGUE

BUFFALO

APRIL	
5-6	at Pawtucket
7-10	at Rochester
11-13	Scranton/Wilkes-Barre
14-15	Pawtucket
16-19	Lehigh Valley
20-22	at Syracuse
23-25	at Lehigh Valley
27-30	Rochester

MAY	
1-4	Syracuse
5-6	at Rochester
7-10	at Gwinnett
11-14	at Charlotte
15-18	Gwinnett
19-22	Indianapolis
24-27	vs. Scranton/W-B at Buffalo
28-31	Columbus

JUNE	
1-4	at Toledo
5-8	at Columbus
9-12	Norfolk
14-17	Pawtucket
18-21	at Norfolk
22-25	at Durham

26-29	Louisville
30	Durham

JULY	
1-3	Durham
4-6	at Syracuse
7-8	vs. Scranton-W-B at Syracuse
12-15	at Pawtucket
16-19	Toledo
20-23	Charlotte
24-27	at Louisville
28-31	at Indianapolis

AUGUST	
2-5	Syracuse
6-7	at Syracuse
8-9	at Lehigh Valley
10-11	Scranton/Wilkes-Barre
12-13	Pawtucket
14-17	Lehigh Valley
18-19	at Pawtucket
20-21	vs. Scranton/W-B at Buffalo
22-24	Scranton/Wilkes-Barre
25-28	Rochester
30-31	at Rochester

SEPTEMBER	
1-3	at Lehigh Valley

CHARLOTTE

APRIL	
5-8	Norfolk
9-11	at Durham
12-15	at Norfolk
16-19	Durham
20-22	Gwinnett
24-26	at Gwinnett
27-30	at Syracuse

MAY	
1-4	at Lehigh Valley
5-6	at Gwinnett
7-10	Toledo
11-14	Buffalo
15-18	at Norfolk
19-22	at Durham
24-27	Lehigh Valley
28-31	Rochester

JUNE	
1-2	at Gwinnett
3-4	Gwinnett
5-8	at Toledo
9-12	at Columbus
14-17	Indianapolis
18-21	Columbus
22-25	at Rochester

26-29	at Pawtucket
30	at Gwinnett

JULY	
1-3	at Gwinnett
4-5	Gwinnett
6-8	Norfolk
12-15	Durham
16-19	vs. Scranton/W-B at Rochester
20-23	at Buffalo
24-27	Scranton/Wilkes-Barre
28-31	Gwinnett

AUGUST	
2-5	at Louisville
6-9	at Indianapolis
10-13	Norfolk
14-17	Louisville
18-19	at Norfolk
20-21	at Durham
23-26	Pawtucket
27-30	Syracuse
31	at Durham

SEPTEMBER	
1	at Durham
2-3	Durham

COLUMBUS

APRIL	
5-8	Louisville
9-12	Indianapolis
13-16	at Louisville
17-20	at Indianapolis
21-23	at Toledo
24-25	Toledo
27-30	Pawtucket

MAY	
1-4	Gwinnett
5-6	at Toledo
7-10	vs. Scranton/W-B at Rochester
11-14	at Pawtucket
15-18	Syracuse
19-22	Scranton/Wilkes-Barre
24-27	at Syracuse
28-31	at Buffalo

JUNE	
1-4	at Rochester
5-8	Buffalo
9-12	Charlotte
14-17	at Gwinnett
18-21	at Charlotte
22-25	Lehigh Valley

26-29	Norfolk
30	Toledo

JULY	
1	Toledo
2-5	at Toledo
6-8	Indianapolis
12-15	at Indianapolis
16-19	Louisville
20-23	at Lehigh Valley
24-27	Toledo
28-31	Rochester

AUGUST	
2-5	at Norfolk
6-9	at Durham
10-12	Indianapolis
14-17	Durham
18-21	at Louisville
22-24	Toledo
25-27	at Indianapolis
28-29	at Louisville
30-31	Louisville

SEPTEMBER	
1	Louisville
2-3	at Toledo

DURHAM

APRIL	
5-8	Gwinnett
9-11	Charlotte
12-15	at Gwinnett
16-19	at Charlotte
20-23	at Pawtucket
24-25	at Norfolk
27-30	Indianapolis

MAY	
1-4	Louisville
5-6	Norfolk
7-10	at Syracuse
11-14	vs. Scranton/W-B at Rochester
15-18	Pawtucket
19-22	Charlotte
24-25	Norfolk
26-27	at Norfolk
28-31	at Indianapolis

JUNE	
1-4	at Louisville
5-8	Scranton/Wilkes-Barre
9-12	Toledo
14-17	at Lehigh Valley
18-21	at Rochester
22-25	Buffalo

26-29	Syracuse
30	at Buffalo

JULY	
1-3	at Buffalo
4-5	Norfolk
6-8	at Gwinnett
12-15	at Charlotte
16-19	Lehigh Valley
20-23	Rochester
24-27	at Gwinnett
28-31	at Norfolk

AUGUST	
2-5	Gwinnett
6-9	Columbus
10-13	at Toledo
14-17	at Columbus
18-19	Gwinnett
20-21	Charlotte
22-26	Norfolk
28-30	at Norfolk
31	Charlotte

SEPTEMBER	
1	Charlotte
2-3	at Charlotte

GWINNETT

APRIL
5-8	. . . . .at Durham
9-11	. . . . at Norfolk
12-15	. . . . Durham
16-19	. . . . .Norfolk
20-22	. . . . . .at Charlotte
24-26	. . . . . . Charlotte
27-30	. . . . . . .at Toledo

MAY
1-4	. . . . at Columbus
5-6	. . . . Charlotte
7-10	. . . . Buffalo
11-14	. . . . Toledo
15-18	. . . . . . at Buffalo
19-22	. . . . at Rochester
24-27	. . . . . Rochester
28-31	. . . . . Lehigh Valley

JUNE
1-2	. . . . Charlotte
3-4	. . . . at Charlotte
5-8	. . . at Lehigh Valley
9-12	. . . . . at Pawtucket
14-17	. . . . . . .Columbus
18-21	. . . . . .Indianapolis
22-25	. . . . . . at Syracuse

26-29	vs. Scranton/W-B at Rochester
30	. . . . Charlotte

JULY
1-3	. . . . Charlotte
4-5	. . . . . . .at Charlotte
6-8	. . . . Durham
12-15	. . . . . .at Louisville
16-19	. . .at Indianapolis
20-23	Scranton/Wilkes-Barre
24-27	. . . . Durham
28-31	. . . . . .at Charlotte

AUGUST
2-5	. . . . .at Durham
6-9	. . . . Norfolk
10-13	. . . . . . Louisville
14-17	. . . . . . at Norfolk
18-19	. . . . . .at Durham
20-21	. . . . Norfolk
23-26	. . . . Syracuse
27-30	. . . . . .Pawtucket
31	. . . . at Norfolk

SEPTEMBER
1-3	. . . . at Norfolk

INDIANAPOLIS

APRIL
6-8	. . . . .at Toledo
9-12	. . . . . . at Columbus
13-16	. . . . Toledo
17-20	. . . . . . .Columbus
21-23	. . . . . .at Louisville
24-25	. . . . . Louisville
27-30	. . . . . .at Durham

MAY
1-4	. . . . at Norfolk
5-6	. . . . Louisville
7-10	. . . . . Lehigh Valley
11-14	. . . . .Norfolk
15-18	. . . at Lehigh Valley
19-22	. . . . . at Buffalo
24-25	. . . . . Louisville
26-27	. . . . .at Louisville
28-31	. . . . Durham

JUNE
1-4	. . . . Syracuse
5-8	. . . . . at Pawtucket
9-12	. . . . Rochester
14-17	. . . .at Charlotte
18-21	. . . . . .at Gwinnett
22-25	Scranton/Wilkes-Barre

26-29	. . . . Toledo
30	. . . . at Louisville

JULY
1-3	. . . . . .at Louisville
4-5	. . . . Louisville
6-8	. . . . . at Columbus
12-15	. . . . . . Columbus
16-19	. . . . . . Gwinnett
20-23	. . . . . . .at Toledo
24-27	. . . . . .Pawtucket
28-31	. . . . Buffalo

AUGUST
2-5	vs. Scranton/W-B at Rochester
6-9	. . . . Charlotte
10-12	. . . . . at Columbus
14-17	. . . . . at Rochester
18-21	. . . . at Syracuse
22-24	. . . . . . Louisville
25-27	. . . . Columbus
28-30	. . . . . . .at Toledo
31	. . . . Toledo

SEPTEMBER
1	. . . . Toledo
2-3	. . . . at Louisville

LEHIGH VALLEY

APRIL
5-6	. . Scranton/Wilkes-Barre
7	. . . . .at Pawtucket (DH)
9-10	. . . . . at Pawtucket
11-13	. . . . Syracuse

14-15	. . . . Rochester
16-19	. . . . . . at Buffalo
20-22	. . . . . at Rochester
23-25	. . . . Buffalo
26-29	vs. Scranton/W-B at Lehigh Valley

MAY (LEHIGH VALLEY)
1-4	. . . . Charlotte
5-6	. . . . Syracuse
7-10	. . . . . at Indianapolis
11-14	. . . .at Louisville
15-18	. . .Indianapolis
19-22	. . . . . . Louisville
24-27	. . . .at Charlotte
28-31	. . . . . at Gwinnett

JUNE
1-4	. . . . . . .Pawtucket
5-8	. . . . Gwinnett
9-12	. . . . at Syracuse
14-17	. . . . . . Durham
18-21	. . . . . . .at Toledo
22-25	. . . . at Columbus
26-29	. . . . . Rochester
30	. . . . .Pawtucket

JULY
1	. . . . .Pawtucket
2-4	. . Scranton/Wilkes-Barre

5-6	vs. Scranton/W-B at Lehigh Valley
7-8	. . . . at Rochester
12-15	. . . . at Norfolk
16-19	. . . . . . .at Durham
20-23	. . . . Columbus
24-27	. . . . . . .Norfolk
28-31	. . . . . at Syracuse

AUGUST
1-2	. . . . .Pawtucket
3-6	. . . . . . at Pawtucket
8-9	. . . . Buffalo
10-11	. . . . Syracuse
12-13	. . . . . . Rochester
14-17	. . . . . . at Buffalo
18-21	. . . . Toledo
22-24	. . . . at Rochester
25-27	Scranton/Wilkes-Barre
29-30	vs. Scranton/W-B at Lehigh Valley
31	. . . . Syracuse

SEPTEMBER
1-3	. . . . Buffalo

LOUISVILLE

APRIL
5-8	. . . . at Columbus
9-12	. . . . .at Toledo
13-16	. . . . Columbus
17-20	. . . . Toledo
21-23	. . . . . . .Indianapolis
24-25	. . . . at Indianapolis
27-30	. . . . . at Norfolk

MAY
1-4	. . . . .at Durham
5-6	. . . . .Indianapolis
7-10	. . . . .Norfolk
11-14	. . . . . Lehigh Valley
15-18	. . . . at Rochester
19-22	. . at Lehigh Valley
24-25	. . . . at Indianapolis
26-27	. . . . .Indianapolis
28-31	. . . . Syracuse

JUNE
1-4	. . . . Durham
5-8	. . . . at Syracuse
9-11	vs. Scranton/W-B at Rochester
12	vs. Scranton/W-B at Batavia
14-17	. . . . Rochester
18-21	Scranton/Wilkes-Barre

22-25	. . . . . at Pawtucket
26-29	. . . . . . at Buffalo
30	. . . . .Indianapolis

JULY
1-3	. . . . .Indianapolis
4-5	. . . . . .at Indianapolis
6-8	. . . . Toledo
12-15	. . . . Gwinnett
16-19	. . . . at Columbus
20-23	. . . . . . .Pawtucket
24-27	. . . . Buffalo
28-31	. . . . . . .at Toledo

AUGUST
2-5	. . . . Charlotte
6-9	. . . . Toledo
10-13	. . . . at Gwinnett
14-17	. . . . at Charlotte
18-21	. . . . . . Columbus
22-24	. . . . at Indianapolis
25-26	. . . . . . .at Toledo
28-29	. . . . Columbus
30-31	. . . . at Columbus

SEPTEMBER
1	. . . . at Columbus
2-3	. . . . .Indianapolis

NORFOLK

APRIL
5-8	. . . . .at Charlotte
9-11	. . . . Gwinnett
12-15	. . . . Charlotte
16-19	. . . . . .at Gwinnett
20-23	vs. Scranton/W-B at Batavia
24-25	. . . . Durham
27-30	. . . . Louisville

MAY
1-4	. . . . .Indianapolis
5-6	. . . . . . .at Durham
7-10	. . . . . .at Louisville

11-14	. . . .at Indianapolis
15-18	. . . . . . Charlotte
19-22	. . . . . . .Pawtucket
24-25	. . . . . . .at Durham
26-27	. . . . Durham
28-31	. . . . . at Pawtucket

JUNE
1-4	. . Scranton/Wilkes-Barre
5-8	. . . . . . at Rochester
9-12	. . . . at Buffalo
14-17	. . . . Toledo
18-21	. . . . Buffalo

22-25 at Toledo
26-29 at Columbus
30 Syracuse

JULY

1-3 Syracuse
4-5 at Durham
6-8 at Charlotte
12-15 Lehigh Valley
16-19 Rochester
20-23 at Syracuse
24-27 at Lehigh Valley
28-31 Durham

AUGUST

2-5 Columbus
6-9 at Gwinnett
10-13 at Charlotte
14-17 Gwinnett
18-19 Charlotte
20-21 at Gwinnett
22-26 at Durham
28-30 Durham
31 Gwinnett

SEPTEMBER

1-3 Gwinnett

PAWTUCKET

APRIL

5-6 Buffalo
7 Lehigh Valley (DH)
9-10 Lehigh Valley
11-13 at Rochester
14-15 at Buffalo
16-19 at Syracuse
20-23 Durham
24-25 Scranton/Wilkes-Barre
27-30 at Columbus

MAY

1-4 at Toledo
5-6 vs. Scranton/W-B at Batavia
7-10 Rochester
11-14 Columbus
15-18 at Durham
19-22 at Norfolk
24-27 Toledo
28-31 Norfolk

JUNE

1-4 at Lehigh Valley
5-8 Indianapolis
9-12 Gwinnett
14-17 at Buffalo
18-21 at Syracuse
22-25 Louisville
26-29 Charlotte
30 at Lehigh Valley

JULY

1 at Lehigh Valley
2-3 Rochester
4-6 at Rochester
7-8 Syracuse
12-15 Buffalo
16-19 Syracuse
20-23 at Louisville
24-27 at Indianapolis
28-29 Scranton/Wilkes-Barre
30-31 vs. Scranton/W-B at Rochester

AUGUST

1-2 at Lehigh Valley
3-6 Lehigh Valley
8-9 Syracuse
10-11 at Rochester
12-13 at Buffalo
14-17 vs. Scranton/W-B at Pawtucket
18-19 Buffalo
20-21 Rochester
23-26 at Charlotte
27-30 at Gwinnett
31 Scranton/Wilkes-Barre

SEPTEMBER

1-3 Scranton/Wilkes-Barre

ROCHESTER

APRIL

5-6 at Syracuse
7-10 Buffalo
11-13 Pawtucket
14-15 at Lehigh Valley
16-19 vs. Scranton/W-B at Rochester
20-22 Lehigh Valley
24-26 Syracuse
27-30 at Buffalo

MAY

1-4 vs. Scranton/W-B at Rochester
5-6 Buffalo
7-10 at Pawtucket
11-14 at Syracuse
15-18 Louisville
19-22 Gwinnett
24-27 at Gwinnett
28-31 at Charlotte

JUNE

1-4 Columbus
5-8 Norfolk
9-12 at Indianapolis
14-17 at Louisville
18-21 Durham
22-25 Charlotte
26-29 at Lehigh Valley
30 Scranton/Wilkes-Barre

JULY

1 Scranton/Wilkes-Barre
2-3 at Pawtucket
4-6 Pawtucket
7-8 Lehigh Valley
12-15 Toledo
16-19 at Norfolk
20-23 at Durham
24-27 Syracuse
28-31 at Columbus

AUGUST

2-5 at Toledo
6-9 Scranton/Wilkes-Barre
10-11 Pawtucket
12-13 at Lehigh Valley
14-17 Indianapolis
18-19 Scranton/Wilkes-Barre
20-21 at Pawtucket
23-24 Lehigh Valley
25-28 at Buffalo
30-31 Buffalo

SEPTEMBER

1-2 at Syracuse
3 Syracuse

SCRANTON/WILKES-BARRE

APRIL

5-6 at Lehigh Valley
7-10 at Syracuse
11-13 at Buffalo
14-15 vs. Syracuse at Syracuse
16-19 vs. Rochester at Rochester
20-23 vs. Norfolk at Batavia
24-25 at Pawtucket
26-29 vs. Lehigh Valley at Lehigh Valley

MAY

1-4 vs. Rochester at Rochester
5-6 vs. Pawtucket at Batavia
7-10 vs. Columbus at Rochester
11-14 vs. Durham at Rochester
15-18 at Toledo
19-22 at Columbus
24-27 vs. Buffalo at Buffalo
28-31 vs. Toledo at Rochester

JUNE

1-4 at Norfolk
5-8 at Durham
9-11 vs. Louisville at Rochester
12 vs. Louisville at Batavia
14-17 vs. Syracuse at Syracuse
18-21 at Louisville
22-25 at Indianapolis
26-29 vs. Gwinnett at Rochester
30 at Rochester

JULY

1 at Rochester
2-4 at Lehigh Valley
5-6 vs. Lehigh Valley at Lehigh Valley
7-8 vs. Buffalo at Buffalo
12-13 at Syracuse
14-15 vs. Syracuse at Syracuse
16-19 vs. Charlotte at Rochester
20-23 at Gwinnett
24-27 at Charlotte
28-29 at Pawtucket
30-31 vs. Pawtucket at Rochester

AUGUST

2-5 vs. Indianapolis at Rochester
6-9 at Rochester
10-11 at Buffalo
12-13 at Syracuse
14-17 vs. Pawtucket at Pawtucket
18-19 at Rochester
20-21 vs. Buffalo at Buffalo
22-24 at Buffalo
25-27 at Lehigh Valley
29-30 vs. Lehigh Valley at Lehigh Valley
31 at Pawtucket

SEPTEMBER

1-3 at Pawtucket

SYRACUSE

APRIL

5-6 Rochester
7-10 Scranton/Wilkes-Barre
11-13 at Lehigh Valley
14-15 vs. Scranton/W-B at Syracuse
16-19 Pawtucket
20-22 Buffalo
24-26 at Rochester
27-30 Charlotte

MAY

1-4 at Buffalo
5-6 at Lehigh Valley
7-10 Durham
11-14 Rochester
15-18 at Columbus
19-22 at Toledo
24-27 Columbus
28-31 at Louisville

JUNE

1-4 at Indianapolis
5-8 Louisville
9-12 Lehigh Valley
14-17 vs. Scranton/W-B at Syracuse
18-21 Pawtucket
22-25 Gwinnett
26-29 at Durham
30 at Norfolk

JULY

1-3 at Norfolk
4-6 Buffalo
7-8 at Pawtucket
12-13 Scranton/Wilkes-Barre
14-15 vs. Scranton/W-B at Syracuse
16-19 at Pawtucket
20-23 Norfolk
24-27 at Rochester
28-31 Lehigh Valley

AUGUST

2-5 at Buffalo
6-7 Buffalo
8-9 at Pawtucket
10-11 at Lehigh Valley
12-13 Scranton/Wilkes-Barre
14-17 Toledo
18-21 Indianapolis
23-26 at Gwinnett
27-30 at Charlotte
31 at Lehigh Valley

1-2. . . . . Rochester

TOLEDO

APRIL	
6-8. . . . . . . .Indianapolis	30 . . . . at Columbus
9-12. . . . . Louisville	**JULY**
13-16 . . . . at Indianapolis	1 . . . . at Columbus
17-20 . . . . . .at Louisville	2-5. . . . . Columbus
21-23 . . . . Columbus	6-8. . . . . . . .at Louisville
24-25 . . . . . at Columbus	12-15 . . . . . at Rochester
27-30 . . . . Gwinnett	16-19 . . . . . . at Buffalo
MAY	20-23 . . . . . .Indianapolis
1-4. . . . . Pawtucket	24-27 . . . . . at Columbus
5-6. . . . . Columbus	28-31 . . . . Louisville
7-10. . . . . . .at Charlotte	**AUGUST**
11-14 . . . . . at Gwinnett	2-5. . . . . Rochester
15-18 Scranton/Wilkes-Barre	6-9. . . . . . .at Louisville
19-22 . . . . Syracuse	10-13 . . . . Durham
24-27 . . . . at Pawtucket	14-17 . . . . . at Syracuse
28-31 vs. Scranton/W-B at Rochester	18-21 . . at Lehigh Valley
JUNE	22-24 . . . . . at Columbus
1-4. . . . . Buffalo	25-26 . . . . Louisville
5-8. . . . . Charlotte	28-30 . . . . .Indianapolis
9-12. . . . . . . .at Durham	31 . . . . . .at Indianapolis
14-17 . . . . . . at Norfolk	**SEPTEMBER**
18-21 . . . . Lehigh Valley	1 . . . . . . .at Indianapolis
22-25 . . . . .Norfolk	2-3. . . . . Columbus
26-29 . . . . at Indianapolis	

PACIFIC COAST LEAGUE

ALBUQUERQUE

APRIL	
5-8. . . . . at Omaha	19-22 . . . . . New Orleans
9-12. . . . . .at Iowa	23-26 . . . . .Nashville
13-16 . . . . .Omaha	27-29 . . . . . .at Memphis
17-20 . . . . Iowa	30 . . . . at Omaha
21-24 . . . at Oklahoma City	**JULY**
26-29 . . .at New Orleans	1-3. . . . . at Omaha
30 . . . . . .Oklahoma City	4-8. . . . . . . .Round Rock
MAY	12-15 . . . . . at Nashville
1-3. . . . . .Oklahoma City	16-19 . . . . . . Memphis
4-7. . . . . .Nashville	20-23 . . . . Iowa
8-11. . . . . . . at Tacoma	24-27 . . . . at Round Rock
12-15 . . . . at Salt Lake	28-31 . . . . . . at Nashville
17-20 . . . . . .Sacramento	**AUGUST**
21-24 . . . . Fresno	1-4. . . . . Las Vegas
25-28 . . . .Oklahoma City	5-8. . . . . Tucson
29-31 . . . .at New Orleans	10-13 . . . . .at Reno
JUNE	14-17 . .at Colorado Springs
1 . . . . . . .at New Orleans	18-21 . . . . . New Orleans
2-5. . . . . at Round Rock	22-26 . . . . . .at Memphis
7-10. . . . . Memphis	27-30 . . at Oklahoma City
11-13 . . . . . .Round Rock	31 . . . . .Omaha
14-17 . . . . .at Iowa	**SEPTEMBER**
	1-3. . . . . .Omaha

COLORADO SPRINGS

APRIL	
5-8. . . . . .at Reno	19-22 . . . . .Salt Lake
9-12. . . . . . . .at Tacoma	23-26 . . . . .Tacoma
13-16 . . . . . . Las Vegas	27-29 . . . . . . at Tucson
17-20 . . . . Tucson	30 . . . . . . at Sacramento
21-24 . . . . .at Las Vegas	**JULY**
26-29 . . . . .at Fresno	1-3. . . . . . . at Sacramento
30 . . . . . . at Sacramento	4-8. . . . . Reno
MAY	12-15 . . . . . at Tacoma
1-3. . . . . . at Sacramento	16-19 . . . . . . .Salt Lake
4-7. . . . . Fresno	20-23 . . . . .Tacoma
8-11. . . . . . at Nashville	24-27 . . . . . .at Reno
12-15 . . . .at Memphis	28-31 . . . . . . Fresno
17-20 . . . . New Orleans	**AUGUST**
21-24 . . . .Oklahoma City	1-4. . . . . .at Iowa
25-28 . . . . . . .at Fresno	5-8. . . . . . . at Omaha
29-31 . . . . . at Salt Lake	10-13 . . . . . .Round Rock
JUNE	14-17 . . . . Albuquerque
1 . . . . . . at Salt Lake	18-21 . . . . at Salt Lake
2-5. . . . . Tucson	22-26 . . . . . . at Tucson
7-10. . . . . . .Sacramento	27-30 . . .Sacramento
11-13 . . . . Reno	31 . . . . Las Vegas
14-17 . . . . . .at Las Vegas	**SEPTEMBER**
	1-3. . . . . Las Vegas

FRESNO

APRIL	
5-8. . . . . at Tucson	23-26 . . . . Tucson
9-12. . . . . . .at Las Vegas	27-29 . . . . .at Reno
13-16 . . . . .Tacoma	30 . . . . .at Tacoma
17-20 . . . . Reno	**JULY**
21-24 . . . . . at Tacoma	1-3. . . . . .at Tacoma
26-29 . . . Colorado Springs	4-8. . . . . . . .Sacramento
30 . . . . .Salt Lake	12-15 . . . . . at Tucson
MAY	16-19 . . . . .at Las Vegas
1-3. . . . . .Salt Lake	20-23 . . . at Salt Lake
4-7. . . .at Colorado Springs	24-27 . . . . . Las Vegas
8-11. . . . . Iowa	28-31 . .at Colorado Springs
12-15 . . . . .Omaha	**AUGUST**
17-20 . . . . at Round Rock	1-4. . . . . .Nashville
21-24 . . . at Albuquerque	5-8. . . . . Memphis
25-28 . . . Colorado Springs	10-13 . . . .at New Orleans
29-31 . . . . at Sacramento	14-17 . . . at Oklahoma City
JUNE	18-21 . . . . Tucson
1 . . . . . . at Sacramento	22-26 . . . . .at Reno
2-5. . . . . .Salt Lake	27-30 . . . . Reno
7-10. . . . . . . Las Vegas	31 . . . . .Tacoma
11-13 . . . . . .Sacramento	**SEPTEMBER**
14-17 . . . at Salt Lake	1-3. . . . . .Tacoma
19-22 . . . . at Sacramento	

IOWA

APRIL	MAY
5-8. . . . . .Round Rock	1-3. . . . . . . .at Memphis
9-12. . . . . . Albuquerque	4-7. . . . . . . New Orleans
13-16 . . . . at Round Rock	8-11. . . . . .at Fresno
17-20 . . . at Albuquerque	12-15 . . . . at Sacramento
21-24 . . . . Memphis	17-20 . . . . .Salt Lake
26-29 . . . . .Nashville	21-24 . . . . .Tacoma
30 . . . . .at Memphis	25-28 . . . . . .at Memphis

3 . . . . at Rochester

29-31 . . . . at Omaha

JUNE
1 . . . . at Omaha
2-5 . . . . at Oklahoma City
7-10 . . . . .Nashville
11-13 . . . . .Omaha
14-17 . . . . . Albuquerque
19-22 . . . . . at Round Rock
23-26 . . . . .Round Rock
27-29 . . . .Oklahoma City
30 . . . . at Nashville

JULY
1-3 . . . . at Nashville
4-8 . . . . .Omaha
12-15 . . . . at Omaha

LAS VEGAS

APRIL
5-8 . . . . .Sacramento
9-12 . . . . Fresno
13-16 . .at Colorado Springs
17-20 . . . . . at Salt Lake
21-24 . . . Colorado Springs
26-29 . . . . .Tacoma
30 . . . . .at Reno

MAY
1-3 . . . . .at Reno
4-7 . . . . .Salt Lake
8-11 . . . at Oklahoma City
12-15 . . . .at New Orleans
17-20 . . . . Memphis
21-24 . . . . . . .Nashville
25-28 . . . . . . at Salt Lake
29-31 . . . . at Tucson

JUNE
1 . . . . at Tucson
2-5 . . . . Reno
7-10 . . . . .at Fresno
11-13 . . . . Tucson
14-17 . . . Colorado Springs
19-22 . . . . at Tucson

MEMPHIS

APRIL
5-8 . . . . at Oklahoma City
9-12 . . . . .at New Orleans
13-16 . . . .Oklahoma City
17-20 . . . . . New Orleans
21-24 . . . . .at Iowa
26-29 . . . . .Omaha
30 . . . . Iowa

MAY
1-3 . . . . Iowa
4-7 . . . . . . at Round Rock
8-11 . . . . Reno
12-15 . . . Colorado Springs
17-20 . . . . . .at Las Vegas
21-24 . . . . . . at Tucson
25-28 . . . . Iowa
29-31 . . . . . . .Round Rock

16-19 . . . . . New Orleans
20-23 . . . . at Albuquerque
24-27 . . . at Oklahoma City
28-31 . . . .at New Orleans

AUGUST
1-4 . . . . . Colorado Springs
5-8 . . . . Reno
10-13 . . . . . . .at Las Vegas
14-17 . . . . at Tucson
18-21 . . . . Memphis
22-26 . . . .Oklahoma City
27-30 . . . . . . at Nashville
31 . . . . . .at New Orleans

SEPTEMBER
1-3 . . . . . .at New Orleans

23-26 . . . . . .Sacramento
27-29 . . . . . . at Tacoma
30 . . . . .at Reno

JULY
1-3 . . . . .at Reno
4-7 . . . . Tucson
12-15 . . . . at Sacramento
16-19 . . . . Fresno
20-23 . . . . Reno
24-27 . . . . .at Fresno
28-31 . . . . Salt Lake

AUGUST
1-4 . . . . . at Albuquerque
5-8 . . . . . . at Round Rock
10-13 . . . . Iowa
14-17 . . . . .Omaha
18-21 . . . . at Sacramento
22-26 . . . . at Tacoma
27-30 . . . . .Tacoma
31 . . .at Colorado Springs

SEPTEMBER
1-3 . . . .at Colorado Springs

JUNE
1 . . . . .Round Rock
2-5 . . . . at Omaha
7-10 . . . . at Albuquerque
11-13 . . . . .Nashville
14-17 . . . . . New Orleans
19-22 . . . . . . at Omaha
23-26 . . . .at New Orleans
27-29 . . . . . Albuquerque
30 . . . . . at Oklahoma City

JULY
1-3 . . . . . at Oklahoma City
4-8 . . . . .Nashville
12-15 . . . at Round Rock
16-19 . . . at Albuquerque
20-23 . . . .Oklahoma City
24-27 . . . . . . at Nashville
28-31 . . . . . .Round Rock

AUGUST
1-4 . . . . . . at Sacramento
5-8 . . . . .at Fresno
10-13 . . . . .Tacoma
14-17 . . . . Salt Lake
18-21 . . . . at Iowa

NASHVILLE

APRIL
5-8 . . . . . .at New Orleans
9-12 . . . at Oklahoma City
13-16 . . . . . New Orleans
17-20 . . . .Oklahoma City
21-24 . . . . at Omaha
26-29 . . . . .at Iowa
30 . . . . .Omaha

MAY
1-3 . . . . .Omaha
4-7 . . . . . . at Albuquerque
8-11 . . . . Colorado Springs
12-15 . . . . Reno
17-20 . . . . at Tucson
21-24 . . . . . .at Las Vegas
25-28 . . . . . .Round Rock
29-31 . . at Oklahoma City

JUNE
1 . . . . . at Oklahoma City
2-5 . . . . New Orleans
7-10 . . . . .at Iowa
11-13 . . . . .at Memphis
14-17 . . . . .Omaha
19-22 . . . .Oklahoma City

NEW ORLEANS

APRIL
5-8 . . . . .Nashville
9-12 . . . . Memphis
13-16 . . . . . at Nashville
17-20 . . . . Memphis
21-24 . . . . . .Round Rock
26-29 . . . . . Albuquerque
30 . . . . at Round Rock

MAY
1-3 . . . . . . at Round Rock
4-7 . . . . .at Iowa
8-11 . . . . Tucson
12-15 . . . . . . Las Vegas
17-20 . .at Colorado Springs
21-24 . . . . .at Reno
25-28 . . . . .Omaha
29-31 . . . . . Albuquerque

JUNE
1 . . . . Albuquerque
2-5 . . . . at Nashville
7-10 . . . at Oklahoma City
11-13 . . . .Oklahoma City
14-17 . . . . . .at Memphis

22-26 . . . . .Albuquerque
27-30 . . . . .Omaha
31 . . . . at Nashville

SEPTEMBER
1-3 . . . . at Nashville

23-26 . . . . at Albuquerque
27-29 . . . . . at Round Rock
30 . . . . Iowa

JULY
1-3 . . . . Iowa
4-8 . . . . .at Memphis
12-15 . . . . . Albuquerque
16-19 . . . . . . .Round Rock
20-23 . . . .at New Orleans
24-27 . . . . . . Memphis
28-31 . . . . . Albuquerque

AUGUST
1-4 . . . . .at Fresno
5-8 . . . . . at Sacramento
10-13 . . . . Salt Lake
14-17 . . . . .Tacoma
18-21 . . . . . . at Omaha
22-26 . . . . at Round Rock
27-30 . . . . Iowa
31 . . . . Memphis

SEPTEMBER
1-3 . . . . Memphis

19-22 . . . at Alququerque
23-26 . . . . . Memphis
27-29 . . . . . at Omaha
30 . . . . . . at Round Rock

JULY
1-3 . . . . . . at Round Rock
4-8 . . . . . .Oklahoma City
12-15 . . . at Oklahoma City
16-19 . . . . .at Iowa
20-23 . . . . . . .Nashville
24-27 . . . . .Omaha
28-31 . . . . Iowa

AUGUST
1-4 . . . . at Salt Lake
5-8 . . . . at Tacoma
10-13 . . . . Fresno
14-17 . . . . . .Sacramento
18-21 . . . . at Alququerque
22-26 . . . . . . at Omaha
27-30 . . . . . .Round Rock
31 . . . . Iowa

SEPTEMBER
1-3 . . . . Iowa

OKLAHOMA CITY

APRIL
5-8 . . . . Memphis
9-12 . . . . .Nashville
13-16 . . . . . . .at Memphis
17-20 . . . . . . at Nashville
21-24 . . . . . Albuquerque
26-29 . . . . .Round Rock
30 . . . . . at Albuquerque

MAY
1-3 . . . at Albuquerque
4-7 . . . . at Omaha
8-11 . . . . Las Vegas
12-15 . . . . Tucson
17-20 . . . . .at Reno
21-24 . .at Colorado Springs
25-28 . . . at Albuquerque
29-31 . . . . .Nashville

JUNE
1 . . . . .Nashville
2-5 . . . . Iowa
7-10 . . . . New Orleans
11-13 . . . .at New Orleans
14-17 . . . . at Round Rock

OMAHA

APRIL
5-8 . . . . Albuquerque
9-12 . . . . . .Round Rock
13-16 . . . at Albuquerque
17-20 . . . at Round Rock
21-24 . . . . .Nashville
26-29 . . . . . at Memphis
30 . . . . at Nashville

MAY
1-3 . . . . at Nashville
4-7 . . . . .Oklahoma City
8-11 . . . . at Sacramento
12-15 . . . . .at Fresno
17-20 . . . . .Tacoma
21-24 . . . . . . .Salt Lake
25-28 . . . .at New Orleans
29-31 . . . . Iowa

JUNE
1 . . . . Iowa
2-5 . . . . Memphis
7-10 . . . . . .Round Rock
11-13 . . . . .at Iowa
14-17 . . . . . at Nashville

RENO

APRIL
5-8 . . . . Colorado Springs
9-12 . . . . .Salt Lake
13-16 . . . . at Sacramento
17-20 . . . . .at Fresno
21-24 . . . . . .Sacramento
26-29 . . . . at Salt Lake
30 . . . . Las Vegas

19-22 . . . . . . at Nashville
23-26 . . . . .Omaha
27-29 . . . . at Iowa
30 . . . . Memphis

JULY
1-3 . . . . Memphis
4-8 . . . . . .at New Orleans
12-15 . . . . New Orleans
16-19 . . . . at Omaha
20-23 . . . . . at Memphis
24-27 . . . . Iowa
28-31 . . . . .Omaha

AUGUST
1-4 . . . . at Tacoma
5-8 . . . . . . at Salt Lake
10-13 . . . . . .Sacramento
14-17 . . . . Fresno
18-21 . . . . at Round Rock
22-26 . . . . .at Iowa
27-30 . . . . Albuquerque
31 . . . . .Round Rock

SEPTEMBER
1-3 . . . . .Round Rock

19-22 . . . . Memphis
23-26 . . at Oklahoma City
27-29 . . . . . New Orleans
30 . . . . Albuquerque

JULY
1-3 . . . . Albuquerque
4-8 . . . . at Iowa
12-15 . . . . Iowa
16-19 . . . .Oklahoma City
20-23 . . . . at Round Rock
24-27 . . . .at New Orleans
28-31 . . at Oklahoma City

AUGUST
1-4 . . . . Reno
5-8 . . . . Colorado Springs
10-13 . . . . at Tucson
14-17 . . . . . .at Las Vegas
18-21 . . . . .Nashville
22-26 . . . . . New Orleans
27-30 . . . . . .at Memphis
31 . . . . . . at Albuquerque

SEPTEMBER
1-3 . . . . . at Albuquerque

MAY
1-3 . . . . Las Vegas
4-7 . . . . .Tacoma
8-11 . . . . . . .at Memphis
12-15 . . . . . at Nashville
17-20 . . . .Oklahoma City
21-24 . . . . . New Orleans
25-28 . . . . at Sacramento
29-31 . . . . .Tacoma

JUNE
1 . . . . .Tacoma
2-5 . . . . . .at Las Vegas
7-10 . . . . at Tucson
11-13 . .at Colorado Springs
14-17 . . . . Tucson
19-22 . . . . . . at Tacoma
23-26 . . . . . . at Salt Lake
27-29 . . . . Fresno
30 . . . . Las Vegas

JULY
1-3 . . . . Las Vegas
4-8 . . .at Colorado Springs
12-15 . . . . .Salt Lake
16-19 . . . . at Tucson

ROUND ROCK

APRIL
5-8 . . . . .at Iowa
9-12 . . . . . . at Omaha
13-16 . . . . Iowa
17-20 . . . . .Omaha
21-24 . . . .at New Orleans
26-29 . . at Oklahoma City
30 . . . . New Orleans

MAY
1-3 . . . . New Orleans
4-7 . . . . Memphis
8-11 . . . . . . at Salt Lake
12-15 . . . . at Tacoma
17-20 . . . . Fresno
21-24 . . . . . .Sacramento
25-28 . . . . . . at Nashville
29-31 . . . . . . .at Memphis

JUNE
1 . . . . .at Memphis
2-5 . . . . Albuquerque
7-10 . . . . at Omaha
11-13 . . . at Albuquerque
14-17 . . .Oklahoma City

SACRAMENTO

APRIL
5-8 . . . . .at Las Vegas
9-12 . . . . at Tucson
13-16 . . . . Reno
17-20 . . . . .Tacoma
21-24 . . . . .at Reno
26-29 . . . . Tucson
30 . . . . Colorado Springs

MAY
1-3 . . . . Colorado Springs
4-7 . . . . at Tucson
8-11 . . . . .Omaha
12-15 . . . . Iowa
17-20 . . . . at Albuquerque
21-24 . . . at Round Rock
25-28 . . . . Reno
29-31 . . . . Fresno

JUNE
1 . . . . Fresno
2-5 . . . . at Tacoma

20-23 . . . . . .at Las Vegas
24-27 . . . . .Colorado
28-31 . . . . . .Sacramento

AUGUST
1-4 . . . . at Omaha
5-8 . . . . .at Iowa
10-13 . . . . . Albuquerque
14-17 . . . . . .Round Rock
18-21 . . . . at Tacoma
22-26 . . . . Fresno
27-30 . . . . .at Fresno
31 . . . . Tucson

SEPTEMBER
1-3 . . . . Tucson

19-22 . . . . Iowa
23-26 . . . . .at Iowa
27-29 . . . . .Nashville
30 . . . . . . New Orleans

JULY
1-3 . . . . New Orleans
4-8 . . . . . at Albuquerque
12-15 . . . . Memphis
16-19 . . . . . at Nashville
20-23 . . . . .Omaha
24-27 . . . . Albuquerque
28-31 . . . . . .at Memphis

AUGUST
1-4 . . . . Tucson
5-8 . . . . Las Vegas
10-13 . .at Colorado Springs
14-17 . . . . .at Reno
18-21 . . . .Oklahoma City
22-26 . . . . .Nashville
27-30 . . . .at New Orleans
31 . . . . . at Oklahoma City

SEPTEMBER
1-3 . . . at Oklahoma City

7-10 . . .at Colorado Springs
11-13 . . . . .at Fresno
14-17 . . . . .Tacoma
19-22 . . . . Fresno
23-26 . . . .at Las Vegas
27-29 . . . . . . .Salt Lake
30 . . . . . Colorado Springs

JULY
1-3 . . . . Colorado Springs
4-8 . . . . .at Fresno
12-15 . . . . Las Vegas
16-19 . . . . . . at Tacoma
20-23 . . . . Tucson
24-27 . . . . at Salt Lake
28-31 . . . . .at Reno

AUGUST
1-4 . . . . Memphis
5-8 . . . . .Nashville
10-13 . . . at Oklahoma City
14-17 . . . .at New Orleans

18-21 . . . . Las Vegas
22-26 . . . . Salt Lake
27-30 . .at Colorado Springs

SALT LAKE

APRIL	
5-8 . . . . at Tacoma	19-22 . .at Colorado Springs
9-12 . . . . .at Reno	23-26 . . . . Reno
13-16 . . . . Tucson	27-29 . . . . at Sacramento
17-20 . . . . . . Las Vegas	30 . . . . at Tucson
21-24 . . . . . . at Tucson	**JULY**
26-29 . . . . Reno	1-3 . . . . at Tucson
30 . . . . .at Fresno	4-8 . . . . .Tacoma
MAY	12-15 . . . . .at Reno
1-3 . . . . .at Fresno	16-19 . .at Colorado Springs
4-7 . . . . . . .at Las Vegas	20-23 . . . . Fresno
8-11 . . . . .Round Rock	24-27 . . . . . .Sacramento
12-15 . . . . . Albuquerque	28-31 . . . . .at Las Vegas
17-20 . . . . .at Iowa	**AUGUST**
21-24 . . . . at Omaha	1-4 . . . . New Orleans
25-28 . . . . . . Las Vegas	5-8 . . . . . .Oklahoma City
29-31 . . . Colorado Springs	10-13 . . . . . at Nashville
JUNE	14-17 . . . . . .at Memphis
1 . . . . . Colorado Springs	18-21 . . . Colorado Springs
2-5 . . . . .at Fresno	22-26 . . . at Sacramento
7-10 . . . . at Tacoma	27-30 . . . . Tucson
11-13 . . . . .Tacoma	31 . . . . .Sacramento
14-17 . . . . Fresno	**SEPTEMBER**
	1-3 . . . . .Sacramento

TACOMA

APRIL	MAY
5-8 . . . . .Salt Lake	1-3 . . . . at Tucson
9-12 . . . Colorado Springs	4-7 . . . . .at Reno
13-16 . . . . .at Fresno	8-11 . . . . . . Albuquerque
17-20 . . . . at Sacramento	12-15 . . . . . .Round Rock
21-24 . . . . Fresno	17-20 . . . . . . at Omaha
26-29 . . . . . .at Las Vegas	21-24 . . . . .at Iowa
30 . . . . at Tucson	25-28 . . . . Tucson

29-31 . . . . .at Reno

JUNE	
1 . . . . .at Reno	
2-5 . . . . .Sacramento	
7-10 . . . . .Salt Lake	
11-13 . . . . . . at Salt Lake	
14-17 . . . . at Sacramento	
19-22 . . . . Reno	
23-26 . .at Colorado Springs	
27-29 . . . . . . Las Vegas	
30 . . . . Fresno	
JULY	
1-3 . . . . Fresno	
4-8 . . . . at Salt Lake	
12-15 . . . Colorado Springs	

TUCSON

APRIL	
5-8 . . . . Fresno	19-22 . . . . Las Vegas
9-12 . . . . . . .Sacramento	23-26 . . . . .at Fresno
13-16 . . . . . at Salt Lake	27-39 . . . Colorado Springs
17-20 . .at Colorado Springs	30 . . . . .Salt Lake
21-24 . . . . . . .Salt Lake	**JULY**
26-29 . . . . at Sacramento	1-3 . . . . .Salt Lake
30 . . . . .Tacoma	4-7 . . . . .at Las Vegas
MAY	12-15 . . . . Fresno
1-3 . . . . .Tacoma	16-19 . . . . Reno
4-7 . . . . .Sacramento	20-23 . . . at Sacramento
8-11 . . . . .at New Orleans	24-27 . . . . . . at Tacoma
12-15 . . . at Oklahoma City	28-31 . . . . .Tacoma
17-20 . . . . . . .Nashville	**AUGUST**
21-24 . . . . Memphis	1-4 . . . . . . at Round Rock
25-28 . . . . . . at Tacoma	5-8 . . . . . . at Albuquerque
29-31 . . . . . . Las Vegas	10-13 . . . . .Omaha
JUNE	14-17 . . . . Iowa
1 . . . . Las Vegas	18-21 . . . . .at Fresno
2-5 . . .at Colorado Springs	22-26 . . . Colorado Springs
7-10 . . . . Reno	27-30 . . . . . at Salt Lake
11-13 . . . . . .at Las Vegas	31 . . . . .at Reno
14-17 . . . . .at Reno	**SEPTEMBER**
	1-3 . . . . .at Reno

29-31 . . . . .at Reno

JUNE	
1 . . . . .at Reno	16-19 . . . . . .Sacramento
2-5 . . . . .Sacramento	20-23 . .at Colorado Springs
7-10 . . . . .Salt Lake	24-27 . . . . Tucson
11-13 . . . . . . at Salt Lake	28-31 . . . . at Tucson
14-17 . . . . at Sacramento	**AUGUST**
19-22 . . . . Reno	1-4 . . . . . . .Oklahoma City
23-26 . .at Colorado Springs	5-8 . . . . New Orleans
27-29 . . . . . . Las Vegas	10-13 . . . . . .at Memphis
30 . . . . Fresno	14-17 . . . . . .at Nashville
JULY	18-21 . . . . Reno
1-3 . . . . Fresno	22-26 . . . . . . Las Vegas
4-8 . . . . at Salt Lake	27-30 . . . . . .at Las Vegas
12-15 . . . Colorado Springs	31 . . . . .at Fresno
	SEPTEMBER
	1-3 . . . . .at Fresno

DOUBLE-A

EASTERN LEAGUE

AKRON

APRIL	MAY
5-7 . . . . . .at Binghamton	1-3 . . . . Binghamton
9-11 . . . . .at Altoona	4-6 . . . . .at Bowie
12-15 . . . . Trenton	7-9 . . . . Erie
16-18 . . . . .Bowie	10-13 . . . . .Harrisburg
20-22 . . . . . . .at Reading	14-16 . . . . at Erie
23-25 . . . . . . at Bowie	18-20 . . . . . . .Richmond
27-29 . . . . Altoona	21-24 . . . . . . .at Trenton
30 . . . . Binghamton	25-28 . . . . at Erie
	29-31 . . . . .Bowie

JUNE	
1-4 . . . . . . .at Binghamton	16-18 . . . . . . .Harrisburg
5-7 . . . . New Britain	19-22 . . . . . at Richmond
8-10 . . . . Altoona	23-25 . . . . Erie
12-14 . . . . at New Britain	26-29 . . . . .Bowie
15-18 . . . . . . .at Reading	31 . . . . at Portland
19-21 . . . . . Binghamton	**AUGUST**
22-25 . . . . . . .at Altoona	1-2 . . . . at Portland
26-29 . . . . Erie	3-5 . . . . at New Hampshire
30 . . . . Richmond	7-9 . . . . Portland
JULY	10-12 . . . New Hampshire
1-3 . . . . .Richmond	14-16 . . . . at Harrisburg
4-6 . . . . at Erie	17-19 . . . . Reading
7-9 . . . . at Bowie	20-22 . . . . at Erie
12-15 . . . . Altoona	23-26 . . . . Trenton
	27-30 . . . . . . .at Altoona

31 . . . . at Richmond

SEPTEMBER
1-3 . . . . at Richmond

ALTOONA

APRIL	
5-7 . . . . Erie	22-25 . . . . .Akron
9-11 . . . . .Akron	26-29 . . . . . at Harrisburg
12-15 . . . . . at Richmond	30 . . . . . .at Binghamton
16-18 . . . . . at Harrisburg	**JULY**
19-22 . . . . .Richmond	1-3 . . . . . at Binghamton
24-26 . . . . . . .Harrisburg	4-6 . . . . Reading
27-29 . . . . at Akron	7-9 . . . . Binghamton
30 . . . . at Erie	12-15 . . . . . . at Akron
MAY	16-18 . . . . . at Richmond
1-3 . . . . at Erie	19-22 . . . . Erie
4-6 . . . . .Richmond	23-25 . . . . . .at Reading
8-9 . . . . .Bowie	26-29 . . . New Hampshire
10-13 . . . . at Erie	31 . . . . .at Trenton
15-17 . . . . . . at Bowie	**AUGUST**
18-20 . . . . Erie	1-2 . . . . at Trenton
21-24 . . . . . .Harrisburg	3-5 . . . . at New Britain
25-28 . . . . . . at Bowie	6-9 . . . . .Bowie
29-31 . . . . . . .Richmond	10-12 . . . . Trenton
JUNE	14-16 . . . . . at Portland
1-3 . . . . Portland	17-19 . . at New Hampshire
5-7 . . . . .at Reading	20-22 . . . . at Trenton
8-10 . . . . at Akron	23-26 . . . . . . .Richmond
12-14 . . . . Trenton	27-30 . . . . .Akron
15-17 . . . .at Binghamton	31 . . . . at Erie
19-21 . . . . . . New Britain	**SEPTEMBER**
	1-3 . . . . at Erie

BINGHAMTON

APRIL	
5-7 . . . . .Akron	22-25 . . . . at Erie
9-11 . . . . Erie	26-29 . . . . .Bowie
12-15 . . . . . at Portland	30 . . . . Altoona
16-18 . . at New Hampshire	**JULY**
19-22 . . . . Portland	1-3 . . . . Altoona
24-26 . . . . New Hampshire	4-6 . . . . . at Richmond
27-29 . . . . at Erie	7-9 . . . . . . .at Altoona
30 . . . . at Akron	12-15 . . . . Erie
MAY	16-18 . . . . Trenton
1-3 . . . . at Akron	19-22 . . . . at Bowie
4-6 . . . . .Harrisburg	23-25 . . . . . at New Britain
7-9 . . . . New Britain	26-29 . . . . Portland
10-13 . . at New Hampshire	31 . . . . .Harrisburg
15-17 . . . . Trenton	**AUGUST**
18-20 . . . . . . at Portland	1-2 . . . . .Harrisburg
21-24 . . . . at New Britain	3-5 . . . . .at Reading
25-28 . . . . New Hampshire	7-9 . . . . New Britain
29-31 . . . . .at Reading	10-12 . . . . . at Harrisburg
JUNE	14-16 . . at New Hampshire
1-4 . . . . .Akron	17-19 . . . . .Richmond
5-7 . . . . . . at Harrisburg	20-22 . . . New Hampshire
8-10 . . . . at Trenton	23-26 . . . . . . at Portland
12-14 . . . . Reading	27-30 . . . . . . .at Reading
15-17 . . . . Altoona	31 . . . . Trenton
19-21 . . . . at Akron	**SEPTEMBER**
	1-3 . . . . Trenton

BOWIE

APRIL	
5-8 . . . . .Harrisburg	22-25 . . . . Reading
9-11 . . . . Richmond	26-29 . . . .at Binghamton
12-15 . . . . at Erie	30 . . . . . . at New Britain
16-18 . . . . . . at Akron	**JULY**
19-22 . . . . Erie	1-3 . . . . . at New Britain
23-25 . . . . .Akron	4-6 . . . . .Harrisburg
27-29 . . . . . at Harrisburg	7-9 . . . . .Akron
30 . . . . at Richmond	12-15 . . . . . .at Reading
MAY	16-18 . . . . at Erie
1-3 . . . . . . at Richmond	19-22 . . . . . . Binghamton
4-6 . . . . .Akron	23-25 . . . . . . .Richmond
8-9 . . . . . . .at Altoona	26-29 . . . . at Akron
10-13 . . . . at Richmond	31 . . . . New Britain
15-17 . . . . Altoona	**AUGUST**
18-20 . . . at Harrisburg	1-2 . . . . New Britain
21-24 . . . . . . .Richmond	3-5 . . . . Trenton
25-28 . . . . Altoona	6-9 . . . . .at Altoona
29-31 . . . . at Akron	10-12 . . . . . at Richmond
JUNE	14-16 . . . . Erie
1-3 . . . . Reading	17-19 . . . . . . at Trenton
5-7 . . . . at Portland	20-22 . . . . at Richmond
8-10 . . at New Hampshire	23-26 . . . . . . .Harrisburg
12-14 . . . . .Richmond	27-30 . . . . Erie
15-17 . . . . New Hampshire	31 . . . . .at Harrisburg
19-21 . . . . at Erie	**SEPTEMBER**
	1-3 . . . . .at Harrisburg

ERIE

APRIL	
5-7 . . . . .at Altoona	22-25 . . . . . . Binghamton
9-11 . . . . .at Binghamton	26-29 . . . . at Akron
12-15 . . . . .Bowie	30 . . . . .at Harrisburg
16-18 . . . . Trenton	**JULY**
19-22 . . . . . . at Bowie	1-3 . . . . at Harrisburg
24-26 . . . . . at Trenton	4-6 . . . . .Akron
27-29 . . . . . Binghamton	7-9 . . . . .Harrisburg
30 . . . . Altoona	12-15 . . . .at Binghamton
MAY	16-18 . . . . .Bowie
1-3 . . . . Altoona	19-22 . . . . . . .at Altoona
4-6 . . . . .at Reading	23-25 . . . . . . at Akron
7-9 . . . . at Akron	26-29 . . . . . . .Richmond
10-13 . . . . Altoona	31 . . . . at New Hampshire
14-16 . . . . .Akron	**AUGUST**
18-20 . . . . .at Altoona	1-2 . . . . at New Hampshire
21-24 . . . . Reading	3-5 . . . . at Portland
25-28 . . . . .Akron	7-9 . . . . . New Hampshire
29-31 . . . . . . at Trenton	10-12 . . . . Portland
JUNE	14-16 . . . . . . .at Bowie
1-3 . . . . at Richmond	17-19 . . . . . . .Harrisburg
5-7 . . . . Trenton	20-22 . . . . .Akron
8-10 . . . . New Britain	23-26 . . . . . . .at Reading
12-14 . . . . at Harrisburg	27-30 . . . . . . .at Bowie
15-17 . . . . at New Britain	31 . . . . Altoona
19-21 . . . . .Bowie	**SEPTEMBER**
	1-3 . . . . Altoona

HARRISBURG

APRIL	
5-8 . . . . at Bowie	12-15 . . . . Reading
9-11 . . . . . at New Britain	16-18 . . . . Altoona
	19-22 . . . . . . .at Trenton

24-26 . . . . . . .at Altoona	
27-29 . . . . .Bowie	
30 . . . . New Britain	

JULY

1-3 . . . . Erie	
4-6 . . . . at Bowie	
7-9 . . . . at Erie	
12-15 . . . . Richmond	
16-18 . . . . at Akron	
19-22 . . . . . . New Britain	
23-25 . . . . New Hampshire	
26-29 . . . . . . at Trenton	
31 . . . . . .at Binghamton	

MAY

1-3 . . . . New Britain	
4-6 . . . . . .at Binghamton	
7-9 . . . . Richmond	
10-13 . . . . at Akron	
15-17 . . . . . . at Richmond	
18-20 . . . . .Bowie	
21-24 . . . . . . .at Altoona	
25-28 . . . . Reading	
29-31 . . . . Portland	

AUGUST

1-2 . . . . . .at Binghamton	
3-5 . . . . Richmond	
7-9 . . . . . . at Richmond	
10-12 . . . . . Binghamton	
14-16 . . . . .Akron	
17-19 . . . . at Erie	
20-22 . . . . Reading	
23-26 . . . . at Bowie	
27-30 . . . . . at Richmond	
31 . . . . .Bowie	

JUNE

1-3 . . . . . at New Britain	
5-7 . . . . Binghamton	
8-10 . . . . . . .at Reading	
12-14 . . . . Erie	
15-17 . . . . Trenton	
19-21 . . . . . . at Portland	
22-25 . . at New Hampshire	
26-29 . . . . Altoona	
30 . . . . Erie	

SEPTEMBER

1-3 . . . . .Bowie	

NEW BRITAIN

APRIL

5-7 . . . . Richmond	
9-11 . . . . .Harrisburg	
12-15 . . at New Hampshire	
16-18 . . . . . . at Portland	
19-22 . . . New Hampshire	
23-25 . . . . Portland	
27-29 . . . . . . at Richmond	
30 . . . . at Harrisburg	

MAY

1-3 . . . . at Harrisburg	
4-6 . . . . Portland	
7-9 . . . .at Binghamton	
10-13 . . . . Reading	
15-17 . . . New Hampshire	
18-20 . . . . . . .at Reading	
21-24 . . . . . Binghamton	
25-28 . . . . . at Portland	
29-31 . . at New Hampshire	

JUNE

1-3 . . . . .Harrisburg	
5-7 . . . . at Akron	
8-10 . . . . at Erie	
12-14 . . . . .Akron	
15-17 . . . . Erie	
19-21 . . . . . . .at Altoona	

22-25 . . . . . at Richmond	
26-29 . . . . Trenton	
30 . . . . .Bowie	

JULY

1-3 . . . . .Bowie	
4-6 . . . . .at Trenton	
7-9 . . . at New Hampshire	
12-15 . . . . Trenton	
16-18 . . . New Hampshire	
19-22 . . . . . at Harrisburg	
23-25 . . . . . Binghamton	
26-29 . . . . . .at Reading	
31 . . . . at Bowie	

AUGUST

1-2 . . . . at Bowie	
3-5 . . . . Altoona	
7-9 . . . . . .at Binghamton	
10-12 . . . . Reading	
14-16 . . . . Richmond	
17-19 . . . . . . at Portland	
20-22 . . . . Portland	
23-26 . . at New Hampshire	
27-30 . . . . at Trenton	
31 . . . . . New Hampshire	

SEPTEMBER

1-3 . . . . . New Hampshire	

NEW HAMPSHIRE

APRIL

5-7 . . . . at Trenton	
9-11 . . . . .at Reading	
12-15 . . . . . New Britain	
16-18 . . . . . Binghamton	
19-22 . . . . at New Britain	
24-26 . . . .at Binghamton	
27-29 . . . . Trenton	
30 . . . . Reading	

29-31 . . . . . . New Britain	

JUNE

1-4 . . . . at Trenton	
5-7 . . . . Richmond	
8-10 . . . . .Bowie	
12-14 . . . . at Richmond	
15-17 . . . . . . at Bowie	
19-21 . . . . Reading	
22-25 . . . . . . .Harrisburg	
26-29 . . . . . at Portland	
30 . . . . .at Reading	

JULY

1-3 . . . . .at Reading	
4-6 . . . . Portland	
7-9 . . . . . . New Britain	
12-15 . . . . at Portland	
16-18 . . . . at New Britain	

PORTLAND

APRIL

5-7 . . . . .at Reading	
9-11 . . . . at Trenton	
12-15 . . . . . Binghamton	
16-18 . . . . . New Britain	
19-22 . . . .at Binghamton	
23-25 . . . at New Britain	
27-29 . . . . . . Reading	
30 . . . . Trenton	

MAY

1-3 . . . . Trenton	
4-6 . . . . . . New Britain	
7-9 . . . . . New Hampshire	
10-13 . . . . . . .at Trenton	
14-16 . . . . . .at Reading	
18-20 . . . . . Binghamton	
21-24 . . at New Hampshire	
25-28 . . . . . New Britain	
29-31 . . . . at Harrisburg	

JUNE

1-3 . . . . .at Altoona	
5-7 . . . . .Bowie	
8-10 . . . . Richmond	
12-14 . . . . at Bowie	
15-17 . . . . . at Richmond	
19-21 . . . . . . .Harrisburg	

READING

APRIL

5-7 . . . . Portland	
9-11 . . . . . New Hampshire	
12-15 . . . . . at Harrisburg	
16-18 . . . . . at Richmond	
20-22 . . . . .Akron	
24-26 . . . . Richmond	
27-29 . . . . . . at Portland	
30 . . . . at New Hampshire	

MAY

1-3 . . . . at New Hampshire	
4-6 . . . . Erie	
8-9 . . . . Trenton	
10-13 . . . . at New Britain	
14-16 . . . . Portland	

19-22 . . . . Portland	
23-25 . . . . . at Harrisburg	
26-29 . . . . . .at Altoona	
31 . . . . Erie	

AUGUST

1-2 . . . . Erie	
3-5 . . . . .Akron	
7-9 . . . . at Erie	
10-12 . . . . at Akron	
14-16 . . . . . . Binghamton	
17-19 . . . . Altoona	
20-22 . . . .at Binghamton	
23-26 . . . . . New Britain	
27-30 . . . . Portland	
31 . . . . . . at New Britain	

SEPTEMBER

1-3 . . . . . . at New Britain	

22-25 . . . . at Trenton	
26-29 . . . . New Hampshire	
30 . . . . Trenton	

JULY

1-3 . . . . Trenton	
4-6 . . . . at New Hampshire	
7-9 . . . . at Trenton	
12-15 . . . New Hampshire	
16-18 . . . . Reading	
19-22 . . at New Hampshire	
23-25 . . . . Trenton	
26-29 . . . .at Binghamton	
31 . . . . .Akron	

AUGUST

1-2 . . . . .Akron	
3-5 . . . . Erie	
7-9 . . . . at Akron	
10-12 . . . . at Erie	
14-16 . . . . . . Altoona	
17-19 . . . . . New Britain	
20-22 . . at New Britain	
23-26 . . . . . Binghamton	
27-30 . . at New Hampshire	
31 . . . . Reading	

SEPTEMBER

1-3 . . . . Reading	

JUNE

1-3 . . . . at Bowie	
5-7 . . . . Altoona	
8-10 . . . . .Harrisburg	
12-14 . . . .at Binghamton	
15-18 . . . . .Akron	
19-21 . . at New Hampshire	
22-25 . . . . at Bowie	
26-29 . . . . . . Richmond	
30 . . . . . . New Hampshire	

JULY		
1-3 . . . . . New Hampshire	3-5 . . . . Binghamton	
4-6 . . . . .at Altoona	7-9 . . . . .at Trenton	
7-9 . . . . . at Richmond	10-12 . . . at New Britain	
12-15 . . . . .Bowie	13-16 . . . . Trenton	
16-18 . . . . . at Portland	17-19 . . . . at Akron	
19-22 . . . . . . .at Trenton	20-22 . . . . .at Harrisburg	
23-25 . . . . Altoona	23-26 . . . . Erie	
26-29 . . . . . New Britain	27-30 . . . . . Binghamton	
31 . . . . at Richmond	31 . . . . at Portland	

AUGUST	SEPTEMBER
1-2 . . . . at Richmond	1-3 . . . . at Portland

RICHMOND

APRIL		
5-7 . . . . . at New Britain	26-29 . . . . . . .at Reading	
9-11 . . . . at Bowie	30 . . . . at Akron	
12-15 . . . . Altoona		
16-18 . . . . Reading	JULY	
19-22 . . . . . .at Altoona	1-3 . . . . .at Akron	
24-26 . . . . . . .at Reading	4-6 . . . . . . Binghamton	
27-29 . . . . . New Britain	7-9 . . . . Reading	
30 . . . . .Bowie	12-15 . . . . .at Harrisburg	
	16-18 . . . . Altoona	
MAY	19-22 . . . . .Akron	
1-3 . . . . .Bowie	23-25 . . . . . .at Bowie	
4-6 . . . . . . .at Altoona	26-29 . . . . . . at Erie	
7-9 . . . . . . at Harrisburg	31 . . . . Reading	
10-13 . . . . .Bowie		
15-17 . . . . . . .Harrisburg	AUGUST	
18-20 . . . . at Akron	1-2 . . . . Reading	
21-24 . . . . . . at Akron	3-5 . . . . . . at Harrisburg	
25-28 . . . . Trenton	7-9 . . . . .Harrisburg	
29-31 . . . . .at Altoona	10-12 . . . . .Bowie	
	14-16 . . . . at New Britain	
JUNE	17-19 . . .at Binghamton	
1-3 . . . . Erie	20-22 . . . . .Bowie	
5-7 . . at New Hampshire	23-26 . . . . . .at Altoona	
8-10 . . . . . . at Portland	27-30 . . . . . .Harrisburg	
12-14 . . . New Hampshire	31 . . . . .Akron	
15-17 . . . . Portland		
19-21 . . . . . . .at Trenton	SEPTEMBER	
22-25 . . . . . . New Britain	1-3 . . . . .Akron	

TRENTON

APRIL		
5-7 . . . . . New Hampshire	JUNE	
9-11 . . . . Portland	1-4 . . . . New Hampshire	
12-15 . . . . . at Akron	5-7 . . . . at Erie	
16-18 . . . . . . at Erie	8-10 . . . . . Binghamton	
19-22 . . . . . . .Harrisburg	12-14 . . . . .at Altoona	
24-26 . . . . Erie	15-17 . . . . . at Harrisburg	
27-29 . . at New Hampshire	19-21 . . . . . .Richmond	
30 . . . . at Portland	22-25 . . . . . . Portland	
	26-29 . . . . at New Britain	
MAY	30 . . . . at Portland	
1-3 . . . . at Portland		
4-6 . . . . . New Hampshire	JULY	
8-9 . . . . .at Reading	1-3 . . . . at Portland	
10-13 . . . . Portland	4-6 . . . . . . New Britain	
15-17 . . . . . Binghamton	7-9 . . . . Portland	
18-20 . . at New Hampshire	12-15 . . . . at New Britain	
21-24 . . . . .Akron	16-18 . . . . .at Binghamton	
25-28 . . . . . at Richmond	19-22 . . . . . . Reading	
29-31 . . . . Erie	23-25 . . . . . at Portland	
	26-29 . . . . . . .Harrisburg	
	31 . . . . Altoona	

AUGUST	20-22 . . . . Altoona
1-2 . . . . Altoona	23-26 . . . . at Akron
3-5 . . . . at Bowie	27-30 . . . . . New Britain
7-9 . . . . Reading	31 . . . . . .at Binghamton
10-12 . . . . . .at Altoona	
13-16 . . . .at Reading	SEPTEMBER
17-19 . . . . .Bowie	1-3 . . . . . .at Binghamton

SOUTHERN LEAGUE

BIRMINGHAM

APRIL		JULY	
5-9 . . . . . . .at Jackson		1-3 . . . . Huntsville	
10-14 . . . . Huntsville		4-6 . . . . at Pensacola	
15-19 . . . . at Chattanooga		7 . . . . .at Mississippi	
20-24 . . . . . . .Mississippi		9 . . . . .at Mississippi	
26-29 . . . . at Montgomery		11-13 . . . . .Tennessee	
		14-17 . . . . at Huntsville	
MAY		19-22 . . . . . Montgomery	
1-5 . . . . .Jacksonville		24-28 . . . . at Chattanooga	
6-10 . . . . .Tennessee		29-31 . . . . Jackson	
11-15 . . . . . at Pensacola			
16-20 . . . . . Montgomery		AUGUST	
22-26 . . . . at Huntsville		1-2 . . . . Jackson	
28-31 . . . . . Chattanooga		3-7 . . . . Mobile	
		8-12 . . . . .at Mississippi	
JUNE		14-18 . . . . . . .Tennessee	
1 . . . . Chattanooga		19-23 . . . . at Jacksonville	
2-6 . . . . at Mobile		24-28 . . . . at Huntsville	
7-11 . . . . . . Pensacola		30-31 . . . . . Chattanooga	
13-17 . . . . at Tennessee			
21-25 . . . . . .Mississippi		SEPTEMBER	
26-30 . . . . at Tennessee		1-3 . . . . Chattanooga	

CHATTANOOGA

APRIL		JULY	
5-9 . . . . .Tennessee		1-3 . . . . .Tennessee	
10-14 . . . . at Jacksonville		4-6 . . . . at Huntsville	
15-19 . . . . . Birmingham		7-9 . . . . . . at Tennessee	
20-24 . . . . at Tennessee		11-13 . . . . . Pensacola	
25-29 . . . . Mobile		14-17 . . . . .at Mississippi	
		19-22 . . . . . .Tennessee	
MAY		24-28 . . . . . Birmingham	
1-5 . . . . at Huntsville		29-31 . . . . at Huntsville	
6-10 . . . . . . Montgomery			
11-15 . . . . . at Mobile		AUGUST	
17-21 . . . . . Huntsville		1-2 . . . . . at Huntsville	
23-27 . . . . .Jacksonville		3-7 . . . . .Mississippi	
28-31 . . .at Birmingham		8-12 . . . . . . at Pensacola	
		14-18 . . . . .Jacksonville	
JUNE		19-23 . . . . at Tennessee	
1 . . . . . . .at Birmingham		24-28 . . . . Jackson	
2-6 . . . . Jackson		30-31 . . . .at Birmingham	
7-11 . . . at Montgomery			
13-17 . . . . . .at Jackson		SEPTEMBER	
21-25 . . . . . . Pensacola		1-3 . . . . . .at Birmingham	
26-30 . . . at Mississippi			

HUNTSVILLE

APRIL		15-19 . . . . . . .Tennessee
5-9 . . . . . at Jacksonville		20-24 . . . . Jackson
10-14 . . . . .at Birmingham		25-29 . . . . . at Mississippi

MAY
1-5 . . . . Chattanooga
6-10 . . . . at Jackson
11-15 . . . . . . .Mississippi
17-21 . . . . at Chattanooga
22-26 . . . . . Birmingham
28-31 . . . . . at Tennessee

JUNE
1 . . . . at Tennessee
2-6 . . . . .Mississippi
7-11 . . . . at Mobile
13-17 . . . . . Montgomery
21-25 . . . . . . .at Jackson
26-30 . . . . Mobile

JULY
1-3 . . . . .at Birmingham
4-6 . . . . Chattanooga

7-9 . . . . .Jacksonville
11-13 . . . . at Mobile
14-17 . . . . . Birmingham
19-21 . . . . . . .at Jackson
24-28 . . . . . at Pensacola
29-31 . . . . . Chattanooga

AUGUST
1-2 . . . . Chattanooga
3-7 . . . . Pensacola
8-12 . . . . . . at Tennessee
14-18 . . . . . Montgomery
19-23 . . . . .at Mississippi
24-28 . . . . . Birmingham
30-31 . . . . at Montgomery

SEPTEMBER
1-3 . . . . . at Montgomery

JACKSON

APRIL
5-9 . . . . . . Birmingham
10-14 . . . . . at Tennessee
15-19 . . . . . .Mississippi
20-24 . . . . at Huntsville
25-29 . . . . . . .Tennessee

MAY
1-5 . . . . at Pensacola
6-10 . . . . Huntsville
11-15 . . . . . at Tennessee
17-21 . . . . Mobile
23-27 . . . . at Montgomery
28-31 . . . . Pensacola

JUNE
1 . . . . Pensacola
2-6 . . . . . at Chattanooga
7-11 . . . . . at Jacksonville
13-17 . . . . . Chattanooga
21-25 . . . . Huntsville
26-30 . . . . . at Pensacola

JULY
1-3 . . . . Montgomery
4-6 . . . . . .at Mississippi
7-9 . . . . . at Montgomery
11-13 . . . . Mississippi
14-17 . . . . . at Tennessee
19-21 . . . . Huntsville
24-28 . . . . . . Montgomery
29-31 . . . at Birgmingham

AUGUST
1-2 . . . . . .at Birmingham
3-7 . . . . Tennessee
8-12 . . . . . at Montgomery
14-18 . . . . . . .Mississippi
19-23 . . . . . . at Mobile
24-28 . . . . at Chattanooga
30-31 . . . . . . Jacksonville

SEPTEMBER
1-3 . . . . Jacksonville

JACKSONVILLE

APRIL
5-9 . . . . Huntsville
10-14 . . . . . Chattanooga
15-19 . . . . . at Pensacola
20-24 . . . . at Mobile
25-29 . . . . Pensacola

MAY
1-5 . . . . .at Birmingham
6-10 . . . . Mobile
11-15 . . . . at Montgomery
17-21 . . . . Pensacola
23-27 . . . . at Chattanooga
28-31 . . . . Mobile

JUNE
1 . . . . Mobile
2-6 . . . . . at Pensacola
7-11 . . . . Jackson
13-17 . . . . .at Mississippi
21-25 . . . . . . .Tennessee
26-30 . . . . Montgomery

JULY
1-3 . . . . Pensacola
4-6 . . . . at Tennessee
7-9 . . . . at Huntsville
11-13 . . . . . Montgomery
14-17 . . . . . at Pensacola
19-22 . . . . . . .Mississippi
24-28 . . . . . . .Tennessee
29-31 . . . . at Mobile

AUGUST
1-2 . . . . at Mobile
3-7 . . . . Montgomery
8-12 . . . . Mobile
14-18 . . . . at Chattanooga
19-23 . . . . . Birmingham
24-28 . . . . at Montgomery
30-31 . . . . . . .at Jackson

SEPTEMBER
1-3 . . . . .at Jackson

MISSISSIPPI

APRIL
5-9 . . . . Mobile
10-14 . . . . . Montgomery
15-19 . . . . . .at Jackson
20-24 . . . .at Birmingham
25-29 . . . . . . Huntsville

MAY
1-5 . . . . at Mobile
6-10 . . . . Pensacola
11-15 . . . . . at Huntsville
17-21 . . . . .Tennessee
23-27 . . . . . at Pensacola
28-31 . . . . . Montgomery

JUNE
1 . . . . Montgomery
2-6 . . . . . . at Huntsville
7-11 . . . . . . at Tennessee
13-17 . . . . .Jacksonville
21-25 . . .at Birmingham
26-30 . . . . Chattanooga

JULY
1-3 . . . . at Mobile
4-6 . . . . Jackson
7 . . . . Birmingham
9 . . . . Birmingham
11-13 . . . . . . .at Jackson
14-17 . . . . . Chattanooga
19-22 . . . at Jacksonville
24-28 . . . . Mobile
29-31 . . . at Montgomery

AUGUST
1-2 . . . . at Montgomery
3-7 . . . . . at Chattanooga
8-12 . . . . . . Birmingham
14-18 . . . . . . .at Jackson
19-23 . . . . Huntsville
24-28 . . . . . . Pensacola
30-31 . . . . at Mobile

SEPTEMBER
1-3 . . . . at Mobile

MOBILE

APRIL
5-9 . . . . . . at Mississippi
10-14 . . . . . . Pensacola
15-19 . . . at Montgomery
20-24 . . . . Jacksonville
25-29 . . . at Chattanooga

MAY
1-5 . . . . .Mississippi
6-10 . . . . at Jacksonville
11-15 . . . . . Chattanooga
17-21 . . . . . . .at Jackson
22-26 . . . . . . .Tennessee
28-31 . . . at Jacksonville

JUNE
1 . . . . at Jacksonville
2-6 . . . . Birmingham
7-11 . . . . Huntsville
13-17 . . . . . at Pensacola
21-25 . . . . . Montgomery
26-30 . . . . . at Huntsville

JULY
1-3 . . . . .Mississippi
4-6 . . . . . . at Montgomery
7-9 . . . . at Pensacola
11-13 . . . . Huntsville
14-17 . . . . at Montgomery
19-22 . . . . Pensacola
24-28 . . . . at Mississippi
29-31 . . . . . Jacksonville

AUGUST
1-2 . . . . Jackson
3-7 . . . . . .at Birmingham
8-12 . . . . . at Jacksonville
14-18 . . . . Pensacola
19-23 . . . . Jackson
24-28 . . . . . at Tennessee
30-31 . . . . . . .Mississippi

SEPTEMBER
1-3 . . . . .Mississippi

MONTGOMERY

APRIL
5-9 . . . . at Pensacola
10-14 . . . at Mississippi
15-19 . . . . Mobile
20-24 . . . . Pensacola
26-29 . . . . . . Birmingham

MAY
1-5 . . . . at Tennessee
6-10 . . . . . at Chattanooga
11-15 . . . . .Jacksonville
16-20 . . . .at Birmingham
23-27 . . . . Jackson
28-31 . . . . .at Mississippi

JUNE
1 . . . . .at Mississippi
2-6 . . . . .Tennessee
7-11 . . . . . Chattanooga
13-17 . . . . . at Huntsville
21-25 . . . . . . at Mobile
26-30 . . . . .Jacksonville

JULY
1-3 . . . . .at Jackson
4-6 . . . . Mobile
7-9 . . . . Jackson
11-13 . . . . at Jacksonville
14-17 . . . . Mobile
19-22 . . . .at Birmingham
24-28 . . . . . . .at Jackson

29-31 . . . . . . .Mississippi

AUGUST
1-2. . . . . . . .Mississippi
3-7. . . . . . at Jacksonville
8-12. . . . . Jackson
14-18 . . . . . at Huntsville

PENSACOLA

APRIL
5-9. . . . . . . Montgomery
10-14 . . . . at Mobile
15-19 . . . . .Jacksonville
20-24 . . . at Montgomery
25-29 . . . at Jacksonville

MAY
1-5. . . . . Jackson
6-10. . . . . at Mississippi
11-15 . . . . . Birmingham
17-21 . . . . at Jacksonville
23-27 . . . . . . .Mississippi
28-31 . . . . .at Jackson

JUNE
1 . . . . .at Jackson
2-6. . . . . . . .Jacksonville
7-11. . . .at Birmingham
13-17 . . . . Mobile
21-25 . . . at Chattanooga
26-30 . . . . Jackson

TENNESSEE

APRIL
5-9. . . . . at Chattanooga
10-14 . . . . Jackson
15-19 . . . . at Huntsville
20-24 . . . . . Chattanooga
25-29 . . . . .at Jackson

MAY
1-5. . . . . . Montgomery
6-10. . . . .at Birmingham
11-15 . . . . Jackson
17-21 . . . at Mississippi
22-26 . . . . at Mobile
28-31 . . . . Huntsville

JUNE
1 . . . . Huntsville
2-6. . . . . at Montgomery
7-11. . . . . . .Mississippi
13-17 . . . . . Birmingham
21-25 . . . . at Jacksonville
26-30 . . . . . Birmingham

TEXAS LEAGUE
ARKANSAS

APRIL
5-7. . . . . Midland
8-10. . . . . .Frisco

19-23 . . . . . at Pensacola
24-28 . . . . . .Jacksonville
30-31 . . . . Huntsville

SEPTEMBER
1-3. . . . . Huntsville

23-26 . . . . .at Tulsa
27-30at Northwest Arkansas

MAY
1-4. . . . . Tulsa
5-8. . . . . . .at Springfield
10-13 . . . . .at Tulsa
14-17 . . . . . . Springfield
18-21 . Northwest Arkansas
23-25 . . .at Corpus Christi
26-28 . . . . at San Antonio
30-31 . . . . Corpus Christi

JUNE
1 . . . . .Corpus Christ
2-4. . . . . . . San Antonio
6-9. .at Northwest Arkansas
10-13 . . . . .at Springfield
14-17 . . . . Tulsa
18-21 . . . . . . Springfield
22-25at Northwest Arkansas
29-30 . . . . Midland

JULY
1 . . . . Midland

CORPUS CHRISTI

APRIL
5-7. . . Northwest Arkansas
8-10. . . . . Tulsa
12-14at Northwest Arkansas
15-17 . . . . .at Tulsa
19-22 . . . . .Frisco
23-26 . . . . Midland
27-30 . . . . at Frisco

MAY
1-4. . . . . at Midland
5-8. . . . . . . San Antonio
10-13 . . . . .Frisco
14-17 . . . .at San Antonio
18-21 . . . . . . at Midland
23-25 . . . . Arkansas
26-28 . . . . . Springfield
30-31 . . . . . at Arkansas

JUNE
1 . . . . at Arkansas
2-4. . . . . . .at Springfield
6-9. . . . . Midland
10-13 . . . . . San Antonio
14-17 . . . . at Frisco
18-21 . . .at San Antonio
22-25 . . . . at Frisco

FRISCO

APRIL
5-7. . . . . . .at Springfield
8-10. . . . . . . at Arkansas
12-14 . . . . . . Springfield
15-17 . . . . .Arkansas
19-22 . . .at Corpus Christi
23-26 . . . . . San Antonio
27-30 . . . . Corpus Christi

MAY
1-4. . . . . .at San Antonio
5-8. . . . . Midland

2-4. . . . . .Frisco
5-7. . . . . at Midland
8-10. . . . . at Frisco
12-15 . . . . Tulsa
16-19at Northwest Arkansas
20-23 . . . . Tulsa
24-26 . . . . .at Springfield
27-30 . . . . .at Tulsa
31 . . . . Springfield

AUGUST
1-2. . . . . Springfield
3-6. . . Northwest Arkansas
8-10. . . .at Corpus Christi
11-13 . . . .at San Antonio
15-17 . . . Corpus Christi
18-20 . . . . . San Antonio
21-24 . . . . .at Tulsa
25-27 . . . . . .at Springfield
28-31at Northwest Arkansas

SEPTEMBER
1-3. . . . . Springfield

29-30 . Northwest Arkansas

JULY
1-4. . . . . Tulsa
5-7. .at Northwest Arkansas
8-10. . . . . .at Tulsa
12-15 . . . . .Frisco
16-19 . . . . . at Midland
20-23 . . . . .Frisco
24-26 . . . .at San Antonio
27-30 . . . . Midland
31 . . . . San Antonio

AUGUST
1-2. . . . . . San Antonio
3-6. . . . . at Midland
8-10. . . . . . . .Arkansas
11-13 . . . . . Springfield
15-17 . . . . at Arkansas
18-20 . . . .at Springfield
21-24 . . . . Midland
25-27 . . . . San Antonio
28-31 . . . . . . at Frisco

SEPTEMBER
1-3. . . . . .at San Antonio

10-13 . . . .at Corpus Christi
14-17 . . . . . at Midland
18-21 . . . . . San Antonio
23-25 . . . . .at Tulsa
26-28at Northwest Arkansas
30-31 . . . . Tulsa

JUNE
1 . . . . Tulsa
2-4. . . Northwest Arkansas
6-9. . . . . .at San Antonio
10-13 . . . . Midland

JULY
1-3. . . . . at Jacksonville
4-6. . . . . Birmingham
7-9. . . . . Mobile
11-13 . . at Chattanooga
14-17 . . . . . Jacksonville
19-22 . . . . . . at Mobile
24-28 . . . . . . Huntsville
30-31 . . . . at Tennessee

AUGUST
1-2. . . . . at Tennessee
3-7. . . . . at Huntsville
8-12 . . . . . Chattanooga
14-18 . . . . . . at Mobile
19-23 . . . . . Montgomery
24-28 . . . .at Mississippi
30-31 . . . . .Tennessee

SEPTEMBER
1-3. . . . . . . .Tennessee

JULY
1-3. . . . . at Chattanooga
4-6. . . . . . .Jacksonville
7-9. . . . . . Chattanooga
11-13 . . .at Birmingham
14-17 . . . . Jackson
19-22 . . at Chattanooga
24-28 . . . . at Jacksonville
30-31 . . . . . Pensacola

AUGUST
1-2. . . . . . Pensacola
3-7. . . . . . .at Jackson
8-12 . . . . . Huntsville
14-18 . . . .at Birmingham
19-23 . . . . Chattanooga
24-28 . . . . Mobile
30-31 . . . . at Pensacola

SEPTEMBER
1-3. . . . . . at Pensacola

12-14 . . . . . . at Midland
15-17 . . . . at Frisco
19-22 . Northwest Arkansas

14-17 . . . . Corpus Christi
18-21 . . . . . . at Midland
22-25 . . . . Corpus Christi
29-30 . . . . .at Springfield

JULY
1 . . . . .at Springfield
2-4. . . . . at Arkansas
5-7. . . . . . . Springfield
8-10. . . . . .Arkansas
12-15 . . .at Corpus Christi
16-19 . . . . . San Antonio
20-23 . . .at Corpus Christi
24-26 . . . . . . at Midland
27-30 . . . . . . San Antonio

31 . . . . Midland

AUGUST
1-2. . . . . Midland
3-6. . . . . .at San Antonio
8-10 . . . . .at Tulsa
11-13at Northwest Arkansas
15-17 . . . . Tulsa
18-20 . Northwest Arkansas
21-24 . . . .at San Antonio
25-27 . . . . . . at Midland
28-31 . . . . Corpus Christi

SEPTEMBER
1-3. . . . . Midland

MIDLAND

APRIL
5-7. . . . . at Arkansas
8-10. . . . . .at Springfield
12-14 . . . . .Arkansas
15-17 . . . . . Springfield
19-22 . . . at San Antonio
23-26 . . .at Corpus Christi
27-30 . . . . . San Antonio

MAY
1-4. . . . . . Corpus Christi
5-8. . . . . at Frisco
10-13 . . . at San Antonio
14-17 . . . . .Frisco
18-21 . . . . . Corpus Christi
23-25at Northwest Arkansas
26-28 . . . . . . .at Tulsa
30-31 . Northwest Arkansas

JUNE
1 . . . . Northwest Arkansas
2-4. . . . . Tulsa
6-9. . . . . .at Corpus Christi
10-13 . . . . at Frisco
14-17 . . . . . San Antonio
18-21 . . . . .Frisco
22-25 . . . . . San Antonio

29-30 . . . . . . at Arkansas

JULY
1 . . . . at Arkansas
2-4. . . . . . .at Springfield
5-7. . . . . .Arkansas
8-10 . . . . Springfield
12-15 . . .at San Antonio
16-19 . . . . . Corpus Christi
20-23 . . .at San Antonio
24-26 . . . . .Frisco
27-30 . . .at Corpus Christi
31 . . . . at Frisco

AUGUST
1-2. . . . . at Frisco
3-6. . . . . . Corpus Christi
8-10 .at Northwest Arkansas
11-13 . . . . .at Tulsa
15-17 . Northwest Arkansas
18-20 . . . . Tulsa
21-24 . . .at Corpus Christi
25-27 . . . . .Frisco
28-31 . . . . . San Antonio

SEPTEMBER
1-3. . . . . at Frisco

NORTHWEST ARKANSAS

APRIL
5-7. . . .at Corpus Christi
8-10. . . . .at San Antonio
12-14 . . . . Corpus Christi
15-17 . . . . . San Antonio
19-22 . . . . . . at Arkansas
23-26 . . . . . . Springfield
27-30 . . . . . . .Arkansas

MAY
1-4. . . . . . .at Springfield
5-8. . . . . Tulsa
10-13 . . . . . . Springfield
14-17 . . . . .at Tulsa
18-21 . . . . . at Arkansas
23-25 . . . . . . Midland
26-28 . . . . .Frisco
30-31 . . . . . at Midland

JUNE
1 . . . . at Midland

2-4. . . . . at Frisco
6-9. . . . . .Arkansas
10-13 . . . . .at Tulsa
14-17 . . . . .at Springfield
18-21 . . . . Tulsa
22-25 . . . . .Arkansas
29-30 . . . at Corpus Christi

JULY
1 . . . . .at Corpus Christi
2-4. . . . . .at San Antonio
5-7. . . . . Corpus Christi
8-10 . . . . . San Antonio
12-15 . . . . .at Springfield
16-19 . . . . . . .Arkansas
20-23 . . . .at Springfield
24-26 . . . . Tulsa
27-30 . . . . . Springfield
31 . . . . .at Tulsa

AUGUST
1-2. . . . . .at Tulsa
3-6. . . . . . . at Arkansas
8-10 . . . . Midland
11-13 . . . . .Frisco
15-17 . . . . . . at Midland

SAN ANTONIO

APRIL
5-7. . . . . Tulsa
8-10 . . Northwest Arkansas
12-14 . . . . .at Tulsa
15-17at Northwest Arkansas
19-22 . . . . Midland
23-26 . . . . . . at Frisco
27-30 . . . . . . at Midland

MAY
1-4. . . . . .Frisco
5-8. . . . .at Corpus Christi
10-13 . . . . Midland
14-17 . . . . Corpus Christi
18-21 . . . . . . at Frisco
23-25 . . . . . Springfield
26-28 . . . . . . .Arkansas
30-31 . . .at Springfield

JUNE
1 . . . . .at Springfield
2-4. . . . . . . at Arkansas
6-9. . . . . .Frisco
10-13 . . .at Corpus Christi
14-17 . . . . . . at Midland
18-21 . . . . . Corpus Christi
22-25 . . . . . . at Midland

18-20 . . . . at Frisco
21-24 . . . . . Springfield
25-27 . . . . . . .at Tulsa
28-31 . . . . at Arkansas

SEPTEMBER
1-3. . . . . Tulsa

29-30 . . . . Tulsa

JULY
1 . . . . Tulsa
2-4. . . Northwest Arkansas
5-7. . . . . .at Tulsa
8-10 .at Northwest Arkansas
12-15 . . . . Midland
16-19 . . . . . . at Frisco
20-23 . . . . Midland
24-26 . . . . . Corpus Christi
27-30 . . . . . . at Frisco
31 . . . .at Corpus Christi

AUGUST
1-2. . . .at Corpus Christi
3-6. . . . . .Frisco
8-10 . . . . . . Springfield
11-13 . . . . . . .Arkansas
15-17 . . .at Springfield
18-20 . . . . at Arkansas
21-24 . . . . .Frisco
25-27 . . .at Corpus Christi
28-31 . . . . . . at Midland

SEPTEMBER
1-3. . . . . . Corpus Christi

SPRINGFIELD

APRIL
5-7. . . . . .Frisco
8-10 . . . . Midland
12-14 . . . . . . at Frisco
15-17 . . . . . at Midland
19-22 . . . . Tulsa
23-26at Northwest Arkansas
27-30 . . . . .at Tulsa

MAY
1-4. . . Northwest Arkansas
5-8. . . . . .Arkansas
10-13at Northwest Arkansas
14-17 . . . . . . at Arkansas
18-21 . . . . Tulsa
23-25 . . . at San Antonio
26-28 . . . .at Corpus Christi
30-31 . . . . . San Antonio

JUNE
1 . . . . San Antonio
2-4. . . . . . Corpus Christi
6-9. . . . . .at Tulsa
10-13 . . . . . . .Arkansas
14-17 . Northwest Arkansas
18-21 . . . . . at Arkansas
22-25 . . . . . . .at Tulsa

29-30 . . . . .Frisco

JULY
1 . . . . .Frisco
2-4. . . . . Midland
5-7. . . . . at Midland
8-10 . . . . . . at Midland
12-15 . Northwest Arkansas
16-19 . . . . .at Tulsa
20-23 . Northwest Arkansas
24-26 . . . . .Arkansas
27-30at Northwest Arkansas
31 . . . . at Arkansas

AUGUST
1-2. . . . . . . at Arkansas
3-6. . . . . Tulsa
8-10 . . . . .at San Antonio
11-13 . . . .at Corpus Christi
15-17 . . . . . San Antonio
18-20 . . . . Corpus Christi
21-24at Northwest Arkansas
25-27 . . . . . . .Arkansas
28-31 . . . . Tulsa

SEPTEMBER
1-3. . . . . . . at Arkansas

TULSA

APRIL
5-7 . . . . . . at San Antonio
8-10 . . . . .at Corpus Christi
12-14 . . . . . San Antonio
15-17 . . . . . Corpus Christi
19-22 . . . . .at Springfield
23-26 . . . . .Arkansas
27-30 . . . . . . Springfield

MAY
1-4 . . . . at Arkansas
5-8 . .at Northwest Arkansas

10-13 . . . . .Arkansas
14-17 . Northwest Arkansas
18-21 . . . . .at Springfield
23-25 . . . . .Frisco
26-28 . . . . Midland
30-31 . . . . at Frisco

JUNE
1 . . . . at Frisco
2-4 . . . . at Midland
6-9 . . . . Springfield
10-13 . Northwest Arkansas

14-17 . . . . . . at Arkansas
18-21at Northwest Arkansas
22-25 . . . . . . Springfield
29-30 . . . . .at San Antonio

JULY
1 . . . . .at San Antonio
2-4 . . . . .at Corpus Christi
5-7 . . . . . San Antonio
8-10 . . . . . Corpus Christi
12-15 . . . . . at Arkansas
16-19 . . . . . Springfield
20-23 . . . . . . at Arkansas
24-26at Northwest Arkansas
27-30 . . . . .Arkansas

31 . . . Northwest Arkansas

AUGUST
1-2 . . . Northwest Arkansas
3-6 . . . . . . .at Springfield
8-10 . . . . .Frisco
11-13 . . . . Midland
15-17 . . . . at Frisco
18-20 . . . . at Midland
21-24 . . . . . . .Arkansas
25-27 . Northwest Arkansas
28-31 . . . . .at Springfield

SEPTEMBER
1-3 . .at Northwest Arkansas

HIGH CLASS A

CALIFORNIA LEAGUE

BAKERSFIELD

APRIL
5-8 . . . . Visalia
9-11 . . . . Stockton
12-15 . . . . . at San Jose
16-18 . . . . at Visalia
19-22 . . . . . San Jose
23-26 . . . . . at Stockton
27-29 . . . . . at Modesto

MAY
1-3 . . . . Lancaster
4-6 . . . . Modesto
7-9 . . . . . . .at Lancaster
10-12 . .at Inland Empire
14-16 . . . . Stockton
17-19 . . . at Lake Elsinore
20-22 . . . . at Visalia
24-26 . . . . . . San Jose
27-29 . . . . Inland Empire
30-31 . . . . . . at San Jose

JUNE
1 . . . . at San Jose
2-4 . . . . Modesto
5-7 . . . . Visalia
8-10 . . . . . . at Modesto
11-13 . . . . . . at Stockton
14-16 . . . . . Lake Elsinore
21-24at Rancho Cucamonga

HIGH DESERT

APRIL
5-8 . . . . Lancaster
9-11 . . . . San Jose
12-15 . . . .at Inland Empire
16-18 . . . . . .at Lancaster
19-22 . . . . Inland Empire
23-26 . . . . . . at San Jose
27-29 . . . .at Inland Empire

25-27 . . . . .at Visalia
28-30 . . . . .Modesto

JULY
1-3 . . . . at Lake Elsinore
4-6 . . . . Stockton
7-9 . . . . . Lake Elsinore
11-13 . . . . . . at Stockton
14-16 . Rancho Cucamonga
17-19 . . . . at High Desert
20-22 . . . . .at Visalia
24-26 . . . . . . San Jose
27-29 . . . . Stockton
31 . . . . at San Jose

AUGUST
1-2 . . . . at San Jose
3-5 . . . . at Modesto
7-9 . . . . Visalia
10-12 . . . . at High Desert
14-16 . . . . . . at San Jose
17-19 . . . . . .High Desert
20-23 . . . . Inland Empire
24-27 . . . . . . at Modesto
28-30 . . . . Visalia
31 . . . Rancho Cucamonga

SEPTEMBER
1-3 . . . Rancho Cucamonga

MAY
1-3 . . . . . . Lake Elsinore
4-6 . . . . .at Visalia
7-9 . . . . at Lake Elsinore
10-12 . Rancho Cucamonga
14-16 . . . . Visalia
17-19at Rancho Cucamonga
20-22 . . . . . .at Lancaster

24-26 . . . . .Modesto
27-29 . . . . .Stockton
30-31 . . . . . . at Modesto

JUNE
1 . . . . at Modesto
2-4 . . . . . . Inland Empire
5-7 . . . . . Lake Elsinore
8-10 .at Rancho Cucamonga
11-13 . . . at Lake Elsinore
14-16 . Rancho Cucamonga
21-24 . . . .at Inland Empire
25-27 . Rancho Cucamonga
28-30 . . . . Inland Empire

JULY
1-3 . .at Rancho Cucamonga
4-6 . . . . Lake Elsinore
7-9 . . . . .Modesto
11-13 . . at Lake Elsinore
14-16 . . . . . . .Stockton

INLAND EMPIRE

APRIL
5-8 . .at Rancho Cucamonga
9-11 . . . . at Lake Elsinore
12-15 . . . . .High Desert
16-18 . . . . .Modesto
19-22 . . . at High Desert
23-26 . . . Lake Elsinore
27-29 . . . . . .High Desert

MAY
1-3 . .at Rancho Cucamonga
4-6 . . . . at San Jose
7-9 . . . Rancho Cucamonga
10-12 . . . . . . Bakersfield
13 . . . . . at Lake Elsinore
15-16 . . . at Lake Elsinore
17-19 . . . . . Lancaster
20-22 . Rancho Cucamonga
24-26 . . . . . .at Lancaster
27-29 . . . .at Bakersfield
30-31 . . . . .Stockton

17-19 . . . . . . Bakersfield
20-22 . . . . . . at Stockton
24-26 . . . . . at Modesto
27-29 . . . . . . Visalia
31 . . . . . at Lake Elsinore

AUGUST
1-2 . . . . . at Lake Elsinore
3-5 . . . . .at Lancaster
7-9 . . . . Lancaster
10-12 . . . . . Bakersfield
14-16 . . . . . .at Lancaster
17-19 . . . . .at Bakersfield
20-23 . . . . . Lake Elsinore
24-27 . . . .at Inland Empire
28-30at Rancho Cucamonga
31 . . . . Lancaster

SEPTEMBER
1-3 . . . . Lancaster

JUNE
1 . . . . .Stockton
2-4 . . . . . . at High Desert
5-7 . . . . at Modesto
8-10 . . . . Lancaster
11-13 . . . . . . .San Jose
14-16 . . . . . .at Lancaster
21-24 . . . . .High Desert
25-27 . . . . . Lake Elsinore
28-30 . . . . . at High Desert

JULY
1-3 . . . . .at Visalia
4-6 . . . Rancho Cucamonga
7-9 . . . . Visalia
11-13at Rancho Cucamonga
14-16 . . . . Lake Elsinore
17-19 . . . . . . at Stockton
20-22 . . . . . at San Jose
24-26 . Rancho Cucamonga
27-29 . . . . . .at Lancaster
31 . .at Rancho Cucamonga

AUGUST	
1-2. .at Rancho Cucamonga	
3-5. . . . . San Jose	
7-9. . . . . . . Lake Elsinore	
10-12 . . . . at Visalia	
14-16 . . . . at Lake Elsinore	
17-19 . . . . Lancaster	

LAKE ELSINORE

APRIL	
5-8. . . . . .Stockton	
9-11. . . . . Inland Empire	
12-15 . . . . . .at Lancaster	
16-18 . . . . . at Stockton	
19-22 . . . . . . Lancaster	
23-26 . . . .at Inland Empire	
27-29 . Rancho Cucamonga	

MAY	
1-3. . . . . . at High Desert	
4-6. .at Rancho Cucamonga	
7-9. . . . . . . .High Desert	
10-12 . . . . . .at Lancaster	
13 . . . . . . Inland Empire	
15-16 . . . . . Inland Empire	
17-19 . . . . . Bakersfield	
20-22 . . . . at Modesto	
24-26 . Rancho Cucamonga	
27-29 . . . . Lancaster	
30-31at Rancho Cucamonga	

JUNE	
1 . . .at Rancho Cucamonga	
2-4. . . . . Visalia	
5-7. . . . . at High Desert	
8-10. . . . . at Visalia	
11-13 . . . . . .High Desert	
14-16 . . . . .at Bakersfield	

LANCASTER

APRIL	
5-8. . . . . . at High Desert	
9-11 .at Rancho Cucamonga	
12-15 . . . . . Lake Elsinore	
16-18 . . . . . .High Desert	
19-22 . . . . at Lake Elsinore	
23-26 . Rancho Cucamonga	
27-29 . . . . .Stockton	

MAY	
1-3. . . . . . .at Bakersfield	
4-6. . . . . at Stockton	
7-9. . . . . Bakersfield	
10-12 . . . . . Lake Elsinore	
14-16at Inland Empire	
17-19 . . .at Inland Empire	
20-22 . . . . . .High Desert	
24-26 . . . . Inland Empire	
27-29 at Lake Elsinore	
30-31 . . . . at Visalia	

JUNE	
1 . . . . at Visalia	
2-4. . . Rancho Cucamonga	
5-7. . . . . San Jose	
8-10. . . . .at Inland Empire	

20-23 . . . . . .at Bakersfield	
24-27 . . . . . .High Desert	
28-30 . . . . Lancaster	
31 . . . . . at Lake Elsinore	

SEPTEMBER	
1-3. . . . . at Lake Elsinore	

21-24 . . . . Lancaster	
25-27 . . .at Inland Empire	
28-30 . . . . . . at San Jose	

JULY	
1-3. . . . . Bakersfield	
4-6. . . . . at High Desert	
7-9. . . .at Bakersfield	
11-13 . . . . . . .High Desert	
14-16 . . .at Inland Empire	
17-19at Rancho Cucamonga	
20-22 . . . . .Modesto	
24-26 . . . . . . Lancaster	
27-29at Rancho Cucamonga	
31 . . . . .High Desert	

AUGUST	
1-2. . . . . .High Desert	
3-5. . . Rancho Cucamonga	
7-9. . . . . .at Inland Empire	
10-12at Rancho Cucamonga	
14-16 . . . . . Inland Empire	
17-19 . Rancho Cucamonga	
20-23 . . . . at High Desert	
24-27 . . . . . .at Lancaster	
28-30 . . . . San Jose	
31 . . . . Inland Empire	

SEPTEMBER	
1-3. . . . . . Inland Empire	

11-13at Rancho Cucamonga	
14-16 . . . . Inland Empire	
21-24 . . . . at Lake Elsinore	
25-27 . . . . . .Modesto	
28-30 . Rancho Cucamonga	

JULY	
1-3. . . . . at Modesto	
4-6. . . . . Visalia	
7-9. . . . . .Stockton	
11-13 . . . . .at Visalia	
14-16 . . . . .Modesto	
17-19 . . . . San Jose	
20-22at Rancho Cucamonga	
24-26 . . . . at Lake Elsinore	
27-29 . . . . Inland Empire	
31 . . . . at Stockton	

AUGUST	
1-2. . . . . at Stockton	
3-5. . . . . . . .High Desert	
7-9. . . . . . at High Desert	
10-12 . . . . . at San Jose	
14-16 . . . . . .High Desert	
17-19 . . .at Inland Empire	
20-23 . Rancho Cucamonga	

24-27 . . . . . Lake Elsinore	
28-30 . . .at Inland Empire	
31 . . . . at High Desert	

MODESTO

APRIL	
5-8. . . . . San Jose	
9-11. . . . . Visalia	
12-15 . . . . . . at Stockton	
16-18 . . . .at Inland Empire	
19-22 . . . . .Stockton	
23-26 . . . . at Visalia	
27-29 . . . . Bakersfield	

MAY	
1-3. . . . . Visalia	
4-6. . . . .at Bakersfield	
7-9. . . . . San Jose	
10-12 . . . . . at Stockton	
14-16 . . . . at San Jose	
17-19 . . . . .Stockton	
20-22 . . . Lake Elsinore	
24-26 . . . . at High Desert	
27-29at Rancho Cucamonga	
30-31 . . . . .High Desert	

JUNE	
1 . . . . .High Desert	
2-4. . . . . . .at Bakersfield	
5-7. . . . . . Inland Empire	
8-10. . . . . . Bakersfield	
11-13 . . . . at Visalia	
14-16 . . . . at San Jose	
21-24 . . . . .Stockton	

RANCHO CUCAMONGA

APRIL	
5-8. . . . . . Inland Empire	
9-11. . . . . Lancaster	
12-15 . . . . at Visalia	
16-18 . . . . at San Jose	
19-22 . . . . Visalia	
23-26 . . . . . .at Lancaster	
27-29 . . . . at Lake Elsinore	

MAY	
1-3. . . . . . Inland Empire	
4-6. . . . . . . Inland Empire	
7-9. . . . .at Inland Empire	
10-12 . . . . at High Desert	
14-16 . . . . Lancaster	
17-19 . . . . . . .High Desert	
20-22 . . .at Inland Empire	
24-26 . . . at Lake Elsinore	
27-29 . . . . .Modesto	
30-31 . . . . Lake Elsisnore	

JUNE	
1 . . . . Lake Elsinore	
2-4. . . . . . . .at Lancaster	
5-7. . . . . at Stockton	
8-10. . . . . . . .High Desert	
11-13 . . . . Lancaster	
14-16 . . . . at High Desert	
21-24 . . . . . . Bakersfield	

25-27 . . . . . at High Desert	
28-30 . . . . .at Lancaster	

JULY	
1-3. . . . . . . .High Desert	
4-6. . . .at Inland Empire	
7-9. . . . . . . at San Jose	
11-13 . . . . . Inland Empire	
14-16 . . . .at Bakersfield	
17-19 . . . . Lake Elsinore	
20-22 . . . . . . Lancaster	
24-26 . . .at Inland Empire	
27-29 . . . . Lake Elsinore	
31 . . . . Inland Empire	

AUGUST	
1-2. . . . . . Inland Empire	
3-5. . . . at Lake Elsinore	
7-9. . . . . at Modesto	
10-12 . . . Lake Elsinore	
14-16 . . . . .Stockton	
17-19 . . . at Lake Elsinore	
20-23 . . . . . .at Lancaster	
24-27 . . . . . . San Jose	
28-30 . . . . . .High Desert	
31 . . . . .at Bakersfield	

SEPTEMBER	
1-3. . . . . . . .at Bakersfield	

SEPTEMBER	
1-3. . . . . . at High Desert	

SEPTEMBER	
1-3. . . . . at San Jose	

SAN JOSE

APRIL	
5-8	at Modesto
9-11	at High Desert
12-15	Bakersfield
16-18	Rancho Cucamonga
19-22	at Bakersfield
23-26	High Desert
27-29	at Visalia
MAY	
1-3	Stockton
4-6	Inland Empire
7-9	at Modesto
10-12	Visalia
14-16	Modesto
17-19	at Visalia
20-22	at Stockton
24-26	at Bakersfield
27-29	Visalia
30-31	Bakersfield
JUNE	
1	Bakersfield
2-4	at Stockton
5-7	at Lancaster
8-10	Stockton
11-13	at Inland Empire
14-16	Modesto
21-24	at Visalia
25-27	Stockton
28-30	Lake Elsinore
JULY	
1-3	at Stockton
4-6	Modesto
7-9	Rancho Cucamonga
11-13	at Modesto
14-16	Visalia
17-19	at Lancaster
20-22	Inland Empire
24-26	at Bakersfield
27-29	at Modesto
31	Bakersfield
AUGUST	
1-2	Bakersfield
3-5	at Inland Empire
7-9	at Stockton
10-12	Lancaster
14-16	Bakersfield
17-19	at Stockton
20-23	Visalia
24-27	at Rancho Cucamonga
28-30	at Lake Elsinore
31	Modesto
SEPTEMBER	
1-3	Modesto

STOCKTON

APRIL	
5-8	at Lake Elsinore
9-11	at Bakersfield
12-15	Modesto
16-18	Lake Elsinore
19-22	at Modesto
23-26	Bakersfield
27-29	at Lancaster
MAY	
1-3	at San Jose
4-6	Lancaster
7-9	at Visalia
10-12	Modesto
14-16	at Bakersfield
17-19	at Modesto
20-22	San Jose
24-26	Visalia
27-29	at High Desert
30-31	at Inland Empire
JUNE	
1	at Inland Empire
2-4	San Jose
5-7	Rancho Cucamonga
8-10	at San Jose
11-13	Bakersfield
14-16	Visalia
21-24	at Modesto
25-27	at San Jose
28-30	Visalia
JULY	
1-3	San Jose
4-6	at Bakersfield
7-9	at Lancaster
11-13	Bakersfield
14-16	at High Desert
17-19	Inland Empire
20-22	High Desert
24-26	at Visalia
27-29	at Bakersfield
31	Lancaster
AUGUST	
1-2	Lancaster
3-5	at Visalia
7-9	San Jose
10-12	Modesto
14-16	at Rancho Cucamonga
17-19	San Jose
20-23	Modesto
24-27	at Visalia
28-30	at Modesto
31	Visalia
SEPTEMBER	
1-3	Visalia

VISALIA

APRIL	
5-8	at Bakersfield
9-11	at Modesto
12-15	Rancho Cucamonga
16-18	Bakersfield
19-22	at Rancho Cucamonga
23-26	Modesto
27-29	San Jose
MAY	
1-3	at Modesto
4-5	High Desert
7-9	Stockton
10-12	at San Jose
14-16	at High Desert
17-19	San Jose
20-22	Bakersfield
24-26	at Stockton
27-29	at San Jose
30-31	Lancaster
JUNE	
1	Lancaster
2-4	at Lake Elsinore
5-7	at Bakersfield
8-10	Lake Elsinore
11-13	Modesto
14-15	at Stockton
21-24	San Jose
25-27	Bakersfield
28-30	at Stockton
JULY	
1-3	Inland Empire
4-6	at Lancaster
7-9	at Inland Empire
11-13	Lancaster
14-16	at San Jose
17-19	at Modesto
20-22	Bakersfield
24-26	Stockton
27-29	at High Desert
31	Modesto
AUGUST	
1-2	Modesto
3-5	Stockton
7-9	at Bakersfield
10-12	Inland Empire
14-16	Modesto
17-19	at Modesto
20-23	at San Jose
24-27	Stockton
28-30	at Bakersfield
31	at Stockton
SEPTEMBER	
1-3	at Stockton

CAROLINA LEAGUE

CAROLINA

APRIL	
6-8	Winston-Salem
9-11	Wilmington
13-15	at Winston-Salem
16-18	at Wilmington
19-22	Myrtle Beach
23-26	Lynchburg
27-29	at Salem
30	at Lynchburg
MAY	
1-3	at Lynchburg
4-6	Frederick
8-10	at Myrtle Beach
11-13	Potomac
14-17	Salem
18-20	at Potomac
21-23	at Frederick
25-27	Winston-Salem
28-31	Wilmington
JUNE	
1-3	at Winston-Salem
4-7	at Wilmington
8-10	Myrtle Beach
11-13	at Lynchburg
14-17	at Salem
21-23	Wilmington
24-27	Frederick
28-30	at Myrtle Beach
JULY	
1-3	Potomac
4-6	Salem
7-9	at Potomac
12-15	at Frederick
16-19	Winston-Salem
20-22	Lynchburg
23-26	at Winston-Salem
27-29	at Wilmington
31	Myrtle Beach
AUGUST	
1-2	Myrtle Beach
3-5	Lynchburg
7-9	at Salem
10-12	at Lynchburg
13-15	Frederick
16-19	at Myrtle Beach
20-23	at Potomac
24-26	Salem
28-30	Potomac
SEPTEMBER	
1-3	at Frederick

FREDERICK

APRIL
6-8 . . . . .Salem
10-12 . . . .Winston-Salem
13-15 . . . . . at Wilmington
16-18 . . . . .Potomac
19-22 . . . . at Lynchburg
23-26 . . . . at Myrtle Beach
27-29 . . . . . . .Lynchburg
30 . . . . Myrtle Beach

MAY
1-3 . . . . . . Myrtle Beach
4-6 . . . . .at Carolina
8-10 . . . . .Winston-Salem
11-13 . . . . . . Wilmington
14-17 . . . . . . at Potomac
18-20 . . . . at Salem
21-23 . . . . Carolina
25-27 . . . . .Salem
28-31 . . at Winston-Salem

JUNE
1-3 . . . . . . at Wilmington
4-7 . . . . .Potomac
8-10 . . . . . at Lynchburg
11-13 . . . . at Myrtle Beach
14-17 . . . . . . .Lynchburg

21-23 . . . . . Myrtle Beach
24-27 . . . . . .at Carolina
28-30 . . at Winston-Salem

JULY
1-3 . . . . Wilmington
4-6 . . . . at Potomac
7-9 . . . . at Salem
12-15 . . . . Carolina
16-19 . . . . .Salem
20-22 . . at Winston-Salem
23-26 . . . . . at Wilmington
27-29 . . . . .Potomac
31 . . . . at Lynchburg

AUGUST
1-2 . . . . . . at Lynchburg
3-5 . . . . at Myrtle Beach
7-9 . . . . .Lynchburg
10-12 . . . . . Myrtle Beach
13-15 . . . . .at Carolina
16-19 . . . . .Winston-Salem
20-23 . . . . . . Wilmington
24-26 . . . . . . at Potomac
28-31 . . . . at Salem

SEPTEMBER
1-3 . . . . Carolina

LYNCHBURG

APRIL
6-8 . . . . .Potomac
10-12 . . . . .Salem
13-15 . . . . . . at Potomac
16-18 . . . . . . at Salem
19-22 . . . . . . .Frederick
23-26 . . . . . . .at Carolina
27-29 . . . . . at Frederick
30 . . . . Carolina

MAY
1-3 . . . . Carolina
4-6 . . . . . . Myrtle Beach
8-10 . . . . at Wilmington
11-13 . . . .Winston-Salem
14-17 . . . . . . Wilmington
18-20 . . at Winston-Salem
22-24 . . . at Myrtle Beach
25-27 . . . . .Potomac
28-29 . . . . . . at Salem
30-31 . . . . .Salem

JUNE
1-3 . . . . at Potomac
4-7 . . . . . at Myrtle Beach
8-10 . . . . .Frederick
11-13 . . . . Carolina
14-17 . . . . . . at Frederick
21-23 . . . . .Salem

24-27 . . . . . Myrtle Beach
28-30 . . . . . at Wilmington

JULY
1-3 . . . . . .Winston-Salem
4-6 . . . . Wilmington
7-9 . . . . at Winston-Salem
11-12 . . . . at Salem
13-14 . . . . .Salem
16-19 . . . . . at Potomac
20-22 . . . . . . .at Carolina
23-26 . . . . .Potomac
27-29 . . . . . at Salem
31 . . . . .Frederick

AUGUST
1-2 . . . . .Frederick
3-5 . . . . .at Carolina
7-9 . . . . at Frederick
10-12 . . . . Carolina
13-15 . . . . . Myrtle Beach
16-19 . . . . . at Wilmington
20-23 . . . .Winston-Salem
24-26 . . . . . . Wilmington
28-31 . . at Winston-Salem

SEPTEMBER
1-3 . . . . . at Myrtle Beach

MYRTLE BEACH

APRIL
6-8 . . . . Wilmington
10-12 . . . . .Potomac

13-15 . . . . at Salem
16-18 . . .Winston-Salem
19-22 . . . . . . .at Carolina

POTOMAC

APRIL
6-8 . . . . at Lynchburg
10-12 . . . at Myrtle Beach
13-15 . . . . . .Lynchburg
16-18 . . . . . . at Frederick
19-22 . . . . .Salem
23-26 . . at Winston-Salem
27-29 . . . Myrtle Beach
30 . . . . . .Winston-Salem

MAY
1-3 . . . . . .Winston-Salem
4-6 . . . . Wilmington
8-10 . . . . . . at Salem
11-13 . . . . . .at Carolina
14-17 . . . . . .Frederick
18-20 . . . . . Carolina
21-23 . . . . at Wilmington
25-27 . . . at Lynchburg
28-31 . . . . . Myrtle Beach

JUNE
1-3 . . . . .Lynchburg
4-7 . . . . at Frederick
8-10 . . . . .Salem
11-13 . . at Winston-Salem
14-17 . . . at Myrtle Beach

21-23 . . . .Winston-Salem
24-27 . . . . Wilmington
28-30 . . . . at Salem

JULY
1-3 . . . . .at Carolina
4-6 . . . . .Frederick
7-9 . . . . Carolina
11-14 . . . . at Wilmington
16-19 . . . . . .Lynchburg
20-22 . . . . . Myrtle Beach
23-26 . . . at Lynchburg
27-29 . . . . at Frederick
31 . . . . .Salem

AUGUST
1-2 . . . . .Salem
3-5 . . . . at Winston-Salem
7-9 . . . . at Myrtle Beach
10-12 . . . .Winston-Salem
13-15 . . . . . . Wilmington
16-19 . . . . . . at Salem
20-23 . . . . Carolina
24-26 . . . . . .Frederick
28-31 . . . . . . .at Carolina

SEPTEMBER
1-3 . . . . . . at Wilmington

SALEM

APRIL
6-8 . . . . at Frederick
10-12 . . . . at Lynchburg
13-15 . . . . . Myrtle Beach
16-18 . . . . .Lynchburg
19-22 . . . . at Potomac
23-26 . . . . . . Wilmington
27-29 . . . . Carolina
30 . . . . . . at Wilmington

MAY
1-3 . . . . . . at Wilmington

4-6 . . . . at Winston-Salem
8-10 . . . . .Potomac
11-13 . . . at Myrtle Beach
14-17 . . . . . .at Carolina
18-20 . . . . . .Frederick
22-24 . . . .Winston-Salem
25-27 . . . . . at Frederick
28-29 . . . . . . .Lynchburg
30-31 . . . . at Lynchburg

JUNE
1-3 . . . . Myrtle Beach

4-7 . . . . . . Winston-Salem	27-29 . . . . . . .Lynchburg
8-10 . . . . . . at Potomac	31 . . . . at Potomac
11-13 . . . . . at Wilmington	**AUGUST**
14-17 . . . . Carolina	1-2. . . . . at Potomac
21-23 . . . . . at Lynchburg	3-5. . . . . . . Wilmington
24-27 . . at Winston-Salem	7-9. . . . . Carolina
28-30 . . . . .Potomac	10-12 . . . . at Wilmington
JULY	13-15 . . at Winston-Salem
1-3. . . . . at Myrtle Beach	16-19 . . . . Potomac
4-6. . . . . .at Carolina	20-23 . . . at Myrtle Beach
7-9. . . . . .Frederick	24-26 . . . . . . .at Carolina
11-12 . . . . . . .Lynchburg	28-31 . . . . .Frederick
13-14 . . . . . at Lynchburg	**SEPTEMBER**
16-19 . . . . . . at Frederick	1-3. . . . . .Winston-Salem
20-22 . . . . Wilmington	
23-26 . . . . . Myrtle Beach	

WILMINGTON

APRIL	21-23 . . . . . . .at Carolina
6-8. . . . . at Myrtle Beach	24-27 . . . . . . at Potomac
9-11 . . . . .at Carolina	28-30 . . . . . . .Lynchburg
13-15 . . . . .Frederick	**JULY**
16-18 . . . . Carolina	1-3. . . . . at Frederick
19-22 . . at Winston-Salem	4-6. . . . . . at Lynchburg
23-26 . . . . at Salem	7-9. . . . . . Myrtle Beach
27-29 . . . .Winston-Salem	11-14 . . . . Potomac
30 . . . . Salem	16-19 . . . at Myrtle Beach
MAY	20-22 . . . . at Salem
1-3. . . . . .Salem	23-26 . . . . . . .Frederick
4-6. . . . . at Potomac	27-29 . . . . Carolina
8-10 . . . . . . .Lynchburg	31 . . . at Winston-Salem
11-13 . . . . . . at Frederick	**AUGUST**
14-17 . . . . at Lynchburg	1-2. . . . at Winston-Salem
18-20 . . . . Myrtle Beach	3-5. . . . . at Salem
21-23 . . . . . . .Potomac	7-9. . . . . . .Winston-Salem
25-27 . . at Myrtle Beach	10-12 . . . . .Salem
28-31 . . . . . .at Carolina	13-15 . . . . at Potomac
JUNE	16-19 . . . . . . .Lynchburg
1-3. . . . . .Frederick	20-23 . . . . at Frederick
4-7. . . . . Carolina	24-26 . . . at Lynchburg
8-10 . . . at Winston-Salem	27-30 . . . Myrtle Beach
11-13 . . . . .Salem	**SEPTEMBER**
14-17 . . . .Winston-Salem	1-3. . . . . .Potomac

WINSTON-SALEM

APRIL	25-27 . . . . . . .at Carolina
6-8. . . . . . . .at Carolina	28-31 . . . . . . .Frederick
10-12 . . . . . at Frederick	**JUNE**
13-15 . . . . Carolina	1-3. . . . . Carolina
16-18 . . . at Myrtle Beach	4-7. . . . . at Salem
19-22 . . . . . Wilmington	8-10 . . . . . Wilmington
23-26 . . . . .Potomac	11-13 . . . . Potomac
27-29 . . . at Wilmington	14-17 . . . at Wilmington
30 . . . . at Potomac	21-23 . . . . at Potomac
MAY	24-27 . . . . . . .Salem
1-3. . . . . at Potomac	28-30 . . . . . . .Frederick
4-6. . . . . .Salem	**JULY**
8-10 . . . . . at Frederick	1-3. . . . . at Lynchburg
11-13 . . . . at Lynchburg	4-6. . . . . . Myrtle Beach
14-17 . . . . Myrtle Beach	7-9. . . . . . . .Lynchburg
18-20 . . . . . .Lynchburg	11-14 . . . at Myrtle Beach
22-24 . . . . . . at Salem	16-19 . . . . . .at Carolina

20-22 . . . . .Frederick	10-12 . . . . . . at Potomac
23-26 . . . . Carolina	13-15 . . . . .Salem
27-29 . . . at Myrtle Beach	16-19 . . . . . at Frederick
31 . . . . Wilmington	20-23 . . . . . .Lynchburg
AUGUST	24-26 . . . . Myrtle Beach
1-2. . . . . Wilmington	28-31 . . . . . . .Lynchburg
3-5. . . . . .Potomac	**SEPTEMBER**
7-9. . . . at Wilmington	1-3. . . . . at Salem

FLORIDA STATE LEAGUE

BRADENTON

APRIL	21 . . . . Charlotte
5-6. . . . . St. Lucie	22-23 . . . . . .at Charlotte
7 . . . . at St. Lucie	24-27 . . . . . at Dunedin
9-11 . . . . . at Palm Beach	28-30 . . . . . . Palm Beach
12 . . . . . at Fort Myers	**JULY**
13 . . . . .Fort Myers	1 . . . . at Charlotte
14 . . . . . at Fort Myers	2-3. . . . . Charlotte
15-17 . . . . . Palm Beach	4-6. . . . . . Palm Beach
19 . . . . . at Fort Myers	7 . . . . at St. Lucie
20-21 . . . . . . .Fort Myers	8-9. . . . . St. Lucie
22-24 . . . . Jupiter	11-14 . . . . Brevard County
25-27 . . . . .at Charlotte	15-18 . . . . .at Clearwater
28-30 . . . . . at Jupiter	19-22 . . . . Tampa
MAY	23-25 . . . . . at St. Lucie
1-3. . . . . Charlotte	26-29 . . . . Daytona
4-7. . . . . .at Tampa	30-31 . . . . at Lakeland
8-11 . . . . Clearwater	**AUGUST**
12 . . . . St. Lucie	1-2. . . . . at Lakeland
14-16 . . . . at St. Lucie	3-5. . . . . . Palm Beach
17-20 . . . . . .Dunedin	7-9. . . . . . .at Charlotte
22-24 . . . . . . .Lakeland	10-12 . . . at Palm Beach
25-27 . . . . . at Jupiter	14-16 . . . . . . Charlotte
29-31 . . . . . .Fort Myers	17-19 . . . . Jupiter
JUNE	21-23 . . . . at Fort Myers
1-4. . . . .at Brevard County	24-26 . . . . . at Jupiter
5-8. . . . . . at Daytona	27-29 . . . . . .Fort Myers
9-11 . . . . Jupiter	30-31 . . . . . at St. Lucie
12-14 . . . . . at Fort Myers	**SEPTEMBER**
18-20 . . . . St. Lucie	1-2. . . . . St. Lucie

BREVARD COUNTY

APRIL	17-20 . . . . . . .Fort Myers
5 . . . . Daytona	21-24 . . . . . .at Charlotte
6 . . . . at Daytona	25-27 . . . . . at Dunedin
7 . . . . Daytona	29-30 . . . . Daytona
9-11 . . . . at Lakeland	31 . . . . at Daytona
12-14 . . . . . . .Dunedin	**JUNE**
15-17 . . . . . .Lakeland	1-4. . . . . .Bradenton
19-21 . . . . . at Dunedin	5-8. . . . . . . at Jupiter
22-24 . . . . .at Clearwater	9-11 . . . . .Lakeland
25-27 . . . . Tampa	12-13 . . . . Daytona
28-30 . . . . Clearwater	14 . . . . at Daytona
MAY	18-20 . . . . at Lakeland
1-3. . . . . .at Tampa	21-23 . . . . . . Dunedin
4-7. . . . at Palm Beach	24-27 . . . . . . Charlotte
8-11 . . . . St. Lucie	28-30 . . . . Tampa
12 . . . . . at Daytona	**JULY**
14-16 . . . . Daytona	1-3. . . . . . . at Clearwater

4-6 . . . . Tampa
7-9 . . . . Charlotte
11-14 . . . . . at Bradenton
15-18 . . . at St. Lucie
19-22 . . . . . Palm Beach
23 . . . . at Daytona
24 . . . . Daytona
25 . . . . at Daytona
26-29 . . . . . at Fort Myers
30-31 . . . . Jupiter

AUGUST
1-2 . . . . Jupiter

CHARLOTTE

APRIL
5 . . . . Fort Myers
6-7 . . . . . . at Fort Myers
9-11 . . . . . at St. Lucie
12-14 . . . . Jupiter
15-17 . . . . St. Lucie
19-21 . . . . . . at Jupiter
22-24 . . . . at Palm Beach
25-27 . . . . . . Bradenton
28-30 . . . . . Palm Beach

MAY
1-3 . . . . . . at Bradenton
4-7 . . . . . . at Clearwater
8-11 . . . . Daytona
12 . . . . Fort Myers
14 . . . . Fort Myers
15-16 . . . . . at Fort Myers
17-20 . . . . at Tampa
21-24 . . . Brevard County
25-27 . . . . at St. Lucie
29-31 . . . . Jupiter

JUNE
1-4 . . . . Dunedin
5-8 . . . . at Lakeland
9-11 . . . . St. Lucie
12-14 . . . . . . at Jupiter
18-20 . . . . . Palm Beach
21 . . . . at Bradenton
22-23 . . . . . . Bradenton
24-27 . . at Brevard County
28 . . . . Fort Myers

CLEARWATER

APRIL
5 . . . . at Dunedin
6 . . . . Dunedin
7 . . . . at Dunedin
9-11 . . . . Tampa
12-14 . . . . Lakeland
15-17 . . . . at Tampa
19-21 . . . . . at Lakeland
22-24 . . . Brevard County
25-27 . . . . Daytona
28-30 . . at Brevard County

MAY
1-3 . . . . at Daytona
4-7 . . . . Charlotte
8-11 . . . . . at Bradenton
12 . . . . at Dunedin

3-5 . . . . .at Tampa
7-9 . . . . Dunedin
10-12 . . . . Tampa
14-16 . . . . . at Dunedin
17-19 . . . at Clearwater
21-23 . . . . . . .Lakeland
24-26 . . . . . Clearwater
27-29 . . . . at Lakeland
30-31 . . . . . at Daytona

SEPTEMBER
1-2 . . . . at Daytona

29 . . . . at Fort Myers
30 . . . . .Fort Myers

JULY
1 . . . . .Bradenton
2-3 . . . . . . at Bradenton
4 . . . . .Fort Myers
5 . . . . at Fort Myers
6 . . . . .Fort Myers
7-9 . . . . . at Palm Beach
11-14 . . . . .Lakeland
15-18 . . . . . . at Daytona
19-22 . . . . . Clearwater
23 . . . . . at Fort Myers
24-25 . . . . . .Fort Myers
26-29 . . . . . at Dunedin
30-31 . . . . Tampa

AUGUST
1-2 . . . . Tampa
3-5 . . . . at Jupiter
7-9 . . . . .Bradenton
10-12 . . . . Jupiter
14-16 . . . . . at Bradenton
17-19 . . . . St. Lucie
21-23 . . . at Palm Beach
24-26 . . . . at St. Lucie
27-29 . . . . . Palm Beach
30-31 . . . at Fort Myers

SEPTEMBER
1 . . . . at Fort Myers
2 . . . . .Fort Myers

14 . . . . at Dunedin
15-16 . . . . Dunedin
17-20 . . . . Jupiter
21-24 . . . . at Fort Myers
25-27 . . . . . . at Daytona
29 . . . . Tampa
30-31 . . . . . . .at Tampa

JUNE
1-4 . . . . Palm Beach
5-8 . . . . at St. Lucie
9-11 . . . . . . at Dunedin
12 . . . . Tampa
13 . . . . .at Tampa
14 . . . . Tampa
18-20 . . . . Dunedin
21-23 . . . . Daytona

24-27 . . . . at Palm Beach
28-30 . . . . .Lakeland

JULY
1-3 . . . . . Brevard County
4-6 . . . . at Lakeland
7-9 . . . .at Brevard County
11-14 . . . . . . .Fort Myers
15-18 . . . . . . .Bradenton
19-22 . . . . . . at Charlotte
23-24 . . . . .Dunedin
25 . . . . at Dunedin
26-29 . . . . at Jupiter
30-31 . . . . . . at St. Lucie

DAYTONA

APRIL
5 . . . . .at Brevard County
6 . . . . . . Brevard County
7 . . . .at Brevard County
9-11 . . . . Dunedin
12-14 . . . . .at Tampa
15-17 . . . . . at Dunedin
19-21 . . . . Tampa
22-23 . . . . .Lakeland
24 . . . . at Lakeland
25-27 . . . . . at Clearwater
28 . . . . .Lakeland
29-30 . . . . . . at Lakeland

MAY
1-3 . . . . Clearwater
4-7 . . . . Jupiter
8-11 . . . . . . at Charlotte
12 . . . . . . Brevard County
14-16 . . at Brevard County
17-20 . . . . at Palm Beach
21-24 . . . . St. Lucie
25-27 . . . . . . Clearwater
29-30 . . at Brevard County
31 . . . . . Brevard County

JUNE
1-4 . . . . at Fort Myers
5-8 . . . . .Bradenton
9-11 . . . . .at Tampa
12-13 . . .at Brevard County
14 . . . . . . Brevard County

DUNEDIN

APRIL
5 . . . . Clearwater
6 . . . . .at Clearwater
7 . . . . Clearwater
9-11 . . . . at Daytona
12-14 . . .at Brevard County
15-17 . . . . Daytona
19-21 . . . . . Brevard County
22-24 . . . . . . .at Tampa
25-27 . . . . at Lakeland
28-30 . . . . Tampa

MAY
1-3 . . . . .Lakeland

AUGUST
1-2 . . . . St. Lucie
3-5 . . . . at Lakeland
7-9 . . . . Tampa
10-12 . . . . .Lakeland
14-16 . . . . .at Tampa
17-19 . . . . Brevard County
21-23 . . . . Daytona
24-26 . . . . . Brevard County
27-29 . . . . . at Daytona
30 . . . . Dunedin
31 . . . . at Dunedin

SEPTEMBER
1 . . . . Dunedin
2 . . . . at Dunedin

18-20 . . . . Tampa
21-23 . . . . .at Clearwater
24-27 . . . . at St. Lucie
28-30 . . . . Dunedin

JULY
1-3 . . . . .Lakeland
4-6 . . . . at Dunedin
7-9 . . . . at Lakeland
11-14 . . . . . Palm Beach
15-18 . . . . Charlotte
19-22 . . . . Jupiter
23 . . . . . Brevard County
24 . . . . .at Brevard County
25 . . . . . Brevard County
26-29 . . . . . at Bradenton
30-31 . . . . . . .Fort Myers

AUGUST
1-2 . . . . .Fort Myers
3-5 . . . . at Dunedin
7-9 . . . . .Lakeland
10-12 . . . . Dunedin
14-16 . . . . . at Lakeland
17-19 . . . . Tampa
21-23 . . . . .at Clearwater
24-26 . . . . .at Tampa
27-29 . . . . . Clearwater
30-31 . . . Brevard County

SEPTEMBER
1-2 . . . . . Brevard County

4-7 . . . . at St. Lucie
8-11 . . . . .Fort Myers
12 . . . . Clearwater
14 . . . . Clearwater
15-16 . . . . .at Clearwater
17-20 . . . . at Bradenton
21-24 . . . . Jupiter
25-27 . . . . Brevard County
29-31 . . . . .Lakeland

JUNE
1-4 . . . . . . .at Charlotte
5-8 . . . . Palm Beach
9-11 . . . . Clearwater

12-14 . . . . . . at Lakeland
18-20 . . . . at Clearwater
21-23 . . .at Brevard County
24-27 . . . . . . .Bradenton
28-30 . . . . . at Daytona

JULY
1-3 . . . . .at Tampa
4-6 . . . . Daytona
7-9 . . . . Tampa
11-14 . . . . . at Jupiter
15-18 . . . . . at Fort Myers
19-22 . . . . St. Lucie
23-24 . . . . at Clearwater
25 . . . . Clearwater
26-29 . . . . . .at Charlotte
30-31 . . . . at Palm Beach

AUGUST
1-2 . . . . . at Palm Beach
3-5 . . . . Daytona
7-9 . . . .at Brevard County
10-12 . . . . . . at Daytona
14-16 . . . . Brevard County
17-19 . . . . . . at Lakeland
21-23 . . . . .at Tampa
24-26 . . . . . . .Lakeland
27-29 . . . . Tampa
30 . . . . . . .at Clearwater
31 . . . . Clearwater

SEPTEMBER
1 . . . . .at Clearwater
2 . . . . Clearwater

FORT MYERS

APRIL
5 . . . . .at Charlotte
5-7 . . . . Charlotte
9-11 . . . . Jupiter
12 . . . . .Bradenton
13 . . . . . . at Bradenton
14 . . . . .Bradenton
15-17 . . . . . . at Jupiter
19 . . . . .Bradenton
20-21 . . . . . at Bradenton
22-24 . . . . . at St. Lucie
25-28 . . . . . Palm Beach
29-31 . . . . St. Lucie

MAY
1-3 . . . . . . at Palm Beach
4-7 . . . . .Lakeland
8-11 . . . . at Dunedin
12 . . . . . .at Charlotte
14 . . . . . .at Charlotte
15-16 . . . . Charlotte
17-20 . . .at Brevard County
21-24 . . . . . Clearwater
25-27 . . . . . . Palm Beach
29-31 . . . . . at Bradenton

JUNE
1-4 . . . . Daytona
5-8 . . . . .at Tampa
9-11 . . . . . at Palm Beach
12-14 . . . . . .Bradenton
18-20 . . . . at Jupiter
21-23 . . . . . at St. Lucie

24-27 . . . . Tampa
28 . . . . at Charlotte
29 . . . . Charlotte
30 . . . . .at Charlotte

JULY
1-3 . . . . St. Lucie
4 . . . . .at Charlotte
5 . . . . Charlotte
6 . . . . .at Charlotte
7-9 . . . . Jupiter
11-14 . . . .at Clearwater
15-18 . . . . Dunedin
19-22 . . . . . at Lakeland
23 . . . . Charlotte
24-25 . . . . . at Charlotte
26-29 . . . . Brevard County
30-31 . . . . . . at Daytona

AUGUST
1-2 . . . . at Daytona
3-5 . . . . at St. Lucie
7-9 . . . . Jupiter
10-12 . . . . . . St. Lucie
14-16 . . . . . . at Jupiter
17-19 . . . at Palm Beach
21-23 . . . . . . .Bradenton
24-26 . . . . . Palm Beach
27-29 . . . . at Bradenton
30-31 . . . . Charlotte

SEPTEMBER
1 . . . . Charlotte
2 . . . . .at Charlotte

JUPITER

APRIL
5 . . . . Palm Beach
6-7 . . . . . . at Palm Beach
9-11 . . . . . at Fort Myers
12-14 . . . .at Charlotte
15-17 . . . . . . .Fort Myers
19-21 . . . . . . Charlotte
22-24 . . . . at Bradenton
25-27 . . . . St. Lucie
28-30 . . . . . . .Bradenton

MAY
1-3 . . . . at St. Lucie

4-7 . . . . at Daytona
8-11 . . . . Tampa
12 . . . . . . at Palm Beach
14-16 . . . . . Palm Beach
17-20 . . . . .at Clearwater
22-24 . . . . . . at Dunedin
25-27 . . . . . . .Bradenton
29-31 . . . . . .at Charlotte

JUNE
1-4 . . . . .Lakeland
5-8 . . . . . Brevard County
9-11 . . . . . at Bradenton

12-14 . . . . Charlotte
18-20 . . . . .Fort Myers
21-23 . . . . . at Palm Beach
24-27 . . . . . at Lakeland
28-30 . . . . St. Lucie

JULY
1-3 . . . . Palm Beach
4-6 . . . . St. Lucie
7-9 . . . . . at Fort Myers
11-14 . . . . Dunedin
15-18 . . . . . .at Tampa
19-22 . . . . Daytona
23-24 . . . . . . Palm Beach
25 . . . . . . at Palm Beach
26-29 . . . . . . Clearwater

LAKELAND

APRIL
5-6 . . . . .at Tampa
7 . . . . Tampa
9-11 . . . . Brevard County
12-14 . . . .at Clearwater
15-17 . . .at Brevard County
19-21 . . . . . . Clearwater
22-23 . . . . at Daytona
24 . . . . Daytona
25-27 . . . . . . Dunedin
28 . . . . . . at Daytona
29-30 . . . . . . Daytona

MAY
1-3 . . . . . . at Dunedin
4-7 . . . . . at Fort Myers
8-11 . . . . . Palm Beach
12 . . . . .at Tampa
14-16 . . . . . .at Tampa
17-20 . . . . . St. Lucie
21-24 . . . . at Bradenton
25-27 . . . . Tampa
29-31 . . . . . at Dunedin

JUNE
1-4 . . . . at Jupiter
5-8 . . . . Charlotte
9-11 . . . .at Brevard County
12-14 . . . . . . Dunedin
18-20 . . . . Brevard County
21-22 . . . . . .at Tampa

23 . . . . Tampa
24-27 . . . . Jupiter
28-30 . . . . .at Clearwater

JULY
1-3 . . . . at Daytona
4-6 . . . . Clearwater
7-9 . . . . Daytona
11-14 . . . . at Charlotte
15-18 . . . at Palm Beach
19-22 . . . . . .Fort Myers
23 . . . . .at Tampa
24 . . . . Tampa
25 . . . . .at Tampa
26-29 . . . . at St. Lucie
30-31 . . . . . .Bradenton

AUGUST
1-2 . . . . .Bradenton
3-5 . . . . Clearwater
7-9 . . . . . . at Daytona
10-12 . . . . .at Clearwater
14-16 . . . . . . Daytona
17-19 . . . . . . Dunedin
21-23 . . .at Brevard County
24-26 . . . . . at Dunedin
27-29 . . . . Brevard County
30-31 . . . . Tampa

SEPTEMBER
1-2 . . . . Tampa

30-31 . . .at Brevard County

AUGUST
1-2 . . . .at Brevard County
3-5 . . . . Charlotte
7-9 . . . . at Fort Myers
10-12 . . . . .at Charlotte
14-16 . . . . . . .Fort Myers
17-19 . . . . at Bradenton
21-23 . . . . at St. Lucie
24-26 . . . . . .Bradenton
27-29 . . . . St. Lucie
30-31 . . . at Palm Beach

SEPTEMBER
1 . . . . at Palm Beach
2 . . . . Palm Beach

PALM BEACH

APRIL
5 . . . . at Jupiter
6-7 . . . . Jupiter
9-11 . . . . .Bradenton
12-14 . . . . St. Lucie
15-17 . . . at Bradenton
19-21 . . . . . at St. Lucie
22-24 . . . . . . Charlotte
25-27 . . . at Fort Myers
28-30 . . . . . .at Charlotte

MAY
1-3 . . . . .Fort Myers
4-7 . . . . . Brevard County
8-11 . . . . . . at Lakeland

12 . . . . Jupiter
14-16 . . . . . . at Jupiter
17-20 . . . . . . Daytona
21-24 . . . . Tampa
25-27 . . . at Fort Myers
29-31 . . . . . . St. Lucie

JUNE
1-4 . . . . . .at Clearwater
5-8 . . . . at Dunedin
9-11 . . . . . .Fort Myers
12-14 . . . . . at St. Lucie
18-20 . . . . .at Charlotte
21-23 . . . . Jupiter
24-27 . . . . . . Clearwater

28-30 . . . . . . at Bradenton

JULY
1-3 . . . . at Jupiter
4-6 . . . . .Bradenton
7-9 . . . . Charlotte
11-14 . . . . . . at Daytona
15-18 . . . . . . .Lakeland
19-22 . . .at Brevard County
23-24 . . . . at Jupiter
25 . . . . Jupiter
26-29 . . . . .at Tampa
30-31 . . . . .Dunedin

ST. LUCIE

APRIL
5-6 . . . . at Bradenton
7 . . . . .Bradenton
9-11 . . . . Charlotte
12-14 . . . at Palm Beach
15-17 . . . .at Charlotte
19-21 . . . . . . Palm Beach
22-24 . . . . . . .Fort Myers
25-27 . . . . . . at Jupiter
28-30 . . . . . at Fort Myers

MAY
1-3 . . . . Jupiter
4-7 . . . . .Dunedin
8-11 . . . .at Brevard County
12 . . . . at Bradenton
14-16 . . . . . . .Bradenton
17-20 . . . . . . at Lakeland
21-24 . . . . . at Daytona
25-27 . . . . . . Charlotte
29-31 . . . . . at Palm Beach

JUNE
1-4 . . . . Tampa
5-8 . . . . Clearwater
9-11 . . . . . . .at Charlotte
12-14 . . . . Palm Beach
18-20 . . . at Bradenton
21-23 . . . . . .Fort Myers
24-27 . . . . . . Daytona
28-30 . . . . . at Jupiter

JULY
1-3 . . . . at Fort Myers
4-6 . . . . Jupiter
7 . . . . .Bradenton
8-9 . . . . at Bradenton
11-14 . . . . . . .at Tampa
15-18 . . . . Brevard County
19-22 . . . . . at Dunedin
23-25 . . . . . . .Bradenton
26-29 . . . . . . .Lakeland
30-31 . . . . . .at Clearwater

AUGUST
1-2 . . . . Dunedin
3-5 . . . . at Bradenton
7-9 . . . . St. Lucie
10-12 . . . . . . .Bradenton
14-16 . . . . . . at St. Lucie
17-19 . . . . . . .Fort Myers
21-23 . . . . Charlotte
24-26 . . . . at Fort Myers
27-29 . . . . . .at Charlotte
30-31 . . . . Jupiter

SEPTEMBER
1 . . . . Jupiter
2 . . . . at Jupiter

AUGUST
1-2 . . . . . . .at Clearwater
3-5 . . . . .Fort Myers
7-9 . . . . . at Palm Beach
10-12 . . . at Fort Myers
14-16 . . . . . . Palm Beach
17-19 . . . . . . at Charlotte

TAMPA

APRIL
5-6 . . . . .Lakeland
7 . . . . at Lakeland
9-11 . . . . . .at Clearwater
12-14 . . . . Daytona
15-17 . . . . . . Clearwater
19-21 . . . . . . at Daytona
22-24 . . . . Dunedin
25-27 . . .at Brevard County
28-30 . . . . . . at Dunedin

MAY
1-3 . . . . . Brevard County
4-7 . . . . .Bradenton
8-11 . . . . at Jupiter
12 . . . . .Lakeland
14-16 . . . . .Lakeland
17-20 . . . . Charlotte
21-24 . . . at Palm Beach
25-27 . . . . . at Lakeland
29 . . . . .at Clearwater
30-31 . . . . Clearwater

JUNE
1-4 . . . . at St. Lucie
5-8 . . . . .Fort Myers
9-11 . . . . Daytona
12 . . . . . .at Clearwater
13 . . . . Clearwater
14 . . . . .at Clearwater
18-20 . . . . . . at Daytona
21-22 . . . . . . .Lakeland

23 . . . . at Lakeland
24-27 . . . . . at Fort Myers
28-30 . . . . . Brevard County

JULY
1-3 . . . . .Dunedin
4-6 . . . .at Brevard County
7-9 . . . . at Dunedin
11-14 . . . . St. Lucie
15-18 . . . . Jupiter
19-22 . . . . at Bradenton
23 . . . . .Lakeland
24 . . . . at Lakeland
25 . . . . .Lakeland
26-29 . . . . . . Palm Beach
30-31 . . . . . .at Charlotte

AUGUST
1-2 . . . . .at Charlotte
3-5 . . . . . Brevard County
7-9 . . . . . . .at Clearwater
10-12 . . .at Brevard County
14-16 . . . . Clearwater
17-19 . . . . . . at Daytona
21-23 . . . . Dunedin
24-26 . . . . Daytona
27-29 . . . . . at Dunedin
30-31 . . . . . .at Lakeland

SEPTEMBER
1-2 . . . . at Lakeland

21-23 . . . . Jupiter
24-26 . . . . Charlotte
27-29 . . . . . . at Jupiter
30-31 . . . . . . .Bradenton

SEPTEMBER
1-2 . . . . at Bradenton

LOW CLASS A

MIDWEST LEAGUE

BELOIT

APRIL
5-7 . . . . Peoria
9-11 . . . . at Kane County
12-15 . . . . . at Clinton
16-18 . . . . . Kane County
19-21 . . . . at South Bend
22-24 . . . at West Michigan
25-27 . . . .Bowling Green
28-30 . . . . .Dayton

MAY
2-4 . . . . . at Cedar Rapids
5-8 . . . . Kane County

9-11 . . . . .at Peoria
12-15 . . . . .Clinton
16-18 . . . . . . Quad Cities
19-21 . . . . at Burlington
23-25 . . . . . Cedar Rapids
26-29 . . . . at Kane County
30-31 . . . . at Quad Cities

JUNE
1 . . . . at Quad Cities
2-4 . . . . Wisconsin
6-8 . . . . at Burlington
9-11 . . . . . . at Wisconsin

12-14 . . . . Peoria
15-17 . . . . . . .Burlington
22-24 . . . . at Cedar Rapids
25-27 . . . . at Kane County
28-30 . . . . .Clinton

JULY
1-3 . . . . Cedar Rapids
4-6 . . . . at Clinton
7-9 . . . . .Burlington
11-13 . . . . .at Fort Wayne
14-16 . . . . .at Lake County
18-20 . . . . Lansing
21-23 . . . . Great Lakes
25-27 . . . . . at Burlington
28-30 . . . . .at Peoria

31 . . . . Kane County

AUGUST
1-3 . . . . Kane County
4-7 . . . . Wisconsin
8-10 . . . . . at Quad Cities
11-13 . . . . Peoria
15-17 . . . . Wisconsin
18-21 . . . . at Quad Cities
22-24 . . . . Peoria
25-28 . . . . at Cedar Rapids
29-31 . . . . . at Wisconsin

SEPTEMBER
1-3 . . . . Quad Cities

BOWLING GREEN

APRIL
5-7 . . . . South Bend
9-11 . . . . . West Michigan
12-15 . . . . .at Lake County
16-18 . . . . . . Great Lakes
19-21 . . . . . Cedar Rapids
22-24 . . . . . . Quad Cities
25-27 . . . . at Beloit
28-30 . . . . . at Wisconsin

MAY
2-4. . . . . . at South Bend
5-8. . . . . . Lake County
9-11 . . . . .at Lansing
12-15 . . . . . South Bend
16-18 . . . . Dayton
19-21 . . . . .at Fort Wayne
23-25 . . . . at Great Lakes
26-29 . . . . .at Fort Wayne
30-31 . . . . Lansing

JUNE
1 . . . . Lansing
2-4. . . . . Dayton
6-8. . . . . .at Lansing
9-11 . . . . at Dayton
12-14 . . . . West Michigan
15-17 . . . . . . Fort Wayne
22-24 . . . . at Dayton

25-27 . . . at West Michigan
28-30 . . . . Lansing

JULY
1-3. . . . . .Dayton
4-6. . . . . . .at Fort Wayne
7-9. . . . . . . Lake County
11-13 . . . . at Burlington
14-16 . . . . .at Peoria
18-20 . . . . Kane County
21-23 . . . . .Clinton
25-27 . . . . . . .at Lansing
28-30 . . . West Michigan
31 . . . . Great Lakes

AUGUST
1-3. . . . . Great Lakes
4-7. . . . . . .at Fort Wayne
8-10 . . . . South Bend
11-13 . . at West Michigan
15-17 . . . . at Great Lakes
18-21 . . . . . . South Bend
22-24 . . . . Dayton
25-28 . . . . at South Bend
29-31 . . . .at Lake County

SEPTEMBER
1-3. . . . . Fort Wayne

BURLINGTON

APRIL
5-7. . . . . at Clinton
9-11 . . . . Wisconsin
12-15 . . . . . Kane County
16-18 . . . . . at Wisconsin
19-21 . . . . Lansing
22-24 . . . . . . Great Lakes
25-27 . . . . .at Fort Wayne
28-30 . . . .at Lake County

MAY
2-4. . . . . . . Quad Cities
5-8. . . . . at Clinton
9-11 . . . . . .Cedar Rapids
12-15 . . . . . . .at Peoria
16-18 . . . . . at Wisconsin
19-21 . . . . Beloit
23-25 . . . at Kane County
26-29 . . . . Clinton
30-31 . . . . Peoria

JUNE
1 . . . . Peoria
2-4. . . . . . at Quad Cities
6-8. . . . . Beloit
9-11 . . . . Quad Cities
12-14 . . . at Cedar Rapids
15-17 . . . . at Beloit
22-24 . . . . Wisconsin

25-27 . . . . at Cedar Rapids
28-30 . . . . at Kane County

JULY
1-3. . . . . .Clinton
4-6. . . . . .at Peoria
7-9. . . . . at Beloit
11-13 . . . .Bowling Green
14-16 . . . . Dayton
18-20 . . . . at South Bend
21-23 . . at West Michigan
25-27 . . . . .Beloit
28-30 . . . . . Cedar Rapids
31 . . . . 'at Wisconsin

AUGUST
1-3. . . . . . . at Wisconsin
4-7. . . . . Quad Cities
8-10 . . . . Peoria
11-13 . . . . at Quad Cities
15-17 . . . . . . .at Peoria
18 . . . . Kane County
20-21 . . . . Kane County
22-24 . . . . .Clinton
25-27 . . . at Kane County
29-31 . . . . at Clinton

SEPTEMBER
1-3. . . . . Wisconsin

CEDAR RAPIDS

APRIL
5-7. . . . . at Wisconsin
9-11 . . . . .Clinton
12-15 . . . . . . Quad Cities
16-18 . . . . at Peoria
19-21 . . at Bowling Green
22-24 . . . . . . at Dayton
26-28 . . . . . South Bend
29-30 . . . West Michigan

MAY
1 . . . . West Michigan
2-4. . . . . .Beloit
5-8. . . . . . at Wisconsin
9-11 . . . . . . at Burlington
12-15 . . . . at Quad Cities
16-18 . . . . . Kane County
19-21 . . . . Peoria
23-25 . . . . . . at Beloit
26-29 . . . . . Quad Cities
30-31 . . . . Wisconsin

JUNE
1 . . . . Wisconsin
2-4. . . . . at Clinton
6-8. . . . . . . .at Peoria
9-11 . . . . .Clinton
12-14 . . . . . . .Burlington
15-17 . . at Kane County

22-24 . . . . Beloit
25-27 . . . . . .Burlington
28-30 . . . at Quad Cities

JULY
1-3. . . . . at Beloit
4-6. . . . . Wisconsin
7-9. . . . . Peoria
11-13 . . . at Great Lakes
14-16 . . . . . .at Lansing
18-20 . . . . . . Fort Wayne
21-23 . . . . Lake County
25-27 . . . . . . .at Peoria
28-30 . . . at Burlington
31 . . . . .Clinton

AUGUST
1-3. . . . . .Clinton
4-7. . . . . at Kane County
8-10 . . . . . . at Wisconsin
11-13 . . . . Kane County
15-17 . . . . . . Quad Cities
18-21 . . . . . . at Clinton
22-24 . . . . at Wisconsin
25-28 . . . . .Beloit
29-31 . . . . . .at Peoria

SEPTEMBER
1-3. . . . . .Clinton

CLINTON

APRIL
5-7. . . . . .Burlington
9-11 . . . . at Cedar Rapids
12-15 . . . . .Beloit
16-18 . . . . at Quad Cities
19-21 . . . . . Lake County
22-24 . . . . . . Fort Wayne
25-27 . . . at Great Lakes
28-30 . . . .at Lansing

MAY
2-4. . . . . Wisconsin
5-8. . . . . .Burlington
9-11 . . . . .at Kane City
12-15 . . . . at Beloit
16-18 . . . . Peoria
19-21 . . . . . Quad Cities
23-25 . . . . . . .at Peoria
26-29 . . . . at Burlington
30-31 . . . . Kane County

JUNE
1 . . . . Kane County
2-4. . . . . . Cedar Rapids
6-8. . . . . . at Wisconsin
9-11 . . . . at Cedar Rapids
12-14 . . . . Wisconsin
15-17 . . . . . .at Peoria
22-24 . . . . . Kane County

25-27 . . . . Peoria
28-30 . . . . at Beloit

JULY
1-3. . . . . . at Burlington
4-6. . . . . .Beloit
7-9. . . . . at Quad Cities
11-13 . . . West Michigan
14-16 . . . . . . South Bend
18-20 . . . . . . at Dayton
21-23 . . at Bowling Green
25-27 . . . . . Quad Cities
28-30 . . . . Wisconsin
31 . . . . . . at Cedar Rapids

AUGUST
1-3. . . . . at Cedar Rapids
4-7. . . . . at Peoria
8-10 . . . . . Kane County
11-13 . . . . at Wisconsin
15-17 . . . at Kane County
18-21 . . . . . Cedar Rapids
22-24 . . . . at Burlington
25-28 . . . . Quad Cities
29-31 . . . . . .Burlington

SEPTEMBER
1-3. . . . . . at Cedar Rapids

DAYTON

APRIL	
5-7	West Michigan
9-11	Lansing
12-15	at South Bend
16-18	at Fort Wayne
19-21	Quad Cities
22-24	Cedar Rapids
25-27	at Wisconsin
28-30	at Beloit

MAY	
2-4	Lake County
5-8	Fort Wayne
9-11	at Lake County
12-15	Lansing
16-18	at Bowling Green
19-21	Great Lakes
23-25	at Lansing
26-29	at West Michigan
30-31	South Bend

JUNE	
1	South Bend
2-4	at Bowling Green
6-8	Lake County
9-11	Bowling Green
12-14	Great Lakes
15-17	Lake County
22-24	Bowling Green
25-27	Lake County
28-30	at South Bend

JULY	
1-3	at Bowling Green
4-6	South Bend
7-9	Great Lakes
11-13	at Peoria
14-16	at Burlington
18-20	Clinton
21-23	Kane County
25-27	at Great Lakes
28-30	at Lake County
31	Lansing

AUGUST	
1-3	Lansing
4-7	at Great Lakes
8-10	at Lansing
11-13	Fort Wayne
15-17	Lake County
18-21	at Fort Wayne
22-24	at Bowling Green
25-28	West Michigan
29-31	Great Lakes

SEPTEMBER	
1-3	at West Michigan

FORT WAYNE

APRIL	
5-7	Lake County
9-11	at South Bend
12-15	at Great Lakes
16-18	Dayton
19-21	at Kane County
22-24	at Clinton
25-27	Burlington
28-30	Peoria

MAY	
2-4	at West Michigan
5-8	at Dayton
9-11	South Bend
12-15	West Michigan
16-18	at Lansing
19-21	Bowling Green
23-25	at South Bend
26-29	Bowling Green
30-31	Great Lakes

JUNE	
1	Great Lakes
2-4	at Lake County
6-8	at West Michigan
9-11	South Bend
12-14	Lansing
15-17	at Bowling Green
22-24	Lake County
25-27	Lansing
28-30	at Great Lakes

JULY	
1-3	at Lake County
4-6	Bowling Green
7-9	at South Bend
11-13	Beloit
14-16	Wisconsin
18-20	at Cedar Rapids
21-23	at Quad Cities
25-27	South Bend
28-30	Great Lakes
31	at South Bend

AUGUST	
1-3	at South Bend
4-7	Bowling Green
8-10	West Michigan
11-13	at Dayton
15-17	at Lansing
18-21	Dayton
22-24	at West Michigan
25-28	at Lansing
29-31	West Michigan

SEPTEMBER	
1-3	at Bowling Green

GREAT LAKES

APRIL	
6-7	at Lansing
9-11	Lake County
12-15	Fort Wayne
16-18	at Bowling Green
19-21	at Peoria
22-24	at Burlington
25-27	Clinton
28-30	Kane County

MAY	
2-4	Lansing
5-8	at South Bend
9-11	at West Michigan
12-15	at Lake County
16-18	West Michigan
19-21	at Dayton
23-25	Bowling Green
26-29	South Bend
30-31	at Fort Wayne

JUNE	
1	at Fort Wayne
2-4	West Michigan
6-8	at South Bend
9-11	at West Michigan
12-14	Dayton
15-17	Lansing
22-24	at Lansing

JULY	
1-3	West Michigan
4-6	at Lansing
7-9	at Dayton
11-13	Cedar Rapids
14-16	Quad Cities
18-20	at Wisconsin
21-23	at Beloit
25-27	Dayton
28-30	at Fort Wayne
31	at Bowling Green

AUGUST	
1-3	at Bowling Green
4-7	Dayton
8-10	at Lake County
11-13	Lansing
15-17	Bowling Green
18-21	at West Michigan
22-24	Lansing
25-28	Lake County
29-31	at Dayton

SEPTEMBER	
1-3	South Bend

KANE COUNTY

APRIL	
5-7	at Quad Cities
9-11	Beloit
12-15	at Burlington
16-18	at Beloit
19-21	Fort Wayne
22-24	Lake County
25-27	at Lansing
28-30	at Great Lakes

MAY	
2-4	Peoria
5-8	at Beloit
9-11	Clinton
12-15	Wisconsin
16-18	at Cedar Rapids
19-21	at Wisconsin
23-25	Burlington
26-29	Beloit
30-31	at Clinton

JUNE	
1	at Clinton
2-4	Peoria
6-8	Quad Cities
9-11	at Peoria
12-14	at Quad Cities
15-17	Cedar Rapids
22-24	at Clinton

JULY	
1-3	at Peoria
4-6	Quad Cities
7-9	at Wisconsin
11-13	South Bend
14-16	West Michigan
18-20	at Bowling Green
21-23	at Daytona
25-27	Wisconsin
28-30	Quad Cities
31	at Beloit

AUGUST	
1-3	at Beloit
4-7	Cedar Rapids
8-10	at Clinton
11-13	at Cedar Rapids
15-17	Clinton
18	at Burlington
20-21	at Burlington
22-24	at Quad Cities
25-28	Burlington
29-31	at Quad Cities

SEPTEMBER	
1-3	Peoria

LAKE COUNTY

APRIL
5-7 . . . . at Fort Worth
9-11 . . . . . at Great Lakes
12-15 . . . . Bowling Green
16-18 . . . . . West Michigan
19-21 . . . . . . at Clinton
22-24 . . . at Kane County
25-27 . . . . Peoria
28-30 . . . . .Burlington

MAY
2-4 . . . . at Dayton
5-8 . . . . at Bowling Green
9-11 . . . . .Dayton
12-15 . . . . . . Great Lakes
16-18 . . . . at South Bend
19-21 . . . . Lansing
23-26 . . . at West Michigan
27-29 . . . . .at Lansing
30-31 . . . . West Michigan

JUNE
1 . . . . West Michigan
2-4 . . . . Fort Wayne
6-8 . . . . at Dayton
9-11 . . . . . . .at Lansing
12-14 . . . . . . South Bend
15-17 . . . . .Dayton

22-24 . . . . . .at Fort Wayne
25-27 . . . . at Dayton
28-30 . . . . . West Michigan

JULY
1-3 . . . . Fort Wayne
4-6 . . . . at West Michigan
7-9 . . . . at Bowling Green
11-13 . . . . Wisconsin
14-16 . . . . Beloit
18-20 . . . . at Quad Cities
21-23 . . . at Cedar Rapids
25-27 . . . . West Michigan
28-30 . . . . .Dayton
31 . . . . . at West Michigan

AUGUST
1-3 . . . . at West Michigan
4-7 . . . . South Bend
8-10 . . . . Great Lakes
11-13 . . . . at South Bend
15-17 . . . . at Dayton
18-21 . . . . Lansing
22-24 . . . . South Bend
25-28 . . . . at Great Lakes
29-31 . . . .Bowling Green

SEPTEMBER
1-3 . . . . .at Lansing

LANSING

APRIL
6-7 . . . . Great Lakes
9-11 . . . . at Dayton
12-15 . . . at West Michigan
16-18 . . . . South Bend
19-21 . . . . . at Burlington
22-24 . . . . at Peoria
25-27 . . . . Kane County
28-30 . . . . .Clinton

MAY
2-4 . . . . . . at Great Lakes
5-8 . . . . . West Michigan
9-11 . . . . . Bowling Green
12-15 . . . . at Dayton
16-18 . . . . . Fort Wayne
19-21 . . . .at Lake County
23-25 . . . . .Dayton
26-29 . . . . . Lake County
30-31 . . . at Bowling Green

JUNE
1 . . . . . . at Bowling Green
2-4 . . . . . at South Bend
6-8 . . . . . .Bowling Green
9-11 . . . . . . Lake County
12-14 . . . .at Fort Wayne
15-17 . . . . at Great Lakes
22-24 . . . . . . Great Lakes

25-27 . . . . .at Fort Wayne
28-30 . . . at Bowling Green

JULY
1-3 . . . . . . at South Bend
4-6 . . . . Great Lakes
7-9 . . . . at West Michigan
11-13 . . . . . . Quad Cities
14-16 . . . . Cedar Rapids
18-20 . . . . at Beloit
21-23 . . . . . at Wisconsin
25-27 . . . .Bowling Green
28-30 . . . . South Bend
31 . . . . at Dayton

AUGUST
1-3 . . . . at Dayton
4-7 . . . . . . .West Michigan
8-10 . . . . .Dayton
11-13 . . . . at Great Lakes
15-17 . . . . . Fort Wayne
18-21 . . . .at Lake County
22-24 . . . . at Great Lakes
25-28 . . . . . Fort Wayne
29-31 . . . . . at South Bend

SEPTEMBER
1-3 . . . . Lake County

PEORIA

APRIL
5-7 . . . . at Beloit
9-11 . . . . Quad Cities
12-15 . . . . . at Wisconsin
16-18 . . . . Cedar Rapids
19-21 . . . . . . Great Lakes
22-24 . . . . Lansing
25-27 . . . .at Lake County
28-30 . . . . .at Fort Wayne

MAY
2-4 . . . . . at Kane County
5-8 . . . . . at Quad Cities
9-11 . . . . .Beloit
12-14 . . . . .Burlington
16-18 . . . . at Clinton
19-21 . . . at Cedar Rapids
23-25 . . . . .Clinton
26-29 . . . . Wisconsin
30-31 . . . . . at Burlington

JUNE
1 . . . . at Burlington
2-4 . . . . . at Kane County
6-8 . . . . . . Cedar Rapids
9-11 . . . . . . Kane County
12-14 . . . . at Beloit
15-17 . . . . .Clinton
22-24 . . . . . . Quad Cities

25-27 . . . . at Clinton
28-30 . . . . . at Wisconsin

JULY
1-3 . . . . Kane County
4-6 . . . . .Burlington
7-9 . . . . at Cedar Rapids
11-13 . . . . .Dayton
14-16 . . . .Bowling Green
18-20 . . . at West Michigan
21-23 . . . . at South Bend
25-27 . . . . . Cedar Rapids
28-30 . . . . .Beloit
31 . . . . . at Quad Cities

AUGUST
1-3 . . . . . . at Quad Cities
4-7 . . . . .Clinton
8-10 . . . . . . at Burlington
11-13 . . . . at Beloit
15-17 . . . . .Burlington
18-21 . . . . . at Wisconsin
22-24 . . . . at Beloit
25-28 . . . . Wisconsin
29-31 . . . . . Cedar Rapids

SEPTEMBER
1-3 . . . . .at Kane City

QUAD CITIES

APRIL
5-7 . . . . Kane County
9-11 . . . . .at Peoria
12-15 . . . . at Cedar Rapids
16-18 . . . . .Clinton
19-21 . . . . at Dayton
22-24 . . . at Bowling Green
26-28 . . . West Michigan
29-30 . . . . . . South Bend

MAY
1 . . . . South Bend
2-4 . . . . . . at Burlington
5-8 . . . . Peoria
9-11 . . . . . . at Wisconsin
12-15 . . . . . Cedar Rapids
16-18 . . . . at Beloit
19-21 . . . . . . at Clinton
23-25 . . . . Wisconsin
26-29 . . . at Cedar Rapids
30-31 . . . . .Beloit

JUNE
1 . . . . Beloit
2-4 . . . . .Burlington
6-8 . . . . . at Kane County
9-11 . . . . . at Burlington
12-14 . . . . . Kane County
15-17 . . . . Wisconsin

22-24 . . . . .at Peoria
25-27 . . . . . at Wisconsin
28-30 . . . .Cedar Rapids

JULY
1-3 . . . . Wisconsin
4-6 . . . . . at Kane County
7-9 . . . . Clinton
11-13 . . . . . . .at Lansing
14-16 . . . . at Great Lakes
18-20 . . . . . Lake County
21-23 . . . . . Fort Wayne
25-27 . . . . . . at Clinton
28-30 . . . at Kane County
31 . . . . Peoria

AUGUST
1-3 . . . . Peoria
4-7 . . . . . . .at Burlington
8-10 . . . . .Beloit
11-13 . . . . .Burlington
15-17 . . . . at Cedar Rapids
18-21 . . . . Beloit
22-24 . . . . . Kane County
25-28 . . . . . . at Clinton
29-31 . . . . . Kane County

SEPTEMBER
1-3 . . . . at Beloit

SOUTH BEND

APRIL	
5-7 . . . . . at Bowling Green	
9-11 . . . . Fort Wayne	
12-15 . . . . .Dayton	
16-18 . . . . . . .at Lansing	
19-21 . . . . .Beloit	
22-24 . . . . Wisconsin	
26-28 . . . at Cedar Rapids	
30-31 . . . . . at Quad Cities	

MAY	
1 . . . . at Quad Cities	
2-4 . . . . . . Bowling Green	
5-8 . . . . Great Lakes	
9-11 . . . . .at Fort Wayne	
12-15 . . . at Bowling Green	
16-18 . . . . . Lake County	
19-21 . . at West Michigan	
23-25 . . . . . Fort Wayne	
26-29 . . . . at Great Lakes	
30-31 . . . . at Dayton	

JUNE	
1 . . . . at Dayton	
2-4 . . . . Lansing	
5-8 . . . . Great Lakes	
9-11 . . . . . .at Fort Wayne	
12-14 . . . . .at Lake County	
15-17 . . . . . West Michigan	

22-24 . . . at West Michigan
25-27 . . . . . . Great Lakes
28-30 . . . . .Dayton

JULY	
1-3 . . . . Lansing	
4-6 . . . . at Dayton	
7-9 . . . . Fort Wayne	
11-13 . . . at Kane County	
14-16 . . . . at Clinton	
18-20 . . . . . . .Burlington	
21-13 . . . . Peoria	
25-27 . . .at Fort Wayne	
28-30 . . . . . .at Lansing	
31 . . . . Fort Wayne	

AUGUST	
1-3 . . . . Fort Wayne	
4-7 . . . . . .at Lake County	
8-10 . . . at Bowling Green	
11-13 . . . . . Lake County	
15-17 . . . . West Michigan	
18-21 . . . . .Bowling Green	
22-24 . . . at Lake County	
25-28 . . . Bowling Green	
29-31 . . . . Lansing	

SEPTEMBER	
1-3 . . . . . . at Great Lakes	

WEST MICHIGAN

APRIL	
5-7 . . . . at Dayton	
9-11 . . . . . .Bowling Green	
12-15 . . . . Lansing	
16-18 . . . .at Lake County	
19-21 . . . . Wisconsin	
22-24 . . . . Beloit	
26-28 . . . . at Quad Cities	
29-30 . . . at Cedar Rapids	

MAY	
1 . . . . . . at Cedar Rapids	
2-4 . . . . Fort Wayne	
5-8 . . . . .at Lansing	
9-11 . . . . .at Fort Wayne	
12-15 . . . . .at Fort Wayne	
16-18 . . . . at Great Lakes	
19-21 . . . . . South Bend	
23-25 . . . . . Lake County	
26-29 . . . . .Dayton	
30-31 . . . .at Lake County	

JUNE	
1 . . . . . . .at Lake County	
2-4 . . . . . . at Great Lakes	
6-8 . . . . . . Fort Wayne	
9-11 . . . . Great Lakes	
12-14 . . . at Bowling Green	
15-17 . . . . . at South Bend	

22-24 . . . . . . South Bend
25-27 . . . . .Bowling Green
28-30 . . . .at Lake County

JULY	
1-3 . . . . . . at Great Lakes	
4-6 . . . . . . Lake County	
7-9 . . . . Lansing	
11-13 . . . . . . at Clinton	
14-16 . . . at Kane County	
18-20 . . . . Peoria	
21-13 . . . . .Burlington	
25-27 . . . .at Lake County	
28-30 . . . at Bowling Green	
31 . . . . Lake County	

AUGUST	
1-3 . . . . Lake County	
4-7 . . . . .at Lansing	
8-10 . . . . . .at Fort Wayne	
11-13 . . . . .Bowling Green	
15-17 . . . . at South Bend	
18-21 . . . . . . Great Lakes	
22-24 . . . . . Fort Wayne	
25-28 . . . . . . at Dayton	
29-30 . . . . .at Fort Wayne	

SEPTEMBER	
1-3 . . . . .Dayton	

WISCONSIN

APRIL	
5-7 . . . . Cedar Rapids	
9-11 . . . . . . at Burlington	
12-15 . . . . Peoria	
16-18 . . . . . . .Burlington	
19-21 . . at West Michigan	
22-24 . . . at South Bend	
25-27 . . . . .Dayton	
28-30 . . . Bowling Green	

MAY	
2-4 . . . . at Clinton	
5-8 . . . . Cedar Rapids	
9-11 . . . . . . Quad Cities	
12-15 . . . at Kane County	
16-18 . . . . . .Burlington	
19-21 . . . . Kane County	
23-25 . . . at Quad Cities	
26-29 . . . . at Peoria	
30-31 . . . at Cedar Rapids	

JUNE	
1 . . . . . . at Cedar Rapids	
2-4 . . . . at Beloit	
6-8 . . . . .Clinton	
9-11 . . . . .Beloit	
12-14 . . . . at Clinton	
15-17 . . . . at Quad Cities	
22-24 . . . . . at Burlington	

25-27 . . . . . . Quad Cities
28-30 . . . . Peoria

JULY	
1-3 . . . . . . at Quad Cities	
4-6 . . . . . at Cedar Rapids	
7-9 . . . . Kane County	
11-13 . . . .at Lake County	
14-16 . . . . .at Fort Wayne	
18-20 . . . . . . Great Lakes	
21-23 . . . . Lansing	
25-27 . . . at Kane County	
28-30 . . . . . . at Clinton	
31 . . . . .Burlington	

AUGUST	
1-3 . . . . .Burlington	
4-7 . . . . at Beloit	
8-10 . . . . . . Cedar Rapids	
11-13 . . . . .Clinton	
15-17 . . . . at Beloit	
18-21 . . . . Peoria	
22-24 . . . . . Cedar Rapids	
25-28 . . . . at Peoria	
29-31 . . . . .Beloit	

SEPTEMBER	
1-3 . . . . at Burlington	

SOUTH ATLANTIC LEAGUE

ASHEVILLE

5-8 . . . . Delmarva	
9-11 . . . . . West Virginia	
12-15 . . . . . at Hickory	
16-18 . . . . at West Virginia	
19-22 . . . . .Rome	
24-27 . . . . . at Lakewood	
28-30 . . . . . .at Delmarva	

MAY	
2-4 . . . . West Virginia	
5-8 . . . . Lexington	
10-13 . . . . at Rome	
14-16 . . . . at Greenville	
17-20 . . . . .Hickory	
21-23 . . . . . . Greenville	
24-27 . . . . at Rome	
28-30 . . . . . . Charleston	
31 . . . . Augusta	

JUNE	
1-3 . . . . Augusta	
5-7 . . . . . . .at Savannah	
8-10 . . . . . . West Virginia	
11-13 . . . . . at Greenville	
14-17 . . . . Lexington	
21-24 . . . . .Rome	

25-28 . . . . . . at Augusta
29-30 . . . . . at Lexington

JULY	
1-3 . . . . at Lexington	
4-8 . . . . Augusta	
10-13 . . . . .at Charleston	
14-17 . . . . at Rome	
19-22 . . . . . . .Greensboro	
23-26 . . . . Greenville	
27-29 . . . .at Charleston	
30-31 . . . . Lexington	

AUGUST	
1-2 . . . . Lexington	
3-6 . . . . Savannah	
8-11 . . . . .at Hickory	
13-15 . . . . . . Charleston	
16-19 . . . . . . Greenville	
20-22 . . . . . .at Savannah	
23-26 . . . . at Greenville	
28-30 . . . . . . Savannah	
31 . . . . . .at Hagerstown	

SEPTEMBER	
1-3 . . . . . .at Hagerstown	

AUGUSTA

APRIL
5-8	.at Savannah
9-11	.at Charleston
12-15	Savannah
16-18	Charleston
19-22	at Greenville
24-27	Kannapolis
28-30	.Hagerstown

MAY
2-4	.at Kannapolis
5-8	at Hagerstown
10-13	Greenville
14-16	Rome
17-20	.at Savannah
21-23	at Rome
24-27	Savannah
28-30	at Lexington
31	at Asheville

JUNE
1-3	at Asheville
5-7	Greensboro
8-10	at Rome
11-13	Rome
14-17	Greenville
21-24	.at Savannah

25-28	Asheville
29-30	Savannah

JULY
1-3	Savannah
4-8	.Asheville
10-13	Greenville
14-17	West Virginia
19-22	at Hagerstown
23-26	at Lexington
27-29	.Hickory
30-31	at Rome

AUGUST
1-2	at Rome
3-6	Charleston
8-11	.at Delmarva
13-15	Lakewood
16-19	at Charleston
20-22	at Greenville
23-26	Greensboro
27-30	at Rome
31	Charleston

SEPTEMBER
1-3	Charleston

CHARLESTON

APRIL
5-8	Rome
9-11	Augusta
12-15	at Rome
16-18	at Augusta
19-22	West Virginia
24-27	at Lexington
28-30	at Hickory

MAY
2-4	Lakewood
5-8	Delmarva
10-13	at West Virginia
14-16	Savannah
17-20	Rome
21-23	.at Savannah
24-27	Greenville
28-30	at Asheville
31	at Greenville

JUNE
1-3	at Greenville
5-7	.Hickory
8-10	Savannah
11-13	.at Savannah
14-17	at Greensboro

21-24	at Greenville
25-28	Savannah
29-30	Greenville

JULY
1-3	Greenville
4-8	.at Savannah
10-13	.Asheville
14-17	Greenville
19-22	.at Kannapolis
23-26	Rome
27-29	Asheville
30-31	at Greenville

AUGUST
1-2	at Greenville
3-6	at Augusta
8-11	.Hagerstown
13-15	at Asheville
16-19	Augusta
20-22	at West Virginia
23-26	at Lexington
28-30	West Virginia
31	at Augusta

SEPTEMBER
1-3	at Augusta

DELMARVA

APRIL
5-8	at Asheville
9-11	.at Kannapolis
12-15	Greensboro
16-18	.Hagerstown
19-22	at Greensboro

24-27	Greenville
28-30	.Asheville

MAY
2-4	.at Savannah
5-8	at Charleston

GREENSBORO

APRIL
5-8	Lexington
9-11	.Lakewood
12-15	.at Delmarva
16-18	at Lakewood
19-22	Delmarva
24-27	at Hickory
28-30	at West Virginia

MAY
2-4	.Hickory
5-8	West Virginia
10-13	at Lakewood
14-16	Kannapolis
17-20	Lakewood
21-23	at Hagerstown
24-27	.at Delmarva
28-30	.Hagerstown
31	.at Savannah

JUNE
1-3	.at Savannah
5-7	at Augusta
8-10	Lexington
11-13	.at Kannapolis
14-17	Charleston

GREENVILLE

APRIL
5-8	.Lakewood
9-11	.Hickory
12-15	at West Virginia
16-18	at Lexington
19-22	Augusta
24-27	.at Delmarva
28-30	at Lakewood

MAY
2-4	Lexington
5-8	Rome
10-13	at Augusta
14-16	.Asheville
17-20	West Virginia
21-13	at Asheville

Augusta (continued top right)

10-13	Kannapolis
14-16	.Lakewood
17-20	at Hagerstown
21-23	at Lakewood
24-27	Greensboro
28-30	.Hickory
31	at Hagerstown

JUNE
1-3	at Hagerstown
4-6	at West Virginia
8-10	Lakewood
11-13	at Lakewood
14-17	Kannapolis
21-24	.at Lakewood
25-28	.Hagerstown
29-30	West Virginia

JULY
1-3	West Virginia
4-8	at Hickory

Greensboro (continued right)

21-24	at Hickory
25-28	Lexington
29-30	.Hickory

JULY
1-3	.Hickory
4-8	.at Kannapolis
10-13	.Hagerstown
14-17	Kannapolis
19-22	at Asheville
23-26	West Virginia
27-29	Greenville
30-31	.at Savannah

AUGUST
1-2	.at Savannah
3-6	Delmarva
8-11	at Rome
13-15	at West Virginia
16-19	.Lakewood
20-22	at Lexington
23-26	at Augusta
28-30	.Hagerstown
31	at Lakewood

SEPTEMBER
1-3	at Lakewood

Greenville (continued right)

24-27	.at Charleston
28-30	Savannah
31	Charleston

JUNE
1-3	Charleston
5-7	at Rome
8-10	at Hickory
11-13	.Asheville
14-17	at Augusta
21-24	Charleston
25-28	at Rome
29-30	.at Charleston

JULY
1-3	.at Charleston

Delmarva (continued, further down center column)

24-27	Greenville
28-30	.Asheville

MAY
2-4	.at Savannah
5-8	at Charleston

Augusta right column AUGUST
1-2	.Lakewood
3-6	at Greensboro
8-11	Augusta
13-15	.at Kannapolis
16-19	.Hagerstown
20-22	at Lakewood
23-26	at Hagerstown
28-30	.Lakewood
31	at West Virginia

SEPTEMBER
1-3	at West Virginia

4-8 . . . . Rome
10-13 . . . . . at Augusta
14-17 . . . . . at Charleston
19-22 . . . . . . Lexington
23-26 . . . . at Asheville
27-29 . . . . at Greensboro
39-31 . . . . . . Charleston

AUGUST
1-2 . . . . Charleston
3-6 . . . . Hickory

HAGERSTOWN

APRIL
5-8 . . . . West Virginia
9-11 . . . . Lexington
12-15 . . . . . at Lakewood
16-18 . . . . . at Delmarva
19-22 . . . . . . Lakewood
24-27 . . . . at Rome
28-30 . . . . . at Augusta

MAY
2-4 . . . . Rome
5-8 . . . . Augusta
10-13 . . . . at Lexington
14-16 . . . . . at Hickory
17-20 . . . . . . Delmarva
21-23 . . . . . Greensboro
24-27 . . . . at Lakewood
28-30 . . . . at Greensboro
31 . . . . Delmarva

JUNE
1-3 . . . . Delmarva
5-7 . . . . Kannapolis
8-10 . . . . at Kannapolis
11-13 . . . . Hickory
14-17 . . . at West Virginia

HICKORY

APRIL
5-8 . . . . . at Kannapolis
9-11 . . . . . at Greenville
12-15 . . . . Asheville
16-18 . . . . . Kannapolis
19-22 . . . . . at Savannah
24-27 . . . . . Greensboro
28-30 . . . . . Charleston

MAY
2-4 . . . . at Greensboro
5-8 . . . . . at Kannapolis
10-13 . . . . . . Savannah
14-16 . . . . . Hagerstown
17-20 . . . . at Asheville
21-22 . . . . . Kannapolis
24-27 . . . . . Lexington
28-30 . . . . at Delmarva
31 . . . . West Virginia

JUNE
1-3 . . . . . . West Virginia
4 . . . . Kannapolis
5-7 . . . . . at Charleston
8-10 . . . . . . Greenville

8-11 . . . . . at Savannah
13-15 . . . . Rome
16-19 . . . . . at Asheville
20-22 . . . . Augusta
23-26 . . . . . Asheville
28-30 . . . at Kannapolis
31 . . . . Hickory

SEPTEMBER
1-3 . . . . Hickory

21-24 . . . . . . Lakewood
25-28 . . . .at Delmarva
29-30 . . . at Lakewood

JULY
1-3 . . . . . at Lakewood
4-8 . . . . Lexington
10-13 . . at Greensboro
14-17 . . . at Lexington
19-22 . . . . . . Augusta
23-26 . . . . . Lakewood
27-29 . . . at Lexington
30-31 . . at West Virginia

AUGUST
1-2 . . . . at West Virginia
3-6 . . . . Lexington
8-11 . . . at Charleston
13-15 . . . . . . Hickory
16-19 . . . .at Delmarva
20-22 . . . . Kannapolis
23-26 . . . . Delmarva
28-30 . . . at Greensboro
31 . . . . .Asheville

SEPTEMBER
1-3 . . . . Asheville

11-13 . . . at Hagerstown
14-17 . . . at Lakewood
21-24 . . . . Greensboro
25-28 . . . .at Kannapolis
29-30 . . . . Greensboro

JULY
1-3 . . . . at Greensboro
4-8 . . . . Delmarva
10-13 . . . at Lakewood
14-17 . . . .at Delmarva
19-22 . . . . Lakewood
23-26 . . . . Delmarva
27-29 . . . at Augusta
30-31 . . . . Kannapolis

AUGUST
1-2 . . . . . Kannapolis
3-6 . . . . at Greenville
8-11 . . . . . Asheville
13-15 . . . at Hagerstown
16-19 . . . . . Savannah
20-22 . . . . . . Rome
23-26 . . at West Virginia
28-30 . . . . . Lexington

31 . . . . at Greenville

KANNAPOLIS

APRIL
5-8 . . . . .Hickory
9-11 . . . . Delmarva
12-15 . . . . at Lexington
16-18 . . . . . at Hickory
19-22 . . . . . Lexington
24-27 . . . . at Augusta
28-30 . . . . . at Rome

MAY
2-4 . . . . Augusta
5-8 . . . . .Hickory
10-13 . . . . .at Delmarva
14-16 . . . at Greensboro
17-20 . . . . Lexington
21-22 . . . . at Hickory
24-27 . . at West Virginia
28-30 . . . . .Rome
31 . . . . Lakewood

JUNE
1-3 . . . . Lakewood
4 . . . . at Hickory
5-7 . . . . at Hagerstown
8-10 . . . . . .Hagerstown
11-13 . . . . .Greensboro
14-17 . . . . .at Delmarva

LAKEWOOD

APRIL
5-8 . . . . . at Greenville
9-11 . . . . at Greensboro
12-15 . . . . . .Hagerstown
16-18 . . . at Hagerstown
19-22 . . . at Hagerstown
24-27 . . . . . . .Asheville
28-30 . . . . . Greenville

MAY
2-4 . . . .at Charleston
5-8 . . . . Savannah
10-13 . . . . .Greensboro
14-16 . . . . . .at Delmarva
17-20 . . . at Greensboro
21-23 . . . . . Delmarva
24-27 . . . . .Hagerstown
28-30 . . at West Virginia
31 . . . . . . at Kannapolis

JUNE
1-3 . . . .at Kannapolis
5-7 . . . . Lexington
8-10 . . . . . .at Delmarva
11-13 . . . . . Delmarva
14-17 . . . . . . .Hickory

SEPTEMBER
1-3 . . . . at Greenville

21-24 . . . . . . Delmarva
25-28 . . . . .Hickory
29-30 . . . . at Rome

JULY
1-3 . . . . at Rome
4-8 . . . . Greensboro
10-13 . . . . . at Lexington
14-17 . . . at Greensboro
19-22 . . . . . . Charleston
23-26 . . . .at Savannah
27-29 . . . .at Delmarva
30-31 . . . . . . at Hickory

AUGUST
1-2 . . . . .at Hickory
3-6 . . . . .Rome
8-11 . . . . . . at Lakewood
13-15 . . . . . . Delmarva
16-19 . . . . . West Virginia
20-22 . . . at Hagerstown
23-26 . . . . at Lakewood
28-30 . . . . Greenville
31 . . . . Savannah

SEPTEMBER
1-3 . . . . Savannah

21-24 . . . . . at Hagerstown
25-28 . . . . . West Virginia
29-30 . . . . .Hagerstown

JULY
1-3 . . . . .Hagerstown
4-8 . . . . at West Virginia
10-13 . . . . . . .Hickory
14-17 . . . . Savannah
19-22 . . . . . . at Hickory
23-26 . . . at Hagerstown
27-29 . . . West Virginia
30-31 . . . .at Delmarva

AUGUST
1-2 . . . . . . .at Delmarva
3-6 . . . . . at West Virginia
8-11 . . . . . . Kannapolis
13-15 . . . . . . at Augusta
16-19 . . . at Greensboro
20-22 . . . . . Delmarva
23-26 . . . . . Kannapolis
28-30 . . . .at Delmarva
31 . . . . Greensboro

SEPTEMBER
1-3 . . . . Greensboro

LEXINGTON

APRIL
5-8 . . . . . . at Greensboro
9-11 . . . . . at Hagerstown
12-15 . . . . . . Kannapolis
16-18 . . . . Greenville
19-22 . . . . . at Kannapolis
24-27 . . . . . . Charleston
28-30 . . . . Savannah

MAY
2-4 . . . . . . at Greenville
5-8 . . . . at Asheville
10-13 . . . . . .Hagerstown
14-16 . . . at West Virginia
17-20 . . . .at Kannapolis
21-23 . . . . . West Virginia
24-27 . . . . at Hickory
28-30 . . . . Augusta
31 . . . . Rome

JUNE
1-3 . . . . Rome
5-7 . . . . . . at Lakewood
8-10 . . . . . at Greensboro
11-13 . . . . . West Virginia
14-17 . . . . .Asheville

21-24 . . . . at West Virginia
25-28 . . . . at Greensboro
29-30 . . . . .Asheville

JULY
1-3 . . . . .Asheville
4-8 . . . . . at Hagerstown
10-13 . . . . . . Kannapolis
14-17 . . . . . .Hagerstown
19-22 . . . . . at Greenville
23-26 . . . . Augusta
27-29 . . . . . .Hagerstown
30-31 . . . . . . at Asheville

AUGUST
1-2 . . . . at Asheville
3-6 . . . . at Hagerstown
8-11 . . . . . . West Virginia
13-15 . . . .at Savannah
16-19 . . . . at Rome
20-22 . . . . . . Greensboro
23-26 . . . . . . Charleston
28-30 . . . . at Hickory
31 . . . . Rome

SEPTEMBER
1-3 . . . . .Rome

ROME

APRIL
5-8 . . . . . . .at Charleston
9-11 . . . . . . .at Savannah
12-15 . . . . . . Charleston
16-18 . . . . Savannah
19-22 . . . . . . at Asheville
24-27 . . . . .Hagerstown
28-30 . . . . . . Kannapolis

MAY
2-4 . . . . . . at Hagerstown
5-8 . . . . . . at Greenville
10-13 . . . . .Asheville
14-16 . . . . . . at Augusta
17-20 . . . .at Charleston
21-23 . . . . Augusta
24-27 . . . . . . .Asheville
28-30 . . . .at Kannapolis
31 . . . . at Lexington

JUNE
1-3 . . . . . . at Lexington
5-7 . . . . Greenville
8-10 . . . . Augusta
11-13 . . . . . . at Augusta
14-17 . . . . Savannah

21-24 . . . . . . at Asheville
25-28 . . . . Greenville
29-30 . . . . Kannapolis

JULY
1-3 . . . . Kannapolis
4-8 . . . . . . at Greenville
10-13 . . . . . West Virginia
14-17 . . . . . . .Asheville
19-22 . . . . .at Savannah
23-26 . . . . .at Charleston
27-29 . . . . . . Savannah
30-31 . . . . Augusta

AUGUST
1-2 . . . . Augusta
3-6 . . . . . . .at Kannapolis
8-11 . . . . . . Greensboro
13-15 . . . . at Greenville
16-19 . . . . . . Lexington
20-22 . . . . . . at Hickory
23-26 . . . . .at Savannah
28-30 . . . . Augusta
31 . . . . at Lexington

SEPTEMBER
1-3 . . . . at Lexington

SAVANNAH

APRIL
5-8 . . . . Augusta
9-11 . . . . .Rome
12-15 . . . . . . at Augusta
16-18 . . . . at Rome
19-22 . . . . .Hickory
24-27 . . . . at West Virginia
28-30 . . . . . at Lexington

MAY
2-4 . . . . Delmarva
5-8 . . . . Lakewood
10-13 . . . . . . at Hickory
14-16 . . . .at Charleston
17-20 . . . . Augusta
21-23 . . . . . . Charleston
24-27 . . . . . at Augusta
28-30 . . . . at Greenville
31 . . . . Greensboro

JUNE
1-3 . . . . Greensboro
5-7 . . . . .Asheville
8-10 . . . .at Charleston
11-13 . . . . . . Charleston
14-17 . . . . . . at Rome

21-24 . . . . Augusta
25-28 . . . . .at Charleston
29-30 . . . . . at Augusta

JULY
1-3 . . . . at Augusta
4-8 . . . . Charleston
10-13 . . . . . .at Delmarva
14-17 . . . . . at Lakewood
19-22 . . . . .Rome
23-26 . . . . . . Kannapolis
27-29 . . . . at Rome
30-31 . . . . . .Greensboro

AUGUST
1-2 . . . . Greenville
3-6 . . . . at Asheville
8-11 . . . . Greenville
13-15 . . . . Lexington
16-19 . . . . . . at Hickory
20-22 . . . . .Asheville
23-26 . . . . .Rome
28-30 . . . . at Asheville
31 . . . . . . .at Kannapolis

SEPTEMBER
1-3 . . . . . . .at Kannapolis

WEST VIRGINIA

APRIL
5-8 . . . . . .at Hagerstown
9-11 . . . . . . at Asheville
12-15 . . . . Greenville
16-18 . . . . .Asheville
19-22 . . . .at Charleston
24-27 . . . . Savannah
28-30 . . . . . Greensboro

MAY
2-4 . . . . at Asheville
5-8 . . . . . . at Greensboro
10-13 . . . . Charleston
14-16 . . . . Lexington
17-20 . . . . at Greenville
21-23 . . . . . at Lexington
24-27 . . . . . Kannapolis
28-30 . . . . . . Lakewood
31 . . . . at Hickory

JUNE
1-3 . . . . at Hickory
4-6 . . . . Delmarva
8-10 . . . . . .at Asheville
11-13 . . . . . at Lexington
14-17 . . . . . .Hagerstown

21-24 . . . . Lexington
25-28 . . . . . at Lakewood
29-30 . . . . . .at Delmarva

JULY
1-3 . . . . .at Delmarva
4-8 . . . . .Lakewood
10-13 . . . . at Rome
14-17 . . . . at Augusta
19-22 . . . . Delmarva
23-26 . . . . at Greensboro
27-29 . . . . . at Lakewood
30-31 . . . . . .Hagerstown

AUGUST
1-2 . . . . .Hagerstown
3-6 . . . . .Lakewood
8-11 . . . . . at Lexington
13-15 . . . . . Greensboro
16-19 . . . . .at Kannapolis
20-22 . . . . . Charleston
23-26 . . . . .Hickory
28-30 . . . . .at Charleston
31 . . . . Delmarva

SEPTEMBER
1-3 . . . . Delmarva

SHORT SEASON

NEW YORK-PENN LEAGUE

ABERDEEN

JUNE	
18-19	. . . at Hudson Valley
20-21	. . . . . Hudson Valley
22-24	. . . . Brooklyn
25-27	. . . . at Staten Island
28-30	. . . . at Brooklyn
JULY	
1-3	. . . . Staten Island
4-6	. . . . at Mahoning Valley
7-9	. . . . at Tri-City
11-13	. . . . Auburn
14-16	. . . . Batavia
17-18	. . at Staten Island
19-20	. . at Hudson Valley
21-22	. . . . Hudson Valley
23-24	. . . . . at Brooklyn
25-27	. . . . Jamestown

28-30	. . . . Vermont
AUGUST	
1-3	. . . . . .at Williamsport
4-6	. . . . . at State College
7-9	. . . . Tri-City
10-12	. . . . . .Connecticut
15-17	. . . . .at Lowell
18-20	. . . .at Connecticut
21-23	. . . . Lowell
24-26	. . .at Hudson Valley
27-28	. . . . .Brooklyn
29-30	. . . . . Staten Island
31	. . . . . . Hudson Valley
SEPTEMBER	
1-2	. . . . Hudson Valley
3-5	. . . . at Vermont

AUBURN

JUNE	
18	. . . . at Batavia
19	. . . . Batavia
20	. . . . at Batavia
21	. . . . Batavia
22-24	. . .at Williamsport
25-27	. . . . . Jamestown
28-30	. . . . . Williamsport
JULY	
1-3	. . . . . . at Jamestown
4-6	. . . . Lowell
7-9	. . . . . Hudson Valley
11-13	. . . . at Aberdeen
14-16	. . . . at Connecticut
17-18	. . . . . Williamsport
19	. . . . Batavia
20-21	. . . . . at Batavia
22	. . . . Batavia
23-24	. . . . at Jamestown
25-27	. . . . Vermont

28-30	. . . . Tri-City
AUGUST	
1-3	. . . . at Staten Island
4-6	. . . . at Brooklyn
7-8	. . . . Jamestown
9-10	. . . . . State College
11-12	. . .Mahoning Valley
15-16	. at Mahoning Valley
17-18	. . . . at State College
19-20	. . . . Batavia
21-23	. . . . . State College
24-26	. . .Mahoning Valley
27-29	. . . at State College
30-31	. . at Mahoning Valley
SEPTEMBER	
1	. . . . at Mahoning Valley
2-3	. . . . at Batavia
4-5	. . . . . .at Williamsport

BATAVIA

JUNE	
18	. . . . .Auburn
19	. . . . at Auburn
20	. . . . .Auburn
21	. . . . at Auburn
22	. . . . Jamestown
23-24	. . . . . at Jamestown
25-27	. . . . . State College
28	. . . . Jamestown
29	. . . . . . at Jamestown
30	. . . . Jamestown

JULY	
1-3	. . . . . at State College
4-6	. . . . .Connecticut
7-9	. . . . Lowell
11-13	. . .at Hudson Valley
14-16	. . . . . at Aberdeen
17	. . . . Jamestown
18	. . . . . at Jamestown
19	. . . . at Auburn
20-21	. . . . .Auburn
22	. . . . at Auburn

BROOKLYN

JUNE	
18	. . . . Staten Island
19	. . . . . at Staten Island
20	. . . . . . Staten Island
21	. . . . . at Staten Island
22-24	. . . . . at Aberdeen
25	. . . . . . Hudson Valley
26	. . . .at Hudson Valley
27	. . . . . . Hudson Valley
28-30	. . . . Aberdeen
JULY	
1	. . .at Hudson Valley
2	. . . . . Hudson Valley
3	. . . .at Hudson Valley
4-6	. . . . . . Williamsport
7-9	. . . . Jamestown
11-13	. . . . at Connecticut
14-16	. . . at State College
17	. . . . . Hudson Valley
18	. . .at Hudson Valley
19	. . . . . at Staten Island
20	. . . . Staten Island
21	. . . . . at Staten Island

22	. . . . Staten Island
23-24	. . . . . . Aberdeen
25-27	. . . . at Batavia
28-30	. at Mahoning Valley
AUGUST	
1-3	. . . . .Connecticut
4-6	. . . . .Auburn
7-9	. . . . .at Lowell
10-12	. . . . Vermont
15-17	. . . . . . at Tri-City
18-20	. . . . . . at Vermont
21-23	. . . . Tri-City
24	. . . . . at Staten Island
25	. . . . . . Staten Island
26	. . . . . at Staten Island
27-28	. . . . . at Aberdeen
29	. . . . .at Hudson Valley
30	. . . . . . Hudson Valley
31	. . . . Staten Island
SEPTEMBER	
1	. . . . . at Staten Island
2	. . . . . . Staten Island
3-5	. . . . Lowell

CONNECTICUT

JUNE	
18-19	. . . . .at Lowell
20-21	. . . . Lowell
22-24	. . . . .Tri-City
25-27	. . . . . at Vermont
28-30	. . . . at Tri-City
JULY	
1-3	. . . . Vermont
4-6	. . . . at Batavia
7-9	. . . at Mahoning Valley
11-13	. . . . .Brooklyn
14-16	. . . . .Auburn
17-18	. . . . .Vermont
19-20	. . . . .at Lowell
21-22	. . . . Lowell
23-24	. . . . . at Tri-City
25-27	. . . . . State College

28-30	. . . . . . Jamestown
AUGUST	
1-3	. . . . at Brooklyn
4-6	. . . . . .at Williamsport
7-9	. . . . Staten Island
10-12	. . . . . at Aberdeen
15-17	. . . . . Hudson Valley
18-20	. . . . . . Aberdeen
21-23	. . .at Hudson Valley
24-26	. . . . .at Lowell
27-28	. . . . . at Vermont
29-30	. . . . .Tri-City
31	. . . . Lowell
SEPTEMBER	
1-2	. . . . Lowell
3-5	. . . . . at Staten Island

AUGUST

1-3	. . . . at Tri-City
4-6	. . . . at Vermont
7-8	. . . . State College
9-10	. . . .Mahoning Valley
11-12	. . . . . Williamsport
15-16	. . . .at Williamsport
17-18	. . at Mahoning Valley

19-20	. . . . at Auburn
21-23	. . .Mahoning Valley
24-26	. . . . . Williamsport
27-29	. . at Mahoning Valley
30-31	. . . .at Williamsport
SEPTEMBER	
1	. . . . . . .at Williamsport
2-3	. . . . .Auburn
4	. . . . Jamestown
5	. . . . at Jamestown

HUDSON VALLEY

JUNE
18-19	. . . . . . Aberdeen
20-21	. . . . . at Aberdeen
22	. . . . Staten Island
23-24	. . . at Staten Island
25	. . . . at Brooklyn
26	. . . . .Brooklyn
27	. . . . at Brooklyn
28	. . . . Staten Island
20	. . . at Staten Island
30	. . . . . . Staten Island

JULY
1	. . . . .Brooklyn
2	. . . . at Brooklyn
3	. . . . .Brooklyn
4-6	. . . . at Vermont
7-9	. . . . at Auburn
11-13	. . . . Batavia
14-16	. . . .Mahoning Valley
17	. . . . at Brooklyn
18	. . . . .Brooklyn
19-20	. . . . . . Aberdeen
21-22	. . . . . at Aberdeen

23	. . . . Staten Island
24	. . . . . at Staten Island
25-27	. . . . .Tri-City
28-30	. . . . . Williamsport

AUGUST
1-3	. . . . . at State College
4-6	. . . . . . at Jamestown
7-9	. . . . Vermont
10-12	. . . . Lowell
15-17	. . . . at Connecticut
18-20	. . . . .at Lowell
21-23	. . . . . . .Connecticut
24-26	. . . . Aberdeen
27	. . . . at Staten Island
28	. . . . . . Staten Island
29	. . . . .Brooklyn
30	. . . . . . at Brooklyn
31	. . . . at Aberdeen

SEPTEMBER
1-2	. . . . at Aberdeen
3-5	. . . . at Tri-City

JAMESTOWN

JUNE
18-19	. . .Mahoning Valley
20-21	. . at Mahoning Valley
22	. . . . at Batavia
23-24	. . . . .Batavia
25-27	. . . . . . at Auburn
28	. . . . at Batavia
29	. . . . Batavia
30	. . . . at Batavia

JULY
1-3	. . . . .Auburn
4-6	. . . . . at Staten Island
7-9	. . . . . . at Brooklyn
11-13	. . . . Vermont
14-16	. . . . .Tri-City
17	. . . . at Batavia
18	. . . . Batavia
19-20	. . . Mahoning Valley
21-22	. . Mahoning Valley
23-24	. . . . .Auburn

25-27	. . . . . . at Aberdeen
28-30	. . . .at Connecticut

AUGUST
1-3	. . . . Lowell
4-6	. . . . .Mahoning Valley
7-8	. . . . at Auburn
9-10	. . . . . . Williamsport
11-12	. . . . State College
15-16	. . at State College
17-18	. . . .at Williamsport
19-20	. at Mahoning Valley
21-23	. . . . . Williamsport
24-26	. . . at State College
27-29	. . . .at Williamsport
30-31	. . . . State College

SEPTEMBER
1	. . . . State College
2-3	. . . . .Mahoning Valley
4	. . . . at Batavia
5	. . . . Batavia

LOWELL

JUNE
18-19	. . . . . .Connecticut
20-21	. . . . .at Connecticut
22-24	. . . . Vermont
25-27	. . . . . at Tri-City
28-30	. . . . . at Vermont

JULY
1-3	. . . . Tri-City
4-6	. . . . at Auburn
7-9	. . . . at Batavia
11-13	. . . Mahoning Valley
14-16	. . . . . Staten Island

17-18	. . . . . . at Tri-City
19-20	. . . . . .Connecticut
21-22	. . . . at Connecticut
23-24	. . . . . at Vermont
25-27	. . . . Williamsport
28-30	. . . . . State College

AUGUST
1-3	. . . . at Jamestown
4-6	. . . . at Staten Island
7-9	. . . . .Brooklyn
10-12	. .at Hudson Valley
15-17	. . . . Aberdeen
18-20	. . . . Hudson Valley

MAHONING VALLEY

JUNE
18-19	. . . . . at Jamestown
20-21	. . . . . . Jamestown
22-24	. . . at State College
25-27	. . . . . Williamsport
28-30	. . . . . State College

JULY
1-3	. . . . . .at Williamsport
4-6	. . . . Aberdeen
7-9	. . . . .Connecticut
11-13	. . . . . . .at Lowell
14-16	. . .at Hudson Valley
17-18	. . . . State College
19-20	. . . . at Jamestown
21-22	. . . . . Jamestown
23-24	. . .at Williamsport
25-27	. . . . Staten Island
28-30	. . . . .Brooklyn

AUGUST
1-3	. . . . at Vermont
4-6	. . . . at Tri-City
7-8	. . . . Williamsport
9-10	. . . . at Batavia
11-12	. . . . . . at Auburn
15-16	. . . . .Auburn
17-18	. . . . Batavia
19-20	. . . . . . Jamestown
21-23	. . . . . at Batavia
24-26	. . . . . . at Auburn
27-29	. . . . Batavia
30-31	. . . . .Auburn

SEPTEMBER
1	. . . . .Auburn
2-3	. . . . . . at Jamestown
4-5	. . . . . at State College

(Top right — Hudson Valley continued)
21-23	. . . . . . at Aberdeen
24-26	. . . . . .Connecticut
27-28	. . . . Tri-City
29-30	. . . . Vermont

(Hudson Valley AUGUST continued)
31	. . . . . . at Connecticut

SEPTEMBER
1-2	. . . . at Connecticut
3-5	. . . . at Brooklyn

STATE COLLEGE

JUNE
18	. . . . . .at Williamsport
19	. . . . Williamsport
20	. . . . . .at Williamsport
21	. . . . Williamsport
22-24	. . .Mahoning Valley
25-27	. . . . . . at Batavia
28-30	. . at Mahoning Valley

JULY
1-3	. . . . Batavia
4-6	. . . . at Tri-City
7-9	. . . . at Vermont
11-13	. . . . Staten Island
14-16	. . . . Brooklyn
17-18	. . .Mahoning Valley
19	. . . . Williamsport
20	. . . . . .at Williamsport
21	. . . . Williamsport
22	. . . . . .at Williamsport
23-24	. . . . Batavia

25-27	. . . .at Connecticut
28-30	. . . . .at Lowell

AUGUST
1-3	. . . . . . Hudson Valley
4-6	. . . . Aberdeen
7-8	. . . . at Batavia
9-10	. . . . . . at Auburn
11-12	. . . . at Jamestown
15-16	. . . . . Jamestown
17-18	. . . . .Auburn
19-20	. . .at Williamsport
21-23	. . . . . at Auburn
24-26	. . . . . Jamestown
27-29	. . . . . . .Auburn
30-31	. . . . . at Jamestown

SEPTEMBER
1	. . . . at Jamestown
2-3	. . . . Williamsport
4-5	. . . . .Mahoning Valley

STATEN ISLAND

JUNE
18	. . . . at Brooklyn
19	. . . . .Brooklyn
20	. . . . . . at Brooklyn
21	. . . . .Brooklyn
22	. . .at Hudson Valley
23-24	. . . . Hudson Valley
25-27	. . . . . . Aberdeen
28	. . .at Hudson Valley
29	. . . . Hudson Valley
30	. . . . .at Hudson Valley

JULY
1-3	. . . . at Aberdeen
4-6	. . . . Jamestown
7-9	. . . . Williamsport
11-13	. . . at State College
14-16	. . . . .at Lowell
17-18	. . . . . . Aberdeen
19	. . . . .Brooklyn
20	. . . . . . at Brooklyn
21	. . . . .Brooklyn
22	. . . . . . at Brooklyn
23	. . . . .at Hudson Valley

24 . . . . . . Hudson Valley
25-27 . . at Mahoning Valley
28-30 . . . . at Batavia
AUGUST
1-3 . . . . .Auburn
4-6 . . . . Lowell
7-9 . . . . . . at Connecticut
10-12 . . . . Tri-City
15-17 . . . . at Vermont
18-20 . . . . at Tri-City
21-23 . . . . Vermont

24 . . . . .Brooklyn
25 . . . . at Brooklyn
26 . . . . .Brooklyn
27 . . . . Hudson Valley
28 . . . . . .at Hudson Valley
29-30 . . . . . at Aberdeen
31 . . . . at Brooklyn
SEPTEMBER
1 . . . . .Brooklyn
2 . . . . at Brooklyn
3-5 . . . . .Connecticut

21 . . . . . at State College
22 . . . . State College
23-24 . . . .Mahoning Valley
25-27 . . . . .at Lowell
28-30 . . . .at Hudson Valley
AUGUST
1-3 . . . . Aberdeen
4-6 . . . . .Connecticut
7-8 . . . .at Mahoning Valley
9-10 . . . . . at Jamestown
11-12 . . . . . . at Batavia

15-16 . . . . Batavia
17-18 . . . . Jamestown
19-20 . . . . . State College
21-23 . . . . . at Jamestown
24-26 . . . . . . at Batavia
27-29 . . . . Jamestown
30-31 . . . . Batavia
SEPTEMBER
1 . . . . Batavia
2-3 . . . . . . at State College
4-5 . . . . .Auburn

TRI-CITY

JUNE
18-19 . . . . . . at Vermont
20-21 . . . . Vermont
22-24 . . . . at Connecticut
25-27 . . . . Lowell
28-30 . . . . . .Connecticut
JULY
1-3 . . . . .at Lowell
4-6 . . . . State College
7-9 . . . . Aberdeen
11-13 . . . .at Williamsport
14-16 . . . . at Jamestown
17-18 . . . . Lowell
19-20 . . . . . at Vermont
21-22 . . . . Vermont
23-24 . . . . . .Connecticut
25-27 . . .at Hudson Valley

28-30 . . . . at Auburn
AUGUST
1-3 . . . . Batavia
4-6 . . . . . .Mahoning Valley
7-9 . . . . at Aberdeen
10-12 . . . . at Staten Island
15-17 . . . . .Brooklyn
18-20 . . . . . Staten Island
21-23 . . . . . at Brooklyn
24-26 . . . . Vermont
27-28 . . . . . . .at Lowell
29-30 . . . . at Connecticut
31 . . . . at Vermont
SEPTEMBER
1-2 . . . . at Vermont
3-5 . . . . . . Hudson Valley

VERMONT

JUNE
18-19 . . . . Tri-City
20-21 . . . . . . at Tri-City
22-24 . . . . .at Lowell
25-27 . . . . . .Connecticut
28-30 . . . . Lowell
JULY
1-3 . . . . . . at Connecticut
4-6 . . . . . . Hudson Valley
7-9 . . . . . . State College
11-13 . . . . at Jamestown
14-16 . . . .at Williamsport
17-18 . . . . at Connecticut
19-20 . . . . Tri-City
21-22 . . . . . at Tri-City
23-24 . . . . Lowell
25-27 . . . . . . at Auburn

28-30 . . . . . at Aberdeen
AUGUST
1-3 . . . . . .Mahoning Valley
4-6 . . . . Batavia
7-9 . . . . .at Hudson Valley
10-12 . . . . . . at Brooklyn
15-17 . . . . . Staten Island
18-20 . . . . . . .Brooklyn
21-23 . . . at Staten Island
24-26 . . . . . . at Tri-City
27-28 . . . . . .Connecticut
29-30 . . . . .at Lowell
31 . . . . Tri-City
SEPTEMBER
1-2 . . . . Tri-City
3-5 . . . . Aberdeen

WILLIAMSPORT

JUNE
18 . . . . State College
19 . . . . . at State College
20 . . . . . . State College
21 . . . at State College
22-24 . . . . .Auburn
25-27 . . at Mahoning Valley
28-30 . . . . at Auburn

JULY
1-3 . . . . .Mahoning Valley
4-6 . . . . . . at Brooklyn
7-9 . . . . . at Staten Island
11-13 . . . . Tri-City
14-16 . . . . Vermont
17-18 . . . . . . at Auburn
19 . . . . . at State College
20 . . . . State College

NORTHWEST LEAGUE

BOISE

JUNE
15-19 . . . . at Salem-Keiser
20-24 . . . . .Eugene
25-27 . . . . . . at Spokane
28-30 . . . . Spokane
JULY
1-3 . . . . at Tri-City
4-6 . . . . .Tri-City
7-9 . . . . at Yakima
11-15 . . . . . . .Vancouver
16-18 . . . . Yakima
19-23 . . . . . . at Eugene
24-26 . . . . Yakima

27-29 . . . . Tri-City
31 . . . . Spokane
AUGUST
1-2 . . . . Spokane
3-5 . . . . at Spokane
6-10 . . . . at Everett
11-15 . . . . . Salem-Keiser
16-18 . . . . at Tri-City
19-21 . . . . at Yakima
22-26 . . . . . at Vancouver
28-31 . . . . Everett
SEPTEMBER
1 . . . . Everett

EUGENE

JUNE
15-19 . . . . Yakima
20-24 . . . . at Boise
25-27 . . . . at Salem-Keiser
28-30 . . . at Vancouver
JULY
1-3 . . . . at Everett
4-6 . . . . Everett
7-9 . . . . Salem-Keiser
11-15 . . . . . at Spokane
16-18 . . . . . .Vancouver
19-23 . . . . Boise
24-26 . . . . . at Vancouver

27-29 . . . . at Salem-Keiser
31 . . . . Everett
AUGUST
1-2 . . . . Everett
3-5 . . . . .Vancouver
6-10 . . . . at Yakima
11-15 . . . . Tri-City
16-18 . . . . . Salem-Keiser
19-21 . . . . at Everett
22-26 . . . . . . at Tri-City
28-31 . . . . Spokane
SEPTEMBER
1 . . . . Spokane

EVERETT

JUNE
15-19 . . . . at Tri-City
20-24 . . . . Spokane
25-27 . . . . . . .Vancouver
28-30 . . . . at Salem-Keiser
JULY
1-3 . . . . .Eugene
4-6 . . . . at Eugene
7-9 . . . . at Vancouver
11-15 . . . . .Tri-City
16-18 . . . . at Salem-Keiser
19-23 . . . . . . at Yakima
24-26 . . . . . Salem-Keiser

27-29 . . . . . . .Vancouver
31 . . . . at Eugene
AUGUST
1-2 . . . . .at Eugene
3-5 . . . . Salem-Keiser
7-10 . . . . Boise
11-15 . . . . . . at Spokane
16-18 . . . . . at Vancouver
19-21 . . . . Eugene
22-26 . . . . Yakima
28-31 . . . . at Boise
SEPTEMBER
1 . . . . at Boise

SALEM-KEISER

JUNE
15-19 . . . . Boise
20-24 . . . . at Yakima
25-27 . . . . .Eugene
28-30 . . . . Everett

JULY
1-3 . . . . at Vancouver
4-6 . . . . .Vancouver
7-9 . . . . at Eugene
11-15 . . . . Yakima
16-18 . . . . Everett
19-23 . . . . . . at Tri-City
24-26 . . . . . . at Everett
27-29 . . . . .Eugene

31 . . . . at Vancouver

AUGUST
1-2 . . . . at Vancouver
3-5 . . . . at Everett
6-10 . . . . Spokane
11-15 . . . . at Boise
16-18 . . . . at Eugene
19-21 . . . . . . .Vancouver
22-26 . . . . . . at Spokane
28-31 . . . . Tri-City

SEPTEMBER
1 . . . . Tri-City

SPOKANE

JUNE
15-19 . . . . . . .Vancouver
20-24 . . . . . . at Everett
25-27 . . . . Boise
28-30 . . . . at Boise

JULY
1-3 . . . . at Yakima
4-6 . . . . Yakima
7-9 . . . . at Tri-City
11-15 . . . . .Eugene
16-18 . . . . Tri-City
19-23 . . . . . at Vancouver
24-26 . . . . . . at Tri-City
27-29 . . . . Yakima

31 . . . . at Boise

AUGUST
1-2 . . . . at Boise
3-5 . . . . Boise
6-10 . . . . at Salem-Keiser
11-15 . . . . Everett
16-18 . . . . at Yakima
19-21 . . . . Tri-City
22-26 . . . . . Salem-Keiser
28-31 . . . . at Eugene

SEPTEMBER
1 . . . . at Eugene

TRI-CITY

JUNE
15-19 . . . . Everett
20-24 . . . . . at Vancouver
25-27 . . . . Yakima

28-30 . . . . at Yakima

JULY
1-3 . . . . Boise
4-6 . . . . at Boise

7-9 . . . . Spokane
11-15 . . . . at Everett
16-18 . . . . . at Spokane
19-23 . . . . . Salem-Keiser
24-26 . . . . Spokane
27-29 . . . . . . at Boise
31 . . . . at Yakima

AUGUST
1-2 . . . . at Yakima

VANCOUVER

JUNE
15-19 . . . . . at Spokane
20-24 . . . . .Tri-City
25-27 . . . . . . at Everett
28-30 . . . . .Eugene

JULY
1-3 . . . . Salem-Keiser
4-6 . . . . . at Salem-Keiser
7-9 . . . . Everett
11-15 . . . . at Boise
16-18 . . . . . . at Eugene
19-23 . . . . Spokane
24-26 . . . . .Eugene

27-29 . . . . . . at Everett
31 . . . . . . at Salem-Keiser

AUGUST
1-2 . . . . Salem-Keiser
3-5 . . . . at Eugene
6-10 . . . . at Tri-City
11-15 . . . . Yakima
16-18 . . . . Everett
19-21 . . . . at Salem-Keiser
22-26 . . . . Boise
28-31 . . . . . . at Yakima

SEPTEMBER
1 . . . . at Yakima

YAKIMA

JUNE
15-19 . . . . at Eugene
20-24 . . . . . Salem-Keiser
25-27 . . . . . . at Tri-City
28-30 . . . . .Tri-City

JULY
1-3 . . . . Spokane
4-6 . . . . at Spokane
7-9 . . . . Boise
11-15 . . . at Salem-Keiser
16-18 . . . . at Boise
19-23 . . . . Everett
24-26 . . . . . . at Boise

27-29 . . . . . . at Spokane
31 . . . . Tri-City

AUGUST
1-2 . . . . Tri-City
3-5 . . . . at Tri-City
6-10 . . . . .Eugene
11-15 . . . . at Vancouver
16-18 . . . . Spokane
19-21 . . . . Boise
22-26 . . . . . . at Everett
28-31 . . . . . .Vancouver

SEPTEMBER
1 . . . . .Vancouver

3-5 . . . . Yakima
6-10 . . . . .Vancouver
11-15 . . . . at Eugene
16-18 . . . . Boise
19-21 . . . . . . at Spokane
22-26 . . . . .Eugene
28-31 . . . at Salem-Keiser

SEPTEMBER
1 . . . . . . at Salem-Keiser

7-9 . . . . Spokane
11-15 . . . . . . at Everett
16-18 . . . . . at Spokane
19-23 . . . . Salem-Keiser
24-26 . . . . Spokane
27-29 . . . . . . at Boise
31 . . . . at Yakima

AUGUST
1-2 . . . . at Yakima

ROOKIE

APPALACHIAN LEAGUE

BLUEFIELD

JUNE
19-21 . . . . .at Bristol
22-24 . . . . . Johnson City
25-27 . . . . at Burlington
28-30 . . . . at Kingsport

JULY
1-3 . . . . Pulaski
4-6 . . . . Danville

7-9 . . . . . . .at Burlington
11-13 . . . . at Pulaski
14-16 . . . .at Elizabethton
17-19 . . . . Princeton
20 . . . . .at Princeton
21 . . . . Princeton
22-24 . . . . Danville
26-28 . . . . . .at Princeton
29-31 . . . . Greenville

AUGUST
1-3 . . . . . . at Johnson City
4-6 . . . . Bristol
7-9 . . . . .at Princeton
10-12 . . . . . . .Burlington

14-16 . . . . . Elizabethton
17-19 . . . . . . .at Danville
20-22 . . . . Pulaski
23-25 . . . . Kingsport
26-28 . . . . . . at Greenville

BRISTOL

JUNE
19-21 . . . . .Bluefield
22-24 . . . . Danville
25-27 . . . .at Elizabethton

28-30 . . . . Princeton

JULY
1-3 . . . . Johnson City
4-6 . . . . . . .at Burlington

7-9 . . . . at Greenville
11-13 . . . . . Johnson City
14-16 . . . . Greenville
17-19 . . . . . at Kingsport
20 . . . . Pulaski
21-24 . . . . at Pulaski
26-28 . . . . . at Kingsport
29-31 . . . . . . Elizabethton

AUGUST
1-3 . . . . .at Danville
4-6 . . . . at Bluefield
7-9 . . . . Kingsport
10-12 . . . . . Elizabethton
14-16 . . . . . at Greenville
17-19 . . . . Pulaski
20-22 . . . . at Johnson City
23-25 . . . . .at Princeton
26-28 . . . . .Burlington

BURLINGTON

JUNE
19-21 . . . . at Pulaski
22-24 . . . . . Elizabethton
25-27 . . . . .Bluefield
28-30 . . . . at Johnson City

JULY
1-3 . . . . .at Danville
4-6 . . . . Bristol
7-9 . . . . .Bluefield
11-13 . . . . . at Kingsport
14-16 . . . . . .at Princeton
17-19 . . . . Danville
20 . . . . .at Danville
21 . . . . Danville

DANVILLE

JUNE
19-21 . . . . . . Elizabethton
22-24 . . . . .at Bristol
25-27 . . . . Kingsport
28-30 . . . . . at Greenville

JULY
1-3 . . . . .Burlington
4-6 . . . . at Bluefield
7-9 . . . . .at Princeton
11-13 . . . . Princeton
14-16 . . . . Pulaski
17-19 . . . . . at Burlington
20 . . . . .Burlington

ELIZABETHTON

JUNE
19-21 . . . . .at Danville
22-24 . . . . . . at Burlington
25-27 . . . . Bristol
28-30 . . . . Pulaski

JULY
1-3 . . . . .at Princeton
4-6 . . . . Kingsport
7-9 . . . . . at Johnson City
11-13 . . . . . at Greenville
14-16 . . . . .Bluefield
17-19 . . . . . Johnson City
20 . . . . . at Johnson City

21 . . . . at Burlington
22-24 . . . . . . at Bluefield
26-28 . . . . Johnson City
29-31 . . . . Pulaski

AUGUST
1-3 . . . . .at Elizabethton
4-6 . . . . Pulaski
7-9 . . . . .at Danville
10-12 . . . . . at Bluefield
14-16 . . . . . . Princeton
17-19 . . . . . at Greenville
20-22 . . . . . . Kingsport
23-25 . . . . Johnson City
26-28 . . . . . at Bristol

21 . . . . Johnson City
22-24 . . . . . at Kingsport
26-28 . . . . . . Greenville
29-31 . . . . at Bristol

AUGUST
1-3 . . . . .Burlington
4-6 . . . . Danville
7-9 . . . . . at Johnson City
10-12 . . . . . . .at Bristol
14-16 . . . . . . at Bluefield
17-19 . . . . . . Kingsport
20-22 . . . . . Greenville
23-25 . . . . . . at Pulaski
26-28 . . . . Princeton

GREENVILLE

JUNE
19-21 . . . . at Johnson City
22-24 . . . . at Kingsport
25-27 . . . . Princeton
28-30 . . . . Danville

JULY
1-3 . . . . at Kingsport
4-6 . . . . Johnson City
7-9 . . . . Bristol
11-13 . . . . . Elizabethton
14-16 . . . . at Bristol
17-19 . . . . Pulaski
20 . . . . at Kingsport
21 . . . . Kingsport

22-24 . . . . . at Burlington
26-28 . . . .at Elizabethton
29-31 . . . . . . at Bluefield

AUGUST
1-3 . . . . Kingsport
4-6 . . . . Johnson City
7-9 . . . . at Pulaski
10-12 . . . . . .at Princeton
14-16 . . . . Bristol
17-19 . . . . . . .Burlington
20-22 . . . .at Elizabethton
23-25 . . . . . . .at Danville
26-28 . . . . . . .Bluefield

JOHNSON CITY

JUNE
19-21 . . . . Greenville
22-24 . . . . . . at Bluefield
25-27 . . . . at Pulaski
28-30 . . . . . . .Burlington

JULY
1-3 . . . . at Bristol
4-6 . . . . . . at Greenville
7-9 . . . . Elizabethton
11-13 . . . . at Bristol
14-16 . . . . Kingsport
17-19 . . . .at Elizabethton
20 . . . . Elizabethton

21 . . . . . . .at Elizabethton
22-24 . . . . . .at Princeton
26-28 . . . . .at Danville
29-31 . . . . Kingsport

AUGUST
1-3 . . . . .Bluefield
4-6 . . . . . . at Greenville
7-9 . . . . . . Elizabethton
10-12 . . . . Pulaski
14-16 . . . . . at Kingsport
17-19 . . . . . . Princeton
20-22 . . . . Bristol
23-25 . . . . . at Burlington
26-28 . . . . Danville

KINGSPORT

JUNE
19-21 . . . . . .at Princeton
22-24 . . . . Greenville
25-27 . . . . .at Danville
28-30 . . . . .Bluefield

JULY
1-3 . . . . Greenville
4-6 . . . . .at Elizabethton
7-9 . . . . at Pulaski
11-13 . . . . . . .Burlington
14-16 . . . . at Johnson City
17-19 . . . . Bristol
20 . . . . Greenville

21 . . . . at Greenville
22-24 . . . . . Elizabethton
26-28 . . . . Bristol
29-31 . . . . at Johnson City

AUGUST
1-3 . . . . at Greenville
4-6 . . . . Princeton
7-9 . . . . .at Bristol
10-12 . . . . Danville
14-16 . . . . . Johnson City
17-19 . . . .at Elizabethton
20-22 . . . . at Burlington
23-25 . . . . . at Bluefield
26-28 . . . . Pulaski

PRINCETON

JUNE
19-21 . . . . Kingsport
22-24 . . . . Pulaski
25-27 . . . . . at Greenville
28-30 . . . . .at Bristol

JULY
1-3 . . . . Elizabethton
4-6 . . . . at Pulaski
7-9 . . . . Danville

11-13 . . . . . . .at Danville
14-16 . . . . . . .Burlington
17-19 . . . . . at Bluefield
20 . . . . .Bluefield
21 . . . . at Bluefield
22-24 . . . . . Johnson City
26-28 . . . . . . .Bluefield
29-31 . . . . . at Burlington

AUGUST	
1-3 . . . . at Pulaski	14-16 . . . . . at Burlington
4-6 . . . . at Kingsport	17-19 . . . at Johnson City
7-9 . . . . Bluefield	20-22 . . . . Danville
10-12 . . . . Greenville	23-25 . . . . Bristol
	26-28 . . . . .at Elizabethton

PULASKI

JUNE	
19-21 . . . . . . .Burlington	21-24 . . . . Bristol
22-24 . . . . . .at Princeton	26-28 . . . . . .Burlington
25-27 . . . . . Johnson City	29-31 . . . . . .at Danville
28-30 . . . .at Elizabethton	

	AUGUST
JULY	1-3 . . . . Princeton
1-3 . . . . at Bluefield	4-6 . . . . . at Burlington
4-6 . . . . Princeton	7-9 . . . . Greenville
7-9 . . . . Kingsport	10-12 . . . at Johnson City
11-13 . . . . Bluefield	13-15 . . . . Danville
14-16 . . . . . . .at Danville	17-19 . . . . . .at Bristol
17-19 . . . . . at Greenville	20-22 . . . . . at Bluefield
20 . . . . at Bristol	23-25 . . . . . Elizabethton
	26-28 . . . . . at Kingsport

PIONEER LEAGUE

BILLINGS

JUNE	AUGUST
18-21 . . . . . . .Missoula	1-3 . . . . at Helena
22-24 . . . . . at Helena	4-6 . . . . Great Falls
25-26 . . . . at Great Falls	7-9 . . . . . at Great Falls
27-29 . . . . . Great Falls	10-11 . . . . . at Missoula
30 . . . . at Missoula	13-15 . . . . . .Idaho Falls
	16-19 . . . . Ogden
JULY	20-23 . . . at Idaho Falls
1-3 . . . . at Missoula	24-26 . . . . . . at Ogden
4-6 . . . . Helena	28-29 . . . . . . Helena
7-9 . . . . . at Great Falls	30-31 . . . . . . .Missoula
11-13 . . . . .Orem	
14-17 . . . . Grand Junction	SEPTEMBER
19-22 . . . . at Orem	1-2 . . . . .Missoula
23-25 . . .at Grand Junction	3-4 . . . . at Helena
27-29 . . . . . . Helena	5-6 . . . . . . at Missoula
30-31 . . . . . . .Great Falls	

GRAND JUNCTION

JUNE	31 . . . . Orem
18-20 . . . . at Ogden	AUGUST
21-22 . . . . . at Idaho Falls	1-2 . . . . .Orem
23-24 . . . . . . .Idaho Falls	3-5 . . . . Ogden
25-27 . . . . .Orem	6-8 . . . . at Orem
28-30 . . . . at Orem	9-11 . . . . at Ogden
	13-15 . . . . Helena
JULY	16-19 . . . . . . Great Falls
1-2 . . . . at Orem	21-24 . . . . . . at Helena
3-4 . . . . Orem	25-27 . . . . at Great Falls
5-6 . . . . .Idaho Falls	28-29 . . . at Idaho Falls
7-9 . . . . Ogden	30-31 . . . . at Orem
11-13 . . . . . . at Missoula	
14-17 . . . . . . at Billings	SEPTEMBER
19-22 . . . . Missoula	1-4 . . . . .Idaho Falls
23-25 . . . . Billings	5-6 . . . . Ogden
27-30 . . . . . at Idaho Falls	

GREAT FALLS

JUNE	27-29 . . . . . . at Missoula
18-19 . . . . . at Helena	30-31 . . . . . at Billings
20-21 . . . . Helena	AUGUST
22-24 . . . . at Missoula	1-3 . . . . .Missoula
25-26 . . . . Billings	4-6 . . . . at Billings
27-29 . . . . . at Billings	7-9 . . . . Billings
30 . . . . Helena	10-11 . . . . . . at Helena
JULY	13-15 . . . . . . at Orem
1 . . . . Helena	16-19 . . .at Grand Junction
2-3 . . . . at Helena	21-24 . . . . .Orem
4-6 . . . . Missoula	25-27 . . . . Grand Junction
7-9 . . . . Billings	28-29 . . . . . at Missoula
11-13 . . . . . at Ogden	30-31 . . . . Helena
14-17 . . . at Idaho Falls	SEPTEMBER
19-22 . . . . . . Ogden	1-4 . . . . Missoula
23-25 . . . . . .Idaho Falls	5-6 . . . . at Helena

HELENA

JUNE	30-31 . . . . . . at Missoula
18-19 . . . . Great Falls	AUGUST
20-21 . . . . at Great Falls	1-3 . . . . Billings
22-24 . . . . Billings	4-6 . . . . . . at Missoula
25-26 . . . . Missoula	7-9 . . . . Missoula
27-29 . . . . . at Missoula	10-11 . . . . . .Great Falls
30 . . . . at Great Falls	13-15 . . .at Grand Junction
JULY	16-19 . . . . at Orem
1 . . . . at Great Falls	21-24 . . . . Grand Junction
2-3 . . . . . . .Great Falls	25-27 . . . . .Orem
4-6 . . . . at Billings	28-29 . . . . . at Billings
7-9 . . . . .Missoula	30-31 . . . . . at Great Falls
11-13 . . . .at Idaho Falls	SEPTEMBER
14-17 . . . . . . at Ogden	1-2 . . . . . . at Great Falls
19-22 . . . . . .Idaho Falls	3-4 . . . . Billings
23-25 . . . . Ogden	5-6 . . . . .Great Falls
27-29 . . . . . . at Billings	

IDAHO FALLS

JUNE	31 . . . . at Ogden
18-20 . . . . .Orem	AUGUST
21-22 . . . . Grand Junction	1-2 . . . . at Ogden
23-24 . . .at Grand Junction	3-5 . . . . at Orem
25-27 . . . . . at Ogden	6-8 . . . . Ogden
28-29 . . . . . . at Orem	9-11 . . . . Orem
30 . . . . Ogden	13-15 . . . . . . at Billings
JULY	16-19 . . . . . at Missoula
1-4 . . . . Ogden	20-23 . . . . Billings
5-6 . . . .at Grand Junction	24-26 . . . . . . .Missoula
7-9 . . . . at Orem	28-29 . . . Grand Junction
11-13 . . . . Helena	30-31 . . . . . at Ogden
14-17 . . . . . . Great Falls	SEPTEMBER
19-22 . . . . . at Helena	1-4 . . . .at Grand Junction
24-25 . . . . at Great Falls	5-6 . . . . Orem
27-30 . . . . Grand Junction	

MISSOULA

JUNE
18-21 . . . . at Billings
22-24 . . . . Great Falls
25-26 . . . . at Helena
27-29 . . . . Helena
30 . . . . Billings

JULY
1-3 . . . . Billings
4-6 . . . . . . at Great Falls
7-9 . . . . at Helena
11-13 . . . . Grand Junction
14-17 . . . . Orem
19-22 . . at Grand Junction
23-25 . . . . at Orem
27-29 . . . . . . Great Falls
30-31 . . . . Helena

AUGUST
1-3 . . . . . . at Great Falls
4-6 . . . . Helena
7-9 . . . . at Helena
10-11 . . . . Billings
13-15 . . . . Ogden
16-19 . . . . Idaho Falls
20-23 . . . . at Ogden
24-26 . . . . . at Idaho Falls
28-29 . . . . . . Great Falls
30-31 . . . . . . at Billings

SEPTEMBER
1-2 . . . . at Billings
3-4 . . . . . at Great Falls
5-6 . . . . Billings

OGDEN

JUNE
18-20 . . . . Grand Junction
21-24 . . . . at Orem
25-27 . . . . . . Idaho Falls
28-29 . . . . Grand Junction
30 . . . . at Idaho Falls

JULY
1-4 . . . . . . at Idaho Falls
5-6 . . . . Orem
7-9 . . . . at Grand Junction
11-13 . . . . . . Great Falls
14-17 . . . . Helena
19-22 . . . . at Great Falls
23-25 . . . . . . at Helena
27-30 . . . . Orem
31 . . . . Idaho Falls

AUGUST
1-2 . . . . Idaho Falls
3-5 . . . . at Grand Junction
6-8 . . . . . at Idaho Falls
9-11 . . . . Grand Junction
13-15 . . . . at Missoula
16-19 . . . . at Billings
20-23 . . . . Missoula
24-26 . . . . Billings
28-29 . . . . . . at Orem
30-31 . . . . . Idaho Falls

SEPTEMBER
1-2 . . . . Orem
3-4 . . . . at Orem
5-6 . . . at Grand Junction

OREM

JUNE
18-20 . . . . . at Idaho Falls
21-24 . . . . Ogden
25-27 . . at Grand Junction
28-30 . . . . Grand Junction

JULY
1-2 . . . . Grand Junction
3-4 . . . . at Grand Junction
5-6 . . . . at Ogden
7-9 . . . . . . Idaho Falls
11-13 . . . . . . at Billings
14-17 . . . . . at Missoula
19-22 . . . . Billings
23-25 . . . . . . Missoula
27-30 . . . . . . at Ogden
31 . . . . . at Grand Junction

AUGUST
1-2 . . . . at Grand Junction
3-5 . . . . . . Idaho Falls
6-8 . . . . . Grand Junction
9-11 . . . . . at Idaho Falls
13-15 . . . . Great Falls
16-19 . . . . Helena
21-24 . . . . at Great Falls
25-27 . . . . . at Helena
28-29 . . . . Ogden
30-31 . . . . Grand Junction

SEPTEMBER
1-2 . . . . at Ogden
3-4 . . . . Ogden
5-6 . . . . . . at Idaho Falls

ARIZONA LEAGUE Home games only

ANGELS

JUNE
20 . . . . Athletics
21 . . . . Indians
24 . . . . Giants
26 . . . . Brewers
30 . . . . Padres

JULY
2 . . . . Royals
5 . . . . Cubs
6 . . . . Diamondbacks
11 . . . . Mariners
13 . . . . Dodgers
15 . . . . Athletics
17 . . . . Reds
20 . . . . . . Diamondbacks

ATHLETICS

JUNE
21 . . . . Cubs
22 . . . . Brewers
26 . . . . Indians
27 . . . . . Diamondbacks
30 . . . . Rangers

JULY
2 . . . . Padres
5 . . . . Giants
6 . . . . Reds
12 . . . . Angels
13 . . . . . Diamondbacks
16 . . . . Cubs
18 . . . . Giants
22 . . . . Mariners
23 . . . . Angels

JUNE
25 . . . . Dodgers
28 . . . . Royals
31 . . . . Padres

AUGUST
2 . . . . Brewers
5 . . . . Mariners
6 . . . . Giants
10 . . . . Reds
12 . . . . . Diamondbacks
15 . . . . Rangers
16 . . . . Giants
19 . . . . Indians
20 . . . . Angels
26 . . . . Cubs
27 . . . . . Diamondbacks

BREWERS

JUNE
21 . . . . Dodgers
24 . . . . . Diamondbacks
28 . . . . Reds
29 . . . . Athletics

JULY
3 . . . . Cubs
4 . . . . Indians
6 . . . . Dodgers
9 . . . . Angels
12 . . . . Mariners
13 . . . . Padres
19 . . . . Royals
20 . . . . Indians
23 . . . . Cubs

JUNE
25 . . . . Giants
28 . . . . Angels
30 . . . . Reds

AUGUST
1 . . . . Athletics
4 . . . . Reds
8 . . . . . Diamondbacks
9 . . . . Indians
11 . . . . Dodgers
13 . . . . Royals
18 . . . . Padres
19 . . . . Reds
22 . . . . Rangers
24 . . . . Indians
26 . . . . Mariners
27 . . . . Dodgers

CUBS

JUNE
20 . . . . Giants
22 . . . . . Diamondbacks
25 . . . . Indians
27 . . . . Angels
30 . . . . Royals

JULY
1 . . . . Athletics
7 . . . . Giants
8 . . . . Brewers
11 . . . . Padres
13 . . . . Rangers
18 . . . . Dodgers
19 . . . . Mariners
22 . . . . Reds

JUNE
24 . . . . Indians
27 . . . . Athletics
28 . . . . . Diamondbacks
31 . . . . Royals

AUGUST
2 . . . . Angels
6 . . . . Brewers
8 . . . . Dodgers
10 . . . . Rangers
11 . . . . Angels
16 . . . . Reds
17 . . . . Athletics
21 . . . . Mariners
22 . . . . . Diamondbacks
25 . . . . Giants
28 . . . . . Diamondbacks

DIAMONDBACKS

JUNE
21 . . . . Giants
23 . . . . Padres
26 . . . . Mariners
28 . . . . Cubs

JULY
1 . . . . Angels
2 . . . . Brewers
7 . . . . Athletics
8 . . . . Indians
14 . . . . Royals
15 . . . . Giants
17 . . . . Brewers
18 . . . . Rangers
24 . . . . Dodgers
25 . . . . Padres

JUNE
27 . . . . Mariners
29 . . . . Dodgers

AUGUST
3 . . . . Cubs
4 . . . . Athletics
7 . . . . Royals
9 . . . . Rangers
13 . . . . Indians
14 . . . . Giants
16 . . . . Angels
18 . . . . Reds
21 . . . . Athletics
23 . . . . Cubs
26 . . . . Giants
29 . . . . Angels

AUGUST
1 . . . . Reds
5 . . . . Royals
7 . . . . Cubs
9 . . . . Dodgers
12 . . . . Padres
14 . . . . Rangers
19 . . . . . Diamondbacks
22 . . . . Giants
24 . . . . . Diamondbacks
25 . . . . Athletics

DODGERS

JUNE
22	Rangers
23	Reds
26	Cubs
29	Diamondbacks

JULY
1	Brewers
3	Royals
4	Mariners
7	Angels
9	Indians
12	Reds
17	Indians
20	Athletics
22	Brewers
23	Giants
27	Reds
28	Padres

AUGUST
1	Giants
4	Indians
6	Diamondbacks
7	Brewers
12	Brewers
13	Padres
17	Angels
19	Royals
22	Athletics
23	Indians
28	Rangers
29	Reds

GIANTS

JUNE
22	Angels
25	Rangers
27	Brewers

JULY
1	Mariners
2	Dodgers
4	Padres
6	Cubs
9	Reds
12	Cubs
16	Angels
17	Athletics
21	Athletics
22	Diamondbacks
26	Royals
28	Rangers
30	Diamondbacks

AUGUST
2	Dodgers
4	Angels
5	Cubs
10	Indians
11	Mariners
15	Reds
17	Brewers
19	Padres
21	Angels
24	Athletics
27	Cubs
29	Athletics

INDIANS

JUNE
20	Reds
23	Brewers
24	Athletics
28	Dodgers
30	Giants

JULY
3	Mariners
5	Rangers
11	Royals
12	Diamondbacks
14	Reds
15	Dodgers
19	Diamondbacks
21	Cubs
26	Padres
27	Brewers
30	Rangers

AUGUST
1	Cubs
3	Dodgers
6	Mariners
8	Reds
11	Athletics
15	Royals
16	Brewers
20	Giants
21	Dodgers
25	Reds
26	Angels
29	Brewers

MARINERS

JUNE
20	Padres
24	Royals
25	Reds
29	Angels
30	Reds

JULY
6	Indians
8	Rangers
9	Athletics
14	Dodgers
15	Padres
17	Cubs
20	Royals
21	Rangers
24	Brewers
26	Angels
31	Giants

AUGUST
1	Diamondbacks
3	Royals
4	Rangers
9	Athletics
10	Padres
14	Brewers
16	Dodgers
18	Cubs
20	Rangers
24	Royals
25	Padres
28	Indians

PADRES

JUNE
22	Royals
25	Angels
27	Dodgers
29	Giants

JULY
3	Diamondbacks
5	Mariners
7	Rangers
9	Royals
14	Cubs
16	Mariners
18	Brewers
20	Reds
23	Rangers
24	Royals
29	Indians
30	Dodgers

AUGUST
2	Diamondbacks
5	Indians
7	Giants
8	Mariners
14	Athletics
15	Mariners
17	Rangers
20	Cubs
23	Reds
24	Rangers
27	Angels
28	Royals

RANGERS

JUNE
20	Royals
23	Mariners
24	Dodgers
28	Padres
29	Indians

JULY
2	Cubs
4	Angels
9	Diamondbacks
11	Athletics
14	Brewers
16	Royals
19	Padres
20	Giants
24	Reds
26	Cubs
29	Mariners
31	Angels

AUGUST
3	Padres
5	Reds
7	Athletics
8	Royals
12	Giants
13	Mariners
18	Dodgers
19	Mariners
23	Brewers
25	Royals
29	Padres

REDS

JUNE
21	Mariners
24	Padres
26	Giants
29	Royals

JULY
1	Indians
3	Rangers
4	Diamondbacks
8	Dodgers
11	Giants
15	Brewers
16	Indians
19	Dodgers
21	Angels
25	Rangers
26	Athletics
29	Cubs
31	Indians

AUGUST
3	Brewers
6	Angels
9	Padres
11	Diamondbacks
13	Cubs
14	Indians
20	Royals
21	Brewers
24	Dodgers
26	Dodgers
28	Brewers

ROYALS

JUNE
23	Cubs
25	Athletics
27	Rangers
28	Mariners

JULY
4	Athletics
5	Reds
7	Brewers
8	Padres
13	Giants
15	Rangers
18	Angels
21	Padres
23	Diamondbacks
25	Indians
29	Brewers
30	Mariners

AUGUST
2	Rangers
4	Padres
9	Giants
10	Angels
12	Cubs
14	Dodgers
17	Diamondbacks
18	Indians
22	Padres
23	Mariners
27	Rangers
29	Mariners

GULF COAST LEAGUE Home games only

ASTROS

JUNE	
18	.Cardinals
20	.Marlins
22	Nationals
26	.Cardinals
28	.Marlins
30	Nationals

JULY	
2	.Marlins
4	.Cardinals
6	Nationals
10	.Marlins
12	.Cardinals
14	Nationals
16	.Cardinals
18	.Marlins
20	Nationals

24	.Cardinals
26	.Marlins
28	Nationals
30	.Marlins

AUGUST	
1	.Cardinals
3	Nationals
7	.Marlins
9	.Cardinals
11	Nationals
13	.Cardinals
15	.Marlins
17	Nationals
21	.Cardinals
23	.Marlins
25	Nationals

BLUE JAYS

JUNE	
19	Pirates
20	Yankees
23	.Tigers
25	Braves
28	Phillies
29	Pirates

JULY	
3	Yankees
4	.Tigers
7	Braves
9	Phillies
12	Pirates
13	Yankees
17	.Tigers
18	Braves
21	Phillies

23	Pirates
26	Yankees
27	.Tigers
31	Braves

AUGUST	
1	Phillies
4	Pirates
6	Yankees
9	.Tigers
10	Braves
14	Phillies
15	Pirates
18	Yankees
20	.Tigers
23	Braves
24	Phillies

BRAVES

JUNE	
18	Yankees
20	Phillies
22	Pirates
26	.Blue Jays
27	.Tigers
30	Yankees

JULY	
3	Phillies
5	Pirates
7	.Blue Jays
10	.Tigers
11	Yankees
13	Phillies
16	Pirates
19	.Blue Jays
20	.Tigers

24	Yankees
26	Phillies
28	Pirates
30	.Blue Jays

AUGUST	
2	.Tigers
3	Yankees
6	Phillies
8	Pirates
11	.Blue Jays
13	.Tigers
16	Yankees
18	Phillies
21	Pirates
22	.Blue Jays
25	.Tigers

CARDINALS

JUNE	
19	.Astros
20	Nationals
23	.Marlins
25	.Astros
28	Nationals
29	.Marlins

JULY	
2	Nationals
5	.Astros
7	.Marlins
10	Nationals
11	.Astros
13	.Marlins
17	.Astros
18	Nationals
21	.Marlins

23	.Astros
26	Nationals
27	.Marlins
30	Nationals

AUGUST	
2	.Astros
4	.Marlins
7	Nationals
8	.Astros
10	.Marlins
14	.Astros
15	Nationals
18	.Marlins
20	.Astros
23	Nationals
24	.Marlins

MARLINS

JUNE	
18	Nationals
21	.Astros
22	.Cardinals
26	Nationals
27	.Astros
30	.Cardinals

JULY	
3	.Astros
4	Nationals
6	.Cardinals
9	.Astros
12	Nationals
14	.Cardinals
16	Nationals
19	.Astros
20	.Cardinals

24	Nationals
25	.Astros
28	.Cardinals
31	.Astros

AUGUST	
1	Nationals
3	.Cardinals
6	.Astros
9	Nationals
11	.Cardinals
13	Nationals
16	.Astros
17	.Cardinals
21	Nationals
22	.Astros
25	.Cardinals

NATIONALS

JUNE	
19	.Marlins
21	.Cardinals
23	.Astros
25	.Marlins
27	.Cardinals
29	.Astros

JULY	
3	.Cardinals
5	.Marlins
7	.Astros
9	.Cardinals
11	.Marlins
13	.Astros
17	.Marlins
19	.Cardinals
21	.Astros

23	.Marlins
25	.Cardinals
27	.Astros
31	.Cardinals

AUGUST	
2	.Marlins
4	.Astros
6	.Cardinals
8	.Marlins
10	.Astros
14	.Marlins
16	.Cardinals
18	.Astros
20	.Marlins
22	.Cardinals
24	.Astros

ORIOLES

JUNE	
18	Twins
20	Red Sox
23	Rays
26	Twins
28	Red Sox
29	Rays

JULY	
3	Red Sox
4	Twins
7	Rays
9	Red Sox
10	Rays
12	Twins
16	Twins
18	Red Sox
21	Rays

24	Twins
26	Red Sox
27	Rays
30	Red Sox

AUGUST	
1	Twins
4	Rays
7	Red Sox
9	Twins
10	Rays
13	Twins
15	Red Sox
18	Rays
20	Red Sox
22	Twins
24	Rays

RAYS

JUNE	
19	Red Sox
21	Twins
23	Orioles
25	Red Sox
27	Twins
30	Orioles

JULY	
2	Twins
5	Red Sox
6	Orioles
12	Red Sox
13	Twins
14	Orioles
17	Red Sox
19	Twins
20	Orioles

23	Red Sox
25	Twins
28	Orioles
31	Twins

AUGUST	
2	Red Sox
3	Orioles
6	Twins
8	Red Sox
11	Orioles
14	Red Sox
16	Twins
17	Orioles
21	Twins
22	Red Sox
25	Orioles

PHILLIES

JUNE	
18	Tigers
21	Braves
23	Yankees
26	Pirates
27	Blue Jays
30	Tigers

JULY	
2	Braves
5	Yankees
6	Pirates
10	Blue Jays
11	Tigers
14	Braves
16	Yankees
19	Pirates
20	Blue Jays

24	Tigers
25	Braves
28	Yankees
30	Pirates

AUGUST	
2	Blue Jays
3	Tigers
7	Braves
8	Yankees
11	Pirates
13	Blue Jays
16	Tigers
17	Braves
21	Yankees
22	Pirates
25	Blue Jays

RED SOX

JUNE	
18	Rays
21	Orioles
22	Twins
26	Rays
27	Orioles
30	Twins

JULY	
2	Orioles
4	Rays
6	Twins
11	Rays
13	Orioles
14	Twins
16	Rays
19	Orioles
20	Twins

24	Rays
25	Orioles
28	Twins
31	Orioles

AUGUST	
1	Rays
3	Twins
6	Orioles
9	Rays
11	Twins
13	Rays
16	Orioles
17	Twins
21	Orioles
23	Rays
25	Twins

PIRATES

JUNE	
18	Blue Jays
20	Tigers
23	Braves
25	Phillies
27	Yankees
30	Blue Jays

JULY	
3	Tigers
4	Braves
7	Phillies
10	Yankees
11	Blue Jays
13	Tigers
17	Braves
18	Phillies
20	Yankees

24	Blue Jays
26	Tigers
27	Braves
31	Phillies

AUGUST	
2	Yankees
3	Blue Jays
6	Tigers
9	Braves
10	Phillies
13	Yankees
16	Blue Jays
18	Tigers
20	Braves
23	Phillies
25	Yankees

TIGERS

JUNE	
19	Phillies
21	Pirates
22	Blue Jays
25	Yankees
28	Braves
29	Phillies

JULY	
2	Pirates
5	Blue Jays
7	Yankees
9	Braves
12	Phillies
14	Pirates
16	Blue Jays
18	Yankees
21	Braves

23	Phillies
25	Pirates
28	Blue Jays
31	Yankees

AUGUST	
1	Braves
4	Phillies
7	Pirates
8	Blue Jays
10	Yankees
14	Braves
15	Phillies
17	Pirates
21	Blue Jays
23	Yankees
24	Braves

TWINS

JUNE	
19	Orioles
20	Rays
23	Red Sox
25	Orioles
28	Rays
29	Red Sox

JULY	
3	Rays
5	Orioles
7	Red Sox
9	Rays
10	Red Sox
11	Orioles
17	Orioles
18	Rays
21	Red Sox

23	Orioles
26	Rays
27	Red Sox
30	Rays

AUGUST	
2	Orioles
4	Red Sox
7	Rays
8	Orioles
10	Red Sox
14	Orioles
15	Rays
18	Red Sox
20	Rays
23	Orioles
24	Red Sox

YANKEES

JUNE	
19	Braves
21	Blue Jays
23	Phillies
26	Tigers
28	Pirates
29	Braves

JULY	
2	Blue Jays
4	Phillies
6	Tigers
9	Pirates
12	Braves
14	Blue Jays
17	Phillies
19	Tigers
21	Pirates

23	Braves
25	Blue Jays
27	Phillies
30	Tigers

AUGUST	
1	Pirates
4	Braves
7	Blue Jays
9	Phillies
11	Tigers
14	Pirates
15	Braves
17	Blue Jays
20	Phillies
22	Tigers
24	Pirates

INDEPENDENT

Home Games Only

AMERICAN ASSOCIATION

AMARILLO SOX

MAY	
18-20	Winnipeg
21-13	Fargo-Moorhead
24-27	Laredo

JUNE	
4-6	El Paso
15-17	Gary SouthShore
25-27	Laredo

JULY	
3-6	Worcester

7-10	Wichita
16-18	El Paso
19-22	Laredo
30-31	Wichita

AUGUST	
1	Wichita
3-5	El Paso
14-16	Grand Prairie
24-26	Grand Prairie
28-31	Kansas City

EL PASO DIABLOS

MAY	
17-20	Fargo-Moorhead
24-26	Winnipeg
28-30	Kansas City

JUNE	
7-10	Grand Prairie
11-13	Amarillo
22-24	Laredo

JULY	
3-6	Laredo
7-10	Worcester

20-22	Lincoln
27-29	Amarillo
31	Grand Prairie

AUGUST	
1-2	Grand Prairie
7-9	Laredo
10-12	Sioux City
21-23	Wichita
31	Sioux Falls

SEPTEMBER	
1-3	Sioux Falls

FARGO-MOORHEAD REDHAWKS

MAY	
25-27	Sioux Falls
28-30	Wichita

JUNE	
4-7	Kansas City
8-10	Winnipeg
18-20	Sioux City
26-28	Lincoln
29-30	St. Paul

JULY	
1	St. Paul

7-10	Kansas City
12-15	Grand Prairie
24-26	Sioux Falls

AUGUST	
3-5	Lincoln
7-9	St. Paul
13-16	Winnipeg
17-19	Rockland
21-23	at Grand Prairie
28-31	Laredo

GARY SOUTHSHORE RAILCATS

MAY	
25-27	Wichita
28-30	Sioux Falls

JUNE	
7-10	Newark
11-13	Wichita
22-24	Lincoln
25-28	Kansas City

JULY	
7-10	Lincoln

24-26	Sioux City
27-29	Fargo-Moorhead

AUGUST	
3-6	St. Paul
7-9	Amarillo
17-19	Sioux Falls
21-23	Winnipeg
28-31	St. Paul

SEPTEMBER	
1-3	Laredo

GRAND PRAIRIE AIR HOGS

MAY	
21-23	El Paso
25-27	Kansas City

JUNE	
4-6	Laredo
11-13	Laredo
14-16	Newark

29-30	. . . . Amarillo

JULY	
1-2	. . . . Amarillo
3-6	. . . . .Wichita
20-23	. . . . . . Kansas City
24-26	. . . . El Paso

AUGUST	
3-6	. . . . Laredo
7-9	. . . . Sioux City
17-20	. . . . El Paso
21-23	. .Fargo-Moorhead
28-30	. . . . . . .Sioux Falls

SEPTEMBER	
1-3	. . . . Amarillo

JULY	
1	. . . . El Paso
3-6	. . . . Gary SouthShore
12-15	. . . . . .Sioux Falls
20-23	. . . . .St. Paul
31	. . . . . Gary SouthShore

AUGUST	
1-2	. . . . Gary SouthShore
3-5	. . . . Winnipeg
14-16	. . . . Rockland
21-23	. . . . Kansas City

SEPTEMBER	
1-3	. . . . Kansas City

KANSAS CITY T-BONES

MAY	
17-20	. . . . . . New Jersey
21-23	. . . Gary SouthShore

JUNE	
1-3	. . . . Amarillo
8-10	. . . . .Wichita
11-13	. . . . .Newark
18-20	. . . . El Paso
21-24	. . . . Amarillo

JULY	
3-6	. . . . .Sioux Falls

13-14	. . . . .Wichita
16-18	. . . . Sioux City
24-26	. . . . .St. Paul
27-29	. . . . . Grand Prairie
31	. . . . Winnipeg

AUGUST	
1-2	. . . . Winnipeg
14-16	. . . . Lincoln
17-19	. . . . Laredo
24-26	. . .Fargo-Moorhead

SIOUX FALLS PHEASANTS

MAY	
17-18	. . . . Sioux City
20	. . . . Sioux City
22-24	. . . . .St. Paul
31	. . . . Lincoln

JUNE	
1-3	. . . . .Lincoln
4-6	. . . . Gary SouthShore
13	. . . . Sioux City
15-17	. . . . .St. Paul
18-20	. . . . Winnipeg
26-28	. . . . El Paso

29-30	. . . Gary SouthShore

JULY	
1-2	. . . . Gary SouthShore
16-18	. . .Fargo-Moorhead
19-22	. . . . Winnipeg
30-31	. . . . Quebec

AUGUST	
1-2	. . . . Quebec
3-5	. . . . .Wichita
10-12	. . .Fargo-Moorhead
14-16	. . . . Laredo
24-26	. . . . . . Sioux City

LAREDO LEMURS

MAY	
17-20	. . . Grand Prairie
21-23	. . . . Winnipeg

JUNE	
1-3	. . . . El Paso
7-10	. . . . Amarillo
14-16	. . . . El Paso
18-20	. . . Gary SouthShore
29-30	. . . . Worcester

JULY	
1	. . . . Worcester
7-10	. . . . . Grand Prairie
11-14	. . . . Amarillo
15-17	. . . . .Wichita
23-25	. . . . Lincoln
27-29	. . . . .Wichita

AUGUST	
10-12	. . . . . Grand Prairie
21-23	. . . . Amarillo
24-26	. . . . El Paso

ST. PAUL SAINTS

MAY	
17-20	. . . Gary SouthShore
25-27	. . . . Sioux City

JUNE	
8-10	. . . . . . .Sioux Falls
11-13	. . .Fargo-Moorhead
22-24	. . . . Sioux Falls

JULY	
3-6	. . . . .Lincoln
7-10	. . . . Sioux Falls
16-18	. . . . . Grand Prairie

27-29	. . . . Quebec
30-31	. . .Fargo-Moorhead

AUGUST	
1-2	. . . . .Fargo-Moorhead
10-12	. . . . Amarillo
13-15	. . . Gary SouthShore
20-22	. . . . . . Rockland
24-27	. . . . Winnipeg

SEPTEMBER	
1-3	. . . . .Wichita

LINCOLN SALTDOGS

MAY	
23	. . . . Sioux City
25-27	. . . . . . New Jersey
28-30	. . . . Laredo

JUNE	
4-7	. . . . Winnipeg
8-10	. . . . Sioux City
14-16	. . .Fargo-Moorhead
18-20	. . . . .St. Paul
29-30	. . . . . Kansas City

JULY	
1-2	. . . . Kansas City
12-15	. . . . El Paso
16-18	. . . . Winnipeg
27-29	. . . . . . Sioux City
31	. . . . Laredo

AUGUST	
1-2	. . . . Laredo
6-8	. . . . .Wichita
10-12	. . Gary SouthShore
17-19	. . . . Amarillo
20-23	. . . . . . .Sioux Falls

WICHITA WINGNUTS

MAY	
17-20	. . . . .Lincoln
21-23	. . . . . New Jersey

JUNE	
1-3	. . . . . . Grand Prairie
4-7	. . . . Sioux City
15-17	. . . . . Kansas City
18-20	. . . . Amarillo
26-28	. . . . .St. Paul
29-30	. . . . . . Winnipeg

JULY	
1	. . . . Winnipeg
11-12	. . . . . . Kansas City
19-22	. . .Fargo-Moorhead
23-26	. . . . Amarillo

AUGUST	
13-16	. . . . El Paso
17-19	. . . . Sioux City
24-26	. . . Gary SouthShore
27-30	. . . . El Paso

SIOUX CITY EXPLORERS

MAY	
19	. . . . .Sioux Falls
21-22	. . . . .Lincoln
24	. . . . .Lincoln
29-31	. . . . . Grand Prairie

JUNE	
1-3	. . . . .Fargo-Moorhead
11-12	. . . . . . .Sioux Falls
14-17	. . . . Winnipeg
21-24	. . . . .Wichita
29-30	. . . . El Paso

WINNIPEG GOLDEYES

MAY	
29-31	. . . . Amarillo

JUNE	
1-3	. . . Gary SouthShore
11-13	. . . . .Lincoln
21-24	. . .Fargo-Moorhead
25-27	. . . . Sioux City

JULY	
3-6	. . . . .Fargo-Moorhead
7-10	. . . . . . .Sioux Falls
12-15	. . . . .St. Paul
24-26	. . . . Quebec
27-29	. . . . . . .Sioux Falls

AUGUST
6-8 . . . . Sioux Falls
9-11 . . . . Wichita
17-19 . . . . St. Paul

28-31 . . . . Sioux City
SEPTEMBER
1-3 . . . . . .Fargo-Moorhead

ATLANTIC LEAGUE Home games only

BRIDGEPORT BLUEFISH

APRIL	
26-29 . . . . Camden	
MAY	
1-3 . . . . Long Island	
18-20 . . . . . . Sugar Land	
21-23 . . Southern Maryland	
28-31 . . . . York	
JUNE	
8-10 . . . . Lancaster	
11-13 . . . . Camden	
14-17 . . . . Lancaster	
22-24 . . . . Somerset	
25-27 . . . . York	

JULY	
2-4 . . . . Sugar Land	
13-15 . . . . . Long Island	
23-25 . . . . York	
26-29 . . . . . . Long Island	
AUGUST	
10-12 . . . . Camden	
16-19 . . . . . . Somerset	
20-23 . . Southern Maryland	
31 . . . . Somerset	
SEPTEMBER	
1-2 . . . . Somerset	
11-13 . . Southern Maryland	
14-16 . . . . . . Sugar Land	
18-20 . . . . Lancaster	

CAMDEN RIVERSHARKS

MAY	
9-10 . . . . Lancaster	
11-12 . . . . . . Bridgeport	
15-17 . . . . Lancaster	
22-23 . . Southern Maryland	
28-21 . . . . . . Long Island	
JUNE	
1-3 . . . Southern Maryland	
14-17 . . . . . . Sugar Land	
19-21 . . . . . . Long Island	
28-30 . . Southern Maryland	
JULY	
1 . . . . Southern Maryland	
5-6 . . . . York	
20-22 . . . . York	

23-25 . . . . Lancaster	
30-31 . . . . Lancaster	
AUGUST	
3-5 . . . . Sugar Land	
13-15 . . . . . . Bridgeport	
18-19 . . . . York	
20-23 . . . . . . Somerset	
24-26 . . Southern Maryland	
31 . . . . Sugar Land	
SEPTEMBER	
1-2 . . . . Sugar Land	
7-10 . . . . . . Bridgeport	
11-13 . . . . York	
18-20 . . Southern Maryland	
21-23 . . . . . . Long Island	

LANCASTER BARNSTORMERS

MAY	
1-3 . . . . Somerset	
4-6 . . . . Sugar Land	
7-8 . . . . Camden	
11-13 . . Southern Maryland	
18-20 . . . . York	
28-31 . . . . Somerset	
JUNE	
1-3 . . . . Sugar Land	
11-13 . . . . . . Long Island	
19-21 . . . . . . Bridgeport	
28-30 . . . . York	
JULY	
1 . . . . York	
2-4 . . . . Camden	

5-8 . . . . Long Island	
17-19 . . . . Camden	
20-22 . . . . . . Bridgeport	
AUGUST	
1-2 . . . . Camden	
3-5 . . . . Somerset	
7-9 . . . . York	
20-23 . . . . . . Sugar Land	
24-26 . . . . . . Long Island	
31 . . . . Southern Maryland	
SEPTEMBER	
1-2 . . . Southern Maryland	
3-6 . . . . Bridgeport	
14-16 . . Southern Maryland	

LONG ISLAND DUCKS

MAY	
4-6 . . . . Camden	
8-10 . . . . York	
18-20 . . . . St. Paul	
21-23 . . . . Lancaster	
24-27 . . . . . . Bridgeport	
JUNE	
1-3 . . . . York	
5-7 . . . . Bridgeport	
14-16 . . Southern Maryland	
28-30 . . . . . . Sugar Land	
JULY	
1 . . . . Sugar Land	
2-4 . . . Southern Maryland	

16-19 . . . . St. Paul	
20-22 . . . . . . Sugar Land	
23-25 . . Southern Maryland	
AUGUST	
3-5 . . . . Bridgeport	
6-8 . . . . Sugar Land	
10-12 . . . . York	
16-19 . . . . . . Lancaster	
27-29 . . . . Camden	
SEPTEMBER	
3-5 . . . . St. Paul	
11-13 . . . . . . Lancaster	
14-16 . . . . Camden	

SOMERSET PATRIOTS

APRIL	
26-29 . . . . . . Long Island	
MAY	
4-6 . . . Southern Maryland	
7-10 . . . . Sugar Land	
15-17 . . . . . . Bridgeport	
24-27 . . . . Camden	
JUNE	
5-7 . . . . Lancaster	
14-17 . . . . York	
25-27 . . . . . . Long Island	
28-30 . . . . . . Bridgeport	
JULY	
1 . . . . Bridgeport	

13-15 . . . . Camden	
23-25 . . . . . . Sugar Land	
26-29 . . Southern Maryland	
AUGUST	
7-9 . . . . Camen	
10-12 . . Southern Maryland	
13-15 . . . . York	
24-26 . . . . York	
27-30 . . . . Lancaster	
SEPTEMBER	
7-9 . . . . Lancaster	
12-13 . . . . . . Sugar Land	
18-20 . . . . . . Long Island	
21-23 . . . . . . Bridgeport	

SOUTHERN MARYLAND BLUE CRABS

APRIL	
26-29 . . . . Lancaster	
MAY	
1-3 . . . . Sugar Land	
7-10 . . . . Bridgeport	
15-17 . . . . York	
18-20 . . . . Camden	
JUNE	
1-3 . . . . Bridgeport	
4-6 . . . . Sugar Land	
8-10 . . . . Camden	
19-21 . . . . . . Somerset	
22-24 . . . . . . Long Island	
25-27 . . . . . . Lancaster	

JULY	
5-8 . . . . Somerset	
20-22 . . . . Somerset	
30-31 . . . . . . Long Island	
AUGUST	
1-2 . . . . Long Island	
7-9 . . . . Bridgeport	
13-15 . . . . . . Long Island	
16-19 . . . . . . Sugar Land	
27-29 . . . . York	
SEPTEMBER	
3-6 . . . . Camden	
7-10 . . . . York	
21-23 . . . . Lancaster	

SUGAR LAND SKEETERS

APRIL	
26-29 . . . . York	
MAY	
11-16 . . . . . . Long Island	
24-27 . . . . . . Lancaster	
28-31 . . Southern Maryland	

JUNE	
8-12 . . . . Somerset	
22-27 . . . . Camden	
JULY	
5-8 . . . . Bridgeport	
13-18 . . Southern Maryland	
26-29 . . . . Camden	

30-31 . . . . Somerset	24-29 . . . . . . Bridgeport

AUGUST

1-2 . . . . Somerset	
10-15 . . . . Lancaster	

SEPTEMBER

7-10 . . . . . . Long Island	
18-23 . . . . York	

YORK REVOLUTION

MAY

1-3 . . . . Camden	13-15 . . . . Lancaster
4-6 . . . . Bridgeport	16-19 . . . . . . Bridgeport
11-13 . . . . Somerset	26-29 . . . . . . Lancaster
21-23 . . . . . Sugar Land	31 . . . . Bridgeport
24-27 . . Southern Maryland	

AUGUST

JUNE	1-2 . . . . Bridgeport
5-7 . . . . Camden	4-5 . . . Southern Maryland
8-10 . . . . Long Island	16-17 . . . . Camden
11-13 . . Southern Maryland	20-23 . . . . . . Long Island
18-20 . . . . . . Sugar Land	31 . . . . Long Island
22-24 . . . . Lancaster	

SEPTEMBER

JULY	1-2 . . . . Long Island
2-4 . . . . Somerset	3-6 . . . . Sugar Land
7-8 . . . . Camden	14-16 . . . . Somerset

CAN-AM LEAGUE Home games only

NEWARK BEARS

JUNE

1-3 . . . . St. Paul	18 . . . . Rockland
4-6 . . . . Rockland	25 . . . . Rockland
18-21 . . . . . . New Jersey	27-29 . . . . . . New Jersey
25-28 . . . . Rockland	
29-30 . . . . . . New Jersey	**AUGUST**

	6-8 . . . . Kansas City
JULY	17-19 . . . . Quebec
1-2 . . . . New Jersey	20-22 . . . . . . Worcester
11-14 . . . . Quebec	24-26 . . . . Lincoln
16 . . . . Rockland	

SEPTEMBER

1-3 . . . . Worcester	

NEW JERSEY JACKALS

MAY

29-31 . . . . Rockland	10 . . . . Newark
	11-14 . . . . Rockland
JUNE	19-22 . . . Gary SouthShore
4-7 . . . . St. Paul	23-25 . . . . . . Worcester
12 . . . . Rockland	
14 . . . . Rockland	**AUGUST**
15-17 . . . . Quebec	3-5 . . . . Newark
22-24 . . . . . Grand Prairie	6-8 . . . . Worcester
25-27 . . . . Quebec	12 . . . . Rockland
	13-16 . . . . Quebec
JULY	17-19 . . . . . . Worcester
6 . . . . Rockland	28 . . . . Newark
7-8 . . . . Newark	30-31 . . . . Newark

QUEBEC LES CAPITALES

MAY	**JUNE**
17-20 . . . . Rockland	5-7 . . . . Worcester
29-31 . . . . St. Paul	8-10 . . . . . . New Jersey

18-21 . . . . . . Worcester	
29-30 . . . . . . Rockland	**AUGUST**
	3-5 . . . . Worcester
JULY	6-8 . . . . Rockland
1 . . . . Rockland	10-12 . . . . Newark
3-6 . . . . Newark	21-23 . . . . . New Jersey
16-18 . . . Gary SouthShore	28-31 . . . . Lincoln
19-22 . . . . Newark	

SEPTEMBER

1-3 . . . . New Jersey	

ROCKLAND BOULDERS

MAY

22-24 . . . . Newark	17 . . . . Newark
25-27 . . . . . . Worcester	19-22 . . . . . . Worcester
	24 . . . . Newark
JUNE	26 . . . . Newark
1-3 . . . . Quebec	30-31 . . . . Newark
15-17 . . . . . . Worcester	
18-21 . . . . . Grand Prairie	**AUGUST**
22-24 . . . . Quebec	1-2 . . . . Newark
	3-5 . . . . Kansas City
JULY	9-11 . . . . . . New Jersey
3-5 . . . . . . New Jersey	24-26 . . . . . . New Jersey
7-10 . . . . Quebec	
15 . . . . New Jersey	**SEPTEMBER**
	1-3 . . . . Lincoln

WORCESTER TORNADOES

MAY

21-22 . . . . Quebec	**JULY**
29-31 . . . . Newark	12-15 . . Gary SouthShore
	16-18 . . . . . . New Jersey
JUNE	27-29 . . . . . . Rockland
1-3 . . . . New Jersey	30-31 . . . . . . New Jersey
8-10 . . . . Rockland	
11-14 . . . . Quebec	**AUGUST**
22-24 . . . . Newark	1-2 . . . . New Jersey
25-27 . . . . . Grand Prairie	9-11 . . . . . . Kansas City
	13-16 . . . . Newark
	24-26 . . . . Quebec
	27-30 . . . . Rockford

FRONTIER LEAGUE Home games only

EVANSVILLE OTTERS

MAY

18-20 . . . . . Washington	13-15 . . . . Rockford
21-23 . . . . Southern Illinois	22-23 . . . . . . River City
	25-27 . . . . Southern Illinois
JUNE	31 . . . . Joliet
5-7 . . . . Lake Erie	
14-16 . . . . London	**AUGUST**
17-19 . . . . . . River City	1-2 . . . . Joliet
23-24 . . . . Florence	3-5 . . . . Normal
30 . . . . Windy City	7-9 . . . . . Traverse City
	17-19 . . . . . . Gateway
JULY	31 . . . . Florence
1-2 . . . . Windy City	
3-5 . . . . . . Schaumburg	**SEPTEMBER**
	1-2 . . . . Florence

FLORENCE FREEDOM

MAY
17-19 . . . . . Traverse City
22-24 . . . . Rockford

JUNE
1-3 . . . . Normal
5-7 . . . . River City
11-13 . . . . London
14-16 . . . . . Washington
27-29 . . . . Gateway
30 . . . . Lake Erie

JULY
1 . . . . Lake Erie
6-8 . . . . Evansville
22-24 . . . . Lake Erie
28-29 . . . . Evansville
31 . . . . Schaumburg

AUGUST
1-2 . . . . Schaumburg
7-9 . . . . Windy City
17-19 . . . Southern Illinois
21-23 . . . . Joliet
24-26 . . . . . . Washington

GATEWAY GRIZZLIES

MAY
9 . . . . . Southern Illinois
12-13 . . . . River City
18-20 . . . . Joliet
29-31 . . . . . . Evansville

JUNE
1-3 . . . . . . Traverse City
11-13 . . . . . . River City
23-25 . . . Southern Illinois
30 . . . . Southern Illinois

JULY
1-2 . . . . . Southern Illinois
3-5 . . . . Windy City

JULY (col 2)
12-14 . . . . Florence
19-21 . . . . . . Schaumburg
22-24 . . . . Rockford
31 . . . . London

AUGUST
1-2 . . . . London
3-5 . . . . River City
7-9 . . . . Lake Erie
14-16 . . . . . . Washington
24-26 . . . . Normal
31 . . . . Rockford

SEPTEMBER
1-2 . . . . Rockford

JOLIET SLAMMERS

MAY
23-24 . . . . . Traverse City
25-27 . . . . Evansville

JUNE
1-3 . . . . Washington
11-13 . . . . . Schaumburg
17-19 . . . . . Traverse City
20-22 . . . . . Schaumburg
27-29 . . . Southern Illinois

JULY
3-5 . . . . Florence
6-8 . . . . Normal
16-18 . . . . Gateway
19-21 . . . . . Windy City
28-30 . . . . . Windy City

AUGUST
7-9 . . . . London
10-12 . . . . Rockford
17-19 . . . . . . Lake Erie
24-26 . . . . . . River City

LAKE ERIE CRUSHERS

MAY
18-20 . . . . . Schaumburg
29-31 . . . . Joliet

JUNE
1-3 . . . . Windy City
8-10 . . . . Gateway
11-13 . . . . . Washington
17-19 . . . . Florence
27-29 . . . . . . River City

JULY
3-5 . . . . London

JULY (col 2)
6-8 . . . . . Southern Illinois
19-21 . . . . . . Evansville
28-30 . . . . Washington
31 . . . . Rockford

AUGUST
1-2 . . . . Rockford
10-12 . . . . . . Florence
14-16 . . . . Normal
21-23 . . . . London
24-26 . . . . Traverse City

LONDON RIPPERS

MAY
25-27 . . . . Gateway

JUNE
5-7 . . . . Normal
8-10 . . . . Joliet
17-19 . . . . . Washington
20-22 . . . . . Lake Erie
27-29 . . . . Windy City
30 . . . . Washington

JULY
1-2 . . . . Washington

JULY (col 2)
6-8 . . . . . . Traverse City
16-18 . . . Southern Illinois
25-27 . . . . . Lake Erie
28-30 . . . . . Traverse City

AUGUST
3-5 . . . . Florence
14-16 . . . . . River City
17-19 . . . Schaumburg
24-26 . . . . . Evansville
28-30 . . . . . . Rockford

NORMAL CORNBELTERS

MAY
10 . . . . River City
18-20 . . . . . . Windy City
22-24 . . . . Lake Erie
25-27 . . . Southern Illinois

JUNE
11-13 . . . . . Evansville
14-16 . . . . . Gateway
20-22 . . . . . Rockford
27-29 . . . Schaumburg

JULY
19-21 . . . . . . London

MAY (col 2)
22-24 . . . . Southern Illinois
28-29 . . . . . River City

AUGUST
7-9 . . . . . . Washington
10-12 . . . . . River City
17-19 . . . . . Rockford
21-23 . . . . Traverse City
28-30 . . . . . Florence
31 . . . . Joliet

SEPTEMBER
1-2 . . . . Joliet

RIVER CITY RASCALS

MAY
18-20 . . . . . Rockford
22-24 . . . . London
29-31 . . . . Traverse City

JUNE
1-3 . . . . . . Evansville
14-16 . . . . . . Joliet
20-22 . . . . Gateway
23-25 . . . . . Normal
30 . . . . Normal

JULY
1-2 . . . . Normal

MAY (col 2)
13-15 . . . . . Lake Erie
19-21 . . . . . Florence
25-27 . . . . Gateway
31 . . . . . Washington

AUGUST
1-2 . . . . Washington
7-9 . . . . . Schaumburg
21-23 . . . Southern Illinois
28-30 . . . Evansville
31 . . . . . . Windy City

SEPTEMBER
1-2 . . . . . Windy City

ROCKFORD RIVERHAWKS

MAY
25-27 . . . . . . Lake Erie
29-31 . . . . Normal

JUNE
1-3 . . . . London
8-10 . . . . Southern Illinois
11-13 . . . . . Windy City
17-19 . . . . . Gateway
27-29 . . . . . Evansville
30 . . . . Joliet

JULY
1-2 . . . . Joliet
6-8 . . . . Gateway
16-18 . . . . River City
19-21 . . . . Traverse City
25-27 . . . . . Normal
28-30 . . . Schaumburg

AUGUST
14-16 . . . . . Florence
21-23 . . . . Washington
24-26 . . . Schaumburg

SCHAUMBURG BOOMERS

MAY	
25-27 . . . . Florence	
29-31 . . . . London	

JUNE	
5-7 . . . . Gateway	
8-10 . . . . River City	
14-16 . . . . Rockford	
17-19 . . . . . Windy City	
23-25 . . . . Rockford	
30 . . . . Traverse City	

JULY	
1-2 . . . . Traverse City	
6-8 . . . . .Washington	
13-15 . . . . .Normal	
16-18 . . . . Lake Erie	
25-27 . . . . Joliet	

AUGUST	
3-5 . . . . Joliet	
14-16 . . . . . . Windy City	
21-23 . . . . . . Evansville	
28-30 . . . . Southern Illinois	

SOUTHERN ILLINOIS MINERS

MAY	
28-20 . . . . London	
29-31 . . . . Florence	

JUNE	
1-3 . . . . Schaumburg	
11-13 . . . . . Traverse City	
17-19 . . . . .Normal	
20-22 . . . . .Evansvlle	

JULY	
3-5 . . . . River City	
13-15 . . . . Joliet	
19-21 . . . . . .Washington	

28-30 . . . . Gateway	
31 . . . . Normal	

AUGUST	
1-2 . . . . .Normal	
7-9 . . . . .Rockford	
10-12 . . . . Gateway	
14-16 . . . . . . Evansville	
24-26 . . . . . Windy City	
31 . . . . .Lake Erie	

SEPTEMBER	
1-2 . . . . .Lake Erie	

TRAVERSE CITY BEACH BUMS

MAY	
25-27 . . . . . . Windy City	

JUNE	
5-7 . . . . .Rockford	

8-10 . . . . Evansville	
14-16 . . . . .Lake Erie	
23-25 . . . .'. London	
27-29 . . . . . .Washington	

JULY	
3-5 . . . . .Normal	
16-18 . . . . Florence	
22-24 . . . . Joliet	
31 . . . . Windy City	

AUGUST	
1-2 . . . . Windy City	
3-5 . . . . Southern Illinois	

10-12 . . . . . Schaumburg	
14-16 . . . . Joliet	
17-19 . . . . . . River City	
28-30 . . . . Gateway	
31 . . . . London	

SEPTEMBER	
1-2 . . . . London	

WASHINGTON WILD THINGS

MAY	
22-24 . . . . Gateway	
25-27 . . . . River City	

JUNE	
5-7 . . . . . Southern Illinois	
8-10 . . . . .Normal	
20-22 . . . . Florence	
23-25 . . . . .Lake Erie	

JULY	
3-5 . . . . .Rockford	
13-15 . . . . . Traverse City	

16-18 . . . . Evansville	
22-24 . . . . London	
25-27 . . . . .Florence	

AUGUST	
3-5 . . . . .Lake Erie	
10-12 . . . . London	
17-19 . . . . . Windy City	
28-30 . . . . Joliet	
31 . . . . Schaumburg	

SEPTEMBER	
1-2 . . . . Schaumburg	

WINDY CITY THUNDERBOLTS

MAY	
17 . . . . Joliet	
22-24 . . . . . Schaumburg	
29-31 . . . . . .Washington	

JUNE	
6-7 . . . . Joliet	
8-10 . . . . Florence	
14-16 . . . Southern Illinois	
20-22 . . . . . Traverse City	
23-25 . . . . Joliet	

JULY	
6-8 . . . . River City	
13-15 . . . . London	
16-18 . . . . .Normal	
22-24 . . . . . Schaumburg	
25-27 . . . . . Traverse City	

AUGUST	
3-5 . . . . .Rockford	
10-12 . . . . Evansville	
21-23 . . . . Gateway	
28-30 . . . . .Lake Erie	

SPRING TRAINING SCHEDULES

ARIZONA CACTUS LEAGUE

ARIZONA DIAMONDBACKS

MARCH	
3 . . . . . . at San Francisco	
3 . . . . at Colorado	
4 . . . . .San Francisco	
5 . . . . at Colorado	
6 . . . . Texas	
7 . . . . Cleveland	
9 . . . . at Seattle	
10 . . . . Seattle	
11 . . . . . at San Diego	
12 . . . . . . at Cleveland	
13 . . . . .Los Angeles (AL)	
14 . . . . . San Diego	
14 . . . . at Colorado	
15 . . . . . .at Chicago (NL)	
16 . . . . . Chicago (AL)	
17 . . . . at Texas	
18 . . . . at Cincinnati	
18 . . . . Oakland	

19 . . . . at Oakland	
20 . . . . . . .San Francisco	
21 . . . . Milwaukee	
23 . . . . . .at Chicago (AL)	
24 . . . . Kansas City	
25 . . . . . at San Diego	
26 . . . . . Chicago (NL)	
27 . . . . .Colorado	
28 . . . . . .at Milwaukee	
29 . . . . Cleveland	
30 . . . at Los Angeles (AL)	
31 . . . . . at Kansas City	
31 . . . . . .Los Angeles (NL)	

APRIL	
1 . . . . at Los Angeles (NL)	
2 . . . . Chicago (NL)	
3 . . . . Brewers	
4 . . . . Brewers	

CHICAGO CUBS

MARCH	
4 . . . . Oakland	
5 . . . . Oakland	
6 . . . . .Colorado	
7 . . . . . at Kansas City	
8 . . . . Seattle	
9 . . . .at Chicago (AL)	
10 . . . .at Milwaukee	
11 . . . at Los Angeles (NL)	
12 . . . . Cincinnati	
13 . . . . at San Francisco	
14 . . . . Milwaukee	
15 . . . . .Arizona	
15 . . . . . . at Colorado	
16 . . . . .San Francisco	
17 . . . . Texas	
17 . . . . at Oakland	
18 . . . . Texas	
18 . . . . . Chicago (AL)	

19 . . . . at Seattle	
20 . . . . at Oakland	
20 . . . . Texas	
22 . . . . at Texas	
23 . . . . . .at Colorado	
24 . . . . San Diego	
25 . . . . . at Cleveland	
26 . . . . San Diego	
26 . . . . at Arizona	
27 . . . . . . at Cincinnati	
28 . . . . Cleveland	
29 . . . . . at San Diego	
30 . . . . .Los Angeles (NL)	
31 . . . . .Los Angeles (AL)	

APRIL	
1 . . . . at Los Angeles (AL)	
2 . . . . at Arizona	
3 . . . . Milwaukee	

CHICAGO WHITE SOX

MARCH
5 . . . . . Los Angeles (NL)
6 . . . . at Los Angeles (AL)
7 . . . . Milwaukee
8 . . . . at Texas
9 . . . . Chicago (NL)
10 . . . . Texas
10 . . . Los Angeles (NL)
11 . . . . at Colorado
12 . . . . Oakland
13 . . . . . at San Diego
14 . . . . . Los Angeles (AL)
15 . . . . . . at Cleveland
16 . . . . at Arizona
17 . . . . Seattle
18 . . . . . .at Chicago (NL)

19 . . . . Cincinnati
21 . . . . at Seattle
22 . . . . Kansas City
23 . . . . .Arizona
24 . . . . . . .at Milwaukee
25 . . . . . . .San Francisco
26 . . . at Los Angeles (NL)
27 . . . . Cleveland
28 . . . . San Diego
28 . . . . at Colorado
29 . . . . at Los Angeles (NL)
30 . . . . . . at Kansas City
31 . . . . .Colorado

APRIL
1 . . . . at Cincinnati
2 . . . . Milwaukee

CINCINNATI REDS

MARCH
3 . . . . Cleveland
4 . . . . at Cleveland
5 . . . . Cleveland
6 . . . . at Seattle
7 . . . . San Diego
8 . . . . . . .at Milwaukee
9 . . . . at San Francisco
9 . . . . Kansas City
10 . . . . at Oakland
11 . . . Los Angeles (AL)
12 . . . . . .at Chicago (NL)
13 . . . . . at Kansas City
14 . . . . San Diego
14 . . . . Los Angeles (NL)
15 . . . at Los Angeles (AL)
16 . . . . .Colorado
17 . . . . at Cleveland

18 . . . . .Arizona
19 . . . . .at Chicago (AL)
20 . . . . Seattle
22 . . . . Texas
23 . . . . . . at San Diego
24 . . . . .San Francisco
24 . . . . . . at San Diego
25 . . . . . . at Colorado
26 . . . . at Texas
27 . . . . Chicago (NL)
28 . . . Los Angeles (AL)
29 . . . . . . .at Milwaukee
30 . . . . Cleveland
31 . . . . at San Francisco

APRIL
1 . . . . Chicago (AL)
2 . . . . at Cleveland

CLEVELAND INDIANS

MARCH
3 . . . . . . at Cincinnati
4 . . . . Cincinnati
5 . . . . . . at Cincinnati
6 . . . . Kansas City
7 . . . . at Arizona
8 . . . Los Angeles (AL)
9 . . . .at Milwaukee
10 . . . . San Diego
11 . . . at Los Angeles (AL)
11 . . . . . . at Texas
12 . . . . .Arizona
13 . . . . Texas
14 . . . . at San Francisco
15 . . . . . Chicago (AL)
16 . . at Los Angeles (AL)
17 . . . . . Cincinnati

18 . . . . . at Kansas City
19 . . . Los Angeles (NL)
21 . . . . . . .San Francisco
22 . . . . . . at San Diego
23 . . . Los Angeles (AL)
24 . . . at Los Angeles (NL)
25 . . . . . . Chicago (AL)
26 . . . . Milwaukee
27 . . . . . .at Chicago (AL)
28 . . . . .at Chicago (AL)
29 . . . . .Colorado
29 . . . . at Arizona
30 . . . . . . at Cincinnati
31 . . . . Texas

APRIL
1 . . . . at Colorado
2 . . . . Cincinnati

COLORADO ROCKIES

MARCH
3 . . . . .Arizona
5 . . . . .Arizona
6 . . . . . .at Chicago (NL)
7 . . . . . at San Francisco
8 . . . . Kansas City
9 . . . . Oakland

10 . . . . . . at Kansas City
11 . . . . . . .at Milwaukee
11 . . . . Chicago (AL)
12 . . . . San Diego
13 . . at Los Angeles (AL)
14 . . . . at Texas
14 . . . . .Arizona

15 . . . . Chicago (NL)
16 . . . . . . at Cincinnati
17 . . . . .Los Angeles (NL)
18 . . . . at Seattle
19 . . . . .Los Angeles (AL)
20 . . . . . . at San Diego
22 . . . . . .San Francisco
23 . . . . Chicago (NL)
24 . . . . at San Francisco
25 . . . . Cincinnati
26 . . at Los Angeles (NL)

27 . . . . at Arizona
28 . . . . . . Chicago (AL)
29 . . . . . . at Cleveland
30 . . . . Texas
31 . . . . . . .at Chicago (AL)

APRIL
1 . . . . Cleveland
2 . . . . at Seattle
3 . . . . Seattle
4 . . . . Seattle

KANSAS CITY ROYALS

MARCH
4 . . . . at Texas
5 . . . . Texas
6 . . . . . . at Cleveland
6 . . . . .San Diego
7 . . . . Chicago (NL)
8 . . . at Colorado
9 . . . . . . at Cincinnati
10 . . . . .Colorado
11 . . . . . . at Oakland
12 . . . .San Francisco
13 . . . . . . Cincinnati
14 . . . . . . at Seattle
15 . . at Los Angeles (NL)
16 . . . . Milwaukee
17 . . at San Diego
18 . . . . Cleveland

20 . . . . . Los Angeles (AL)
21 . . . . Oakland
22 . . at Los Angeles (AL)
22 . . . . . .at Chicago (AL)
23 . . . Los Angeles (NL)
24 . . . . at Arizona
25 . . . . Milwaukee
26 . . . . at San Francisco
27 . . . . . .at Milwaukee
28 . . . . Texas
29 . . . at Los Angeles (AL)
30 . . . . Chicago (AL)
31 . . . . .Arizona

APRIL
1 . . . . at Seattle

LOS ANGELES ANGELS

MARCH
5 . . . . at Oakland
6 . . . . Chicago (AL)
7 . . . . Seattle
8 . . . . . . at Cleveland
9 . . . . . . .San Diego
10 . . . . . .San Francisco
11 . . . . . . at Cincinnati
11 . . . . Cleveland
12 . . . . .Los Angeles (NL)
13 . . . . at Arizona
14 . . .at Chicago (AL)
15 . . . . Cincinnati
16 . . . . Cleveland
16 . . . . . at San Diego
17 . . . . Milwaukee

18 . . . at Los Angeles (NL)
19 . . . . . . at Colorado
20 . . . . . at Kansas City
22 . . . . . . Kansas City
23 . . . . . .at Milwaukee
23 . . . . . at Cleveland
24 . . . . at Texas
25 . . . . Texas
26 . . . . .Colorado
27 . . . . at San Francisco
28 . . . . . . at Cincinnati
29 . . . . . Kansas City
30 . . . . .Arizona
31 . . . .at Chicago (NL)

APRIL
1 . . . . Chicago (NL)

LOS ANGELES DODGERS

MARCH
5 . . . . .at Chicago (AL)
6 . . . . . .San Francisco
7 . . . . . . at Oakland
8 . . . . Oakland
9 . . . . at Texas
10 . . . . . . at Seattle
10 . . . .at Chicago (AL)
11 . . . . . Chicago (NL)
12 . . at Los Angeles (AL)
13 . . . . .Colorado
14 . . . . at Cincinnati
15 . . . . . Kansas City
16 . . . . Texas
17 . . . . . .at Colorado
17 . . . . .San Francisco

18 . . . . . Los Angeles (AL)
19 . . . . . at Cleveland
20 . . . . Milwaukee
21 . . . . . . .San Diego
23 . . . . . at Kansas City
24 . . . . Cleveland
25 . . . . . .at Milwaukee
26 . . . .at Chicago (AL)
27 . . . . . at San Diego
28 . . . . at San Francisco
29 . . . . . . Chicago (AL)
30 . . .at Chicago (NL)
30 . . . . Milwaukee
31 . . . . at Arizona

APRIL
1 . . . . .Arizona

MILWAUKEE BREWERS

MARCH
4 . . . . .San Francisco
5 . . . . . . at San Francisco
6 . . . . Oakland
7 . . . . .at Chicago
8 . . . . Cincinnati
9 . . . . Cleveland
10 . . . . Chicago (NL)
10 . . . . at San Francisco
11 . . . . .Colorado
13 . . . . at Oakland
13 . . . . Seattle
14 . . . .at Chicago (NL)
15 . . . . San Diego
16 . . . . . at Kansas City
17 . . at Los Angeles (AL)
18 . . . . Texas
19 . . . . at Texas

APRIL
20 . . . . at Los Angeles (NL)
21 . . . . at Arizona
23 . . . . . .Los Angeles (AL)
24 . . . . Chicago (AL)
25 . . . . . .Los Angeles (NL)
25 . . . . . . at Kansas City
26 . . . . . . at Cleveland
27 . . . . Kansas City
28 . . . . .Arizona
29 . . . . Cincinnati
30 . . . at Los Angeles (NL)
31 . . . . at San Diego

APRIL
1 . . . . .San Francisco
2 . . . . . .at Chicago (AL)
3 . . . . . .at Chicago (NL)
3 . . . . at Arizona
4 . . . . at Arizona

OAKLAND ATHLETICS

MARCH
2 . . . . Seattle
3 . . . . at Seattle
4 . . . . .at Chicago (NL)
5 . . . .Los Angeles (AL)
5 . . . . .at Chicago (NL)
6 . . . . . . at Milwaukee
7 . . . .Los Angeles (NL)
8 . . . . at Los Angeles (NL)
9 . . . . at Colorado
10 . . . . Cincinnati

MARCH (cont.)
11 . . . . Kansas City
12 . . . . . .at Chicago (AL)
13 . . . . Milwaukee
15 . . . . at Texas
16 . . . . Seattle
17 . . . . . . Chicago (NL)
17 . . . . at San Francisco
18 . . . . .at Arizona
19 . . . . .Arizona
20 . . . . . . Chicago (NL)
21 . . . . . at Kansas City

SAN DIEGO PADRES

MARCH
4 . . . . at Seattle
5 . . . . Seattle
6 . . . . . . at Kansas City
7 . . . . . . at Cincinnati
7 . . . . Texas
8 . . . . .San Francisco
9 . . . . at Los Angeles (AL)
10 . . . . . . at Cleveland
11 . . . . .Arizona
12 . . . . . . at Colorado
13 . . . . . Chicago (AL)
14 . . . . . . at Cincinnati
14 . . . . at Arizona
15 . . . . .at Milwaukee
16 . . . . .Los Angeles (AL)
17 . . . . Kansas City
18 . . . . . at San Francisco

MARCH (cont.)
20 . . . . .Colorado
21 . . . at Los Angeles (NL)
22 . . . . Cleveland
23 . . . . Cincinnati
24 . . . . Cincinnati
24 . . . .at Chicago (NL)
25 . . . . .Arizona
26 . . . . . .at Chicago (NL)
27 . . . .Los Angeles (NL)
27 . . . . at Texas
28 . . . .at Chicago (AL)
29 . . . . . Chicago (NL)
30 . . . . . . .San Francisco
31 . . . . Milwaukee
31 . . . . . . at Seattle

APRIL
1 . . . . at Texas

SAN FRANCISCO GIANTS

MARCH
3 . . . . .Arizona
4 . . . . .at Milwaukee
4 . . . . at Arizona
5 . . . . Milwaukee
6 . . . at Los Angeles (NL)
7 . . . . .Colorado
8 . . . . at San Diego
9 . . . . Cincinnati
10 . . . . Milwaukee
10 . . . .at Los Angeles (AL)
11 . . . . Seattle
12 . . . . . at Kansas City

MARCH (cont.)
13 . . . . Chicago (NL)
14 . . . . Cleveland
15 . . . . at Seattle
16 . . . . . .at Chicago (NL)
17 . . . . Oakland
17 . . at Los Angeles (NL)
18 . . . . San Diego
20 . . . . at Arizona
21 . . . . . . at Cleveland
22 . . . . . . at Colorado
23 . . . . Texas
24 . . . . . . at Cincinnati
24 . . . . .Colorado

SEATTLE MARINERS

MARCH
25 . . . . . .at Chicago (AL)
26 . . . . Kansas City
27 . . . .Los Angeles (AL)
28 . . . .Los Angeles (NL)
29 . . . . at Texas

MARCH
2 . . . . . . at Oakland
3 . . . . Oakland
4 . . . . San Diego
5 . . . . at San Diego
6 . . . . Cincinnati
7 . . . . at Los Angeles (AL)
8 . . . .at Chicago (NL)
9 . . . . .Arizona
10 . . . .Los Angeles (NL)
10 . . . . at Arizona
11 . . . . at San Francisco
12 . . . . Texas
13 . . . . . .at Milwaukee

MARCH (cont.)
14 . . . . Kansas City
15 . . . . . .San Francisco
16 . . . . at Oakland
17 . . . . .at Chicago (AL)
18 . . . . .Colorado
19 . . . . . . Chicago (NL)
20 . . . . . at Cincinnati
21 . . . . . Chicago (AL)
31 . . . . San Diego

APRIL
1 . . . . Kansas City
2 . . . . .Colorado
3 . . . . at Colorado
4 . . . . at Colorado

TEXAS

MARCH
4 . . . . . . Kansas City
5 . . . . . at Kansas City
6 . . . . at Arizona
7 . . . . . at San Diego
8 . . . . . . Chicago (AL)
9 . . . .Los Angeles (NL)
10 . . . .at Chicago (AL)
11 . . . . Cleveland
12 . . . . at Seattle
13 . . . . . at Cleveland
14 . . . . .Colorado
15 . . . . Oakland
16 . . . . at Los Angeles (NL)
17 . . . .at Chicago (NL)
17 . . . . .Arizona
18 . . . .at Chicago (NL)

MARCH (cont.)
18 . . . . . .at Milwaukee
19 . . . . Milwaukee
20 . . . .at Chicago (NL)
21 . . . . Chicago (NL)
22 . . . . . at Cincinnati
23 . . . . at San Francisco
24 . . . . .Los Angeles (AL)
25 . . at Los Angeles (AL)
26 . . . . Cincinnati
27 . . . . at San Diego
28 . . . . at Kansas City
29 . . . . . .San Francisco
30 . . . . . . at Colorado
31 . . . . at Cleveland

APRIL
1 . . . . San Diego

FLORIDA GRAPEFRUIT LEAGUE

ATLANTA BRAVES

MARCH
3 . . . . Detroit
4 . . . . at Detroit
5 . . . . at Houston
6 . . . . . . .Washington
7 . . . . at Detroit
8 . . . . .at Baltimore
9 . . . . at New York (AL)
9 . . . . . New York (NL)
10 . . . . New York (AL)
11 . . . . .at Toronto
11 . . . . Toronto
12 . . . . .at St. Louis
13 . . . . at Miami
14 . . . . . .Washington
15 . . . .at Philadelphia
16 . . . . Houston
17 . . . . Toronto

MARCH (cont.)
17 . . . . .at New York (NL)
18 . . . . Baltimore
19 . . . . St. Louis
20 . . . . at Detroit
21 . . . . . at Washington
22 . . . . Miami
23 . . . . . New York (NL)
24 . . . . . . .at Toronto
25 . . . . Houston
27 . . . .at New York (NL)
28 . . . . . New York (AL)
29 . . . . . at Washington
30 . . . . at Houston
30 . . . . Houston
31 . . . . Detroit

APRIL
1 . . . . Philadelphia
2 . . . . New York (NL)

BALTIMORE ORIOLES

MARCH
5 . . . . .at Tampa Bay

5 . . . . .Pittsburgh
6 . . . . at Boston

7 . . . . .Minnesota
8 . . . . .Atlanta
9 . . . . at Tampa Bay
10 . . . . . .at Philadelphia
11 . . . . Boston
12 . . . . at Toronto
13 . . . . Tampa Bay
14 . . . . .Pittsburgh
15 . . . . at Detroit
16 . . . . . . at Minnesota
17 . . . . Boston
17 . . . . at Boston
18 . . . . at Atlanta
18 . . . . . . New York (AL)

20 . . . . Philadelphia
21 . . . . Toronto
22 . . . . . . at Minnesota
23 . . . . Boston
24 . . . . .Washington
25 . . . .at Philadelphia
26 . . . . . . at Pittsburgh
27 . . . . .Minnesota
28 . . . . at Toronto
29 . . . . .at New York (AL)
30 . . . . Detroit
31 . . . . . at Pittsburgh

28 . . . . Miami
29 . . . . .at New York (NL)
30 . . . . Atlanta
30 . . . . at Atlanta

31 . . . . . . New York (AL)

APRIL
1 . . . . at Detroit

MIAMI MARLINS

APRIL
1 . . . . Tampa Bay

BOSTON RED SOX

MARCH
4 . . . . .Minnesota
5 . . . . . . at Minnesota
6 . . . . Baltimore
7 . . . . at Toronto
8 . . . . .at St. Louis
9 . . . . .Pittsburgh
10 . . . . . . Tampa Bay
11 . . . . . . .at Baltimore
12 . . . . Miami
13 . . . .at New York (AL)
15 . . . . St. Louis
16 . . . . .Minnesota
17 . . . . . . .at Baltimore
17 . . . . Baltimore
18 . . . . . .at Tampa Bay
19 . . . . .Minnesota

20 . . . . Tampa Bay
21 . . . . . . at Pittsburgh
22 . . . . . . New York (AL)
23 . . . . . . .at Baltimore
24 . . . . at Miami
24 . . . . Philadelphia
25 . . . . at Toronto
26 . . . .at Philadelphia
27 . . . . Tampa Bay
29 . . . . Tampa Bay
30 . . . . . . at Minnesota
31 . . . . . at Tampa Bay

APRIL
1 . . . . .Minnesota
2 . . . . .Washington

MARCH
5 . . . . .at St. Louis
6 . . . . .Detroit
7 . . . . . . New York (NL)
8 . . . . .at New York (NL)
9 . . . . .Washington
10 . . . . St. Louis
11 . . . .at New York (NL)
12 . . . . at Boston
13 . . . . Atlanta
14 . . . . . .at Tampa Bay
15 . . . . . . New York (NL)
16 . . . . . . .at St. Louis
17 . . . . at Washington
17 . . . . .Minnesota
18 . . . . . . .at St. Louis

19 . . . . Houston
20 . . . . Tampa Bay
22 . . . . at Atlanta
23 . . . . St. Louis
24 . . . . Boston
25 . . . . .at Tampa Bay
26 . . . . at Detroit
27 . . . . .Washington
28 . . . . at Houston
29 . . . . St. Louis
30 . . . . at Washington
31 . . . . . New York (NL)

APRIL
1 . . . . New York (AL)
2 . . . . New York (AL)

MINNESOTA TWINS

MARCH
3 . . . . Tampa Bay
4 . . . . . at Tampa Bay
4 . . . . at Boston
5 . . . . Boston
6 . . . . . at Tampa Bay
7 . . . . . .at Baltimore
8 . . . . Tampa Bay
9 . . . . St. Louis
10 . . . . . . at Pittsburgh
11 . . . . . New York (AL)
12 . . . . .at Tampa Bay
13 . . . . Toronto
14 . . . .at Philadelphia
15 . . . . .Pittsburgh
16 . . . . Baltimore
16 . . . . . . at Boston
17 . . . . at Miami

18 . . . . .Pittsburgh
19 . . . . at Boston
21 . . . . at Detroit
22 . . . . Baltimore
23 . . . . . .at New York
24 . . . . . . Tampa Bay
25 . . . . . .at St. Louis
26 . . . . . . Tampa Bay
27 . . . .at Baltimore
28 . . . . . . Philadelphia
29 . . . . at Pittsburgh
30 . . . . Boston
30 . . . . . . at Toronto
31 . . . . .Pittsburgh

APRIL
1 . . . . at Boston
2 . . . . .at Tampa Bay
3 . . . . Tampa Bay

DETROIT TIGERS

MARCH
3 . . . . at Atlanta
4 . . . . Atlanta
5 . . . . Toronto
6 . . . . at Miami
7 . . . . Atlanta
8 . . . . . . .at Tampa Bay
9 . . . . Philadelphia
10 . . . . . . .Washington
11 . . . . . . at Houston
11 . . . .at Philadelphia
12 . . . . . New York (NL)
13 . . . . at Washington
14 . . . . . New York (NL)
15 . . . . Baltimore
16 . . . .at New York (NL)
17 . . . . St. Louis
18 . . . . . at Washington

19 . . . . .at Philadelphia
20 . . . . Atlanta
21 . . . . .Minnesota
23 . . . . . . at Pittsburgh
24 . . . . . New York (AL)
25 . . . .at New York (AL)
25 . . . . . . Philadelphia
26 . . . . Miami
27 . . . . . . at Houston
28 . . . . . .at St. Louis
29 . . . . . . .Washington
30 . . . . . . at Houston
31 . . . . at Atlanta

APRIL
1 . . . . Houston
1 . . . .at New York (NL)
2 . . . . Toronto
3 . . . . at Toronto

HOUSTON ASTROS

MARCH
3 . . . . .Washington
4 . . . . . . at Washington
5 . . . . Atlanta
6 . . . . . . New York (NL)
7 . . . . . .at Philadelphia
8 . . . . . . at Washington
9 . . . . Toronto
10 . . . . . . at Toronto
11 . . . . Detroit
12 . . . .at New York (AL)
13 . . . . Philadelphia
14 . . . . . . .at St. Louis

15 . . . . Toronto
16 . . . . at Atlanta
17 . . . . .at New York (AL)
18 . . . . . New York (AL)
19 . . . . at Miami
20 . . . . St. Louis
22 . . . .at New York (AL)
23 . . . . . . .Washington
24 . . . . . . at Pittsburgh
25 . . . . .Pittsburgh
25 . . . . at Atlanta
26 . . . . . at Washington
27 . . . . Detroit

NEW YORK METS

MARCH
5 . . . . .Washington
6 . . . . at Houston
6 . . . . St. Louis
7 . . . . .at Miami
8 . . . . Miami
9 . . . . at Atlanta
10 . . . . at Washington
11 . . . . Miami
12 . . . . . . at Detroit
13 . . . . St. Louis
14 . . . . at Detroit
15 . . . . . . .at Miami
16 . . . . Detroit
17 . . . . Atlanta
18 . . . . . . at Houston
20 . . . . . . .Washington

21 . . . . . . .at St. Louis
22 . . . . Houston
23 . . . . at Atlanta
24 . . . . St. Louis
25 . . . at Washington
26 . . . . . .at St. Louis
27 . . . . Atlanta
28 . . . . . . .Washington
29 . . . . Houston
30 . . . . . .at St. Louis
31 . . . . .at Miami

APRIL
1 . . . . Detroit
2 . . . . at Atlanta
3 . . . . . . New York (AL)
4 . . . . . .at New York (AL)

NEW YORK YANKEES

MARCH
3 . . . . . .at Philadelphia
4 . . . . Philadelphia

5 . . . . . .at Philadelphia
6 . . . . at Pittsburgh
7 . . . . Tampa Bay

8	at Toronto
9	Atlanta
10	at Atlanta
11	at Minnesota
11	Philadelphia
12	Houston
13	Boston
14	at Toronto
15	at Washington
16	Washington
17	Houston
18	at Baltimore
20	Pittsburgh
21	at Tampa Bay
22	at Boston

23	Minnesota
23	at Philadelphia
24	at Detroit
25	Detroit
27	Toronto
28	at Atlanta
29	Baltimore
30	Philadelphia
31	at Houston

APRIL

1	at Miami
2	at Miami
3	at New York (NL)
4	New York (NL)

25	Minnesota
26	New York (NL)
28	Detroit
20	at Miami
30	New York (NL)

31	at Washington

APRIL

1	Washington

PHILADELPHIA PHILLIES

MARCH

3	New York (AL)
4	at New York (AL)
5	New York (AL)
6	at Toronto
7	Houston
8	Pittsburgh
9	at Detroit
10	Baltimore
11	Detroit
11	at New York (AL)
12	at Pittsburgh
13	at Houston
14	Minnesota
15	Atlanta
15	at Tampa Bay
16	at Pittsburgh
17	Toronto

18	at Toronto
19	Detroit
20	at Baltimore
22	at Toronto
23	New York (AL)
24	at Boston
25	Baltimore
25	at Detroit
26	Boston
27	Pittsburgh
28	at Minnesota
29	Tampa Bay
30	at New York (AL)
31	Toronto

APRIL

1	at Atlanta

TAMPA BAY RAYS

MARCH

3	at Minnesota
4	Minnesota
5	Baltimore
6	Minnesota
7	at New York (AL)
8	Detroit
8	at Minnesota
9	Baltimore
10	at Boston
11	Pittsburgh
12	Minnesota
13	at Baltimore
14	Miami
15	Philadelphia
16	at Toronto
17	at Pittsburgh

18	Boston
20	at Miami
21	New York (AL)
22	at Pittsburgh
23	Toronto
24	at Minnesota
25	Miami
26	at Minnesota
27	at Boston
28	Pittsburgh
29	at Philadelphia
30	at Pittsburgh
31	Boston

APRIL

1	at Baltimore
2	Minnesota
3	at Minnesota

TORONTO BLUE JAYS

MARCH

3	Pittsburgh
4	at Pittsburgh
5	at Detroit
6	Philadelphia
7	at Pittsburgh
7	Boston
8	New York (AL)
9	at Houston
10	Houston
11	Atlanta
11	at Atlanta
12	Baltimore
13	at Minnesota
14	New York (AL)
15	at Houston
16	Tampa Bay
17	at Atlanta

17	at Philadelphia
18	Philadelphia
20	at Boston
21	at Baltimore
22	Philadelphia
23	at Tampa Bay
24	Atlanta
25	Boston
27	at New York (AL)
28	Baltimore
29	at Boston
30	Minnesota
31	at Philadelphia

APRIL

1	Pittsburgh
2	at Detroit
3	Detroit

PITTSBURGH PIRATES

MARCH

3	at Toronto
4	Toronto
5	at Baltimore
6	New York (AL)
7	Toronto
8	at Philadelphia
9	at Boston
10	Minnesota
11	at Tampa Bay
12	Philadelphia
14	at Baltimore
15	at Minnesota
16	Philadelphia
17	Tampa Bay
18	at Minnesota

20	at New York (AL)
21	Boston
22	Tampa Bay
23	Detroit
24	Houston
25	at Houston
26	Baltimore
27	at Philadelphia
28	at Tampa Bay
29	Minnesota
30	Tampa Bay
31	Baltimore
31	at Minnesota

APRIL

1	at Toronto

ST. LOUIS CARDINALS

MARCH

5	Miami
6	at New York (NL)
7	at Washington
8	Boston
9	at Minnesota
10	at Miami
11	Washington
12	Atlanta
12	at Washington
13	at Miami

14	Houston
15	at Boston
16	Miami
17	at Detroit
18	Miami
19	at Atlanta
20	at Houston
21	New York (NL)
22	Washington
23	at Miami
24	at New York (NL)

WASHINGTON NATIONALS

MARCH

3	at Houston
4	Houston
5	at New York (NL)
6	at Atlanta
7	St. Louis
8	Houston
9	at Miami
10	New York (NL)
10	at Detroit
11	at St. Lois
12	St. Louis
13	Detroit
14	at Atlanta
15	New York (AL)
16	at New York (NL)
17	Miami
18	Detroit

20	at New York (NL)
21	Atlanta
22	at St. Louis
23	at Houston
24	at Baltimore
25	New York (NL)
26	Houston
27	at Miami
28	at New York (NL)
29	Atlanta
29	at Detroit
30	Miami
31	St. Louis

APRIL

1	at St. Louis
2	at Boston

COLLEGES

COLLEGE ORGANIZATIONS

NATIONAL COLLEGIATE ATHLETIC ASSOCIATION

Mailing Address: PO Box 6222, Indianapolis, IN 46206. **Telephone:** (317) 917-6222. **Fax:** (317) 917-6826 (championships), 917-6710 (baseball). **E-Mail Addresses:** dpoppe@ncaa.org (Dennis Poppe), dleech@ncaa.org (Damani Leech), jhamilton@ncaa.org (JD Hamilton), ctolliver@ncaa.org (Chad Tolliver), ryurk@ncaa.org (Russ Yurk), aholman@ncaa.org (Anthony Holman). **Websites:** www.ncaa.org, www.ncaa.com.

President: Dr. Mark Emmert. **Vice President, Division I Baseball/Football:** Dennis Poppe. **Director, Division I Baseball/Football:** Damani Leech. **Assistant Director, Division I Baseball/Football:** Chad Tolliver. **Division II Assistant Director, Championships:** Russ Yurk. **Division III Assistant Director, Championships:** Anthony Holman. **Media Contact, Division I College World Series:** JD Hamilton. **Contacts, Statistics:** Jeff Williams (Division I and RPI); Gary Johnson (Division II); Sean Straziscar (Division III).

Chairman, Division I Baseball Committee: Kyle Kallander (Commissioner, Big South Conference). **Vice-Chair, Division I Baseball Committee:** Dennis Farrell (Commissioner, Big West Conference). **Division I Baseball Committee:** Larry Gallo Jr (Senior Associate Athletic Director, North Carolina); John Hardt (Director of Athletics, Bucknell); Dave Heeke (Director of Athletics, Central Michigan); Eric Hyman (Director of Athletics, South Carolina); Mark LaBarbera (athletic director, Valparaiso); Chris Monasch (Athletics Director, St. John's); Dr. Gary Overton (Assistant Athletics Director, East Carolina); TBA.

Chairman, Division II Baseball Committee: Jim Givens (Associate Athletic Director, University of Findlay, Ohio). **Chairman, Division III Baseball Committee:** Gregg Kaye (Commissioner, Commonwealth Coast Conference).

2013 National Convention: Jan. 16-19 at Grapevine, Texas.

2012 CHAMPIONSHIP TOURNAMENTS

NCAA DIVISION I
66th College World Series . . . . .Omaha, June 15-25/26
Super Regionals (8) . . . . .Campus sites, June 8-11
Regionals (16). . . . . .Campus sites, June 1-4

NCAA DIVISION II
45th annual World Series . . . USA Baseball National Training Complex, Cary, N.C., May 26-June 2.
Regionals (8) . . . . Campus sites, May 17-21.

NCAA DIVISION III
37th annual World Series . . . . . Appleton, Wis., May 25-29
Regionals (8) . . . . Campus sites, May 16-20

NATIONAL ASSOCIATION OF INTERCOLLEGIATE ATHLETICS

Mailing Address: 1200 Grand Blvd, Kansas City, MO 64106. **Telephone:** (816) 595-8000. **Fax:** (816) 595-8200. **E-Mail Address:** cwaller@naia.org. **Website:** www.naia.org.

President/CEO: Jim Carr. **Manager, Championship Sports:** Scott McClure. **Director, Sports Information:** Chad Waller. **President, Coaches Association:** Lou Yacinich, (Grand View, Iowa, College).

2012 CHAMPIONSHIP TOURNAMENT

Opening round: May 10-14, campus locations.
Avista-NAIA World Series: May 25-June 1, Lewiston, Idaho.

NATIONAL JUNIOR COLLEGE ATHLETIC ASSOCIATION

Mailing Address: 1631 Mesa Ave, Suite B, Colorado Springs, CO 80906. **Telephone:** (719) 590-9788. **Fax:** (719) 590-7324. **E-Mail Address:** mkrug@njcaa.org. **Website:** www.njcaa.org.

Executive Director: Mary Ellen Leicht.
Director, Division I Baseball Tournament: Jamie Hamilton. **Director, Division II Baseball Tournament:** Billy Mayberry. **Director, Division III Baseball Tournament:** Tim Drain. **Director, Media Relations:** Mark Krug.

2012 CHAMPIONSHIP TOURNAMENTS

DIVISION I
World Series: . . . . Grand Junction, Colo., May 26-June 2

DIVISION II
World Series: . . . . Enid, Okla., May 26-June 2

DIVISION III
World Series: . . . . Tyler, Texas, May 19-25

CALIFORNIA COMMUNITY COLLEGE COMMISSION ON ATHLETICS

Mailing Address: 2017 O St, Sacramento, CA 95811-5211. **Telephone:** (916) 444-1600. **Fax:** (916) 444-2616. **E-Mail Addresses:** ccarter@cccaasports.org, jboggs@cccaasports.org. **Website:** www.cccaasports.org.

Executive Director: Carlyle Carter. **Director, Membership Services:** Debra Wheeler. **Director, Championships:** George Mategakis. **Assistant Director, Sports Information/Communications:** Jason Boggs.

2012 CHAMPIONSHIP TOURNAMENT

State Championship . . . . Bakersfield, Calif., May 18-20

NORTHWEST ATHLETIC ASSOCIATION OF COMMUNITY COLLEGES

Mailing Address: Clark College TGB 121, 1933 Fort Vancouver Way, Vancouver, WA 98663-3598. **Telephone:** (360) 992-2833. **Fax:** (360) 696-6210. **E-Mail Address:** nwaacc@clark.edu. **Website:** www.nwaacc.org.

Executive Director: Marco Azurdia. **Executive Assistant:** Carol Hardin. **Director, Marketing:** Charles Warner. **Sports Information Director:** Tracy Swisher.

2012 CHAMPIONSHIP TOURNAMENT

NWAACC Championship,. . . . . Lower Columbia CC, Longview, Wash., May 24-28

AMERICAN BASEBALL COACHES ASSOCIATION

Office Address: 108 S University Ave, Suite 3, Mount Pleasant, MI 48858-2327. **Telephone:** (989) 775-3300. **Fax:** (989) 775-3600. **E-Mail Address:** abca@abca.org. **Website:** www.abca.org.

Executive Director: Dave Keilitz. **Assistant to Executive Director:** Betty Rulong. **Coordinator:** Nick Phillips. **Marketing Director:** Juahn Clark. **Associate Membership/Convention Coordinator:** Jeff Franklyn.

Chairman: Jack Kaiser. **President:** John Schaly (Ashland University, Ohio).

2013 National Convention: Jan. 3-6 at Hyatt Regency in Chicago.

NCAA DIVISION I CONFERENCES

AMERICA EAST CONFERENCE

Mailing Address: 215 First Street, Suite 140, Cambridge, MA 02142. **Telephone:** (617) 695-6369. **Fax:** (617) 695-6380. **E-Mail Address:** casey@americaeast.com. **Website:** www.americaeast.com.

Baseball Members (First Year): Albany (2002), Binghamton (2002), Hartford (1990), Maine (1990), Maryland-Baltimore County (2004), Stony Brook (2002).

Associate Director, Communications: Leslie Casey

2012 Tournament: Four teams, double-elimination. May 23-25 at highest-seeded team.

ATLANTIC COAST CONFERENCE

Office Address: 4512 Weybridge Lane, Greensboro, NC 27407. **Mailing Address:** 4512 Weybridge Lane, Greensboro, NC 27407. **Telephone:** (336) 851-6062. **Fax:** (336) 854-8797. **E-Mail Address:** sphillips@theacc.org. **Website:** www.theacc.com.

Baseball Members (First Year): Boston College (2006), Clemson (1954), Duke (1954), Florida State (1992), Georgia Tech (1980), Maryland (1954), Miami (2005), North Carolina (1954), North Carolina State (1954), Virginia (1955), Virginia Tech (2005), Wake Forest (1954).

Associate Director, Communications: Steve Phillips.

2012 Tournament: Eight teams, group play. May 23-27 at Newbridge Bank Park, Greensboro, N.C.

ATLANTIC SUN CONFERENCE

Mailing Address: 3370 Vineville Ave, Suite 108-B, Macon, GA 31204. **Telephone:** (478) 474-3394. **Fax:** (478) 474-4272. **E-Mail Addresses:** pmccoy@atlanticsun.org. **Website:** www.atlanticsun.org.

Baseball Members (First Year): Belmont (2002), East Tennessee State (2006), Florida Gulf Coast (2008), Jacksonville (1999), Kennesaw State (2006), Lipscomb (2004), Mercer (1979), North Florida (2006), South Carolina-Upstate (2008), Stetson (1986).

Director, Sports Information: Patrick McCoy.

2012 Tournament: Six teams, double-elimination. May 23-26 at DeLand, Fla. (Stetson).

ATLANTIC 10 CONFERENCE

Mailing Address: 11827 Canon Blvd., Suite 200, Newport News, VA 23606. **Telephone:** (757) 706-3059. **Fax:** (757) 706-3042. **E-Mail Address:** mkristofak@atlantic10.org. **Website:** www.atlantic10.org.

Baseball Members (First Year): Charlotte (2006), Dayton (1996), Fordham (1996), George Washington (1977), LaSalle (1996), Massachusetts (1977), Rhode Island (1981), Richmond (2002), St. Bonaventure (1980), Saint Joseph's (1983), Saint Louis (2006), Temple (1983), Xavier (1996).

Commissioner: Bernadette V. McGlade. **Director of Communications:** Drew Dickerson. **Assistant Director of Communications/Baseball Contact:** Melissa Kristofak.

2012 Tournament: Six teams, double elimination. May 23-26 at Houlihan Park (Fordham).

BIG EAST CONFERENCE

Mailing Address: 15 Park Row West, Providence, RI 02903. **Telephone:** (401) 453-0660. **Fax:** (401) 751-8540. **E-Mail Address:** csullivan@bigeast.org. **Website:** www.bigeast.org.

Baseball Members (First Year): Cincinnati (2006), Connecticut (1985), Georgetown (1985), Louisville (2006), Notre Dame (1996), Pittsburgh (1985), Rutgers (1996), St. John's (1985), Seton Hall (1985), South Florida (2006),

Villanova (1985), West Virginia (1996).

Director, Communications: Chuck Sullivan.

2012 Tournament: Eight teams, double-elimination. May 23-27 at Clearwater, Fla.

BIG SOUTH CONFERENCE

Mailing Address: 7233 Pineville-Matthews Rd., **Suite 100, Charlotte, NC 28226. Telephone:** (704) 341-7990. **Fax:** (704) 341-7991. **E-Mail Address:** marks@bigsouth.org. **Website:** www.bigsouthsports.com.

Baseball Members (First Year): Campbell (2012), Charleston Southern (1983), Coastal Carolina (1983), Gardner-Webb (2009), High Point (1999), Liberty (1991), UNC Asheville (1985), Presbyterian (2009), Radford (1983), Virginia Military Institute (2004), Winthrop (1983).

Assistant Commissioner, Public Relations: Mark Simpson.

2012 Tournament: Eight teams, double-elimination. May 22-26 at High Point.

BIG TEN CONFERENCE

Mailing Address: 1500 W Higgins Rd, Park Ridge, IL 60068. **Telephone:** (847) 696-1010. **Fax:** (847) 696-1110. **E-Mail Addresses:** vtodryk@bigten.org. **Website:** www.bigten.org.

Baseball Members (First Year): Illinois (1896), Indiana (1906), Iowa (1906), Michigan (1896), Michigan State (1950), Minnesota (1906), Nebraska (2012), Northwestern (1898), Ohio State (1913), Penn State (1992), Purdue (1906).

Associate Director, Communications: Valerie Todryk Krebs.

2012 Tournament: Six teams, double-elimination. May 23-26 at Huntington Park in Columbus, Ohio.

BIG 12 CONFERENCE

Mailing Address: 400 E John Carpenter Freeway, Irving, TX 75062. **Telephone:** (469) 524-1000. **E-Mail Address:** lrasmussen@big12sports.com. **Website:** www.big12sports.com.

Baseball Members (First Year): Baylor (1997), Kansas (1997), Kansas State (1997), Missouri (1997), Oklahoma (1997), Oklahoma State (1997), Texas (1997), Texas A&M (1997), Texas Tech (1997).

Assistant Director, Communications: Laura Rasmussen

2012 Tournament: Double-elimination division play. May 23-27 at RedHawks Ballpark, Oklahoma City.

BIG WEST CONFERENCE

Mailing Address: 2 Corporate Park, Suite 206, Irvine, CA 92606. **Telephone:** (949) 261-2525. **Fax:** (949) 261-2528. **E-Mail Address:** jstcyr@bigwest.org. **Website:** www.bigwest.org.

Baseball Members (First Year): Cal Poly (1997), UC Davis (2008), UC Irvine (2002), UC Riverside (2002), UC Santa Barbara (1970), Cal State Fullerton (1975), Cal State Northridge (2001), Long Beach State (1970), Pacific (1972).

Director, Communications: Julie St. Cyr.

2012 Tournament: None.

COLONIAL ATHLETIC ASSOCIATION

Mailing Address: 8625 Patterson Ave., Richmond, VA 23229. **Telephone:** (804) 754-1616. **Fax:** (804) 754-1830. **E-Mail Address:** rwashburn@caasports.com. **Website:** www.caasports.com.

Baseball Members (First Year): Delaware (2002), George Mason (1986), Georgia State (2006), Hofstra (2002), James Madison (1986), UNC Wilmington (1986),

Northeastern (2006), Old Dominion (1992), Towson (2002), Virginia Commonwealth (1996), William & Mary (1986).

Associate Commissioner/Communications: Rob Washburn.

2012 Tournament: Six teams, double-elimination. May 23-26 at Harrisonburg, Va. (James Madison).

CONFERENCE USA

Mailing Address: 5201 N. O'Connor Blvd., Suite 300, Irving, TX 75039. **Telephone:** (214) 774-1300. **Fax:** (214) 496-0055. **E-Mail Address:** rdanderson@c-usa.org. **Website:** www.conferenceusa.com.

Baseball Members (First Year): Alabama-Birmingham (1996), Central Florida (2006), East Carolina (2002), Houston (1997), Marshall (2006), Memphis (1996), Rice (2006), Southern Miss (1996), Tulane (1996).

Assistant Commissioner, Baseball Operations: Russell Anderson.

2012 Tournament: Eight-team, two-division pool play. May 23-27 at Pearl, Miss.

GREAT WEST CONFERENCE

Mailing Address: PO Box 9344, Naperville, IL 60567. **Telephone:** (630) 428-4492. **Fax:** (630) 548-0705. **E-Mail Address:** martin@gwconference.org. **Website:** www.greatwestconference.org.

Baseball Members (First Year): Chicago State (2010), Houston Baptist (2010), New Jersey Tech (2010), New York Tech (2010), North Dakota (2010), Northern Colorado (2010), Texas-Pan American (2010), Utah Valley (2010).

Media Relations Assistant Director: Cliff Martin.

2012 Tournament: Eight teams, double-elimination, May 22-26 at Utah Valley.

HORIZON LEAGUE

Mailing Address: 201 S Capitol Ave, Suite 500, Indianapolis, IN 46225. **Telephone:** (317) 237-5604. **Fax:** (317) 237-5620. **E-Mail Address:** chammel@horizonleague.org. **Website:** www.horizonleague.org.

Baseball Members (First Year): Butler (1979), Cleveland State (1994), Illinois-Chicago (1994), Wisconsin-Milwaukee (1994), Valparaiso (2008), Wright State (1994), Youngstown State (2002).

Assistant Director, Communications: Craig Hammel.

2012 Tournament: Six teams, double-elimination. May 23-26 at Illinois-Chicago.

IVY LEAGUE

Mailing Address: 228 Alexander Rd., Second Floor, Princeton, NJ 08544. **Telephone:** (609) 258-6426. **Fax:** (609) 258-1690. **E-Mail Address:** trevor@ivyleaguesports.com. **Website:** www.ivyleaguesports.com.

Baseball Members (First Year): Rolfe—Brown (1948), Dartmouth (1930), Harvard (1948), Yale (1930). Gehrig—Columbia (1930), Cornell (1930), Pennsylvania (1930), Princeton (1930).

Interim Assistant Executive Director, Communications/Championships: Trevor Rutledge-Leverenz.

2012 Tournament: Best-of-three series between division champions. May 5-6 at team with best overall record.

METRO ATLANTIC ATHLETIC CONFERENCE

Mailing Address: 712 Amboy Ave, Edison, NJ 08837. **Telephone:** (732) 738-5455. **Fax:** (732) 738-8366. **E-Mail Address:** edward.clinton@maac.org. **Website:** www.maacsports.com.

Baseball Members (First Year): Canisius (1990), Fairfield (1982), Iona (1982), Manhattan (1982), Marist (1998), Niagara (1990), Rider (1998), St. Peter's (1982),

Siena (1990).

Associate Commissioner, External Relations: Ed Clinton.

2012 Tournament: Four teams, double-elimination. May 24-27 at Joseph L Bruno Stadium, Troy, N.Y.

MID-AMERICAN CONFERENCE

Mailing Address: 24 Public Square, 15th Floor, Cleveland, OH 44113. **Telephone:** (216) 566-4622. **Fax:** (216) 858-9622. **E-Mail Address:** jguy@mac-sports.com. **Website:** www.mac-sports.com.

Baseball Members (First Year): Akron (1992), Ball State (1973), Bowling Green State (1952), Buffalo (2001), Central Michigan (1971), Eastern Michigan (1971), Kent State (1951), Miami (1947), Northern Illinois (1997), Ohio (1946). Toledo (1950), Western Michigan (1947).

Director, Communications: Jeremy Guy.

2012 Tournament: Eight teams (top three in each division and two teams with the next-best overall records, regardless of division), double-elimination. May 23-26 at All Pro Freight Stadium (Avon, Ohio).

MID-EASTERN ATHLETIC CONFERENCE

Mailing Address: 2730 Ellsmere Avenue, Norfolk, VA 23513. **Telephone:** (757) 951-2055. **Fax:** (757) 951-2077. **E-Mail Address:** rashids@themeac.com; porterp@themeac.com. **Website:** www.meacsports.com.

Baseball Members (First Year): Bethune-Cookman (1979), Coppin State (1985), Delaware State (1970), Florida A&M (1979), Maryland Eastern Shore (1970), Norfolk State (1998), North Carolina A&T (1970), North Carolina Central (1970-1977; 2012), Savannah State (2012).

Assistant Director, Media Relations/Baseball Contact: Sahar Abdur-Rashid.

2012 Tournament: Eight teams, double-elimination. May 17-20 at Norfolk, Va. (Norfolk State).

MISSOURI VALLEY CONFERENCE

Mailing Address: 1818 Chouteau Ave, St. Louis, MO 63103. **Telephone:** (314) 444-4300. **Fax:** (314) 421-3505. **E-Mail Address:** kbriscoe@mvc.org. **Website:** www.mvc-sports.com.

Baseball Members (First Year): Bradley (1955), Creighton (1976), Evansville (1994), Illinois State (1980), Indiana State (1976), Missouri State (1990), Southern Illinois (1974), Wichita State (1945).

Director, Communications/Sports Administration: Kelli Briscoe.

2012 Tournament: Eight-team tournament with two four-team brackets mirroring the format of the College World Series, with the winners of each four-team bracket meeting in a single championship game. May 22-26 at Hammons Field (Missouri State).

MOUNTAIN WEST CONFERENCE

Mailing Address: 15455 Gleneagle Dr., Suite 200, Colorado Springs, CO 80921. **Telephone:** (719) 488-4052. **Fax:** (719) 487-7241. **E-Mail Address:** jwilson@themwc.com. **Website:** www.themwc.com.

Baseball Members (First Year): Air Force (2000), Nevada-Las Vegas (2000), New Mexico (2000), San Diego State (2000), Texas Christian (2006).

Director, Communications: Judy Wilson.

2012 Tournament: Four teams, double-elimination. May 24-27 at UNLV.

NORTHEAST CONFERENCE

Mailing Address: 399 Campus Drive, Somerset, NJ 08873. **Telephone:** (732) 469-0440. **Fax:** (732) 469-0744. **E-Mail Address:** rventre@northeastconference.org.

Website: www.northeastconference.org.

Baseball Members (First Year): Bryant (2010), Central Connecticut State (1999), Fairleigh Dickinson (1981), Long Island (1981), Monmouth (1985), Mount St. Mary's (1989), Quinnipiac (1999), Sacred Heart (2000), Wagner (1981).

Assistant Commissioner: Ralph Ventre.

2012 Tournament: Four teams, double-elimination. May 17-19. **Site:** Norwich, Conn.

OHIO VALLEY CONFERENCE

Mailing Address: 215 Centerview Dr., Suite 115, Brentwood, TN 37027. **Telephone:** (615) 371-1698. **Fax:** (615) 371-1788. **E-Mail Address:** kschwartz@ovc.org. **Website:** www.ovcsports.com.

Baseball Members (First Year): Austin Peay State (1962), Eastern Illinois (1996), Eastern Kentucky (1948), Jacksonville State (2003), Morehead State (1948), Murray State (1948), Southeast Missouri State (1991), Southern Illinois-Edwardsville (2012), Tennessee-Martin (1992), Tennessee Tech (1949).

Assistant Commissioner: Kyle Schwartz.

2012 Tournament: Six teams, double-elimination. May 23-27 at Jackson, Tenn.

PACIFIC-12 CONFERENCE

Mailing Address: 1350 Treat Blvd., Suite 500. **Telephone:** (925) 932-4411. **Fax:** (925) 932-4601. **E-Mail Address:** skezele@pac-12.org. **Website:** www.pac-12.org.

Baseball Members (First Year): Arizona (1979), Arizona State (1979), California (1916), UCLA (1928), Oregon (1916-1981, 2009) Oregon State (1916), Southern California (1923), Stanford (1918), Utah (2012), Washington (1916), Washington State (1919).

Public Relations Contact: Sarah Kezele.

2012 Tournament: None.

PATRIOT LEAGUE

Mailing Address: 3773 Corporate Pkwy, Suite 190, Center Valley, PA 18034. **Telephone:** (610) 289-1960. **Fax:** (610) 289-1951. **E-Mail Address:** jjohnson@patriotleague.com. **Website:** www.patriotleague.org.

Baseball Members (First Year): Army (1993), Bucknell (1991), Holy Cross (1991), Lafayette (1991), Lehigh (1991), Navy (1993).

Coordinator, Multimedia: Jimmy Johnson.

2012 Tournament: Four teams, May 12-13 and May 19-20 at site of higher seeds.

SOUTHEASTERN CONFERENCE

Mailing Address: 2201 Richard Arrington Blvd. N., Birmingham, AL 35203. **Telephone:** (205) 458-3000. **Fax:** (205) 458-3030. **E-Mail Address:** cdunlap@sec.org. **Website:** www.secsports.com.

Baseball Members (First Year): East—Florida (1933), Georgia (1933), Kentucky (1933), South Carolina (1992), Tennessee (1933), Vanderbilt (1933). West—Alabama (1933), Arkansas (1992), Auburn (1933), Louisiana State (1933), Mississippi (1933), Mississippi State (1933).

Associate Director, Media Relations: Chuck Dunlap.

2012 Tournament: Ten teams, modified double-elimination. May 22-27 at Hoover, Ala.

SOUTHERN CONFERENCE

Mailing Address: 702 N. Pine St., Spartanburg, SC 29303. **Telephone:** (864) 591-5100. **Fax:** (864) 591-4282. **E-Mail Address:** jcaskey@socon.org. **Website:** www.soconsports.com.

Baseball Members (First Year): Appalachian State (1971), College of Charleston (1998), The Citadel (1936), Davidson (1991), Elon (2004), Furman (1936), Georgia

Southern (1991), UNCG (1997), Samford (2009), Western Carolina (1976), Wofford (1997).

Media Relations: Jonathan Caskey.

2012 Tournament: Eight teams, double-elimination. May 23-27 at Fluor Field, Greenville, S.C.

SOUTHLAND CONFERENCE

Mailing Address: 2600 Network Blvd., Suite 150, Frisco, Texas 75034. **Telephone:** (972) 422-9500. **Fax:** (972) 422-9225. **E-Mail Address:** tlamb@southland.org. **Website:** www.southland.org.

Baseball Members (First Year): Central Arkansas (2007), Lamar (1999), McNeese State (1973), Nicholls State (1992), Northwestern State (1988), Sam Houston State (1988), Southeastern Louisiana (1998), Stephen F. Austin (2006), Texas-Arlington (1964), Texas-San Antonio (1992), Texas A&M-Corpus Christi (2007), Texas State (1988).

Baseball Contact/Assistant Commissioner: Todd Lamb.

2012 Tournament: Two four-team brackets, double-elimination. May 23-26 at San Marcos, Texas (Texas State).

SOUTHWESTERN ATHLETIC CONFERENCE

Mailing Address: 2101 6th Avenue North, Suite 700, Birmingham, AL 35203. **Telephone:** (205) 251-7573. **Fax:** (205) 297-9820. **E-Mail Address:** t.galbraith@swac.org. **Website:** www.swac.org.

Baseball Members (First Year): East—Alabama A&M (2000), Alabama State (1982), Alcorn State (1962), Jackson State (1958), Mississippi Valley State (1968). West—Arkansas-Pine Bluff (1999), Grambling State (1958), Prairie View A&M (1920), Southern (1934), Texas Southern (1954).

Assistant Commissioner, Communications: Tom Galbraith.

2012 Tournament: Eight teams, double-elimination. May 16-20 at Baton Rouge, La.

SUMMIT LEAGUE

Mailing Address: 340 W Butterfield Rd, Suite 3-D, Elmhurst, IL 60126. **Telephone:** (630) 516-0661. **Fax:** (630) 516-0673. **E-Mail Address:** mette@thesummitleague.org. **Website:** www.thesummitleague.org.

Baseball Members (First Year): IPFW (2008), North Dakota State (2008), Oakland (2000), Oral Roberts (1998), South Dakota State (2008), Southern Utah (2000), Western Illinois (1984).

Associate Director, Communications (baseball contact): Greg Mette.

2012 Tournament: Four teams, double-elimination. May 24-26 at Tulsa, Okla. (Oral Roberts).

SUN BELT CONFERENCE

Mailing Address: 601 Poydras St, Suite 2355, New Orleans, LA 70130. **Telephone:** (504) 299-9066. **Fax:** (504) 299-9068. **E-Mail Address:** nunez@sunbeltsports.org. **Website:** www.sunbeltsports.org.

Baseball Members (First Year): Arkansas-Little Rock (1991), Arkansas State (1991), Florida Atlantic (2007), Florida International (1999), Louisiana-Lafayette (1991), Louisiana-Monroe (2007), Middle Tennessee State (2001), South Alabama (1976), Troy (2006), Western Kentucky (1982).

Assistant Commissioner, Media Relations: Keith Nunez.

2012 Tournament: Eight-team, two-division pool play. May 23-27 at Bowling Green, Ky. (Western Kentucky).

WEST COAST CONFERENCE

Mailing Address: 1111 Bayhill Dr, Suite 405, San Bruno, CA 94066. **Telephone:** (650) 873-8622. **Fax:** (650) 873-7846. **E-Mail Addresses:** jtourial@westcoast.org. **Website:** www.wccsports.com.

Baseball Members (First Year): Brigham Young (2012), Gonzaga (1996), Loyola Marymount (1968), Pepperdine (1968), Portland (1996), Saint Mary's (1968), San Diego (1979), San Francisco (1968), Santa Clara (1968).

Director, Communications: Jeff Tourial. **Associate Director, Communications:** James Vega.

2012 Tournament: None.

WESTERN ATHLETIC CONFERENCE

Mailing Address: 9250 East Costilla Ave., Suite 300, Englewood, CO 80112. **Telephone:** (303) 799-9221. **Fax:** (303) 799-3888. **E-Mail Address:** jerickson@wac.org. **Website:** www.wacsports.com.

Baseball Members (First Year): Fresno State (1993), Hawai'i (1980), Louisiana Tech (2002), Nevada (2001), New Mexico State (2006), Sacramento State (2006), San Jose State (1997).

Commissioner: Karl Benson. **Senior Associate Commissioner:** Jeff Hurd. **Director of Media Relations:** Jason Erickson.

2012 Tournament: Six teams, double elimination. May 23-27 at Hohokam Stadium, Mesa, Ariz.

NCAA DIVISION I TEAMS
*Recruiting coordinator

AIR FORCE FALCONS

Conference: Mountain West.
Mailing Address: 2169 Field House Drive, USAFA, CO 80840. **Website:** goairforcefalcons.com.
Head Coach: Mike Kazlausky. **Telephone:** (719) 333-0835. **Baseball SID:** Nick Arseniak. **Telephone:** (719) 333-9251. **Fax:** (719) 333-3798.
Assistant Coaches: Toby Bicknell, *Tim Dixon. **Telephone:** (719) 333-7539.
Home Field: Falcon Field. **Seating Capacity:** 1,000. **Press Box Telephone:** (719) 333-3472.

AKRON ZIPS

Conference: Mid-American (East).
Mailing Address: University of Akron, Rhodes Arena, Akron, OH 44325. **Website:** www.GoZips.com.
Head Coach: *Rick Rembielak. **Telephone:** (330) 972-7290. **Baseball SID:** Nick VanDemark. **Telephone:** (330) 972-7171. **Fax:** (330) 374-8844.
Assistant Coaches: Fred Worth. **Telephone:** (330) 972-7290.
Home Field: Lee R. Jackson Baseball Field. **Seating Capacity:** 1,500. **Press Box Telephone:** (419) 769-3544.

ALABAMA CRIMSON TIDE

Conference: Southeastern (West).
Mailing Address: Coleman Coliseum, Rm 170, 323 Bryant Drive, Tuscaloosa, AL 35401. **Website:** www.rollti-de.com.
Head Coach: Mitch Gaspard. **Telephone:** (205) 348-4029. **Baseball SID:** Rich Davi. **Telephone:** (205) 348-3550. **Fax:** (205) 348-6084.
Assistant Coaches: *Dax Norris, Andy Phillips. **Telephone:** (205) 348-4029.
Home Field: Sewell-Thomas Stadium. **Seating Capacity:** 6,541. **Press Box Telephone:** (205) 348-4927.

ALABAMA A&M BULLDOGS

Conference: Southwestern Athletic.
Mailing Address: 4900 Meridian St, Normal, AL 35762. **Website:** www.aamusports.com.
Head Coach: Michael Tompkins. **Telephone:** (256) 372-4004. **Baseball SID:** Brandon Willis. **Telephone:** (256) 372-4005. **Fax:** (256) 372-5919.
Assistant Coaches: Preston Potter. **Telephone:** (256) 372-4004.
Home Field: Bulldog Baseball Field. **Seating Capacity:** 500.

ALABAMA STATE HORNETS

Conference: Southwestern Athletic.
Mailing Address: 915 South Jackson Street, Montgomery, AL 36104. **Website:** www.bamastatesports.com.
Head Coach: Mervyl Melendez. **Telephone:** (334) 229-8899. **Baseball SID:** Duane Lewis. **Telephone:** (334) 229-5230. **Fax:** (334) 262-2971.
Assistant Coaches: Drew Clark, *Jose Vazquez. **Telephone:** (334) 229-8899.
Home Field: Hornets Stadium. **Seating Capacity:** 1,000. **Press Box Telephone:** (334) 229-8899.

ALABAMA-BIRMINGHAM BLAZERS

Conference: Conference USA.
Mailing Address: 1212 University Blvd, U236, Birmingham, AL 35294. **Website:** www.uabsports.com.
Head Coach: Brian Shoop. **Telephone:** (205) 934-5181. **Baseball SID:** Ben Warnick. **Telephone:** (205) 934-0725. **Fax:** (205) 934-7505.
Assistant Coaches: Josh Hopper, *Perry Roth. **Telephone:** (205) 934-5182.
Home Field: Jerry D Young Memorial Field. **Seating Capacity:** 1,000. **Press Box Telephone:** (205) 934-0200.

ALBANY GREAT DANES

Conference: America East.
Mailing Address: 1400 Washington Ave, PE Bldg 123, Albany, NY 12222. **Website:** www.ualbanysports.com.
Head Coach: Jon Mueller. **Telephone:** (518) 442-3014. **Baseball SID:** Brianna LaBrecque. **Telephone:** (518) 442-5733. **Fax:** (518) 442-3139.
Assistant Coaches: Garett Baron, *Drew Pearce. **Telephone:** : (518) 442-3014.
Home Field: Varsity Field. **Seating Capacity:** 1,000.

ALCORN STATE BRAVES

Conference: Southwestern Athletic.
Mailing Address: 1000 ASU Dr, #510, Alcorn State, MS 39096. **Website:** www.alcornsports.com.
Head Coach: Barret Rey. **Telephone:** (601) 877-4090. **Baseball SID:** LaToya Shields. **Telephone:** (601) 877-6501. **Fax:** (601) 877-3821.
Assistant Coaches: *David Gomez, Kevin Vital. **Telephone:** (601) 877-4090.
Home Field: Willie "Rat" McGowan, Sr Stadium/Bill Foster Field. **Seating Capacity:** 500. **Press Box Telephone:**(601) 443-1087.

APPALACHIAN STATE MOUNTAINEERS

Conference: Southern.
Mailing Address: Smith Baseball Stadium, ASU Box 32159, Boone, NC 28608. **Website:** www.goasu.com.
Head Coach: Chris Pollard. **Telephone:** (828) 262-6097. **Baseball SID:** Mike Flynn. **Telephone:** (828) 262-2845. **Fax:** (828) 262-6106.
Assistant Coaches: *Josh Jordan, Chris Moore.

Telephone: (828) 262-7165.
Home Field: Beaver Field at Jim and Bettie Smith Stadium. **Seating Capacity:** 1,000. **Press Box Telephone:** (828) 262-2016.

ARIZONA WILDCATS

Conference: Pacific-12.
Mailing Address: 1 National Championship Drive, Tucson, AZ 85721-0096. **Website:** www.arizonaathletics. com.
Head Coach: Andy Lopez. **Telephone:** (520) 621-4102. **Baseball SID:** Blair Willis. **Telephone:** (520) 621-0914. **Fax:** (520) 621-2681.
Assistant Coaches: *Shaun Cole, Matt Siegel. **Telephone:** (520) 621-4714.
Home Field: Hi Corbett Field. **Seating Capacity:** 9,500.

ARIZONA STATE SUN DEVILS

Conference: Pacific-12.
Mailing Address: 500 East Veteran's Way, Tempe, AZ 85287. **Website:** www.TheSunDevils.com.
Head Coach: Tim Esmay. **Telephone:** (480) 965-3677. **Baseball SID:** Randy Policar. **Telephone:** (480) 965-6592. **Fax:** (480) 965-5408.
Assistant Coaches: *Travis Jewett, Ken Knutson. **Telephone:** (480) 965-3677.
Home Field: Packard Stadium. **Seating Capacity:** 4,371. **Press Box Telephone:** (480) 727-7253.

ARKANSAS RAZORBACKS

Conference: Southeastern (West).
Mailing Address: 1255 S Razorback, Fayetteville, AR 72701. **Website:** www.arkansasrazorbacks.com.
Head Coach: Dave Van Horn. **Telephone:** (479) 575-3655. **Baseball SID:** Chad Crunk. **Telephone:** (479) 575-2753. **Fax:** (479) 575-7481.
Assistant Coaches: *Todd Butler, Dave Jorn. **Telephone:** (479) 575-3552.
Home Field: Baum Stadium. **Seating Capacity:** 10,737. **Press Box Telephone:** (479) 575-4141.

ARKANSAS STATE RED WOLVES

Conference: Sun Belt.
Mailing Address: Box 1000, State University, AR 72467. **Website:** www.astateredwolves.com.
Head Coach: Tommy Raffo. **Telephone:** (870) 972-2700. **Baseball SID:** Anthony Reynolds. **Telephone:** (870) 972-2707. **Fax:** (870) 972-3367.
Assistant Coaches: *Chris Cook, Tighe Dickinson. **Telephone:** (870) 972-2700.
Home Field: Tomlinson Stadium Kell Field. **Seating Capacity:** 1,500. **Press Box Telephone:** (870) 972-3383.

ARKANSAS-LITTLE ROCK TROJANS

Conference: Sun Belt.
Mailing Address: 2801 S University Avenue, Little Rock, AR 72204. **Website:** www.ualrtrojans.com.
Head Coach: Scott Norwood. **Telephone:** (501) 663-8095. **Baseball SID:** Joe Angolia. **Telephone:** (501) 569-3449. **Fax:** (501) 683-7002.
Assistant Coaches: Jeremy Haworth, *Brandon Rowan. **Telephone:** (501) 280-0759.
Home Field: Gary Hogan Field. **Press Box Telephone:** (501) 351-1060.

ARKANSAS-PINE BLUFF GOLDEN LIONS

Conference: Southwestern Athletic.
Mailing Address: 1200 N University Drive, Mail Slot 4891, Pine Bluff, AR 71601. **Website:** www.uapblionsroar.com.

Head Coach: Carlos James. **Telephone:** (870) 575-8995. **Baseball SID:** Andrew Roberts. **Telephone:** (870) 575-7949. **Fax:** (870) 575-4655.
Assistant Coaches: *Marc MacMillan, Jon Tatum. **Telephone:** (870) 575-8995.
Home Field: Torii Hunter Baseball Complex. **Seating Capacity:** 1,500.

ARMY BLACK KNIGHTS

Conference: Patriot.
Mailing Address: 639 Howard Road, West Point, NY 10996. **Website:** www.goarmysports.com.
Head Coach: Joe Sottolano. **Telephone:** (845) 938-3712. **Baseball SID:** Christian Anderson. **Telephone:** (845) 938-3303. **Fax:** (845) 446-2556.
Assistant Coaches: Anthony DeCicco, *Matt Reid. **Telephone:** (845) 938-3712.
Home Field: Johnson Stadium at Doubleday Field. **Seating Capacity:** 880. **Press Box Telephone:** (845) 938-8168.

AUBURN TIGERS

Conference: Southeastern (West).
Mailing Address: PO Box 351, Auburn, AL 36849. **Website:** www.auburntigers.com.
Head Coach: John Pawlowski. **Telephone:** (334) 844-9758. **Baseball SID:** Dan Froehlich. **Telephone:** (334) 844-9803. **Fax:** (334) 844-9807.
Assistant Coaches: *Scott Foxhall, Link Jarrett. **Telephone:** (334) 844-9767.
Home Field: Plainsman Park. **Seating Capacity:** 4,096. **Press Box Telephone:** (334) 844-4138.

AUSTIN PEAY STATE GOVERNORS

Conference: Ohio Valley.
Mailing Address: Austin Peay Baseball Office, Box 4515, Clarksville, TN 37044. **Website:** www.letsgopeay. com.
Head Coach: Gary McClure. **Telephone:** (931) 221-6266. **Baseball SID:** Cody Bush. **Telephone:** (931) 221-7561. **Fax:** (931) 221-7389.
Assistant Coaches: Derrick Dunbar, *Joel Mangrum. **Telephone:** (931) 221-7902.
Home Field: Raymond C Hand Park. **Seating Capacity:** 2,000. **Press Box Telephone:** (931) 221-7406.

BALL STATE CARDINALS

Conference: Mid-American (West).
Mailing Address: HP 245, Muncie, IN 47306. **Website:** www.ballstatesports.com.
Head Coach: Alex Marconi. **Telephone:** (765) 285-1425. **Baseball SID:** Matt McCollester. **Telephone:** (765) 285-8242. **Fax:** (765) 285-8929.
Assistant Coaches: Pete Milas, *Jeremy Plexico. **Telephone:** (765) 285-2862.
Home Field: Ball Diamond. **Seating Capacity:** 1,500.

BAYLOR BEARS

Conference: Big 12.
Mailing Address: 1612 S University Parks Dr, Waco, TX 76712. **Website:** www.baylorbears.com.
Head Coach: Steve Smith. **Telephone:** (254) 710-3097. **Baseball SID:** David Kaye. **Telephone:** (254) 710-4389. **Fax:** (254) 710-1369.
Assistant Coaches: Steve Johnigan, *Mitch Thompson. **Telephone:** (254) 710-3044.
Home Field: Baylor Ballpark. **Seating Capacity:** 5,000. **Press Box Telephone:** (254) 754-5546.

BELMONT BRUINS

Conference: Atlantic Sun.
Mailing Address: 1900 Belmont Blvd, Nashville, TN 37212. **Website:** www.belmontbruins.com.
Head Coach: Dave Jarvis. **Telephone:** (615) 460-6166. **Baseball SID:** Dan Forcella. **Telephone:** (615) 460-8023. **Fax:** (615) 460-5584.
Assistant Coaches: Matt Barnett, *Scott Hall. **Telephone:** (615) 460-5586.
Home Field: ES Rose Park.

BETHUNE-COOKMAN WILDCATS

Conference: Mid-Eastern Athletic.
Mailing Address: Bethune Cookman Baseball, 640 Dr Mary McLeod Bethune Blvd, Daytona Beach, FL 32114. **Website:** www.bccathletics.com.
Head Coach: Jason Beverlin. **Telephone:** (386) 481-2224. **Baseball SID:** Michael Stambaugh. **Telephone:** (386) 481-2278. **Fax:** (386) 481-2238.
Assistant Coaches: *Barrett Shaft, Kenny Smith. **Telephone:** (386) 481-2242.
Home Field: Jackie Robinson. **Seating Capacity:** 5,000.

BINGHAMTON BEARCATS

Conference: America East.
Mailing Address: Binghamton University, Events Center Office #110, Binghamton, NY, 13902. **Website:** www.bubearcats.com.
Head Coach: Tim Sinicki. **Telephone:** (607) 777-2525. **Baseball SID:** John Hartrick. **Telephone:** (607) 777-6800. **Fax:** (607) 777-4597.
Assistant Coaches: *Ryan Hurba, Dustin Johnson. **Telephone:** (607) 777-5808, (607) 777-4552.
Home Field: Under Construction.

BOSTON COLLEGE EAGLES

Conference: Atlantic Coast (Atlantic).
Mailing Address: 140 Commonwealth Ave Conte Forum, Chestnut Hill, MA 02467. **Website:** bceagles.cstv.com.
Head Coach: Mike Gambino. **Telephone:** (617) 552-2674. **Baseball SID:** Zanna Ollove. **Telephone:** (617) 552-3004. **Fax:** (617) 552-4903.
Assistant Coaches: *Scott Friedholm, Steve Englert. **Telephone:** (617) 552-1131.
Home Field: Eddie Pellagrini Diamond at Commander Shea Field. **Seating Capacity:** 1,000.

BOWLING GREEN STATE FALCONS

Conference: Missouri Valley.
Mailing Address: Bowling Green State University, Sebo Athletic Center - Baseball, Bowling Green, OH 43403. **Website:** www.bgsufalcons.com.
Head Coach: Danny Schmitz. **Telephone:** (419) 372-7065. **Baseball SID:** Scott Swegan. **Telephone:** (419) 372-7105. **Fax:** (419) 372-6969.
Assistant Coaches: *Rick Blanc, Spencer Schmitz. **Telephone:** (419) 372-7095, (419) 372-7641.
Home Field: Warren E Steller. **Seating Capacity:** 1,100 (seats), 300 (grass). **Press Box Telephone:** (419) 372-1234.

BRADLEY BRAVES

Conference: Missouri Valley.
Mailing Address: 1501 W Bradley Ave, Peoria, IL 61625. **Website:** www.bubraves.com.
Head Coach: Elvis Dominguez. **Telephone:** (309) 677-2684. **Baseball SID:** Bobby Parker. **Telephone:** (309) 677-

2624. **Fax:** (309) 677-2626.
Assistant Coaches: *John Corbin, Sean Lyons. **Telephone:** (309) 677-4583.
Home Field: O'Brien Field. **Seating Capacity:** 7,500. **Press Box Telephone:** (309) 680-4045.

BRIGHAM YOUNG COUGARS

Conference: West Coast.
Mailing Address: 30 SFH, BYU, Provo, UT 84602. **Website:** www.byucougars.com.
Head Coach: Vance Law. **Telephone:** (801) 422-5049. **Baseball SID:** Ralph Zobell. **Telephone:** (801) 422-9769. **Fax:** (801) 422-0633.
Assistant Coaches: Wally Ritchie, *Ryan Roberts. **Telephone:** (801) 422-5064.
Home Field: Larry H. **Miller Field. Seating Capacity:** 2,204. **Press Box Telephone:** (801) 422-4041.

BROWN BEARS

Conference: Ivy League (Rolfe).
Mailing Address: 235 Hope St, Providence, RI 02912. **Website:** www.brownbears.com.
Head Coach: Marek Drabinski. **Telephone:** (401) 863-3090. **Baseball SID:** Michael Gambardella. **Telephone:** (401) 863-6069. **Fax:** (401) 863-1436.
Assistant Coaches: *Brian Murphy, Michael O'Malley. **Telephone:** (401) 863-3090.
Home Field: Murray Stadium. **Seating Capacity:** 2,000. **Press Box Telephone:** (401) 863-9427.

BRYANT BULLDOGS

Conference: Northeast.
Mailing Address: 1150 Douglas Pike, Smithfield, RI 02917. **Website:** www.bryantbulldogs.com.
Head Coach: Steve Owens. **Telephone:** (401) 232-6397. **Baseball SID:** Tristan Hobbes. **Telephone:** (401) 232-6558 Ext. 2. **Fax:** (401) 319-5153.
Assistant Coaches: *Ryan Fecteau, Michael Gedman. **Telephone:** (401) 232-6967.
Home Field: Conaty Park. **Seating Capacity:** 500.

BUCKNELL BISON

Conference: Patriot.
Mailing Address: Moore Ave, Lewisburg, PA 17837. **Website:** www.bucknellbison.com.
Head Coach: Gene Depew. **Telephone:** (570) 577-3593. **Baseball SID:** Todd Merriett. **Telephone:** (570) 577-3488. **Fax:** (570) 577-1660.
Assistant Coaches: Jim Gulden, *Scott Heather. **Telephone:** (570) 577-1059.
Home Field: Depew Field. **Seating Capacity:** 500.

BUFFALO BULLS

Conference: Mid-American (East).
Mailing Address: University at Buffalo, Division of Athletics, 175 Alumni Arena, Buffalo, NY 14260. **Website:** www.buffalobulls.com.
Head Coach: Ron Torgalski. **Telephone:** (716) 645-6834. **Baseball SID:** Joe Kepler. **Telephone:** (716) 645-5523. **Fax:** .
Assistant Coaches: *Brad Cochrane, Steve Ziroli. **Telephone:** (716) 645-3437.
Home Field: Amherst Audubon Field. **Press Box Telephone:** (716) 867-1908.

BUTLER BULLDOGS

Conference: Horizon.
Mailing Address: 510 W 49th St, Indianapolis, IN 46208. **Website:** www.butlersports.com.
Head Coach: Steve Farley. **Telephone:** (317) 940-9721.

Baseball SID: Josh Rattray. **Telephone:** (317) 940-9994. **Fax:** 317) 940-9808.
Assistant Coaches: Michael Dalton, *DJ Throneburg. **Telephone:** (317) 940-6536.
Home Field: Bulldog Park. **Seating Capacity:** 500. **Press Box Telephone:** (317) 945-8943.

CALIFORNIA GOLDEN BEARS

Conference: Pacific-12.
Mailing Address: Haas Pavilion, Berkeley, CA 94720. **Website:** www.calbears.com.
Head Coach: David Esquer. **Telephone:** (510) 642-9026. **Baseball SID:** Scott Ball. **Telephone:** (510) 643-1741. **Fax:** (510) 643-7778.
Assistant Coaches: Tony Arnerich, *Mike Neu. **Telephone:** (510) 643-6006.
Home Field: Evans Diamond. **Seating Capacity:** 2,500. **Press Box Telephone:** (510) 642-3098.

UC DAVIS AGGIES

Conference: Big West.
Mailing Address: One Shields Ave Davis, CA 95616. **Website:** ucdavisaggies.com.
Head Coach: Matt Vaughn. **Telephone:** (530) 752-7513. **Baseball SID:** Amanda Piechowski. **Telephone:** (530) 752-2663. **Fax:** (530) 752-6681.
Assistant Coaches: Jason Armstrong, *Tony Schifano. **Telephone:** (530) 752-7513.
Home Field: Dobbins Stadium. **Seating Capacity:** 3,500. **Press Box Telephone:** (530) 752-3673.

UC IRVINE ANTEATERS

Conference: Big West.
Mailing Address: UC Irvine Athletics, 903 W Peltason Drive, Irvine, CA 92697. **Website:** www.ucirvinesports.com.
Head Coach: Mike Gillespie. **Telephone:** (949) 824-4292. **Baseball SID:** Fumi Kimura. **Telephone:** (949) 824-9474. **Fax:** (949) 824-5260.
Assistant Coaches: Jason Dietrich, *Pat Shine. **Telephone:** (949) 824-1154.
Home Field: Anteater Ballpark. **Seating Capacity:** 3,200. **Press Box Telephone:** (949) 824-9905.

UCLA BRUINS

Conference: Pacific-12.
Mailing Address: J.D. Morgan Center, 325 Westwood Plaza, Los Angeles, CA 90095. **Website:** www.uclabruins.com.
Head Coach: John Savage. **Telephone:** (310) 794-2470. **Baseball SID:** Alex Timiraos. **Telephone:** (310) 206-0524. **Fax:** (310) 825-8664.
Assistant Coaches: *TJ Bruce, Rex Peters. **Telephone:** (310) 794-2473.
Home Field: Jackie Robinson Stadium. **Seating Capacity:** 1,820. **Press Box Telephone:** (310) 792-8231.

UC RIVERSIDE HIGHLANDERS

Conference: Big West.
Mailing Address: 900 University Ave, Riverside, CA 92521. **Website:** www.gohighlanders.com.
Head Coach: Doug Smith. **Telephone:** (951) 827-5441. **Baseball SID:** John Maxwell. **Telephone:** (951) 827-5438. **Fax:** (951) 827-3569.
Assistant Coaches: *Bobby Applegate, Bryson LeBlanc. **Telephone:** (951) 236-8527.
Home Field: UC Riverside Sports Center. **Seating Capacity:** 1,900.

UC SANTA BARBARA GAUCHOS

Conference: Big West.
Mailing Address: ICA Building, UC Santa Barbara, Santa Barbara, CA 93106-5200. **Website:** www.ucsbgauchos.com.
Head Coach: Andrew Checketts. **Telephone:** (805) 893-3690. **Baseball SID:** Matt Hurst. **Telephone:** (805) 893-8603. **Fax:** (805)893-5477.
Assistant Coaches: *Eddie Cornejo, Jason Hawkins. **Telephone:** (805) 893-2021.
Home Field: Caesar Uyesaka Stadium. **Seating Capacity:** 1,000. **Press Box Telephone:** (805) 893-4671.

CAL POLY MUSTANGS

Conference: Big West.
Mailing Address: 1 Grand Avenue, San Luis Obispo, CA 93407-0388. **Website:** www.GoPoly.com.
Head Coach: Larry Lee. **Telephone:** (805) 756-6367. **Baseball SID:** Eric Burdick. **Telephone:** (805) 756-6550. **Fax:** (805) 756-2650.
Assistant Coaches: Jason Kelly, *Teddy Warrecker. **Telephone:** (805) 756-1201.
Home Field: Baggett Stadium. **Seating Capacity:** 1,734. **Press Box Telephone:** (805) 756-7456.

CAL STATE BAKERSFIELD ROADRUNNERS

Conference: Independent.
Mailing Address: 9001 Stockdale Highway, GYM 08, Bakersfield, CA 93311. **Website:** www.csub.edu.
Head Coach: Bill Kernen. **Telephone:** (661) 335-1058. **Baseball SID:** Matt Turk. **Telephone:** (661) 654-3071. **Fax:** (661) 654-6978.
Assistant Coaches: *Jody Robinson. **Telephone:** (661) 654-2678.
Home Field: Hardt Field. **Seating Capacity:** 500.

CAL STATE FULLERTON TITANS

Conference: Big West.
Mailing Address: 800 N State College Blvd, Fullerton, CA 92834. **Website:** www.fullertontitans.com.
Head Coach: Rick Vanderhook. **Telephone:** (657) 278-3780. **Baseball SID:** Mike Greenlee. **Telephone:** (657) 278-3081. **Fax:** (657) 279-3141.
Assistant Coaches: *Mike Kirby, Kirk Saarloos. **Telephone:** (657) 278-2492.
Home Field: Goodwin Field. **Seating Capacity:** 3,500. **Press Box Telephone:** (657) 278-5327.

CAL STATE NORTHRIDGE MATADORS

Conference: Big West.
Mailing Address: 18111 Nordhoff St, Northridge, CA 91330-8301. **Website:** www.gomatadors.cstv.com.
Head Coach: Matt Curtis. **Telephone:** (818) 677-7055. **Baseball SID:** Kevin Strauss. **Telephone:** (818) 677-3860. **Fax:** (818) 677-4762.
Assistant Coaches: *Shaun Larkin, Dennis Machado. **Telephone:** (818) 677-3218.
Home Field: Matador Field. **Seating Capacity:** 1,000. **Press Box Telephone:** (818) 677-4292.

CAMPBELL FIGHTING CAMELS

Conference: Atlantic Sun.
Mailing Address: PO Box 10, Buies Creek, NC 27506. **Website:** www.gocamels.com.
Head Coach: Greg Goff. **Telephone:** (910) 893-1354. **Baseball SID:** Daniel Smith. **Telephone:** (910) 893-1529. **Fax:** (910) 893-1330.
Assistant Coaches: *Justin Haire, Rick McCarty. **Telephone:** (910) 893-1338, (910) 814-4335.

Home Field: Taylor Field. **Seating Capacity:** 1,000. **Press Box Telephone:** (910) 814-4781.

CANISIUS GOLDEN GRIFFINS

Conference: Metro Atlantic.
Mailing Address: 2001 Main St, Buffalo, NY 14208.
Website: www.gogriffs.com.
Head Coach: Mike McRae. **Telephone:** (716) 888-8485.
Baseball SID: Matt Lozar. **Telephone:** (716) 888-8266. **Fax:** (716) 888-8444.
Assistant Coaches: *Matt Mazurek, Perry Silverman. **Telephone:** (716) 888-8479.
Home Field: Demske Sports Complex. **Seating Capacity:** 1,200. **Press Box Telephone:** (440) 477-3777.

CENTRAL ARKANSAS BEARS

Conference: Southland.
Mailing Address: 2401 College Ave, Conway, AR 72034.
Website: www.ucasports.com.
Head Coach: Allen Gum. **Telephone:** (501) 450-3147.
Baseball SID: Steve East. **Telephone:** (501) 450-5743. **Fax:** (501) 450-5740.
Assistant Coaches: *Dallas Black, Kirk Kelley. **Telephone:** (501) 339-0101.
Home Field: Bear Stadium. **Seating Capacity:** 2,000. **Press Box Telephone:** (501) 450-5972.

CENTRAL CONNECTICUT STATE BLUE DEVILS

Conference: Northeast.
Mailing Address: 16151 Stanley St, New Britain, CT 06050. **Website:** www.ccsubluedevils.com.
Head Coach: Charlie Hickey. **Telephone:** (860) 832-3074. **Baseball SID:** Tom Pincince. **Telephone:** (860) 832-3089. **Fax:** (860) 832-3754.
Assistant Coaches: *Pat Hall, James Ziogas. **Telephone:** (860) 832-3075.
Home Field: Balf Savin Baseball Field.

CENTRAL FLORIDA KNIGHTS

Conference: Conference USA.
Mailing Address: 4000 Central Florida Blvd, Orlando, FL 32816. **Website:** www.ucfathletics.com.
Head Coach: Terry Rooney. **Telephone:** (407) 823-0140. **Baseball SID:** Eric DeSalvo. **Telephone:** (407) 823-6489. **Fax:** (407) 823-5266.
Assistant Coaches: Ryan Klosterman, *Joe Mercadante. **Telephone:** (407) 823-4320.
Home Field: Jay Bergman Field. **Seating Capacity:** 3,000. **Press Box Telephone:** (407) 823-4487.

CENTRAL MICHIGAN CHIPPEWAS

Conference: Mid-American (West).
Mailing Address: 100 Rose Center, Mount Pleasant, MI 48859. **Website:** www.cmuchippewas.com.
Head Coach: Steve Jaksa. **Telephone:** (989) 774-4392.
Baseball SID: Kyle Kelley. **Telephone:** (989) 774-1128. **Fax:** (989) 774-1763.
Assistant Coaches: Brett Haring, *Jeff Opalewski. **Telephone:** (989) 774-2123.
Home Field: Theunissen Stadium. **Seating Capacity:** 2,046. **Press Box Telephone:** (989) 774-3579.

CHARLESTON SOUTHERN BUCCANEERS

Conference: Big South.
Mailing Address: 9200 University Blvd, Charleston, SC 29406. **Website:** www.csusports.com.
Head Coach: Stuart Lake. **Telephone:** (843) 863-7591.
Baseball SID: Ashley Bailey. **Telephone:** (843) 863-7688. **Fax:** (843) 863-7676.
Assistant Coaches: *Sid Fallaw, Adam Ward.

Telephone: (843) 863-7764.
Home Field: CSU Ballpark. **Seating Capacity:** 1,500. **Press Box Telephone:** (843) 863-7591.

CHARLOTTE 49ERS

Conference: Atlantic 10.
Mailing Address: 9201 University City Blvd Charlotte, NC 28223. **Website:** www.charlotte49ers.com.
Head Coach: Loren Hibbs. **Telephone:** (704) 687-0726.
Baseball SID: Ryan Rose. **Telephone:** (704) 687-6312. **Fax:** (704) 687-4918.
Assistant Coaches: *Brandon Hall, Kris Rochelle. **Telephone:** (704) 687-0728.
Home Field: Robert and Mariam Hayes Stadium. **Seating Capacity:** 1,100 (seat), 3,300 (stand). **Press Box Telephone:** (704) 687-5959.

CHICAGO STATE COUGARS

Conference: Great West.
Mailing Address: 9501 S King Dr, Chicago, IL 60628. **Website:** www.csu.edu/athletics.
Head Coach: Michael Caston. **Telephone:** (773) 995-3659. **Baseball SID:** Corey Miggins. **Telephone:** (773) 995-2217. **Fax:** (773) 995-3656.
Assistant Coach: *Neal Frendling. **Telephone:** (773) 995-2817.
Home Field: Gwendolyn Brooks Field. **Seating Capacity:** 2,000.

CINCINNATI BEARCATS

Conference: Big East.
Mailing Address: 2751 O'Varsity Way, Suite 764 Cincinnati, OH 45221. **Website:** gobearcats.com.
Head Coach: Brian Cleary. **Telephone:** (513) 556-1577.
Baseball SID: Jeff Geiser. **Telephone:** (513) 556-0618. **Fax:** (513) 556-0619.
Assistant Coaches: *J.D. Heilmann, Greg Mamula. **Telephone:** (513) 556-1577.
Home Field: Marge Schott Stadium. **Seating Capacity:** 3,085. **Press Box Telephone:** (513) 556-9645.

CITADEL BULLDOGS

Conference: Big South.
Mailing Address: McAlister Field House, 171 Moultrie Street, Charleston, SC 29409. **Website:** www.citadelsports.com.
Head Coach: Fred Jordan. **Telephone:** (843) 953-5901.
Baseball SID: Ben Waring. **Telephone:** (843) 953-5120. **Fax:** (843) 953-6727.
Assistant Coaches: *David Beckley, Britt Reames. **Telephone:** (843) 953-7265.
Home Field: Joseph P. Riley, Jr. Park. **Seating Capacity:** 6,000. **Press Box Telephone:** (843) 965-4151.

CLEMSON TIGERS

Conference: Atlantic Coast (Atlantic).
Mailing Address: Jervey Athletic Center; 100 Perimeter Road, Clemson, SC 29633. **Website:** clemsontigers.com.
Head Coach: Jack Leggett. **Telephone:** (864) 656-1947.
Baseball SID: Brian Hennessy. **Telephone:** (864) 656-1921. **Fax:** (864) 656-0299.
Assistant Coaches: *Bradley LeCroy, Dan Pepicelli. **Telephone:** (864) 656-1948.
Home Field: Doug Kingsmore Stadium. **Seating Capacity:** 6,346. **Press Box Telephone:** (864) 656-7731.

COASTAL CAROLINA CHANTICLEERS

Conference: Big South.
Mailing Address: PO Box 261954 Conway, SC 29528. **Website:** www.GoCCUSports.com.

Head Coach: Gary Gilmore. **Telephone:** (843) 349-2816. **Baseball SID:** Mike Cawood. **Telephone:** (843) 349-2822. **Fax:** (843) 349-2819.
Assistant Coaches: *Kevin Schnall, Drew Thomas. **Telephone:** (843) 349-2849.
Home Field: Watson Stadium. **Press Box Telephone:** (843) 234-3474.

COLLEGE OF CHARLESTON COUGARS

Conference: Southern.
Mailing Address: 66 George Street, Charleston, SC 29424. **Website:** www.cofcsports.com.
Head Coach: Monte Lee. **Telephone:** (843) 953-5916. **Baseball SID:** Will Bryan. **Telephone:** (843) 953-3683. **Fax:** (843) 953-6534.
Assistant Coaches: *Matt Heath, Chris Morris. **Telephone:** (943) 953-7013.
Home Field: Patriots Point Field. **Seating Capacity:** 2,000. **Press Box Telephone:** (843) 953-9141.

COLUMBIA LIONS

Conference: Ivy League (Gehrig).
Mailing Address: 3030 Broadway, Mail Code 1930, New York, NY 10027. **Website:** www.gocolumbialions.com.
Head Coach: Brett Boretti. **Telephone:** (212) 854-8448. **Baseball SID:** Pete McHugh. **Telephone:** (212) 854-7064. **Fax:** (212) 854-8168.
Assistant Coaches: *Pete Maki, Jim Walsh. **Telephone:** (212) 854-7772.
Home Field: Robertson Field at Satow Stadium. **Seating Capacity:** 600. **Press Box Telephone:** (917) 678-3621.

CONNECTICUT HUSKIES

Conference: Big East.
Mailing Address: 2095 Hillside Road Unit 1173, Storrs, CT 06269. **Website:** www.UConnHuskies.com.
Head Coach: Jim Penders. **Telephone:** (860) 486-4089. **Baseball SID:** Brendan Flynn. **Telephone:** (860) 486-1496. **Fax:** (860) 486-5085.
Assistant Coaches: *Jeff Hourigan, Josh MacDonald. **Telephone:** (860) 486-5771.
Home Field: J.O. Christian Field. **Seating Capacity:** 2,000. **Press Box Telephone:** (860) 486-2018.

COPPIN STATE EAGLES

Conference: Mid-Eastern Athletic.
Mailing Address: 2500 W North Avenue, Baltimore, MD 21216. **Website:** www.coppinstatesports.com.
Head Coach: *Sherman Reed, Sr. **Telephone:** (410) 951-3723. **Baseball SID:** Roger McAfee. **Telephone:** (410) 951-3729. **Fax:** (410) 951-3717.
Assistant Coaches: Gregory Beckman, Charles Chaffin. **Telephone:** (410) 951-6941.
Home Field: Joe Cannon Stadium. **Seating Capacity:** 1,500. **Press Box Telephone:** (410) 222-6652.

CORNELL BIG RED

Conference: Ivy League (Rolfe).
Mailing Address: Cornell Baseball, Teagle Hall, Campus Rd, Ithaca, NY 14853. **Website:** www.cornellbigred.com.
Head Coach: Bill Walkenbach. **Telephone:** (607) 255-3812. **Baseball SID:** Brandon Thomas. **Telephone:** (607) 255-5627. **Fax:** (607) 255-9791.
Assistant Coaches: Tom Ford, *Scott Marsh. **Telephone:** (607) 255-6604.
Home Field: David F. Hoy Field. **Seating Capacity:** 1,000.

CREIGHTON BLUEJAYS

Conference: Missouri Valley.
Mailing Address: 2500 California Plaza, Omaha, NE 68178. **Website:** www.gocreighton.com.
Head Coach: Ed Servais. **Telephone:** (402) 280-2483. **Baseball SID:** Shannon Pivovar. **Telephone:** (402) 280-5801. **Fax:** (402) 280-2495.
Assistant Coaches: Craig Moore, *Rob Smith. **Telephone:** (402) 280-2628.
Home Field: TD Ameritrade Park Omaha. **Seating Capacity:** 24,000.

DALLAS BAPTIST PATRIOTS

Conference: Independent.
Mailing Address: 3000 Mountain Creek Pkwy, Dallas, TX 75211. **Website:** www.dbu.edu.
Head Coach: Dan Heefner. **Telephone:** (214) 333-5324. **Baseball SID:** Nate Frieling. **Telephone:** (214) 333-5590. **Fax:** (214) 333-5306.
Assistant Coaches: *Jim Blair, Wes Johnson. **Telephone:** (214) 333-6957.
Home Field: Patriot Field. **Seating Capacity:** 1,500. **Press Box Telephone:** (214) 333-5542.

DARTMOUTH BIG GREEN

Conference: Ivy League (Rolfe).
Mailing Address: 6083 Alumni Gym, Hanover, NH 03755. **Website:** www.dartmouthsports.com.
Head Coach: Bob Whalen. **Telephone:** (603) 646-2477. **Baseball SID:** Rick Bender. **Telephone:** (603) 646-1030. **Fax:** (603) 646-3348.
Assistant Coaches: Jonathan Anderson, *Nicholas Enriquez. **Telephone:** (603) 646-2765.
Home Field: Red Rolfe Field at Biondi Park. **Seating Capacity:** 2,000. **Press Box Telephone:** (603) 646-6937.

DAVIDSON WILDCATS

Conference: Southern.
Mailing Address: Box 7158 Davidson College, Davidson, NC 28035. **Website:** www.davidsonwildcats.com.
Head Coach: Dick Cooke. **Telephone:** (704) 894-2368. **Baseball SID:** Mark Brumbaugh. **Telephone:** (704) 894-2931. **Fax:** (704) 894-2636.
Assistant Coaches: *Tod Gross. **Telephone:** (707) 894-2772.
Home Field: Wilson Field. **Seating Capacity:** 700. **Press Box Telephone:** (704) 894-2740.

DAYTON FLYERS

Conference: Atlantic 10.
Mailing Address: Baseball Office 300 College Park, Dayton, OH 45469. **Website:** www.daytonflyers.com.
Head Coach: Tony Vittorio. **Telephone:** (937) 229-4456. **Baseball SID:** Brian Karst. **Telephone:** (937) 229-4431. **Fax:** (937) 229-4461.
Assistant Coaches: Todd Linklater. **Telephone:** (937) 229-4481.
Home Field: Time Warner Cable Stadium. **Seating Capacity:** 500. **Press Box Telephone:** (937) 229-2255.

DELAWARE FIGHTIN' BLUE HENS

Conference: Colonial Athletic.
Mailing Address: 116 Delaware Field House, Newark, DE 19716. **Website:** www.bluehens.com.
Head Coach: Jim Sherman. **Telephone:** (302) 831-8596. **Baseball SID:** TBA. **Telephone:** (302) 831-6439. **Fax:** (302) 831-8653.
Assistant Coaches: *Dan Hammer, Mike Ranson.

Telephone: (302) 831-2723, (302) 831-3097.
Home Field: Bob Hannah Stadium. Seating Capacity: 1,300.

DELAWARE STATE HORNETS

Conference: Mid-Eastern Athletic.
Mailing Address: 1200 N Dupont Hwy, Dover, DE 19901. Website: www.dsuhornets.com.
Head Coach: JP Blandin. Telephone: (302) 857-6035. Baseball SID: Dennis Jones. Telephone: (302) 857-6068. Fax: (302) 857-6069.
Assistant Coaches: *Russ Steinhorn. Telephone: (302) 857-7809.
Home Field: Soldier Field. Seating Capacity: 500.

DUKE BLUE DEVILS

Conference: Atlantic Coast (Coastal).
Mailing Address: 118 Cameron Indoor Stadium, Durham, NC 27708. Website: www.goduke.com.
Head Coach: Sean McNally. Telephone: (919) 668-0255. Baseball SID: Lee Aldridge. Telephone: (919) 668-4543. Fax: (919) 684-2489.
Assistant Coaches: Sean Snedeker, *Edwin Thompson. Telephone: (919) 668-2535.
Home Field: Jack Coombs Field. Seating Capacity: 2,000. Press Box Telephone: (919) 812-4436.

EAST CAROLINA PIRATES

Conference: Conference USA.
Mailing Address: 102 Clark-LeClair Stadium, Greenville, NC 27858. Website: www.ecupirates.com.
Head Coach: Billy Godwin. Telephone: (252) 737-1985. Baseball SID: Malcolm Gray. Telephone: (252) 737-4523. Fax: (252) 737-4528.
Assistant Coaches: Dan Roszel, *Nick Schnabel. Telephone: (252) 737-1985.
Home Field: Clark-LeClair Stadium. Seating Capacity: 5,000. Press Box Telephone: (252) 328-0068.

EAST TENNESSEE STATE BUCCANEERS

Conference: Atlantic Sun.
Mailing Address: PO Box 70707, Johnson City, TN 37614. Website: www.etsubucs.com.
Head Coach: Tony Skole. Telephone: (423) 439-4496. Baseball SID: Ryan Dunn. Telephone: (423) 439-8212. Fax: (423) 439-6138.
Assistant Coaches: *Xan Barksdale, Kyle Bunn. Telephone: (423) 439-4485.
Home Field: Thomas Stadium. Seating Capacity: 500.

EASTERN ILLINOIS PANTHERS

Conference: Ohio Valley.
Mailing Address: 600 Lincoln Ave, Charleston, IL 61920. Website: www.EIUpanthers.com.
Head Coach: Jim Schmitz. Telephone: (217) 581-2522. Baseball SID: Greg Lautzenheiser. Telephone: (217) 581-7020. Fax: (217)-581-6434.
Assistant Coaches: Jason Belk, *Skylar Meade. Telephone: (217) 581-8510.
Home Field: Coaches Stadium. Seating Capacity: 600.

EASTERN KENTUCKY COLONELS

Conference: Ohio Valley.
Mailing Address: 521 Lancaster Ave, Richmond, KY 40475. Website: www.ekusports.com.
Head Coach: Jason Stein. Telephone: (859) 622-2128. Baseball SID: Steve Fohl. Telephone: (859) 622-1253. Fax: (859) 622-5108.
Assistant Coaches: *Jerry Edwards, John Peterson. Telephone: (859) 622-8295.

Home Field: Turkey Hughes Field. Seating Capacity: 1,500. Press Box Telephone: (859) 200-1958.

EASTERN MICHIGAN EAGLES

Conference: Mid-American (West).
Mailing Address: 799 Hewitt Rd, Ypsilanti, MI 48197. Website: www.emueagles.com.
Head Coach: Jay Alexander. Telephone: (734) 487-0315. Baseball SID: Chris Puzzuoli. Telephone: (734) 487-0317. Fax: (734) 485-3840.
Assistant Coaches: *Drew Maki, Aaron Hepner. Telephone: (734) 487-1985, (734) 487-0315.
Home Field: Oestrike Stadium. Seating Capacity: 1,400. Press Box Telephone: (734) 481-9328.

ELON PHOENIX

Conference: Southern.
Mailing Address: 2500 Campus Box, 100 Campus Drive, Elon, NC 27244. Website: www.elonphoenix.com.
Head Coach: Mike Kennedy. Telephone: (336) 278-6741. Baseball SID: Chris Rash. Telephone: (336) 278-6712. Fax: (336) 278-6768.
Assistant Coaches: Robbie Huffstetler, *Greg Starbuck. Telephone: (336) 278-6794.
Home Field: Latham Park. Seating Capacity: 2,000. Press Box Telephone: (336) 278-6788.

EVANSVILLE PURPLE ACES

Conference: Missouri Valley.
Mailing Address: 1800 Lincoln Ave, Evansville, IN 47722. Website: www.gopurpleaces.com.
Head Coach: Wes Carroll. Telephone: (812) 488-2059. Baseball SID: Lizzie Barlow. Telephone: (812) 488-1152. Fax: (812) 488-2199.
Assistant Coaches: Mike Gilner, *Marc Wagner. Telephone: (812) 488-2764.
Home Field: Braun Stadium. Seating Capacity: 1,200. Press Box Telephone: (812) 479-2587.

FAIRFIELD STAGS

Conference: Metro Atlantic.
Mailing Address: 1073 North Benson Rd, Fairfield, CT 06824. Website: www.fairfieldstags.com.
Head Coach: Bill Currier. Telephone: (203) 254-4000 EXT 2605. Baseball SID: Kelly McCarthy. Telephone: (203) 254-4000. Fax: (203) 254-4117.
Assistant Coaches: *Trevor Brown. Telephone: (203) 254-4000 EXT 3178.
Home Field: Alumni Diamond.

FAIRLEIGH DICKINSON KNIGHTS

Conference: Northeast.
Mailing Address: 1000 River Road, Teaneck, NJ 07666. Website: www.fduknights.com.
Head Coach: Gary Puccio. Telephone: (201) 692-2245. Baseball SID: Chris Strauch. Telephone: (201) 692-2499. Fax: (201) 692-9361.
Assistant Coaches: Enver Lopez, *Justin McKay. Telephone: (201) 692-2245.
Home Field: Naimoli Family Baseball Complex. Seating Capacity: 500.

FLORIDA GATORS

Conference: Southeastern.
Mailing Address: University Athletic Association PO Box 14485, Gainesville, FL 32604. Website: www.GatorZone.com.
Head Coach: Kevin O'Sullivan. Telephone: (352) 375-4457. Baseball SID: John Hines. Telephone: . Fax: (352) 375-4809.

Assistant Coaches: *Craig Bell, Brad Weitzel. Telephone: (352) 375-4457.
Home Field: Alfred A. McKethan Stadium. Seating Capacity: 5,500.

FLORIDA A&M RATTLERS

Conference: Mid-Eastern Athletic.
Mailing Address: 1835 Wahnish Way, Tallahassee, FL 32307. Website: www.famu.edu/athletics.
Head Coach: Willie Brown. Telephone: (850) 599-3202.
Baseball SID: Ronnie Johnson. Telephone: (850) 599-3200. Fax: (850) 599-3206.
Home Field: Moore-Kittles Field. Seating Capacity: 500.

FLORIDA ATLANTIC OWLS

Conference: Sun Belt.
Mailing Address: 777 Glades Rd, Boca Raton, FL 33431. Website: www.fausports.com.
Head Coach: John Mc Cormack. Telephone: (561) 297-1055. Baseball SID: Katrina Mc Cormack. Telephone: (561) 297-3163. Fax: (561) 291-3956.
Assistant Coaches: *Jason Jackson, Ben Sanderson. Telephone:(561) 297-1055.
Home Field: FAU Baseball Stadium. Seating Capacity: 2,500. Press Box Telephone: (561) 297-3455.

FLORIDA GULF COAST EAGLES

Conference: Atlantic Sun.
Mailing Address: 10501 FGCU Boulevard South, Fort Myers, Fla. 33965. Website: www.fgcuathletics.com.
Head Coach: Dave Tollett. Telephone: (239) 590-7051.
Baseball SID: Patrick Pierson. Telephone: (239) 590-7061. Fax: (239) 590-7014.
Assistant Coaches: Forrest Martin, *Rusty McKee. Telephone: (239) 590-7059.
Home Field: Swanson Stadium. Seating Capacity: 1,500. Press Box Telephone: (239) 357-2390.

FLORIDA INTERNATIONAL PANTHERS

Conference: Sun Belt.
Mailing Address: 11200 SW 8th St, Miami, FL 33199. Website: www.fiusports.com.
Head Coach: Turtle Thomas. Telephone: (305) 348-3166. Baseball SID: Mat Ratner. Telephone: (305) 348-1496. Fax: (305) 348-2963.
Assistant Coaches: *Frank Damas, Drew French. Telephone: (305) 348-2145.
Home Field: FIU Baseball Stadium. Seating Capacity: 2,000. Press Box Telephone: (561) 441-8057.

FLORIDA STATE SEMINOLES

Conference: Atlantic Coast (Atlantic).
Mailing Address: 403 Stadium Drive West, Room D0107, Tallahassee, FL 32316. Website: www.seminoles.com.
Head Coach: Mike Martin. Telephone: (850) 644-1073.
Baseball SID: Jason Leturmy. Telephone: (850) 644-3920. Fax: (850) 644-3820.
Assistant Coaches: Mike Bell, *Mike Martin Jr. Telephone: (850) 644-1072.
Home Field: Dick Howser Stadium. Seating Capacity: 6,700. Press Box Telephone: (850) 644-1553.

FORDHAM RAMS

Conference: Atlantic 10.
Mailing Address: 441 East Fordham Road, Bronx, NY 10458. Website: www.fordhamsports.com.
Head Coach: Kevin Leighton. Telephone: (718) 817-4292. Baseball SID: Scott Kwiatkowski. Telephone: (718)

817-4219. Fax: (718) 817-4244.
Assistant Coaches: *Jimmy Jackson, Jerry DeFabbia. Telephone: (718) 817-4292.
Home Field: Houlihan Park. Seating Capacity: 1,000. Press Box Telephone: (718) 817-0773.

FRESNO STATE BULLDOGS

Conference: Western Athletic.
Mailing Address: 1620E Bulldog Lane, OF 87, Fresno, CA 93740. Website: www.gobulldogs.com.
Head Coach: Mike Batesole. Telephone: (559) 278-2178. Baseball SID: Jennifer Jones. Telephone: (559) 278-2509. Fax: (559) 278-4689.
Assistant Coaches: Steve Rousey, *Pat Waer. Telephone: (559) 278-6648.
Home Field: Beiden Field. Seating Capacity: 3,575. Press Box Telephone: (559) 278-7678.

FURMAN PALADINS

Conference: Southern.
Mailing Address: 3300 Poinsett Ave, Greenville, SC 29613. Website: www.furmanpaladins.com.
Head Coach: Ron Smith. Telephone: (864) 294-2146.
Baseball SID: Hunter Reid. Telephone: (864) 294-2061. Fax: (864) 294-3061.
Assistant Coaches: Chris Edwards, *Jeff Whitfield. Telephone: (864) 294-2243.
Home Field: Latham Stadium/Flour Field. Seating Capacity: 1,500/7,000.

GARDNER-WEBB RUNNIN' BULLDOGS

Conference: Atlantic Sun.
Mailing Address: PO Box 877, Boiling Springs, NC 28017. Website: www.gwusports.com.
Head Coach: Rusty Stroupe. Telephone: (704) 406-4421. Baseball SID: Marc Rabb. Telephone: (704) 406-4355. Fax: (704) 406-4739.
Assistant Coaches: *Kent Cox, Ray Greene. Telephone: (704) 406-3557.
Home Field: Moss Stadium/Masters Field. Seating Capacity: 800.

GEORGE MASON PATRIOTS

Conference: Colonial Athletic.
Mailing Address: 4400 University Dr MS 3A5, Fairfax, VA 22030. Website: www.gomason.com.
Head Coach: Bill Brown. Telephone: (703) 993-3282.
Baseball SID: Rachel Buck. Telephone: (703) 993-3264. Fax: (703) 993-3259.
Assistant Coaches: *Stephen Hay, Lucas Jones. Telephone: (703) 993-3281.
Home Field: Hap Spuler. Seating Capacity: 2,000.

GEORGE WASHINGTON COLONIALS

Conference: Atlantic 10.
Mailing Address: 600 22nd Street NW, Washington DC 20052. Website: www.gwsports.cstv.com.
Head Coach: Steve Mrowka. Telephone: (202) 994-7399. Baseball SID: Dan DiVeglio. Telephone: (202) 994-0339. Fax: (202) 994-2713.
Assistant Coaches: *Tim Brown, Jon Greenwich. Telephone: (202) 994-5933.
Home Field: Barcroft Park. Seating Capacity: 1,000. Press Box Telephone: (703) 671-2151.

GEORGETOWN HOYAS

Conference: Big East.
Mailing Address: Baseball Office, McDonough Arena, Washington DC 20057. Website: www.guhoyas.com.
Head Coach: Pete Wilk. Telephone: (202) 687-2462.

Baseball SID: Mex Carey. **Telephone:** (202) 687-2475. **Fax:** (202) 687-2491.
Assistant Coaches: Grant Achilles, *Curtis Brown. **Telephone:** (202) 687-2384.
Home Field: Shirley Povich Field. **Seating Capacity:** 800.

GEORGIA BULLDOGS

Conference: Southeastern (East).
Mailing Address: PO Box 1472, Athens, GA 30603-1472. **Website:** www.georgiadogs.com.
Head Coach: David Perno. **Telephone:** (706) 542-7971. **Baseball SID:** Christopher Lakos. **Telephone:** (706) 542-7994. **Fax:** (706) 542-9339.
Assistant Coaches: *Jason Eller, Allen Osborne. **Telephone:** (706) 542-7971.
Home Field: Foley Field. **Seating Capacity:** 3,291. **Press Box Telephone:** (706) 542-6161.

GEORGIA SOUTHERN EAGLES

Conference: Southern.
Mailing Address: Hanner Fieldhouse, 590 Herty Drive, Room 1125, Statesboro, GA 30460. **Website:** www.georgiasoutherneagles.com.
Head Coach: Rodney Hennon. **Telephone:** (912) 478-7360. **Baseball SID:** Barrett Gilham. **Telephone:** (912) 478-5448. **Fax:** (912) 478-1063.
Assistant Coaches: B.J. Green, *Mike Tidick. **Telephone:** (912) 478-1331.
Home Field: J.I. Clements Stadium. **Seating Capacity:** 3,000. **Press Box Telephone:** (912) 478-5764.

GEORGIA STATE PANTHERS

Conference: Colonial Athletic.
Mailing Address: Intercollegiate Athletics, PO Box 3975, Atlanta, GA 30302-3975. **Website:** www.georgiastatesports.com.
Head Coach: Greg Frady. **Telephone:** (404) 413-4078. **Baseball SID:** Ned Colegrove. **Telephone:** (404) 413-4166. **Fax:** (404) 413-4035.
Assistant Coaches: *Jason Arnold, Willie Stewart. **Telephone:** (404) 413-4078.
Home Field: Field at Panthersville. **Seating Capacity:** 1,092. **Press Box Telephone:** (518) 817-3564.

GEORGIA TECH YELLOW JACKETS

Conference: Atlantic Coast (Coastal).
Mailing Address: 150 Bobby Dodd Way NW, Atlanta, GA 30332. **Website:** www.ramblinwreck.com.
Head Coach: Danny Hall. **Telephone:** (404) 894-5471. **Baseball SID:** Mike DeGeorge. **Telephone:** (404) 894-5445. **Fax:** (404) 894-1248.
Assistant Coaches: Tom Kinkelaar, *Bryan Prince. **Telephone:** (404) 894-5081.
Home Field: Russ Chandler Stadium. **Seating Capacity:** 4,157. **Press Box Telephone:** (404) 894-3167.

GONZAGA BULLDOGS

Conference: West Coast.
Mailing Address: 502 E Boone Ave, Spokane, WA 99258. **Website:** www.gozags.com.
Head Coach: Mark Machtolf. **Telephone:** (509) 313-4209. **Baseball SID:** Ricky Hoskin. **Telephone:** (509) 313-4227. **Fax:** (509) 313-5730.
Assistant Coaches: Steve Bennett, *Danny Evans. **Telephone:** (509) 313-3597.
Home Field: Patterson Baseball Complex & Washington Trust Field. **Seating Capacity:** 3,000. **Press Box Telephone:** (509) 313-4224.

GRAMBLING STATE TIGERS

Conference: Southwestern Athletic.
Mailing Address: 403 Main St, PO Box 4252 Grambling, LA 71245. **Website:** www.gsutigers.com.
Head Coach: James Cooper. **Telephone:** (318) 274-6566. **Baseball SID:** Unavailable.
Assistant Coaches: Davin Pierre. **Telephone:** (318) 274-2416.
Home Field: Jones Field at Ellis Park. **Seating Capacity:** 3,000.

HARTFORD HAWKS

Conference: America East.
Mailing Address: 200 Bloomfield Avenue, West Hartford, CT 06117. **Website:** www.hartfordhawks.com.
Head Coach: Justin Blood. **Telephone:** (860) 768-5760. **Baseball SID:** Dan Ruede. **Telephone:** (860) 768-4501.
Assistant Coaches: John Delaney, *Steve Malinowski. **Telephone:** (860) 768-4972.
Home Field: Fiondella Field. **Seating Capacity:** 2,000.

HARVARD THE CRIMSON

Conference: Ivy League (Rolfe).
Mailing Address: 65 North Harvard Street, Boston, MA 02163. **Website:** www.gocrimson.com.
Head Coach: Joe Walsh. **Telephone:** (617) 495-2629. **Baseball SID:** Kurt Svoboda. **Telephone:** (617) 495-2206. **Fax:** (617) 495-2130.
Assistant Coaches: John Birtwell, *Tom LoRicco. **Telephone:** (617) 496-1435.
Home Field: O'Donnell Field. **Seating Capacity:** 1,600.

HAWAII RAINBOWS

Conference: Western Athletic.
Mailing Address: 1337 Lower Campus Rd, Honolulu, HI 96822. **Website:** www.hawaiiathletics.com.
Head Coach: Mike Trapasso. **Telephone:** (808) 956-6247. **Baseball SID:** John Barry. **Telephone:** (808) 956-7506. **Fax:** (808) 956-4470.
Assistant Coaches: *Chad Konishi, Rusty McNamara. **Telephone:** (808) 956-6247.
Home Field: Les Murakami Stadium. **Seating Capacity:** 4,312.

HIGH POINT PANTHERS

Conference: Big South.
Mailing Address: 833 Montlieu Ave, High Point, NC 27262. **Website:** www.highpointpanthers.com.
Head Coach: Craig Cozart. **Telephone:** (336) 841-9190. **Baseball SID:** Erika Carruba. **Telephone:** (336) 841-4640. **Fax:** (336) 841-9182.
Assistant Coaches: *Bryan Peters, Rich Wallace. **Telephone:** (336) 841-4628.
Home Field: Williard Stadium. **Seating Capacity:** 800. **Press Box Telephone:** (336) 841-9192.

HOFSTRA PRIDE

Conference: Colonial Athletic.
Mailing Address: 240 Hofstra University, Hempstead, NY 11549. **Website:** www.gohofstra.com.
Head Coach: Patrick Anderson. **Telephone:** (516) 463-5065. **Baseball SID:** Len Skoros. **Telephone:** (516) 463-4602. **Fax:** (516) 463-5033.
Assistant Coaches: Kelly Haynes, *John Russo. **Telephone:** (516) 463-3759.
Home Field: University Field. **Seating Capacity:** 600. **Press Box Telephone:** (516) 463-1896.

HOLY CROSS CRUSADERS

Conference: Patriot.
Mailing Address: 1 College Street, Worcester, MA 01610. **Website:** www.goholycross.com.
Head Coach: Greg DiCenzo. **Telephone:** (508) 793-2753. **Baseball SID:** Meredith Cook. **Telephone:** (508) 793-2780. **Fax:** (508) 793-2309.
Assistant Coaches: *Jeff Kane, Ron Rakowski. **Telephone:** (508) 793-2753.
Home Field: Fitton Field. **Seating Capacity:** 3,000.

HOUSTON COUGARS

Conference: Conference USA.
Mailing Address: 3100 Cullen Blvd, Houston, TX 77204. **Website:** www.UHCougars.com.
Head Coach: Todd Whitting. **Telephone:** (713) 743-9416. **Baseball SID:** Jamie Zarda. **Telephone:** (713) 743-9406. **Fax:** (713) 743-9411.
Assistant Coaches: *Trip Couch, Jack Cressend. **Telephone:** (713) 743-9415.
Home Field: Cougar Field. **Seating Capacity:** 3,500. **Press Box Telephone:** (713) 743-0840.

HOUSTON BAPTIST HUSKIES

Conference: Great West.
Mailing Address: 7502 Fondren, Houston, TX 77074. **Website:** www.hbuhuskies.com.
Head Coach: Jared Moon. **Telephone:** (281) 649-3332. **Baseball SID:** Russ Reneau. **Telephone:** (281) 649-3098. **Fax:** (281) 649-3496.
Assistant Coaches: *Xavier Hernandez, Russell Stockton. **Telephone:** (281) 649-3264.
Home Field: Husky Field. **Seating Capacity:** 500. **Press Box Telephone:** (281) 923-0813.

ILLINOIS FIGHTING ILLINI

Conference: Big Ten.
Mailing Address: 1700 S Fourth St, Champaign, IL 61820. **Website:** www.fightingillini.com.
Head Coach: Dan Hartleb. **Telephone:** (217) 244-8144. **Baseball SID:** Ben Taylor. **Telephone:** (217) 244-5045. **Fax:** (217) 333-5540.
Assistant Coaches: Drew Dickinson, *Eric Snider. **Telephone:** (217) 244-5539.
Home Field: Illinois Field. **Seating Capacity:** 1,500. **Press Box Telephone:** (217) 333-1227.

ILLINOIS STATE REDBIRDS

Conference: Missouri Valley.
Mailing Address: 211 Horton Field House, Campus Box 7130, Normal, IL, 61790-7130. **Website:** www.GoRedbirds.com.
Head Coach: Mark Kingston. **Telephone:** (309) 438-5709. **Baseball SID:** John Twork. **Telephone:** (309) 438-5746. **Fax:** (309) 438-5634.
Assistant Coaches: *Bo Durkac, Bill Mohl. **Telephone:** (309) 438-5151.
Home Field: Duffy Bass Field. **Seating Capacity:** 1,500.

ILLINOIS-CHICAGO FLAMES

Conference: Horizon.
Mailing Address: 839 W Roosevelt Road Chicago, IL 60608. **Website:** www.uicflames.cstv.com.
Head Coach: Mike Dee. **Telephone:** (312) 996-8645. **Baseball SID:** Mike Laninga. **Telephone:** (312) 996-5881. **Fax:** (312) 996-8349.
Assistant Coaches: *John Flood, Sean McDermott. **Telephone:** (312) 355-1757.

Home Field: Les Miller Field. **Seating Capacity:** 1,500. **Press Box Telephone:** (312) 355-1190.

INDIANA HOOSIERS

Conference: Big Ten.
Mailing Address: 1001 E 17th St, Bloomington, IN 47408. **Website:** www.iuhoosiers.com.
Head Coach: Tracy Smith. **Telephone:** (812) 855-1680. **Baseball SID:** Kyle Kuhlman. **Telephone:** (812) 855-4770. **Fax:** (812) 855-9401.
Assistant Coaches: Ben Greenspan, *Ty Neal. **Telephone:** (812) 855-9790.
Home Field: Sembower Field. **Seating Capacity:** 1,500. **Press Box Telephone:** (419) 308-8292.

INDIANA STATE SYCAMORES

Conference: Missouri Valley.
Mailing Address: 401 N 4th St, ISU Arena, Terre Haute, IN 47809. **Website:** www.gosycamores.com.
Head Coach: Rick Heller. **Telephone:** (812) 237-4051. **Baseball SID:** Danny Pfrank. **Telephone:** (812) 237-4159. **Fax:** (812) 237-4157.
Assistant Coaches: *Tyler Herbst, Brian Smiley. **Telephone:** (812) 237-4630.
Home Field: Bob Warn Field at Sycamore Stadium. **Seating Capacity:** 2,000. **Press Box Telephone:** (812) 237-4498.

IONA GAELS

Conference: Metro Atlantic.
Mailing Address: 715 North Ave, New Rochelle, NY 10801. **Website:** www.icgaels.com.
Head Coach: Pat Carey. **Telephone:** (914) 633-2319. **Baseball SID:** Brian Beyrer. **Telephone:** (914) 633-2334. **Fax:** (914) 633-2072.
Assistant Coaches: Rob DiToma, James LaSala. **Telephone:** (914) 633-2319.
Home Field: Salesian Field. **Seating Capacity:** 450. **Press Box Telephone:** (914) 497-3136.

IOWA HAWKEYES

Conference: Big Ten.
Mailing Address: 1 Elliott Drive, Iowa City, IA. **Website:** www.hawkeyesports.com.
Head Coach: Jack Dahm. **Telephone:** (319) 335-9390. **Baseball SID:** Patrick Sojka. **Telephone:** (319) 335-9411.
Assistant Coaches: *Ryan Brownlee, Chris Maliszewski. **Telephone:** (319) 335-9389.
Home Field: Duane Banks Field. **Seating Capacity:** 3,000. **Press Box Telephone:** (319) 335-9520.

IPFW MASTODONS

Conference: Summit.
Mailing Address: 2101 E Coliseum Blvd, Fort Wayne, IN 46805. **Website:** www.gomastodons.com.
Head Coach: Bobby Pierce. **Telephone:** (260) 481-5480. **Baseball SID:** Bill Salyer. **Telephone:** (260) 481-0729.
Assistant Coaches: *Grant Birely, Alex Rinearson. **Telephone:** (260) 481-5455.
Home Field: Mastodon Field. **Seating Capacity:** 500. **Press Box Telephone:** (260) 402-6599.

JACKSON STATE TIGERS

Conference: Southwestern Athletic.
Mailing Address: JSU Box 18060, Jackson, MS 39217-0660. **Website:** www.jsutigers.com.
Head Coach: Omar Johnson. **Telephone:** (601) 979-3930. **Baseball SID:** Wesley Peterson. **Telephone:** (601) 979-5899.
Assistant Coach: Ryan Goodwin, Ralph Johnson.

Telephone: (601) 979-3930.
Home Field: Robert "Bob" Braddy Sr Field. **Seating Capacity:** 800.

JACKSONVILLE DOLPHINS

Conference: Atlantic Sun.
Mailing Address: 2800 University Blvd N, Jacksonville, FL 32211. **Website:** www.judolphins.com.
Head Coach: Terry Alexander. **Telephone:** (904) 256-7412. **Baseball SID:** Brian DeLettre. **Telephone:** (904) 256-7478. **Fax:** (904) 256-7424.
Assistant Coaches: *Tim Montez, Tommy Murphy. **Telephone:** (904) 256-7414.
Home Field: John Sessions Stadium. **Seating Capacity:** 3,000. **Press Box Telephone:** (904) 256-7588.

JACKSONVILLE STATE GAMECOCKS

Conference: Ohio Valley.
Mailing Address: 700 Pelham Road North, Jacksonville, AL 36265. **Website:** www.jsugamecocksports.com.
Head Coach: Jim Case. **Telephone:** (256) 782-5367. **Baseball SID:** Greg Seitz. **Telephone:** (256) 782-5279. **Fax:** (256) 782-5958.
Assistant Coaches: *Steve Gillispie, Mike Murphree. **Telephone:** (256) 782-8141.
Home Field: Rudy Abbott Field. **Seating Capacity:** 3,500. **Press Box Telephone:** (256) 782-5533.

JAMES MADISON DUKES

Conference: Colonial Athletic.
Mailing Address: 395 South High Street, Harrisonburg, VA 22812. **Website:** www.jmusports.com.
Head Coach: Spanky McFarland. **Telephone:** (540) 568-5510. **Baseball SID:** Kevin Warner. **Telephone:** (540) 568-4263. **Fax:** (540) 568-3703.
Assistant Coaches: Brandon Cohen, *Ted White. **Telephone:** (540) 568-5510.
Home Field: Eagle Field. **Seating Capacity:** 1,200. **Press Box Telephone:** (540) 568-6545.

KANSAS JAYHAWKS

Conference: Big 12.
Mailing Address: 1651 Naismith Drive, Lawrence, KS 66045. **Website:** www.kuathletics.com.
Head Coach: Ritch Price. **Telephone:** (785) 864-7907. **Baseball SID:** Michael Cummings. **Telephone:** (785) 864-3575. **Fax:** (785) 864-7944.
Assistant Coaches: Ryan Graves, *Ritchie Price. **Telephone:** (785) 864-7908.
Home Field: Hoglund Ballpark. **Seating Capacity:** 2,500. **Press Box Telephone:** (785) 864-4037.

KANSAS STATE WILDCATS

Conference: Big 12.
Mailing Address: 1800 College Ave, Manhattan, KS 66502. **Website:** www.kstatesports.com.
Head Coach: Brad Hill. **Telephone:** (785) 532-3926. **Baseball SID:** Ryan Lackey. **Telephone:** (785) 532-7708. **Fax:** (785) 532-6093.
Assistant Coaches: Josh Reynolds, *John Szefc. **Telephone:** (785) 532-3926.
Home Field: Tointon Family Stadium. **Seating Capacity:** 2,331. **Press Box Telephone:** (785) 532-5801.

KENNESAW STATE OWLS

Conference: Atlantic Sun.
Mailing Address: 1000 Chastain Road, Building 2, Kennesaw, GA 30144. **Website:** ksuowls.com.
Head Coach: Mike Sansing. **Telephone:** (770) 423-6264. **Baseball SID:** Brian Harper. **Telephone:** (770) 794-

7789. **Fax:** (770) 423-6665.
Assistant Coaches: *Derrick Tucker, Kevin Erminio. **Telephone:** (678) 797-2098, (678) 797-2099.
Home Field: Stillwell Stadium. **Seating Capacity:** 1,200.

KENT STATE GOLDEN FLASHES

Conference: Mid-American (East).
Mailing Address: 234 MACC, Kent, OH 44242. **Website:** www.kentstatesports.com.
Head Coach: Scott Stricklin. **Telephone:** (330) 672-8432. **Baseball SID:** Mike Ashcraft. **Telephone:** (330) 672-2110. **Fax:** (330) 672-2112.
Assistant Coaches: Mike Birkbeck, *Scott Daeley. **Telephone:** (330) 672-8433.
Home Field: Schoonover Stadium. **Seating Capacity:** 1,100. **Press Box Telephone:** (330) 672-2112.

KENTUCKY WILDCATS

Conference: Southeastern (East).
Mailing Address: Commonwealth Stadium, Lexington, KY 40506. **Website:** www.ukathletics.com.
Head Coach: Gary Henderson. **Telephone:** (859) 257-8052. **Baseball SID:** Brent Ingram. **Telephone:** (859) 257-8504. **Fax:** (859) 323-4310.
Assistant Coaches: *Brad Bohannon, Brian Green. **Telephone:** (859) 257-8502.
Home Field: Cliff Hagan Stadium. **Seating Capacity:** 3,000. **Press Box Telephone:** (859) 257-9011.

LA SALLE EXPLORERS

Conference: Atlantic 10.
Mailing Address: 1900 Olney Avenue, Philadelphia, PA 19141. **Website:** www.goexplorers.com.
Head Coach: Mike Lake. **Telephone:** (215) 951-1995. **Baseball SID:** Kevin Bonner. **Telephone:** (215) 951-1513. **Fax:** (215) 951-1694.
Assistant Coaches: John Duffy, Eric Smith. **Telephone:** (215) 951-1995
Home Field: Hank DeVincent Field. **Seating Capacity:** 1,000.

LAFAYETTE LEOPARDS

Conference: Patriot.
Mailing Address: Kirby Sports Center, Pierce & Hamilton Streets, Easton, PA 18042. **Website:** www.goleopards.com.
Head Coach: Joe Kinney. **Telephone:** (610) 330-5476. **Baseball SID:** Drew Kingsley. **Telephone:** (610) 330-5518. **Fax:** (610) 330-5519.
Assistant Coaches: *Ian Law, Greg Durrah. **Telephone:** (610) 330-5945.
Home Field: Kamine Stadium. **Seating Capacity:** 1,000.

LAMAR CARDINALS

Conference: Southland.
Mailing Address: PO Box 10066, Beaumont, TX 77710. **Website:** lamarcardinals.com.
Head Coach: Jim Gilligan. **Telephone:** (409) 880-8315. **Baseball SID:** Rush Wood. **Telephone:** (409) 880-7845. **Fax:** (409) 880-2338.
Assistant Coaches: Scott Hatten, *Jim Ricklefson. **Telephone:** (409) 880-8315
Home Field: Vincent-Beck Stadium. **Seating Capacity:** 3,500. **Press Box Telephone:** (409) 880-8327.

LEHIGH MOUNTAIN HAWKS

Conference: Patriot.
Mailing Address: 641 Taylor St, Bethlehem, PA 18015.

Website: www.lehighsports.com.
Head Coach: *Sean Leary. **Telephone:** (610) 758-4315.
Baseball SID: Ben Masur. **Telephone:** (610) 758-5101.
Fax: (610) 758-6629.
Assistant Coaches: Ben Krentzman. **Telephone:** (610) 758-6629.
Home Field: Lehigh Field. **Seating Capacity:** 250.

LIBERTY FLAMES

Conference: Big South.
Mailing Address: 1971 University Blvd, Lynchburg, VA 24502. **Website:** www.libertyflames.com.
Head Coach: Jim Toman. **Telephone:** (434) 582-2305.
Baseball SID: Ryan Bomberger. **Telephone:** (434) 582-2605. **Fax:** (434) 582-2205.
Assistant Coaches: *Jason Murray, Garrett Quinn. **Telephone:** (434) 582-2119.
Home Field: Worthington Stadium. **Seating Capacity:** 1,000. **Press Box Telephone:** (434) 582-2914.

LIPSCOMB BISONS

Conference: Atlantic Sun.
Mailing Address: One University Park Drive, Nashville, TN 37204. **Website:** www.lipscombsports.com.
Head Coach: Jeff Forehand. **Telephone:** (615) 966-5716. **Baseball SID:** Jamie Gilliam. **Telephone:** (615) 966-5166. **Fax:** (615) 966-1806.
Assistant Coaches: *Chris Collins, Tyler Shrout. **Telephone:** (615) 966-5879.
Home Field: Ken Dugan Field. **Seating Capacity:** 1,500. **Press Box Telephone:** (615) 479-6133.

LONG BEACH STATE DIRTBAGS

Conference: Big West.
Mailing Address: 1250 Bellflower Blvd, Long Beach, CA 90840. **Website:** www.longbeachstate.com.
Head Coach: Troy Buckley. **Telephone:** (562) 985-8125.
Baseball SID: Roger Kirk. **Telephone:** (562) 985-7565. **Fax:** (562) 985-1549.
Assistant Coaches: Shawn Gilbert, *Jesse Zepeda. **Telephone:** (562) 985-7548.
Home Field: Blair Field. **Seating Capacity:** 3,000. **Press Box Telephone:** (562) 433-8605.

LONG ISLAND-BROOKLYN BLACKBIRDS

Conference: Northeast.
Mailing Address: 1 University Plaza, Brooklyn, NY 11201. **Website:** www.liuathletics.com.
Head Coach: Donald Maines. **Telephone:** (718) 488-1538. **Baseball SID:** Shawn Sweeney. **Telephone:** (718) 488-1030. **Fax:** (718) 488-1669.
Assistant Coaches: *Craig Noto, Jesse Marsh. **Telephone:** (718)488-1000 Ext 3034.
Home Field: "The Bird Cage" at LIU Field. **Seating Capacity:** 500.

LONGWOOD LANCERS

Conference: Independent.
Mailing Address: 201 High Street, Farmville, VA 23909. **Website:** www.longwoodlancers.com.
Head Coach: *Buddy Bolding. **Telephone:** (434) 395-2352. **Baseball SID:** Greg Prouty. **Telephone:** (434) 395-2097. **Fax:** (434) 395-2568.
Assistant Coaches: Brett Mooney. **Telephone:** (434) 395-2351.
Home Field: Charles Buddy Bolding Stadium. **Seating Capacity:** 500. **Press Box Telephone:** (434) 395-2710.

LOUISIANA STATE FIGHTING TIGERS

Conference: Southeastern (West).

Mailing Address: PO Box 25095 Baton Rouge, LA 70894-5095. **Website:** www.LSUsports.net.
Head Coach: Paul Mainieri. **Telephone:** (225) 578-7393. **Baseball SID:** Bill Franques. **Telephone:** (225) 578-8226. **Fax:** (225) 578-1861.
Assistant Coaches: Alan Dunn, *Brian Rountree. **Telephone:** (225) 578-2524.
Home Field: Alex Box Stadium. **Seating Capacity:** 10,150. **Press Box Telephone:** (225) 578-4149.

LOUISIANA TECH BULLDOGS

Conference: Western Athletic.
Mailing Address: Thomas Assembly Center, Room 161, Ruston, LA, 71270. **Website:** www.latechsports.com.
Head Coach: Wade Simoneaux. **Telephone:** (318) 257-5318. **Baseball SID:** Kevin Queliz. **Telephone:** (318) 257-5314. **Fax:** (318) 257-3757.
Assistant Coaches: Fran Andermann, *Brian Rountree. **Telephone:** (318) 257-5312.
Home Field: JC Love Field at Pat Patterson Park. **Seating Capacity:** 3,000. **Press Box Telephone:** (318) 257-3144.

LOUISIANA-LAFAYETTE RAGIN' CAJUNS

Conference: Sun Belt.
Mailing Address: 201 Reinhardt Dr, Lafayette, LA 70506. **Website:** www.ragincajuns.com.
Head Coach: Tony Robichaux. **Telephone:** (337) 482-6189. **Baseball SID:** Matt Hebert. **Telephone:** (337) 482-6331. **Fax:** (337) 482-6529.
Assistant Coaches: Anthony Babineaux, *Mike Trahan. **Telephone:** (337) 482-6093.
Home Field: M.L.'Tigue' Moore Field. **Seating Capacity:** 3,600. **Press Box Telephone:** (337) 851-2255.

LOUISIANA-MONROE WARHAWKS

Conference: Sun Belt.
Mailing Address: 308 Warhawk Way, Monroe, LA 71209. **Website:** www.ulmwarhawks.com.
Head Coach: Jeff Schexnaider. **Telephone:** (318) 342-3591. **Baseball SID:** Adam Prendergast. **Telephone:** (318) 342-5463.
Assistant Coaches: *Cory Barton, Justin Hill. **Telephone:** (318) 342-5391.
Home Field: Warhawk Field. **Seating Capacity:** 2,000. **Press Box Telephone:** (318) 342-5476.

LOUISVILLE CARDINALS

Conference: Big East.
Mailing Address: 215 Central Ave, Louisville, KY 40292. **Website:** www.UofLSports.com.
Head Coach: Dan McDonnell. **Telephone:** (502) 852-0103. **Baseball SID:** Garett Wall. **Telephone:** (502) 852-3088. **Fax:** (502) 852-7401.
Assistant Coaches: *Chris Lemonis, Roger Williams. **Telephone:** (502) 852-3929.
Home Field: Jim Patterson Stadium. **Seating Capacity:** 2,500. **Press Box Telephone:** (502) 852-3700.

LOYOLA MARYMOUNT LIONS

Conference: West Coast.
Mailing Address: 1 LMU Drive, Los Angeles, CA 90045. **Website:** lmulions.com.
Head Coach: Jason Gill. **Telephone:** (310) 338-2949. **Baseball SID:** Tyler Geivett. **Telephone:** (310) 338-7638. **Fax:** (310) 338-2703.
Assistant Coaches: Dan Ricabal, *Bryant Ward. **Telephone:** (310) 338-4511.
Home Field: Page Stadium. **Seating Capacity:** 600. **Press Box Telephone:** (310) 338-3046.

MAINE BLACK BEARS

Conference: America East.
Mailing Address: 5747 Memorial Gym, Orono, ME 04469. **Website:** www.goblackbears.com.
Head Coach: Steve Trimper. **Telephone:** (207) 581-1090. **Baseball SID:** Laura Reed. **Telephone:** (207) 581-3646. **Fax:** (207) 581-3297.
Assistant Coaches: Billy Cather, *Jason Spaulding. **Telephone:** (207) 581-1097.
Home Field: Mahaney Diamond. **Seating Capacity:** 4,400. **Press Box Telephone:** (207) 581-1049.

MANHATTAN JASPERS

Conference: Metro Atlantic.
Mailing Address: 4513 Manhattan College Parkway, Riverdale, NY 10471. **Website:** www.gojaspers.com.
Head Coach: Jim Duffy. **Telephone:** (718) 862-7936. **Baseball SID:** Stephen Dombroski. **Telephone:** (718) 862-7228. **Fax:** (718) 862-8020.
Assistant Coaches: Elvys Quezada, *Rene Ruiz. **Telephone:** (718) 862-7815.
Home Field: Van Cortland Park. **Seating Capacity:** 1,000.

MARIST RED FOXES

Conference: Metro Atlantic.
Mailing Address: 3399 North Road, Poughkeepsie, NY 12601. **Website:** www.goredfoxes.com.
Head Coach: Chris Tracz. **Telephone:** (845) 575-3000 Ext 2570. **Baseball SID:** Mike Ferraro. **Telephone:** (845) 575-3321.
Assistant Coaches: Justin Haywood, *Thomas Seay. **Telephone:** (845) 575-3000 Ext 7583.
Home Field: McCann Field. **Seating Capacity:** 1,000. **Press Box Telephone:** (914) 456-3447.

MARSHALL THUNDERING HERD

Conference: Conference USA.
Mailing Address: PO Box 1360, Huntington, WV 25715. **Website:** www.herdzone.com.
Head Coach: Jeff Waggoner. **Telephone:** (304) 696-5277. **Baseball SID:** Ty Osborne. **Telephone:** (304) 696-6160. **Fax:** (304) 696-2325.
Assistant Coaches: Tim Donnelly, *Joe Renner. **Telephone:** (304) 696-3885.
Home Field: Power Park. **Seating Capacity:** 5,000.

MARYLAND TERRAPINS

Conference: Atlantic Coast (Atlantic).
Mailing Address: 1 Terrapin Tr, College Park, MD 20742. **Website:** umterps.com.
Head Coach: Erik Bakich. **Telephone:** (301) 314-1845. **Baseball SID:** Justin Moore. **Telephone:** (301) 314-7068. **Fax:** (301) 314-9094.
Assistant Coaches: *Dan Burton, Sean Kenny. **Telephone:** (301) 314-1286.
Home Field: Bob Turtle Smith Stadium. **Seating Capacity:** 2,500. **Press Box Telephone:** (301) 314-0379.

MARYLAND-BALTIMORE COUNTY RETRIEVERS

Conference: America East.
Mailing Address: 1000 Hilltop Circle, Baltimore, MD 21250. **Website:** www.umbcretrievers.com.
Head Coach: Bob Mumma. **Telephone:** (410) 455-2239. **Baseball SID:** Daniel LaHatte. **Telephone:** (410) 455-1530. **Fax:** (410) 455-3994.
Assistant Coaches: Tim O'Brien, Jeff Moore. **Telephone:** (410) 455-5845.
Home Field: Baseball Factory Field. **Seating**

Capacity: 1000.

MARYLAND-EASTERN SHORE HAWKS

Conference: Mid-Eastern.
Mailing Address: 1 College Backbone Road William P Hytche Athletic Center, Princess Anne, MD 21853. **Website:** www.umeshawks.com.
Head Coach: Will Gardner. **Telephone:** (410) 651-8158. **Baseball SID:** Dave Vatz. **Telephone:** (410) 621-1108. **Fax:** (410) 651-7514.
Assistant Coaches: *Robbie Bailey, John O'Neil. **Telephone:** (410) 651-8908.
Home Field: Hawks Stadium. **Seating Capacity:** 1,000.

MASSACHUSETTS MINUTEMEN

Conference: Atlantic 10.
Mailing Address: 131 Commonwealth Ave, Amherst, MA 01003. **Website:** umassathletics.com.
Head Coach: Mike Stone. **Telephone:** (413) 545-3120. **Baseball SID:** Jillian Jakuba. **Telephone:** (413) 577-0053. **Fax:** (413) 545-1404.
Assistant Coaches: *Mike Sweeney. **Telephone:** (413) 545-3766.
Home Field: Earl Lorden Field. **Seating Capacity:** 1,500. **Press Box Telephone:** (413) 420-3116.

MCNEESE STATE COWBOYS

Conference: Southland.
Mailing Address: Box 92735, McNeese State, Lake Charles, LA 70609. **Website:** mcneesesports.com.
Head Coach: Terry Burrows. **Telephone:** (337) 475-5484. **Baseball SID:** Louis Bonnette. **Telephone:** (337) 475-5207. **Fax:** (337) 475-5202.
Assistant Coaches: *Bubbs Merrill, Matt Collins. **Telephone:** (337) 475-5903, (337) 475-5904.
Home Field: Cowboy Diamond. **Seating Capacity:** 2,000. **Press Box Telephone:** (337) 475-8007.

MEMPHIS TIGERS

Conference: Conference USA.
Mailing Address: 207 Athletic Office Bldg, Memphis, TN 38152. **Website:** www.gotigersgo.com.
Head Coach: Darren Schoenrock. **Telephone:** (901) 734-8889. **Baseball SID:** Mark Taylor. **Telephone:** (901) 678-5108. **Fax:** (901) 678-4134.
Assistant Coaches: Fred Corral, *Clay Greene. **Telephone:** (901) 678-4139.
Home Field: Fed Ex Park. **Seating Capacity:** 2,000.

MERCER BEARS

Conference: Atlantic Sun.
Mailing Address: 1400 Coleman Ave, Macon, GA 31207. **Website:** www.mercerbears.com.
Head Coach: Craig Gibson. **Telephone:** (478) 301-2396. **Baseball SID:** Jason Farhadi. **Telephone:** (478) 301-5218. **Fax:** (478) 301-5350.
Assistant Coaches: Justin Holmes, *Brent Shade. **Telephone:** (478) 301-2738.
Home Field: Claude Smith Field. **Seating Capacity:** 500. **Press Box Telephone:** (478) 301-2339.

MIAMI HURRICANES

Conference: Atlantic Coast (Coastal).
Mailing Address: 6201 San Amaro Dr, Coral Gables, FL 33146. **Website:** www.hurricanesports.com.
Head Coach: Jim Morris. **Telephone:** (305) 284-4171. **Baseball SID:** Bryan Harvey. **Telephone:** (305) 284-3249. **Fax:** (305) 284-2807.
Assistant Coaches: *JD Arteaga, Gino Dimare.

Telephone: (305) 284-4236.
Home Field: Alex Rodriguez Park. **Seating Capacity:** 5,000. **Press Box Telephone:** (305) 284-8192.

MIAMI (OHIO) REDHAWKS

Conference: Mid-American (East).
Mailing Address: 120 Withrow Court, Oxford, OH 45056. **Website:** www.muredhawks.com.
Head Coach: Dan Simonds. **Telephone:** (513) 529-6631. **Baseball SID:** Jim Stephan. **Telephone:** (513) 529-4330. **Fax:** (513) 529-6729.
Assistant Coaches: *Ben Bachmann, Jeremy Ison. **Telephone:** (513) 529-7293.
Home Field: McKie Field@Hayden Park. **Seating Capacity:** 1,000. **Press Box Telephone:** (513) 529-4331.

MICHIGAN WOLVERINES

Conference: Big Ten.
Mailing Address: 1114 S State St, Ann Arbor, MI 48104. **Website:** www.mgoblue.com.
Head Coach: Rich Maloney. **Telephone:** (734) 647-4550. **Baseball SID:** Kent Reichert. **Telephone:** (734) 647-1726. **Fax:** (734) 647-1188.
Assistant Coaches: *Matt Husted, Steve Merriman. **Telephone:** (734) 647-4555.
Home Field: Wilpon Complex/Ray Fisher Stadium. **Seating Capacity:** 4,000. **Press Box Telephone:** (734) 647-1283.

MICHIGAN STATE SPARTANS

Conference: Big Ten.
Mailing Address: 304 Jenison Field House, East Lansing,MI 48824. **Website:** msuspartans.com.
Head Coach: Jake Boss. **Telephone:** (517) 353-0816. **Baseball SID:** Ben Phlegar. **Telephone:** (517) 355-2271. **Fax:** (517) 353-9636.
Assistant Coaches: Graham Sikes, *Mark Van. **Telephone:** (517) 353-0816.
Home Field: Kobs Field at McLane Baseball Stadium. **Seating Capacity:** 2,500. **Press Box Telephone:** (517) 353-3009.

MIDDLE TENNESSEE STATE BLUE RAIDERS

Conference: Sun Belt.
Mailing Address: MTSU Box 20, Murfreesboro, TN 37132. **Website:** www.goblueraiders.com.
Head Coach: Steve Peterson. **Telephone:** (615) 898-2450. **Baseball SID:** Leslie Wilhite. **Telephone:** (615) 904-8115. **Fax:** (615) 898-5626.
Assistant Coaches: *Jim McGuire, Mike McLaury. **Telephone:** (615) 898-5495.
Home Field: Reese Smith Jr. Field. **Seating Capacity:** 2,100. **Press Box Telephone:** (615) 898-2117.

MINNESOTA GOLDEN GOPHERS

Conference: Big Ten.
Mailing Address: University of Minnesota 516 15th Avenue SE, Minneapolis, MN 55455. **Website:** www.gophersports.com.
Head Coach: John Anderson. **Telephone:** (612) 625-4057. **Baseball SID:** Michelle Traen. **Telephone:** (612) 624-0522.
Assistant Coaches: *Rob Fornasiere, Todd Oakes. **Telephone:** (612) 625-3568.
Home Field: Metrodome. **Seating Capacity:** 48,000. **Press Box Telephone:** (612) 627-4400.

MISSISSIPPI OLE MISS REBELS

Conference: Southeastern (West).
Mailing Address: Ole Miss Baseball Office, University Place, University, MS 38677. **Website:** www.OleMissSports.com.
Head Coach: Mike Bianco. **Telephone:** (662) 915-6643. **Baseball SID:** Bill Bunting. **Telephone:** (662) 915-1083. **Fax:** (662) 915-7006.
Assistant Coaches: Cliff Godwin, *Carl Lafferty. **Telephone:** (662) 915-2013.
Home Field: O-U Stadium/Swayze Field. **Seating Capacity:** 10,323. **Press Box Telephone:** (662) 915-7858.

MISSISSIPPI STATE BULLDOGS

Conference: Southeastern (West).
Mailing Address: Box 5327, Mississippi State, MS 39762. **Website:** www.mstateathletics.com.
Head Coach: John Cohen. **Telephone:** (662) 325-3597. **Baseball SID:** Joe Dier. **Telephone:** (662) 325-8040. **Fax:** (662) 325-3600.
Assistant Coaches: Lane Burroughs, *Butch Thompson. **Telephone:** (662) 325-3597.
Home Field: Dudy Noble Field, Polk-DeMent Stadium. **Seating Capacity:** 15,000. **Press Box Telephone:** (662) 325-3776.

MISSISSIPPI VALLEY STATE DELTA DEVILS

Conference: Southwestern Athletic.
Mailing Address: 14000 Highway 82 West, #7246, Itta Bena, MS 38941. **Website:** www.mvsu.edu/athletics.
Head Coach: Doug Shanks. **Telephone:** (662) 254-3834. **Baseball SID:** William Bright Jr. **Telephone:** (662) 254-3011. **Fax:** (662) 254-3639.
Assistant Coach: Aaron Stevens. **Telephone:** (662) 254-3834.

MISSOURI TIGERS

Conference: Big 12.
Mailing Address: 100 MATC, Columbia, MO 65211. **Website:** mutigers.com.
Head Coach: Tim Jamieson. **Telephone:** (573) 882-1917. **Baseball SID:** Shawn Davis. **Telephone:** (573) 882-0711.
Assistant Coaches: Matt Hobbs, *Kerrick Jackson. **Telephone:** (573) 882-0731.
Home Field: Simmons Field. **Seating Capacity:** 3,031. **Press Box Telephone:** (573) 884-8912.

MISSOURI STATE BEARS

Conference: Missouri Valley.
Mailing Address: 901 S National, Springfield, MO 65897. **Website:** www.missouristatebears.com.
Head Coach: Keith Guttin. **Telephone:** (417) 836-4497. **Baseball SID:** Eric Doennig. **Telephone:** (417) 836-4584. **Fax:** (417) 836-4868.
Assistant Coaches: *Paul Evans, Brent Thomas. **Telephone:** (417) 836-6196.
Home Field: Hammons Field. **Seating Capacity:** 8,000. **Press Box Telephone:** (417) 832-3029.

MONMOUTH HAWKS

Conference: Northeast.
Mailing Address: 400 Cedar Ave, West Long Branch, NJ 07764. **Website:** www.gomuhawks.com.
Head Coach: Dean Ehehalt. **Telephone:** (732) 263-5186. **Baseball SID:** Jarred Weiss. **Telephone:** (732) 263-5557. **Fax:** (732) 571-3535.
Assistant Coaches: *Jimmy Belanger, Rick Oliveri. **Telephone:** (732) 263-5524.
Home Field: MU Baseball Field. **Seating Capacity:** 500. **Press Box Telephone:** (732) 263-5401.

MOREHEAD STATE EAGLES

Conference: Ohio Valley.
Mailing Address: Allen Field, Morehead, KY 40351.
Website: www.msueagles.com.
Head Coach: Jay Sorg. **Telephone:** (606) 783-2882.
Baseball SID: Matt Segal. **Telephone:** (606) 783-2557.
Fax: (606) 783-5035.
Assistant Coaches: Dillon Lawson, *Jason Neal.
Telephone: (606) 207-2881.
Home Field: Allen Feld. **Seating Capacity:** 1,100.

MOUNT ST. MARY'S MOUNTAINEERS

Conference: Northeast.
Mailing Address: 16300 Old Emmitsburg Rd, Emmitsburg, MD 21727. **Website:** www.mountathletics.com.
Head Coach: Scott Thomson. **Telephone:** (301) 447-3806. **Baseball SID:** Mark Vandergrift. **Telephone:** (301) 447-5384. **Fax:** (301) 447-5300.
Assistant Coach: *Scott Biesecker, Greg White. **Telephone:** (301) 447-3806.
Home Field: ET Straw Family Stadium.

MURRAY STATE TOUROUGHBREDS

Conference: Ohio Valley.
Mailing Address: 217 Stewart Stadium, Murray, KY. **Website:** goracers.com.
Head Coach: Rob McDonald. **Telephone:** (270) 809-4892. **Baseball SID:** John Brush. **Telephone:** (270) 809-7044. **Fax:** (270) 809-6814.
Assistant Coaches: *Chris Cole, Dan Skirka. **Telephone:** (270) 809-3475.
Home Field: Johnny Reagan Field. **Seating Capacity:** 800. **Press Box Telephone:** (270) 809-5650.

NAVY MIDSHIPMEN

Conference: Patriot.
Mailing Address: 566 Brownson Rd, Annapolis, MD 21402. **Website:** navysports.com.
Head Coach: Paul Kostacopoulos. **Telephone:** (410) 293-5571. **Baseball SID:** Jeff Barnes. **Telephone:** (410) 293-8771. **Fax:** (410) 293-8954.
Assistant Coaches: Ryan Mau, *Matt Reynolds. **Telephone:** (410) 293-5428.
Home Field: Terwilliger Brothers Field at Max Bishop Stadium. **Seating Capacity:** 1,500. **Press Box Telephone:**(410) 293-5430.

NEBRASKA CORNHUSKERS

Conference: Big Ten.
Mailing Address: 403 Line Drive Circle, Lincoln, NE. **Website:** huskers.com.
Head Coach: Darin Erstad. **Telephone:** (402) 472-2269. **Baseball SID:** Jeremy Foote. **Telephone:** (402) 472-7778. **Fax:** (402) 472-2005.
Assistant Coaches: Will Bolt, *Ted Silva. **Telephone:** (402) 472-2269.
Home Field: Hawks Field at Haymarket Park. **Seating Capacity:** 8,486. **Press Box Telephone:** (402) 434-6861.

NEBRASKA-OMAHA MAVERICKS

Conference: Summit League.
Mailing Address: 6001 Dodge Street, Omaha, NE 68182. **Website:** www.omavs.com
Head Coach: Bob Herold. **Telephone:** (402) 554-3388. **Baseball SID:** Bonnie Ryan. **Telephone:** (402) 554-3267. **Fax:** (402) 554-3694.
Assistant Coaches: Chris Gadsden, Dan McGinn. **Telephone:** (402) 554-2141.

Home Field: Ballpark at Boys Town.

NEVADA WOLF PACK

Conference: Western Athletic.
Mailing Address: 1664 N Virginia Street, Reno, NV 89557. **Website:** www.nevadawolfpack.com.
Head Coach: Gary Powers. **Telephone:** (775) 682-6978. **Baseball SID:** Jack Kuestermeyer. **Telephone:** (775) 682-6984. **Fax:** (775) 784-4386.
Assistant Coaches: Buddy Gouldsmith, *Chris Pfatenhauer. **Telephone:** (775) 682-6979.
Home Field: Peccole Park. **Seating Capacity:** 3,000. **Press Box Telephone:** (775) 784-1585.

NEVADA-LAS VEGAS REBELS

Conference: Mountain West.
Mailing Address: 4505 S Maryland Parkway, Las Vegas, NV 89154. **Website:** www.unlvrebels.com.
Head Coach: Tim Chambers. **Telephone:** (702) 895-3499. **Baseball SID:** Paul Pancoe. **Telephone:** (702) 895-3764. **Fax:** (702) 895-0989.
Assistant Coaches: Kevin Higgins, *Stan Stolte. **Telephone:** (702) 895-3802.
Home Field: Wilson Stadium. **Seating Capacity:** 3,500. **Press Box Telephone:** (702) 895-1585.

NEW JERSEY TECH HIGHLANDERS

Conference: Great West.
Mailing Address: NJIT University Heights, Newark, NJ 07102. **Website:** www.njithighlanders.com.
Head Coach: Mike Cole. **Telephone:** (973) 596-5827.
Baseball SID: Tim Camp. **Telephone:** (973) 596-8461. **Fax:** (973) 596-8295.
Assistant Coaches: *Brian Guiliana, Trevor Marcotte. **Telephone:** (973) 596-8396.
Home Field: Riverfront Stadium. **Seating Capacity:** 6,500.

NEW MEXICO LOBOS

Conference: Mountain West.
Mailing Address: Colleen J. Maloof Administration Building, MSC04 2680, 1 University of New Mexico, Albuquerque, NM 87131-0001. **Website:** golobos.com.
Head Coach: Ray Birmingham. **Telephone:** (505) 925-5720. **Baseball SID:** Taylor Stern. **Telephone:** (505) 925-5520. **Fax:** (505) 925-5734.
Assistant Coaches: *Ken Jacome, David Martinez. **Telephone:** (505) 925-5721.
Home Field: Isotopes Park. **Seating Capacity:** 12,000. **Press Box Telephone:** (505) 222-4093.

NEW MEXICO STATE AGGIES

Conference: Western Athletic.
Mailing Address: PO Box 30001, Dept 3145, Las Cruces, NM 88011. **Website:** nmstatesports.com.
Head Coach: Rocky Ward. **Telephone:** (575) 646-5813. **Baseball SID:** Eddie Morelos. **Telephone:** (575) 646-3269.
Assistant Coaches: *Mike Evans, Gary Ward. **Telephone:** (575) 646-7693.
Home Field: Presley Askew Field. **Seating Capacity:** 1,000. **Press Box Telephone:** (575) 646-5700.

NEW YORK TECH BEARS

Conference: Great West.
Mailing Address: Sports Complex, Northern Blvd, Old Westbury, NY 11568-8000. **Website:** www.nyit.edu/athletics.
Head Coach: TBD. **Telephone:** (516) 686-7513.
Baseball SID: Sabrina Polidoro. **Telephone:** (516) 686-7504. **Fax:** (516) 686-1219.

Assistant Coaches: Chris Rojas, Mike MacMillan. **Telephone:** (516) 686-7513.

Home Field: President's Field. **Seating Capacity:** 500. **Press Box Telephone:** (516) 686-7886.

NIAGARA PURPLE EAGLES

Conference: Metro Atlantic.
Mailing Address: PO Box 2009, UL Gallagher Ctr, Niagara University, NY 14109. **Website:** www.purpleeagles.com.
Head Coach: Rob McCoy. **Telephone:** (716) 286-7361. **Baseball SID:** Derek Thornton. **Telephone:** (716) 286-8588. **Fax:** (716) 286-8609.
Assistant Coaches: *Eric Peterson, Jeff Ziemecki. **Telephone:** (716) 286-8624.
Home Field: Sal Maglie Stadium. **Seating Capacity:** 5,000.

NICHOLLS STATE COLONELS

Conference: Southland.
Mailing Address: PO Box 2032, Thibodaux, LA 70310. **Website:** geauxcolonels.com.
Head Coach: Seth Thibodeaux. **Telephone:** (985) 449-7149. **Baseball SID:** Clyde Verdin. **Telephone:** (985) 448-4282. **Fax:** (985) 448-4814.
Assistant Coaches: Rudy Darrow, *Chris Prothro. **Telephone:** (985) 448-4807.
Home Field: Ray E Didier Field. **Seating Capacity:** 2,500. **Press Box Telephone:** (985) 448-4834.

NORFOLK STATE Spartans
Conference: Mid-Eastern Athletic.
Mailing Address: 700 Park Ave, Norfolk, VA 23504. **Website:** www.nsuspartans.com.
Head Coach: *Claudell Clark. **Telephone:** (757) 676-3082. **Baseball SID:** Matt Michalec. **Telephone:** (757) 823-2628. **Fax:** (757) 823-8218.
Assistant Coaches: A.J. Corbin. **Telephone:** (757) 823-9533.
Home Field: Marty L. Miller Field. **Seating Capacity:** 1,500. **Press Box Telephone:** (757) 823-8196.

NORTH CAROLINA TAR HEELS

Conference: Atlantic Coast (Coastal).
Mailing Address: PO Box 2126, Chapel Hill, NC 27515. **Website:** tarheelblue.com.
Head Coach: Mike Fox. **Telephone:** (919) 962-2351. **Baseball SID:** Dave Schmidt. **Telephone:** (919) 962-0084. **Fax:** (919) 962-0612.
Assistant Coaches: Scott Forbes, *Scott Jackson. **Telephone:** (919) 962-5451.
Home Field: Boshamer Stadium. **Seating Capacity:** 4,200. **Press Box Telephone:** (919) 962-3509.

NORTH CAROLINA A&T AGGIES

Conference: Mid-Eastern Athletic.
Mailing Address: 1601 E Market St, Greensboro, NC 27411. **Website:** www.ncataggies.com.
Head Coach: Joel Sanchez. **Telephone:** (336) 285-4272. **Baseball SID:** Kristin Pratt. **Telephone:** (336) 334-7141. **Fax:** (336) 334-7181.
Assistant Coaches: Jeremy Jones, *Austin Love. **Telephone:** (336) 285-4272.
Home Field: War Memorial Stadium. **Seating Capacity:** 2,000. **Press Box Telephone:** (336) 328-6710.

NORTH CAROLINA CENTRAL EAGLES

Conference: Independent.
Mailing Address: 1801 Fayetteville St, Durham, NC 27707. **Website:** www.nccueaglepride.com.
Head Coach: Jim Koerner. **Telephone:** (919) 530-6723.

Baseball SID: Chris Hooks. **Telephone:** (919) 530-6017. **Fax:** (919) 530-5426.
Assistant Coaches: Tyler Hanson, *Jerry Shank. **Telephone:** (919) 530-5439.
Home Field: Durham Athletic Park. **Seating Capacity:** 3,000.

NORTH CAROLINA STATE WOLFPACK

Conference: Atlantic Coast (Atlantic).
Mailing Address: 1081 Varsity Drive, Raleigh, NC 27695. **Website:** gopack.com.
Head Coach: Elliott Avent. **Telephone:** (919) 515-3613. **Baseball SID:** Bruce Winkworth. **Telephone:** (919) 515-1182. **Fax:** (919) 515-3624.
Assistant Coaches: Chris Hart, *Tom Holliday. **Telephone:** (919) 515-3613.
Home Field: Doak Field at Dail Park. **Seating Capacity:** 3,000. **Press Box Telephone:** (919) 819-3035.

UNC ASHEVILLE BULLDOGS

Conference: Big South.
Mailing Address: One University Heights, Asheville, NC 28804. **Website:** www.uncabulldogs.com.
Head Coach: Tom Smith. **Telephone:** (828) 251-6920. **Baseball SID:** Matt Pellegrin. **Telephone:** (828) 251-6931. **Fax:** (828) 251-6386.
Assistant Coaches: *Aaron Rembert, Matt Henson. **Telephone:** (828) 251-6903.
Home Field: Greenwood Field. **Seating Capacity:** 500.

UNC GREENSBORO SPARTANS

Conference: Southern.
Mailing Address: 1408 Walker Ave, HHP 337, Greensboro, NC 27402. **Website:** www.uncgspartans.com.
Head Coach: Mike Gaski. **Telephone:** (336) 334-3247. **Baseball SID:** David Percival. **Telephone:** (336) 334-5615. **Fax:** (336) 334-3182.
Assistant Coaches: *Jamie Athas, Jarrett Santos. **Telephone:** (336) 334-3247.
Home Field: UNCG Baseball Stadium. **Seating Capacity:** 3,500. **Press Box Telephone:** (336) 334-3885.

UNC WILMINGTON SEAHAWKS

Conference: Colonial Athletic.
Mailing Address: 601 South College Road, Wilmington, NC 28403. **Website:** www.uncwsports.com.
Head Coach: Mark Scalf. **Telephone:** (910) 962-3570. **Baseball SID:** Tom Riordan. **Telephone:** (910) 962-4099. **Fax:** (910) 962-3001.
Assistant Coaches: *Randy Hood, Jason Howell. **Telephone:** (910) 962-7471.
Home Field: Brooks Field. **Seating Capacity:** 3,500. **Press Box Telephone:** (910) 395-5141.

NORTH DAKOTA FIGHTING SIOUX

Conference: Great West.
Mailing Address: Hyslop Sports Center Rm 120, 2751 2nd Ave N, Stop 9013, Grand Forks, ND 58202. **Website:** www.fightingsioux.com.
Head Coach: Jeff Dodson. **Telephone:** (701) 777-4038. **Baseball SID:** Ryan Powell. **Telephone:** (701) 777-2986. **Fax:** (702) 777-3385.
Assistant Coaches: Brian DeVillers, *JC Field. **Telephone:** (701) 777-2352.
Home Field: Kraft Field. **Seating Capacity:** 2,000.

NORTH DAKOTA STATE BISON

Conference: Summit.
Mailing Address: NDSU Dept 1200, PO Box 6050, Fargo, ND 58108-6050. **Website:** www.gobison.com.
Head Coach: Tod Brown. **Telephone:** (701) 231-8853. **Baseball SID:** Ryan Perreault. **Telephone:** (701) 231-8331. **Fax:** (701) 231-8022.
Assistant Coaches: Jake Angier, *David Pearson. **Telephone:** (701) 231-7817.
Home Field: Newman Outdoor Field. **Seating Capacity:** 4,422. **Press Box Telephone:** (701) 235-5204.

NORTH FLORIDA OSPREYS

Conference: Atlantic Sun.
Mailing Address: 1 UNF Drive, Jacksonville, FL 32224. **Website:** www.unfospreys.com.
Head Coach: Smoke Laval. **Telephone:** (904) 620-1556. **Baseball SID:** Chris Whitehead. **Telephone:** (904) 620-4029. **Fax:** (904) 620-3943.
Assistant Coaches: *Judd Loveland, Tim Parenton. **Telephone:** (904) 620-2556.
Home Field: Harmon Stadium. **Seating Capacity:** 1,000. **Press Box Telephone:** (904) 620-1557.

NORTHEASTERN HUSKIES

Conference: Colonial Athletic.
Mailing Address: 360 Huntington Ave, Boston, MA 02115. **Website:** www.gonu.com.
Head Coach: Neil McPhee. **Telephone:** (617) 373-3657. **Baseball SID:** Jack Grinold. **Telephone:** (617) 373-2691. **Fax:** (617) 373-3152.
Assistant Coaches: *Mike Glavine, Kevin Cobb. **Telephone:** (617) 373-5256.
Home Field: Freidman Diamond. **Seating Capacity:** 3,000.

NORTHERN COLORADO BEARS

Conference: Great West.
Mailing Address: 270 Butler-Hancock Sports Pavilion, Greeley, CO 80639. **Website:** uncbears.com.
Head Coach: Carl Iwasaki. **Telephone:** (970) 351-1714. **Baseball SID:** Heather Kennedy. **Telephone:** (970) 351-1065. **Fax:** (970) 351-2018.
Assistant Coaches: Patrick Perry, *RD Spiehs. **Telephone:** (970) 351-1203.
Home Field: Jackson Field. **Seating Capacity:** 1,500. **Press Box Telephone:** (970) 978-0675.

NORTHERN ILLINOIS HUSKIES

Conference: Mid-American (West).
Mailing Address: 1525 West Lincoln Highway, DeKalb, IL 60115. **Website:** niuhuskies.com.
Head Coach: Ed Mathey. **Telephone:** (815) 753-2225. **Baseball SID:** Matt Scheerer. **Telephone:** (815) 753-1708. **Fax:** (815) 753-7700.
Assistant Coaches: *Steve Joslyn, Ray Napientek. **Telephone:** (815) 753-0147.
Home Field: Ralph McKinzie Field. **Seating Capacity:** 2,000. **Press Box Telephone:** (815) 753-8094.

NORTHWESTERN WILDCATS

Conference: Southland.
Mailing Address: 1501 Central St, Evanston, IL 60208. **Website:** nusports.com.
Head Coach: Paul Stevens. **Telephone:** (847) 491-4652. **Baseball SID:** Nick Brilowski. **Telephone:** (847) 467-3831. **Fax:** (847) 491-8818.
Assistant Coaches: *Jon Mikrut, Tim Stoddard. **Telephone:** (847) 491-4651.

Home Field: Rocky Miller Park. **Seating Capacity:** 1,000. **Press Box Telephone:** (847) 491-4200.

NORTHWESTERN STATE DEMONS

Conference: Southland.
Mailing Address: Athletic Fieldhouse, Natchitoches, LA 71497. **Website:** www.nsudemons.com.
Head Coach: Jon Paul Davis. **Telephone:** (318) 357-4139. **Baseball SID:** Matthew Bonnette. **Telephone:** (318) 357-6467. **Fax:** (318) 357-4515.
Assistant Coaches: *Jeff McCannon, Andy Morgan. **Telephone:** (318) 357-4176, (318) 357-4134.
Home Field: Brown-Stroud Field. **Seating Capacity:** 1,200. **Press Box Telephone:** (318) 357-4606.

NOTRE DAME FIGHTING IRISH

Conference: Big East.
Mailing Address: 202 Joyce Center, Notre Dame, IN 46556. **Website:** und.com.
Head Coach: Mik Aoki. **Telephone:** (574) 631-8466. **Baseball SID:** Michael Bertsch. **Telephone:** (574) 631-8642. **Fax:** (574) 631-7941.
Assistant Coaches: *Joe Hastings, Jesse Woods. **Telephone:** (574) 631-3375.
Home Field: Frank Eck Stadium. **Seating Capacity:** 2,500. **Press Box Telephone:** (574) 631-9018.

OAKLAND GOLDEN GRIZZLIES

Conference: Summit.
Mailing Address: 2200 N E Squirrell Road, Rochester, MI 48309. **Website:** www.ougrizzlies.com.
Head Coach: John Musachio. **Telephone:** (248) 370-4059. **Baseball SID:** Scott Dunford. **Telephone:** (248) 370-3123. **Fax:** (248) 370-3138.
Assistant Coaches: Damon Lessler, *Matt PLante. **Telephone:** (248) 370-4228.
Home Field: OU Baseball Field. **Seating Capacity:** 500. **Press Box Telephone:** (248) 688-7646.

OHIO BOBCATS

Conference: Mid-American (East).
Mailing Address: N117 Convocation Center, Athens, OH 45701. **Website:** www.ohiobobcats.com.
Head Coach: Joe Carbone. **Telephone:** (740) 593-1180. **Baseball SID:** Tom Symonds. **Telephone:** (740) 593-1298.
Assistant Coaches: Scott Malinowski, *Andrew See. **Telephone:** (740) 593-1207.
Home Field: Bob Wren Stadium. **Seating Capacity:** 5,000. **Press Box Telephone:** (740) 593-0526.

OHIO STATE BUCKEYES

Conference: Big Ten.
Mailing Address: 650 Borror Dr, Columbus, OH 43210. **Website:** www.ohiostatebuckeyes.com.
Head Coach: Greg Beals. **Telephone:** (614) 292-1075. **Baseball SID:** Brett Ryback. **Telephone:** (614) 292-1112. **Fax:** (614) 292-8547.
Assistant Coaches: *Chris Holick, Mike Stafford. **Telephone:** (614) 292-1075.
Home Field: Nick Swisher Field at Bill Davis Stadium. **Seating Capacity:** 4,450. **Press Box Telephone:** (614) 292-0021.

OKLAHOMA SOONERS

Conference: Big 12.
Mailing Address: 401 W Imhoff, Norman, OK 73019. **Website:** www.soonersports.com.
Head Coach: Sunny Golloway. **Telephone:** (405) 325-8354. **Baseball SID:** Craig Moran. **Telephone:** (405) 325-6449. **Fax:** (405) 325-7623.

Assistant Coaches: Jack Giese, *Aric Thomas. Telephone: (405) 325-8354.
Home Field: L. Dale Mitchell Park. Seating Capacity: 2,900. Press Box Telephone: (405) 325-8363.

OKLAHOMA STATE COWBOYS

Conference: Big 12.
Mailing Address: 220 Athletics Center, Stillwater, OK 74078. Website: www.okstate.com.
Head Coach: Frank Anderson. Telephone: (405) 744-5849. Baseball SID: Wade McWhorter. Telephone: (405) 744-7853. Fax: (405) 744-7754.
Assistant Coaches: Greg Evans, *Billy Jones. Telephone: (405) 744-5849.
Home Field: Allie P. Reynolds Stadium. Seating Capacity: 4,000. Press Box Telephone: (405) 744-5757.

OLD DOMINION MONARCHS

Conference: Colonial Athletic.
Mailing Address: Athletic Dept Norfolk, Va. 23529. Website: www.odusports.com.
Head Coach: Chris Finwood. Telephone: (757) 683-4230. Baseball SID: Carol Hudson. Telephone: (757) 683-3395. Fax: (757) 683-3119.
Assistant Coaches: Tim LaVigne, *Karl Nonemaker. Telephone: (757) 683-4230.
Home Field: Bud Metheny Complex. Seating Capacity: 2.500. Press Box Telephone: (757) 683-5036.

ORAL ROBERTS GOLDEN EAGLES

Conference: Summit.
Mailing Address: 7777 S, Lewis Ave, Tulsa, OK 74171. Website: www.orugoldeneagles.com.
Head Coach: Rob Walton. Telephone: (918) 495-7205. Baseball SID: Eli Linton. Telephone: (918) 495-6646.
Assistant Coaches: Ryan Folmar, *Ryan Neil. Telephone: (918) 495-7639.
Home Field: J.L. Johnson Stadium. Seating Capacity: 2,418. Press Box Telephone: (918) 495-7165.

OREGON DUCKS

Conference: Pacific-12.
Mailing Address: 2727 Leo Harris Parkway, Eugene, OR 97401. Website: www.goducks.com.
Head Coach: George Horton. Telephone: (541) 346-5235. Baseball SID: Andria Wenzel. Telephone: (541) 346-0962. Fax: (541) 346-5449.
Assistant Coaches: Jay Uhlman, *Mark Wasikowski. Telephone: (541) 346-5768.
Home Field: PK Park. Seating Capacity: 4,000. Press Box Telephone: (541) 346-6309.

OREGON STATE BEAVERS

Conference: Pacific-12.
Mailing Address: 114 Gill Coliseum, Corvallis, OR 97331. Website: www.osubeavers.com.
Head Coach: Pat Casey. Telephone: (541) 737-2825. Baseball SID: Hank Hager. Telephone: (541) 737-7472. Fax: (541) 737-3072.
Assistant Coaches: Pat Bailey, *Marty Lees. Telephone: (541) 737-7484, (541) 737-5738.
Home Field: Goss Stadium at Coleman Field. Seating Capacity: 3,248. Press Box Telephone: (541) 737-7475.

PACIFIC TIGERS

Conference: Big West.
Mailing Address: 3601 Pacific Ave, Stockton, CA 95211. Website: pacifictigers.com.
Head Coach: Ed Sprague. Telephone: (209) 946-2389. Baseball SID: Kevin Wilkinson. Telephone: (209) 946-

2289. Fax: (209) 946-2757.
Assistant Coaches: *Don Barbara, Mike McCormick. Telephone: (209) 946-2386.
Home Field: Klein Family Field. Seating Capacity: 2500. Press Box Telephone: (209) 946-2722.

PENN STATE NITTANY LIONS

Conference: Big Ten.
Mailing Address: Medlar Field at Lubrano Park Suite 230, University Park, PA 16802. Website: www.GoPSUsports.com.
Head Coach: Robbie Wine. Telephone: (814) 863-0239. Baseball SID: Greg Kincaid. Telephone: (814) 865-1757. Fax: (814) 863-3165.
Assistant Coaches: Jason Bell, *Eric Folmar. Telephone: (814) 865-8605.
Home Field: Medlar Field at Lubrano Park. Seating Capacity: 5,406.

PENNSYLVANIA QUAKERS

Conference: Ivy League (Gehrig).
Mailing Address: 235 S 33rd St, Philadelphia, PA 19104. Website: www.pennathletics.com.
Head Coach: John Cole. Telephone: (215) 898-6282. Baseball SID: Alex Keil. Telephone: (215) 898-6128. Fax: (215) 898-1747.
Assistant Coaches: Mike Santello, *John Yurkow. Telephone: (215) 746-2325.
Home Field: Meiklejohn Stadium. Seating Capacity: 1,000.

PEPPERDINE WAVES

Conference: West Coast.
Mailing Address: 24255 Pacific Coast Highway, Malibu, CA 90263. Website: www.PepperdineSports.com.
Head Coach: Steve Rodriguez. Telephone: (310) 506-4371. Baseball SID: Rachel Caton. Telephone: (310) 506-4333. Fax: (310) 506-7459.
Assistant Coaches: Rick Hirtensteiner, *Jon Strauss. Telephone: (310) 506-4404.
Home Field: Eddy D. Field Stadium. Seating Capacity: 2,000. Press Box Telephone: (310) 506-4598.

PITTSBURGH PANTHERS

Conference: Big East.
Mailing Address: 212 Fitzgerald Fieldhouse, Pittsburgh, PA 15261. Website: pittsburghpanthers.com.
Head Coach: Joe Jordano. Telephone: (412) 648-8208. Baseball SID: Matt Jackson. Telephone: (412) 648-8245. Fax: (412) 648-8248.
Assistant Coaches: Tom Lipari, *Danny Lopaze. Telephone: (412) 648-3825.
Home Field: Charles L. Cost Field at Petersen Sports Complex. Seating Capacity: 1,000.

PORTLAND PILOTS

Conference: West Coast.
Mailing Address: 5000 North Willamette Blvd, Portland, OR 97203. Website: www.portlandpilots.com.
Head Coach: Chris Sperry. Telephone: (503) 943-7707. Baseball SID: Adam Linnman. Telephone: (503) 943-7731. Fax: (503) 943-7242.
Assistant Coaches: Tucker Brack, *Larry Casian. Telephone: (503) 943-7732, (503) 943-7745.
Home Field: Joe Etzel Field. Seating Capacity: 1,000.

PRAIRIE VIEW A&M PANTHERS

Conference: Southwestern Athletic.
Mailing Address: PO Box 519 MS 1500, Prairie View, TX 77446. Website: sports.pvamu.edu.

Head Coach: Waskyla Cullivan. **Telephone:** (936) 261-9121. **Baseball SID:** Ryan McGinty. **Telephone:** (936) 261-9140. **Fax:** (936) 261-9159.

Assistant Coach: *Byron Carter. **Telephone:** (936) 261-9115.

PRESBYTERIAN BLUE HOSE

Conference: Big South.
Mailing Address: 105 Ashland Ave, Clinton, SC, 29325.
Website: www.gobluehose.com.
Head Coach: Elton Pollock. **Telephone:** (864) 833-8236. **Baseball SID:** Ryan Real. **Telephone:** (864) 833-7095. **Fax:** (864) 833-8323.
Assistant Coaches: Cody Church, *Josh Davis. **Telephone:** (864) 833-7134.
Home Field: PC Baseball Complex. **Seating Capacity:** 500. **Press Box Telephone:** (864) 833-8527.

PRINCETON TIGERS

Conference: Ivy League (Gehrig).
Mailing Address: Jadwin Gym, Princeton University, Princeton, NJ 08544. **Website:** www.GoPrincetonTigers.com.
Head Coach: Scott Bradley. **Telephone:** (609) 258-5059. **Baseball SID:** Diana Schmoro. **Telephone:** (609) 258-4849. **Fax:** (609) 258-2399.
Assistant Coaches: *Lloyd Brewer, Hank Coogan. **Telephone:** (609) 258-5059.
Home Field: Clarke Field. **Seating Capacity:** 750. **Press Box Telephone:** (609) 462-0248.

PURDUE BOILERMAKERS

Conference: Big Ten.
Mailing Address: Ross-Ade Pavilion, 850 Beering Drive, West Lafayette, IN 47907. **Website:** purduesports.com.
Head Coach: Doug Schreiber. **Telephone:** (765) 494-3998. **Baseball SID:** Ben Turner. **Telephone:** (765) 494-3198. **Fax:** (765) 494-5447.
Assistant Coaches: *Jeff Duncan, Tristan McIntyre. **Telephone:** (765) 496-3442.
Home Field: Lambert Field/Alexander Field. **Seating Capacity:** 1,500. **Press Box Telephone:** (217) 549-7965.

QUINNIPIAC BOBCATS

Conference: Northeast.
Mailing Address: 275 Mount Carmel Ave, Hamden, CT 06518. **Website:** quinnipiacbobcats.com.
Head Coach: *Dan Gooley. **Telephone:** (203) 582-8966. **Baseball SID:** Ken Sweeten. **Telephone:** (203) 582-8625. **Fax:** (203) 582-5385.
Assistant Coaches: Tim Binkoski, Marc Stonaha. **Telephone:** (203) 582-8966
Home Field: Quinnipiac Field. **Seating Capacity:** 1,000. **Press Box Telephone:** (203) 859-8529.

RADFORD HIGHLANDERS

Conference: Big South.
Mailing Address: PO Box 6913, Radford, VA 24142.
Website: www.ruhighlanders.com.
Head Coach: Joe Raccuia. **Telephone:** (540) 831-5881. **Baseball SID:** Patrick Reed. **Telephone:** (540) 831-5574. **Fax:** (540) 831-6095.
Assistant Coaches: *Brian Anderson, Kyle Werman. **Telephone:** (540) 831-6581.
Home Field: RU Baseball Stadium. **Seating Capacity:** 800. **Press Box Telephone:** (540) 831-6062.

RHODE ISLAND RAMS

Conference: Atlantic 10.
Mailing Address: 3 Keaney Road Suite One, Kingston,

RI 02881. **Website:** gorhody.com.
Head Coach: Jim Foster. **Telephone:** (401) 874-4550. **Baseball SID:** Jodi Pontbriand. **Telephone:** (401) 874-5356. **Fax:** (401) 874-5354.
Assistant Coaches: *Raphael Cerrato, Eric Cirella. **Telephone:** (401) 874-4888.
Home Field: Bill Beck Field. **Press Box Telephone:** (401) 874-4888.

RICE OWLS

Conference: Conference USA.
Mailing Address: 6100 Main, Houston, TX. **Website:** www.riceowls.com.
Head Coach: Wayne Graham. **Telephone:** (713) 348-8864. **Baseball SID:** John Sullivan. **Telephone:** (713) 348-5636. **Fax:** (713) 348-6019.
Assistant Coaches: Pat Hallmark, *Mike Taylor. **Telephone:** (713) 348-8862.
Home Field: Reckling Park. **Seating Capacity:** 5,368. **Press Box Telephone:** (713) 348-4931.

RICHMOND SPIDERS

Conference: Atlantic 10.
Mailing Address: The Robins Center, Richmond, VA 23173. **Website:** RichmondSpiders.com.
Head Coach: Mark McQueen. **Telephone:** (804) 287-1933. **Baseball SID:** open. **Telephone:** (804) 287-6313. **Fax:** (804) 289-8820.
Assistant Coaches: Charlie Goens, *Tag Montague. **Telephone:** (804) 289-8391.
Home Field: Pitt Field. **Seating Capacity:** 600. **Press Box Telephone:** (804) 289-8714.

RIDER BRONCS

Conference: Metro Atlantic.
Mailing Address: 2083 Lawrenceville Road, Lawrenceville, NJ. **Website:** www.gobroncs.com.
Head Coach: Barry Davis. **Telephone:** (609) 896-5055. **Baseball SID:** Bud Focht. **Telephone:** (609) 896-5138. **Fax:** (609) 896-0341.
Assistant Coaches: Jaime Steward. **Telephone:** (609) 895-5703.
Home Field: Sonny Pittaro Field. **Seating Capacity:** 1,000.

RUTGERS SCARLET KNIGHTS

Conference: Big East.
Mailing Address: 83 Rockafeller Rd, Piscataway, NJ 08854. **Website:** www.scarletknights.com.
Head Coach: Fred Hill. **Telephone:** (732) 445-7833. **Baseball SID:** Jimmy Gill. **Telephone:** (732) 445-4200. **Fax:** (732) 445-3063.
Assistant Coaches: Joe Litterio, Rick Freeman. **Telephone:** (732) 445-7834.
Home Field: Bainton Field. **Seating Capacity:** 1,500. **Press Box Telephone:** (732) 921-1067.

SACRAMENTO STATE HORNETS

Conference: Western Athletic.
Mailing Address: 600 J Street, Sacramento, CA 95819-6099. **Website:** www.hornetsports.com.
Head Coach: Reggie Christiansen. **Telephone:** (916) 278-4036. **Baseball SID:** Joe Waltasti. **Telephone:** (916) 278-6896. **Fax:** (916) 278-5429.
Assistant Coaches: Thad Johnson, *Tommy Nicholson. **Telephone:** (916) 278-4036.
Home Field: John Smith Field. **Seating Capacity:** 1,050. **Press Box Telephone:** (916) 889-6643.

SACRED HEART PIONEERS

Conference: Northeast.
Mailing Address: 5151 Park Ave, Fairfield, CT 06825.
Website: www.sacredheartpioneers.com.
Head Coach: Nick Giaquinto. **Telephone:** (203) 365-7632. **Baseball SID:** Randal Brochu. **Telephone:** (203) 396-8127. **Fax:** (203) 371-7889.
Assistant Coaches: *Tyler Kavanaugh, Wayne Mazzoni. **Telephone:** (203) 365-7632, (203) 365-4469.
Home Field: Ballpark at Harbor Yard. **Seating Capacity:** 5,500.

ST. BONAVENTURE BONNIES

Conference: Atlantic 10.
Mailing Address: PO Box G, Reilly Center, St. Bonaventure, NY 14778. **Website:** gobonnies.com.
Head Coach: Larry Sudbrook. **Telephone:** (716) 375-2641. **Baseball SID:** Jason MacBain. **Telephone:** (716) 375-4019. **Fax:** (716) 375-2383.
Assistant Coaches: Jamie Wallschlaeger, Nick LaBella. **Telephone:** (716) 375-2699.
Home Field: Fred Handler Park.

ST. JOHN'S RED STORM

Conference: Big East.
Mailing Address: 8000 Utopia Parkway, Queens, NY 11439. **Website:** www.redstormsports.com.
Head Coach: Ed Blankmeyer. **Telephone:** (718) 990-6148. **Baseball SID:** Tim Brown. **Telephone:** (718) 990-1521. **Fax:** (718) 969-8468.
Assistant Coaches: Scott Brown, *Mike Hampton. **Telephone:** (718) 990-7523.
Home Field: Jack Kaiser Stadium. **Seating Capacity:** 3,500. **Press Box Telephone:** (718) 990-2724.

ST. JOSEPH'S HAWKS

Conference: Atlantic 10.
Mailing Address: 5600 City Ave, Philadelphia, PA 19131. **Website:** sjuhawks.com.
Head Coach: Fritz Hamburg. **Telephone:** (610) 660-1718. **Baseball SID:** Joe Greenwich. **Telephone:** (610) 660-1738. **Fax:** (610) 660-1724.
Assistant Coaches: *Jacob Gill, Greg Manco. **Telephone:** (610) 660-1704.
Home Field: Campbell's Field. **Seating Capacity:** 6,425.

ST. PETER'S PEACOCKS

Conference: Metro Atlantic.
Mailing Address: 2641 Kennedy Blvd, Jersey City, NJ 07306. **Website:** www.spc.edu.
Head Coach: Derek England. **Telephone:** (201) 761-7319. **Baseball SID:** Scott Johnson. **Telephone:** (201) 761-7315. **Fax:** (201) 761-7317.
Assistant Coaches: Sean Cashman, Joe Romano. **Telephone:** (201) 761-7318.

SAINT LOUIS BILLIKENS

Conference: Atlantic 10.
Mailing Address: 3330 Laclede Ave, St Louis, MO 63103. **Website:** www.slubillikens.com.
Head Coach: Darin Hendrickson. **Telephone:** (314) 977-3172. **Baseball SID:** Jake Gossage. **Telephone:** (314) 977-2524. **Fax:** (314) 977-3178.
Assistant Coaches: Will Bradley, *Kevin Moulder. **Telephone:** (314) 977-3260.
Home Field: Billiken Sports Center. **Seating Capacity:** 500. **Press Box Telephone:** (314) 956-1265.

ST. MARY'S GAELS

Conference: West Coast.
Mailing Address: 1928 Saint Mary's Road, Moraga, CA 94575. **Website:** www.smcgaels.com.
Head Coach: Jedd N Soto, Sr. **Telephone:** (925) 631-4637. **Baseball SID:** Matt Fontenont. **Telephone:** (925) 631-4950. **Fax:** (925) 376-0829.
Assistant Coaches: *Lloyd Acosta, Gabe Zappin-. **Telephone:** (925) 631-4637.
Home Field: Louis Guisto Field. **Seating Capacity:** 1,000. **Press Box Telephone:** (925) 376-3906.

SAM HOUSTON STATE BEARKATS

Conference: Southland.
Mailing Address: 620 Bowers Blvd, Huntsville, TX 77341 Website: gobearkats.com.
Head Coach: David Pierce. **Telephone:** (936) 294-1731. **Baseball SID:** Paul Ridings. **Telephone:** (936) 294-1764. **Fax:** (936) 294-3538.
Assistant Coaches: *Sean Allen, Philip Miller. **Telephone:** (936) 294-4435.
Home Field: Don Sanders. **Seating Capacity:** 1,463. **Press Box Telephone:** (936) 294-4132.

SAMFORD BULLDOGS

Conference: Southern.
Mailing Address: 800 Lakeshore Dr, Birmingham AL 35229. **Website:** samfordsports.cstv.com.
Head Coach: Casey Dunn. **Telephone:** (205) 726-2134. **Baseball SID:** Joey Mullins. **Telephone:** (205) 726-2799. **Fax:** (205) 726-2132.
Assistant Coaches: *Tony David, Mick Fieldbinder. **Telephone:** (205) 726-4095.
Home Field: Joe Lee Griffin Field. **Seating Capacity:** 1,000. **Press Box Telephone:** (205) 726-4167.

SAN DIEGO TOREROS

Conference: West Coast.
Mailing Address: 5998 Alcala Park, San Diego, CA 92110. **Website:** usdtoreros.cstv.com.
Head Coach: Rich Hill. **Telephone:** (619) 260-5953. **Baseball SID:** Chris Loucks. **Telephone:** (619) 260-7930. **Fax:** (619) 260-2213.
Assistant Coaches: *Jay Johnson, Tyler Kincaid. **Telephone:** (619) 260-5989.
Home Field: Cunningham Stadium. **Seating Capacity:** 1,200. **Press Box Telephone:** (619) 260-8829.

SAN DIEGO STATE AZTECS

Conference: Mountain West.
Mailing Address: Athletic Dept 5402 55th Street, San Diego, CA 92182. **Website:** www.goaztecs.com.
Head Coach: Tony Gwynn. **Telephone:** (619) 594-6889. **Baseball SID:** Dave Kuhn. **Telephone:** (619) 594-5242. **Fax:** (619) 582-6541.
Assistant Coaches: Mark Martinez, *Eric Valenzuela. **Telephone:** (619) 594-3357.
Home Field: Tony Gwynn Stadium. **Seating Capacity:** 3,000. **Press Box Telephone:** (619) 594-4103.

SAN FRANCISCO DONS

Conference: West Coast.
Mailing Address: 2130 Fulton Street, San Francisco, CA 94118. **Website:** www.usfdons.com.
Head Coach: Nino Giarratano. **Telephone:** (415) 422-2933. **Baseball SID:** Ryan McCrary. **Telephone:** (415) 422-6162. **Fax:** (415) 422-2510.
Assistant Coaches: Greg Moore, *Troy Nakamura. **Telephone:** (415) 422-2393.

Home Field: Benedetti Diamond. **Seating Capacity:** 1,500. **Press Box Telephone:** (415) 422-2919.

SAN JOSE STATE SPARTANS

Conference: Western Athletic.
Mailing Address: 1393 South 7th Street, San Jose, CA 95112. **Website:** www.sjsuspartans.com.
Head Coach: Sam Piraro. **Telephone:** (408) 924-1255. **Baseball SID:** Mark Rivera. **Telephone:** (408) 924-1211. **Fax:** (408) 924-1291.
Assistant Coaches: Mark O'Brien, *Jeff Pritchard. **Telephone:** (408) 924-1467.
Home Field: Municipal Stadium. **Seating Capacity:** 5,200. **Press Box Telephone:** (408) 924-7276.

SANTA CLARA BRONCOS

Conference: West Coast.
Mailing Address: 500 El Camino Real, Santa Clara, CA 95053. **Website:** www.santaclarabroncos.com.
Head Coach: Dan O'Brien. **Telephone:** (408) 554-4882. **Baseball SID:** Joey Karp. **Telephone:** (408) 554-4670. **Fax:** (408) 554-6969.
Assistant Coaches: *Gabe Ribas, Eddie Smith. **Telephone:** (408) 554-4151.
Home Field: Stephen Schott Stadium. **Seating Capacity:** 1,500. **Press Box Telephone:** (408) 554-5587.

SAVANNAH STATE TIGERS

Conference: Independent.
Mailing Address: 3219 College St, Savannah, GA 31404. **Website:** www.ssuathletics.com.
Head Coach: Carlton Hardy. **Telephone:** (912) 358-3082. **Baseball SID:** Opio Mashariki. **Telephone:** (912) 356-2446. **Fax:** (912) 353-5287.
Assistant Coach: Anthony Macon, Blake Miller. **Telephone:** (912) 358-3082.

SEATTLE REDHAWKS

Conference: Independent.
Mailing Address: 901 12th Avenue, PO Box 222000, Seattle, WA, 98122. **Website:** www.goseattleu.com.
Head Coach: Donny Harrel. **Assistant Coaches:** *Casey Powell, Dave Wainhouse. **Telephone:** (206) 398-4399. **Baseball SID:** Jason Behenna. **Telephone:** (206) 296-5915. **Fax:** (206) 296-2154.
Home Field: Bannerwood Park. **Seating Capacity:** 1,200.

SETON HALL PIRATES

Conference: Big East.
Mailing Address: 400 South Orange Ave, South Orange, N.J. 07079. **Website:** www.shupirates.com.
Head Coach: Rob Sheppard. **Telephone:** (973) 761-9557. **Baseball SID:** Matt Sweeney. **Telephone:** (973) 761-9493. **Fax:** (973) 761-9061.
Assistant Coaches: *Phil Cundari, Mark Pappas. **Telephone:** (973) 275-6437.
Home Field: Owen T Carroll Field. **Seating Capacity:** 1,800. **Press Box Telephone:** (973) 670-2752.

SIENA SAINTS

Conference: Metro Atlantic.
Mailing Address: 515 Loudon Rd, Loudonville, NY 12211. **Website:** www.sienasaints.com.
Head Coach: Tony Rossi. **Telephone:** (518) 786-5044. **Baseball SID:** Jason Rich. **Telephone:** (518) 783-2411. **Fax:** (518) 783-2992.
Assistant Coaches: *George Brown, Ryan Myers. **Telephone:** (518) 782-6875.
Home Field: Siena Field. **Seating Capacity:** 1,000.

Press Box Telephone: (518) 542-7240.

SOUTH ALABAMA JAGUARS

Conference: Sun Belt.
Mailing Address: 5950 Old Shell Road, Mitchell Center Room 1209, Mobile, AL 36688. **Website:** www.usajaguars.com.
Head Coach: Mark Calvi. **Telephone:** (251) 414-8243. **Baseball SID:** Charlie Nichols. **Telephone:** (251) 414-8017. **Fax:** (251) 460-7297.
Assistant Coaches: Bob Keller, *Jerry Zulli. **Telephone:** (251) 414-8209.
Home Field: Stanky Field. **Seating Capacity:** 3,575. **Press Box Telephone:** (251) 461-1842.

SOUTH CAROLINA GAMECOCKS

Conference: Southeastern (East).
Mailing Address: 431 Williams St, Columbia, SC 29201. **Website:** www.gamecocksonline.com.
Head Coach: Ray Tanner. **Telephone:** (803) 777-5257. **Baseball SID:** Andrew Kitick. **Telephone:** (803) 777-5257. **Fax:** (803) 777-2967.
Assistant Coaches: *Chad Holbrook, Jerry Meyers. **Telephone:** (803) 777-9913.
Home Field: Carolina Stadium. **Seating Capacity:** 8,242. **Press Box Telephone:** (803) 777-6648.

SOUTH CAROLINA-UPSTATE SPARTANS

Conference: Atlantic Sun.
Mailing Address: 800 University Way, Spartanburg, SC, 29303. **Website:** upstatespartans.com.
Head Coach: Matt Fincher. **Telephone:** (864) 503-5135. **Baseball SID:** Alex Edwards. **Telephone:** (864) 503-5166. **Fax:** (864) 503-5127.
Assistant Coaches: Dusty Blake, *Grant Rembert. **Telephone:** (864) 503-5164.
Home Field: Cleveland S Harley Baseball Park. **Seating Capacity:** 500. **Press Box Telephone:** (864) 503-5058.

SOUTH DAKOTA STATE JACKRABBITS

Conference: Summit.
Mailing Address: 2820 HPER Center, Brookings, SD 57007-1497. **Website:** gojacks.com.
Head Coach: Dave Schrage. **Telephone:** (605) 688-5027. **Baseball SID:** Jason Hove. **Telephone:** (605) 688-4623. **Fax:** (605) 688-5999.
Assistant Coaches: *Brian Grunzke, Tyler Oakes. **Telephone:** (605) 688-5778.
Home Field: Erv Huether Field. **Seating Capacity:** 500. **Press Box Telephone:** (605) 695-1827.

SOUTH FLORIDA BULLS

Conference: Big East.
Mailing Address: 4202 E Fowler Ave ATH 100, Tampa, FL 33620. **Website:** www.GoUSFBulls.com.
Head Coach: Lelo Prado. **Telephone:** (813) 974-2504. **Baseball SID:** Ashlee Walker. **Telephone:** (813) 974-4087. **Fax:** (813) 974-4029.
Assistant Coaches: *Chris Heintz, Chuck Hernandez. **Telephone:** (813) 974-2995.
Home Field: USF BASEBALL STADIUM. **Seating Capacity:** 3,211. **Press Box Telephone:** (813) 410-1194.

SOUTHEAST MISSOURI STATE REDHAWKS

Conference: Ohio Valley.
Mailing Address: 1 University Plaza, Cape Girardeau, MO 63701. **Website:** gosoutheast.com.
Head Coach: Mark Hogan. **Telephone:** (573) 986-6002. **Baseball SID:** Nick Seeman. **Telephone:** (573) 651-2294. **Fax:** (573) 651-2810.

Assistant Coaches: *Steve Bieser, Chris Cafalone. Telephone: (573) 986-6002.
Home Field: Capaha Field. Seating Capacity: 2,000. Press Box Telephone: (573) 651-9139.

SOUTHEASTERN LOUISIANA LIONS

Conference: Southland.
Mailing Address: SLU Athletics 800 Galloway Dr, Hammond, LA 70402. Website: www.lionsports.net.
Head Coach: Jay Artigues. Telephone: (985) 549-3566.
Baseball SID: Damon Sunde. Telephone: (985) 549-3774. Fax: (985) 549-3773.
Assistant Coaches: Daniel Latham, *Matt Riser. Telephone: (985) 549-2897.
Home Field: Alumni Field. Seating Capacity: 2,500. Press Box Telephone: (985) 549-2431.

SOUTHERN JAGUARS

Conference: Southwestern Athletic.
Mailing Address: Southern University Harding Boulevar, Baton Rouge, LA 70813. Website: gojagsports.com.
Head Coach: Roger Cador. Telephone: (225) 771-2513.
Baseball SID: Chris Jones. Telephone: (225) 771-3495.
Assistant Coaches: *Fernando Puebla, Chris King. Telephone: (225) 771-3712.
Home Field: Lee-Hines Stadium. Seating Capacity: 1,500.

SOUTHERN CALIFORNIA TROJANS

Conference: Pacific-12.
Mailing Address: 1021 Childs Way, Los Angeles, CA 90089. Website: usctrojans.com.
Head Coach: Frank Cruz. Telephone: (213) 740-5762.
Baseball SID: Chris Roberts. Telephone: (213) 740-3809. Fax: (213) 740-7584.
Assistant Coaches: Gabe Alvarez, *Dan Hubbs. Telephone: (213) 740-8448.
Home Field: Dedeaux Field. Seating Capacity: 2,500. Press Box Telephone: (213) 748 3409.

SOUTHERN ILLINOIS SALUKIS

Conference: Missouri Valley.
Mailing Address: 425 Saluki Dr, Carbondale, IL 62901. Website: siusalukis.com.
Head Coach: Ken Henderson. Telephone: (618) 453-3794. Baseball SID: Scott Gierman. Telephone: (618) 453-5470. Fax: (618) 453-2648.
Assistant Coaches: *PJ Finigan, Ryan Strain. Telephone: (618) 453-7646.
Home Field: Abe Martin Field. Seating Capacity: 2,000. Press Box Telephone: (618) 453-3794.

SOUTHERN ILLINOIS-EDWARDSVILLE COUGARS

Conference: Independent.
Mailing Address: 1 University Drive, Edwardsville, IL 62026. Website: www.siuecougars.com.
Head Coach: Gary Collins. Telephone: (618) 650-2872.
Baseball SID: Joe Pott. Telephone: (618) 650-2860. Fax: (618) 650-3369.
Assistant Coaches: Danny Jackson, *Tony Stoecklin. Telephone: (618) 650-2032.
Home Field: Simmons Baseball Complex. Seating Capacity: 1,000. Press Box Telephone: (314) 707-1712.

SOUTHERN MISSISSIPPI GOLDEN EAGLES

Conference: Conference USA.
Mailing Address: 118 College Dr, #5161, Hattiesburg, MS 39406. Website: www.southernmiss.com.
Head Coach: Scott Berry. Telephone: (601) 266-5821.

Baseball SID: Jack Duggan. Telephone: (601) 266-5947. Fax: (601) 266-4507.
Assistant Coaches: *Chad Caillet, Michael Federico. Telephone: (601) 266-5891.
Home Field: Pete Taylor Park. Seating Capacity: 3,800. Press Box Telephone: (601) 266-5428.

SOUTHERN UTAH THUNDERBIRDS

Conference: Summit.
Mailing Address: 351 West University Blvd, Cedar City, Utah 84720. Website: www.suutbirds.com.
Head Coach: David Eldredge. Telephone: (435) 327-0452. Baseball SID: Kyle Newhouse. Telephone: (435) 586-7758. Fax: (435) 865-8037.
Assistant Coaches: *Chase Hudson, Dustin Wittwer. Telephone: (509) 301-8843.
Home Field: Thunderbird Park. Seating Capacity: 500. Press Box Telephone: (801) 336-8959.

STANFORD CARDINAL

Conference: Pacific-10.
Mailing Address: 641 E Campus Dr, Stanford, CA 94305. Website: gostanford.com.
Head Coach: Mark Marquess. Assistant Coaches: Rusty Filter, *Dean Stotz. Telephone: (650) 723-4528.
Baseball SID: Niall Adler. Telephone: (650) 725-2959. Fax: (650) 725-2957.
Assistant Coaches: Rusty Filter, *Dean Stotz. Telephone: (650) 725-2373, (650) 723-9528.
Home Field: Klein Field at Sunken Diamond. Seating Capacity: 4,000. Press Box Telephone: (650) 723-4629.

STEPHEN F. AUSTIN STATE LUMBERJACKS

Conference: Southland.
Mailing Address: PO Box 13010, SFA Station, Nacogdoches, TX 75962. Website: www.sfajacks.com.
Head Coach: Johnny Cardenas. Telephone: (936) 468-5982. Baseball SID: Ben Rikard. Telephone: (936) 468-5801. Fax: (936) 468-4593.
Assistant Coaches: *Chris Connally, Chad Massengale. Telephone: (936) 559-9957.
Home Field: Jaycees Field. Seating Capacity: 1,000. Press Box Telephone: (036) 559-8344.

STETSON HATTERS

Conference: Atlantic Sun.
Mailing Address: 421 N Woodland Blvd Unit 8359, DeLand, FL, 32723. Website: www.gohatters.com.
Head Coach: Pete Dunn. Telephone: (386) 822-8106.
Baseball SID: Ricky Hazel. Telephone: (386) 822-8130. Fax: (386) 822-7486.
Assistant Coaches: *Mark Leavitt, Chris Roberts. Telephone: (386) 822-8733.
Home Field: Melching Field at Conrad Park. Seating Capacity: 2,500. Press Box Telephone: (386) 736-7360.

STONY BROOK SEAWOLVES

Conference: America East.
Mailing Address: Stony Brook University, Indoor Sports Complex, Stony Brook, NY, 11794-3500. Website: goseawolves.cstv.com.
Head Coach: Matt Senk. Telephone: (631) 632-9226.
Baseball SID: Jeremy Cohen. Telephone: (631) 632-6328. Fax: (631) 632-8841.
Assistant Coaches: Mike Marron, *Joe Pennucci. Telephone: (631) 632-4755.
Home Field: Joe Nathan Field. Press Box Telephone: (860) 690-3482.

TEMPLE OWLS

Conference: Atlantic Sun.
Mailing Address: 1700 North Broad Street, Philadelphia, PA 19122. **Website:** www.owlsports.com.
Head Coach: Ryan Wheeler. **Telephone:** (215) 204-8639. **Baseball SID:** Alex Samuelian. **Telephone:** (215) 204-7445. **Fax:** (215) 933-5257.
Assistant Coaches: *Brian Pugh, Mike Hickey. **Telephone:** (215) 204-8640.
Home Field: Skip Wilson Field. **Seating Capacity:** 1,000. **Press Box Telephone:** (609) 969-0975.

TENNESSEE VOLUNTEERS

Conference: Southeastern (East).
Mailing Address: 1511 Pat Summitt Drive, Knoxville, TN 37996. **Website:** www.UTsports.com.
Head Coach: Dave Serrano. **Telephone:** (865) 974-2057. **Baseball SID:** Cameron Harris. **Telephone:** (865) 974-8876. **Fax:** (865) 974-8875.
Assistant Coaches: Greg Bergeron, *Bill Mosiello. **Telephone:** (865) 974-2057.
Home Field: Lindsey Nelson Stadium. **Seating Capacity:** 3,800. **Press Box Telephone:** (865) 974-3376.

TENNESSEE TECH GOLDEN EAGLES

Conference: Ohio Valley.
Mailing Address: Box 5057 1100 McGee Blvd, Cookeville, TN 38505-0001. **Website:** www.ttusports.com.
Head Coach: Matt Bragga. **Telephone:** (931) 372-3925. **Baseball SID:** Nick Burns. **Telephone:** (931) 372-6139.
Assistant Coaches: Matt Mihoci, *Donnie Suttles. **Telephone:** (931) 372-6546.
Home Field: Bush Stadium at Averitt Express Baseball Complex. **Seating Capacity:** 1100.

TENNESSEE-MARTIN SKYHAWKS

Conference: Ohio Valley.
Mailing Address: 1022 Elam Center, 15 Mt Pelia Road, Martin, TN 38238. **Website:** www.utmsports.com.
Head Coach: *Bubba Cates. **Telephone:** (731) 881-7337. **Baseball SID:** Joe Lofaro. **Telephone:** (731) 881-7632. **Fax:** (731) 881-7624.
Assistant Coaches: Brad Goss. **Telephone:** (731) 881-3691.
Home Field: Skyhawk Field. **Seating Capacity:** 500. **Press Box Telephone:** (270) 703-2601.

TEXAS LONGHORNS

Conference: Big 12.
Mailing Address: 2100 San Jacinto Boulevard, Bellmont Hall 327, Austin, TX 78712. **Website:** www.TexasSports.com.
Head Coach: Augie Garrido. **Telephone:** (512) 471-5732. **Baseball SID:** Thomas Dick. **Telephone:** (512) 471-6039. **Fax:** (512) 471-6040.
Assistant Coaches: *Tommy Harmon, Skip Johnson. **Telephone:** (512) 471-5732.
Home Field: UFCU Disch-Falk Field. **Seating Capacity:** 6,649.

TEXAS A&M AGGIES

Conference: Big 12.
Mailing Address: PO Box 30017, College Station, TX 77842-3017. **Website:** AggieAthletics.com.
Head Coach: Rob Childress. **Telephone:** (979) 845-4810. **Baseball SID:** Adam Quisenberry. **Telephone:** (979) 862-5453. **Fax:** (979) 845-6825.
Assistant Coaches: Andy Sawyers, *Justin Seely. **Telephone:** (979) 845-4810.

Home Field: Olsen Field at Blue Bell Park. **Seating Capacity:** 6,100. **Press Box Telephone:** (979) 458-3604.

TEXAS A&M-CORPUS CHRISTI ISLANDERS

Conference: Southland.
Mailing Address: 6300 Ocean Dr, Unit 5719, Corpus Christi, TX 78412. **Website:** www.goislanders.com.
Head Coach: Scott Malone. **Telephone:** (361) 825-3413. **Baseball SID:** Josh Brown. **Telephone:** (361) 825-3411. **Fax:** (361) 825-3218.
Assistant Coaches: *Chris Ramirez, Marty Smith. **Telephone:** (361) 825-3252.
Home Field: Chapman Field. **Seating Capacity:** 700. **Press Box Telephone:** (337) 302-4722.

TEXAS CHRISTIAN HORNED FROGS

Conference: Mountain West.
Mailing Address: 3500 Berry St, Fort Worth, TX 76129. **Website:** www.gofrogs.com.
Head Coach: Jim Schlossnagle. **Telephone:** (817) 257-5354. **Baseball SID:** Brandie Davidson. **Telephone:** (817) 257-7479. **Fax:** (817) 257-7964.
Assistant Coaches: Randy Mazey, *Tony Vitello. **Telephone:** (817) 257-5656.
Home Field: Lupton Stadium. **Seating Capacity:** 4,500. **Press Box Telephone:** (817) 257-7966.

TEXAS SOUTHERN TIGERS

Conference: Southwestern Athletic.
Mailing Address: 3100 Cleburne Street, Houston, TX 77004. **Website:** www.tsu.edu.
Head Coach: Michael Robertson. **Telephone:** (713) 313-4315. **Baseball SID:** Rodney Bush. **Telephone:** (713) 313-7603. **Fax:** (713) 313-1045.
Assistant Coaches: *Marqus Johnson, Calvin Medlock. **Telephone:** (713) 313-7993.
Home Field: MacGregor Park. **Seating Capacity:** 500.

TEXAS STATE BOBCATS

Conference: Southland.
Mailing Address: 601 University Dr, San Marcos, TX 78666. **Website:** txstatebobcats.com.
Head Coach: Ty Harrington. **Telephone:** (512) 245-7566. **Baseball SID:** Steve Appelhans. **Telephone:** (512) 245-4387. **Fax:** (512) 245-8387.
Assistant Coaches: Jeremy Fikac, *Derek Matlock. **Telephone:** (512) 245-8395.
Home Field: Bobcat Ballpark. **Seating Capacity:** 2,400. **Press Box Telephone:** (512) 245-5739.

TEXAS TECH RED RAIDERS

Conference: Big 12.
Mailing Address: Box 43021, 6th and Boston Ave, Lubbock, TX 79409. **Website:** www.texastech.com.
Head Coach: Dan Spencer. **Telephone:** (806) 742-3355. **Baseball SID:** Blayne Beal. **Telephone:** (806) 742-2770. **Fax:** (806) 742-1970.
Assistant Coaches: Jim Horner, *Tim Tadlock. **Telephone:** (806) 742-3355.
Home Field: Rip Griffin Park.

TEXAS-ARLINGTON MAVERICKS

Conference: Southland.
Mailing Address: 1309 West Mitchell Street, Arlington, TX 76019. **Website:** utamavs.com.
Head Coach: Darin Thomas. **Telephone:** (817) 272-2542. **Baseball SID:** Art Garcia. **Telephone:** (817) 272-2239. **Fax:** (817) 272-5037.
Assistant Coaches: KJ Hendricks, *Jay Sirianni. **Telephone:** (817) 272-0111, (817) 272-7625.

Home Field: Clay Gould Ballpark. **Seating Capacity:** 1,600. **Press Box Telephone:** (817) 462-4225.

TEXAS-PAN AMERICAN BRONCS

Conference: Independent.
Mailing Address: 1201 W University Dr, Edinburg, TX 78539. **Website:** utpabroncs.com.
Head Coach: Manny Mantrana. **Telephone:** (956) 665-2235. **Baseball SID:** Jonah Goldberg. **Telephone:** (956) 665-2240. **Fax:** (956) 665-2261.
Assistant Coaches: Robert Clayton, *Norberto Lopez. **Telephone:** (956) 665-2891.
Home Field: Edinburg Baseball Stadium. **Seating Capacity:** 5,500.

TEXAS-SAN ANTONIO ROADRUNNERS

Conference: Southland.
Mailing Address: One UTSA Circle, San Antonio, TX 78249. **Website:** www.goutsa.com.
Head Coach: Sherman Corbett. **Telephone:** (210) 458-4805. **Baseball SID:** Tony Baldwin. **Telephone:** (210) 458-6460. **Fax:** (210) 458-4813.
Assistant Coaches: Brett Lawler, *Jason Marshall. **Telephone:** (210) 458-4195.
Home Field: Roadrunner Field. **Seating Capacity:** 800. **Press Box Telephone:** (210) 458-4612.

TOLEDO ROCKETS

Conference: Mid-American (West).
Mailing Address: 2801 West Bancroft Street, Toledo, OH 43606. **Website:** utrockets.com.
Head Coach: Cory Mee. **Telephone:** (419) 530-6263. **Baseball SID:** Brian DeBenedictis. **Telephone:** (419) 530-4919. **Fax:** (419) 530-4428.
Assistant Coaches: *Josh Bradford, Nick McIntyre. **Telephone:** (419) 530-3097.
Home Field: Scott Park. **Seating Capacity:** 1,000. **Press Box Telephone:** (419) 530-3089.

TOWSON TIGERS

Conference: Colonial Athletic.
Mailing Address: 8000 York Road, Towson, MD 21252. **Website:** www.towsontigers.com.
Head Coach: Mike Gottlieb. **Telephone:** (410) 704-3775. **Baseball SID:** Dan O'Connell. **Telephone:** (410) 704-3102. **Fax:** (410) 704-3861.
Assistant Coaches: Scott Roane. **Telephone:** (410) 704-4587.
Home Field: John B Schuerholz Park. **Seating Capacity:** 500. **Press Box Telephone:** (410) 704-5810.

TROY TROJANS

Conference: Sun Belt.
Mailing Address: 5000 Veterans Stadium Drive, Troy, AL, 36082. **Website:** www.TroyTrojans.com.
Head Coach: Bobby Pierce. **Telephone:** (334) 670-3489. **Baseball SID:** Tyler Pigg. **Telephone:** (334) 670-5655. **Fax:** (334) 670-5665.
Assistant Coaches: Brad Phillips, *Mark Smartt. **Telephone:** (334) 670-5705.
Home Field: Riddle-Pace Field. **Seating Capacity:** 2,000. **Press Box Telephone:** (334) 670-5701.

TULANE GREEN WAVE

Conference: Conference USA.
Mailing Address: Ben Weiner Drive, New Orleans, LA 70118. **Website:** www.TulaneGreenWave.com.
Head Coach: Rick Jones. **Telephone:** (504) 862-8238. **Baseball SID:** Greg Campbell. **Telephone:** (504) 314-7271. **Fax:** (504) 862-8569.

Assistant Coaches: *Jake Gautreau, Chad Sutter. **Telephone:** (504) 314-7203.
Home Field: Greer Field at Truchin Stadium. **Seating Capacity:** 5,000. **Press Box Telephone:** (504) 615-8059.

UTAH UTES

Conference: Pacific-12.
Mailing Address: 1825 E South Campus Dr, Salt Lake City, UT 84112-0900. **Website:** utahutes.com.
Head Coach: Bill Kinneberg. **Telephone:** (801) 581-3526. **Baseball SID:** Brooke Frederickson. **Telephone:** (801) 493-9254.
Assistant Coaches: *Michael Crawford, Bryan Kinneberg. **Telephone:** (801) 581-3024.
Home Field: Spring Mobile Ballpark. **Seating Capacity:** 15,500.

UTAH VALLEY WOLVERINES

Conference: Independent.
Mailing Address: 800 W University Parkway, Orem, Utah 84058. **Website:** www.WolverineGreen.com.
Head Coach: Eric Madsen. **Telephone:** (801) 863-6509. **Baseball SID:** Clint Burgi. **Telephone:** (801) 863-8644. **Fax:** (801) 863-8813.
Assistant Coaches: *Dave Carter, Mike Martin. **Telephone:** (801) 863-8647, (801) 863-7586.
Home Field: Brent Brown Ballpark. **Seating Capacity:** 5,000. **Press Box Telephone:** (801) 362-1548.

VALPARAISO CRUSADERS

Conference: Horizon.
Mailing Address: 1009 Union Street, Valparaiso, IN 46383. **Website:** www.valpoathletics.com.
Head Coach: *Tracy Woodson. **Telephone:** (219) 464-5239. **Baseball SID:** Ryan Wronkowicz. **Telephone:** (219) 464-5232. **Fax:** (219) 464-5762.
Assistant Coaches: Brian Schmack. **Telephone:** (219) 464-6117.
Home Field: Emory G. Bauer Field. **Seating Capacity:** 500. **Press Box Telephone:** (219) 464-6006.

VANDERBILT COMMODORES

Conference: Southeastern (East).
Mailing Address: 2601 Jess Neely Drive, Nashville, TN 37212. **Website:** www.vucommodores.com.
Head Coach: Tim Corbin. **Telephone:** (615) 322-3716. **Baseball SID:** Kyle Parkinson. **Telephone:** (615) 322-0020. **Fax:** (615) 343-7064.
Assistant Coaches: *Josh Holliday, Derek Johnson. **Telephone:** (615) 322-3074.
Home Field: Hawkins Field. **Seating Capacity:** 3,700. **Press Box Telephone:** (615) 320-0436.

VILLANOVA WILDCATS

Conference: Big East.
Mailing Address: 800 E Lancaster Avenue, Jake Nevin Field House, Villanova, PA 19085. **Website:** villanova.com.
Head Coach: Joe Godri. **Telephone:** (610) 519-4529. **Baseball SID:** David Berman. **Telephone:** (610) 519-4122. **Fax:** (610) 519-7323.
Assistant Coaches: *Jim Carone, Deron Spink. **Telephone:** (610) 519-5520, (610) 519-5520.
Home Field: Villanova Ballpark at Plymouth. **Seating Capacity:** 750. **Press Box Telephone:** (860) 490-6398.

VIRGINIA CAVALIERS

Conference: Atlantic Coast (Coastal).
Mailing Address: PO Box 400853, Charlottesville, VA 22904-4853. **Website:** www.virginiasports.com.
Head Coach: Brian O'Connor. **Telephone:** (434) 982-

4932. **Baseball SID:** Andy Fledderjohann. **Telephone:** (434) 982-5131. **Fax:** (434) 982-5525.

Assistant Coaches: Karl Kuhn, *Kevin McMullan. **Telephone:** (434) 982-5776.

Home Field: Davenport Field. **Seating Capacity:** 5,074. **Press Box Telephone:** (434) 244-4071.

VIRGINIA COMMONWEALTH RAMS

Conference: Colonial Athletic.

Mailing Address: 1300 W Broad St, Richmond, VA 23284. **Website:** www.vcuathletics.com.

Head Coach: Paul Keyes. **Telephone:** (804) 828-4820. **Baseball SID:** Jon Nolan. **Telephone:** (804) 828-9567. **Fax:** (804) 828-9428.

Assistant Coaches: Jeff Palumbo, *Shawn Stiffler. **Telephone:** (804) 828-4821.

Home Field: The Diamond. **Seating Capacity:** 9,750. **Press Box Telephone:** (302) 593-0115.

VIRGINIA MILITARY INSTITUTE KEYDETS

Conference: Big South.

Mailing Address: Cameron Hall, Lexington, VA, 24450. **Website:** Big South.

Head Coach: Marlin Ikenberry. **Telephone:** (540) 464-7609. **Baseball SID:** Brad Salois. **Telephone:** (540) 464-7015. **Fax:** (540) 464-7583.

Assistant Coaches: Travis Beazley, *Jonathan Hadra. **Telephone:** (540) 464-7605.

Home Field: Gray-Minor Stadium. **Seating Capacity:** 1,000. **Press Box Telephone:** (540) 460-6920.

VIRGINIA TECH HOKIES

Conference: Atlantic Coast (Coastal).

Mailing Address: 460 Jamerson Athletic Center, Blacksburg, VA 24061-0502. **Website:** www.hokiesports.com.

Head Coach: Pete Hughes. **Telephone:** (540) 231-3671. **Baseball SID:** Marc Mullen. **Telephone:** (540) 231-1894. **Fax:** (540) 231-6984.

Assistant Coaches: Mike Kunigonis, *Pat Mason. **Telephone:** (540) 231-3671.

Home Field: English Field. **Seating Capacity:** 4,000. **Press Box Telephone:** (540) 231-8974.

WAGNER SEAHAWKS

Conference: Northeast.

Mailing Address: Spiro Sports Center; One Campus Road, Staten Island, NY 10301. **Website:** wagnerathletics.com.

Head Coach: Unavailable. **Telephone:** (718) 390-3154. **Baseball SID:** Kevin Ross. **Telephone:** (718) 390-3215. **Fax:** (718) 420-4015.

Assistant Coaches: Mike Consolmagno, Bill Malloy. **Telephone:** (718) 420-4121, (718) 420-4081.

Home Field: Richmond County Bank Ballpark. **Seating Capacity:** 6,900. **Press Box Telephone:** (716) 969-6126.

WAKE FOREST DEMON DEACONS

Conference: Atlantic Coast (Atlantic).

Mailing Address: 1834 Wake Forest Drive, Winston Salem, NC 27109. **Website:** wakeforestsports.com.

Head Coach: Tom Walter. **Telephone:** (336) 758-5570. **Baseball SID:** Steven Wright. **Telephone:** (336) 758-4120. **Fax:** (336) 758-5140.

Assistant Coaches: Bill Cilento, *Dennis Healy. **Telephone:** (336) 758-5645.

Home Field: Wake Forest Ballpark. **Seating Capacity:** 6,400. **Press Box Telephone:** (336) 759-7373.

WASHINGTON HUSKIES

Conference: Pacific-12.

Mailing Address: Graves Annex Box 354080, Seattle, WA 98195-4080. **Website:** www.gohuskies.com.

Head Coach: Lindsay Meggs. **Telephone:** (206) 543-9365. **Baseball SID:** Jeff Bechthold. **Telephone:** (206) 685-7910. **Fax:** (206) 543-5000.

Assistant Coaches: Dave Dangler, *Dave Nakama. **Telephone:** (206) 685-7016.

Home Field: Husky Ballpark. **Seating Capacity:** 2,200. **Press Box Telephone:** (206) 685-1994.

WASHINGTON STATE COUGARS

Conference: Pacific-12.

Mailing Address: 195 Bohler Athletic Complex, Pullman, WA 99164-1602. **Website:** wsucougars.cstv.com.

Head Coach: Donnie Marbut. **Telephone:** (509) 335-0332. **Baseball SID:** Craig Lawson. **Telephone:** (509) 335-0265. **Fax:** (206) 543-5000.

Assistant Coaches: *Spencer Allen, Gregg Swenson. **Telephone:** (509) 335-0216.

Home Field: Baily-Brayton. **Seating Capacity:** 3,500. **Press Box Telephone:** (509) 335-8291.

WEST VIRGINIA MOUNTAINEERS

Conference: Big East.

Mailing Address: PO Box 0877, Morgantown, WV 26507-0877. **Website:** www.msnsportsnet.com.

Head Coach: Greg Van Zant. **Telephone:** (304) 293-9881. **Baseball SID:** Grant Dovey. **Telephone:** (304) 293-2821. **Fax:** (304) 293-4105.

Assistant Coaches: *Pat Sherald, Jacob Weghorst. **Telephone:** (304) 293-0067.

Home Field: Hawley Field. **Seating Capacity:** 2,500. **Press Box Telephone:** (304) 293-5988.

WESTERN CAROLINA CATAMOUNTS

Conference: Southern.

Mailing Address: Ramsey Center, Cullowhee, NC 28723. **Website:** catamountsports.com.

Head Coach: Bobby Moranda. **Telephone:** (828) 227-7338. **Baseball SID:** Daniel Hooker. **Telephone:** (828) 227-2339. **Fax:** (828) 227-7688.

Assistant Coaches: *Alan Beck, Bruce Johnson. **Telephone:** (828) 227-2022.

Home Field: Childress Field at Hennon Stadium. **Seating Capacity:** 1,500. **Press Box Telephone:** (828) 227-7020.

WESTERN ILLINOIS FIGHTING LEATHERNECKS

Conference: Summit.

Mailing Address: 1 University Circle, Macomb, IL 61455 USA (309) 298-1414. **Website:** www.wiuathletics.com.

Head Coach: Mike Villano. **Telephone:** (309) 298-1521. **Baseball SID:** Cameron Weidenthaler. **Telephone:** (309) 298-1133. **Fax:** (309) 298-1960.

Assistant Coaches: *Shane Davis, Cooper Stewart. **Telephone:** (309) 298-1521.

Home Field: Alfred D. **Boyer Stadium. Seating Capacity:** 502. **Press Box Telephone:** (309) 298-3492.

WESTERN KENTUCKY HILLTOPPERS

Conference: Sun Belt.

Mailing Address: 1605 Avenue of Champions, Bowling Green, KY 42101. **Website:** www.wkusports.com.

Head Coach: Matt Myers. **Telephone:** (270) 745-2277. **Baseball SID:** Melissa Anderson. **Telephone:** (270) 745-3576. **Fax:** (270) 745-2573.

Assistant Coaches: *Blake Allen, Brendan Dougherty.

Telephone: (270) 745-2274.
Home Field: Nick Denes Field. **Seating Capacity:** 1,500. **Press Box Telephone:** (270) 745-6941.

WESTERN MICHIGAN BRONCOS

Conference: Mid-American (West).
Mailing Address: 1903 W Main, Kalamazoo, MI 49008.
Website: www.wmubroncos.com.
Head Coach: Billy Gernon. **Telephone:** (269) 276-3205.
Baseball SID: Kristin Keirns. **Telephone:** (269) 387-4123.
Fax: (269) 387-4122.
Assistant Coaches: Blaine McFerrin, *Bobby Walmsley.
Telephone: (269) 276-3208.
Home Field: Robert J. Bobb Stadium at Hyames Field.
Seating Capacity: 1,400.

WICHITA STATE SHOCKERS

Conference: Missouri Valley.
Mailing Address: 1845 Fairmount, Campus Box 18, Wichita, KS 67260-0018. **Website:** www.goshockers.com.
Head Coach: Gene Stephenson. **Telephone:** (316) 978-3636. **Baseball SID:** Tami Cutler. **Telephone:** (316) 978-5559. **Fax:** (316) 978-3336.
Assistant Coaches: *Brent Kemnitz, Jim Thomas.
Telephone: (316) 978-5303.
Home Field: Eck Stadium. **Seating Capacity:** 7,851.
Press Box Telephone: (316) 978-3390.

WILLIAM & MARY TRIBE

Conference: Colonial Athletic.
Mailing Address: PO Box 399, Williamsburg, VA 23187.
Website: www.tribeathletics.com.
Head Coach: Frank Leoni. **Telephone:** (757) 221-3399.
Baseball SID: Scott Burns. **Telephone:** (757) 221-3344.
Fax: (757) 221-2989.
Assistant Coaches: David Miller, *Jamie Pinzino.
Telephone: (757) 221-3475.
Home Field: Plumeri Park. **Seating Capacity:** 1,000.
Press Box Telephone: (757) 221-3998.

WINTHROP EAGLES

Conference: Big South.
Mailing Address: 1162 Eden Terrace, Rock Hill, SC 29733. **Website:** www.winthropeagles.com.
Head Coach: Tom Riginos. **Telephone:** (803) 323-2129.
Baseball SID: Wesley Herring. **Telephone:** (803) 323-2129. **Fax:** (803) 323-2433.
Assistant Coaches: *Clint Chrysler, Ben Hall.
Telephone: (803) 323-2129.
Home Field: The Winthrop Ballpark. **Seating Capacity:** 1,800. **Press Box Telephone:** (803) 323-2155.

WISCONSIN-MILWAUKEE PANTHERS

Conference: Horizon.
Mailing Address: UW-Milwaukee Baseball, 3409 N Downer Ave, Milwaukee, WI 53211. **Website:** uwmpanthers.com.
Head Coach: Scott Doffek. **Telephone:** (414) 229-5670.
Baseball SID: Chris Zills. **Telephone:** (414) 229-4593. **Fax:** (414) 229-4593.
Assistant Coaches: *Cory Bigler, Mike Goetz.
Telephone: (414) 229-2433.
Home Field: Henry Aaron Field. **Press Box Telephone:** (414) 750-2090.

WOFFORD TERRIERS

Conference: Southern.
Mailing Address: 429 N Church Street, Spartanburg, SC 29303. **Website:** athletics.wofford.edu.
Head Coach: Todd Interdonato. **Telephone:** (864) 597-4497. **Baseball SID:** Brent Williamson. **Telephone:** (864) 597-4093. **Fax:** (864) 597-4129.
Assistant Coaches: *Jason Burke, Phil Disher.
Telephone: (864) 597-4499.
Home Field: Russell C. King Field. **Seating Capacity:** 2500. **Press Box Telephone:** (864) 597-4487.

WRIGHT STATE RAIDERS

Conference: Horizon.
Mailing Address: 3640 Colonel Glenn Highway, Dayton, OH 45435. **Website:** wsuraiders.cstv.com.
Head Coach: Rob Cooper. **Telephone:** (937) 775-3667.
Baseball SID: Matt Zircher. **Telephone:** (937) 775-2831.
Fax: (937) 775-2368.
Assistant Coaches: *Greg Lovelady, Ross Oeder.
Telephone: (937) 775-4188.
Home Field: Nischwitz Stadium. **Seating Capacity:** 750. **Press Box Telephone:** (937) 602-0326.

XAVIER MUSKETEERS

Conference: Atlantic 10.
Mailing Address: 3800 Victory Pkwy, Cincinnati, OH 45207. **Website:** www.goxavier.com.
Head Coach: Scott Googins. **Telephone:** (513) 745-3727. **Baseball SID:** Jason Ashcraft. **Telephone:** (513) 745-3388. **Fax:** (513) 745-2825.
Assistant Coaches: Danny Hayden, *Nick Otte.
Telephone: (513) 745-2890.
Home Field: Hayden Field. **Seating Capacity:** 500.
Press Box Telephone: (513) 598-0327.

YALE BULLDOGS

Conference: Ivy League (Rolfe).
Mailing Address: 20 Tower Parkway, New Haven, CT 06511. **Website:** yalebulldogs.com.
Head Coach: John Stuper. **Telephone:** (203) 432-1466.
Baseball SID: Jon Erickson. **Telephone:** (203) 432-4747.
Assistant Coaches: *Tucker Frawley. **Telephone:** (203) 432-1467.
Home Field: Yale Field. **Seating Capacity:** 6,000.

YOUNGSTOWN STATE PENGUINS

Conference: Horizon.
Mailing Address: One University Plaza, Youngstown, OH, 44555. **Website:** www.ysusports.com.
Head Coach: Rich Pasquale. **Telephone:** (330) 941-3485. **Baseball SID:** John Vogel. **Telephone:** (330) 941-1480. **Fax:** (330) 941-3191.
Assistant Coaches: *Ed Marko, Bobby Pizzuto.
Telephone: (304) 633-8150.
Home Field: Eastwood Field. **Seating Capacity:** 6,000.
Press Box Telephone: (330) 505-0000, ext 229.

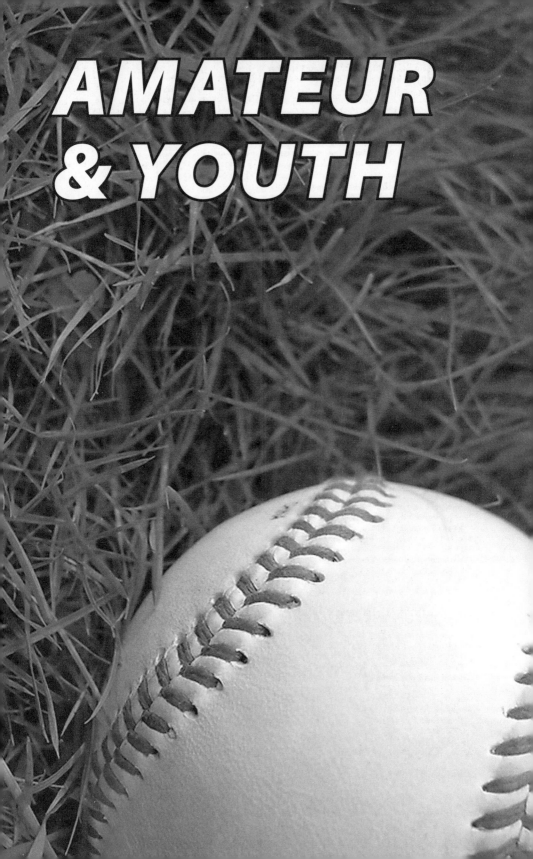

AMATEUR & YOUTH

INTERNATIONAL ORGANIZATIONS

INTERNATIONAL BASEBALL FEDERATION

Headquarters: Maison du Sport International – 54, Avenue de Rhodanie, 1007 Lausanne - Switzerland. **Telephone:** (+41-21) 318-82-40. **Fax:** (41-21) 318-82-41. **Website:** www.ibaf.org. **E-Mail:** ibaf@ibaf.org. **Year Founded:** 1938.
President: Riccardo Fraccari.
1st Vice President: Kazuhiro Tawa. **2nd Vice President:** Alonso Perez Gonzalez. **3rd Vice President:** Antonio Castro. **Secretary General:** Israel Roldan. **Treasurer:** Rene Laforce. **Members at Large:** Luis Melero, Tom Peng, Paul Seiler. **Continental VP, Africa:** Ishola Williams. **Continental VP, Americas:** Eduardo De Bello. **Continental VP, Asia:** Kang Seung Kyoo. **Continental VP, Europe:** Martin Miller. **Continental VP, Oceania:** Rob Finlay. **Continental VP, Africa:** Ishola Williams. **Continental VP, Americas:** Jorge Otsuka. **Assistant, President:** Oscar Lopez. **Assistant, Media Relations/Webmaster:** Philipp Wuerfel. **Manager, Anti-Doping:** Victor Isola. **Marketing/Tournaments:** Masaru Yokoo. **Assistant, Office Operations:** Anna Di Luca. **Coordinator, Administration Department:** Jacques Adrien Clermont. **Assistant, Administration/ Accounting:** Sandrine Pennone.

CONTINENTAL ASSOCIATIONS

CONFEDERATION PAN AMERICANA DE BEISBOL (COPABE)

Mailing Address: Calle 3, Francisco Filos, Vista Hermosa, Edificio 74, Planta Baja Local No. 1, Panama City, Panama. **Telephone:** (507) 229-8684. **Fax:** Unavailable. **Website:** www.copabe.net. **E-Mail:** copabe@sinfo.net.
President: Eduardo De Bello (Panama). **Secretary General:** Hector Pereyra (Dominican Republic).

AFRICAN BASEBALL/SOFTBALL ASSOCIATION

Mailing Address: Paiko Road, Changaga, Minna, Niger State, PMB 150, Nigeria. **Telephone:** (234-66) 224-555. **Fax:** (234-66) 224-555. **E-Mail Address:** absasecretariat@ yahoo.com.
President: Ishola Williams (Nigeria). **Executive Director:** Friday Ichide (Nigeria). **Secretary General:** Mabothobile Shebe (Lesotho).

BASEBALL FEDERATION OF ASIA

Mailing Address: No. 946-16 Dogok-Dong, Kangnam-Gu, Seoul, 135-270 Korea. **Telephone:** (82-2) 572-8413.

Fax: (82-2) 572-8416.
President: Seung-Kyoo Kang (Korea). **Vice Presidents:** Suzuki Yoshinobu (Japan), Chen Tai Cheng (Taipei), Shen Wei (China). **Secretary General:** Sang-Hyun Lee (Korea). **Members At Large:** Allan Mak Nin Fung (Hong Kong), Hector Navasero (Phillippines), Khawar Shah (Pakistan).

EUROPEAN BASEBALL CONFEDERATION

Mailing Address: Otto-FleckSchneise 12, D - 60528 Frankfurt, Germany. **Telephone:** +49-69-6700-284. **Fax:** +49-69-67724-212. **E-Mail Address:** office@baseballeurope.com. **Website:** baseballeurope.com.
President: Martin Miller (Germany). **1st Vice President:** Petr Ditrich (Czech Republic). **2nd Vice President:** Alexander Ratner (Russia). **3rd Vice President:** Mick Manning (Ireland). **Secretary General:** Samuel Pelter (Israel). **Treasurer:** Rene Laforce (Belguim). **Vocals:** Mats Fransson (Sweden), Attila Borbely (Hungary), Monique Schmitt (Switzerland), Juan Garcia (Spain), Rainer Husty (Austria).

BASEBALL CONFERERATION OF OCEANIA

Mailing Address: 48 Partridge Way, Mooroolbark, Victoria 3138, Australia. **Telephone:** 613 9727 1779. **Fax:** 613 9727 5959. **E-Mail Address:** bcosecgeneral@baseballoceania.com. **Website:** www.baseballoceania.com.
President: Ron Finlay (Australia). **1st Vice President:** Bob Steffy (Guam). **2nd Vice President:** Laurent Cassier (New Caledonia). **Secretary General:** Chet Gray (Australia). **Executive Committee:** David Ballinger (New Zealand), Ronald Seeto (Fiji), Rose Igitol (Commonwealth of Northern Mariana Islands).

ORGANIZATIONS

INTERNATIONAL GOODWILL SERIES, INC.

Mailing Address: 982 Slate Drive, Santa Rosa, CA 95405. **Telephone:** (707) 538-0777. **E-Mail Address:** bobw.24@goodwillseries.org. **Website:** www.goodwillseries.org.
President, Goodwill Series, Inc.: Bob Williams.

INTERNATIONAL SPORTS GROUP

Mailing Address: 3135 South Vermont Ave., Milwaukee, WI 53207. **Telephone:** (541) 882-4293. **E-Mail Address:** isgbaseball@yahoo.com. **Website:** www.isgbaseball.com.
President: Jim Jones. **Vice President:** Tom O'Connell. **Secretary/Treasurer:** Randy Town.

NATIONAL ORGANIZATIONS

USA BASEBALL

Mailing Address, Corporate Headquarters: 403 Blackwell St., Durham, NC 27701. **Telephone:** (919) 474-8721. **Fax:** (919) 474-8822. **E-Mail Address:** info@usabaseball.com. **Website:** www.usabaseball.com.
President: Mike Gaski. **Secretary General:** Ernie Young. **Treasurer:** Jason Dobis.
Executive Director/Chief Executive Officer: Paul Seiler. **Director, Operations/Women's National Team:** Ashley Bratcher. **General Manager, National Teams:** Eric Campbell. **Chief Financial Officer:** Ray Darwin. **Director, Media/Public Relations:** Jake Fehling. **Director, 14U National Team:** Nate Logan. **Chief Operating Officer:** David Perkins. **Director, Membership Services:** Adrian

Pringle. **Director, Development:** Rick Riccobono. **Director, Community Relations:** Lindsay Robertson. **Director, 15U National Team:** Jeff Singer. **Director, 18U National Team/Alumni:** Brant Ust. **Director, Travel Services:** Jocelyn Fern.
National Members: Amateur Athletic Union (AAU), American Amateur Baseball Congress (AABC), American Baseball Coaches Association (ABCA), American Legion Baseball, Babe Ruth Baseball, Dixie Baseball, Little League Baseball, National Amateur Baseball Federation (NABF), National Association of Intercollegiate Athletics (NAIA), National Baseball Congress (NBC), National Collegiate Athletic Association (NCAA), National Federation of State High School Athletic Associations, National High School Baseball Coaches Association (BCA), National Junior

College Athletic Association (NJCAA), Police Athletic League (PAL), PONY Baseball, T-Ball USA, United States Specialty Sports Association (USSSA), YMCAs of the USA. **Events:** www.usabaseball.com/events/schedule.jsp.

BASEBALL CANADA

Mailing Address: 2212 Gladwin Cres., Suite A7, Ottawa, Ontario K1B 5N1. **Telephone:** (613) 748-5606. **Fax:** (613) 748-5767. **E-Mail Address:** info@baseball.ca. **Website:** www.baseball.ca.

Director General: Jim Baba. **Head Coach/Director, National Teams:** Greg Hamilton. **Manager, Baseball Operations:** Andre Lachance. **Program Coordinator:** Kelsey McIntosh. **Manager, Media/Public Relations:** Andre Cormier. **Administrative Coordinator:** Denise Thomas.

NATIONAL BASEBALL CONGRESS

Mailing Address: 300 S. Sycamore, Wichita, KS 67213. **Telephone:** (316) 264-6887. **Fax:** (316) 264-2129. **Website:** www.nbcbaseball.com.
Year Founded: 1931.
General Manager: Josh Robertson. **Tournament Director:** Jerry Taylor.

ATHLETES IN ACTION

Mailing Address: 651 Taylor Dr., Xenia, OH 45385. **Telephone:** (937) 352-1000. **Fax:** (937) 352-1245. **E-Mail Address:** baseball@athletesinaction.org. **Website:** www.aiabaseball.org.
Director, AIA Baseball: Jason Lester. **U.S. Teams Director:** Chris Beck. **International Teams Director:** John McLaughlin. **General Manager, Great Lakes:** John Henschen. **Athletic Trainer:** Natalie McLaughlin.

SUMMER COLLEGE LEAGUES

NATIONAL ALLIANCE OF COLLEGE SUMMER BASEBALL

Telephone: (508) 404-7403. **E-Mail Address:** pgalop@comcast.net. **Website:** www.nacsb.org
Executive Directors: Bobby Bennett (Sunbelt Baseball League), Immediate Past, Jeff Carter (Southern Collegiate Baseball League). **Assistant Executive Director:** David Biery (Valley Baseball League). **Treasurer:** Larry Tremitiere (Southern Collegiate Baseball League). **Director, Public Relations/Secretary:** Sara Whiting (Florida Collegiate Summer League). **Compliance Officer:** Tom Bonekemper (Atlantic Collegiate Baseball League).
Member Leagues: Atlantic Collegiate Baseball League, Cal Ripken Collegiate Baseball League, Cape Cod Baseball League, Florida Collegiate Summer League, Great Lakes Summer Collegiate League, New England Collegiate Baseball League, New York Collegiate Baseball League, Prospect League, Southern Collegiate Baseball League, Sunbelt Baseball League, Valley Baseball League.

ALASKA BASEBALL LEAGUE

Mailing Address: PO box 71154, Fairbanks, AK 99707. **Telephone:** (907) 745-6401. **Fax:** (907) 746-5068. **E-Mail Address:** gmminers@gci.net.
Year Founded: 1974 (reunited, 1998)
President: Don Dennis (Fairbanks Alaska Goldpanners). **VP, Scheduling:** James Clark (Peninsula Oilers). **VP, Marketing:** Jon Dyson (Anchorage Glacier Pilots). **VP, Umpiring:** Pete Christopher (Mat-Su Miners). **VP, Secretary:** Shawn Maltby (Anchorage Bucs). **VP, Rules and Membership:** Chris Beck (Chugiak-Eagle River Chinooks). **League Spokesperson:** Mike Baxter. **League Stats:** Dick Lobdell.
Regular Season: 40 league games and approximately 5 non-league games. **2012 Opening Date:** June 10. **Closing Date:** July 31.
Playoff Format: League champion and second-place finisher qualify for National Baseball Congress World Series.
Roster Limit: 26 plus exemption for Alaska residents. **Player Eligibility:** Open except drafted college seniors.

ANCHORAGE BUCS

Mailing Address: PO Box 240061, Anchorage, AK 99524-0061. **Telephone:** (907) 561-2827. **Fax:** (907) 561-2920. **E-Mail Address:** gm@anchoragebucs.com.

Website: www.anchoragebucs.com. **General Manager:** Shawn Maltby. **Head Coach:** Tony Cappuccilli (Irvine Valley CC).

ANCHORAGE GLACIER PILOTS

Mailing Address: 207 East Northern Lights Blvd #125, Anchorage, AK 99503. **Telephone:** (907) 274-3627. **Fax:** (907) 274-3628. **E-Mail Address:** gpilots@alaska.net. **Website:** www.glacierpilots.com. **General Manager:** Jon Dyson. **Head Coach:** Conor Bird (College of Marin).

CHUGIAK-EAGLE RIVER CHINOOKS

Mailing Address: 651 Taylor Dr, Xenia, OH 45385. **Telephone:** (937) 352-1237. **Fax:** (937) 352-1245. **E-Mail Address:** chris.beck@athletesinaction.org. **Website:** www.aiabaseball.org. **General Manager:** Chris Beck. **Head Coach:** Jon Groth (Tyler CC).

FAIRBANKS ALASKA GOLDPANNERS

Mailing Address: PO Box 71154, Fairbanks, AK 99707. **Telephone:** (907) 451-0095, (619) 561-4581. **Fax:** (907) 456-6429, (619) 561-4581. **E-Mail Address:** addennis@cox.net. **Website:** www.goldpanners.com. **General Manager:** Don Dennis. **Assistant GM:** Todd Dennis. **Head Coach:** Jim Dietz.

MAT-SU MINERS

Mailing Address: PO Box 2690, Palmer, AK 99645-2690. **Telephone:** (907) 746-4914; (907) 745-6401. **Fax:** (907) 746-5068. **E-Mail Address:** generalmanager@matsuminers.org. **Website:** www.matsuminers.org. **General Manager:** Pete Christopher. **Assistant GM:** Bob Plumley. **Head Coach:** Chris Gordon (Milligan College)

PENINSULA OILERS

Mailing Address: 601 S Main St, Kenai, AK 99611. **Telephone:** (907) 283-7133. **Fax:** (907) 283-3390. **E-Mail Address:** gm@oilersbaseball.com. **Website:** www.oilersbaseball.com. **General Manager:** James Clark. **Head Coach:** John Stevens (Nipomo, Calif., HS).

ATLANTIC COLLEGIATE BASEBALL LEAGUE

Mailing Address: 1760 Joanne Drive, Quakertown, PA 18951. **Telephone:** (215) 536-5777. **Fax:** (215) 536-5177. **E-Mail:** tbonekemper@verizon.net. **Website:** www.acbl-online.com.

Year Founded: 1967.

Commissioner: Ralph Addonizio. **President/Acting Secretary:** Tom Bonekemper. **Vice President:** Doug Cinella. **Treasurer:** Bob Hoffman.

Division Structure: Wolff—Allentown, Jersey, Lehigh Valley, North Jersey, Quakertown, Trenton. Kaiser—Long Island, Nassau, New York, Staten Island. Hamptons—Center Moriches, North Fork, Riverhead, Sag Harbor, Shelter Island, Southampton, Westhampton.

Regular Season: 40 games. **2012 Opening Date:** June 1. **Closing Date:** August 5. **All-Star Game:** July 18, 7 p.m., MCU Park, Brooklyn, NY.

Roster Limit: 25 (college-eligible players only).

ALLENTOWN RAILERS

Mailing Address: Suite 202, 1801 Union Blvd, Allentown, PA 18109. **E-Mail Address:** ddando@lehighvalleybaseballacademy.com. **Field Manager:** Dylan Dando.

CENTER MORICHES BATTLECATS

Website: www.hamptonsbaseball.org. **President:** Anthony Eadersto. **General Manager:** Ed Morris Sr. **Field Manager:** Bill Batewell.

JERSEY PILOTS

Mailing Address: 401 Timber Dr, Berkeley Heights, NJ 07922. **Telephone:** (908) 464-8042. **E-Mail Address:** bensmookler@aol.com. **President/General Manager:** Ben Smookler. **Field Manager:** Evan Davis.

LEHIGH VALLEY CATZ

Mailing Address: 103 Logan Dr, Easton, PA 18045. **Telephone:** (610) 533-9349. **E-Mail Address:** poconnell@coopersburgsports.com. **Website:** www.lvcatz.com. **General Manager:** Pat O'Connell. **Field Manager:** Dennis Morgan.

LONG ISLAND SHAMROCKS

E-Mail Address: brandon@baseballplayermagazine.com. **General Manager:** Brandon Kurz. **Field Managers:** Rod Steffans, Justin Karn.

NASSAU COLLEGIANS

Mailing Address: 825 East Gate Blvd, Suite 101, Garden City, NY 11530. **E-Mail Address:** butchcaulfield@hotmail.com. **Website:** www.licollegians.com. **General Manager/VP:** Butch Caulfield. **Field Manager:** Brendan Monaghan.

NEW YORK ATLANTICS

Telephone: (516) 526-6820. **E-Mail Address:** keithkenny44@aol.com. **General Manager:** Keith Kenny. **Field Managers:** Dan Luisi, John Garvey.

NORTH FORK OSPREYS

Operated by: Hamptons Collegiate Baseball. **Telephone:** (631) 680-7870. **Website:** www.hamptonsbaseball.org. **General Manager:** Jeff Standish. **Field Manager:** Bill Iannicicllo.

NORTH JERSEY EAGLES

Mailing Address: 107 Pleasant Avenue, Upper Saddle River, NJ 07458. **General Manager:** Brian Casey. **Field Manager:** Jorge Hernandez.

QUAKERTOWN BLAZERS

Telephone: (215) 536-5777. **E-Mail Address:** gbonekemper@yahoo.com. **Website:** www.quakertownblazers.com. **General Manager:** Jerry Mayza. **Field Manager:** Lee Saverio.

RIVERHEAD TOMCATS

Operated by: Hamptons Collegiate Baseball. **Website:** www.hamptonsbaseball.org. **General Manager:** Bob Furlong. **Field Manager:** Randy Cadin.

SAG HARBOR WHALERS

Operated by: Hamptons Collegiate Baseball. **Website:** www.hamptonsbaseball.org. **General Manager:** Sandi Kruel. **Head Coach:** Jim Buckley.

SHELTER ISLAND BUCKS

Website: www.hamptonsbaseball.org. **E-Mail Address:** cocass@optonline.com. **General Manager:** Cori Cass. **Field Manager:** Joe Burke.

SOUTHAMPTON BREAKERS

Operated by: Hamptons Collegiate Baseball. **Website:** www.hamptonsbaseball.org. **General Managers:** John Venturella, Skip Norsic. **Field Manager:** Rob Cafiero.

STATEN ISLAND TIDE

Website: www.statenislandtide.com. **General Manager:** Gary Sutphen. **Field Manager:** Tommy Weber.

TRENTON GENERALS

E-Mail Address: gally22@aol.com. **General Manager:** Dave Gallagher. **Field Manager:** Jim Maher.

WESTHAMPTON AVIATORS

Operated by: Hamptons Collegiate Baseball. **Telephone:** (631) 466-4393. **Website:** www.hamptonsbaseball.org. **General Manager:** Henry Bramwell. **Field Manager:** Jeff Quiros.

CALIFORNIA COLLEGIATE LEAGUE

Mailing Address: 806 W Pedregosa St, Santa Barbara, CA 93101. **Telephone:** (805) 680-1047. **Fax:** (805) 684-8596. **Email Address:** burns@calsummerball.com. **Website:** www.calsummerball.com.

Year Founded: 1993.

Commissioner: Pat Burns.

Member Clubs: Academy Barons, Conejo Oaks, Glendale Angelenos, Orange County Pioneers, San Luis Obispo Blues, Santa Barbara Foresters. **Participating Non-Member:** Team Vegas Baseball Club.

Regular Season: 36 games. **2012 Opening Date:** June 1. **Closing Date:** July 31. **Playoff Format:** None.

Roster Limit: 33.

ACADEMY BARONS

Address: 901 E. Artesia Blvd, Compton, CA 90221. **Telephone:** (310) 635-2967. **Website:** www.academybarons.org. **Email Adress:** tavelli08@gmail.com.

Director: Ike Hampton. **Field Manager:** Josh Tavelli.

CONEJO OAKS

Address: 1710 N. Moorpark Rd., #106, Thousand Oaks, CA 91360. **Telephone:** (805) 797-7889. **Fax:** (805) 529-9862. **Email Address:** oaksbaseball@roadrunner.com. **Website:** www.oaksbaseball.org.

General Managers: Randy Riley, Verne Merrill. **Field Manager:** David Soilz.

GLENDALE ANGELENOS

Address: 6361 West 5th Street, Los Angeles, CA 90048. **Telephone:** (213) 344-8600. **Email Address:** tonyriviera@hotmail.com. **Website:** www.angelenosbaseball.com. **General Manager/Field Manager:** Tony Riviera.

ORANGE COUNTY PIONEERS

Address: 2312 Park Ave., #413, Tustin CA 92626. **Telephone:** (949) 278-2458. **Email Address:** jwicks@piosbaseball.org. **Website:** www.piosbaseball.org. **General Manager/Field Manager:** Jameson Wicks.

SAN LUIS OBISPO BLUES

Address: 241-B Prado Rd., San Luis Obispo, CA 93401. **Telephone:** (805) 215-6660. **Fax:** (805) 528-1146. **Email Address:** chal@bluesbaseball.com. **Website:** www.bluesbaseball.com. **General Manager:** Adam Stowe. **Field Manager:** Chal Fanning.

SANTA BARBARA FORESTERS

Address: 4299 Carpinteria Ave., Suite 201, Carpinteria, CA 93013. **Telephone:** (805) 684-0657. **Email Address:** foresters19@dock.net. **Website:** www.sbforesters.org. **General Manager/Field Manager:** Bill Pintard.

TEAM VEGAS BASEBALL CLUB

Address: 9265 Euphoria Rose Ave., Las Vegas NV 89166. **Telephone:** (702) 575-9394. **Email Address:** rangerbuck2002@yahoo.com. **Website:** www.teamvegasbaseball.com. **General Manager/Field Manager:** Buck Thomas.

CAL RIPKEN COLLEGIATE LEAGUE

Address: 12 Silver Fox Court, Cockeysville, MD 21030. **Telephone:** (410) 746-1829. **E-Mail:** robertmdouglas@hotmail.com. **Website:** www.calripkenleague.org. **Year Founded:** 2005.

Commissioner: Robert Douglas. **Deputy Commissioner:** Jerry Wargo. **Executive Director:** Pat Malone.

Regular Season: 42 games. **2012 Opening Date:** June 6. **Closing Date:** July 30. **All-Star Game:** July 13 at Bethesda, MD. **Playoff Format:** Four-team, double-elimination tournament, Aug. 1-4.

Roster Limit: 30 (college-eligible players 22 and under).

ALEXANDRIA ACES

Address: 600 14th Street NW, Suite 400, Washington, DC 20005. **Telephone:** (202) 265-0200. **E-Mail:** ddinan@ralaw.com. **Website:** www.alexandriaaces.org. **President/General Manager:** Donald Dinan. **Head Coach:** Corey Haines.

BALTIMORE REDBIRDS

Address: 2208 Pine Hill Farms Lane, Cockeysville, MD 21030. **Telephone:** (410) 802-2220. **Fax:** (410) 785-6138. **E-Mail:** johntcarey@hotmail.com. **Website:** baltimoreredbirds.pointstreaksites.com. **President:** John Carey. **Head Coach:** Frank Velleggia.

BETHESDA BIG TRAIN

Address: PO Box 30306, Bethesda, MD 20824. **Telephone:** (301) 983-1006. **Fax:** (301) 652-0691. **E-Mail:** faninfo@bigtrain.org. **Website:** www.bigtrain.org. **General Manager:** Jordan Henry. **Head Coach:** Sal Colangelo.

D.C. GRAYS

Address: 900 19th Street NW, 8th floor, Washington, DC 20006. **Telephone:** (202) 327-8116. **Fax:** 202-327-8101. **Website:** www.dcgrays.com. **E-Mail Address:** Barbera@acgre.com. **President/Chairman:** Michael Barbera. **General Manager:** Antonio Scott. **Head Coach:** Arlan Freeman.

HERNDON BRAVES

Address: 1305 Kelly Court, Herndon, VA 20170-2605. **Telephone:** (703) 973-4444. **Fax:** (703) 783-1319. **E-Mail:** herndonbraves@cox.net. **Website:** www.herndonbraves.com. **General Manager:** Chris Smith. **Trainer:** Lisa Lombardozzi. **Head Coach:** Eric Williams.

ROCKVILLE EXPRESS

Address: PO Box 10188, Rockville, MD 20849. **Telephone:** (301) 928-6608. **E-Mail:** info@rockvilleexpress.org. **Website:** www.rockvilleexpress.org. **President/GM:** Jim Kazunas. **Vice President:** Brad Botwin. **Head Coach:** Angelo Nicolosi.

SILVER SPRING-TAKOMA T-BOLTS

Address: 906 Glaizewood Court, Takoma Park, MD 20912. **Telephone:** (301) 270-0794. **E-Mail:** tboltsbaseball@gmail.com. **Website:** www.tbolts.org. **General Manager:** David Stinson. **Head Coach:** Jason Walck.

SOUTHERN MARYLAND NATIONALS

Address: 2243 Garrity Rd, Saint Leonard, MD 20685. **Telephone:** (301) 751-6299. **E-Mail:** winegard@erols.com. **President/Head Coach:** Chuck Winegardner. **General Manager:** Don Herbert.

VIENNA RIVER DOGS

Address: 12703 Hitchcock Ct, Reston, VA 201919. **Telephone:** (703) 904-0548. **Fax:** (703) 904-1723. **E--Mail Address:** coach @viennariverdogs.org. **Website:** www.viennariverdogs.org. **President/General Manager/Head Coach:** Bruce Hall.

YOUSE'S ORIOLES

Address: 3 Oyster Court, Baltimore, MD 21219. **Telephone:** (410) 477-3764. **E-Mail:** tnt017@comcast.net. **Website:** www.youseorioles.org. **General Manager/Head Coach:** Tim Norris.

CAPE COD LEAGUE

Mailing Address: PO Box 266, Harwich Port, MA 02646. **Telephone:** (508) 432-6909. **E-Mail:** info@capecodbaseball.org. **Website:** www.capecodbaseball.org. **Year Founded:** 1885

Commissioner: Paul Galop. **President:** Judy Walden Scarafile. **Senior Vice President:** Jim Higgins. **Vice Presidents:** Peter Ford, Bill Bussiere. **Deputy Commissioner:** Richard Sullivan. **Deputy Commissioner/Umpire in Chief:** Sol Yas. **Treasurer/Webmaster:** Steven Wilson. **Secretary:** Kim Wolfe. **Director, Memorabilia:** Dan Dunn. **Director, Public Relations/Broadcasting:** John Garner Jr. **Director, Communications:** Jim McGonigle. **Director, Publications:** Lou Barnicle. **Website Editor and Senior Writer:** Geoff Converse. **Director, Special Projects/Senior Web Editor:** Joe Sherman. **Publications Editor/Senior Writer, Website:** Rob Duca.

Division Structure: Eastern—Brewster, Chatham, Harwich, Orleans, Yarmouth-Dennis. Western—Bourne, Cotuit, Falmouth, Hyannis, Wareham.

Regular Season: 44 games

2012 Opening Date: June 14. **Closing Date:** August 15. **All-Star Game:** July 28. **Playoff Format:** Top four teams in each division qualify. Three rounds of best-of-three series.

Roster Limit: 25 (college-eligible players only).

BOURNE BRAVES

Mailing Address: PO Box 895, Monument Beach, MA 02553. **Telephone:** (508) 345-1013. **E-Mail Address:** bournebravesgm@hotmail.com. **Website:** www.bournebraves. org. **President:** Thomas Fink. **General Manager:** Chuck Sturtevant. **Head Coach:** Harvey Shapiro.

BREWSTER WHITECAPS

Mailing Address: PO Box 2349, Brewster, MA 02631. **Telephone:** (508) 896-8500, ext. **147. Fax:** (508) 896-9845. **E-Mail Address:** PABlatz@comcast.net. **Website:** www. brewsterwhitecaps.com. **President:** Peter Blatz. **General Manager:** Ned Monthie. **Head Coach:** John Altobelli.

CHATHAM ANGLERS

Mailing Address: PO Box 428, Chatham, MA 02633. **Telephone:** (508) 241-8382. **Fax:** (508) 430-8382. **Website:** www.chathamas.com. **President:** Doug Grattan. **General Manager:** Charlie Thoms. **Head Coach:** John Schiffner.

COTUIT KETTLEERS

Mailing Address: PO Box 411, Cotuit, MA 02635. **Telephone:** (508) 428-3358. **Fax:** (508) 420-5584. **E-Mail Address:** info@kettleers.org. **Website:** www.kettleers.org. **President:** Paul Logan. **General Manager:** Bruce Murphy. **Head Coach:** Mike Roberts.

FALMOUTH COMMODORES

Mailing Address: PO Box 808 Falmouth, MA 02541. **Telephone:** (508) 472-7922. **Fax:** (508) 862-6011. **Website:** www.falcommodores.org. **President:** Christine Clark. **General Manager:** Bob Clark. **Head Coach:** Jeff Trundy.

HARWICH MARINERS

Mailing Address: PO Box 201, Harwich Port, MA 02646. **Telephone:** (508) 432-2000. **Fax:** (508) 432-5357. **E-Mail Address:** mehendy@comcast.net. **Website:** www.har-wichmariners.org. **President:** Mary Henderson. **General Manager:** Ben Layton. **Head Coach:** Steve Englert (Boston College).

HYANNIS HARBOR HAWKS

Mailing Address: PO Box 852, Hyannis, MA 02601. **Telephone:** (508) 364-3164. **Fax:** (508) 534-1270. **E-Mail Address:** bbussiere@harborhawks.org. **Website:** www.harborhawks.org. **President:** Tino DiGiovanni. **General Manager:** Michael Letseizen. **Head Coach:** Chad Gassman.

ORLEANS FIREBIRDS

Mailing Address: PO Box 504, Orleans, MA 02653. **Telephone:** (508) 255-0793. **Fax:** (508) 255-2237. **Website:** www.orleansfirebirds.com. **President:** Don LeSieur. **General Manager:** Bill Scheier. **Head Coach:** Kelly Nicholson.

WAREHAM GATEMEN

Mailing Address: PO Box 287, Wareham, MA 02571. **Telephone:** (508) 748-0287. **Fax:** (508) 880-2602. **E-Mail Address:** sheri.gay4gatemen@comcast.net. **Website:** www.gatemen.org. **President/General Manager:** Thomas Gay. **Head Coach:** Cooper Farris.

YARMOUTH-DENNIS RED SOX

Mailing Address: PO Box 814, South Yarmouth, MA 02664. **Telephone:** (508) 394-9387. **Fax:** (508) 398-2239. **E-Mail Address:** jimmartin321@yahoo.com. **Website:** www.ydredsox.org. **President:** Steve Faucher. **General Manager:** Jim Martin. **Head Coach:** Scott Pickler (Cypress, Calif., CC).

COASTAL PLAIN LEAGUE

Mailing Address: 125 Quantum Street, Holly Springs, NC 27540. **Telephone:** (919) 852-1960. **Fax:** (919) 516-0852. **Email Address:** justins@coastalplain.com. **Website:** www.coastalplain.com.

Year Founded: 1997.

Chairman/CEO: Jerry Petitt. **President/Commissioner:** Pete Bock. **Assistant Commissioner:** Justin Sellers. **Director, On-Field Operations:** Jeff Bock.

Division Structure: East—Edenton, Fayetteville, Morehead City, Peninsula, Petersburg, Wilmington, Wilson. West—Asheboro, Columbia, Florence, Forest City, Gastonia, Martinsville, Thomaville.

Regular Season: 56 games (split schedule). **2012 Opening Date:** May 28. **Closing Date:** August 14. **All-Star Game:** July 23. **Playoff Format:** Three rounds, best of three in each round.

Roster Limit: 27 (college-eligible players only).

ASHEBORO COPPERHEADS

Mailing Address: PO Box 4006, Asheboro, NC 27204. **Telephone:** (336) 460-7018. **Fax:** (336) 629-2651. **E-Mail Address:** info@teamcopperhead.com. **Website:** www.teamcopperhead.com. **Owners:** Ronnie Pugh, Steve Pugh, Doug Pugh, Mike Pugh. **General Manager:** David Camp. **Head Coach:** Donnie Wilson (College of the Sequoias, Calif.).

COLUMBIA BLOWFISH

Mailing Address: PO Box 1328, Columbia, SC 29202. **Telephone:** (803) 254-3474. **Fax:** (803) 254-4482. **E-Mail Address:** info@blowfishbaseball.com. **Website:** www.blowfishbaseball.com. **Owner:** HWS Baseball V (Michael Savit, Bill Shanahan). **General Manager:** Skip Anderson. **Head Coach:** Brian Buscher.

EDENTON STEAMERS

Mailing Address: PO Box 86, Edenton, NC 27932. **Telephone:** (252) 482-4080. **Fax:** (252) 482-1717. **E-Mail Address:** edentonsteamers@hotmail.com. **Website:** www.edentonsteamers.com. **Owner:** Edenton Steamers Inc. **President/General Manager:** Katy Ebersole. **Head Coach:** Steve Moritz (Georgia College and State).

FAYETTEVILLE SWAMPDOGS

Mailing Address: PO Box 64691, Fayetteville, NC 28306. **Telephone:** (910) 426-5900. **Fax:** (910) 426-3544. **E-Mail Address:** info@fayettevilleswampdogs.com. **Website:** www.goswampdogs.com. **Owners:** Lew Handelsman, Darrell Handelsman. **Head Coach/General Manager/Director, Operations:** Darrell Handelsman.

FLORENCE REDWOLVES

Mailing Address: PO Box 809, Florence, SC 29503. **Telephone:** (843) 629-0700. **Fax:** (843) 629-0703. **E-Mail Address:** jamie@florenceredwolves.com. **Website:** www.florenceredwolves.com. **Owners:** Kevin Barth, Donna Barth. **General Manager:** Jamie Young. **Head Coach:** Jared Barkdoll (Francis Marion).

FOREST CITY OWLS

Mailing Address: PO Box 1062, Forest City, NC 28043. **Telephone:** (828) 245-0000. **Fax:** (828) 245-6666. **E-Mail Address:** forestcitybaseball@yahoo.com. **Website:** www.forestcitybaseball.com. **Owner/President:** Ken Silver. **Managing Partner:** Jesse Cole. **General Manager:** Jeremy Boler. **Head Coach:** Phil Disher (Wofford).

GASTONIA GRIZZLIES

Mailing Address: PO Box 177, Gastonia, NC 28053. **Telephone:** (704) 866-8622. **Fax:** (704) 864-6122. **E-Mail Address:** jesse@gastoniagrizzlies.com. **Website:** www.gastoniagrizzlies.com. **President:** Ken Silver. **Managing Partner/General Manager:** Jesse Cole. **Head Coach:** Kyle Surprenant.

MARTINSVILLE MUSTANGS

Mailing Address: PO Box 1112, Martinsville, VA 24114. **Telephone:** (276) 403-5250. **Fax:** (276) 403-5387. **E-Mail Address:** jtaipalus@ci.martinsville.va.us. **Website:** www.martinsvillemustangs.com. **Owner:** City of Martinsville. **General Manager:** Jim Taipalus. **Head Coach:** Matt Duffy.

MOREHEAD CITY MARLINS

Mailing Address: 1921 Oglesby Road, Morehead City, NC 28557. **Telephone:** (252) 269-9767. **Fax:** (252) 727-9402. **E-Mail Address:** chris@mhcmarlins.com. **Website:** www.mhcmarlins.com. **President:** Buddy Bengel. **General Manager:** Chris Marmo. **Head Coach:** Brian McRae.

PENINSULA PILOTS

Mailing Address: PO Box 7376, Hampton, VA 23666. **Telephone:** (757) 245-2222. **Fax:** (757) 245-8030. **E-Mail Address:** jeffscott@peninsulapilots.com. **Website:** www.peninsulapilots.com. **Owner:** Henry Morgan. **General Manager:** Jeffrey Scott. **Head Coach/Vice President:** Hank Morgan.

PETERSBURG GENERALS

Mailing Address: 1981 Midway Ave, Petersburg, VA 23803. **Telephone:** (804) 722-0141. **Fax:** (804) 733-7370. **E-Mail Address:** petggenerals@earthlink.net. **Website:** www.generals.petersburgsports.com. **Owner:** City of Petersburg. **General Manager:** Ryan Massenburg. **Head Coach:** Bob Smith.

THOMASVILLE HI-TOMS

Mailing Address: PO Box 3035, Thomasville, NC 27361. **Telephone:** (336) 472-8667. **Fax:** (336) 472-7198. **E-Mail Address:** info@hitoms.com. **Website:** www.hitoms.com. **Owner:** Richard Holland. **President:** Greg Suire. **General Manager:** John Massey. **Head Coach:** Sean Walsh (Brevard College).

WILMINGTON SHARKS

Mailing Address: PO Box 15233, Wilmington, NC 28412. **Telephone:** (910) 343-5621. **Fax:** (910) 343-8932. **E-Mail Address:** info@wilmingtonsharks.com. **Website:** www.wilmingtonsharks.com. **Owners:** Lew Handelsman, Darrell Handelsman. **President:** Greg Suire. **General Manager:** Andrew Aguilar. **Head Coach:** Ryan McCleney (UNC Pembroke).

WILSON TOBS

Mailing Address: PO Box 633, Wilson, NC 27894. **Telephone:** (252) 291-8627. **Fax:** (252) 291-1224. **E-Mail Address:** wilsontobs@gmail.com. **Website:** www.wilsontobs.com. **Owner:** Richard Holland. **President:** Greg Suire. **Head Coach:** Jason Immekus (Missouri Southern).

FLORIDA COLLEGIATE SUMMER LEAGUE

Mailing Address: 55 West Crystal Lake Street, Suite 50, Orlando, FL 32806. **Telephone:** (321) 206-9174. **Fax:** (407) 574-7926. **E-Mail Address:** info@floridaleague.com. **Website:** www.floridaleague.com.

Year Founded: 2004.
CEO: Sara Whiting. **President/COO:** Rob Sitz. **Vice President:** Stefano Foggi. **League Operations:** Phil Chinnery.
Regular Season: 45 games. **2012 Opening Date:** June 7. **Closing Date:** Aug. 1. **All-Star Game:** July 10. **Playoff Format:** Five teams, No. 4 and No. 5 seed play-in game. Second round features two best-of-three series, with winners meeting in winner-take-all championship game.
Roster Limit: 27 (college-eligible players only).

DELAND SUNS

Operated through league office. **E-Mail Address:** delandsuns@floridaleague.com. **Head Coach:** Rick Hall.

LEESBURG LIGHTNING

Mailing Address: 318 South 2nd St, Leesburg, FL 34748. **Telephone:** (352) 728-9885. **E-Mail Address:** leesburglightning@floridaleague.com. **President:** Bruce Ericson. **Head Coach:** Dave Therneau.

ORLANDO FREEDOM

Operated through league office. **E-Mail Address:** orlandofreedom@floridaleague.com. **Head Coach:** Scott Makarewicz.

ORLANDO MONARCHS

Operated through league office. **E-Mail Address:** orlandomonarchs@floridaleague.com. **President:** Rickie Weeks Sr. **Head Coach:** Unavailable.

SANFORD RIVER RATS

Operated through league office. **E-Mail Address:** sanfordriverrats@floridaleague.com. **Head Coach:** Steve Piercefield.

WINTER HAVEN LOGGERHEADS

Operated through league office. **E-Mail Address:** winterhavenloggerheads@floridaleague.com. **Head Coach:** Nick Vera.

WINTER PARK DIAMOND DAWGS

Operated through league office. **E-Mail Address:** winterparkdiamonddawgs@floridaleague.com. **Head Coach:** Kevin Davidson.

FUTURES COLLEGIATE LEAGUE OF NEW ENGLAND

Mailing Address: 46 Chestnut Hill Rd, Chelmsford, MA 01824. **Telephone:** (617) 593-2112. **E-Mail Address:** futuresleague@yahoo.com. **Website:** www.thefuturesleague.com.
Year Founded: 2010.
Commissioner: Chris Hall.
Member Clubs: Martha's Vineyard Sharks, Nashua Collegiate Baseball, Old Orchard Beach Collegiate Baseball, Pittsfield Collegiate Baseball, Seacoast Mavericks, Torrington Titans, Wachusett Dirt Dogs.
Regular Season: 54 games. **2012 Opening Date:** June 7. **Closing Date:** Aug. 9. **Playoff Format:** Four teams with best overall records meet in best-of-three semifinals; winners meet in best-of-three championship series.
Roster Limit: 30. Half must be from New England or play collegiately at a New England college.

GREAT LAKES SUMMER COLLEGIATE LEAGUE

Mailing Address: 133 W Winter St, Delaware, OH

43015. **Telephone:** (740) 368-3527. **Fax:** (740) 368-3999. **E-Mail Address:** kalance@owu.edu. **Website:** www.great-lakesleague.org.
Year Founded: 1986.
President/Commissioner: Kim Lance.
Regular Season: 40 games. **2012 Opening Date:** June 8. **Closing Date:** July 29. **All-Star Game:** July 11 at All Pro Freight Stadium, Avon, Ohio. **Playoff Format:** Top six teams meet in playoffs.
Roster Limit: 30 (college-eligible players only).

CINCINNATI STEAM

Mailing Address: 2745 Anderson Ferry Rd, Cincinnati, OH 45238. **Telephone:** (513) 922-4272. **Website:** www.cincinnatisteam.com. **General Manager:** Max McLeary. **Head Coach:** Billy O'Connor.

DAYTON DOCS

Mailing Address: Dayton Docs Baseball Club, PO Box 773, Greenville, OH 45331. **Telephone:** (937) 423-3053. **Website:** www.docsbaseball.com. **President/General Manager:** Joe Marker. **Head Coach:** Burt Davis.

GRAND LAKE MARINERS

Mailing Address: 1460 James Drive, Celina, OH 45822. **Telephone:** (419) 586-3187. **Website:** www.grandlakemariners.com. **General Manager:** Betty Feliciano. **Head Coach:** Mike Goldschmidt.

HAMILTON JOES

Mailing Address: 6218 Greens Way, Hamilton, OH 45011. **Telephone:** (513) 267-0601. **E-mail address:** darrelgrissom@fuse.net. **Website:** www.hamiltonjoes.com. **General Manager:** Josh Manley. **Head Coach:** Darrel Grissom.

LAKE ERIE MONARCHS

Mailing Address: 2220 West Sigler Road, Carleton, MI 48117. **Telephone:** (734) 626-1166. **Website:** www.lakeeriemonarchs.com. **General Manager:** Jim DeSana. **Head Coach:** Mike Montgomery.

LEXINGTON HUSTLERS

Mailing Address: 2061 Lexington Road, Nicholasville, KY 40356. **Telephone:** (859) 335-0928. **Fax:** (859) 881-0598. **Website:** lexingtonhustlers.wordpress.com. **Email Address:** lexigntonhustlers@gmail.com. **General Manager:** Adam Revelette. **Head Coach:** Bobby Wright.

LICKING COUNTY SETTLERS

Mailing Address: 958 Camden Dr, Newark, OH 43055. **Telephone:** (678) 367-8686. **Website:** www.settlersbaseball.com. **General Manager:** Sean West. **Head Coach:** Devin McIntosh.

LIMA LOCOS

Mailing Address: 3588 South Conant Rd, Spencerville, OH 45887. **Telephone:** (419) 647-5242. **Website:** www.limalocos.com. **General Manager:** Steve Meyer. **Head Coach:** Gene Stechshulte.

SOUTHERN OHIO COPPERHEADS

Mailing Address: PO Box 442, Athens, OH 45701. **Telephone:** (740) 541-9284. **Website:** www.copperheadsbaseball.com. **General Manager:** David Palmer. **Head Coach:** Chris Moore.

STARK COUNTY TERRIERS

Mailing Address: 1019 35th St Northwest, Canton, OH, 44709. **Telephone:** (330) 492-9220. **Website:** www.ter-

riersbaseballclub.com. **General Manager:** Greg Trbovich. **Head Coach:** Trent McIlvain.

XENIA SCOUTS

Mailing Address: 651 Taylor Dr, Xenia, OH 45385. **Telephone:** (937) 352-1000. **E-Mail Address:** john.henschen@athletesinaction.org **Website:** www.aiabaseball.org. **General Manager:** John Henschen. **Head Coach:** J.D. Arndt.

JAYHAWK LEAGUE

Mailing Address: 865 Fabrique, Wichita, KS 67218
Telephone: (316) 942-6333. **Fax:** (316) 942-2009. **Website:** www.jayhawkbaseballleague.org
Year Founded: 1976
Commissioner: Jim Foltz. **President:** J.D. Schneider. **Vice President:** Frank Leo. **Public Relations/Statistician:** Gary Karr. **Secretary:** Cheryl Kastner
Regular Season: 32 games. **2012 Opening Date:** June 3. **Closing Date:** July 25.
Playoff Format: Top two teams qualify for National Baseball Congress World Series
Roster Limit: 30 to begin season; 28 at midseason.

DERBY TWINS

Mailing Address: 1245 N. Pine Grove, Wichita, KS 67212. **Telephone:** (316) 992-3623. **E-mail Address:** jwells@riadatrading.com, jwells53@att.net. **Website:** www.derbytwins.com. **General Manager:** Jeff Wells. **Head Coach:** Billy Hall.

DODGE CITY A'S

Mailing Address: 1715 Central Ave., Dodge City, KS 67801. **Telephone:** 620-225-0238. **Website:** www.dodgecityas.com. **General Manager/Head Coach:** Phil Stevenson.

EL DORADO BRONCOS

Mailing Address: Box 168, El Dorado, KS 67042. **Telephone:** (316) 323-5098. **Website:** www.360eldorado.com. **General Manager:** Doug Bell. **Head Coach:** Pat Hon.

HAYS LARKS

Mailing Address: 2715 Walnut, Hays, KS 67601. **Telephone:** (785) 259-1430. **Fax:** (630) 848-2236. **Website:** www.hdnews.net/larks. **General Manager:** Frank Leo. **Head Coach:** Frank Leo.

LIBERAL BEE JAYS

Mailing Address: PO Box 793, Liberal, KS 67901. **Telephone:** (620) 629-1162. **Fax:** (620) 624-1906. **Head Coach:** Mike Silva.

HAYSVILLE HEAT

Mailing Address: 417 Apple Ct., Haysville, KS 67060. **Telephone:** (928) 854-4092. **Website:** www.haysvilleheat.com. **Email Address:** haysvilleheat@yahoo.com. **General Manager:** Jim Agne. **Owner/Head Coach:** Rick Twyman.

M.I.N.K. LEAGUE

(Missouri, Iowa, Nebraska, Kansas)
Mailing Address: PO Box 1155, Chillicothe, MO 64601. **Telephone:** (660) 646-2165. **Fax:** (660) 646-6933. **E-mail Address:** lfechtig@midwestglove.com. **Website:** www.minkleaguebaseball.com.
Year Founded: 1995.
Commissioner: Bob Steinkamp. **President:** Liz Fechtig. **Vice President:** Jeff Post. **Secretary:** Edwina Rains.

Regular Season: 48 games. **2012 Opening Date:** May 31. **Closing Date:** July 17. **Playoff Format:** Top team qualifies for National Baseball Congress World Series.
Roster Limit: 30.

CHILLICOTHE MUDCATS

Mailing Address: 426 E. Jackson, Chillicothe, MO 64601. **Telephone:** (660) 646-2165. **Fax:** (660) 646-6933. **E-Mail Address:** lfechtig@midwestglove.com. **Website:** www.chillicothemudcats.com. **General Manager:** Liz Fechtig. **Head Coach:** Eric Peterson.

CLARINDA A'S

Mailing Address: 225 East Lincoln, Clarinda, IA 51632. **Telephone:** (712) 542-4272. **E-Mail Address:** m.everly@mchsi.com. **Website:** www.clarindaiowa-as-baseball.org. **General Manager:** Merle Eberly. **Head Coach:** Ryan Eberly.

JOPLIN OUTLAWS

Mailing Address: 5860 North Pearl, Joplin, MO 64801. **Telephone:** (417) 825-4218. **E-Mail Address:** merains@mchsi.com. **Website:** www.joplinoutlaws.com. **President/General Manager:** Mark Rains. **Head Coach:** Rob Vessell.

NEVADA GRIFFONS

Mailing Address: PO Box 601, Nevada, MO 64772. **Telephone:** (417) 667-6159. **E-Mail Address:** jpost@morrisonpost.com. **Website:** www.nevadagriffons.org. **President:** Pedro Claudio. **General Manager/Stats:** Jeff Post. **Head Coach:** Ryan Mansfield.

OMAHA DIAMOND SPIRIT

Mailing Address: 4618 N 135th Ave, Omaha, NE 68164. **Telephone:** (402) 679-0206. **E-Mail Address:** arkaosky@cox.net. **Website:** www.scorebook.com/spirit2006. **General Manager/Head Coach:** Arden Rakosky.

OZARK GENERALS

Mailing Address: 1336 W Farm Road 182, Springfield, MO 65810. **Telephone:** (417) 832-8830. **Fax:** (417) 877-4625. **E-Mail Address:** rda160@yahoo.com. **Website:** www.generalsbaseballclub.com. **General Manager/Head Coach:** Rusty Aton.

ST. JOSEPH MUSTANGS

Mailing Address: 2600 SW Parkway, St. Joseph, MO 64503. **Telephone:** (816) 279-7856. **Fax:** (816) 749-4082. **E-Mail Address:** rmuntean717@gmail.com. **Website:** www.stjoemustangs.com. **President:** Dan Gerson. **General Manager:** Rick Muntean. **Manager/Director, Player Personnel:** Matt Johnson.

SEDALIA BOMBERS

Mailing Address: 2201 S Grand, Sedalia, MO 65301. **Telephone:** (660) 287-4722. **E-Mail Address:** jkindle@knobnoster.k12.mo.us. **Website:** www.sedaliabombers.com. **President/General Manager/Head Coach:** Jud Kindle. **Vice President:** Ross Dey.

MOUNTAIN COLLEGIATE LEAGUE

E-mail Address: info@mcbl.net. **Website:** www.mcbl.net. **Year Founded:** 2005.
Directors: Kurt Colicchio, Ron Kailey, Nicko Kleppinger. **Director of Umpires:** Gary Weibert.
Regular Season: 42 games. **2012 Opening Date:** June 3. **Closing Date:** July 29. **Playoff Format:** Second- and third-place teams meet in one-game playoff; winner advances to best-of-three championship series against

first-place team. **All-Star Game:** July 7 in Fort Collins, Colo.
Roster limit: 31 total, 25 active (college-eligible players only).

CHEYENNE GRIZZLIES

Telephone: (307) 631-7337. **E-mail Address:** rkaide@aol.com. **Website:** www.cheyennegrizzlies.com. **Owner/General Manager:** Ron Kailey. **Head Coach:** Nick Signaigo (Cal Lutheran University, Calif.).

FORT COLLINS FOXES

Telephone: (970) 225-9564. **E-Mail Address:** info@fortcollinsfoxes.com. **Website:** www.fortcollinsfoxes.com. **Owner/General Manager:** Kurt Colicchio. **Head Coach:** Brad Averitte.

LARAMIE COLTS

Telephone: (307) 760-0544. **E-Mail Address:** laramiecolts@msn.com. **Website:** www.laramiecolts.com. **Owners:** Kent & Nicko Kleppinger. **Head Coach:** Marty Berson.

NEW ENGLAND COLLEGIATE LEAGUE

Mailing Address: 37 Grammar School Dr, Danbury, CT 06811. **Telephone:** (203) 241-9392. **Fax:** (203) 643-2230. **Website:** www.necbl.com.
Year founded: 1993.
Commissioner: Mario Tiani. **Deputy Commissioner:** Everts "Eph" Mangan. **President:** John DeRosa. **Executive President:** Dick Murray. **Treasurer:** Brigid Schaffer. **Secretary:** Richard Rossiter.
Regular Season: 42 games. **2012 Opening Date:** June 7. **Closing Date:** Aug. 1. **All-Star Game:** July 22 at Montpelier, Vt.
Roster Limit: 30 (college-eligible players only).

DANBURY WESTERNERS

Mailing Address: 5 Old Hayrake Rd, Danbury, CT 06810. **Telephone:** (203) 313-3024. **Fax:** (203) 792-6177. **E-Mail Address:** westerners1@aol.com. **Website:** www.danburywesterners.com. **President:** Paul Schaffer. **General Manager:** Terry Whalen. **Field Manager:** Jamie Shevchik.

HOLYOKE BLUE SOX

Mailing Address: 19 Cranberry Lane, Dedham, MA 01026. **Telephone:** (413) 652-9014. **E-Mail Address:** karen@wadsworthsports.net. **Website:** www.holyokesox.com. **Chairman/CEO:** Karen Wadsworth-Rella. **General Manager:** Kirk Fredriksson. **Head Coach:** Darryle Morhardt.

KEENE SWAMP BATS

Mailing Address: PO Box 160, Keene, NH 13431. **Telephone:** (603) 357-5464. **Fax:** (603) 357-5090. **Website:** www.swampbats.com. **President:** Kevin Watterson. **Field Manager:** Marty Testo.

LACONIA MUSKRATS

Mailing Address: 134 Stevens Rd, Lebanon, NH 03766. **Telephone:** (864) 380-2873. **E-Mail Address:** noah@laconiamuskrats.com. **Website:** www.laconiamuskrats.com. **President:** Jonathan Crane. **General Manager:** Noah Crane. **Field Manager:** Matt Alison.

MYSTIC SCHOONERS

Mailing Address: 6 Forest Park Dr, Farmington, CT 06032. **Telephone:** (860) 558-6870. **Website:** www.

mysticbaseball.org. **President:** Kevin Kelleher. **General Manager:** Dennis Long. **Field Manager:** Phil Orbe.

NEW BEDFORD BAY SOX

Mailing Address: 17 Sawmill Road, Jericho, VT 05465. **Telephone:** (802) 578-9935. **E-Mail Address:** accormier@nbbaysox.com. **Website:** www.nbbaysox.com. **President:** Pat O'Connor. **General Manager:** Andrew Cormier. **Field Manager:** Rick Miller.

NEWPORT GULLS

Mailing Address: PO Box 777, Newport, RI 02840. **Telephone:** (401) 845-6832. **Website:** www.newport-gulls.com. **President:** Chuck Paiva. **Field Manager:** Mike Coombs.

NORTH ADAMS STEEPLECATS

Mailing Address: PO Box 540, North Adams, MA 01247. **Telephone:** (413) 652-1031. **E-Mail Address:** steeplecats_gm@roadrunner.com. **Website:** www.steeplecats.com. **President:** Dan Bosley. **General Manager:** Sean McGrath. **Field Manager:** Unavailable.

NORTH SHORE NAVIGATORS

Mailing Address: 365 Western Ave, PO Box 8188, Lynn MA 01904. **Telephone:** (781) 595-9400. **E-Mail Address:** sal@nsnavs.com. **Website:** www.nsnavs.com. **President:** Tim Haley. **General Manager:** Sal Accardi. **Field Manager:** Jeff Waldron.

SANFORD MAINERS

Mailing Address: PO Box 26, 4 Washington St, Sanford, ME 04073. **Telephone:** (207) 324-0010. **Fax:** (207) 324-2227. **E-Mail Address:** jwebb@nicholswebb.com. **Website:** www.sanfordmainers.com. **CEO:** Steve Cabana. **General Manager:** John Webb. **Field Manager:** Aaron Izaryk.

VERMONT MOUNTAINEERS

Mailing Address: PO Box 57, East Montpelier, VT 05651. **Telephone:** (802) 223-5224. **E-Mail Address:** gmcbaseballvt@aol.com. **Website:** www.thevermontmountaineers.com. **President:** Katheran Thayer. **General Manager:** Brian Gallagher. **Field Manager:** John Russo.

NEW YORK COLLEGIATE BASEBALL LEAGUE

Mailing Address: 4 Creekside Ln, Rochester, NY 14624-1059. **Telephone:** (585) 314-1122. **E-Mail Address:** slehman@nycbl.com. **Website:** www.nycbl.com.

Year founded: 1978.

President/Commissioner/Executive Director: Stan Lehman. **Vice President:** Cal Kern. **Treasurer:** Dan Russo. **Secretary:** Paul Welker. **Director of Baseball Operations:** Jake Dennstedt. **Franchise Development:** Cal Kern.

Franchises: East—Geneva Red Wings, Utica Brewers, Rome Thunderbolts, Sherrill Silversmiths, Syracuse Salt Cats, Syracuse Junior Chiefs. West—Geneva Yankees, Niagara Power, Alfred Thunder, Allegany County Nitros, Hornell Dodgers, Oleans Oilers.

Regular season starts: June 3. **Regular season ends:** July 26. **All-Star Game/Scout Day:** July 11 at Sal Maglie Field, Niagara Falls, New York. **Playoff Format:** Round 1 is one playoff game between the second- and third-place teams in each division. Round 2 is a three-game playoff between first-place team and the winner of Round 1 in each division. The championship is the East Division winner versus the West Division winner

Roster Limit: 30 (college-eligible players only)

NORTHWOODS LEAGUE

Office Address: 2900 4th St. SW, Rochester, MN 55902. **Telephone:** (507) 536-4579. **Fax:** (507) 536-4597. **E-Mail Address:** info@northwoodsleague.com. **Website:** www.northwoodsleague.com.

Year Founded: 1994.

President: Dick Radatz Jr. **Director of Operations:** Curt Carstensen.

Division Structure: North—Alexandria, Duluth, Mankato, Rochester, St. Cloud, Thunder Bay, Waterloo, Willmar. South—Battle Creek, Eau Claire, Green Bay, La Crosse, Lakeshore, Madison, Rochester, Wisconsin, Wisconsin Rapids.

Regular Season: 70 games (split schedule)

2012 Opening Date: May 30. **Closing Date:** August 12. **All-Star Game:** July 24 at Madison. **Playoff Format:** First-half and second-half division winners meet in best-of-three series. **Winners meet in best-of-three series for league championship.**

Roster Limit: 26 (college-eligible players only).

ALEXANDRIA BEETLES

Mailing Address: 1210 Broadway, Suite 100, Alexandria, MN 56308. **Telephone:** (320) 763-8151. **Fax:** (320) 763-8152. **E-Mail Address:** shawn@alexandriabeetles.com, alex@alexandriabeetles.com. **Website:** www.alexandria-beetles.com. **General Manager:** Shawn Reilly. **Assistant General Manager:** Josh Swanson. **Field Manager:** Drew Saberhagen (Newberry College, South Carolina).

BATTLE CREEK BOMBERS

Mailing Address: 189 Bridge Street, Battle Creek, MI 49017. **Telephone:** (269) 962-0735. **Fax:** (269) 962-0741. **Email Address:** info@battlecreekbombers.com Website: www.battlecreekbombers.com. **General Manager:** Brian Colopy. **Field Manager:** Brandon Higelin.

DULUTH HUSKIES

Mailing Address: 207 W Superior St, Suite 206, Holiday Center Mall, Duluth, MN 55802. **Telephone:** (218) 786-9909. **Fax:** (218) 786-9001. **E-Mail Address:** huskies@duluthhuskies.com. **Website:** www.duluthhuskies.com. **Owners:** Andy Karon, Michael Rosenzweig. **General Manager:** Craig Smith. **Assistant General Manager:** Bill Olson. **Field Manager:** Daniel Hersey (Central Florida CC).

EAU CLAIRE EXPRESS

Mailing Address: 108 E. Grand Ave, Eau Claire, WI 54701. **Telephone:** (715) 839-7788. **Fax:** (715) 839-7676. **E-Mail Address:** info@eauclaireexpress.com. **Website:** www.eauclaireexpress.com. **Owner:** Bill Rowlett. **General Manager:** Andy Neborak. **Director of Operations/Field Manager:** Dale Varsho.

GREEN BAY BULLFROGS

Mailing Address: 1306 Main Street, Green Bay, WI 54302. **Telephone:** (920) 497-7225. **Fax:** (920) 437-3551. **Email Address:** info@greenbaybullfrogs.com. **Website:** www.greenbaybullfrogs.com. **President:** Jeffrey L Royle. **Field Manager:** Jordan Bischel (Northwest Missouri State).

LA CROSSE LOGGERS

Mailing Address: 1225 Caledonia St, La Crosse, WI 54603. **Telephone:** (608) 796-9553. **Fax:** (608) 796-9032. **E-Mail Address:** info@lacrosseloggers.com. **Website:** www.lacrosseloggers.com. **Owner:** Dan Kapanke. **General Manager:** Chris Goodell. **Assistant General Manager:** Ben Kapanke. **Field Manager:** Andy McKay (Sacramento CC).

LAKESHORE CHINOOKS

Mailing Address: PO Box 227, 995 Badger Circle, Grafton, WI 53024. **Telephone:** (262) 618-4659. **Fax:** (262) 618-4362. **E-Mail Address:** info@lakeshorechinooks. com. **Website:** www.lakeshorechinooks.com. **Owner:** Jim Kacmarcik. **General Manager:** Dean Rennicke. **Assistant General Manager:** Chad Bauer. **Field Manager:** John Vodenlich (Wisconsin-Whitewater).

MADISON MALLARDS

Mailing Address: 2920 N Sherman Ave, Madison, WI 53704. **Telephone:** (608) 246-4277. **Fax:** (608) 246-4163. **E-Mail Address:** conor@mallardsbaseball.com. **Website:** www.mallardsbaseball.com. **Owner:** Steve Schmitt. **President:** Vern Stenman. **General Manager:** Conor Caloia. **Field Manager:** Greg Labbe (Eagle's View Academy, Jacksonville).

MANKATO MOONDOGS

Mailing Address: 1221 Caledonia Street, Mankato, MN 56001. **Telephone:** (507) 625-7047. **Fax:** (507) 625-7059. **E-Mail Address:** office@mankatomoondogs. com. **Website:** www.mankatomoondogs.com. **Owner/President:** Joe Schwei. **General Manager:** Kyle Mrozek. **Assistant General Manager:** Greg Weis. **Field Manager:** Mike Orchard (Central Arizona JC).

ROCHESTER HONKERS

Mailing Address: PO Box 482, Rochester, MN 55903. **Telephone:** (507) 289-1170. **Fax:** (507) 289-1866. **E-Mail Address:** honkers@rochesterhonkers.com. **Website:** www.rochesterhonkers.com. **Owner/General Manager:** Dan Litzinger. **Field Manager:** Zach Etheredge (UC Santa Barbara).

ST. CLOUD RIVER BATS

Mailing Address: PO Box 5059, St. Cloud, MN 56302. **Telephone:** (320) 240-9798. **Fax:** (320) 255-5228. **E-Mail Address:** info@riverbats.com. **Website:** www.riverbats. com. **Field Manager:** Unavailable.

THUNDER BAY BORDER CATS

Mailing Address: PO Box 29105, Thunder Bay, Ontario P7B 6P9. **Telephone:** (807) 766-2287. **Fax:** (807) 345-8299. **E-Mail Address:** baseball@tbaytel.net. **Website:** www. bordercatsbaseball.com. **President/General Manager:** Brad Jorgenson. **Field Manager:** Andy Judkins (Central Arizona).

WATERLOO BUCKS

Mailing Address: PO Box 4124, Waterloo, IA 50704. **Telephone:** (319) 232-0500. **Fax:** (319) 232-0700. **E-Mail Address:** waterloobucks@waterloobucks.com. **Website:** www.waterloobucks.com. **General Manager:** Dan Corbin. **Field Manager:** Travis Kiewiet.

WILLMAR STINGERS

Mailing Address: PO Box 201, Willmar, MN, 56201. **Telephone:** (320) 222-2010. **E-Mail Address:** ryan@willmarstingers.com. **Website:** www.willmarstingers.com. **Owners:** Marc Jerzak, Ryan Voz. **General Manager:** Ryan Voz. **Field Manager:** Matt Hollod (Southern Utah).

WISCONSIN WOODCHUCKS

Mailing Address: PO Box 6157, Wausau, WI 54402. **Telephone:** (715) 845-5055. **Fax:** (715) 845-5015. **E-Mail Address:** info@woodchucks.com. **Website:** www.wood-chucks.com. **Owner/President:** Clark Eckhoff. **General Manager:** Ryan Treu. **Field Manager:** Erik Supplee

(Lynchburg College, Virginia).

WISCONSIN RAPIDS

Mailing Address: 521 Lincoln St., Wisconsin Rapids, WI 54494. **Telephone:** (715) 424-5400. **E-Mail Address:** info@ rapidsbaseball.com. **Website:** www.rapidsbaseball.com. **Owner/President:** Vern Stenman. **General Manager:** Liz Kern. **Field Manager:** Jake Martin (Coffeyville CC, Kansas).

PACIFIC INTERNATIONAL LEAGUE

Mailing Address: 4400 26th Ave W, Seattle, WA 98199. **Telephone:** (206) 623-8844. **Fax:** (206) 623-8361. **E-Mail Address:** spotter@potterprinting.com. **Website:** www. pacificinternationalleague.com.

Year Founded: 1992.

President: Mike MacColloch. **Vice President:** David Laing. **Commissioner:** Brian Gooch. **Secretary:** Steve Potter. **Treasurer:** Mark Dow.

Member Clubs: Northwest Honkers, Burnaby Bulldogs, Coquitlam Angels, Everett Merchants, Kamloops Sundevils, Kelowna Jays, Langley Blaze, Nanaimo Coal Miners, Seattle Studs, Trail (BC) franchise, Burnaby Collegiate.

Regular Season: 20 league games. **2012 Opening Date:** June 1. **Closing Date:** July 31. **Playoff Format:** The top team is invited to NBC World Series.

Roster Limit: 30; 25 eligible for games (players must be at least 18 years old).

PROSPECT LEAGUE

Mailing Address: 12268 Longleaf Oak Trail, Arlington, TN 38002. **Telephone:** (901) 218-3386. **Fax:** (480) 247-5068. **E-Mail Address:** commissioner@prospectleague. com. **Website:** www.prospectleague.com.

Year Founded: 1963 as Central Illinois Collegiate League; 2009 as Prospect League.

Commissioner: Dave Chase.

Regular Season: 56 games. **2012 Opening Date:** May 29. **Closing Date:** Aug. 6. **All-Star Game:** July 13 at Linda K. Epling Stadium, Beckley, W.V. **Championship Game:** Aug 12.

Roster Limit: 26

BUTLER BLUESOX

Mailing Address: 6 West Diamond Street, Butler, PA 16001. **Telephone:** (724) 282-2222. **Fax:** (724) 282-6565. **E-Mail Address:** frontoffice@butlerbluesox.net. **Website:** www.butlerbluesox.com. **General Manager:** Matt Cunningham. **Field Manager:** Anthony Rebyanski.

CHILLICOTHE PAINTS

Mailing Address: 59 North Paint Street, Chillicothe, OH 45601. **Telephone:** (740) 773-8326. **Fax:** (740) 773-8338. **E-Mail Address:** paints@bright.net. **Website:** www. chillicothepaints.com. **General Manager:** Bryan Wickline. **Field Manager:** Brian Mannino.

DANVILLE DANS

Mailing Address: 138 East Raymond, Danville, IL 61832. **Telephone:** (217) 9183401. **Fax:** (217) 446-9995. **E-Mail Address:** danvilledans@comcast.net. **Website:** www.danvilledans.com. **General Manager:** Jeanie Cooke. **Field Manager:** Unavailable.

DUBOIS COUNTY BOMBERS

Mailing Address: PO Box 332, Huntingburg, IN 47542. **Telephone:** (812) 683-3700. **E-Mail Address:** dcbombers@psci.net. **Website:** www.dcbombers.com. **President:** John Bigness. **General Manager:** Gary Freymiller. **Field

Manager: Ryan Anderson.

HANNIBAL CAVEMEN

Mailing Address: 403 Warren Barrett Drive, Hannibal, MO 63401. **Telephone:** (573) 221-1010. **Fax:** (573) 221-5269. **E-Mail Address:** hannibalbaseball@sbcglobal.com. **Website:** www.hannibalcavemen.com. **President:** Robert Hemond. **General Manager:** John Civitate. **Field Manager:** Jay Hemond.

LORAIN COUNTY IRONMEN

Mailing Address: 2840 Meister Road, Lorain, OH 44052. **Telephone:** (440) 552-9549. **Email Address:** info@lcironmentbaseball.com. **Website:** www.lcironmenbaseball.com. **President:** Robert Schenosky. **General Manager:** Brian McCrodden. **Field Manager:** Unavailable.

QUINCY GEMS

Mailing Address: 300 Civic Center Plaza, Quincy, IL 62301. **Telephone:** (217) 223-1000. **Fax:** (217) 223-1330. **E-Mail Address:** rebbing@quincygems.com. **Website:** www.quincygems.com. **General Manager:** Rob Ebbing. **Field Manager:** Chris Martin.

RICHMOND RIVERRATS

Mailing Address: McBride Stadium, 201 NW 13th Street, Richmond, IN 47374. **Telephone:** (765) 935-7287. **Fax:** (765) 935-7529. **E-Mail Address:** dbeaman@richmondriverrats.com. **Website:** www.richmondriverrats.com. **General Manager:** Deanna Beaman. **Field Manager:** Tyler Lairson.

SLIPPERY ROCK SLIDERS

Mailing Address: PO Box 496, Slippery Rock, PA 16057. **Telephone:** (724) 458-8831. **E-Mail Address:** mbencic@zoominternet.net. **Website:** www.theslipperyrocksliders.com. **General Manager:** Mike Bencic. **Field Manager:** Unavailable.

SPRINGFIELD SLIDERS

Mailing Address: 1415 North Grand Avenue East, Suite B, Springfield, IL 62702. **Telephone:** (217) 679-3511. **Fax:** (217) 679-3512. **E-Mail Address:** jb@springfieldsliders.com. **Website:** www.springfieldsliders.com. **Assistant General Manager:** Dana Plummer. **Head Coach:** Danny Cox.

TERRE HAUTE REX

Mailing Address: 30 North 5th Street, Terre Haute, IN 47807-2929. **Telephone:** (812) 514-8557. **Fax:** (812) 514-8551. **E-mail Address:** threxbaseball@indianastatefoundation.org. **Website:** www.threxbaseball.com. **General Manager:** Roland Shelton. **Field Manager:** Brian Dorsett.

WEST VIRGINIA MINERS

Mailing Address: 476 Ragland Road, Suite 1, Beckley, WV 25801. **Telephone:** (304) 252-7233. **Fax:** (304) 253-1998. **E-mail Address:** wvminers@wvminersbaseball.com. **Website:** www.wvminersbaseball.com. **President:** Douglas M. **Epling. General Manager:** Tim Epling. **Field Manager:** Tim Epling.

SOUTHERN COLLEGIATE BASEBALL LEAGUE

Mailing Address: 9723 Northcross Center Court, Huntersville, NC 28078. **Telephone:** (704) 635-7126. **Fax:** (704) 234-8448. **E-Mail Address:** SCBLCommissioner@aol.com. **Website:** www.scbl.org.

Year Founded: 1999.

Commissioner: Bill Capps. **President:** Jeff Carter. **Executive Vice President:** Brian Swords. **Secretary:** James Bradley. **Treasurer:** Brenda Templin. **League Historian:** Larry Tremitiere. **Umpire in Chief:** Tom Haight.

Regular Season: 42 games. **2012 Opening Date:** June 4. **Closing Date:** July 30. **Playoff Format:** Six-team double-elimination tornament, July 26-30.

Roster Limit: 30 (College-eligible players only).

ASHEVILLE REDBIRDS

Mailing Address: PO Box 17637, Asheville, NC 28816. **Telephone:** (828) 691-3679. **Email Address:** billstewart210@charter.net. **General Manager:** Bill Stewart. **Head Coach:** Ryan Smith.

BALLANTYNE SMOKIES

Mailing Address: 31014 Executive Point, Fort Mill, SC 29708. **Telephone:** (704) 996-1367. **Email Address:** jspencer@ballantynesmokies.com. **General Manager/Head Coach:** John Spencer.

CAROLINA CHAOS

Mailing Address: 142 Orchard Drive, Liberty, SC 29657. **Telephone:** (864) 843-3232, (864) 901-4331. **E-Mail Address:** brian_swords@carolinachaos.com. **Website:** www.carolinachaos.com. **General Manager:** Brian Swords (Southern Wesleyan, S.C.). **Head Coach:** Guy Howard.

LAKE NORMAN COPPERHEADS

Mailing Address: PO Box 9723, Northcross Center Court, Huntersville, NC 28078. **Telephone:** (704) 892-1041, (704) 564-9211. **E-Mail Address:** jcarter@copperheadsports.org. **Website:** www.copperheadsports.org. **General Manager:** Jeff Carter. **Head Coach:** Derek Shoe.

MORGANTON AGGIES

Mailing Address: PO Box 3448, Morganton, NC 28680. **Telephone:** (828) 438-5351. **Fax:** (828) 438-5350. **E-Mail Address:** gleonhardt@ci.morganton.nc.us. **General Manager:** Gary Leonhardt. **Head Coach:** Travis Howard.

PINEVILLE PIONEERS

Mailing Address: 1108-F Continental Boulevard, Charlotte, NC 28273. **Telephone:** (704) 264-4523. **E-Mail Address:** dave@cbcbaseball.net. **General Manager:** Dave Collins. **Head Coach:** Terry Brewer.

STATESVILLE OWLS

Mailing Address: 8680 Shallowford Road, Lewisville, NC 27023. **Telephone:** (336) 408-1516. **E-Mail Address:** keith.bray@statesvilleowls.net. **President:** Jeff Young. **General Manager:** Keith Bray.

TEXAS COLLEGIATE LEAGUE

Mailing Address: 735 Plaza Blvd, Suite 200, Coppell, TX 75019. **Telephone:** (979) 985-5198. **Fax:** (979) 779-2398. **E-Mail Address:** info@tclbaseball.com. **Website:** www.texascollegiateleague.com.

Year Founded: 2004.

President: Uri Geva.

Regular Season: 56 games (split schedule). **2011 Opening Date:** June 1. **Closing Date:** August 15. **Playoff Format:** The first- and second-half champions will be joined in the TCL playoffs by two wild card teams. Winners of the best-of-three divisional round meet in the three-game TCL Championship Series.

Roster Limit: 30 (College-eligible players only)

ACADIANA CANE CUTTERS

Telephone: (337) 237-2923. **Website:** www.canecuttersbaseball.com. **Owner/General Manager:** Richard Chalmers. **Head Coach:** Lonny Landry.

ALEXANDRIA ACES

Mailing Address: 1 Babe Ruth Dr, Alexandria, LA 71301. **Telephone:** (318) 473-2273. **Website:** www.myacesbaseball.com. **President/Chief Executive Officer:** Eric Moran. **Head Coach:** Mike Byrnes.

BRAZOS VALLEY BOMBERS

Mailing Address: 405 Mitchell St, Bryan, TX 77801. **Telephone:** (979) 799-7529. **Fax:** (979) 779-2398. **E-Mail Address:** info@bvbombers.com. **Website:** www.bvbombers.com. **Owners:** Uri Geva, Kfir Jackson. **General Manager:** Chris Clark. **Head Coach:** Brent Alumbaugh.

EAST TEXAS PUMP JACKS

Physical Address: 1100 Stone Rd, Suite 120, Kilgore, TX 75662. **Mailing Address:** PO Box 2369, Kilgore, TX 75663. **Telephone:** (903) 218-4638. **Fax:** (866) 511-5449. **E-mail Address:** info@pumpjacksbaseball.com. **Website:** www.pumpjacksbaseball.com. **General Manager:** Mike Lieberman. **Head Coach:** Stan Phelps.

MCKINNEY MARSHALS

Mailing Address: 6151 Alma Rd, McKinney, TX 75070. **Telephone:** (972) 747-8248. **E-Mail Address:** info@tclmarshals.com. **Website:** www.tclmarshals.com. **Director, General Operations:** David Apple. **Director, Finance:** Steve Pratt. **Director, Baseball Operations:** Mike Henneman.

COPPELL COPPERHEADS

Mailing Address: 735 Plaza Blvd, Suite 200, Coppell, TX 75019. **Telephone:** (972) 745-2929. **Fax:** (972) 315-1955. **Website:** www.tclmarshals.com. **General Manager:** Kyleigh Callender. **Director of Baseball Operations:** John Marston. **Head Coach:** Barry Rose.

TEXAS TOMCATS

Mailing Address: 3708 N Navarro St, Suite A, Victoria, TX 77901. **Telephone:** (361) 485-9522. **Fax:** (361) 485-0936. **E-Mail Address:** info@baseballinvictoria.com. **President:** Tracy Young. **General Manager:** Blake Koch.

VICTORIA GENERALS

Mailing Address: 3708 N Navarro St, Suite A, Victoria, TX 77901. **Telephone:** (361) 485-9522. **Fax:** (361) 485-0936. **E-Mail Address:** info@baseballinvictoria.com. **Website:** www.victoriagenerals.com. **President:** Tracy Young. **General Manager:** Blake Koch. **Head Coach:** Chris Clemons.

VALLEY BASEBALL LEAGUE

Mailing Address: Valley Baseball League, 58 Bethel Green Rd, Staunton, VA 24401. **Telephone:** (540) 213-8254. **Fax:** (540) 213-8295. **E-Mail Addresses:** dmbiery@wildblue.net, davidb@fisherautoparts.com. **Website:** www.valleyleaguebaseball.com.

Year Founded: 1961.

President: David Biery. **Assistant to the President:** Donald Lemish. **Executive Vice President:** Bruce Alger. **Media Relations Director:** Scott Musa. **Secretary:** Megan Smith. **Treasurer:** Gene Davis.

Regular Season: 44 games. **2012 Opening Date:** June 1. **Closing Date:** July 23. **All-Star Game:** North vs South, July 8 at Front Royal. **Playoff Format:** Eight teams; best-of-three quarterfinals and semifinals; best-of-five finals.

Roster Limit: 28 (college eligible players only)

COVINGTON LUMBERJACKS

Mailing Address: PO Box 30, Covington, VA 24426. **Telephone:** (540) 969-9923, (540) 962-1155. **Fax:** (540) 962-7153. **E-Mail Address:** covingtonlumberjacks@valleyleaguebaseball.com. **Website:** www.lumberjacksbaseball.com. **President:** Dizzy Garten. **Head Coach:** Dan Scott.

FRONT ROYAL CARDINALS

Mailing Address: 382 Morgans Ridge Road, Front Royal, VA 22630. **Telephone:** (703) 244-6662, (540) 631-9201. **Fax:** (703) 696-0583. **E-Mail Address:** frontroyalcardinals@valleyleaguebaseball.com. **Website:** www.frontroyalcardinals.com. **President:** Donna Settle. **Head Coach:** Clayton Kuklick.

HARRISONBURG TURKS

Mailing Address: 1489 S Main St, Harrisonburg, VA 22801. **Telephone:** (540) 434-5919. **Fax:** (540) 434-5919. **E-Mail Address:** turksbaseball@hotmail.com. **Website:** www.harrisonburgturks.com. **Operations Manager:** Teresa Wease. **General Manager/Head Coach:** Bob Wease.

HAYMARKET SENATORS

Mailing Address: 42020 Village Center Plaza, Suite 120-50, Stoneridge, VA 20105. **Telephone:** (703) 542-2110, (703) 989-5009. **Fax:** (703) 327-7435. **E-Mail Address:** haymarketsenators@valleyleaguebaseball.com. **Website:** www.haymarketbaseball.com. **President:** Scott Newell. **General Manager:** Bernie Schaffler. **Head Coach:** Justin Aspegren.

LURAY WRANGLERS

Mailing Address: 1203 E. Main St, Luray, VA 22835. **Telephone:** (540) 743-3338, (540) 843-4472. **Fax:** (540) 743-4251. **E-Mail Address:** luraywranglers@hotmail.com. **Website:** www.luraywranglers.com. **President:** Bill Turner. **Recruiting Coordinator:** Gerland Harman. **Head Coach:** Mike Bocock.

NEW MARKET REBELS

Mailing Address: PO Box 902, New Market, VA 22844. **Telephone:** (540) 740-4247, (540) 435-8453. **Fax:** (540) 740-9486. **E-Mail Address:** nmrebels@shentel.net. **Website:** www.rebelsbaseball.biz. **President/General Manager:** Bruce Alger. **Head Coach:** John Combs.

ROCKBRIDGE RAPIDS

Mailing Address: PO Box 600, Lexington, VA 24450. **Telephone:** (540) 460-7502, (540) 462-7521. **E-Mail Address:** rockbridgerapids@valleyleaguebaseball.com. **Website:** www.rockbridgerapids.com. **General Manager:** Ken Newman. **Head Coach:** Evan Wise.

STAUNTON BRAVES

Mailing Address: 14 Shannon Place, Staunton, VA 24401. **Telephone:** (540) 886-0987, (540) 885-1645. **Fax:** (540) 886-0905. **E-Mail Address:** stauntonbraves@valleyleaguebaseball.com. **Website:** www.stauntonbravesbaseball.com. **General Manager:** Steve Cox. **Head Coach:** Paul LaMarr.

STRASBURG EXPRESS

Mailing Address: PO Box 417, Strasburg, VA 22657. **Telephone:** (540) 325-5677, (540) 459-4041. **Fax:** (540) 459-3398. **E-Mail Address:** neallaw@shentel.net. **Website:** www.strasburgexpress.com. **General manager:** Jay Neal. **Head coach:** Butch Barnes.

WAYNESBORO GENERALS

Mailing Address: 435 Essex Ave., Suite 105, Waynesboro VA 22980. **Telephone:** (540) 932-2300. **Fax:** (540) 932-2322. **E-Mail Address:** waynesborogenerals@valleyleaguebaseball.com. **Website:** www.waynesboro-generals.com. **Chairman:** David T Gauldin II. **Head Coach:** Derek McDaniel.

WINCHESTER ROYALS

Mailing Address: PO Box 2485, Winchester, VA 22604. **Telephone:** (540) 539-8888, (540) 664-3978. **Fax:** (540) 662-1434. **E-Mail Addresses:** winchesterroyals@valley-leaguebaseball.com, jimphill@shentel.net. **Website:** www.winchesterroyals.com. **President:** Todd Thompson. **Head Coach:** Steve Sabins.

WOODSTOCK RIVER BANDITS

Mailing Address: 2044 Palmyra Rd, Edinburg, VA 22824. **Telephone:** (540) 481-0525. **Fax:** (540) 459-8227. **E-Mail Address:** woodstockriverbandits@valleyleague-baseball.com. **Website:** www.woodstockriverbandits.org. **President:** R.W. Bowman Jr. **Head Coach:** Phil Betterly.

WEST COAST LEAGUE

Mailing Address: PO Box 8395, Portland, OR 97207. **Telephone:** (503) 764-9510. **E-Mail Address:** wilson@westcoastleague.com. **Website:** www.westcoastleague.com.

Year Founded: 2005.

President: Ken Wilson. **Vice Presidents:** Jim Corcoran, Eddie Poplawski. **Secretary:** Dan Segel. **Treasurer:** Tony Bonacci. **Supervisor of Umpires:** Dave Perez

Division Structure: East—Bellingham, Kelowna, Walla Walla, Wenatchee. West—Bend, Corvallis, Cowlitz, Kitsap, Klamath Falls.

Regular Season: 54 games. **2012 Opening Date:** June 1. **Closing Date:** August 9. **All-Star Game:** July 24 at Walla Walla. **Playoff Format:** First- and second-place teams in each division meet in best-of-three semifinal series; winners advance to best-of-three championship series.

Roster Limit: 25 (college-eligible players only).

BELLINGHAM BELLS

Mailing Address: 1221 Potter Street, Bellingham, WA 98229. **Telephone:** (360) 746-0406. **E-Mail Address:** info@bellinghambells.com. **Website:** www.bellinghambells.com. **Owner:** Eddie Poplawski. **General Manager:** Nick Caples. **Head Coach:** Gary Hatch.

BEND ELKS

Mailing Address: PO Box 9009, Bend, OR 97708. **Telephone:** (541) 312-9259. **E-Mail Address:** richardsj@bendcable.com. **Website:** www.bendelks.com. **Owner/General Manager:** Jim Richards. **Head Coach:** Sean Kinney (Whitman College, Wash.).

CORVALLIS KNIGHTS

Mailing Address: PO Box 1356, Corvallis, OR 97339. **Telephone:** (541) 752-5656. **E-Mail Address:** dan.segel@corvallisknights.com. **Website:** www.corvallisknights.com. **President:** Dan Segel. **General Manager/Head Coach:** Brooke Knight.

COWLITZ BLACK BEARS

Mailing Address: PO Box 1255, Longview, WA 98632. **Telephone:** (360) 703-3195. **E-Mail Address:** gwilsonagm@gmail.com. **Website:** www.cowlitzblackbears.com. **Owner:** Tony Bonacci. **General Manager:** Grant Wilson. **Head Coach:** Tim Matz (Santa Ana College).

KELOWNA FALCONS

Mailing Address: 201-1014 Glenmore Dr, Kelowna, BC, V1Y 4P2. **Telephone:** (250) 763-4100. **E-Mail Address:** mark@kelownafalcons.com. **Website:** www.kelownafalcons.com. **Owner:** Dan Nonis. **General Manager:** Mark Nonis. **Head Coach:** Al Cantwell.

KITSAP BLUEJACKETS

Mailing Address: PO Box 68, Silverdale, WA 98383. **Telephone:** (360) 692-5566. **E-Mail Address:** rsmith@kitsapbluejackets.com. **Website:** www.kitsapbluejackets.com. **Managing Partner/General Manager:** Rick Smith. **Head Coach:** Ryan Parker (Olympic College).

KLAMATH FALLS GEMS

Mailing Address: 2001 Crest Street, Klamath Falls, Oregon 97603. **Telephone:** (541) 883-4367. **E-Mail Address:** chuck@klamathfallsgems.com. **Website:** www.klamathfallsgems.com. **General Manager:** Chuck Heeman. **Head Coach:** Josh Hogan (Oregon).

WALLA WALLA SWEETS

Mailing Address: 109 E Main Street, Walla Walla, WA 99362. **Telephone:** (509) 522-2255. **E-Mail Address:** Zachary.Fraser@pacificbaseballventures.com. **Website:** www.wallawallabaseball.com. **Owner:** Pacific Baseball Ventures, LLC. **General Manager:** Zachary Fraser. **Head Coach:** J.C. Biagi (Walla Walla CC, Wash.)

WENATCHEE APPLESOX

Mailing Address: PO Box 5100, Wenatchee, WA 98807. **Telephone:** (509) 665-6900. **E-Mail Address:** sales@applesox.com. **Website:** www.applesox.com. **Owner/General Manager:** Jim Corcoran. **Head Coach:** Ed Knaggs.

WCL PORTLAND

Mailing Address: 2811 NE Holman, Portland, Oregon 97211. **Telephone:** (503) 280-8691. **E-Mail Address:** rvance@cu-portland.edu. **Website:** www.wccbl.com/portland.

Year Founded: 2009.

Commissioner: Rob Vance.

Regular Season: 25 games. **2011 Opening Date:** June 4. **Closing Date:** August 7. **All-Star Game:** None. **Playoff Format:** First-place team faces fourth-place team and second-place team faces third-place team in first round. **Winners advance to championship game.**

Roster Limit: 25 (college-eligible players only)

Teams: Bucks, Dukes, Lobos, Ports, Stars, Toros.

HIGH SCHOOL BASEBALL

NATIONAL FEDERATION OF STATE HIGH SCHOOL ASSOCIATIONS

Mailing Address: P.O. Box 690, Indianapolis, IN 46206. **Telephone:** (317) 972-6900. **Fax:** (317) 822-5700. **E-Mail Address:** baseball@nfhs.org. **Website:** www.nfhs.org.

Executive Director: Bob Gardner. **Chief Operating Officer:** James Tenopir. **Assistant Director/Baseball Rules Editor:** Elliot Hopkins. **Director, Publications/Communications:** Bruce Howard.

NATIONAL HIGH SCHOOL BASEBALL COACHES ASSOCIATION

Mailing Address: P.O. Box 12843, Tempe, AZ 85284. **Telephone:** (602) 615-0571. **Fax:** (480) 838-7133. **E-Mail Address:** rdavini@cox.net. **Website:** www.baseballcoaches.org. **Executive Director:** Ron Davini. **President:** Phil Clark (Bartlett, Tenn, HS). **First Vice President:** Art Griffith (Winslow, Ariz, HS). **Second Vice President:** John Lowery Sr. (Jefferson HS, Shepherdstown, W.Va.).

2012 National Convention: Nov. 29-Dec. 2, at St. Louis.

NATIONAL TOURNAMENTS

IN-SEASON

HORIZON NATIONAL INVITATIONAL

Mailing Address: Horizon High School, 5653 Sandra Terrace, Scottsdale, AZ 85254. **Telephone:** (602) 867-9003. **E-mail:** huskycoach1@yahoo.com Website: www.horizonbaseball.com.

Tournament Director: Eric Kibler.
2012 Tournament: March 19-22.

INTERNATIONAL PAPER CLASSIC

Mailing Address: 4775 Johnson Rd., Georgetown, SC 29440. **Telephone:** (843) 527-9606, (843) 546-3807. **Fax:** (843) 546-8521. **Website:** www.ipclassic.com.

Tournament Director: Alicia Johnson.
2012 Tournament: March 8-11 (eight teams).

LIONS INVITATIONAL

Mailing Address: 3502 Lark St., San Diego CA 92103. **Telephone:** (619) 602-8650. **Fax:** (619) 239-3539. **Website:** www.anaheimlionsbaseball.org.

Tournament Director: Rod Wallace.
2012 Tournament: April 2, 4-6.

NATIONAL CLASSIC BASEBALL TOURNAMENT

Mailing Address: P.O. Box 338, Placentia, CA 92870. **Telephone:** (714) 993-2838. **Fax:** (714) 993-5350. **E-Mail Address:** placentiamustang@aol.com. **Website:** www.national-classic.com

Tournament Director: Marcus Jones.
2012 Tournament: April 9-12 (16 teams).

USA BASEBALL NATIONAL HIGH SCHOOL INVITATIONAL

Mailing Address: 403 Blackwell St., Durham, NC 27701. **Telephone:** (919) 474-8721. **Fax:** (919) 474-8822. **Email:** rickriccobono@usabaseball.com. **Website:** www.usabaseball.com.

Tournament Director: Rick Riccobono.
2012 Tournament: March 28-31 at USA Baseball National Training Complex, Cary, NC (16 teams).

USA CLASSIC NATIONAL HIGH SCHOOL INVITATIONAL

Mailing Address: P.O. Box 247, Millington, TN 38043. **Telephone:** (901) 873-5880. **Fax:** (901) 873-5885. **Email:** jwaits@cityofmillington.org. **Website:** www.millingtontn.gov.

Tournament Organizers: Jeff Waits, Johnny Ray.
2012 Tournament: April 4-7 at USA Baseball Stadium, Millington, TN (16 teams).

POSTSEASON

SUNBELT BASEBALL CLASSIC SERIES

Mailing Address: 505 North Blvd., Edmond, OK 73034. **Telephone:** (405) 348-3839. **Fax:** (405) 340-7538. **Email:** lyngor@aol.com. **Website:** www.sunbeltclassicbaseball.com.

Chairman: John Schwartz.
2012 Senior Series: Unavailable.
2012 Junior Series: Unavailable.
2012 Sophomore Series: Unavailable.

ALL-STAR GAMES/AWARDS

PERFECT GAME ALL-AMERICAN CLASSIC

Mailing Address: 1932 Wynnton Road, Columbus, Georgia 31999. **Telephone:** (706) 763-2827. **Fax:** (706) 320-2288. **Event Organizer:** Blue Ridge Sports & Entertainment. **Vice President, Events:** Lou Lacy. **2012 Game:** Unavailable.

UNDER ARMOUR ALL-AMERICA GAME, POWERED BY BASEBALL FACTORY

Mailing Address: 9212 Berger Rd., Suite 200, Columbia, MD 21046. **Telephone:** 410-715-5080. **E-Mail Address:** jason@baseballfactory.com. **Website:** baseballfactory.com. **Event Organizers:** Baseball Factory, Team One Baseball. **2012 Game:** August.

GATORADE CIRCLE OF CHAMPIONS

(National HS Player of the Year Award)

Mailing Address: The Gatorade Company, 321 N. Clark St., Suite 24-3, Chicago, IL, 60610. **Telephone:** 312-821-1000. **Website:** www.gatorade.com.

SHOWCASE EVENTS

ALL-AMERICAN BASEBALL TALENT SHOWCASES

Mailing Address: 333 Preston Ave., Unit 1, Voorhees, NJ 08043. **Telephone:** (856) 354-0201. **Fax:** (856) 354-0818. **E-Mail Address:** hitdoctor@thehitdoctor.com. **Website:** thehitdoctor.com. **National Director:** Joe Barth.

AREA CODE GAMES

Mailing Address: 23954 Madison Street, Torrance, CA 90505. **Telephone:** 310-791-1142 x 7166. **Email address:** Andrew.Knepper@espn.com. **Website:** areacodebaseball.com

Event Organizer: Andrew Knepper
2012 Area Code Games: August 5th-10th at Blair Field in Long Beach, Calif.

ARIZONA FALL CLASSIC

Mailing Address: 6102 W. Maui Lane, Glendale, AZ 85306. **Telephone:** (602) 978-2929. **Fax:** (602) 439-4494. **E-Mail Address:** azbaseballted@msn.com. **Website:** www.azfallclassic.com.

Directors: Ted Heid, Tracy Heid.

2012 Events

Four Corner Classic	Peoria, AZ, May 31-June 2
Arizona Summer Classic	Peoria, AZ, July 12-15
Arizona Summer Classic (16U)	July 19-22
Arizona Fall Invitational	Oct. 5-7
Arizona Fall Classic (16U)	Oct. 5-7
AZ Senior Fall Classic (HS seniors)	Peoria, AZ, Oct. 11-14
AZ Junior Fall Classic (HS juniors)	Peoria, AZ, Oct. 18-21
AZ Sophomore Fall Classic. (HS soph. and under)	Peoria, AZ, Oct. 25-28

BASEBALL FACTORY

Office Address: 9212 Berger Rd., Suite 200, Columbia, MD 21046. **Telephone:** (800) 641-4487, (410) 715-5080. **Fax:** (410) 715-1975. **E-Mail Address:** info@baseballfactory.com. **Website:** www.baseballfactory.com.

Chief Executive Officer: Steve Sclafani. **President:** Rob Naddelman. **Executive VP, Baseball Operations:** Steve Bernhardt. **Senior VP, Finance:** Matt Frese. **Senior VP, Operations/Marketing:** Jason Budden. **VP, On-Field Events:** Jim Gemler. **VP, Creative:** Matt Kirby. **VP, Player Development:** Dan Forester. **Senior Director, Baseball Operations:** Andy Ferguson. **Senior Director, Instruction:** Matt Schilling. **Senior Director, College Recruiting:** Dan Mooney. **Senior Director, Youth Baseball:** Jeff Brazier. **Senior Multimedia Producer:** Brian Johnson.

Player Development Coordinators: Steve Nagler, Dave Packer, John Perko, Patrick Wuebben, Chris Brown, Adam Darvick, Will Bach, Will Bowers, Ronald Greene, Rob Onolfi, Scott Ritter, Ryan Schweikert. **Client Services Coordinator:** Cecile Banas. **Lessons Coordinator:** Joe Lake. **Director, PVP Program/National Tryouts:** Bryan Dunkel. **Director, College Recruiting Operations:** Woody Wingfield.

Under Armour Pre-Season All-America Tournament: January 13-15 in Tucson, AZ (Kino Sports Complex).
Under Armour All-America Game: August 2012.
2012 Under Armour Baseball Factory National Tryouts & Premium Video Program: Various locations across the country. Year round. Open to high school players, ages 14–18 and a separate division for pre-high school players, ages 12–13. Check www.baseballfactory.com/tryouts for full schedule.

BLUE-GREY CLASSIC

Mailing address: 68 Norfolk Road, Mills MA 02054. **Telephone:** (508) 376-1250. **E-Mail address:** impact-prospects@comcast.net. **Website:** www.impactprospects.com.

2012 events: Various dates, locations June-Sept. 2012.

BOBBY VALENTINE ALL-AMERICAN CAMPS

Address: 72 Camp Avenue, Stamford, CT 06907. **Telephone:** (203) 517-1277. **Fax:** (203) 517-1377. **Website:** www.allamericanfoundation.com

COLLEGE SELECT BASEBALL

Mailing Address: P.O. Box 783, Manchester, CT 06040. **Telephone:** (800) 645-9854. **E-Mail Address:** TRhit@msn.com. **Website:** www.collegeselect.org. **Consulting Director:** Tom Rizzi.

IMPACT BASEBALL

Mailing Address: P.O. Box 47, Sedalia, NC 27342. **E-Mail Address:** andypartin@aol.com. **Website:** impactbaseball.com. **Operator:** Andy Partin.
2012 Showcases: June 11-12, Wingate University; June 26-26, Mount Olive College; Aug. 10-12, TBA; August 25, Appalachian State.

EAST COAST PROFESSIONAL SHOWCASE

Website: www.eastcoastproshowcase.com. **Tournament Directors:** John Castleberry. **Tournament Coordinator:** Shannon Follett.
2012 Showcase: Aug. 1-4, Syracuse, N.Y.

PACIFIC NORTHWEST CHAMPIONSHIPS

Mailing Address: 42783 Deerhorn Road, Springfield, Or. 97478. **Telephone:** (541) 896-0841. **E-Mail Address:** mckay@baseballnorthwest.com. **Website:** www.baseballnorthwest.com. **Tournament Organizer:** Jeff McKay.

PERFECT GAME USA

Mailing Address: 1203 Rockford Road SW, Cedar Rapids, IA 52404. **Telephone:** (319) 298-2923 **Fax:** (319) 298-2924. **E-Mail Address:** jerry@perfectgame.org. **Website:** www.perfectgameusa.com.

President/Director: Jerry Ford. **Vice Presidents:** Andy Ford, Jason Gerst, Tyson Kimm, Allan Simpson. **International Director:** Kentaro Yasutake. **National Showcase Director:** Jim Arp. **National Tournament Director:** Taylor McCollough. **Scouting Director:** David Rawnsley. **National BCS Director:** Ben Ford. **Iowa League Director:** Steve James. **Northeast Director/Showcase Director:** Dan Kennedy. **West Coast Director:** Mike Spiers. **Scouting Coordinators:** Jeff Simpson, Greg Sabers, Kyle Noesen, Jason Piddington, Anup Sinha. **National Coordinator:** Frank Fulton.

2012 Showcase/Tournament Events: Sites across the United States, Jan. 9-Nov. 7.

PROFESSIONAL BASEBALL INSTRUCTION—BATTERY INVITATIONAL

(for top HS pitchers and catchers)

Mailing Address: 107 Pleasant Avenue, Upper Saddle River NJ 07458. **Telephone:** (800) 282-4638. **Fax:** (201) 760-8720. **E-Mail Address:** info@baseballclinics.com. **Website:** www.baseballclinics.com/batteryinvitational. html.

President: Doug Cinnella.

Senior Staff Administrator: Greg Cinnella. **General Manager/PR/Marketing:** Jim Monaghan.

SELECTFEST BASEBALL

Mailing Address: 60 Franklin Pl., Morris Plains, NJ 07950. **Telephone:** (862) 222-6404. **E-Mail Address:** selectfest@optonline.net. **Website:** www.selectfestbaseball.org. **Camp Directors:** Bruce Shatel.

2012 Showcase: June 29-July 1.

TEAM ONE BASEBALL

(A division of Baseball Factory)

Office Address: 1000 Bristol Street North, Box 17285, Newport Beach, CA 92660. **Telephone:** (800) 621-5452, (805) 451-8203. **Fax:** (949) 209-1829. **E-Mail Address:** jroswell@teamonebaseball.com. **Website:** www.teamonebaseball.com.

Senior Director: Justin Roswell. **Executive VP, Baseball Operations:** Steve Bernhardt. **VP, On-Field Events:** Jim Gemler. **National Recruiting Coordinator:** Vince Sacco.

2012 Under Armour Showcases: Team One Florida: June 13 in Jupiter, FL (Roger Dean Sports Complex); Team One West: July 8–9 in Costa Mesa, CA (Vanguard University); Team One South: July 13–14 in Atlanta, GA (Emory University); Team One Midwest: July 16–17 in River Forest, IL (Concordia University); Team One Northeast: July 23–24 in Trenton, NJ (Waterfront Park); Team One Futures East: September 22 in Jupiter, FL (Roger Dean Stadium); Team One Futures West: Oct 19 in Peoria, AZ (Peoria Stadium).

2012 Under Armour Tournaments: Under Armour Memorial Day Classic: May 25-28 in Jupiter, FL (Roger Dean Sports Complex), Under Armour Southeast Tournament: June 8–12 in Jupiter, FL (Roger Dean Sports Complex), Under Armour Firecracker Classic: July 2–6 in Jupiter, FL (Roger Dean Sports Complex), Under Armour Southwest Tournament: July 31 – August 4 in Azusa, CA (Azusa Pacific University/Citrus College), Under Armour Fall Classic: September 21–23 in Jupiter, FL (Roger Dean Sports Complex), Under Armour Invitational: Oct 12–14 in St. Petersburg, FL (Walter Fuller Complex. **Under Armour SoCal Classic:** Oct 26–28 in Azusa, CA (Azusa Pacific University/Citrus College).

TOP 96 COLLEGE COACHES CLINICS

Mailing Address: 6 Foley Dr. Southboro, MA 01772. **Telephone:** 508-481-5935.

E-Mail Address: doug.henson@top96.com. **Website:** www.top96.com.

Directors: Doug Henson, Dave Callum.

2012 Clinics: Various clinics throughout the United States; see website for schedule.

YOUTH BASEBALL

ALL AMERICAN AMATEUR BASEBALL ASSOCIATION

Mailing Address: 331 Parkway Dr., Zanesville, OH 43701. **Telephone:** (740) 453-8531. **E-Mail Address:** clw@aol.com. **Website:** www.aaaba.us.
Year Founded: 1944.
President: Lou Tiberi. **Executive Director/Secretary:** Bob Wolfe.
2012 Events: Dates unavailable.

AMATEUR ATHLETIC UNION OF THE UNITED STATES, INC.

Mailing Address: P.O. Box 22409, Lake Buena Vista, FL 32830. **Telephone:** (407) 934-7200. **Fax:** (407) 934-7242. **E-Mail Address:** oldpro77@msn.com, debra@aausports.org. **Website:** www.aaubaseball.org.
Year Founded: 1982. **Sports Manager, Baseball:** Debra Horn.

AMERICAN AMATEUR BASEBALL CONGRESS

National Headquarters: 100 West Broadway, Farmington, NM 87401. **Telephone:** (505) 327-3120. **Fax:** (505) 327-3132. **E-Mail Address:** aabc@aabc.us. **Website:** www.aabc.us.
Year Founded: 1935.
President: Richard Neely.

AMERICAN AMATEUR YOUTH BASEBALL ALLIANCE

Mailing Address: 1703 Koala Drive, Wentzville, MO 63385. **Telephone:** (636) 332-7799. **E-Mail Address:** clwjr28@aol.com. **Website:** www.aayba.com.
President, Baseball Operations: Carroll Wood. **President, Business Operations:** Greg Moore.

AMERICAN LEGION BASEBALL

National Headquarters: American Legion Baseball, 700 N. Pennsylvania St., Indianapolis, IN 46204. **Telephone:** (317) 630-1213. **Fax:** (317) 630-1369. **E-Mail Address:** baseball@legion.org **Website:** www.baseball.legion.org/baseball.
Year Founded: 1925.
Program Coordinator: Jim Quinlan.
2012 World Series (19 and under): Aug. 17-21 at Veteran's Field, Shelby, N.C.
2011 Regional Tournaments (Aug. 4-13): Northeast—Old Orchard Beach, Maine; Mid-Atlantic—West Lawn, Pa.; Southeast—Sumter, S.C.; Mid-South—New Orleans, La; Great Lakes—Midland, Mich.; Central Plains—Dickinson, N.D.; Northwest—Billings, Mont.; Western—Fairfield, Calif.

BABE RUTH BASEBALL

International Headquarters: 1770 Brunswick Pike, P.O. Box 5000, Trenton, NJ 08638. **Telephone:** (609) 695-1434. **Fax:** (609) 695-2505. **E-Mail Address:** info@baberuthleague.org. **Website:** www.baberuthleague.org.
Year Founded: 1951.
President/Chief Executive Officer: Steven Tellefsen.

CONTINENTAL AMATEUR BASEBALL ASSOCIATION

Mailing Address: 1173 French Court, Maineville, Ohio 45039. **Telephone:** (513) 677-1580. **Fax:** 513-677-2586. **E-Mail Address:** lred-wine@cababaseball.com. **Website:** www.cababaseball.com.
Year Founded: 1984.
Executive Director: Larry Redwine. **Commissioner:** John Mocny. **Executive Vice President:** Fran Pell.

DIXIE YOUTH BASEBALL

Mailing Address: P.O. Box 877, Marshall, TX 75671. **Telephone:** (903) 927-2255. **Fax:** (903) 927-1846. **E-Mail Address:** dyb@dixie.org. **Website:** www.dixie.org.
Year Founded: 1955.
Commissioner: Wes Skelton.

DIXIE BOYS BASEBALL

Mailing Address: P.O. Box 8263, Dothan, Alabama 36304. **Telephone:** (334) 793-3331. **E-Mail Address:** jjones29@sw.rr.com. **Website:** www. http://baseball.dixie.org.
Commissioner/Chief Executive Officer: Sandy Jones

DIZZY DEAN BASEBALL

Mailing Address: P.O. Box 856, Hernando, MS 38632. **Telephone:** (662) 429-4365, (423) 596-1353. **E-Mail Address:** DPhil10513@aol.com, jimmywahl@bellsouth.net, Bdunn39270@comcast.net, hsuggsdizzydean@aol.com. **Website:** www.dizzydeanbbinc.org.
Year Founded: 1962.
Commissioner: Danny Phillips. **President:** Jimmy Wahl. **VP:** Bobby Dunn. **Secretary:** Billy Powell. **Treasurer:** Houston Suggs.

HAP DUMONT YOUTH BASEBALL

(A Division of the National Baseball Congress)
E-Mail Address: bruce@prattrecreation.com,gbclev@hapdumontbaseball.com. **Website:** www.hapdumont-baseball.com.
Year Founded: 1974.
President: Bruce Pinkall

LITTLE LEAGUE BASEBALL

International Headquarters: P.O. Box 3485, Williamsport, PA 17701. **Telephone:** (570) 326-1921. **Fax:** (570) 326-1074. **Website:** www.littleleague.org.
Year Founded: 1939.
Chairman: Dennis Lewin.
President/Chief Executive Officer: Stephen D. Keener. **Chief Financial Officer:** David Houseknecht. **Vice President, Operations:** Patrick Wilson. **Treasurer:** Melissa Singer. **Senior Communications Executive:** Lance Van Auken.

NATIONAL AMATEUR BASEBALL FEDERATION

Mailing Address: P.O. Box 705, Bowie, MD 20718. **Telephone:** (410) 721-4727. **Fax:** (410) 721-4940. **E-Mail Address:** nabf1914@aol.com. **Website:** www.nabf.com.
Year Founded: 1914.
Executive Director: Charles Blackburn.

NATIONAL ASSOCIATION OF POLICE ATHLETIC LEAGUES

Mailing Address: 658 W Indiantown Road #201, Jupiter, FL 33458. **Telephone:** (561) 745-5535. **Fax:** (561) 745-3147. **E-Mail Address:** copnkid@nationalpal.org. **Website:** www.nationalpal.org.
Year Founded: 1914.
President: L.B. Scott.

PONY BASEBALL

International Headquarters: P.O. Box 225, Washington, PA 15301. **Telephone:** (724) 225-1060. **Fax:** (724) 225-9852. **E-Mail Address:** info@pony.org. **Website:** www.pony.org.
Year Founded: 1951.
President: Abraham Key.

REVIVING BASEBALL IN INNER CITIES

Mailing Address: 245 Park Ave., New York, NY 10167. **Telephone:** (212) 931-7800. **Fax:** (212) 949-5695. **Year Founded:** 1989. **Director, Reviving Baseball in Inner Cities:** David James (David.James@mlb.com). **Vice President, Community Affairs:** Thomas C. **Brasuell.** **Email:** rbi@mlb.com. **Website:** www.mlb.com/rbi.

SUPER SERIES BASEBALL OF AMERICA

National Headquarters: 3449 East Kael Street., Mesa, AZ 85213-1773. **Telephone:** (480) 664-2998. **Fax:** (480) 664-2997. **E-Mail Address:** info@superseriesbaseball.com. **Website:** www.superseriesbaseball.com.
President: Mark Mathew.

TRIPLE CROWN SPORTS

Mailing Address: 3930 Automation Way, Fort Collins, CO 80525. **Telephone:** (970) 223-6644. **Fax:** (970) 223-3636. **Websites:** www.triplecrownsports.com. **E-Mail:** thad@triplecrownsports.com. **Director, Baseball Operations:** Thad Anderson.

U.S. AMATEUR BASEBALL ASSOCIATION

E-Mail Address: usaba@usaba.com. **Website:** www.usaba.com.
Year Founded: 1969.

U.S. AMATEUR BASEBALL FEDERATION

Mailing Address: PO Box 531216, San Diego, CA 92153. **Telephone:** (619) 934-2551. **Fax:** (619) 271-6659. **E-Mail Address:** usabf@cox.net. **Website:** www.usabf.com.
Year Founded: 1997.
Senior Chief Executive Officer/President: Tim Halbig.

UNITED STATES SPECIALTY SPORTS ASSOCIATION

Executive Vice President, Baseball: Don DeDonatis III, 33600 Mound Rd., Sterling Heights, MI 48310. **Telephone:** (810) 597-6410. **E-Mail Address:** michusssa@aol.com.
Executive Vice President, Baseball Operations: Rick Fortuna, 6324 N. Chatham Ave., #136, Kansas City,

MO 64151. **Telephone:** (816) 587-4545. **E-Mail Address:** rick@kcsports.org. **Website:** www.usssabaseball.org. **Year Founded:** 1965/Baseball 1996.

WORLD WOOD BAT ASSOCIATION

(A Division of Perfect Game USA)
Mailing Address: 1203 Rockford Road SW, Cedar Rapids, IA 52404. **Telephone:** (319) 298-2923. **Fax:** (319) 298-2924. **E-Mail Address:** taylor@perfectgame.org. **Website:** www.worldwoodbat.com.
Year Founded: 1997.
President: Jerry Ford. **National Director:** Taylor McCollough. **Scouting Director:** David Rawnsley.

BASEBALL USA

Mailing Address: 2626 W. Sam Houston Pkwy. N., Houston, TX 77043. **Telephone:** (713) 690-5055. **E-Mail Address:** info@baseballusa.com. **Website:** www.baseballusa.com.
Tournament Director: Steve Olson

CALIFORNIA COMPETITIVE YOUTH BASEBALL

Mailing Address: P.O. Box 338, Placentia, CA 92870. **Telephone:** (714) 993-2838. **E-Mail Address:** ccybnet@aol.com. **Website:** www.ccyb.net.
Tournament Director: Todd Rogers.

COCOA EXPO SPORTS CENTER

Mailing Address: 500 Friday Road, Cocoa, FL 32926. **Telephone:** (321) 639-3976. **Fax:** (407) 390-9435. **E-Mail Address:** athleticdirector@cocoaexpo.com. **Website:** www.cocoaexpo.com.
Athletic Director: Matt Yurish.
Activities: Spring training program, spring & fall leagues, instructional camps, team training camps, youth tournaments.

COOPERSTOWN BASEBALL WORLD

Mailing Address: P.O. Box 646, Allenwood, NJ 08723. **Telephone:** (888) CBW-8750. **Fax:** (888) CBW-8720. **E-Mail:** cbw@cooperstownbaseballworld.com. **Website:** www.cooperstownbaseballworld.com.
Complex Address: Cooperstown Baseball World, SUNY-Oneonta, Ravine Parkway, Oneonta, NY 13820.
President/Chairman: Eddie Einhorn. **Vice President:** Debra Sirianni.
2012 Tournaments (15 Teams Per Week): Open to 11U, 12U, 13U, 14U, 15U, 16U

COOPERSTOWN DREAMS PARK

Mailing Address: 330 S. Main St., Salisbury, NC 28144. **Telephone:** (704) 630-0050. **Fax:** (704) 630-0737. **E-Mail Address:** info@cooperstowndreamspark.com. **Website:** www.cooperstowndreamspark.com.
Complex Address: 4550 State Highway 28, Cooperstown, NY 13807.
Chief Executive Officer: Lou Presutti. **Program Director:** Geoff Davis.
2012 Tournaments: Weekly June 2–Aug. 31.

COOPERSTOWN ALL STAR VILLAGE

Mailing Address: P.O. Box 670, Cooperstown, NY 13326. **Telephone:** (800) 327-6790. **Fax:** (607) 432-1076. **E-Mail Address:** info@cooperstownallstarvillage.com. **Website:** www.cooperstownallstarvillage.com.
Team Registrations: Jim Rudloff. **Hotel Room**

Reservations: Shelly Yager. **Presidents:** Martin and Brenda Patton.

DISNEY'S WIDE WORLD OF SPORTS

Mailing Address: P.O. BOX 470847, Celebration, Fl 34747. **Telephone:** (407) 938-3802. **Fax:** (407) 938-3442. **E-mail address:** wdw.sports.baseball@disneysports.com. **Website:** www.disneybaseball.com.

Manager, Sports Events: Scott St George. **Senior Sports Manager:** Emily Moak. **Tournament Director:** Al Schlazer.

KC SPORTS TOURNAMENTS

Mailing Address: KC Sports, 6324 N. Chatham Ave., No. 136, Kansas City, MO 64151.
Telephone: (816) 587-4545. **Fax:** (816) 587-4549.
E-Mail Address: info@kcsports.org. **Website:** www.kcsports.org.
Activities: USSSA Youth tournaments (ages 6-18).

U.S. AMATEUR BASEBALL FEDERATION

Mailing Address: P.O. Box 531216, San Diego, CA 92153. **Telephone:** (619) 934-2551. **Fax:** (619) 271-6659. **E-Mail Address:** usabf@cox.net. **Website:** www.usabf.com.
Year Founded: 1997. **Senior Chief Executive Officer/President:** Tim Halbig.

INSTRUCTIONAL SCHOOLS/ PRIVATE CAMPS

ACADEMY OF PRO PLAYERS

Mailing Address: 140 5th Avenue, Hawthorne, NJ 07506. **Telephone:** (973) 304-1470. **Fax:** (973) 636-6375. **E-Mail Address:** proplayer@nji.com. **Website:** www.academypro.com. **Camp Director:** Dan Gilligan.

ALL-STAR BASEBALL ACADEMY

Mailing Addresses: 650 South Parkway Blvd., Broomall, PA 19008; 52 Penn Oaks Dr., West Chester, PA 19382, 3 Esterbrook Lane, Cherry Hill, NJ 08003, 417 Boot Rd., Downington, PA 19335, 1537 Campus Drive, Warminster, PA 18974. **Telephone:** (610) 355-2411, (856) 433-8312, (610) 518-7400, (215) 672-1826, (610) 399-8050. **Fax:** (610) 355-2414. **E-Mail Address:** basba@allstarbaseballacademy.com. **Website:** www.allstarbaseballacademy.com. **Directors:** Mike Manning, Jim Freeman.

AMERICAN BASEBALL FOUNDATION

Mailing Address: 2660 10th Ave. South, Suite 620, Birmingham, AL 35205. **Telephone:** (205) 558-4235. **Fax:** (205) 918-0800. **E-Mail Address:** abf@asmi.org. **Website:** www.americanbaseball.org. **Executive Director:** David Osinski.

THE BASEBALL ACADEMY

Mailing Address: IMG Academies, 5500 34th St. W., Bradenton, FL 34210. **Telephone:** (941) 739-7480. **Fax:** (941) 739-7484. **E-Mail Address:** acad_baseball@imgworld.com. **Website:** www.imgacademies.com.

AMERICA'S BASEBALL CAMPS

Mailing Address: Ben Boulware, 3020 ISSQ. Pine Lake Road #12, Sammamish, WA 98075. **Telephone:** (800) 222-8152. **Fax:** (888) 751-8989. **E-Mail Address:** info@baseballcamps.com. **Website:** www.baseballcamps.com.

BUCKY DENT'S BASEBALL SCHOOL

Mailing Address: 490 Dotterel Road, Delray Beach, FL 33444. **Telephone:** (561) 265-0280. **Fax:** (561) 278-6679. **E-Mail Address:** staff@dentbaseball.com. **Website:** www.buckydentbaseballschool.com. **Director of Baseball Operations:** Luis Alicea. **Operations Manager:** Kelli Morse.

CHAMPIONS BASEBALL ACADEMY

Mailing Address: 5994 Linneman Street Cincinatti, OH 45228. **Telephone:** (513) 831-8873. **Fax:** (513) 247-0040. **E-Mail Address:** championsbaseball@ymail.com. **Website:** www.championsbaseball.net.

DOYLE BASEBALL ACADEMY

Mailing Address: P.O. Box 9156, Winter Haven, FL 33883. **Telephone:** (863) 439-1000. **Fax:** (863) 294-8607. **E-Mail Address:** info@doylebaseball.com.
Website: www.doylebaseball.com. **President:** Denny Doyle. **CEO & CFO:** Blake Doyle.

FROZEN ROPES TRAINING CENTERS

Mailing Address: 24 Old Black Meadow Rd., Chester, NY 10918. **Telephone:** (845) 469-7331. **Fax:** (845) 469-6742. **E-Mail Address:** info@frozenropes.com. **Website:** www.frozenropes.com. **Corporate Director of Operations:** Tony Abbatine.

MARK CRESSE BASEBALL SCHOOL

Mailing Address: 58 Fulmar Lane, Aliso Viego, CA 92656. **Telephone:** (714) 892-6145. **Fax:** (949) 600-9807. **E-Mail Address:** info@markcresse.com. **Website:** www.markcresse.com. **Owner/Founder:** Mark Cresse. **Executive Director:** Jeff Sears.

US SPORTS CAMPS

Mailing Address: 750 Lindaro Street, Suite 220, San Rafael, CA 94901. **Telephone:** (415) 479-6060. **Fax:** (415) 479-6061. **E-Mail Address:** baseball@ussportscamps.com. **Website:** www.ussportscamps.com.

MOUNTAIN WEST BASEBALL ACADEMY

Mailing Address: 389 West 10000 South, South Jordan, UT 84095. **Telephone:** (801) 561-1700. **Fax:** (801) 561-1762. **E-Mail Address:** kent@utahbaseballacademy.com. **Website:** www.mountainwestbaseball.com. **Director:** Bob Keyes

NORTH CAROLINA BASEBALL ACADEMY

Mailing Address: 1137 Pleasant Ridge Road, Greensboro, NC 27409. **Telephone:** (336) 931-1118. **E-Mail Address:** info@ncbaseball.com. **Website:** www.ncbaseball.com.
Owner/Director: Scott Bankhead.

PENNSYLVANIA DIAMOND BUCKS

Mailing Address: 2320 Whitetail Court, Hellertown, PA 18055. **Telephone:** (610) 838-1219, (610) 442-6998. **E-Mail Address:** janciganick@yahoo.com. **Camp Director:** Jan Ciganick. **Head of Instruction:** Chuck Ciganick.

PROFESSIONAL BASEBALL INSTRUCTION

Mailing Address: 107 Pleasant Ave., Upper Saddle River, NJ 07458. **Telephone:** (800) 282-4638 (NY/NJ), (877) 448-2220 (rest of U.S.). **Fax:** (201) 760-8820. **E-Mail Address:** info@baseballclinics.com. **Website:** www.baseballclinics.com. **President:** Doug Cinnella.

RIPKEN BASEBALL CAMPS

Mailing Address: 1427 Clarkview Rd., Suite 100, Baltimore, MD 21209. **Telephone:** (410) 823-0808. **Fax:** (410) 823-0850. **E-Mail Address:** information@ripken-baseball.com. **Website:** www.ripkenbaseball.com.

SHO-ME BASEBALL CAMP

Mailing Address: P.O. Box 2270, Branson West, MO 65737. **Telephone:** (417) 338-5838. **Fax:** (417) 338-2610. **E-Mail Address:** info@shomebaseball.com. **Website:** www.shomebaseball.com.

COLLEGE CAMPS

Almost all of the elite college baseball programs have summer/holiday instructional camps. Please consult the college section for listings.

SENIOR BASEBALL

MEN'S SENIOR BASEBALL LEAGUE

(25 and Over, 35 and Over, 45 and Over, 55 and Over)
Mailing Address: One Huntington Quadrangle, Suite 3NO7, Melville, NY 11747. **Telephone:** (631) 753-6725. **Fax:** (631) 753-4031.
President: Steve Sigler. **Vice President:** Gary D'Ambrisi.
E-Mail Address: info@msblnational.com. **Website:** www.msblnational.com.

MEN'S ADULT BASEBALL LEAGUE

(18 and Over)
Mailing Address: One Huntington Quadrangle, Suite 3NO7, Melville, NY 11747. **Telephone:** (631) 753-6725. **Fax:** (631) 753-4031.
E-Mail Address: info@msblnational.com. **Website:** www.msblnational.com.
President: Steve Sigler. **Vice President:** Gary D'Ambrisi.

NATIONAL ADULT BASEBALL ASSOCIATION

Mailing Address: 3609 S. Wadsworth Blvd., Suite 135, Lakewood, CO 80235. **Telephone:** (800) 621-6479. **Fax:** (303) 639-6605. **E-Mail:** nabanational@aol.com. **Website:** www.dugout.org.
President: Shane Fugita.

NATIONAL AMATEUR BASEBALL FEDERATION

Mailing Address: P.O. Box 705, Bowie, MD 20718. **Telephone:** (410) 721-4727. **Fax:** (410) 721-4940. **E-Mail Address:** nabf1914@aol.com. **Website:** www.nabf.com.
Year Founded: 1914.
Executive Director: Charles Blackburn.

ROY HOBBS BASEBALL

Open (28-over), Veterans (38-over), Masters (48-over), Legends (55-over); Classics (60-over), Seniors (65-over), Timeless (70-over), Women's open.
Mailing Address: 2048 Akron Peninsula Rd., Akron, OH 44313. **Telephone:** (330) 923-3400. **Fax:** (330) 923-1967. **E-Mail Address:** rhbb@royhobbs.com. **Website:** www.royhobbs.com.
President: Tom Giffen. **Vice President:** Ellen Giffen.

DIRECTORIES
- **AGENT**
- **SERVICE**

ACES, INC
188 Montague St
Brooklyn, NY 11201
Phone: 718-237-2900
Fax: 718-522-3906
aces@acesinc.com
Seth Levinson, Esq: Sam Levinson,
Keith Miller, Peter Pedalino, Esq: Mike
Zimmerman, Brandon O'Hearn, Jamie
Appel

FRANK A. BLANDINO, LLC
204 Towne Centre Dr
Hillsbrough, NJ 08844
Phone: 908-217-3226
Fax: 908-281-0596
frank@blandinolaw.com
Frank A. Blandino

METIS SPORTS MANAGEMENT
132 North Old Woodward Ave
Birmingham, MI 48009
Phone: 248-594-1070
Fax: 248-281-5150
www.metissports.com
storm@metissports.com/
hector@metissports.com
Storm T. Kirshenbaum ESQ/Hector Faneytt

OAK SPORTS MANAGEMENT
41 Morton Ave East
Brantford, ON N3R7J5
Phone: 905-462-3001
Fax: 519-753-9495
oaksportsmanagement.com
info@oaksportsmanagement.com
Michael Bonanno, Jeffrey Cordova

PETER E. GREENBERG & ASSOCIATES, LTD
200 Madison Ave Ste 2225
New York, NY 10016
Phone: 212-334-6880
Fax: 212-334-6895
www.petergreenbergsports.com
Peter E Greenberg Esq, Edward L
Greenberg, Chris Leible

PRO AGENTS, INC
90 Woodbridge Centere Ste 901
Woodbridge, NJ 07095
Phone: 800-795-3454
Fax: 732-726-6688
pepeda@wilentz.com
David P. Pepe, Billy Martin Jr

PRO STAR MANAGEMENT, INC.
1600 Scripps Center, 312 Walnut Street
Cincinnati, OH 45202
Phone: 513-762-7676
Fax: 513-721-4628
www.prostarmanagement.com
prostar@fuse.net
Joe Bick, President: Brett Bick: Executive
Vice President: Ryan Bick, Vice President

SOSNICK COBBE SPORTS
712 Bancroft Rd 510
Walnut Creek, CA 94598
Phone: 925-890-5283
Fax: 925-476-0130
www.sosnickcobbesports.com
paulcobbe@me.com
Matt Sosnick, Paul Cobbe, Adam Karon,
Matt Hofer, Tripper Johnson, Jonathan
Pridie

VERRILL DANA SPORTS LAW GROUP
David S. Abramson, Esq.
One Portland Square
Portland, ME 04101
Phone: 207-774-4000
Fax: 207-774-7499
www.verrilldana.com
dabramson@verrilldana.com

ACCESSORIES

BWP BATS, LLC
80 Womeldorf Lane
Brookville, PA 15825
Phone: 814-849-0089
Fax: 814-849-8584
www.bwpbats.com
sales@bwpbats.com

SHUTTLE BASEBALL
"Put more blast in your swing!"
8698 Elk Grove Blvd Ste 3174
Elk Grove, CA 95624
Phone: 855-55-BASEBALL
Fax: 916-405-3867
www.shuttlebaseball.com
info@shuttlebaseball.com

WILSON SPORTING GOODS
8750 West Bryn Mawr Ave
13th Floor
Chicago IL 60631
Phone: 800-333-8326
Fax: 773-714-4565
www.wilson.com
askwilson@wilson.com

APPAREL

MINOR LEAGUES, MAJOR DREAMS
P.O. Box 6098
Anaheim, CA 92816
Phone: 800-345-2421
Fax: 714-939-0655
www.minorleagues.com
mlmd@minorleagues.com

MV SPORT
88 Spence St.
Bay Shore, NY 11706
Phone: 800-367-7900
Fax: 631-435-8018
www.mvsport.com
terry@wpmv.com

APPRAISERS

HERITAGE AUCTIONS
3500 Maple Ave,
17th Floor
Dallas, TX 75219
Phone: 800-872-6467
Fax: 214-409-1425
www.ha.com/sports
sports@ha.com

AUCTIONS

HERITAGE AUCTIONS
3500 Maple Ave,
17th Floor
Dallas, TX 75219
Phone: 800-872-6467
Fax: 214-409-1425
www.ha.com/sports
sports@ha.com

BAGS

DIAMOND SPORTS COMPANY
1880 E. St. Andrew Place
Santa Ana, CA 92705
Phone: 714-415-7600
Fax: 714-415-7601
www.diamond-sports.com
info@diamond-sports.com

GERRY COSBY AND COMPANY
11 Pennsylvania Plaza
New York, NY 10001
Phone: 877-563-6464
Fax: 212-967-0876
www.cosbysports.com
gcsmsg@cosbysports.com

LOUISVILLE SLUGGER
800 W Main St
Louisville, KY 40202
Phone: 800-282-2287
Fax: 502-585-1179
www.slugger.com
customer.service@slugger.com

SCHUTT SPORTS
710 S. Industrial Drive
Litchfield, IL 62025
Phone: 217-324-2712
www.schuttsports.com
sales@schutt-sports.com

WILSON SPORTING GOODS
8750 West Bryn Mawr Ave
13th Floor
Chicago IL 60631
Phone: 800-333-8326
Fax: 773-714-4565
www.wilson.com
askwilson@wilson.com

BASEBALLS

DIAMOND SPORTS COMPANY
1880 E. St. Andrew Place
Santa Ana, CA 92705
Phone: 714-415-7600
Fax: 714-415-7601
www.diamond-sports.com
info@diamond-sports.com

PICKLE-BALL INC.
810 NW 45th St.
Seattle, WA 98072
Phone: 800-377-9915
Fax: 206-632-0126
www.pickleball.com
info@pickleball.com

WILSON SPORTING GOODS
8750 West Bryn Mawr Ave
13th Floor
Chicago IL 60631
Phone: 800-333-8326
Fax: 773-714-4565
www.wilson.com
askwilson@wilson.com

BASES

BEAM CLAY
One Kelsey Park
Great Meadows, NJ 07838
Phone: 800-247-BEAM (2326)
Fax: 908-637-8421
www.beamclay.com
sales@partac.com

See our ad on page 312!

C&H BASEBALL, INC
10615 Technology Terrace, #100
Bradenton, FL 34211
Phone: 800-248-5192
Fax: 941-727-0588
www.chbaseball.com
info@chbaseball.com

SOUTH PADRE ISLAND NETS, INC
2001 Amistad Drive
San Benito, TX 78586
Phone: 956-276-9598
Fax: 956-276-9691
www.spinets.net/
joer@spinets.net

BATS

B45 BATS–THE FIRST & BEST YELLOW BIRCH BATS
281 Edward-Assh
Ste-Catherine-de-la-Jacques-Cartier,
QC Canada G3N 1A3
Phone: 1-888-669-0145
www.b45online.com
info@b45online.com
*Pro/MLB Contact – Rick Kramer
301-346-1046
rkramer@b45online.com

BRETT BROS. SPORTS
East 9516 Montgomery Ave.
BLDG #14
Spokane Valley, WA 99206
Phone: 509-891-6435
Fax: 509-891-4156
www.brettbros.com
brettbats@aol.com

BWP BATS, LLC
80 Womeldorf Lane
Brookville, PA 15825
Phone: 814-849-0089
Fax: 814-849-8584
www.bwpbats.com
sales@bwpbats.com

DEMARINI
6435 NW Croeni Rd
Hillsboro, OR 97124
Phone: 800-937-BATS (2287)
Fax: 503-531-5506
www.demarini.com

DIAMOND SPORTS COMPANY
1880 E. St. Andrew Place
Santa Ana, CA 92705
Phone: 714-415-7600
Fax: 714-415-7601
www.diamond-sports.com
info@diamond-sports.com

HOOSIER BAT CO.
P.O. Box 432
4511 Evans Ave
Valparaiso, IN 46383
Phone: 800-228-3787
Fax: 219-465-0877
www.hoosierbat.com
baseball@netnitco.net

LOUISVILLE SLUGGER
800 W Main St
Louisville, KY 40202
Phone: 800-282-2287
Fax: 502-585-1179
www.slugger.com
customer.service@slugger.com

MIKEN SPORTS, LLC
131 Bissen Street
Caledonia, MN 55921
Phone: 877-807-5291
Fax: 507-725-3675
www.mikensports.com
info@mikensports.com

"MINE" BY MINELLI USA
CA 91335
Phone: 877-MINE-BAT
www.minebats.com
mine@minebats.com

OLD HICKORY BAT COMPANY
P.O. Box 588
White House, TN 37188
Phone: 615-285-0588
Fax: 615-285-0512
www.oldhickorybats.com
mail@oldhickorybats.com

PHOENIX BATS
7801 Corprate Blvd
Ste E
Plain City, OH 43064
Phone: 877-598-2287
Fax: 614-873-7796
www.phoenixbats.com
lefty@phoenixbats.com

RX SPORT/ CRAFTSMAN OF THE CHANDLER BAT
670 W. Washington St.
Norristown, PA 19401
Phone: 877-497-(BATS) 2287 ext 501
www.CHANDLERBATS.com
angela@rxsport.com

SAM BAT - THE ORIGINAL MAPLE BAT CORPORATION
110 Industrial Ave
Carleton Place, ON K7C3T2
Phone: 1-888-SAM-BATS
Fax: 613-725-3299
www.sambat.com
bats@sambat.com

ZORIAN
960 Reservoir Avenue
Suite 30
Cranston, RI 02910
Phone: 781-266-8188
Fax: 401-884-1535
www.zorianbats.com
rob@zorianbats.com

X-BATS
1930 Village Center Circle
#3-812
Las Vegas, NV 89134
Phone: 702-419-0404
Fax: 702-974-0695
www.xbats.com
customerservice@xbats.com

BATTING CAGES

BEAM CLAY
One Kelsey Park
Great Meadows, NJ 07838
Phone: 800-247-BEAM (2326)
Fax: 908-637-8421
www.beamclay.com
sales@partac.com

See our ad on page 312!

C&H BASEBALL, INC
10615 Technology Terrace, #100
Bradenton, FL 34211
Phone: 800-248-5192
Fax: 941-727-0588
www.chbaseball.com
info@chbaseball.com

DIAMOND SPORTS COMPANY
1880 E. St. Andrew Place
Santa Ana, CA 92705
Phone: 714-415-7600
Fax: 714-415-7601
www.diamond-sports.com
info@diamond-sports.com

GOLF RANGE NETTING INC
40351 US Hwy 19 N, #303
Tarpon Springs, FL 34689
Phone: 727-938-4448
Fax: 727-938-4135
www.golfrangenetting.com
infor@golfrangenetting.com

JUGS SPORTS
11885 SW Herman Rd
Tualatin, OR 97062
Phone: 1-800-547-6843
Fax: 503-691-1100
www.jugssports.com
stevec@jugssports.com

NATIONAL SPORTS PRODUCTS
3441 S 11th Ave
Eldridge, IA 52748
Phone: 800-478-6497
Fax: 800-443-8907
wwws.nationalsportsproducts.com
sales@nationalsportsproducts.com

NETEX NETTING INC
5128 Central Ave
Delta, BC V4K 2H2
Phone: 800-936-6388
Fax: 604-946-8690
www.netexnetting.ca
m.wilson@dccnet.com

See our ad on the inside back cover!

PROMATS ATHLETICS
P.O. Box 2489
Salisbury, NC 28145
Phone: 800-617-7125
Fax: 704-603-4138
www.promatsathletics.com
mcross@promatsathletics.com

SOUTH PADRE ISLAND NETS, INC
2001 Amistad Drive
San Benito, TX 78586
Phone: 956-276-9598
Fax: 956-276-9691
www.spinets.net/
joer@spinets.net

WEST COAST NETTING
5075 Flightline Dr.
Kingman, AZ 86401
Phone: 928-692-1144
Fax: 928-692-1501
www.westcoastnetting.com
info@westcoastnetting.com

BATTING HELMETS

SCHUTT SPORTS
710 S. Industrial Drive
Litchfield, IL 62025
Phone: 217-324-2712
www.schuttsports.com
sales@schutt-sports.com

CAMPS/SCHOOLS

I.T.S. BASEBALL
602 Cornerstone Ct.
Hillsborough, NC 27278
Phone: 919-245-1181
www.itsbaseball.net
www.drivedeveloper.com
www.hittingrebelion.com
chas@itsbaseball.net

PROFESSIONAL BASEBALL INSTRUCTION
107 Pleasant Ave.
Upper Saddle River, NJ 07458
Phone: 800-282-4638
Fax: 201-760-8820
www.baseballclinics.com
info@baseballclinics.com

CAPS/HEADWEAR

MINOR LEAGUES, MAJOR DREAMS
P.O. Box 6098
Anaheim, CA 92816
Phone: 800-345-2421
Fax: 714-939-0655
www.minorleagues.com
mlmd@minorleagues.com

OC SPORTS
1200 Melissa Drive
Bentonville, AR 72712
Phone: 800-823-6047
Fax: 800-200-0329
www.ocsports.com
sales@outdoorcap.com

CARTS & KIOSKS

B-R CARTS + KIOSKS, INC
1360 County Rd 8
P.O. Box 25338
Farmington, NY 14425
Phone: 585-398-2190
Fax: 585-398-2143
www.brcarts.com
nancyrole@brcarts.com

CONCESSION OPERATIONS

CONCESSION SOLUTIONS INC
16022 - 26th Ave NE
Shoreline, WA 98155
Phone: 206-440-9203
Fax: 206-440-9213
www.concessionsolutions.com
theresa@concessionsolutions.com

TEXAS DIGITAL SYSTEMS
400 Technology Parkway
College Station, TX 77845
Phone: 979-693-9378
Fax: 979-764-8650
www.txdigital.com
smedlin@txdigital.com

CONSULTING/PRODUCTION

TOTAL SPORTS ENTERTAINMENT
2414 State Rd
La Crosse, WI 54601
Phone: 800-962-2471
Fax: 608-782-4655
www.totalsportsentertainment.com
info@totalsportsentertainment.com

EMBROIDERED EMBLEMS

THE EMBLEM SOURCE
4575 Westgrove Dr #500
Addison, TX 75001
Phone: 972-248-1909
Fax: 972-248-1615
www.theemblemsource.com
larry@theemblemsource.com

ENTERTAINMENT

BIRDZERK!
P.O. Box 36061
Louisville, KY 40233
Phone: 800-219-0899/502-458-4020
Fax: 502-458-0867
www.birdzerk.com
dom@birdzerk.com

BREAKIN' BBOY McCOY
P.O. Box 36061
Louisville, KY 40233
Phone: 800-219-0899/502-458-4020
Fax: 502-458-0867
www.bboymccoy.com
dom@theskillvillegroup.com

COYOTE PROMOTIONS
300 Worthern Blvd, #26
Great Neck, NY 11021
Phone: 800-726-9683
Fax: 516-482-7425
www.coyotepromtions.com
info@coyotepromotions.com

INFLATAMANIACS
8004 Sycamore Creek
Louisville, KY 40222
Phone: 502-417-8659
Fax: 502-566-1896
www.inflatamaniacs.com
steven@inflatamaniacs.com

MYRON NOODLEMAN
P.O. Box 36061
Louisville, KY 40233
Phone: 800-219-0899/502-458-4020
Fax: 502-458-0867
www.myronnoodleman.com
dom@theskillvillegroup.com

SCOLLON PRODUCTIONS/ SCOLLON LIVE EVENTS
P.O. Box 486
White Rock, SC 29177
Phone: 803-345-3922
Fax: 803-345-9313
www.scollon.com
rick@scollon.com

TOTAL SPORTS ENTERTAINMENT
2414 State Rd
La Crosse, WI 54601
Phone: 800-962-2471
Fax: 608-782-4655
www.totalsportsentertainment.com
info@totalsportsentertainment.com

VIRTUS STUNTS, LLC TED A. BATCHELOR
16320 Snyper Road
Chagrin Falls, OH 44023
Phone: 216-402-8705
Fax: 440-247-1909
www.tedbatchelor.com
stuntma488@aol.com
"Running the Bases on Fire!"

ZOOPERSTARS!
P.O. Box 36061
Louisville, KY 40233
Phone: 800-219-0899/502-458-4020
Fax: 502-458-0867
www.zooperstars.com
dom@zooperstars.com

FIELD COVERS/TARPS

BEAM CLAY
One Kelsey Park
Great Meadows, NJ 07838
Phone: 800-247-BEAM (2326)
Fax: 908-637-8421
www.beamclay.com
sales@partac.com

See our ad on page 312!

C&H BASEBALL, INC
10615 Technology Terrace, #100
Bradenton, FL 34211
Phone: 941-727-1533
Fax: 941-727-0588
www.chbaseball.com
info@chbaseball.com

COVERMASTER INC
100 Westmore Dr. 11-D
Rexdale, ON M9V 5C3
Phone: 800-387-5808
Fax: 416-742-6837
www.covermaster.com
info@covermaster.com

NATIONAL SPORTS PRODUCTS
3441 S 11th Ave
Eldridge, IA 52748
Phone: 800-478-6497
Fax: 800-443-8907
wwws.nationalsportsproducts.com
sales@nationalsportsproducts.com

REEF INDUSTRIES, INC.
9209 Almeda Genoa Rd.
Houston, TX 77075
Phone: 713-507-4251
Fax: 713-507-4295
www.reefindustries.com
myoung@reefindustries.com

SOUTH PADRE ISLAND NETS, INC
2001 Amistad Drive
San Benito, TX 78586
Phone: 956-276-9598
Fax: 956-276-9691
www.spinets.net/
joer@spinets.net

FIELD EQUIPMENT

DIAMOND SPORTS COMPANY
1880 E. St. Andrew Place
Santa Ana, CA 92705
Phone: 714-415-7600
Fax: 714-415-7601
www.diamond-sports.com
info@diamond-sports.com

FIELD WALL PADDING

BEAM CLAY
One Kelsey Park
Great Meadows, NJ 07838
Phone: 800-247-BEAM (2326)
Fax: 908-637-8421
www.beamclay.com
sales@partac.com

See our ad on page 312!

C&H BASEBALL, INC
10615 Technology Terrace, #100
Bradenton, FL 34211
Phone: 800-248-5192
Fax: 941-727-0588
www.chbaseball.com
info@chbaseball.com

COVERMASTER INC
100 Westmore Dr. 11-D
Rexdale, ON M9V 5C3
Phone: 800-387-5808
Fax: 416-742-6837
www.covermaster.com
info@covermaster.com

NATIONAL SPORTS PRODUCTS
3441 S 11th Ave
Eldridge, IA 52748
Phone: 800-478-6497
Fax: 800-443-8907
wwws.nationalsportsproducts.com
sales@nationalsportsproducts.com

NETEX NETTING INC
5128 Central Ave
Delta, BC V4K 2H2
Phone: 800-936-6388
Fax: 604-946-8690
www.netexnetting.ca
m.wilson@dccnet.com

See our ad on the inside back cover!

PROMATS ATHLETICS
P.O. Box 2489
Sailisbury, NC 28145
Phone: 800-617-7125
Fax: 704-603-4138
www.promatsathletics.com
mcross@promatsathletics.com

SOUTH PADRE ISLAND NETS, INC
2001 Amistad Drive
San Benito, TX 78586
Phone: 956-276-9598
Fax: 956-276-9691
www.spinets.net/
joer@spinets.net

WEST COAST NETTING
5075 Flightline Dr.
Kingman, AZ 86401
Phone: 928-692-1144
Fax: 928-692-1501
www.westcoastnetting.com
info@westcoastnetting.com

FIREWORKS

PYROTECNICO
P.O. Box 149
New Castle, PA 16103
Phone: 800-854-4705
Fax: 724-652-1288
www.pyrotecnico.com
vlaurenza@pyrotecnico.com

GAME MANAGEMENT SOFTWARE

TOTAL SPORTS ENTERTAINMENT
2414 State Rd
La Crosse, WI 54601
Phone: 800-962-2471
Fax: 608-782-4655
www.totalsportsentertainment.com
info@totalsportsentertainment.com

GIVEAWAY ITEMS

COYOTE PROMOTIONS
300 Worthern Blvd, #26
Great Neck, NY 11021
Phone: 800-726-9683
Fax: 516-482-7425
www.coyotepromtions.com
info@coyotepromotions.com

RICO INDUSTRIES, INC/ TAG EXPRESS
7000 N. Austin
Niles, IL 60714
Phone: 1-800-423-5856
Fax: 312-427-0190
www.ricoinc.com
jimz@ricoinc.com

GLOVE BREAK-IN SERVICE

BERGEN BATTING CENTER
3 New Bridge Road
River Edge, NJ 07661
Phone: 201-525-1888
Fax: 201-525-1887
www.bergenbattingcenter.com
bergenbatting@aol.com,
sales@bergenbattingcenter.com

GLOVES

ALL-STAR DIVISION— AMPAC ENTERPRISES INC.
P.O. Box 1356
Shirley, MA 01404
Phone: 978-425-6266
Fax: 978-425-4068
www.all-starsports.com
customerservice@all-starsports.com

BERGEN BATTING CENTER
3 New Bridge Road
River Edge, NJ 07661
Phone: 201-525-1888
Fax: 201-525-1887
www.bergenbattingcenter.com
bergenbatting@aol.com,
sales@bergenbattingcenter.com

BRETT BROS. SPORTS
East 9516 Montgomery Ave.
BLDG #14
Spokane Valley, WA 99206
Phone: 509-891-6435
Fax: 509-891-4156
www.brettbros.com
brettbats@aol.com

FRANK'S SPORT SHOP
430 E. Tremont Ave
Bronx, NY 10457
Phone: 718-299-5223, 212-945-0020
Fax: 718-583-1653
www.frankssportsshop.com

See our ad on the insert!

LOUISVILLE SLUGGER
800 W Main St
Louisville, KY 40202
Phone: 800-282-2287
Fax: 502-585-1179
www.slugger.com
customer.service@slugger.com

OLD HICKORY BAT COMPANY
P.O. Box 588
White House, TN 37188
Phone: 615-285-0588
Fax: 615-285-0512
www.oldhickorybats.com
mail@oldhickorybats.com

WILSON SPORTING GOODS
8750 West Bryn Mawr Ave
13th Floor
Chicago IL 60631
Phone: 800-333-8326
Fax: 773-714-4565
www.wilson.com
askwilson@wilson.com

GRAPHIC DESIGN

PROMATS ATHLETICS
P.O. Box 2489
Salisbury, NC 28145
Phone: 800-617-7125
Fax: 704-603-4138
www.promatsathletics.com
mcross@promatsathletics.com

HIGHER EDUCATION

SAINT LEO UNIVERSITY ONLINE MBA/SPORT BUSINESS
33701 State Road 52
P.O. Box 6665/MC 2011
Saint Leo, FL 33574
Phone: 352-588-7326
Fax: 352-588-8923
www.saintleo.edu
eric.schwarz@saintleo.edu

INSURANCE

K&K INSURANCE
1712 Magnavox Way
Fort Wayne, IN 46804
Phone: 800-441-3994
Fax: 260-459-5120
www.kandkinsurance.com
kk-sports@kandkinsurance.com

See our ad on the inside front cover!

LIGHTING

GOLF RANGE NETTING INC
40351 US Hwy 19 N, #303
Tarpon Springs, FL 34689
Phone: 727-938-4448
Fax: 727-938-4135
www.golfrangenetting.com
infor@golfrangenetting.com

MASCOT COSTUMES

ALINCO COSTUMES
5505 S Riley Lane
Murray, UT 84107
Phone: 801-266-6337
jill@alincocostumes.com
www.alincocostumes.com

MASCOTS

OLYMPUS GROUP
9000 West Heather Ave
Milwaukee, WI 53224
Phone: 414-355-2010
Fax: 414-355-1931
www.olympusgrp.com
sales@olympusgrp.com

SCOLLON PRODUCTIONS/ SCOLLON LIVE EVENTS
P.O. Box 486
White Rock, SC 29177
Phone: 803-345-3922
Fax: 803-345-9313
www.scollon.com
rick@scollon.com

MANAGMENT SOLUTIONS

TOTAL SPORTS ENTERTAINMENT
2414 State Rd
La Crosse, WI 54601
Phone: 800-962-2471
Fax: 608-782-4655
www.totalsportsentertainment.com
info@totalsportsentertainment.com

MUSIC/SOUND EFFECTS

SOUND DIRECTOR, INC
2918 SW Royal Way
Gresham, OR 97080
Phone: 503-665-6869
Phone: 888-276-0078
Fax: 503-914-1812
www.sounddirector.com
info@sounddirector.com

NETTING/POSTS

BEAM CLAY
One Kelsey Park
Great Meadows, NJ 07838
Phone: 800-247-BEAM (2326)
Fax: 908-637-8421
www.beamclay.com
sales@partac.com

See our ad on page 312!

C&H BASEBALL, INC
10615 Technology Terrace, #100
Bradenton, FL 34211
Phone: 800-248-5192
Fax: 941-727-0588
www.chbaseball.com
info@chbaseball.com

GOLF RANGE NETTING INC
40351 US Hwy 19 N, #303
Tarpon Springs, FL 34689
Phone: 727-938-4448
Fax: 727-938-4135
www.golfrangenetting.com
infor@golfrangenetting.com

L.A. STEELCRAFT PRODUCTS, INC
1975 Lincoln Ave
Pasadena, CA 91103
Phone: 800-371-2438
Fax: (626)-798-1482
www.lasteelcraft.com
info@lasteelcraft.com

NATIONAL SPORTS PRODUCTS
3441 S 11th Ave
Eldridge, IA 52748
Phone: 800-478-6497
Fax: 800-443-8907
wwws.nationalsportsproducts.com
sales@nationalsportsproducts.com

WEST COAST NETTING
5075 Flightline Dr.
Kingman, AZ 86401
Phone: 928-692-1144
Fax: 928-692-1501
www.westcoastnetting.com
info@westcoastnetting.com

NETEX NETTING INC
5128 Central Ave
Delta, BC V4K 2H2
Phone: 800-936-6388
Fax: 604-946-8690
www.netexnetting.ca
m.wilson@dccnet.com

See our ad on the inside back cover!

PROMATS ATHLETICS
P.O. Box 2489
Salisbury, NC 28145
Phone: 800-617-7125
Fax: 704-603-4138
www.promatsathletics.com
mcross@promatsathletics.com

SOUTH PADRE ISLAND NETS, INC
2001 Amistad Drive
San Benito, TX 78586
Phone: 956-276-9598
Fax: 956-276-9691
www.spinets.net/
joer@spinets.net

NOVELTY ITEMS

COYOTE PROMOTIONS
300 Worthern Blvd, #26
Great Neck, NY 11021
Phone: 800-726-9683
Fax: 516-482-7425
www.coyotepromtions.com
info@coyotepromotions.com

PATCHES

THE EMBLEM SOURCE
4575 Westgrove Dr #500
Addison, TX 75001
Phone: 972-248-1909
Fax: 972-248-1615
www.theemblemsource.com
larry@theemblemsource.com

PENNANTS, FOAM HANDS AND NOVELTY GIFTS

RICO INDUSTRIES, INC/ TAG EXPRESS
7000 N. Austin
Niles, IL 60714
Phone: 1-800-423-5856
Fax: 312-427-0190
www.ricoinc.com
jimz@ricoinc.comr

PITCHING AIDS

THROWTHECURVE.COM
107 Pleasant Ave.
Upper Saddle River, NJ 07458
Phone: 1-800-282-4638
Fax: 201-760-8820
www.throwthecurve.com

PITCHING MACHINES

ATHLETIC TRAINING EQUIPMENT COMPANY— ATEC
655 Spice Island Dr.
Sparks, NV 89431
Phone: 800-998-ATEC (2832)
Fax: 800-959-ATEC (2832)
www.atecsports.com
askATEC@wilson.com

C&H BASEBALL, INC
10615 Technology Terrace, #100
Bradenton, FL 34211
Phone: 800-248-5192
Fax: 941-727-0588
www.chbaseball.com
info@chbaseball.com

JUGS SPORTS
11885 SW Herman Rd
Tualatin, OR 97062
Phone: 1-800-547-6843
Fax: 503-691-1100
www.jugssports.com
stevec@jugssports.com

PICKLE-BALL INC.
810 NW 45th St.
Seattle, WA 98072
Phone: 800-377-9915
Fax: 206-632-0126
www.pickleball.com
info@pickleball.com

PROBATTER SPORTS
49 Research Dr, Ste A
Milford, CT 06460
Phone: 203-874-2500
Fax: 203-878-9019
www.probatter.com
abattersby@probatter.com

SPORTS TUTOR, INC
3300 Winona Ave
Burbank, CA 91504
Phone: (818)-972-2772
Fax: (818)-972-9651
www.sportsmachines.com
orders@sportstutor.com

PLAYING FIELD PRODUCTS

BEAM CLAY
One Kelsey Park
Great Meadows, NJ 07838
Phone: 800-247-BEAM (2326)
Fax: 908-637-8421
www.beamclay.com
sales@partac.com

See our ad on page 312!

C&H BASEBALL, INC
10615 Technology Terrace, #100
Bradenton, FL 34211
Phone: 800-248-5192
Fax: 941-727-0588
www.chbaseball.com
info@chbaseball.com

DIAMOND PRO
1341 West Mockingbird Lane
Dallas, TX 75247
Phone: 800-228-2987
Fax: 800-640-6735
www.diamondpro.com
diamondpro@txi.com

See our ad on the inside back cover!

SOUTH PADRE ISLAND NETS, INC
2001 Amistad Drive
San Benito, TX 78586
Phone: 956-276-9598
Fax: 956-276-9691
www.spinets.net/
joer@spinets.net

STALKER RADAR (APPLIED CONCEPTS)
2609 Technology Dr.
Plano, TX 75074
Phone: 1-888-stalker
www.stalkerradar.com
sales@stalkerradar.com

See our ad on page 7!

POINT OF SALES

GERRY COSBY AND COMPANY
11 Pennsylvania Plaza
New York, NY 10001
Phone: 877-563-6464
Fax: 212-967-0876
www.cosbysports.com
gcsmsg@cosbysports.com

MICROS SYSTEMS, INC.
7031 Columbia Gateway Dr
Columbia, MD 21046
Phone: 866-287-4736
Fax: 443-583-2505
www.micros.com
info@micros.com

PROFESSIONAL SERVICES

GERRY COSBY AND COMPANY
11 Pennsylvania Plaza
New York, NY 10001
Phone: 877-563-6464
Fax: 212-967-0876
www.cosbysports.com
gcsmsg@cosbysports.com

PROMOTIONAL ITEMS

C&H BASEBALL, INC
10615 Technology Terrace, #100
Bradenton, FL 34211
Phone: 800-248-5192
Fax: 941-727-0588
www.chbaseball.com
info@chbaseball.com

COYOTE PROMOTIONS
300 Worthern Blvd, #26
Great Neck, NY 11021
Phone: 800-726-9683
Fax: 516-482-7425
www.coyotepromtions.com
info@coyotepromotions.com

RICO INDUSTRIES, INC/
TAG EXPRESS
7000 N. Austin
Niles, IL 60714
Phone: 1-800-423-5856
Fax: 312-427-0190
www.ricoinc.com
jimz@ricoinc.com

VIRTUS STUNTS, LLC
TED A. BATCHELOR
16320 Snyper Road
Chagrin Falls, OH 44023
Phone: 216-402-8705
Fax: 440-247-1909
www.tedbatchelor.com
stuntma488@aol.com
"Running the Bases on Fire!"

PROMOTIONS

COYOTE PROMOTIONS
300 Worthern Blvd, #26
Great Neck, NY 11021
Phone: 800-726-9683
Fax: 516-482-7425
www.coyotepromotions.com
info@coyotepromotions.com

INFLATAMANIACS
8004 Sycamore Creek
Louisville, KY 40222
Phone: (502)-417-8659
Fax: 502-566-1896
www.inflatamaniacs.com
steven@inflatamaniacs.com

TOTAL SPORTS
ENTERTAINMENT
2414 State Rd
La Crosse, WI 54601
Phone: 800-962-2471
Fax: 608-782-4655
www.totalsportsentertainment.com
info@totalsportsentertainment.com

VIRTUS STUNTS, LLC
TED A. BATCHELOR
16320 Snyper Road
Chagrin Falls, OH 44023
Phone: 216-402-8705
Fax: 440-247-1909
www.tedbatchelor.com
stuntma488@aol.com
"Running the Bases on Fire!"

PROTECTIVE EQUIPMENT

ALL-STAR DIVISION —
AMPAC ENTERPRISES INC.
P.O. Box 1356
Shirley, MA 01404
Phone: 978-425-6266
Fax: 978-425-4068
www.all-starsports.com
customerservice@all-starsports.com

BEAM CLAY
One Kelsey Park
Great Meadows, NJ 07838
Phone: 800-247-BEAM (2326)
Fax: 908-637-8421
www.beamclay.com
sales@partac.com

See our ad on page 312!

C&H BASEBALL, INC
10615 Technology Terrace, #100
Bradenton, FL 34211
Phone: 800-248-5192
Fax: 941-727-0588
www.chbaseball.com
info@chbaseball.com

DIAMOND SPORTS COMPANY
1880 E. St. Andrew Place
Santa Ana, CA 92705
Phone: 714-415-7600
Fax: 714-415-7601
www.diamond-sports.com
info@diamond-sports.com

EVOSHIELD
300 Commerce Blvd
Bogart, GA 30622
Phone: 770-725-2724
www.evoshield.com

JUGS SPORTS
11885 SW Herman Rd
Tualatin, OR 97062
Phone: 1-800-547-6843
Fax: 503-691-1100
www.jugssports.com
stevec@jugssports.com

LOUISVILLE SLUGGER
800 W Main St
Louisville, KY 40202
Phone: 800-282-2287
Fax: 502-585-1179
www.slugger.com
customer.service@slugger.com

SCHUTT SPORTS
710 S. Industrial Drive
Litchfield, IL 62025
Phone: 217-324-2712
www.schuttsports.com
sales@schutt-sports.com

SOUTH PADRE
ISLAND NETS, INC
2001 Amistad Drive
San Benito, TX 78586
Phone: 956-276-9598
Fax: 956-276-9691
www.spinets.net/
joer@spinets.net

WEST COAST NETTING
5075 Flightline Dr.
Kingman, AZ 86401
Phone: 928-692-1144
Fax: 928-692-1501
www.westcoastnetting.com
info@westcoastnetting.com

WILSON SPORTING GOODS
8750 West Bryn Mawr Ave
13th Floor
Chicago IL 60631
Phone: 800-333-8326
Fax: 773-714-4565
www.wilson.com
askwilson@wilson.com

RADAR EQUIPMENT

DIAMOND PRO
1341 West Mockingbird Lane
Dallas, TX 75247
Phone: 800-228-2987
Fax: 800-640-6735
www.diamondpro.com
diamondpro@txi.com

JUGS SPORTS
11885 SW Herman Rd
Tualatin, OR 97062
Phone: 1-800-547-6843
Fax: 503-691-1100
www.jugssports.com
stevec@jugssports.com

STALKER RADAR
(APPLIED CONCEPTS)
2609 Technology Dr.
Plano, TX 75074
Phone: 1-888-stalker
www.stalkerradar.com
sales@stalkerradar.com

See our ad on page 7!

SCOREBOARD

TOTAL SPORTS
ENTERTAINMENT
2414 State Rd
La Crosse, WI 54601
Phone: 800-962-2471
Fax: 608-782-4655
www.totalsportsentertainment.com
info@totalsportsentertainment.com

SEATING

STURDISTEEL CO.
131 Ava Drive
Hewitt, TX 76643
Phone: 800-433-3116
Fax: 254-666-4472
www.sturdisteel.com
rgroppe@sturdisteel.com

SHOES

FRANK'S SPORT SHOP
430 E. Tremont Ave
Bronx, NY 10457
Phone: 718-299-5223, 212-945-0020
Fax: 718-583-1653
www.frankssportsshop.com

See our ad on the insert!

SHOWCASES/
PLAYER DEVELOPMENT

PROFESSIONAL
BASEBALL INSTRUCTION
BATTERY INVITATIONAL
(pitchers/catchers–early November)
107 Pleasant Ave
Upper Saddle River, NJ 07458
Phone: 800-282-4638
Fax: 201-760-8820
greg@baseballclinics.com

SPORTING GOODS

JUGHEAD SPORTS
107 Pleasant Ave.
Upper Saddle River, NJ 07458
Phone: 800-282-4638
Fax: 201-760-8820
www.jugheadsports.com

SPORTS MEMORABILIA

HERITAGE AUCTIONS
3500 Maple Ave,
17th Floor
Dallas, TX 75219
Phone: 800-872-6467
Fax: 214-409-1425
www.ha.com/sports
sports@ha.com

STADIUM ARCHITECTS

360 ARCHITECTURE
300 W 22nd Street
Kansas City, MO 64108
Phone: 816-472-3360
Fax: 816-472-2100
www.360architects.com
clamberth@360architects.com

TICKETS

INDIANA TICKET CO.
P.O. Box 823
Muncie, IN 47308
Phone: 800-428-8640
Fax: 888-428-8640
www.indianaticket.com
info@indianaticket.com

NATIONAL TICKET CO.
P.O. Box 547
Shamokin, PA 17872
Phone: 800-829-0829
Fax: 800-829-0888
www.nationalticket.com
ticket@nationalticket.com

TRAINING EQUIPMENT

ATHLETIC TRAINING EQUIPMENT COMPANY— ATEC
655 Spice Island Dr.
Sparks, NV 89431
Phone: 800-998-ATEC (2832)
Fax: 800-959-ATEC (2832)
www.atecsports.com
askATEC@wilson.com

I.T.S. BASEBALL
602 Cornerstone Ct.
Hillsborough, NC 27278
Phone: 919-245-1181
www.itsbaseball.net
www.drivedeveloper.com
www.hittingrebelion.com
chas@itsbaseball.net

JUGS SPORTS
11885 SW Herman Rd
Tualatin, OR 97062
Phone: 1-800-547-6843
Fax: 503-691-1100
www.jugssports.com
stevec@jugssports.com

LOUISVILLE SLUGGER
800 W Main St
Louisville, KY 40202
Phone: 800-282-2287
Fax: 502-585-1179
www.slugger.com
customer.service@slugger.com

PICKLE-BALL INC.
810 NW 45th St.
Seattle, WA 98072
Phone: 800-377-9915
Fax: 206-632-0126
www.pickleball.com
info@pickleball.com

WEST COAST NETTING
5075 Flightline Dr.
Kingman, AZ 86401
Phone: 928-692-1144
Fax: 928-692-1501
www.westcoastnetting.com
info@westcoastnetting.com

TRAVEL

BROACH BASEBALL TOURS
3235 South Blvd
Charlotte, NC 28209
Phone: 800-849-6345
Fax: 704-365-3800
www.baseballtoursusa.com
info@broachsportstours.com

SPORTS TRAVEL AND TOURS
60 Main Street
P. O. Box 50
Hatfield, MA 01038
Phone: 1-800-662-4424
Fax: 413-247-5700
www.sportstravelandtours.com
info@sportstravelandtours.com

See our ad on page 6!

UNIFORMS

AIS ATHLETIC UNIFORMS
2202 Anderson Street
Vernon, CA 90058
Phone: 323-582-3005
Fax: 323-582-2831
www.aisathleticuniforms.com
allan@aisathleticuniforms.com

WILSON SPORTING GOODS
8750 West Bryn Mawr Ave
13th Floor
Chicago IL 60631
Phone: 800-333-8326
Fax: 773-714-4565
www.wilson.com
askwilson@wilson.com

WINDSCREENS

BEAM CLAY
One Kelsey Park
Great Meadows, NJ 07838
Phone: 800-247-BEAM (2326)
Fax: 908-637-8421
www.beamclay.com
sales@partac.com

See our ad on page 312!

C&H BASEBALL, INC
10615 Technology Terrace, #100
Bradenton, FL 34211
Phone: 800-248-5192
Fax: 941-727-0588
www.chbaseball.com
info@chbaseball.com

GOLF RANGE NETTING INC
40351 US Hwy 19 N, #303
Tarpon Springs, FL 34689
Phone: 727-938-4448
Fax: 727-938-4135
www.golfrangenetting.com
infor@golfrangenetting.com

NATIONAL SPORTS PRODUCTS
3441 S 11th Ave
Eldridge, IA 52748
Phone: 800-478-6497
Fax: 800-443-8907
wwws.nationalsportsproducts.com
sales@nationalsportsproducts.com

PROMATS ATHLETICS
P.O. Box 2489
Salisbury, NC 28145
Phone: 800-617-7125
Fax: 704-603-4138
www.promatsathletics.com
mcross@promatsathletics.com

SOUTH PADRE ISLAND NETS, INC
2001 Amistad Drive
San Benito, TX 78586
Phone: 956-276-9598
Fax: 956-276-9691
www.spinets.net/
joer@spinets.net

WEST COAST NETTING
5075 Flightline Dr.
Kingman, AZ 86401
Phone: 928-692-1144
Fax: 928-692-1501
www.westcoastnetting.com
info@westcoastnetting.com

WRISTBANDS

NATIONAL TICKET CO.
P.O. Box 547
Shamokin, PA 17872
Phone: 800-829-0829
Fax: 800-829-0888
www.nationalticket.com
ticket@nationalticket.com

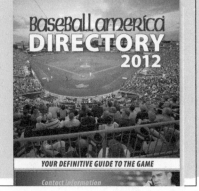

MAJOR LEAGUE TEAMS

MINOR LEAGUE TEAMS

INDEPENDENT TEAMS

OTHER ORGANIZATIONS